Tocqueville
and His America

TOCQUEVILLE
AND HIS AMERICA

A Darker Horizon

Arthur Kaledin

Yale

UNIVERSITY

PRESS

New Haven & London

Published with assistance from the Mary Cady Tew Memorial Fund.

Yale University Press books may be purchased in quantity for
educational, business, or promotional use. For information,
please e-mail sales.press@yale.edu (U.S. office)
or sales@yaleup.co.uk (U.K. office).

Set in Electra type by IDS Infotech Ltd., Chandigarh, India.
Printed in the United States of America by Sheridan Books, Ann Arbor, Michigan.

Library of Congress Cataloging-in-Publication Data
Kaledin, Arthur, 1930–
Tocqueville and his America: a darker horizon/ Arthur Kaledin.
p. cm.
Includes bibliographical references and index.
ISBN 978-0-300-11931-2 (cloth: alk. paper) 1. Tocqueville, Alexis de, 1805–1859.
2. Historians—France—Biography. 3. Tocqueville, Alexis de, 1805–1859—Philosophy.
4. Tocqueville, Alexis de, 1805–1859. De la démocratie en Amérique. I. Title.
JC229.T8K35 2011
320.973—dc22
2011008450

A catalogue record for this book is available from the British Library.

This paper meets the requirements of
ANSI/NISO Z39.48–1992 (Permanence of Paper).

10 9 8 7 6 5 4 3 2 1

To the Memory of
Paul Gagnon
Historian, Teacher, Steadfast Friend
Passionate, untiring advocate of the education that our
democracy needs if it is to become a fully free and just society
and to
My Sons and Daughter and my Grandchildren
who know how to be
citizens of a free and just society

I have no doubt that the social and political structure of a nation predisposes a people in favor of certain tastes and beliefs which then flourish carefree, and the same reason, without deliberate striving and indeed almost unconsciously, keeps other opinions and inclinations out of mind.

The essence of the lawgiver's art is by anticipation to appreciate those natural bents of human societies in order to know where the citizens' efforts need support and where there is more need to hold them back. For different times make different demands. The goal alone is fixed, to which humanity should press forward; the means of getting there forever change.

Governments must study means to give men back that interest in the future which neither religion nor social conditions any longer inspire and, without specifically saying so, give daily practical examples to the citizens proving that wealth, renown, and power are the rewards of work, that great success comes when it has been long desired, and that nothing of lasting value is achieved without trouble.

*　　*　　*

If the citizens continue to shut themselves up more and more narrowly in the little circle of petty domestic interests and keep themselves constantly busy therein, there is a danger that they may in the end become practically out of reach of those great and powerful public emotions which do indeed perturb peoples but which also make them grow and refresh them. Seeing property change hands so quickly, and love of property become so anxious and eager, I cannot help fearing that people may reach a point where they look on every new theory as a danger, every innovation as a toilsome trouble, every social advance as a first step toward revolution, and that they may absolutely refuse to move at all for fear of being carried off their feet. The prospect really does frighten me that they finally may become so engrossed in a cowardly love of immediate pleasures that their interest in their own future and in that of their descendants may vanish, and that they may prefer tamely to follow the course of their destiny rather than make a sudden energetic effort necessary to set things right.
> —Alexis de Tocqueville, *Democracy in America*

CONTENTS

PREFACE

By the time he finished writing *Democracy in America* in 1839 Tocqueville's view of the future of democracy, especially its American version, had grown dim. By the 1850s, toward the end of his life, his hopes for America's prospects had become even darker. Why had his once guarded hopefulness faded into pessimism?

While writing *Democracy in America* he had gradually noted certain qualities inherent in democratic culture and especially American culture—its refusal to acknowledge limits and its tendency to excess—that he feared would in the long run undermine the strengths of mind and character needed to maintain liberty and a truly democratic politics. These weaknesses he discussed in the second volume of *Democracy in America*, his remarkable exploration of the inner life of democracy that was in effect a second journey to America. (Tocqueville's ideas about democratic culture and politics are discussed mainly in part IV of this book, especially in chapters 7–9.) Even before 1839 he had noted a strain of violence and lawlessness in American life, both of which by the 1850s were fueling the increasingly violent struggle over slavery as well as the Republic's chaotic economic life. (His thoughts about the growing violence and lawlessness of American life are discussed in chapter 10 of part I and throughout part IV of this book.) These developments further darkened his already dim view of the prospects for the Republic of Liberty he had hoped would disprove the claim of the autocratic powers of Europe that democracy was bound to fail.

This book is a study of the character and thought of Alexis de Tocqueville. Its aim is to see how his life helps to illuminate the meaning and the art of *Democracy in America* and account for his growing pessimism about the

American future. It is a thematic biography that moves from topic to topic, each chapter exploring an aspect of his life and thought. Each chapter is in effect an essay that can stand on its own, but all are linked and present a full portrait of Tocqueville, a narrative of his life, and a fuller understanding of his ever-relevant book. Since Tocqueville the man usually disappears in discussions of his ideas, I have sought to bring him as vividly to life as I can, believing that his ideas and his literary art cannot be fully understood apart from the man.

We are living in the Age of Tocqueville. After a long period of relative obscurity (following his death in 1859) during which he enjoyed the esteem mostly of scholars and intellectuals, his repute began in mid-twentieth century to rise until he has now become a world figure, something of a modern prophet. *Democracy in America* (1835, 1840) has acquired the uncanny glamour of scripture, cited by all who wish to say something about democracy and its prospects or America and its destiny. It is as if his name were invoked to legitimate arguments by laying on some of the aura of moral earnestness and historical clairvoyance that is part of his peculiar grace. He has even given his name to a school of historical and political thought: Tocquevillian now stands alongside Marxian as shorthand for a mode of social analysis. Unfortunately, the complexity of his analysis has made it possible for ideologues of every persuasion to shanghai him in support of arguments he would have rejected as simplistic.

Even though the inadequacies of *Democracy in America* are now well known, Tocqueville's authority remains undiminished because of the continuing pertinence of the questions he asked and the issues he underscored. So do some central aspects of his analysis of the democratic political system in the United States, for example, the crucial importance of local government and of the right of association. His views about the power and hazards of public opinion in democratic societies have found new meaning in the era of mass culture. His analysis of the alienating, socially isolating tendencies of the hyperindividualism bred by democracy is ever more relevant as the United States plunges on into the historically unprecedented affluence which has become a hothouse of dreamy individual utopias. No one has better analyzed the many paradoxes of American culture.

In our time what has become especially relevant in Tocqueville's work is his analysis of the relationship of culture to politics, his insight into the qualities of democratic culture and their *political* consequences. He was right about the strengths of democratic culture, such as the participatory enthusiasm it nurtures and its success in increasing the general competence and political savoir-faire of the American people (in this respect he called the Americans "the most enlightened in the world"), but he was also prescient about the moral and intellectual weaknesses of that culture. His ideas about how those weaknesses would develop in the future, especially when combined with the passion for acquisition and the affluence likely to be produced by dynamic egalitarianism, now seem prophetic. He would not be surprised to find that democratic America had become a self-indulgent society in which instant self-gratification, an over-whelming quest for comfort and security, and carelessness about the future were its dominant traits—a society that might ultimately consume itself. He would not be surprised to find a culture in which everything is commodified and monetized, including the past and even religion, that lacks a sense of limits, and that nourishes the belief that identities can be discarded, remade, and transformed. In effect he foresaw the birth of a born-again culture, an everything-is-possible culture with an insatiable thirst for the New. "Every day in America is new," he wrote, not with Emersonian enthusiasm but with astonishment and dismay.

Tocqueville was apprehensive about the American Dream—not the quest for individual freedom but its unrestrained pursuit, which he thought would produce a society of self-regarding, alienated individuals with a weakened sense of the common good, less and less able to distinguish between dream and reality, between the virtual and the real. He saw the beginnings of a culture of anxiety and anger produced by expectations that could not be met. He pointed ahead to the development of a culture of illusion, entertainment, and specta-cle, one in which even politics would become carnival. It would be a culture of excess that increasingly lacked the restraints and the understanding that make men free. He would have found the economic collapse of 2008 the result of the fantastic the-sky's-the-limit element in American culture, its thoughtlessness about the future, its disregard for rules and moral bounds, its passionate con-sumerism and single-minded pursuit of wealth. It would also remind him of his own devastating experience of the wildness of American economic life. Having invested in American railroad bonds, he lost heavily, perhaps one-quarter of his investments, in the collapses of 1837 and 1857. "Ces voleurs de banquiers" was his pithy judgment. He had been a victim of an early incarnation of the "bankster."

If it were possible to ask Tocqueville what he thought the major problem facing American democracy and freedom now is, he would say that it lies in cultural weaknesses and confusions intrinsic to the American character and the American Dream (about which he was deeply skeptical) as well as in certain tendencies inherent in any democratic culture. Why he would say so is what I have sought to explain.

Would Tocqueville's pessimism have been moderated by the extraordinary election in 2008 of Barack Hussein Obama to the presidency of the American Republic, a man whose moral and intellectual qualities fulfill what he looked for in his Ideal Legislator? Would President Obama's call for a new realism in American expectations, for what in effect would be the transformation of a culture with fantastic notions of what is possible, have much relieved his doubts? How would he interpret "Yes We Can"? What would he have to say about the chastening message of Obama's Inaugural Address? Surely he would have been impressed by evidence of advances toward equality in a multicultural, multiethnic society as well as by the continuing vociferous defense of liberty and rights endangered by war, preparation for war, and the subsequent increase in the powers of government, a danger he had much to say about in *Democracy in America*.

Perhaps the election of 2008 would have somewhat revived his hopes that with strength of will and character a nation might transcend its limits and weaknesses. But the current political and cultural disarray of American life would only corroborate his analysis of the disintegrative tendencies inherent in democratic culture. There is much in his character that suggests he would at best have remained caught in the doubt that seemed to be his fate.

Tocqueville's biography is essential to understanding *Democracy in America*. I have sought to link his social and political thought as well as his judgments about history, literature and religion, vocation and friendship to his uncertain sense of identity and to his quest to locate himself in society and history. *Democracy in America* is crucially informed by Tocqueville's struggle to make sense of and to reintegrate the shattered world into which he was born and in which he always felt displaced. In effect he created a History that was a context for his personal drama. He was a protagonist in all his books. He believed that history had made his class and his family superfluous and that it threatened to do the same to him. This was a fate he would not accept. His profound need for personal independence in every aspect of his life as a means of escaping the grasp of history and of becoming his own master explains much about his thought and art. In a sense it is illuminating to read his book as a bildungsroman in which he transforms what began as a fact-finding expedition, an adventure, and also a flight from political difficulties and personal anguish into a historical and sociological study that was on some level a search for himself.

Tocqueville's interpreters have often tied themselves in knots trying to understand him too much on the level of ideas, but it has remained notoriously difficult to make him coherent. Far more than occasional contradictions and illogic in his thinking, the problem lies in the unresolved issues of identity that underlay much of what he said and wrote and created the ambiguities, ambivalences, and tentativeness that have often puzzled his interpreters and have led to the view that there were many Tocquevilles. But there was one Tocqueville. His contemporaries knew him as a sharply defined personality, yet they also found him puzzling and were often baffled by what seemed to be his excessive need for independence.

The same is true of many mysteries and questions about this driven man. To understand his uncertainty about his identity sheds light on his confusions about the aristocracy and makes it easier to grasp the tentativeness and contradictions of his moderate progressive liberalism. It helps explain the extent to which he masked his indebtedness to other writers, especially historians, exceeding even the careless citation practices of his time. He hid important borrowings and failed to mention the names of historians and scholars whose work he had relied on or been influenced by. In my study of Tocqueville's intellectual life it has proven difficult to know what he read, even to know what he knew and when he knew it. It would appear, on reading Tocqueville, that he had thought through everything himself and had pulled his work like a golden thread from his head. It was enormously important to him to appear not only independent but also original, that is, self-generated.

To know the whole Tocqueville is to understand how his uncertainty about identity accounts for his thoroughgoing skepticism. To what should he commit himself? He longed for belief and certainty, but for many reasons, including his relentless rationality, these always lay beyond his reach. He was never able to escape the doubt, rooted in his self-doubt, which he regarded as the plague of his life. His urgently felt need to define his identity and to free himself from social and political definition makes it easier to understand his constant insistence on independence.

Ultimately, to know the whole man is to see how deeply his judgments about all social and political issues as well as about history, literature, and religion were moral. And it was his sense of the moral shortcomings of American culture that accounts in large measure for the growing pessimism of *Democracy in America*.

To understand the various ways in which Tocqueville's self-imagination—his powerful sense of displacement, his dream of the redemptive role he hoped to play in French political life, and his powerfully critical responses to the newly dominant bourgeois culture of his time—shaped all his work is to read *Democracy in America* in an unexpected light. To do so makes it easier to understand the complexities and apparent shifts in his thought as well the tentativeness that is another quality of his mind. His ideas are sometimes examined as if they were Revelation—the thoughts of St. Alexis—or as if he were simply a mind. His America was in fact a place in his mind: it was the creation of a complicated imagination that was deeply preoccupied as much with questions about himself and his personal destiny as with the new world of democracy. He traveled through America sometimes open-eyed but often with his gaze turned inward on France, with a distressing sense of his displacement, and with questions about where he belonged in the new world of democracy.

I have also sought to read *Democracy in America* not only as a work that is at once a sociological, political, and philosophical study, but also as a work of literary art and to see this aspect of the book in the man. Tocqueville's true vocation was not political but as a writer and as a sociopolitical philosopher. He ruefully came to understand this after his political career was ended in 1851 by the advent of Napoleon III's Second Empire. To examine *Democracy in America* as a work of literary art and to see how it was shaped by Tocqueville's literary and personal imagination is to bring more sharply into focus certain aspects of the book too easily overlooked, for example, its dramatic qualities and strategies, the personal turmoil that occasionally bursts through its orderly, classically structured prose, its dialogic tensions and subtextual intellectual struggles such as that about doubt and belief. *Democracy in America* is a dramatic work, a modern morality play. To read it thus, as the work of the whole man, and to place it in the various intellectual contexts of his life is to experience more consciously some of the qualities that continue to make it a compelling book into this second century of its life. *Democracy in America* can be read as a revelation of Tocqueville's inner life as well as a work of literature and a book of ideas.

My major aim has been to explore Tocqueville's ideas about the two great questions that preoccupied him as he visited the United States and as he wrote *Democracy in America*. The first and most important was how democratic culture would affect democratic political life and individual freedom. The second was the question of what kind of society would be possible in the onrushing age of individualism and multiplicity. What new social contract might take the place of the one now canceled?

Though writing about an America that has largely vanished and before the technological revolutions that have created modern mass society, Tocqueville remarkably managed to see what America would become. His accomplishment is as much a triumph of theory as it is a result of his observations of early nineteenth-century American culture and his forebodings about tendencies of middle-class French culture in his time. His increasingly bleak view was also shaped by his ironic view of human rationality and aspiration and by his melancholy sense of the impermanance of human accomplishment, the fragility of human dreams. *Democracy in America* begins with a vision of the traces of past civilizations whose ruined monuments could still be found in the most fertile regions of America.

What Tocqueville foresaw as possibly the greatest hazard looming for democracy was how the culture bound to develop in a free, energetic, egalitarian society could weaken political democracy and subvert liberty. In America he had witnessed the culture of "whirl is King": a culture that was constantly changing, experimental, intensely materialistic, and radically individualistic, a culture that promised permanent instability and normlessness.

Tocqueville's deepening apprehensions about the prospects for democracy are clearly related to his view that the central impulses of democratic culture, that is, its chronic excessiveness, its disregard for limits, its present-mindedness, its loss of a sense of order and form, would too much weaken the moral and intellectual strengths he believed democracy and freedom require to flourish. Such weaknesses would make a democratic people psychologically and culturally vulnerable to management and manipulation by a despotic state. The benevolent despotism he summons up in the second volume of *Democracy in America* would encourage the people's willingness to surrender freedom for the sake of peace, security, and comfort.

In many ways, his forebodings are being borne out, certainly in the United States, red-hot incubator and marketplace of democratic culture where barely restrained individual freedom and what Tocqueville called a "trading taste" for ideas and cultural products have created a dynamic culture of the always new, a culture that leaves the past behind in a kind of flotsam and jetsam wake. Modern democratic culture in the United States is now dominated by an increasingly ill-informed and manipulated (and one might also say a willingly gullible and misled) mass opinion and taste. It is a culture of entertainment and trivial pursuits, a culture shaped by a cynical dumbing down by political and commercial interests, lulled by the Orwellian euphemisms of public discourse, weakened intellectually by an education that does not encourage critical powers and independent thought. Americans are befuddled by the substitution of slogans for complex ideas, suspicious of individuals who challenge the status quo and threaten to disrupt the single-minded pursuit of well-being and comfort. Oddly, all this is despite the fact that the United States, thanks to its extraordinary colleges, universities, professional schools, research institutions, and dedicated laboratories, has a great many exceptionally well educated men and women and a brilliant professional class, undoubtedly the largest, in comparison to the general population, in human history. However, the gradual softening of the general intellectual culture continues to weaken the society and make it more and more resemble that soft-willed, comfort-seeking society of easily led ruminants Tocqueville feared he saw lying ahead in the democratic future. President Jimmy Carter learned to his great cost the dangers of warning Americans about their character-softening addiction to comfort and consumption. The occasion of his famous speech of 1977 was the energy crisis of that moment: Carter said that the crisis was really a "test of the American character"; that Americans had to stop identifying well-being with consumption; and that they had to make sacrifices for the sake of future generations. He warned that they were living in a dream world and had to wake up to reality. He knew *Democracy in America* and no doubt had read the chapters in which Tocqueville writes of his fears for a people "so entranced by a contemptible love of present pleasures that their interest in their own future and the future of their offspring might disappear." Carter lost the presidency in 1980 to Ronald Reagan for many reasons, but one of them was that he had challenged Americans to wake up from their dream life. They responded by voting for the Great American Dreamer.

In the darkest and most despairing chapter of *Democracy in America*, "Why Great Revolutions Will Become Rare," Tocqueville wrote,

> When I see property becoming so mobile, and love of property so restless and ardent, I cannot overcome my fear that men may come to the point of look-ing upon every new theory as a danger, every innovation as a vexing distur-bance, and every sign of social progress as a first step toward revolution, and that they may refuse to change altogether lest they be induced to change more than they wish. I tremble, I confess, that they might eventually allow themselves to become so entranced by a contemptible love of present plea-sures that their interest in their own future and the future of their offspring might disappear, and that they might choose to acquiesce in their fate with-out offering any resistance rather than make a sudden and energetic effort to set it right.

What Tocqueville feared was not just a softening of will but also the domi-nant intellectual and cultural tendencies of democratic culture that he thought would lead to a kind of intellectual laxness and a tendency to self-deception in the common culture. There is little that would have surprised Tocqueville about the readiness with which Americans have increasingly lived in the fantasy world created by modern mass media, deceiving themselves about their true condition and ignoring the reality-based complexities of their lives. Just as he well understood at the dawn of the modern American capitalist–industrialist system the spirit that would drive the machine once it was built, so too he clearly saw the utopian impulses in American culture. These have been given full rein by the astonishing power of modern technology, managed by mass media, to create an alternative world, a virtual reality, which has become a utopian fulfillment even for those who suffer and who are far from enjoying the American promise.

Many of his observations remain startlingly pertinent and cast brilliant light on contemporary American culture and politics. In this, he stands alongside his contemporary and friend John Stuart Mill as a prophet of the major issues of modern democratic politics, above all the increasingly central issue: how to create and maintain an informed, discerning, critical, engaged people and a responsible, courageous, honest leadership. On this score, Americans are losing ground.

An equally profound question Tocqueville confronts in *Democracy in America* is the question intensely debated at the start of the modern era, that of how society will be possible when all the ancient and traditional ligaments of social order, already greatly weakened, will have vanished. How will community be possible, what will hold human beings together, in the age of democracy? What will replace old forms of the social contract? Here too America was a testing ground. This great question lies behind all of Tocqueville's writing about democracy and politics. The problem of society had become, by Tocqueville's time, a matter of intense concern, provoking a great variety of critiques, strategies, and utopian proposals, especially in France. The age was felt by all, as Mill noted, to be a time of transition between the old order and a new one not yet defined or understood. The overwhelming sense that the West was in the midst of a radical social transformation is the context for Tocqueville's social thought, made poignant by his personal dilemma. His views about what it is that divides and also about what might yet continue to bind a society of culturally deracinated, exuberant, striving individualists who believe that all is possible, that happiness is their right and their destiny, and whose social imaginations and sympathies have been weakened by the extraordinary mobility of modern life uncannily say much about the United States in the first decades of the twenty-first century, a society seething with aggressively self-centered individuals and interest groups (which behave like individuals). It is a far more diverse, unsettled, and bizarre society than the one he encountered in 1831 in the midst of the age of Andrew Jackson. What indeed can prevent this potentially explosive society from becoming a social supernova? Will it develop a sense of the common good? (I consider Tocqueville's reflections on these issues in part IV.)

A few other prefatory remarks are needed here, starting with comments on the book's structure. Part I, mainly biographical, offers a portrait of Tocqueville's thought and character. Part II is more specifically focused on his political thought and career; III deals with the genesis and writing of *Democracy in America* and with its literary and intellectual aspects; IV focuses on his first responses to the politics and culture of the United States and how his initial views were suppressed, modified, and developed by the time he finished writing *Democracy in America*. Each part consists of chapters concerned with a specific aspect of Tocqueville's life and thought, and each chapter begins with a précis meant to serve as a summary guide to what follows.

The literature on Tocqueville is now immense and growing almost exponentially. It would require a great deal of specialized study simply to keep up with it. Much of it consists of commentary on commentary: a lengthening, complex debate about his ideas, most of which is useful and engaging but often loses sight of the man and what he initially said. My work has been informed by the best contemporary writing on Tocqueville and on the history of his time. I am much beholden to several outstanding studies, but I have not spent much time participating in the debates among Tocqueville scholars and have instead focused on connecting the man with his ideas. Tocqueville's ideas had blood in them. Hence my book is very heavily based on his own writing, not only his major works and political papers but also, especially, his voluminous correspondence, and on what he says about himself. His letters constitute a chronicle of his life: they are a passionate, revealing commentary on his political, literary, and personal struggles. Taken together they make a full, candid self-portrait. Without making this book an anthology, I have quoted Tocqueville liberally because I have thought it important for the reader to hear his voice (its complex tone, which one hears even in translation) as much as possible. The whole person comes through no matter what he is talking about. Thus I have occasionally included rather long passages from his letters and his political writings and speeches. I hope the reader will not skip over these but read them carefully and savor them. I have also wanted to make sure that I have said as little as possible that was not warranted, with perhaps a little defensible spin, by what he said himself, especially about himself.

In an era in which people have become skeptical about self-presentation and about ostensible meanings, it may seem innocent always to take Tocqueville's professions at face value, but though he may not have fully or even well understood himself, he was as candid and as honest as he could be, of that I am certain. He was not a self-conscious prevaricator or a dissimulator, or a Rousseauian performer and provocateur.

I also read subtexts when that seems called for, not as elaborately and as schematically as Hayden White does in his stimulating chapters on Tocqueville in *Metahistory*, but to illuminate other ways in which Tocqueville was engaged by the America he was experiencing. I do so especially during his more literary moments when his fantasy, that instrument of our inner broodings, was fully in flight, as for example in the astonishing first chapter of *Democracy in America*, at first glance simply a bird's-eye view of the terrain of North America but on closer reading quite unmistakably a philosophical and moral meditation on the meaning of America and a soliloquy on History and historical change; or in his various accounts of his adventures in the wilderness, in which at first silent religious and philosophical preoccupations become explicit as subsequent versions of those adventures become more elaborate; or in his encounters with American Indians, who are wonderfully transformed in his writing from debauched beggars to proud aristocrats as he moves west in the United States and then as he steps back to consider the whole sweep and meaning of the history of the native Americans. I also listen with a third ear when he writes about himself either to construct a persona to aid his own self-understanding or, as was usually the case, to report to others on his obsessive and pitiless (his term) journey down (the direction he always said his self-searching took) into the melancholy, dim depth of his psyche. There are also many passages in his more formal writing in which deeper, unarticulated sentiments and anxieties well up to tinge his thought, and I try to give these fuller voice.

It may appear that I present too static a picture of Tocqueville's mind, and that my focus on him is so intense that I scant his engagement with the intellectual issues of his time as well as what he shared of the general sensibility and preoccupations of his generation. As for the last matter, I do note how remarkably much Tocqueville, despite his intellectual and psychological isolation, shared with the generation analyzed by Alan Spitzer in *The French Generation of 1820*. Perhaps *separateness* would be a better way to put it: for though he no doubt, one must assume, was thoroughly familiar with the intellectual developments and issues of his time, it is remarkable how seldom or how cursorily he mentions them and how infrequently he writes about the intellectual and literary achievements of his contemporaries, even those he frequently encountered. In his correspondence he rarely or only briefly mentions, with the exception of François Guizot, any of the historians, for example, Augustin Thierry, who were so productive during the booming historical renaissance of early nineteenth-century France. He appears not to have been much engaged by the historiographical issues that concerned his contemporaries. If he read or knew the work of any of the outstanding legal historians of his time or read any of the major journals of legal historiography like *Themis*, one simply does not know. He seems to have been indifferent to all such matters, even though his imagination was powerfully historical, and he did read histories, especially English historians like George Grote and Thomas Macaulay. Charles de Rémusat, an astute literary and political man who sat in the Chamber of Deputies with Tocqueville and knew him well, once wrote that Tocqueville's ideas seemed to have been self-generated, in that he paid no attention to what his contemporaries and colleagues said and wrote. This view of Tocqueville has been repeated by many, including the foremost student of Tocqueville's work in the twentieth century, the historian François Furet. Doris Goldstein, in her illuminating study of Tocqueville's religious thought *Trial of Faith*, argues that the study of external influences and contemporary discourse, at least as far as religious thought and attitudes are concerned, is not the best way to get at his religious ideas: "One discovers that to a far greater extent than might be expected in dealing with an *erudit* . . . [his ideas were] derived from a few premises, barely articulated but strongly felt, and ultimately from his own temperament and personality. . . . These premises . . . underwent no perceptible degree of change throughout his life." Françoise Mélonio has said of Tocqueville's mind that it was "profound but narrow." He was intent on exploring his own perceptions and ideas and was aiming at complete originality.

To me it has seemed that there was something terribly isolated about Tocqueville, and that there was little that was truly tentative or exploratory about his thinking even when he professed to be on a voyage of discovery. And it has seemed to me that his basic ideas changed very little despite his broadening experience and knowledge. Even with regard to his American experience there was little change to the intellectual baggage he carried to the United States. His life was an immense intellectual journey, but it was a journey within, an exhaustive exploration of the implications of his ideas and insights. Late in life (in 1855) he wrote to his oldest friend and soul mate Louis de Kergorlay, "There is hardly one of the views of our youth the justice of which the passage of time has not demonstrated, and if I had illusions at 25 I have completely conserved them at 50." He made the same proud, defiant declaration to Gustave de Beaumont: "As for most of my ideas, my sentiments and even my actions, I would change nothing. I would note also how little I have changed my views of men in general during this time."

There is something about his worldview that tempts one to believe he had been born with it. In writing about Tocqueville and his ideas, I have therefore felt free to draw on what he had to say on a particular topic without much regard for when he said it, assuming that his accumulated utterances reveal not a mind that changed much or was capable of it but a fixed point of view. It has been rather like putting together an elaborate jigsaw puzzle or painting a landscape in which all that changed was the light. His ideas about America did develop, but the development was something like connecting the dots. What seems to be development in Tocqueville is often a relentless opening up of his ideas, a kind of Cartesian social science. It is quite striking that his remarks about American life and culture and politics become less empirical as *Democracy in America* unfolds and increasingly the logical extensions of his "idées mères"—hence the notable deductive quality of his book. Even before he had set foot in the United States he said that while everyone was talking about America, no one really knew it. How could he have known that? Did he think so because he sensed that somehow he already knew it?

What did change were his views about the prospects for democracy and what lay ahead for America, changes based on how he drew out the implications of his theory of cultural and political change as he applied them to his observations of American politics and culture and to his experience of French democratic politics and culture.

I have not hesitated to point out Tocqueville's shortcomings and failures of perception and understanding, but it has not been my primary intent to do so. I have tried to bring him to life, to present the whole man along with his ideas, and to understand him: to recover him, as it were, from his academification, which has been brilliantly done. His bicentennial was well celebrated in scholarly conferences in France and in the United States, but there was little public debate about his ideas. I have tried to see how his ideas were rooted in his life. That they also were in part shaped by the contradictions and confusions of that life does not diminish what is true and useful in them.

I have to admit that there are aspects of Tocqueville's politics and character I have found less than admirable. He and I would almost always have taken opposite sides in debates concerning issues of social justice. But I continue to admire strongly his personal and intellectual courage and his great literary accomplishment. I have preferred to focus on what is insightful and still useful and provocative in his thought, especially concerning American culture and politics. He raises questions about the future of democratic culture and politics that call for the most serious and urgent thought—that is, if you believe, as Tocqueville wanted to believe, that Americans still have a chance, even if only slim one, to determine their destiny and to make democracy work to the b⟨ of all.

ACKNOWLEDGMENTS

This book was read at many stages of its writing by Paul Gagnon, whose great knowledge of the history of France and whose unsparing criticism, never muted by the sentiments of friendship, immensely improved it. In many ways he embodied Tocqueville's spirit. Others also have helped, advised, and encouraged me along the way, but I owe special thanks to Roger Emerson, Richard Sewell, and Eugenia Kaledin, who read major portions of the manuscript and offered incisive, knowledgeable, and sometimes stern critiques. Thanks also to Emily Dalgarno, who read a portion of the manuscript with a discerning literary eye. I owe thanks also to Georges Borchardt, who is as much a critic as he is a literary agent. I am grateful to my colleague John Dower for having prompted me to take Tocqueville out of the desk drawer in which he had been languishing for too many years as I sought to teach history in a way that illuminates the conditions and choices that make us a more, or a less, free and just society. Such was Tocqueville's aim for the study of history, as it was for Paul Gagnon, to whom this book is rightly dedicated.

I want to thank Lawrence Kenney, whose meticulous, thoughtful editing made this a better book. I am also obliged to the anonymous readers whose thorough reports to Yale University Press offered helpful detailed criticism and suggestions.

In the front ranks of the many whose help has been invaluable are the librarians at the Massachusetts Institute of Technology, especially Theresa Tobin of the Humanities Library as well as the staff of the Dewey Library. The history department at MIT provided a stimulating and supportive community of scholars for almost four decades as well as many diverting challenges—among them how to teach history to young men and women whose time and passions were devoted to the study of science and engineering as well as the compelling challenge of teaching those aspects of American history and culture that promised to shed light on the many issues and crises of the turbulent last decades of the twentieth century and the beginning of ours.

My sons, Nicholas and Jonathan, and my daughter, Elizabeth, have sustained me with their unfailing love. My grandchildren, Luke, Clay, Nina, Noelle, Sarah, and Toby—and now Austin—give me hope for the future. They have also given me much present joy. Christine Horigan, Jon Dohlin, and Catherine Claman have offered both constant friendship and affection. I want to express my gratitude to Eugenia Kaledin for many years of support, challenge, intellectual stimulation, and adventure. I am grateful also to Emily Dalgarno for her sustaining friendship. The friendship and good conversation for a half century of Richard Sewell and Roger Emerson have been an anchor against the winds of change. I owe thanks to Drs. Michael Kane and Peter Jenney, whose skillful and thoughtful care over many decades has returned me to the battle again and again. I want to thank Patricia LeDoux, whose help and cheer at a crucial time have been important, and Myron Vernick, for constant help and moral support. Laura Davulis and Ann-Marie Imbornoni of the Yale University Press have skillfully and cheerfully guided the book every step of the way.

Introduction: A Brief Life of Alexis de Tocqueville

Alexis de Tocqueville's family, on both sides from the old French nobility, was shattered by the Revolution of 1789. Some, among them his mother's parents, her sister and brother-in-law, and her illustrious grandfather Guillaume-Chrétien de Lamoignon de Malesherbes, had been executed during the Terror of 1793–94. Some had been driven into exile or had sought rural sanctuary. Many had been traumatized; while imprisoned in the Conciergerie in 1794, his father, Hervé de Tocqueville, then twenty-two, had turned white-haired; and his mother, Louise, also twenty-two, fell into the melancholy that eventually submerged her completely. They had barely avoided the guillotine thanks to the execution of Robespierre and the end of the bloody Terror. It is small wonder that, brought up on stories of such misery and terror, Alexis was full of anxieties and self-doubt, torn by conflicts and confusions about his society, and afflicted with a constant sense of menace and a strongly felt need to isolate himself to secure his endangered self.

Though during Napoleon's empire the old social order seemed largely intact, its legal basis had been abolished, and the authority and power of the old aristocracy had begun to fade, to be somewhat revived during the Bourbon Restoration of 1814–30, after which it was eclipsed by a triumphant bourgeoisie. Tocqueville was born into an ultraroyalist noble family and was brought up among the ultraroyalist nobility. If he eventually abandoned the deeply engrained legitimism of his family and in other ways distanced himself from his class, he never fully lost a certain aristocratic anger at a bourgeoisie that he felt had become a pseudoaristocracy and that had seized—usurped, was more like it—the power and authority of the nobility but did not have what he thought were the qualities that had made the old aristocracy fit to govern: a certain disdain for material values, a tradition of public service, a sense of duty to France, and a readiness to serve it selflessly, even to the sacrifice of life.

All through his life the earthquake that had struck France in 1789 would continue to shake and transform the political and social landscape, sometimes violently. It is easy to understand why Tocqueville, heir to all the values, the culture, and the manners of a world that was disappearing, yet convinced also that the past was indeed past and that change and reform were not only inevitable but also necessary, would be a seriously conflicted individual, so full of uncertainties and ambivalences that his sense of identity sometimes wavered. Choices that once would usually have been prescribed for someone of his class were now difficult and complicated. So situated between the past and the onrushing future, he sought to reunite the two. Where and to what did he belong, and what was his duty? what was the relevance of the past to him, and what were his obligations to it? what role was he to play, what role could he play, in the new France? He was constantly aware of a radical disharmony between his sentiments and his realistic acceptance of the new order of things as well as between his instinctive conservatism and the enlightenment liberalism that was also his heritage. John Stuart Mill believed that it was all the ambivalences felt by Tocqueville as a man suspended between past and present—his divided consciousness, as it were—that made him so acute a critic of the tendencies and shifting values of the great transitional era they both struggled to understand and to guide. He was a displaced person in his time and country, lacking a settled sense of self, full of anxieties and confusions, constantly preoccupied by questions about his identity, troubled by a sense of personal and historical jeopardy. Where did he belong?

My book is a portrait of the inner man, of his self-understanding and his character, his views about the major intellectual and cultural issues of his time and about his place in a society in which he felt increasingly alien. The facts of his life and the events of his time nevertheless structure my account of his inner life. Apart from various studies of the history and culture of eighteenth- and nineteenth-century France as well as interpretations of Tocqueville's thought, I have especially relied on André Jardin's authoritative, detailed, and scrupulous biography, Tocqueville's only complete biography until the recent publication of Hugh Brogan's fine *Tocqueville: A Life*, which appeared after this book had been substantially completed. Tocqueville's splendidly annotated correspondence, published in the *Oeuvres Complètes*, has been essential.

Alexis-Charles-Henri-Clérel de Tocqueville was born in Paris on July 24, 1805, the youngest and third son of Hervé-Louis-François-Jean-Bonaventure Clérel de Tocqueville (1772–1856) and Louise-Madeleine Le Peletier de Rosanbo

(1772–1836), both of ancient noble families. Until the collapse of Napoleon's empire in 1815 he was raised at home by his ultraroyalist parents, whose loyalty to the Bourbons and to the divine-right monarchy never wavered through the Revolution (1789–1805), Napoleon's empire (1805–15), the Bourbon Restoration (1815–30), and the bourgeois monarchy of Louis-Philippe (1830–48).

Tocqueville was educated by the archconservative family priest and tutor as well as by private tutors until he entered the lycée in Metz in 1821, when he was sixteen. There, he received a quite traditional and conservative education, the curriculum (stressing Latin and rhetoric) having been redesigned to stifle liberal tendencies in the first postrevolutionary generation. When he was young he lived much of the time with his father, who traveled from one appointment to another as prefect, that is, royally appointed agent of royal power, in various départements, mostly in the north and west of France; his invalid mother remained in Paris. Hervé de Tocqueville's constant struggle to defend and extend royal power and prerogative wherever he served, by fair means and foul, along with his efforts to collaborate with local bourgeois interests to improve the economic infrastructure as well as the educational system of whatever département he was governing provided the young Tocqueville with a thorough political education. As his father's occasional secretary, he must have gained insight into the nitty-gritty of the continuing, often bitter struggles between royal–noble and bourgeois interests. The example of the father's commanding energy and decisiveness as well as his pragmatic, moderately liberal approach to needed economic and social reforms despite his unbending legitimism surely shaped the son.

Nevertheless, by his midtwenties Tocqueville's politics had become considerably more moderate and liberal than his father's. His political liberation, or independence, especially in view of the continuing powerful conservatism of his family, relatives, and most of his intimate friends, is both notable and difficult to account for. It is the first of the puzzles around which this biographical sketch is organized. It was so striking and unexpected a transformation that he was constantly called upon to explain himself and defend his politics to conservative relatives and friends. Though he remained determined to be as independent as possible and with considerable courage succeeded in doing so, he always explained himself thoroughly and with great delicacy as well as with obvious anxiety, fearing the loss of their affection.

Little in his education accounts for this liberal transformation or for his subsequent striking political and intellectual independence. His education all the way through law school in Paris from 1824 to 1826 was quite conservative, the legal curriculum having been purged of any liberal tendencies when it became suspected that law schools had served as recruiting grounds for radical societies like the Carbonari. From the start, Tocqueville seems always to have been inclined to think for himself and to follow his own path. In some ways he was prompted to do so by the family priest and tutor, a deeply conservative man who urged him to choose a career that would use his mind. His deeply felt need to secure a self endangered by onrushing history nurtured his critical independence. It may be that a precocious reading of the French philosophes, whose works he found in his father's prefectorial library, undermined not only his inherited religious faith but his ascribed political faith as well by inducing critical habits of mind and distrust of arbitrary authority. From then on, the notion of a fixed order of things existed only as a shadowy, though tenacious, assumption in his mind. And though his wife, Marie (Mary Mottley before their marriage in 1835), whom he met in Versailles in 1828, is usually not thought to have had much, if any, influence on his intellectual and political ideas (his family evidently thought otherwise and blamed her for his shift toward liberalism) other than to strengthen his fragile self-confidence, it is difficult to believe that this intelligent, morally stern, middle-class Englishwoman did not in some way bring a broader, an English, sense of justice into his life, conventional though she was in many ways.

His intense encounter in 1831–32 with the culture and politics of the dazzling New Republic across the Atlantic unquestionably encouraged the liberal tendencies of his mind, though it did not have much effect on his practice of politics. His American experience did not transform him into a convinced democrat, but it loosened the hold of traditional assumptions and expectations on him. His journey to America touched him with a cautious sense of possibility and of the transformability of societies, politics, and culture. It also made it clearer to him that France badly lacked what made a republic possible: widespread political enlightenment acquired through experience, the vital tradition of self-governance, and a vigorous regard for rights, all of which greatly impressed him about democratic America.

It was during Tocqueville's brief, inauspicious legal career in 1827–32, served unhappily as an unsalaried, apprentice assistant investigative judge in Versailles passed over for promotion, that he went on his much-celebrated journey with Gustave de Beaumont to the United States, the fruit of which was *Democracy in America*. Here is a second puzzle about Tocqueville, much vexed by subsequent students of Tocqueville's thought. What were the sources of this startling, influential book? out of what did it grow? The journey to America, undertaken to study the American prison system, had been concocted largely as an escape from vocational, personal, and political miseries, though Tocqueville and

Beaumont also had in mind a Big Book about the amazing New World republic that had long fascinated France as an augury of the future. At first they had thought of a collaborative work, but they eventually abandoned that idea. Whatever their intentions, they took their officially approved but unpaid mission, for which they had been granted a leave of absence, quite seriously and after much diligent fieldwork eventually produced a well-read, influential book, *On the Penitentiary System of the United States* (1833). How and why did the journey also produce *Democracy in America*? Apart from the intention of writing something large about America as well as examining close-up the still poorly understood democratic transformation of society and politics, he had only a vague idea of what his big book would be about. In fact, as late as 1839 he confessed that he still was unclear about what he was aiming at even as he drew close to finishing it.

The years from late 1833 through 1839 were largely devoted to the writing of *Democracy in America*—the first volume of which appeared early in 1835, the second early in 1840—to preparing for his political career, and then to campaigning for office. His sudden distinction and notoriety along with his ambitious campaigning swept him into France's most notable intellectual institutions, the Académie des sciences morales et politiques in 1838 and—crowning glory—the august Académie française in 1841. After inheriting, in 1836, the ancient family seat of Tocqueville and its dilapidated chateau on the Cotentin peninsula in Normandy, he set about establishing a political base to prepare for his long-dreamt-of political career. No less important at this time was his marriage to Mary Mottley, after seven years of hesitant courtship complicated by the strong opposition of family and friends to what they felt was a misalliance. Her companionship and her political intelligence were important sources of strength for his political career. After failing in his first campaign, in 1837, for a seat in the Chamber of Deputies, he was elected in 1839 and was victorious in every subsequent election, against sometimes unscrupulous opposition and despite continuing local antipathy toward the old nobility. He won decisively even after the suffrage had been considerably broadened in 1848 but refused to run again after Louis Napoleon's coup of December 1851 brought an end to the Second Republic (1848–51). It may be too much to call his political career a disaster, though in a way it was; to pursue it, he put his work as historian and writer, his true calling, on hold for nearly fifteen years. In terms of his dreams, ambitions, and practical goals it was a failure, with many bitter disappointments and only a few achievements and moments of intellectual distinction to show for his efforts.

Considering his thoroughly informed knowledge of the political situation in France and his deep understanding of the dynamics of the still-unresolved

French Revolution, how does one account for his political ineffectiveness? — a third puzzle. Certainly not much was possible during the politically sluggish years of the July Monarchy, dominated by struggles for power and reward between interests almost monolithic in their likeness, when only republican and radical threats frightened bourgeois politicos out of their inertia. Tocqueville endlessly lamented the poverty of the political life of his time.

One might rightly say that the intellectual in politics is almost always an onlooker and a commentator — essentially Tocqueville's fate. But there was more to his failure than that. Adolphe Thiers, whom he detested, and the historian François Guizot, prime minister from 1840 to 1848, also were intellectuals. Both were members of the Académie française, as were a number of other deputies. Thiers and Guizot, however, were shrewd politicos. For all its sluggishness, the Chamber of Deputies during Tocqueville's years was home to many men of considerable accomplishment, some of them distinguished. Tocqueville's brooding, passionate temperament, his intense, sometimes paralyzing, self-consciousness, his aloof and condescending personal bearing, his inhibitions as an orator, and his high-minded refusal to play the game of political bargaining to ensure modest advance toward political goals, as well as his much-noted iciness, conspired to make him ineffective even if he was in some ways admired. He had few political skills and certainly had not returned from the United States prepared to play the democratic political game.

He did valuable work in the 1840s as rapporteur for several significant parliamentary committees (on the abolition of slavery, on prison reform, and on the Algerian question), and gave a number of astute, admired, and widely read speeches which instructed many but moved few. Otherwise he accomplished little. Perhaps his greatest failure, apart from not fulfilling his impossible dream of bringing about a moral revival in politics, was his inability to create a party of idealistic young liberals free of the corruptions of ambition who would work toward an orderly, that is, a nonrevolutionary, nonradical, progressivism. He was less interested in any agenda of progressive change than in the restoration of a principled politics informed by great passions, though he did have a number of realistic, useful, moderate reforms in mind.

The last seven years of his life, following his retreat from politics in 1852, was a time of increasing despair, resulting from the relentless decline of his health and his view that France had once again surrendered its freedom to a Bonaparte in exchange for order, security, and material progress. He was also depressed by the increasing disorder and violence of American life and by the possibility that the intensifying struggle over slavery might destroy the Republic, still the best hope for democracy and liberty. Nevertheless, during this time of deepening shadows he summoned the physical and intellectual strength to write *L'Ancien Régime et la Révolution*, his second great literary accomplishment, published in 1856 to great acclaim in France and in England as well. Like *Democracy in America*, it has been enduringly influential. After its publication he undertook a last journey (1857) to England—a melancholy, lonely month even though he was wined and dined and was able to carry on his research in the rich collections in various British archives of material on the French Revolution, preparing the second volume of *L'Ancien Régime*, which he did not live to complete. The chapters he had completed and the abundant notes and commentaries he had accumulated were eventually edited and published after his death by Beaumont, despite his wishes that nothing of his writing, if imperfect and incomplete, be made public but should remain in his archive for scholars to consult.

Tocqueville's rapidly failing health—he had long suffered from a complex of problems mostly pulmonary and gastric—forced him and Marie in late 1858 to seek sanctuary in Cannes, in balmy Provence, where he was visited seriatim by only a few friends and by his brothers. It was to no avail; he died there in April of 1859, in fact voiceless, for his illness had almost completely deprived him of the power to speak. He was buried at Tocqueville in Normandy. Marie died in 1864, as did Beaumont.

Part I

—————————◆◆◆—————————

TRIPLE-ALIENATED MAN

Identity in a Time of Historical Transition

All through Tocqueville's life the earthquake that had struck France in 1789 would continue to shake and transform the social and political landscape, sometimes violently. It is easy to understand why he, though heir to all the values, culture, and manners of world that was fast disappearing, yet convinced that change and reform were inevitable and necessary and that he too would have to change if he were to lead an effective political life, would be a seriously conflicted individual. Hovering between the old order and the new, he was in many ways a displaced person in his time and country, constantly preoccupied by questions about his identity and troubled by a sense of personal and historical jeopardy. This and the following chapters deal with the various strategies by which he tried to resolve the issue of identity and how his uncertainties and ambivalences shaped every aspect of his life and thought. This was the Tocqueville who wrote *Democracy in America*, which is equally a subject of this book.

Alexis de Tocqueville liked to describe himself as a man above parties, politics, and prejudice, committed neither to the vanishing old order of things nor to the emerging new one, neither to aristocracy nor to democracy. He was, he said, an impartial, objective analyst seeking only to understand the inexorable drift of history and to provide moral guidance to democracy, which without doubt owned the future. He was not a democrat but bowed before its inevitability and sought to instruct it. His only passion was "the love of liberty and of human dignity."

In a long letter of 1837 to his English translator and friend Henry Reeve he commented on those critics of *Democracy in America* (including Reeve) who had found him partial to democracy:

> I am always seen as a party man, and I am not at all; I am given passions and I have only convictions, or rather I have only one passion, the love of liberty and of human dignity. All forms of government are, to my eyes, only more or

less perfect means for achieving this holy and legitimate passion. Alternatively, I am given democratic or aristocratic prejudices; perhaps I would have had one or the other had I been born in another century and in another country. But the accident of my birth has made it easy for me to resist one or the other. I came into the world at the end of a long revolution which, after having destroyed the old order had not yet created anything lasting. The aristocracy was already dead when I began life, and democracy did not yet exist. My instincts could not lead me blindly to one or the other. I have lived in a country which for forty years has tried a bit of everything without definitively settling on anything; I am therefore not facile with political illusions. Belonging myself to the ancient aristocracy of my country, I have neither jealousy for nor hatred of it; and that aristocracy having been destroyed, I do not any longer have a love for it because one can be attached strongly only to that which is alive. I am therefore close enough to it to know it well, distant enough to judge it without attachment. I can say as much about democracy. No family memory, no personal interest gives me a natural or expedient leaning toward democracy. I have not been injured by it; I have no motive either to love it or hate it, independently of those furnished by my Reason. In a word, I am in such equilibrium between the past and the future that I do not feel myself naturally and instinctively attracted to one or the other, and I have not needed a great effort calmly to observe both sides.[1]

If he claimed to view the past and the future calmly and rationally, he still regarded the present with great anguish.

What is notable about this denial of bias is not the familiar authorial claim of objectivity, but Tocqueville's view of himself as a man who has risen above history and politics, free to look coolly both back and ahead in time, with no natural inclination toward any political or social system. He saw himself as an unprejudiced man, totally disengaged, purely rational. He attributes his serene impartiality to "la hazard de ma naissance" (on July 29, 1805) at a moment of historical disjunction when the old, prerevolutionary order lay in ruins while the new one had not yet clearly emerged. His sociopolitical self-levitation was thus, according to Tocqueville, not simply a rational act, but also, more impressively, a matter of destiny as well. For someone whose stormy historical moment had shattered the ancient social and political order and compelled all thoughtful Frenchmen and women to deal with the most profound questions of allegiance and identity, this was either a spectacular fantasy or a remarkable act of self-deception.

He had come, he said, from "l'ancienne aristocratie" of France and felt neither hatred nor jealousy for it. Since this aristocracy had been destroyed he felt no "amour naturel" for it, for one could be attached only to "that which is living," an untruth he should have felt the moment he said it. He was close enough to the aristocracy, he said, to know it well, distant enough to judge it without passion. As for "la démocratie," since he had no inherited or natural inclination toward it and had never been personally injured by it, another patent untruth, he had no reason either to hate it or love it except for "those furnished by my Reason." He saw himself, in effect, as a being of pure reason, poised above history, "in such equilibrium between the past and the future" that he felt naturally and instinctively attached to neither. Anyone undertaking a comprehensive analysis of democracy should have a better understanding of himself than Tocqueville offers here.

This persona was not the creation of a momentary flight of literary fantasy but was central to Tocqueville's self-understanding, curiously existing, as we will see, with another view of himself as a melancholy man tormented by self-doubt, ambition, turbulent passions and by the dream, which he called his "beau rêve," of helping France escape the moral morass into which it was sinking. In many ways throughout his life he described himself as an autonomous man free to choose his commitments rationally. He persistently saw himself as an independent being committed only to certain moral principles and to the cause of humanity—and to France as well but to a France that was as much moral idea as it was a homeland. He was able to sustain this fantasy because he was a man without an unquestioned sense of identity.

He described himself in almost exactly the same terms at yet another significant moment, thirteen years later in 1850, when the idea of *L'Ancien Régime* began to take shape: "I am proud enough to believe that I am better suited than anyone else to bring to such a subject great freedom of mind and to speak without passion and without reticence about men and events. As for individuals, though they are still among us today I assuredly do not feel either love or hate for them, and as for formal matters such as constitutions, laws, dynasties, classes, they do not have, so to speak, I won't say worth but existence in my eyes independent of their consequences. I have no traditions, I have no cause at all if it isn't that of liberty and human dignity."[2] This self-assessment as a man of imperturbable objectivity and equanimity of spirit was written at precisely the same time he was writing his *Recollections* (his memoir of the Revolution of 1848, not intended for publication), a book full of passionate, sometimes angry judgments and bristling with acid comments about nearly everyone, most notably with contempt for a bourgeoisie that through its timidity, fearfulness, and crassly self-centered politics was primarily responsible, he thought, for the catastrophe of 1848. The mask of dispassionate judgment had slipped at that moment.

Tocqueville was far from being the serenely rational, detached, suprahistorical figure that remained his ideal persona. He in fact felt all the contradictions and conflicts of the historical moment, was borne along by all the turbulent psychological undercurrents of his culture. The deeper sense of self that emerges from his writing reveals not the rational self-mastery he claimed but great uncertainty and ambivalence, sentiments which drove him toward both a painfully intense self-consciousness and a sense of alienation. His ideal self-image reflects not an achieved detachment but an effort to transcend the inner contradictions he experienced as a historical being. The notions of willfully detaching oneself from class and past and of being guided solely by reason, moral principle, and one's independent judgment remind one, in fact, of a cultural fantasy Tocqueville himself criticized: the dream of the philosophes of the eighteenth century that they could simply jettison their "ridiculous ramshackle institutions, survivals of an earlier age," and "remold society on entirely new lines traced . . . in the sole light of reason."[3] It reminds one as well of the equally ahistorical view of the romantics that truth was to be found by searching one's heart and exploring one's sensibility.

To see oneself as a rational construct, as an idea, or similarly as an autonomous source of truth, is itself a dramatic refusal of history and at the same time an effort to control it. The psychological function of such a view of identity, especially for someone whose sense of identity and place had been so profoundly dislocated by shocking historical and family discontinuities, was to preserve a feeling of personal integrity and significance. In this light, Tocqueville's passionate attachment to the idea of freedom, which he saw as the indispensable source of individual creativity, power, and moral worth, takes on additional meaning. Living on the level of abstract reason, one can remain master of one's fate. The self-fashioned man escapes the judgment of history.

Another, very different version of identity emerges from Tocqueville's more intimate writings, especially his immense correspondence. This other Tocqueville reflects the multiple ambivalences, the puzzlements about identity, the deep sense of displacement—all the varied psychological anxieties of his era—and the strategies of imagination he fashioned to deal with them. These made him a peculiarly sensitive and adept analyst of the democratic psyche, free but uprooted and anxious. His unremitting fascination with his own emotional life made him an acute observer of the inner lives of others and of the psychic dramas of private and public life. When, in *Democracy in America*, he describes the social atomization that has occurred in democratic America and discusses the inevitable decline of class awareness and loyalty, the weakening and even the disintegration of all connections and loyalties beyond those to family and friends, and the keen sense of isolation and alienation that is part of the inner life of individualism, Tocqueville is drawing on his own experiences as well as relying on observations of American social life. Social and cultural analysis has become subtle autobiography.

In a way he was, surprisingly, "democratic man" himself, even though obviously aristocratic to his bones. In his own life he experienced the great shift of affect, analyzed in *Democracy in America*, from the larger world of class, institutions, and politics—from the great community—to the world of intimate personal relations, which increasingly bore the greatest meaning for him. While he spoke and wrote about the importance of resurrecting the public man by recreating a sense of civic responsibility and of identity with the larger community, that is, the nation, his own strongest emotional life increasingly shifted into a small world of intimate relations. He found much to praise in the warmer, more natural social and family relationships he observed in democratic America.

If his imagination was too tightly constrained by the weight of experience and responsibility in France, it found necessary freedom in America, where it could escape the personal burden of the past as well as the impinging complexities of familiar circumstances. Little wonder that his journey to America was so exuberant a time for him: he was borne along by a surging energy that at times even the more robust Beaumont could not match. He had found himself. In the literal New World his imagination found radical release. America was the scene where he could most freely work out the meaning of his personal experience and trace his destiny, not literally but metaphorically and in terms of a deeper self-feeling and understanding. America gave him a means of self-definition, especially in the dark last decade of his life when, an exile in his own country, he felt he was once again in the "dark forests of America" in which, when he was there in 1831, a year after the July Revolution of 1830, he had powerfully reexperienced the emotions he had felt—he could almost smell the gunpowder—at that turning point of his life

The land of self-made men anxiously experiencing all the psychological effects of radical cultural and historical change was for him a simpler, clearer, yet more fully developed version of his own reality. He was so imaginative an analyst of the anxieties, the fantasies, the uncertainties, and the modes of self-perception of men experiencing all the disconnections of modernity, men for whom society and culture had to be found or made, because he had experienced all these tensions so fully and so self-consciously himself. America was the terrain on which his own inner drama was played out and where his social and political imagination found fullest scope.

The new society provided Tocqueville with the remarkable example of uprooted individuals who, like him, had experienced shocking social and historical discontinuities and were refashioning their identities, as it were rationally deciding who they were to be. It was not long after he had arrived in the United States that he started to call the Americans a rational, coldly logical people who by an extraordinary exercise of reason and choice were demonstrating a freedom so profound that it was difficult for him to grasp its meaning fully. When he arrived and for months after that he was persuaded that race, or physiognomy, as he called it, was destiny and that the imprint of race and culture on the individual was so deep that whatever the circumstances there was no escaping heritage. A Frenchman in the New World would remain French, an Englishman, English. By the end of his visit, however, in late 1831 early 1832, he had come to believe that the Americans were exercising the most remarkable freedom of all: they were transcending the destinies fixed for them by race and history and had learned how to transform themselves. He had encountered one manifestation of the born-again culture.

In astonishment Tocqueville had written that "every generation of Americans is new." The spectacle of radical self-transformation, of rational self-shaping, and of liberation from the grasp of history profoundly impressed him, though he recognized that the loss of one's inherited culture, one's roots, was costly, and he traced some of the consequences of that loss in various aspects of the new American character. His musings about the tenacity of what people now call ethnic and national culture and his recognition of the emergence of an American character run through all his American notebooks.

His gradual recognition of the extraordinary and quite unexpected freedom enjoyed by the Americans, who were becoming, as Hector St. John de Crèvecoeur a half century before him had thought, new men in a new world, conceivably had personal and moral meaning for him. Had his American experience suggested to him that he too might rise above history and decide which aspects of his culture and his past would be integral to his identity? The long funk he evidently fell into on his return to France suggests that he had been changed in ways that made it difficult for him to feel at home and that he had begun to think of and to feel about himself differently.

In calling Tocqueville a triple-alienated man, I mean first that he was self-alienated. He was beside himself. His self-alienation was an expression of the intellectual's inescapable burden of self-consciousness, in which both the mind and the emotions become the objects of relentless, close observation. For Tocqueville, such extreme awareness of the self was especially difficult because other aspects of his identity were also problematic. His constant self-scrutiny became a source of great unease and anguish. That he was never able to resolve his dilemmas frequently plunged him into melancholy. Tellingly, he called his relentless self-probing unpitying. He suffered also from a perpetual inner tension resulting from his chronic skeptical undercutting of his will to believe — of his religious craving. His skepticism allowed him only the vaguest and least satisfying of affirmations.

He was also socially alienated in that he persistently felt there was no place for him in French society. He was a man with strong class feelings, but he also felt that he had to distance himself from his birthright, ascribed class. He was almost anthropological in his detachment from his society, observing it with that sense of strangeness that can make even familiar behavior and customs seem new. Though he had been invested with the riches of French culture, he had been brought up largely in privileged isolation and did not have an intimate knowledge of social worlds beyond his noble milieu. Perhaps it would be better to say, to continue the analogy, that he became, as anthropologist, a participant-observer.

He was also alienated from the intellectual life and the culture of his time, whether the newly hegemonic bourgeois culture or the lively romantic and bohemian cultures of midcentury France so plainly linked to the former. If he was a romantic in spite of himself and at the same time a philosophe, he was also deeply critical of both intellectual movements. If he thought he was defining a new political science and claimed that it was an empirical science, he refused finally to be confined to any system, especially if its fundamental assumptions were determinist. He insisted on leaving room in his science for the unpredictable and for the force of belief, or faith. The new science he had in mind had to account for moral facts as well as the empirical.

He was a disharmonious man, full of disunited passions and impulses. Yet he was also profoundly French: as one contemporary put it, he was, in the new age of democracy, an almost perfect French *gentilhomme*.[4]

At the same time, he was also very much a man of his time and his culture. He was an intensely ambitious writer and politician, ironically bourgeois in his entrepreneurial energy and shrewdness in promoting his literary and political careers. In both he managed his "image" with great care. He craved influence and was warned by his chosen mentor, Pierre-Paul Royer-Collard, about being too eager a courtier of public opinion. He believed firmly in the supremacy of European civilization and justified its imperial conquests as the historically fated imposition of superior order and culture on less advanced peoples. He was not as alienated as his bohemian and reactionary contemporaries were from the customs and rituals of his society or from the emerging middle-class culture of nineteenth-century France. It may be something of a strain to see a member of the Académie française, that holy circle of cultural deities, as a significantly alienated figure. But one can adhere to cultural norms, deliver acceptable cultural messages, and clothe oneself in the appropriate cultural style and nonetheless see oneself as a marginal man. Yet even his apparent cultural normality and conventionality poignantly accent his sense of isolation and marginality. He was on the edge in many ways.

Tocqueville never knew quite where he belonged and increasingly felt alone until, by the time he was in his late forties (he died when he was fifty-four, in 1859), he could say that he was attached to life by only one person, his wife. His transcendental Self was a work of his imagination. His isolation was the felt experience of his historical self.

2

CLASS: BETWEEN TWO WORLDS

Class had provided the fundamental frame for every aspect of French life before the Revolution, and it continued to do so in the era of democracy. It was the major means of self-definition even in the age of choice, when prescriptive identities were rapidly fading. Tocqueville still applied the old template of class to all his political and social thought, but his views of the aristocracy—and to a lesser degree of the bourgeoisie—were deeply affected by his own identity uncertainties and ambivalences. He distanced himself from both the aristocracy and the bourgeoisie and was sharply critical of both. Though he remained an aristocrat to the bone, he was a man without a class.

If there is illusion in Tocqueville's self-imagination as a man above it all, there is some truth to it as well. With regard to that fundamental context of self-definition, class, he was detached not only from the middle classes, for the culture of which he felt deep repugnance, but also in some ways from his own class, which he persistently thought of as historically dead and no longer consequential in the life of France. His critical intellect distanced him from all classes, communities, and groups. He was self-consciously a man apart, a man whose social identity and social place were constantly problematic. At times he seems to have felt socially and intellectually more at ease in England than in France. England was a society in which a still-flourishing aristocracy had played the progressive and unifying role that the impotent, doomed French aristocracy should have played. Henry James thought Tocqueville was the "most Anglican" of all Frenchmen.[1] As he slipped into deeper isolation in the 1850s, he seemed increasingly to identify with the English aristocracy, attempting even to refashion his estate at Tocqueville into something resembling an English country manor complete with sheep park.

Though 1789 had thrown the old social order into disarray and it wasn't yet clear what new social structure or social categories would replace the old, the old social template still very much shaped everyone's thought, Tocqueville's as well. As late as the 1850s, well after he had begun to think about the culture and politics of individualism, he would write (in the notes to *L'Ancien Régime*) that history is interested only in classes and not in individuals.[2] At the same time, classes seem to have acquired as much moral as social meaning for him. If the idea of class remained analytically useful it was because it was as much a way of thinking about the moral qualities of a social group, a community or a society, as it was a tool of social and economic analysis. In *Democracy in America* he dramatically structures his argument by contrasting the moral and cultural values of aristocracy and democracy. In that book, what had once been the struggle of classes for privilege becomes a question of what qualities will prevail in a society in which the old class structure has disappeared—or, as in the case of the United States, had had only an ephemeral existence. What had been class struggle—and what for Marx powerfully remained a matter of class struggle—for Tocqueville became competing systems of values between which he suggests a people must choose. For Tocqueville, this cultural–moral struggle was more important than the class struggle for economic and political power: he believed that the future of liberty depended on its outcome.

Tocqueville's contempt for the bourgeoisie—expressed in many ways, including even a refusal to see his middle-class colleagues in the Chamber of Deputies as more than two-dimensional figures, to remember their names, or to acknowledge what they had written (Beaumont pleaded with him to treat them decently at least for the sake of political effectiveness)—was rarely a matter of personal repugnance.[3] It was far more a matter of moral judgment leveled against a class, or rather against certain values and behaviors.

His sweeping judgment in the *Recollections* about the reckless, self-centered behavior of a smug, acquisitive bourgeoisie that had disastrously ignored the well-being of the nation was certainly not a nuanced account that recognized differences among individuals, but was, rather, a condemnation of values easily attributed to a class long associated with aggressive striving, social climbing, and a preoccupation with material values. He loathed the bourgeoisie because it lacked the virtues he believed had animated the old aristocracy. His romance of his class's past deeply shaped his thinking about his own time.[4]

Even worse, the ascendant bourgeoisie was pushing the old aristocracy aside. A bourgeois had replaced his father as prefect of the Oise-et-Seine. Indeed, virtually all, some 87 percent, of the aristocratic prefects serving during the Restoration had been replaced by middle-class bureaucrats after 1830.[5] Was Tocqueville as rational about social and political change as he claimed to be? or so detached from the fate of his class that he was above being angered by this affront to his father and by this usurpation of dignity? His aristocratic sense of honor was keen and easily provoked, leading even to a duel (then forbidden by law) and later to a challenge, from which the offender backed down.[6]

Tocqueville's loathing of the bourgeoisie, not always expressed discreetly or subtly, was one aspect of his conviction that France was lost in a moral swamp. The bourgeoisie was to him much less a social group or a system of economic power than a moral condition. In all that he wrote about it he rarely distinguishes between diverse elements of that many-leveled class. Petty ambition had replaced great and noble aspiration, the limited contractual obligation of the businessman had replaced noble honor, self-seeking had replaced noble willingness to serve. Even the American middle class, which he grudgingly admitted was proof that the middle classes could govern effectively, lacked true virtue. It was true virtue that Tocqueville thought it was his mission to restore to political life in France.

He could not divest himself of his heritage and of his class feelings as a man of aristocratic sensibility and values. Thus his relationship to his class and to his heritage was considerably more complicated than he usually described it to be. He was decidedly ambivalent about the aristocracy and his relationship to it. Such conflicted feelings thread through his life and remained a source of the acute social awareness he brought to bear on his analysis of social relations in the new world of democracy.

One may imagine that the sadness from which he chronically suffered stemmed in part from his sense of belonging to a class that was, as he believed, doomed and whose suffering was vividly and painfully felt by his family. In France, he wrote John Stuart Mill, "l'égalité" had triumphed irrevocably, while the aristocracy was "in the dust."[7] The sense of loss that filled his life and that is so strong a tone in all his writing, as well as his continual striving to relocate himself in history and even his occasional passionate and exaggerated patriotism, are all expressions of his feeling that the revolutionary rupture of history and the death of old France had left him marooned in an alien world—a view of himself he expressed in many ways and at many times.

Claiming that he could dispassionately assess democracy because it had done him no harm was psychologically untrue. The Revolution had been cruel to his family. His mother's grandfather, father, mother, a sister and brother-in-law had been executed in 1793; his father, Comte Hervé de Tocqueville, who barely escaped revolutionary justice, had turned white-haired during his imprisonment in the Conciergerie in 1793–94 and had continued all his life to nap between three and four in the afternoon, the hour when prisoners usually were led away to the guillotine. His mother, shattered by the catastrophe of 1793, had never fully recovered her equilibrium and seems to have spent the rest of her life withdrawn in a state of tearful piety. It is impossible to believe that Tocqueville was not deeply and permanently affected by her melancholy. In fact he did attribute his own enduring and sometimes severe depression in part to hers.[8]

He could happily recall the wit and éclat of the society in which he grew up, which he constantly contrasted with the heavy, monochromatic, money-preoccupied, *terre-à-terre* culture of the bourgeoisie dominant during his maturity, yet he also strongly felt the underlying sadness of a class that knew its way of life was vanishing. Though he had been strongly critical of Charles X's reactionary policies, he had wept to watch the last Bourbon king flee Versailles, the emblems of the royal coach shrouded. He never lost his capacity for a kind of sentimental devotion to "le race royal," which he justified as a basis for disinterested service to the state. He admired the English for perpetuating such loyalty, dead among the young of France and fading from the world. He recalled this sentiment, a vestige of feudal sensibility, with a certain "douceur de souvenir."[9]

Nor would the world permit him to forget he was an aristocrat. In Normandy, his family's ancestral home, where he finally settled in 1836 after having inherited Tocqueville, one of the family estates, he was constantly reminded that he was a member of the nobility. "Point de nobles!" had been the cry raised against him in his first campaign for a seat in the Chamber of Deputies (1837); and next to his chateau stood the ruins of a stone pigeon tower, sacked during the Revolution as a symbol of feudal privilege. Yet there were also evidences of continuing local fidelity and trust. These always moved him and gratified him, as his due. Though he learned, reluctantly, to campaign for office in democratic style by venturing into what must have seemed to him the French version of the stumps, he liked to claim that the office had sought him and that he was admired and trusted because of his quality. Yet even in the midst of the most strenuous political campaigns, during which he carefully managed his candidacy, shook many Norman hands, speechified, and endangered his fragile health on the essential circuit of dinners, he would play the role of seigneur when the opportunity presented itself.[10]

He had in fact chosen to live at Tocqueville because it connected him to his ancestry, yet characteristically his feeling about such filiopiety was ambivalent. "Here I am finally at Tocqueville," he wrote Beaumont, "in the ancient ruins of my family. I have in view, a league away, the port from which William sailed to conquer England. I am surrounded by Normans whose names one can find on the list of the conquerors. All this, I must confess to you, thrills my heart with a foolish pride and sometimes gives rise to stirrings of childish enthusiasm for which I am later ashamed."[11]

Nonetheless, sentiment and pride dominated; Tocqueville was for him a place where the past lived vividly: "This place is full of memories for me: I live here in a world of shadows."[12] "I live here in a world of shadows" might have served as his motto. Throughout his life but especially in the 1850s, when he finally found himself living in profound isolation on every level, he increasingly took pleasure in tangible emblems of the past and spent much to restore and improve his estate at Tocqueville.

The emblems of the past also awoke a sense of loss and regret. His descriptions of the ruined monuments of the nobility are sometimes melodramatic. At Tourlaville, another family estate around which he guided Henry Reeve on a tour of noble ruins, the cannons placed around the chateau by his aristocratic military forebears were "useful now only for tying up the animals";[13] and Chamarande, an old chateau where he once rented an apartment near Paris, had declined from great glory:

> The place we live in recalls the entire history of the French aristocracy. The chateau is immense, and was built by LeNôtre in the time of Louis XIV. It was the seat of an immense family. . . . The chateau and its park have fallen into the hands of a merchant from Paris who has not demolished it because it is made of brick and the debris would be worth nothing. But he rents apartments in it. He has cut down the ancient trees [les arbres seculaires] and grows potatoes in the paths. Statues of the goddesses of mythology still stand in a field of cabbages. One stubs one's feet on broken and overturned marble benches. Running water meant to make waterfalls now turns a mill for grain. Gone is the splendor of a privileged leisure class, but it is not yet the picture of a productive industrial economy. It is the vision of the ravages of revolutions: a melancholy tableau unknown to people who should sometimes think about it.[14]

At Tocqueville he took increasing pleasure in playing the role of benevolent patron and "father" of his people, seeking not to eradicate distinctions between classes but to rebuild links of sentiment and obligation between them. He attempted, that is, in his own life and milieu to re-create the harmony he believed, despite the evidence to the contrary provided by the class savagery of the Revolution, had once existed between the noblesse and the people. He sought to take precisely those steps that would, in his view, have saved the aristocracy, which by the eighteenth century had lost itself in proud isolation. Indeed, while he gradually retreated to the countryside from the city for many reasons, one of them no doubt was his awareness, vividly expressed in *L'Ancien Régime*, that the old nobility had lost its influence and power, in fact its understanding of what had happened to France and its people when it abandoned the countryside for Paris and lives of empty display. Though he did not use his title and abandoned the few remaining symbols of old seigneurial privilege, "transforming the former family patriciate into a truly democratic patronage," as his first modern biographer, Antoine Redier, put it, he nonetheless continued to play the role of seigneur. He founded a school for boys and girls in the hamlet of Tocqueville; reinstituted the formal ceremonies of almsgiving at Tocqueville; and assisted at Sunday Mass and at Vespers in the church at Saint-Pierre Église, a gesture of noblesse oblige rather than of true piety, for he was not a believing and practicing Catholic but felt it imperative to set an example for the people, who, he believed, needed faith and dogmatic belief (a point he emphasizes in *Democracy in America*).

After his first election to the Chamber of Deputies in 1839 (he had been defeated in 1837), a crowd escorted him back to his chateau "with a great roar of acclaim," and he briefly spoke to the crowd "from a window above." The moment was a fine blend of the democratic and the seigneurial.[15] A similar moment occurred in 1848 as he accompanied the newly enfranchised voters of Tocqueville to the polls in Valognes. The procession paused on a hilltop on the way to the town to receive instructions from Tocqueville on proper behavior, such as not stopping in taverns, after which he took his place "in the ranks."[16]

One suspects that whatever pleasure he took in local politics from his long service on the Conseil de la Manche resulted more from the deference he was shown and from his felt obligations as a local notable than from the work of local governance, which he usually found tedious and too concerned with patronage and local interests and passions. As a matter of principle, however, he acknowledged its importance: the experience and practice of self-governance in the United States had shown him how vital it was in a democratic society. And it was with an aristocratic independence that he represented the people of his arrondissement in the Chamber of Deputies, in a style that can only be called paternal. Occasionally he acknowledged that it was also his duty to serve their local interests, which he sometimes did not fully understand until instructed. But he always had something much greater in mind, namely, the good of the nation.[17]

Late in life he more deeply identified with his forebears, finding satisfaction not only in proofs of continuity, but also in the evidence he discovered "of the sweet and paternal relationships that still existed in those days between upper and lower classes, relationships that have been replaced so widely by feelings of jealousy, distrust and often hatred."[18] Though he knew that the old aristocratic social order could not be revived and was critical of those who sought to do so, it was the aristocratic past, not the democratic future, that embodied the ideals and values he most cherished.

Tocqueville's self-characterization as a man poised between two worlds, between two ideal types of social order, judiciously examining the advantages and disadvantages of each, was not wholly or even largely true, though John Stuart Mill thought that Tocqueville was thereby able to understand both. For him, democracy was *faute de mieux*. One may to some degree accept his frequently repeated claim that he wrote as a "friend of democracy" anxious to help guide it to its best possible fulfillment and prevent it from taking a debased form, but even the best democratic scenario fell short of his ideal, which was essentially aristocratic in every respect, whether it was a question of social structure or inner spirit. The analytic device that structures the whole of *Democracy in America*—Tocqueville's constant contrasting of aristocratic and democratic social structures, intellectual styles, manners, political systems, and values while asking readers to choose between the two—finally serves to illuminate his own values and preferences, which he fails to disguise despite his effort to appear neutral. What he saw as essential to the aristocratic spirit at its best and to aristocratic societies was a greater spirituality, a more intense ardor for liberty, tighter social bonds, a broader tolerance for diversity, bolder aspiration, a sharper sense of honor, a more intense and disinterested intellectuality, a stronger sense of form, greater social harmony, and a stronger sense of community than was likely to be found in the age of democracy. These were qualities he highly prized that he saw fading from contemporary life. He was candid about the characteristic failings of aristocracy and fair enough in his assessment of the creative potential of democratic culture; indeed his overall judgment of democratic culture and society is complex and full of subtleties. But it is not possible to read *Democracy in America* carefully without recognizing that Tocqueville's heart was attached to a past, to a system of values, and to an ideal of order that were all vanishing. In accepting democracy he was making the best of what was inevitable, not embracing what he preferred.

Yet his understanding of the history of the French aristocracy was surprisingly ill-informed, and his account of its past condition, especially in the eighteenth century, was full of contradictions. His understanding of the culture of the French aristocracy was intimate. In that he was brought up sequestered in the world of a wounded nobility mourning its losses and lamenting its eclipse, his sensibility was deeply rooted in the past. One of the sad ironies of his life is that in many respects he represented a final, autumnal fulfillment of the aristocratic ideal even as he declared that the aristocracy was finished. He was, it was noted, a perfect example of "a nobleman of the ancien régime." Yet as François

Furet, one of Tocqueville's most insightful modern interpreters, pointed out in a harsh critique of *L'Ancien Régime*, his picture of the eighteenth-century French aristocracy was full of inaccuracies, a result of an inadequate understanding of the structure of eighteenth-century French society; and his sketch of the development of the nobility from the feudal era on was more fable than informed history. "The French nobility," Furet comments, "was never that 'aristocracy' of which Tocqueville dreamed [that is, vigilant, independent protectors of local liberties]."[19] Guizot, Tocqueville's major historical and political antagonist, who saw the feudal aristocracy as villains of violence and chaos, was closer to the truth. Tocqueville's view of the past of the French aristocracy was a mixture of fantasy, nostalgia, historical misunderstanding, and ideology. It was increasingly shaped by his personal resentments, by his dismaying political encounters with the self-aggrandizing bourgeoisie that was now governing France, whom he continued to think of as usurpers, and by his own complicated political ambitions.

His views of the old aristocracy were shaped perhaps most of all by the growing conviction that the loss of aristocratic leadership in the age of democratic ascendancy, the loss, that is, of the independent, courageous, selfless leadership he believed an aristocracy was likely to provide, would prove a disaster.[20] As Tocqueville's thinking about democracy became darker, and as his experience of democratic politics became increasingly dismaying, his views about the old French aristocracy and its virtues became increasingly idealized and semimythical. As his conviction grew that an aristocracy, even a moral aristocracy, was essential to save democracy from its worst instincts (a central theme of the second volume of *Democracy in America*), his thinking about aristocracy at times became even more typological and less historical and particular, a fault for which Mill rebuked him in his first review of *Democracy in America*, reminding Tocqueville that there were many different aristocracies and that specificity was essential in social analysis.[21] Nevertheless, Mill shared Tocqueville's conviction that leadership by an elite of intellect, merit, and virtue would be crucial in the democratic future. For Tocqueville the matter was more complicated than it was for Mill: he never emotionally accepted the demise of the aristocracy. For him the question of finding a functional equivalent of the old aristocracy was in part a way of mourning its loss.

Consequently, what Tocqueville said about the French aristocracy, past and present, was full of contradictions. His ideal view of the prerevolutionary aristocracy's virtues in the long struggle to advance liberty was not only historically confused, it conflicted even with the critical comments he sometimes vented about its decline and failure in the eighteenth century. He thought it had abandoned its historical role and become a caste of irresponsible courtiers. Yet while walking with the English economist and political chronicler William Nassau Senior at the splendid chateau of Azay-le-Rideau, he spoke rhapsodically of the virtues of that irresponsible eighteenth-century aristocracy that were lacking not only in the heavy-footed bourgeoisie but also in the legitimists of his time, who were not the true successors of the old aristocracy: "The legitimists are not their successors either in culture, intellect or force, and consequently in influence. Between them and the bourgeoisie exists a gulf that shows no sign of collapsing. . . . The loss of our aristocracy . . . is a misfortune from which we have not begun to recover."[22] While he celebrated the old aristocracy for the virtues it had once possessed, he quite consciously distanced himself from his class, or from what remained of it in its decayed and toothless condition. He felt as little at home among the demoralized aristocracy as he did among the bourgeoisie, in part for the same reason, a lack of moral compatibility. He refused to be identified with a class that was now in history's dustbin. If the aristocracy would not adjust to the modern world, he at least would refuse to be dragged to the same historical death. Tocqueville's independence also reflected a deep passion for autonomy, an intense personal need to stand alone, and a vigilant jealousy for the integrity of his conscience. He would not be guided by the interests and ideology of a class or by those of a political party, though his aristocratic passions at times ruled his judgment.

Whatever the psychological roots of his persistent quest for autonomy—plausibly an endangered and threatened sense of self enhanced by the constant sight of "noble ruins" and the vague but tangible antiaristocratic menace still in the air—in every aspect of his life Tocqueville displayed an exaggerated, almost pathological concern for his independence. It was a concern so intense, for example, that he refused even to read what his contemporaries had said or were saying about matters about which he was writing, for fear that his judgment would be affected by their opinions or that he would appear to have been influenced by them. While writing *Democracy in America*, he read Pascal, Rousseau, and Machiavelli but nothing new on America.

The same jealous regard for his independence colored his whole political life, all through which he remained a lonely, critical, somewhat Olympian figure. Perhaps he was less isolated in local politics, where the demands of practical politics called for constant personal negotiating, handshaking, fulfilling the duties of a notable, and the setting aside of theory and the grand view. Yet even in local politics he was anxious to avoid any act or gesture that might make it even appear that he wasn't his own man. He believed that his constituents kept returning him to office because they knew he was independent. He worked hard and consciously to cultivate and protect that image. He would not be seen as "ministeriel," a committed vote. But whom did he think he represented?

He seems to have recognized that there was something excessive about his striving for autonomy and purity. While debating whether to accept nomination to the Legion of Honor in 1837, which might appear to be a kind of co-option, he asked his political mentor Royer-Collard if there wasn't something pathological about his drawn-out hesitation and reservations: "Are these the ideas of a malade? Do you see here misplaced pride, too much spirit of independence?"[23]

The same quest for independence appeared in all aspects of his life. At high personal cost he often defied the wishes of his family and the conventions of his class, especially in those decisions in which customary expectations were clear. Perhaps his choice of a judicial career despite some criticism from relatives who reminded him that his ancestors had usually been "gens de l'épée" required little personal struggle. In fact he had briefly tried a military career. Both of his brothers, Hippolyte, the eldest son, and Edouard, the next eldest, and his most intimate friend (and cousin), Louis de Kergorlay, and initially even his father were military men, as had been the towering François René de Chateaubriand. But his politics sometimes painfully divided him from some of his closest friends and from his family. His father and brothers had resigned their administrative and military commissions in 1830, as had Lieutenant Kergorlay, rather than take the required oath of loyalty to Louis-Philippe. Tocqueville took the oath despite pressure from friends and family. "I have finally sworn it," he wrote to Mary Mottley, "my conscience has nothing to reproach me, but I am no less profoundly wounded and I shall number this day among the unhappiest of my life."[24] His act had been coerced—it was the price he paid to keep alive the possibility of effective action in the world. He dreaded the impotent isolation of those who had fallen from history. After this, for a while he could not discuss politics with his deeply conservative, legitimist family, which remained firmly opposed to the July Monarchy.

He constantly feared that politics would destroy some of his friendships, especially with Eugene Stoffels and Kergorlay, both of whom were critical of his liberalism, mild as it was. He struggled not to offend or alienate his revered, old ultraroyalist uncle Louis de Rosanbo, to whom he attempted to explain himself. His correspondence with friends and family and with others as well reveals a touching effort to sustain intimacies or family ties that seemed to him sometimes to bend dangerously under the weight of political disagreement. But he would not abandon his views or mask them.

Tocqueville most dramatically displayed his independence and flouted class expectations when he married Mary Mottley ("Marie"), a middle-class

Englishwoman undistinguished by beauty, wealth, or social status and six years older than he. Ignoring such values, he had chosen her for her moral qualities. From the point of view of his class and of those who believed that his talents promised a brilliant future, the marriage was a misalliance, and he was vigorously advised against it. Here too he resisted family pressures and class expectations and followed his own judgment. Though his family finally accepted the marriage, its effect was to increase the distance between him and his family and friends and to intensify his social isolation, especially as Marie's strangeness, her jealousies, and, easy to imagine, her moral rigidity and hauteur kept the two of them if not isolated then socially remote. One sometimes hears in Tocqueville's letters to his touchy middle-class English wife quiet dismay about familial coolness and obvious relief during those few moments when the strain lessened.

Beaumont felt that Tocqueville's marriage, more than any other act of his life, revealed "the real nature [le fond] of his character." Though the family struggle over the marriage remains discreetly obscure, Beaumont, who himself initially had doubts about it, suggests that it was opposed largely because of Mottley's poverty, an objection he claims Tocqueville could not take seriously precisely because he was so much the aristocrat:

> Although Alexis de Tocqueville understood democratic ideas, he had retained aristocratic values; there is nothing so aristocratic as disdain for money. While well understanding the importance of money as a means of action in life, Alexis de Tocqueville nonetheless found it only of secondary importance. He did not think that one should risk honor and happiness for wealth; and unlike those who in marrying aspire to above all *une bonne affaire*, he followed his good judgment and his pride to marry his reason to his heart. He many times said to the one writing these lines that his marriage, advised against by a number of sages, had been the most sensible act of his life.[25]

Whatever truth there is in Beaumont's view of the matter, what seems most striking about Tocqueville's marriage is not that it showed an aristocratic disdain for money (he showed little such disdain throughout his life), but that it constituted a disregard for all his class norms. Such a marriage must have had many meanings for Tocqueville, who had inherited his class's sensitivity to the slightest nuances of social behavior, especially regarding liaisons. He was always an acute interpreter of social semiotics, one of his great strengths as an observer of American social life. His analyses of the complex symbolism of marriage in his travel notebooks, in *Democracy in America*, and in much of his correspondence, especially of the ways in which marriage illuminates the moral as well as the political condition of society means that his own must have carried a very

complicated burden of meaning for him. One suspects that, apart from its intimate and sexual basis, it was also for Tocqueville a deliberate symbolic and
social gesture. It was an act of self-definition, like his refusal to use his title and
his abandoning of his family's old seigneurial pew in the church at Saint-Pierre
Église. His life was a series of gestures and declarations of independence.
Whatever else it meant to him his marriage was also a social gesture, an act of
reason that distanced him from a dying aristocracy and located him in a realm
of enduring moral values.

    Whatever else united Tocqueville and Mary Mottley, including sexual attrac-
tion, theirs was also a marriage made not in heaven but in that abstract realm of
mind in which he felt most at home. Perhaps it was a marriage of true minds.
The fact that they had no children symbolizes its ideal meaning, though his
letters to Marie suggest that their marriage did not lack for physical intimacy.
He apparently had wanted children, yet even here his desires seemed to be
partly conceptual. To Edouard he wrote about his childlessness this way: "It's
true, my dear friend, that I have a thousand reasons for being contented; for,
independent of all the causes for happiness you have enumerated, there is one
you have not mentioned and that must be added; it is to have found a wife who
suits me the best. I lack a number of things the absence of which would make
most men unhappy and that I would somewhat enjoy: such as great wealth and
even, I confess, children. I would greatly like to have children such as I can
imagine; but I do not have a very keen desire to risk the grand lottery of paternity."[26] Apart from revealing the fact that his brother evidently did not think
Tocqueville's marriage worth mentioning as something to be happy about, what
is remarkable about this fragment of self-revelation is that it points to the degree
to which Tocqueville lived in the realm of the mind. Platonic marriage may be
possible; Platonic children are not. That is not to say the marriage was Platonic.
Tocqueville's letters to Marie throughout their marriage show that for him, at
least, there was also an erotic attachment, which evidently was also a source
of strain since she seems to have been somewhat repressed and prudish enough
to have scratched out passionate and physically suggestive passages in her
husband's letters to her.

    Tocqueville's marriage was a gesture that vividly symbolized his alienation
from his class. He could not have found a more dramatic way of demonstrating
his independence or his determination to save himself from historical irrele-
vance, despite the sad, unforeseen irony of his failure to have children. The
criticism he constantly leveled at the French aristocracy was that it had lost its
will and capacity to govern, refused to adjust to the times, remained socially
isolated and thus had become almost purely ornamental. The same would not

be true of him. What had saved the English aristocracy, he believed, was its flexibility. It was an open class, not a rigidly isolated one, which he mistakenly believed the eighteenth-century French aristocracy had become. Above all, it had continued to govern. It had formed an alliance with the middle class "to protect society and lead it liberally together."[27] The French nobility had by the time of the Revolution abandoned its social and political responsibilities. It had deserted the countryside for the cities, had lost touch with rural France, which Tocqueville thought was the soul of France, and was no longer a credible or effective ruling class. It was a fatal fall that Tocqueville described with regret and bitterness in *L'Ancien Régime*, in 1856, when he himself was suffering political powerlessness and isolation in the early years of Napoleon III's empire.

The old aristocracy, a caricature of a ruling nobility, had preserved, it was true, a gallant willingness to die for France, but this had simply fostered the delusion that military service alone, along with the demonstration of feudal honor, would create power and a raison d'être. "It isn't only through military service that an aristocracy preserves itself," he wrote in 1855; "if that were so, ours would not be in the dust, as it is. For who has less bargained over his life than the aristocrat of France, the lesser as well as the greater, in all times." This truth was borne out by his family history: "My grandfather and my great uncle died in battle or of the wounds they had received. The same was true for their father and grandfather, and there is not one family in the neighborhood that cannot say as much; and yet no trace of their power remains." It had been an aristocracy that "knew how to die, but not how to govern."[28] The English aristocracy had not made the same mistake. It knew how to do both, "which is why it endures, though the climate of this century is not at all favorable to plants of that species."

No one of Tocqueville's intellectual intensity and ambition could have felt at home in a world as frivolous and pointless as that of the nineteenth-century French aristocracy, whatever its graces. He felt estranged from a class that either had become a fashionable and empty haute monde or had maintained a narrow, rigid notion of suitable noble vocations. In this world he knew he was seen as "a sad, bizarre creature who, with no career, writes to kill the time." "People of our class," he wrote Kergorlay, shared the general mistrust of "the life of the mind." His awareness of his oddness fired his need to succeed at his deviant métier: "I feel very strongly that one who lives unlike others must bend all his strength to be more than they or silently conform to conventional standards. Now that my book has almost had the success I would wish, I see that I am allowed peacefully to pursue my own ways without being troubled."[29] The pointless life of social display and gossip that most of his class now led was meaningless to him. His brother Hippolyte's pursuit of happiness in the giddy world of fashion constantly grieved and angered him: "Hippolyte's tastes, and especially those of his wife drift more and more from simple and inexpensive pleasures toward the fashionable, the kind that as you know are the most costly if they weren't also increasingly meaningless and boring."[30] When in 1857 Hippolyte considered selling his Norman estate to buy a "joli chateau" near Paris, "where they can be distracted from morning to night by those they call their friends," Tocqueville blasted the scheme: "Isn't that pitiful? Can one find a better example of human wretchedness and stupidity? I spoke to them about it. At first the husband was enraged but concluded by saying that I was right. The wife assuredly thought nothing about it. Beyond a circle of three or four idiots and as many contemptible bitches who come to tea in Paris every day to gossip and to retail the trivial scandal of the day, there is nothing at all redeeming about it. That has not at all stopped them from becoming devoted to it. As for Hippolyte, it has been a long while since I've seen his spirit so off balance."[31]

Tocqueville's idea of the proper use of a life called for a strenuous and stoic fulfillment of one's talents and duties. He was bound to find the world of wasted privilege doubly repelling, since it encouraged not only a frivolous and futile pursuit of happiness but also irresponsibility. That world in turn saw him as a severe presence. "We live among people who scarcely understand us," he wrote to Kergorlay.[32] Even among those with whom he shared traditions, memories, and a class culture, he strongly felt a certain marginality. He praised the aristocracy for having redeemed itself in some ways from the dissoluteness of its eighteenth-century forebears; in fact he thought, perhaps inconsistently, that in his time it was the least corrupt class in France while "lax morals" had "spread through the middle and lower classes," and thus concluded that democracy ironically seemed to have "improved the moral standards of the aristocracy only." But he was referring, in this passage in *Democracy in America*, to family life, which, while laudable in itself, was also a sign of retreat from the world, a kind of self-immolating walling in.[33] In all its behavior his class seemed to have accepted its impotence and futility, which to Tocqueville was morally repugnant and personally threatening. He was ambitious for a life of effective action and moral influence, if not in politics, then as a writer. He wished to seize history and shape it, not to retreat from it, to lead his society, not live sequestered from it. But the latter was ultimately to be his fate.

His attitude toward the bourgeoisie and its culture was considerably less complicated than his views of the aristocracy. He constantly expressed a repugnance for middle-class values and pretensions. That Parisian merchant who refrained from destroying Chamarande only because he couldn't sell the rubble represented the whole spirit of the class to Tocqueville. His bitter remarks in his

Recollections about the timidity, narrow self-interest, and money-mindedness of the bourgeoisie repeat a refrain that runs through all his writing. It is a judgment that, somewhat muted, also runs throughout *Democracy in America*.

Tocqueville located the major cause of France's political lethargy and moral confusion in the character and spirit of the middle class, which, he said, had dominated France since 1830 as no class had dominated it before. He lay major responsibility for the Revolution of 1848 not on the masses or on the social theorists who had beguiled and misled the people with "false notions of political economy," but on the bourgeoisie, which had so choked and paralyzed political life with its selfish and visionless rule that the eruption had become inevitable. "The great and real cause of the Revolution," he wrote in the *Recollections*, "was the detestable spirit which animated the government during this long reign, a spirit of trickery, of baseness and bribery, which has enervated and degraded the middle classes, destroyed their public spirit, and filled them with a selfishness so blind as to induce them to separate their interests entirely from those of the lower classes whence they sprung."[34]

"The middle classes," he wrote in 1847, "have gradually assumed toward the nation the position of a little aristocracy, and without its higher feelings: one feels shamed of being led by such a vulgar and corrupt aristocracy."[35] Barely masked by this sharp political judgment lay an aristocratic animus against money grubbing, anger about the aristocracy's loss of authority and power, and some of the social rage always expressed by displaced classes. The bourgeoisie was dominated by the spirit of speculation. Getting and spending, comfort and security were its preoccupations, instead of worthy, spiritual goals. Cabbages and potatoes, "chemins-de-fer et la bourse," had replaced national honor and statues of Greek goddesses. The "higher feelings" could not survive in the age of business and industry. "I have insurmountable prejudices against industrial work," he wrote, "even the grandest. I have almost always found that industrial preoccupations exercise an influence which in the long run has not been good on the feelings and on the ideas of those who have devoted themselves to such work."[36]

Even in America, where vast freedom and relatively widespread enlightenment or "enlightened self-interest" somewhat vitiated the worst tendencies of egalitarianism, the middle class's preoccupation with material well-being and money had already debased the culture. Though he admitted that the case of America proved that the middle-class could govern, the Americans' lust for wealth formed the basis of one of his sharpest criticisms of the American character:

> When one considers the chastity of their morals, the simplicity of their manners, their habits of work and the religious and settled spirit which prevails in

the United States, one is tempted to believe that the Americans are a virtuous people; but when one considers the commercial fervor which seems to
devour the whole society, the thirst for gain, the respect for money and the
bad faith in business which appears on every side, one is soon led to think
that this pretended virtue is only the absence of certain vices, and if the
number of human passions seems restricted here, it is because they have
been all absorbed in just one: the love of wealth.[37]

The overwhelming dominance of the middle class in America had many
woeful cultural consequences. It had led to a trivializing of ambition, to a narrowing and a debasing of vision, to a loss of "prévoyance" (the long view), to the
triumph of self-interest as the chief law of politics and of life, and to a rampant
individualism that greatly narrowed social awareness and was steadily leading to
a disastrous social indifference. Its appalling effect on cultural life was spelled
out by Tocqueville in many ways in the second volume of *Democracy in America*.

These consequences of the triumph of the bourgeois spirit in America were
offset to a degree by the impressive development of enlightened self-interest,
which saved the society from the most destructive effects of radical individualism, and by the opening of all aspects of cultural life to the participation of the
many, not simply of a privileged, permanent elite, which at least ensured vitality, if not quality. If bourgeois culture seemed to lower and narrow ambition and
to ground the imagination in a materialist vision of life, it also freed and stirred
the imaginations of the many who had formerly been excluded from cultural
life, unable to participate even as consumers. This paradox of middle-class culture is central to Tocqueville's analysis of the cultural consequences of equality
and democracy in *Democracy in America*.

But his somewhat more detached exploration of the complexities of bourgeois culture in democratic America did not lessen his harsh judgment of the
growing dominance of the bourgeoisie in France. In fact he became increasingly persuaded that, even in the fortunate new American Republic, which
seemed in many ways to have freed itself from the grip of history, the dynamic
of middle-class culture would eventually bring on a darkness that that culture
would not be able to foresee or avert. In a society in which the centralization of
state power prevailed, fostered by both democracy and technology, the blending of the soft, hedonistic, and uncritical democratic culture with the increasingly overwhelming "social power," strengthened and extended in every possible
way by new technologies, spelled disaster. It would mean the appearance of the
"tutelary State," in which the passive masses, like contented ruminants, were
managed by centralized power more interested in control, order, and equality

than in liberty—a new kind of benevolent despotism. Tocqueville may have thought that the United States, where to his astonishment he found almost no government, might longer avert this nightmarish fate, but he thought that sooner or later such would be the destiny of all democratic societies, whatever their traditions and institutions. Such was the future being fashioned by the bourgeoisie.

Tocqueville saw his era not only as politically squalid and empty but also as a time of cultural decay. In this respect, too, France had lapsed from its former glory, another result of the ascendancy of the bourgeoisie, which brought the same deadening touch to culture as to politics. He was not alone in lamenting the supposed decadence of modern culture. His dismayed recognition of France's cultural and moral decay under the new bourgeois hegemony was as important in shaping his views about the future of democratic culture as his observations of bourgeois culture in America or his theoretical analysis of the social foundations of culture. He once described how, when he was a child at Tocqueville, everything had been the occasion for a poem; such wit, irony, and gaiety had now disappeared from French life, smothered by the spirit of the bourse. He commented on the loss of esprit in cultural life to Reeve: "What did our fathers talk about fifty years ago? Remove politics from our discourse and nothing remains but monosyllables and gestures that are often better [than politics]. They found a hundred things to talk about, while we think about only one thing. They knew how to make light of serious matters; it's quite different with us, who talk so sadly about follies."[38] He exempted no aspect of cultural life from his indictment. Literature, too, was in decline. He regarded the late seventeenth century as the golden age of French literature. "If Bossuet and Pascal were to come to life," he remarked to Nassau Senior in conversation, "they would think us receding into semibarbarianism; they would be unable to enter into the ideas of our most fashionable writers; they would be disgusted with their style, and be puzzled even by their language."[39] He was speaking also for himself. He attributed the greatness of seventeenth-century French literature to authors who "wrote solely for fame . . . and addressed a public small and highly cultivated"; while in his time the increased competition for distinction and preferment as well as the attention of a larger, less discriminating audience had led to the corruption of classical French into something ornamental and grotesque.[40] This also was the result of middle-class culture. The age seemed to Tocqueville to be suffering from a "somnolence intellectuelle" which he attributed to the exhaustion following the intellectual turbulence and vivacity of the eighteenth century, the endless revolution that began in 1789, and also to the leaden, leveling influence of Louis-Philippe, the bourgeois monarch.

The severity of Tocqueville's judgment of the cultural life of France as the romantic era flowered is startling, especially since he shared so much of the critical reaction both to the Enlightenment and to bourgeois culture that was a major informing impulse of the great romantic movement in the art, music, and literature of Louis-Philippe's France. How much of the literature of his time he had read and knew well is not at all clear, though he must at least have been au courant. When he was responsible for the literary pages of *Le Commerce* he tried to persuade Balzac to contribute a serial to that journal—without success. He rarely mentions contemporary writers or artists in his correspondence, though he was acquainted with many of them through literary salons, the Académie, and by way of mutual friendships. The flowering of French romantic music seems to have escaped his attention. Had he ever heard Hector Berlioz's astonishing *Symphonie Fantastique*, which had overwhelmed Paris in 1830?

The self-indulgent individualism of romanticism, bursting the formal restraints of the classical culture he prized, seemed to him to be part of the pathology of that middle-class spirit which had lost a sense of form and seemed to recognize no limits. It was this experience of a culture of self-indulgence lacking a sense of restraint and limits, the culture of romanticism and also of democracy, that was one source of the dark vision of how democratic culture was spinning out of order that he dramatically elaborates in the second volume of *Democracy in America*.

The 1830s also saw the birth of Bohemia in France. Nothing more foreign to his temper and taste and to his view of the social responsibilities of the intellectual than this early countercultural movement can be imagined. He was not likely to have much sympathy for a cultural movement that sought to establish itself in opposition to or in isolation from society, no matter how isolated he felt himself. Charles Baudelaire, the dyspeptic *flâneur*, stood for all Tocqueville detested, though Baudelaire's critique of bourgeois life and culture was equally harsh. Yet at the same time he criticized the efforts of the July Monarchy and the reigning bourgeoisie to incorporate intellectuals and academics into the ruling class, fearing that such co-option would result in the loss of intellectual independence. He was, as it were, caught between the romantics and the Rotarians, but to him both simply represented radically opposed wings of bourgeois culture.

At times Tocqueville seemed to see lurking behind this political and cultural disaster the crafty figure of the middle-class wife. He constantly attributed great cultural and moral influence to women. Well known is his eulogy of the American woman in *Democracy in America* as the rational, disciplined, self-sacrificing, spiritual force that made middle-class society in America as chaste and orderly as he believed it was despite all the powerful tendencies in the culture that constantly pressed beyond order and limits.[41] The moral condition of women seems to have been for him the most significant indicator of the moral condition of society. Women were the canaries in the cultural mines, though they were agents of cultural change and health as well.

He was sharply critical of the new aristocratic woman. In his comments she is usually lost either in the vagueness of sentimental religion or in the game of lightheaded gossip and display. Such was his view, even though he was a familiar figure at literary salons held by aristocratic bluestockings. The middle-class woman was a dark, almost malign figure, one whose thirst for status and success turned men away from nobler goals like the ideal of self-denying, disinterested public service. The curse of calculating, careerist politics originated in the middle-class bedroom. The most significant cultural mover and shaker was no longer the inspiring mistress of the salon, but the ambitious middle-class wife anxiously promoting her husband's career. Late in his life he summed up this view, which he had constantly maintained:

> Here is what I would want to make clear to men and, I will add, especially to women. Nothing has struck me more in my long experience of public life than the influence women always exercise in it; an influence all the greater because it is indirect. I don't doubt that it is the women especially who give every society a certain moral temperament, which eventually affects political life. I could cite by name a great many examples who would serve to illustrate what I mean. A hundred times in the course of my life I have seen weak men display true public courage because one encountered by their side a woman who has sustained them in that path, not by advising them to undertake specific acts, but by exerting a strengthening influence on the way in which they ought to think in general about their duty or even about their ambition. Even more often, it must be said, I have seen private domestic transactions [le travail intérieur et domestique] gradually transform a man naturally generous, disinterested, and of great vision, into an ambitious, lazy, vulgar egoist who in the affairs of his country ends up by thinking of nothing more than how to make his own condition wealthy and comfortable.[42]

One can only guess whose names he would have offered had he chosen to be indiscreet about the negative instances he had in mind. Some of his most prominent political colleagues, married to middle-class women (Alphonse de Lamartine and Odilon Barrot had married middle-class Englishwomen, as had Tocqueville), had experienced notable seizures of ambition. Apart from what this says of Tocqueville's conviction that women wielded enormous power over men, such a comment makes it clear that he thought the general influence of bourgeois women was to narrow and privatize ambitions, to focus them on success and the pursuit of wealth. In the United States, however, the influence of the middle-class wife was different. There, she provided moral restraint and a calm domestic order that was the basis of what he seemed to believe was the remarkable orderliness of democratic politics in the United States.

Tocqueville's ideas about the proper roles of women were not class-bound but almost wholly conventional. The American girl may have enjoyed breathtaking freedom, but what he found noteworthy about women in democratic America was the way they changed. Despite their remarkably free, happily unconstrained education and their cherry-cheeked vivacity and bold independence while young and single, once married they decisively renounced such freedom and thoroughly devoted themselves to the domestic roles of affording a tranquil refuge and moral support for their husbands and moral education to their children. He attributed what he perceived as the extraordinary chasteness and orderliness of American life to the powerful moral influence of the self-denying American wife.

In the chapter of the second volume of *Democracy in America* devoted to the effect of democracy on the relations of men and women in America, he moved far beyond observation to warm praise. There is no mistaking his view that the Americans had got it right. In France, where the "crude, disorderly fancy of our age" had made "so coarse a jumble of nature's works," the assumption was that men and women were "not equal only, but actually similar." The Americans "more than anywhere else" had accepted the equality of men and women but had kept separate the roles they were to play. His somewhat incongruous argument was that the purpose of this separation of function was, first, to ensure "that the great work of society may be better performed" and, second but more important, to make sure that men remained men and women remained women. The Americans recognized that men and women are so different in both physical and moral makeup that to confound the two would degrade both and "produce nothing but feeble men and unseemly women." American women, though "they sometimes show the minds and hearts of men . . . usually preserve great delicacy of personal appearance and always have the manners of women." More important, they accepted "with pride" their sequestered, subordinate role in the family.[43] One of his objections to the writings of George Sand was that she wrote like a man. He also later repeated the gossip that it was her sexual libertinism, a result of the creed of total equality, that had led one of her lovers, Alfred de Musset, to drink himself to death.

The gender equality Tocqueville admired was equality of esteem. Men and women were creatures of equal worth. In Europe, where men were exceptionally skilled at flattering and seducing women, they at the same time felt a certain contempt for females as "seductive but incomplete beings." In America, women were deeply and truly respected. It was not acceptable even to use coarse language in their presence. Implicitly and sometimes openly Tocqueville's remarkable, overheated, and ill-informed chapter offers an ominous view of the moral chaos that was already spreading as a result of the ill-conceived quest for complete equality between the sexes and from the simultaneous failure of Europe to accept women as moral equals. The focus of his argument tightens on sexual morality. In a curious remark he implies that French feminists were clamoring for sexual freedom while deranging the sacred institution of the family: "In the United States one never hears an adulterous wife noisily proclaiming the rights of women while stamping the most hallowed duties underfoot." In France, a double standard of sexual morality prevailed. There, for example, the penalty for rape was "much milder . . . it is difficult to find a jury that will convict." The Americans punished rape by death because the "seducer is as much dishonored as the victim." He concluded with a comment many times quoted: "If anyone asks me what I think the chief cause of the extraordinary prosperity and the growing power of this nation, I should answer that it is due to the superiority of their women."[44]

The ideal he had in mind is illustrated by the counsel he offered the oldest daughter of his brother Edouard, Denise, just after she turned seventeen:

> Continue to think of others more than of yourself. Dream of being amiable and thoughtful more than just appearing such; and above all, remain simple, honest, spontaneous and natural . . . be thus because you know it is right, and when you will have acquired the experience you still lack, you will discover that all this is at the same time also very useful. You yourself will see with pleasure that you have become almost without being aware of it more noted than most of the women one encounters in life, not only more respected but more treasured, loved and sought after because, chère Denise, true charm is not found in manners but in character and especially in the heart.[45]

This is not a prescription for the development of talent or for the nurturing of dreams or of the mind. There is nothing here about the self-fulfillment that equality was beginning to open up to more than the exceptionally gifted and outspoken woman. It is the old prescription for how to be loved and useful by being a good, self-effacing heart. Nine months after receiving this letter, Denise married Count Philippe Emmanuel de Blic of Burgundy. Tocqueville learned about the marriage more than a year later. Denise and Philippe would have seven children.

Although he admired the female impresarios whose salons were the intellectual exchange places—or showrooms—of Paris during the July Monarchy, with a few exceptions he did not regard them as intellectuals or writers. Though he had eagerly joined the happy few who courted Mme Récamier's nods and smiles and may even have felt a half-suppressed sexual frisson upon receiving a sign of approval from that beautiful woman, he uncharitably, though perhaps honestly, said after her death that he had never heard her say anything memorable. He no doubt would have said the same about almost all the women whose salons he attended. Such women were acceptable because they were in fact not violating conventional gender rules. They were supplying what one might call support services as intellectual and political facilitators. Just as important, they had remained female, skilled at displaying the charms of their sex while spreading sweetness and light, as if they were Muses shared by those who came to play what Tocqueville called "un jeu des coulisses," the game of glances.

There were some exceptions. He regularly attended the salon of the duchesse de Dino, Talleyrand's niece by marriage and a close friend of Royer-Collard.[46] He also attended the mysterious salon of Sophie Swetchine, an exiled Russian savant and a general's widow from a scholarly family, who had become, by dint of extraordinary study undertaken to settle her doubts about the truth claims of the Catholic Church, an authority on Catholic theology. From their first encounter in the early 1850s until his death, he carried on an intense, confessional correspondence with Swetchine in which he seems at times to be kneeling humbly before her.[47] For a time he also attended the Paris salon of the even more formidably accomplished writer and scholar the princess de Belgiojoso, who in 1844 published her French translation of Giambattista Vico's *La Scienza Nuova*, for which she had written a lengthy overview of Vico's thought. Tocqueville's letter of thanks for the gift copy she sent concludes with what he must have thought was a compliment: "I have already read and admired your book, and at each page I have wondered how a spirit full of all the feminine graces has been able to penetrate and throw in relief the manliest genius there ever was."[48] Belgiojoso had previously published (anonymously, for it was not thought fit for women to write about theology) the first volume of a four-volume commentary on Catholic theology, which Tocqueville greeted with warm praise: "A masterpiece, profoundly thoughtful and admirable in style. You have not only written beautifully in our language [she was Italian], you have recovered the style of the great era of our literature, which is truly marvelous."[49] Such literary women were acceptable because while formidable writers they were nonetheless fulfilling their vocation by dealing with spiritual matters and because they had remained, as he said to

Belgiojoso, "full of all the feminine graces." Female writers who wrote like men, such as Sand, he cast into outer darkness.

Such attitudes were not simply expressions of class values and conventions. They were general, as strongly maintained by the bourgeoisie as by the aristocracy and by intellectuals and academics too. For the Great Positivist Auguste Comte, the Utopia into which he was about to lead benighted humanity was to be unified and kept harmonious by a beaming Goddess before whom all were to genuflect. Such was Comte's view of the major function of the female. Tocqueville's professed astonishment at the femininity of the interpreter of the virile Vico was expressed also by Victor Cousin, the leading philosopher and educational theorist in France, who wrote to Belgiojoso, "'Femina sexu, genio vir.' Philosophy is not the work of women."[50]

However, alongside the thoroughly alienated Tocqueville who so keenly felt himself displaced from his culture even though he shared the conventions and social expectations of his time, there was also the skeptical Tocqueville whose relentless rationality could at times lead him to ignore or criticize conventional mores and expectations. He was an intellectual who highly valued originality, intellectual passion, and accomplishment, whether in men or women. This was the Tocqueville who agreed that the main redeeming value of equality was that it opened the door to individual self-fulfillment. Some such transcending of convention occurred when he invited the very bluestockinged Comtesse d'Agoult (Franz Liszt's mistress and mother of three of his children, notorious as the radical republican historian, novelist, and pamphleteer Daniel Stern, and a friend of Sand) to dinner at his home in Paris in May of 1848 along with the visiting American transcendentalist Ralph Waldo Emerson. Perhaps she had been invited because Tocqueville knew she was among the French writers and academics, including Edgar Quinet and Jules Michelet, who had discovered Emerson and because he needed an interlocutor or a translator at the table. Regrettably, this extraordinary encounter, apparently the only time Tocqueville met Emerson, was one of the silent encounters of Tocqueville's life. Nothing about what was spoken of at the dinner was recorded, either by Tocqueville or by Emerson, and one is left to imagine what was discussed. The celebrated American writer and philosopher, the quintessential American democrat, drinks wine and spends hours with the celebrated French student of American politics and culture—and the record is silent.[51] Had they failed to understand one another? The pity of the silence aside, the fact that Tocqueville was host to an unconventional, bohemian literary female whose politics were anathema to him suggests that his intellectually curious, enlightened self sometimes broke out of the cocoon of convention.

His view of the roots of the supreme passion of the bourgeoisie, for equality, was not generous. He saw it as the expression not of a desire for social justice, a principled devotion to rights, or a conviction based on religious belief, but of social jealousy and of a hatred of distinctions. Though the Revolution had destroyed the "system of privilege," it had not been able to "destroy the social distinctions which depend upon manners. It could not enable the bourgeois to feel himself the equal of the gentilhomme." "Equality," he said, "is the expression of envy. It means in the heart of every republican, 'no one shall be better off than I am,' and while this is preferred to good government, good government is impossible." This bitter view of the animus that informed egalitarianism reveals much about Tocqueville's animus toward the bourgeoisie. Behind democracy he saw the force of destructive, jealous, and selfish passions, not principle or a larger sentiment for justice.[52]

Envy had been the passion that corrupted the French Revolution. Envy and something else. His discussion of the modern passion for equality colors it with a tinge of menace. As he wrote about equality in *Democracy in America*, especially in the crucial chapter "Why Democratic Nations Show a More Ardent and Enduring Love for Equality Than for Liberty," it becomes an irrational force driving men beyond any recognition of the natural order of things. It was an overpowering impulse that swept all restraints from its path and blinded them from what they are losing, above all, freedom:

> Democratic peoples always like equality, but there are times when their passion for it turns to delirium. This happens when the old social hierarchy, long menaced, finally collapses after severe inner struggle and the barriers of rank are at length thrown down. At such times men pounce on their booty and cling to it as a treasure they fear to have snatched away. The passion for equality seeps into every corner of the human heart, expands and fills the whole. It is of no use telling them that by their blind surrender to an exclusive passion they are compromising their dearest interests; they are deaf. It is of no use pointing out that freedom is slipping from their grasp while they look the other way: they are blind, or rather they can see but one thing to covet in the whole world.[53]

This condescending, overheated remark comes at the end of the first chapter of the concluding book of volume 2 of *Democracy in America*, written as Tocqueville slipped into deeper gloom about the prospects of democracy. "It is of no use . . . it is of no use": despair is replacing calm analysis. Equality, here presented as a passion of manic intensity, overwhelms the old guardians of order ("the old social hierarchy"). It has the power to make men blind and deaf, that is to say, irrational. It knows no barriers, no limits, no fixed order. It is an insatiable source of disorder. Whatever Tocqueville believed to be the etiology of this "delirium," it is clear that equality was for him not simply an uncontrollable, irrational drive but also a force inimical to that inherited sense of order and to that clarity of mind he believed to be essential conditions of freedom. Not only liberty but also the passion for equality was an unsettling force in the modern world. It was a demonic impulse that threatened to disrupt all patterns of control and exchange, all the languages and symbols of unity and order, and all the social rituals that had hitherto made both community and liberty possible at the same time.

As a legal and political goal, the mind and even the heart might support egalitarianism, but as delirium it always threatened to drive beyond the moral notion of equality before the law and undermine the diversity Tocqueville believed was the natural order of things. Efforts to achieve full equality would perpetually lead to bitter disappointment, distress, unrest, and malaise, the kind of chronic restlessness that he perceived even among the Americans, who already enjoyed what to him was an astonishing equality. Even they were not satisfied, and their example proved that in any democratic society the quest for equality would become "more insatiable in proportion as equality is more complete." In reading *L'Ancien Régime* it is striking to note what weight Tocqueville places on the growing passion for equality and on the hatreds and the envy produced by legally established distinctions within classes in accounting for the origins of the French Revolution.[54] Beyond that, the drive for equality, along with the astonishing dream of creating a new society out of whole cloth, had upset the Revolution's balanced aspirations and had thrown liberty in jeopardy.

He acknowledged equality's benefits. The comparative inventories of the merits and deficiencies of democracy and aristocracy that occasionally appear in *Democracy in America* like a chorus reciting the basic moral issue of the tale make it clear that he understood the quest for equality even though he disdained it as an ideal. But he thought it was a futile quest that would forever roil society. He believed that some degree of political equality was essential for maintaining moderation and for averting revolutionary passions. He thus accepted the very gradual extension of suffrage, after the careful education of the qualified, as a regrettable necessity. With regard to political equality, he would always be, as he was when campaigning in 1839, the seigneur lecturing new voters on their responsibilities.

The bourgeoisie was the carrier of this illness. He knew, of course, how powerful and durable class feelings were. In his view, the ongoing Revolution had not "cured" or "much palliated" distinctions and animosities of caste, which he said constituted "a kind of freemasonry." He acknowledged that he felt them strongly himself: "When I talk to a gentilhomme, though we have not two ideas in common, though all his wishes and thoughts are very opposed to mine, yet I feel at once that we belong to the same family, that we speak the same language. I may like a bourgeois better, but he is a stranger."[55] He barely disguised his disdain for his bourgeois colleagues in the Chamber of Deputies, hardly knew their names, could rarely attach names to faces, called them oafs. He somewhat transcended such class hauteur when serving on the Conseil de la Manche, where some amiability was needed for effectiveness, but he also bent a bit because, as noted above, he enjoyed the deference shown him, knew the rules of noblesse oblige, and actually learned to value "honnêtes hommes" whatever their class. At home he was also playing the traditional role of local notable, as described by André-Jean Tudesq.[56]

It was in part class feeling that underlay his attachment to Arthur de Gobineau, a young aristocrat befriended and mentored by the older Tocqueville. Gobineau's ideas and wishes were almost totally the opposite of Tocqueville's. Several times in their correspondence he had to ask Gobineau to stop discussing matters about which their views sharply differed. Yet they remained close. Tocqueville accepted Gobineau as one accepts a difficult, errant family member. "I regard Gobineau as a good fellow and a man of honor," he wrote to Kergorlay, adding, "he was born into our class."[57] And despite his own marriage to a middle-class Englishwoman, he advised Kergorlay during his protracted search for a suitable wife "to choose . . . only from a family that belongs on both sides from what we would have called our class."[58]

3

INTIMACY

Tocqueville highly valued friendship, about which he wrote a great deal. He found in friendship all those qualities of heart and honesty that were fading from the modern world, which he thought was becoming cold, calculating, contractual. Though he had only a small circle of friends, he was capable of passionate and enduring friendships. He was too complicated a man to be an easy friend— he expected too much of his friends, and his candor sometimes stung. His family and especially his marriage were at times difficult for the demanding, ambivalent Tocqueville. All aspects of his intimate life, especially his marriage, were affected by his deep uncertainties about identity and the psychic turmoil in which he often found himself.

The terminal irony of Tocqueville's comment to Kergorlay—"what we would have called our class"—illuminates the fact that his relationship to the aristocracy was too laced with ambiguities to offer him a secure sense of community. He was a man of class feelings without a class. He had to look elsewhere for his true community, which he found in a society of friendship based on a shared moral sensibility and on shared goals, more the sensibility than the goals. Like other moralists alienated to a degree from their society and culture, Tocqueville dreamed of forming "alongside the great society, a small, ideal community inhabited by those I respect and love, and living there" while working for the moral transformation of the larger society.[1] His dream of a morally satisfying intimate society never led him to attempt to create anything resembling the utopian communities beginning to appear at that time as nodes of regeneration in a decadent Western culture, or even to form a sustained intellectual interest in them. Much in *Democracy in America* does, however, anticipate the era of intentional communities and the general retreat in democratic societies to more intimate milieus of family, friendship, and love, a retreat that characterized his life as well. No more than his historical contemporary Emerson, who also found his ideal society in a circle of friends but could never live in or join a utopia and in fact mocked them, could Tocqueville have joined the kind of Bohemia of the culturally and socially marginal just then forming in France.

He increasingly sought meaning and satisfaction in friendship, the art of which he cultivated with great intensity. It was in his small circle of friends that he most fully overcame his many alienations, though even there he retained a certain critical detachment that expressed itself in the challenging candor with which he spoke and wrote to them. His affection for them did not permit him to ignore or remain still about their failings. He recoiled from the calculating divisiveness and the instrumentalism that touched all relations in the political and social worlds, which he constantly described as a wasteland of deception, petty self-interest, and ego display. The honest, direct, warm relationships he found lacking in political life he sought all the more ardently among his friends, with whom one could create the ideal, moral society that an amoral politics made impossible. His friendships had for him a moral meaning, though to be sure the fundamental joys of intimacy and affection were part of them as well. When he signs off his letters to close friends with "de tout mon coeur" or "du fond de mon coeur," one feels he meant it. Friendship afforded him a refuge in a disorderly, morally chaotic world drifting without purpose.

He nourished his friendships carefully and analyzed their quality and meaning with the same relentless scrutiny he gave to the study of his psyche. No subject in all his correspondence is more thoroughly or more passionately explored in all its nuances. His letters to his friends are warm, open, frank, confessional, pleading, sometimes anxious and imperious. They could be as demanding and as ardent as any lover's letters. When, for example, a new judicial assignment shifted Beaumont to Paris from Versailles, where they had been sharing an apartment, Tocqueville sent the following poignant message, full of feeling and wit:

> Our true friendship, my dear Beaumont, this constant intimacy, this trust without any limit whatever, all that constitutes in a word the charm of our shared life, all that is ended. This reflection will seem a small thing to you: I know and understand that what you are giving up is replaced by something so promising that for most men the comparison would be ridiculous (not for you, however). An immense future opens itself before you; the circle in which you are known will henceforth be extended indefinitely. But for me, for whom all is suddenly lost, the thought . . . is singularly painful. There is no compensation for me, poor devil who will return to dwell in the lodgings in which I was bored to death when I stayed there a week without you; who would seek you out in the evening for a walk, during the day for our work; who will feel weighed down by my thoughts; who will not be able to ask

anyone's counsel in the midst of all the petty difficulties, all the small weari-
nesses of which our condition is full. That, however, is my future as I see it,
perhaps my very long future.[2]

He was generous, ardent, even importunate in his friendships. The warmth
of his loyalty and affection is manifest in his letters, full of the intimate detail of
his outer and inner lives. He was frankly chagrined when his letters were not
answered or when replies went astray. Nothing gave him greater satisfaction
than to gather one or more of his friends at Tocqueville, which he even redesigned with their tastes and needs in mind. One of the reconstructed towers of
the chateau became the "tour d'Ampère," named for his friend Jean-Jacques
Ampère, the son of the famous physicist André-Marie Ampère. He pressed
them with invitations, would carefully plan Ampère's visits so that the two of
them could enjoy their intimacy in tranquility without having to worry about
local politics or neighborhood affairs. "I like to gather you tranquilly," he wrote
Ampère, "with one or two intimate friends like you, within four walls; that's
what I call the way really to enjoy one another." What he called his "theory of
friendship" required long periods of shared solitude in which to savor the pleasures of intimacy and intellectual exchange: to Ampère he wrote "The summer
is the time when one should receive acquaintances in the country; but for true
good friends, the autumn and even the winter are the seasons I love, with their
long evenings in the corner of a large flaming hearth. If you can't come in
October or later, come as soon as possible."[3]

In the despairing, deep isolation of his last years, his community of friends
became his last refuge. As he lay dying in Cannes in the spring of 1859, he
summoned Beaumont and Ampère to be with him and Kergorlay as well,
along with his brothers. Though he had feared that the solicitous and emotionally intense Ampère would be shattered by his condition and had insisted at
first that he not visit, his last letter to Ampère concluded with the following
plea: "Come, come; because nothing is more selfish than true friendship,
like another sentiment that one can no longer utter, especially in my actual
condition."[4]

He placed extraordinary value on the experience of friendship because it
seemed to him to strengthen values that modern life was eroding. As relations
between men became more and more manipulative in the universal struggle
for place and power it was necessary to cultivate sentiment, loyalty, affection,
and generosity. In friendship one found it easiest to accept another as an end
in himself. Though Tocqueville greatly prized intellect and true individuality, what he cherished most of all in others was heart, by which he meant the

capacity to love but also uncalculating spontaneity of sentiment, force of passion, personal generosity, moral seriousness, independence of spirit, originality, and integrity—everything Emerson meant when he spoke of character. Such, for example, was the basis of his relationship to Eugene Stoffels, a friend from school days in Metz with whom he had little in common socially, politically, or intellectually. Though Stoffels was a man of "sound judgment and considerable knowledge," in Beaumont's view it was "his moral qualities, his integrity, his fidelity and his sympathy" that bound Tocqueville to him.[5] "What a great heart in a life so constrained," Tocqueville wrote sadly when Stoffels died.

Friendship was that realm of experience in which he could give freest rein to his passions and in which he came closest to escaping the shadow of doubt that chilled his life. He spoke often of the freedom he experienced in friendship, sometimes calling it virile. Perhaps even more than family, which was after all in some ways as subject to the lottery of life as paternity, friendship seemed to him the only solid reality on which one could rely in a world of chance and instability. Friendship alone, he wrote Kergorlay, "is strong and stable in life." "Only the sentiments of the heart," he said to Stoffels, "have any durability in life."[6] His attitude toward friends was linked increasingly to his ideas about the place of emotions, or heart, in life. To Ampère he expressed his view that the passionate life was growing weaker in their time:

> The more distant I become from my youth, I have more regard, I will almost say respect, for the passions. I approve of them when they are positive, and I'm not really sure I disapprove of them when they are negative. They are power, and power, whenever one finds it seems to have the advantage in the midst of the general feebleness that surrounds us. I encounter only cowards who tremble at the slightest stirring of the heart and who speak only about the dangers the passions threaten us with. Such are in my opinion useless chatterboxes. In our time we too little find the passions, true and solid passions, seizing and guiding life. We no longer know how nor want to either love or hate. Doubt and philanthropy make us incapable of anything, of great evil as well as great good, and we circle heavily around a multitude of petty matters none of which attract us or repel us strongly and which we never resolve.[7]

Friendship represented the antithesis of the calculating impersonality and the cautious prudence of bourgeois culture, from which the capacity for heroic and passionate commitment to ideals of any sort seemed to be vanishing. If Tocqueville's plea for a bolder passionate life sounds like a call that has welled up out of an aristocratic–feudal imagination full of memories of chivalric heroism, it also draws very much on the same impulses and ideas that underlay the romantic critique of a mechanized, impersonal culture from which cold reason was chasing warm fancy. His version of the wasteland was a world of "universal feebleness" in which men flitted about without conviction, preoccupied with a "multitude of petty objects," ultimately indifferent to everything, an image that appears again and again in *Democracy in America*.

In his experience, the polar reality of friendship was politics, a cold, abstract, manipulative world all the forces of which were poised in opposition to the values friendship embodied. Politics seemed to be the enemy of love, and he struggled not to allow it to damage his personal relationships. He was deeply distressed by the strain that their small political differences occasionally raised between him and Beaumont. To the conservative Stoffels he patiently and solicitously explained his ideas, offering in his letters one of the most eloquent statements of his political credo. He anxiously sought not to allow his and Kergorlay's sometimes radically divergent political views to spoil their old friendship. "You return again and again to the subject of the July Revolution," he wrote Kergorlay in 1836:

> To put it in one word, I fear that politics may finally cool our friendship, which I would regard as one of the great misfortunes of my life. If ever I thought that because of some differences of opinion your feelings about me had changed, I would feel deeply distressed. For there is something in our friendship that nothing could replace and that has no room for the ordinary. It's an open spirit, generous, manly, free, which always lifts the mind. At the moment our feelings become commonplace, our affection a matter of familiarity, the magic [le prestige] will have vanished. Let us struggle then with all our strength against the common enemy, the only enemy we have to fear.[8]

He was not an easy friend but candid and critical when a more easygoing temperament would have remained tactfully silent or gently reproachful. When Beaumont left him in Versailles, Tocqueville warned him that his facile *bonhommerie* was a danger. In his plea to Kergorlay not to allow politics to disrupt their friendship he argued that the problem lay in Kergorlay's untamed passions: "I don't doubt that that will happen because of yours, not mine. Independent of your reason, when it's a question of politics, you have an instinct, that is to say an inner force that makes you feel and act independently of your will. I cannot stop myself from fearing that it is against that force that our intimacy will crash . . . I fear your instinct."[9]

He reproved his friends for all their failings, whether it was a matter of their prose style or working habits, sometimes quite sharply criticizing them for wasting their talents when he thought that was the case. He was relentlessly harsh with Kergorlay for failing to use his outstanding abilities in the service of France. He often lectured his friends, offered prudential advice, and at times could be cruelly deflating.[10] In turn, he did not hesitate to write frankly about personal, even intimate, issues in his own life, sometimes thoroughly and radically deconstructing his psyche and acknowledging his failures and flaws. He recognized that he was often too severe with his friends and thought he knew why: it was that the more he identified with them, the more strongly he felt "the profound distrust of self that is my great malady . . . when it is a question of me."

His family and his marriage provided other experiences of intimacy. In *Democracy in America* he contrasts at considerable length the differences between families in aristocratic and democratic societies. (He writes only about fathers and sons, and says nothing about mothers, daughters, sisters in his chapter about democratic families.) He describes how the once-unquestioned authority of the father, almost a divine right king within his family, vanishes in democracies, where the former patriarch becomes just the chief among equals, perhaps respected for his wisdom and his great years but no longer as the awesome, revered figure he once was. The democratic father is now closer to his sons, if not quite intimate. Brothers within the democratic family are also closer; here too a truer fraternity replaces the old aristocratic structure of seniority, authority, and power. With the abolition of primogeniture the eldest brother is no longer a minor father.

What Tocqueville says about the authority of the father and the relationships between patriarch and sons as well as between sons in aristocratic societies undoubtedly reflects his own cultural experience, but his family life seems to have been somewhat less formal than the aristocratic model he presents in *Democracy in America*. Even so, it seems to have been more reserved and less intimate than his relationships with his friends. He was a difficult, sometimes painfully candid brother—a prickly presence in the family bosom. His letters to his brothers, of which there are many more to Edouard than to Hippolyte, were much less confessional and dealt much less with intellectual issues than the ones he wrote to his friends, even though he saw his friends more often. His correspondence with his father and mother, perhaps understandably sparse, was polite, full of expressions of filial devotion and fondness that seem conventional. There are few signs that he regarded Hervé as the authoritative aristocratic patriarch described in *Democracy in America*, whose word was law and whose views were always to be consulted and followed. In fact Tocqueville père was rather more like a respected old man, a democratic father to his very independent son. Tocqueville's grief and sense of profound loss at Hervé's death in

1856 are unmistakable, expressed in moving homage sent to his friends. Nevertheless, there was some distance between them: the correspondence of the mature Alexis with his father is superficial, its personal focus and tone thin.

If with members of his legitimist family Tocqueville sought to separate the personal from the political, there was little of either in his letters to Hervé, especially after he had begun his literary and political careers. And although the senior Tocqueville late in life wrote histories of the reigns of Louis XV and Louis XVI, the son never mentioned them in correspondence with his father or with friends. Did he ever congratulate the old man for his perseverance and accomplishment, whatever he thought of the books?[11] He occasionally discussed *Democracy in America* with his father and brothers and asked them to read portions of both volumes, but he regarded such family consultations as perfunctory and obligatory and said they were a waste of time. He may have felt that they were, yet judging from the detailed, often insightful critical notes Hervé offered on much of volume 1 of *Democracy in America*, Tocqueville père took the family literary responsibilities seriously.

It is easy to understand why his brother Edouard exploded in anger in 1852 after receiving a wrathful letter of admonition from Alexis for having expressed support for Napoleon III in which his younger brother forbade further discussion of politics because there was too great a gulf between them. Edouard sharply replied that he was tired of being talked down to and that he would no longer tolerate being treated like a political infant with whom one could seriously discuss neither political ideas nor anything profound.[12] In fact, according to Tocqueville, he and Edouard had begun to drift apart after his political career began.[13] He also found Edouard's religious ideas distressing: Edouard "had allowed himself, in a way that disturbs me, to drift slowly toward mystical ideas," and this subject too became off-limits.[14] The breach healed somewhat only when Tocqueville lay dying in 1859.

He was also constantly lecturing Hippolyte, a mercurial, embarrassingly opportunistic military man of wobbly judgment, despairing over his superficial life as socialite and boulevardier. And he had savage things to say about the vanity and crass love of money of Hippolyte's wife, Émilie, as well as about her family's materialistic culture.[15]

But the major source of strain between Alexis and his brothers was the result of Marie's growing hostility to both, especially to their wives. His family had not been happy about his marriage, and he had the bad judgment of often leaving Marie alone for long stretches in the bosom of a family that had been less than enthusiastic about her. Their correspondence in 1837 reveals the beginnings of a rift between Marie and Edouard's wife, Alexandrine, that widened as the years passed. Marie felt disliked and apparently believed that the Tocquevilles thought she had influenced his shift to a more liberal politics. Moreover, she herself felt such incompatibility. From the start she complained about Alexandrine's limitations, and Tocqueville agreed that Marie's mind and soul were much larger and that she and his sister-in-law should not long stay together under the same roof. By Tocqueville's death she had drifted so far from Edouard and Alexandrine that she cut off relations.[16] Her relationship to Hervé de Tocqueville was uneasy, and she did not get along well with Hervé's companion, Mme Guermarquer. From the start Marie could not abide Émilie. Marie's life as an awkward, sensitive, middle-class English member of the Tocqueville family is described by André Jardin, one of the editors of the family correspondence and Tocqueville's biographer, as follows: "We are left with the impression of a persistent hostility, more or less veiled. . . . She was not very comfortable or well-liked in the family circle. . . . Her own bitter obstinacy also seems to have played a large part in it."[17] According to Jardin, she was also "a misfit in Tocqueville's social circle," and, except for a few of his close friends like Beaumont, Francisque de Corcelle, Kergorlay, and Ampère, she preferred Tocqueville's middle-class acquaintances.[18] If his life with Marie was a source of stability and support for his anxious and uncertain spirit, it was also a source of family and social strain.

How does one account for this boldly unconventional, improbable marriage? and what was its quality? They were an odd couple. What kind of intimacy did they enjoy? Not much is known about Marie. Her letters to Alexis have vanished, and many of his to her exist in copies she made, passages in some of them deleted for motives not clear. She no doubt was determined to protect not only Tocqueville's reputation but hers as well. She evidently had not lived with her family since quite young, and when Tocqueville met her—she was then close to thirty, he about twenty-three—she was living in Versailles with her aunt, Mrs. Belam. What was she doing there? or rather, why had she left her family and England? She was bright and well-read and a better linguist than her husband: she knew German before he started to study it in the 1850s. Her correspondence with Francis Lieber, a German-American social scientist, academic, and journalist, while he was the American correspondent to *Le Commerce*, reveals how strong and informed (and conservative) her views of French politics and culture were.[19] Beaumont testified to her prudent judgment and good sense. However, she also had a difficult temperament, again alleged by Jardin, who writes that while "very few opinions of her have been handed down," she seems to have been given to fits of jealousy, sulking, and obstinacy, which meant that she "ruled the roost."[20] She often complained about being left alone or left behind when Tocqueville was in Paris or traveling or politicking.

His letters to her before 1843 are heavy with reassurances ("on my honor") of his fidelity. Such professions of fidelity had become necessary because of Marie's growing suspicions that her husband was enjoying amorous adventures while he was in Paris or elsewhere and she was alone in Normandy. These suspicions led to increasing coldness and anger on her part and to a yearlong rift, eventually forcing Tocqueville to confess that he had not always been true to her. His confession swept away years of denial. In it he writes of "the inexpressible tenderness" that fills his heart when he thinks of her, of the happiness he owes her, of the terror he feels at the thought of losing her, all of which sentiments he experiences "a hundred times more vividly and more deeply than I can say, and yet I distress you constantly and wound a heart that lives only for me. When I think of this I look at myself with horror. I can't escape the poignant sorrow that tears my spirit. I know, mon amie chérie, that I have no way of convincing you that I will hurt you no longer. I have so often committed this inexcusable fault that I have no assurance to give."[21]

Two days after that confession and after having received what evidently was a gentle letter instead of the rebuke he had been anticipating (he was traveling in Normandy, not far from their home, inspecting prisons), he wrote the following:

How could I ever have feared that your letters would cause me chagrin and trouble, mon amie chérie, how could I ever have doubted that your affection for me is inexhaustible? Hasn't experience shown me a hundred times that when you feel I am unhappy and sad your heart suffers and that you draw from your treasury of consolations? That is what I have again said to myself on reading your last letter, which I received yesterday. You have chosen with adorable art from all that you might have said to me those things which would soften and make less painful my thoughts. You have put aside those of yours that would have awakened or revived some cruel memory. Oh, mon amie, you must believe that all such care, all such effort, is not in vain. The memory of it is engraved in ineffaceable lines in my heart; it joins all those which make you a unique being, my guardian angel, my all. Because what would I be without you? Experience has begun to show me limited horizons in every direction; the more I see the more I pause and abide in the thought that the only real and solid good that I possess on earth is our mutual attachment, the union so extraordinary of our two spirits, that grace with which you fill my life. For me, all the true *jouissances* of life lies in that. Experience has shown me more and more that beyond that there are only pleasures of pride followed always by regrets; fleeting excitements mixed with gall. If you could read deep within my heart, you would see that what I am saying to you is profoundly felt and true; you would finally understand what an immense and singular place you occupy in my life. And yet, I torment you; I grieve a heart that is my only refuge; I trouble that source of goodness and tenderness in which I can always find the only real consolations that can soften for me the setbacks and vexations of life. How can one understand that? Isn't man the most incomprehensible and irrational of beings?[22]

One might uncharitably say that this explanation was an instance of philosophical special pleading—transferring his guilt to the drooping shoulders of an "incomprehensible and irrational" humanity—but Tocqueville always thought in such terms. Life for him was on every level an unending drama best understood as a struggle of moral forces. His profession of psychological dependence was completely honest.

Between the letter just quoted, of August 25, 1843, and the following one of July 24, 1844, almost a full year later, there are only two letters from Alexis to Marie. The intensity of the sentiments and poignancy of their relationship can best be conveyed by once more quoting him at length. What he says about this particular moment and about what she means to him, a refrain in all his letters to her, suggests something about the drama and the emotional tenor of their marital intimacy. Here he writes about what he felt after putting her in a carriage that would carry her back to Tocqueville. They had had a "petty quarrel":

> You were scarcely in the carriage, mon amie chérie, and I had seen the last pleat of your dress disappear behind the closing door, when my bad mood suddenly disappeared, and I ran like a madman to the side door of *l'hôtel des Postes*, hoping I might once again catch your glance. I saw a part of your hat, but you did not know I was there and you passed by without looking toward me. I was sure that a glance rapidly exchanged would tell us that all was already forgotten and that the memory of that miserable petty quarrel had disappeared in the midst of all the vivid and profound feelings that a separation of even a few days inspires in us. It would be senseless for us to be chagrined about such miseries when we possess in full the greatest good in the world, that good so rare that wherever I look I can see it nowhere but between us, the profound, intimate, total, and indissoluble union of two souls. As for me, Marie, I have complete confidence in only one being in the world, and that being is you. There is only one heart I count on absolutely, and that heart is yours. I see the possibility of my friendships ending in the future. But to separate my mind from yours, my heart from yours, I imagine only death. In truth, I count on you as I count on myself—more than on myself.[23]

The breach between the two had been mediated by Kergorlay, who had attempted to persuade Marie that there was a difference between "les mauvaises habitudes et l'infidelité du coeur." Were these "bad habits" simply a matter of indulging in suggestive attentiveness and erotic flirting? Or something beyond that? Through much of Tocqueville's marriage Kergorlay was an indispensable intermediary between Alexis and Marie. For years there are in the *Oeuvres Complètes* many more surviving letters from Kergorlay to Marie than there are between the two old friends.

Marie was often not well, suffering from lumbago, rheumatism, and respiratory ailments. When in 1858 Tocqueville went to Cannes in very bad health, en route to his death, she was nearly as ill as he. She suffered as well from "mental disturbances" during which, according to Jardin, "her reason would become unhinged."[24] Whether that was in fact so, she undoubtedly was a high-strung, moody woman with what used to be called female nervous ailments, now better understood as the consequences of suppressed ambition and repressed sexuality, among other reasons for human unhappiness.

What was the basis of their marriage? What was the nature of the intimacy Tocqueville prized so highly and wrote about incessantly? It is difficult to believe that both Tocqueville and Marie were driven by romantic passion or simply by pheromones, though Tocqueville was a passionate man, hot-tempered enough to have fought a duel and to have challenged someone else for a political attack. His letters to his wife are full of mildly erotic passages and expressions of sensual longing, most of which she scratched out. There is abundant evidence in Tocqueville's letters to Marie to suggest that the strength of their relationship was based largely on moral and intellectual compatibility and that despite her reputed emotional spikiness and his demanding emotional instability—and the bitter experience of his unfaithfulness—it was a kind of spiritual harmony that kept their marriage meaningful. So did a deepening mutual attachment to life at Tocqueville, where she preferred to be, as eventually he would too, although initially he had said he was chilled by the prospect of living the "life of a potato."

For all their social and cultural differences, they were much alike. She was alienated herself, having said goodbye to England forever. She had to be reminded by Nassau William Senior that she would not be an alien in England, as she had said she was, because one couldn't ever give up English citizenship. Apparently she never returned to her native country: she did not accompany Tocqueville on his trips there. Was that because the aristocratic English social world through which Tocqueville moved while traveling there would have made her, or him, uncomfortable? They were both marginal individuals with little taste for social life, though Tocqueville tried to maintain connections with aristocratic and literary circles. Both much enjoyed seclusion and solitude. Their social isolation provided them with a vantage point and with a sense of superiority and purity that comes with self-imposed separateness, from which it is easier to hand down moral judgments. Despite Tocqueville's frequent philosophical claims that he was part of vulgar humanity, he and his wife undoubtedly felt very much above it all.

The strains in their marriage notwithstanding, she provided him with the emotional calm, the reassurance, and the validation he often desperately needed as he swung from moods of grandiosity to longer and more frequent spells of paralyzing melancholy, during which he was overwhelmed by self-doubt, by that "profound distrust of self" that he called his greatest malady. If his letters constantly praise her moral qualities, they even more steadily profess how crucial she was to his well-being and his psychological tranquility. His gratitude for her life-giving nurturance was not always matched by an equivalent concern for her well-being. The exchange of gifts seems one-way. In this respect, their marriage was quite conventional.

The following lengthy excerpt from a letter Tocqueville sent to Marie in late 1837, when they had been married for almost two years, is representative of their whole correspondence. It had become clear that she was miserable living with Edouard's family at Baugy (his father was there also) while he was away. He says much about what she means to him in words that he repeated almost like a formula; his plaintive effort to overcome her doubts about his love would become a sad refrain. It is not a happy letter. Beginning by lamenting their misunderstandings of the moment, recalling the closeness and the happiness they had formerly enjoyed, insisting that it will be recaptured, he professes that her unhappiness is his unhappiness. And then he characteristically continues at great length about how much his happiness and equilibrium, in fact his attachment to life itself, depend on her:

> I know very well that we torment ourselves too much over small matters and that we are not joyful enough about the great good we possess, our mutual love. All the rest is nothing in my eyes, that alone remains. We are too often concerned with secondary matters and forget the primary. If you knew how full my heart is with tenderness for you at this moment. Oh, if we were not separated, I am sure that it would not be long before our spirits returned to oneness and that we would fully enjoy the happiness of loving and of being loved. You believe that I have somewhat reproached you about your conduct toward my family; yet again, a thousand times, you are mistaken. . . .
>
> Marie, mon amie chérie, let us not allow miseries to make us bitter with one another. As soon as I have returned, when our spirits are truly united once again, one with the other, we will discuss frankly and without reservation what will be best to do in the interest of our happiness. You will look into your heart and tell me if it will truly be painful for you to remain in the

country [at Baugy]. In that case, very well, we will return to Paris in a few days. If you truly believe that to remain another two months at Baugy does not seem to you too great a sacrifice, that it will be possible for you to remain there and to be happy—because that's the important thing—we will remain. It is in my interest too to talk with sincerity, because if you will be unhappy at Baugy I will without fail be unhappy myself. Your soul is so much part of mine that I suffer when you suffer, and cannot enjoy repose when you are not tranquil. Such is my great happiness and my great misery. They are linked together—I can't have one without the other.

As you have suspected, Marie, I have just spent here [he was in Paris, not a great distance from his brother's chateau] one of the saddest times of my life. To the depth of my being I have been in perpetual turmoil. I have constantly been prey to unreasonable discouragement, to sadness without cause, to restless activity without aim. All this is quite distressing. But what is to be done, Marie, heaven has made me this way. I was born never to be happy and to trouble constantly the happiness of those around me. Haven't you discovered that by now, mon amie? Didn't you know that when you linked my destiny forever to yours? Are you weary of the task you have undertaken? There are moments when it seems to me that you bend under the burden and I can foresee that I will become a responsibility.

I do not know what lies ahead for me in this world. In vain am I told that I am surrounded by all the conditions of happiness. That is true, except for the primary one, which is peace of spirit. I lack that, and I especially lack it in proportion to how close I live to my fellow human beings. Who will ever understand the incessant tumult of my heart, who will ever take the trouble to listen to it, if it isn't you? Who will understand the many pettinesses that fill my spirit as well as the immoderate, immense taste for grandeur that pulls it ceaselessly? I have a thousand times wished that God had not allowed me to know the miseries and the limits of our nature, or that he had allowed me to see them with some detachment. But no, I am part of humanity, the vulgarest and most ordinary humanity, and yet I see something above and beyond the human condition. I forever pursue in all things an ideal that is always beyond reach. I aspire to a perfection and a wholeness that doesn't exist. For me it is all or nothing, and I struggle everyday between the feebleness of my powers and the immensity of my desires. That is the whole of me, the most unfinished and incoherent of all the members of a species that is itself the most unfinished and incoherent of all that have been created; feebler than all my fellow beings in some ways, as capable as any of them in others, poorly put together, unintegrated, constitutionally unable even to hold on to the good I have.

Haven't you known all this, Marie? Is that the man you have loved, or is it someone else? Have you misjudged your strength in thinking that you could live with him without winding up worn out or displeased? Sometimes I believe so, Marie, and that thought is the bitterest of all. Because what would become of me now without you? Who will ever listen to me, if not you? Who will know how to care for my spirit, soothe it, put it at ease, if not you? Who will be better able to tolerate my faults for my virtues? Along with the miseries of my nature. Providence seems to have sent you to relieve them.

I know that task is most difficult to bear, mon amie, I know, but if you could read my deepest heart you would see the profound gratitude that has been born there. I love you as my greatest treasure, my only consolation, my ultimate and surest strength.[25]

4

AMBITION

Tocqueville's persistent, painful self-doubt along with his great need to be independent and his consuming ambitiousness inevitably made him dissatisfied with prosaic, technical vocations. He was ill-suited for working within institutions. He needed a stage—or an occasion—for heroic action and accomplishment. He brooded much about the question of ambition, and characteristically analyzed his own to a fare-thee-well. A good aristocrat, he did not wish to appear ambitious, for him a bourgeois vice, the product of a culture that fostered grasping, self-centered self-promoting individuals with no sense of a larger good or the capacity for disinterested action. His own ambitiousness tormented him. Yet it is not surprising that someone with his complicated psychological needs would fail to be satisfied with any ordinary vocation requiring the slow development of mastery.

The "défiance de moi-même," the troubled and complicated sense of self which was a lifelong distracting interest for Tocqueville, remains at variance with his self-portrait as an individual serenely poised above history, class, and party, rationally in possession of himself. Tocqueville was in fact a restless, dissatisfied individual who lived in an almost unremitting state of interior agitation and self-doubt. He never felt fully composed or at ease in anything he undertook in any social milieu or in any vocation. His was not simply a case of the social and self-alienation customarily experienced by any critical consciousness. His "vie errant et agitée," as he called it, a formulaic phrase he used again and again in his correspondence with friends—his "mécontentement de moi-même"—showed all the signs of a spirit in radical disequilibrium, however lucid his mind. He was kept in constant turmoil and uneasy restlessness by chronic self-doubt, intense and even morbid self-consciousness, impatience with ordinary routine, a thirst for large-scale, even holistic, views and solutions, a strong dissatisfaction with the limitations of any vocation, and unease in any conventional community, which led to reclusiveness. He experienced sharp swings between euphoria and melancholy. He always saw himself at the edge of things. At the center of any sketch of his life is the blur of his often distressed and puzzled self-consciousness.

A fascinated, relentless student of his psyche, he, like Michel de Montaigne, could well have said with as much justification that whatever he was studying, he was studying himself. In view of his warnings about the multiple pathologies of individualism there is a keen irony to his self-absorption; and though he professed to be bored by his endless self-study, he pursued it to the end of his life. To Sophie Swetchine, his last confidante, in whose friendship he found some solace and to whom he sent endless, woe-laden self-analyses while apologizing for being so self-centered, he would write after giving yet another account of the sources of his melancholy and his "mécontentement de moi-même," that he found self-study increasingly fruitless and tedious: "One rightly says that you never know yourself; that is true in that you do not often discover the source of the motives that guide you; but as for the effects produced by the unknown impulses in your heart and mind, after a time you know them all too well; they appear endlessly the same way so that you are finally weary of them and turn away to other matters."[1] Like Rousseau, whom he had read well, he retreated to the calm of rural isolation to defend his identity from the dissonances of an urban intellectual world he found too stressful for his composure. His incessant auto-analysis was not self-justifying, however, but candidly self-critical. He was always examining "my motives minutely and unpityingly,"[2] and the self-critiques he shared with friends in his rich correspondence are fragments of a confession that can be unified. Of its honesty there can be no doubt. In his intimate community there was no need for him to manage his image. He may not have ransacked his psyche quite as pitilessly or as thoroughly as we moderns have learned to do, and his self-understanding, rather old-fashionedly moralistic, does not appear to have been shaped by any of the new psychological or psychiatric theories current in his time—except perhaps for the new interest in monomania, then a popular preoccupation thanks to the work of the psychiatrist Jean Etienne Esquirol, founder of the psychiatric hospital at Charenton, to which, Tocqueville jested, his family might have him sent because of his "monomanie" about America.[3]

He was not self-sparing. His *Recollections* makes no effort to magnify his virtues or to hide his failings. It is a bitter history of human failure and self-delusion, and the self-irony with which he writes of himself makes him fully part of the farce, though it is true that his almost uniform contempt for all the actors has the effect of more sharply separating the narrating consciousness from the historical moment than a more charitable tone would have done. In this drama of futility, ineptitude, and confusion, he does not give himself a heroic role.

The main elements of his ongoing confessional, self-portrait as opposed to his ideal self, a godlike figure judging history calmly, rationally, and selflessly, suggest a radical degree of self-perplexity and alienation. He saw himself fated to perpetual unhappiness and dissatisfaction by the discordant elements of his character, by overreaching ambition, and by frailty of body and will. Just before his marriage he sent a devastating self-portrait to Marie, which for all its extravagance and morbidity was, in a way, a fair assessment of the trials she would face as companion to so hypercritical and intense a character. She would frequently hear this self-critique in the years ahead:

> I shall never be happy, Marie, that is certain. Nothing is in agreement within me. With a limited and incomplete capacity, I have immense desires; with delicate health, an inexpressible need of activity and emotion; with a taste for the good, passions which lead astray; with enough intelligence to see what I ought to desire, enough folly to wish the contrary. I am of mediocre strength and mind, at the extremity in my passions and my weakness.
>
> For a man thus organized there is not the slightest chance ever, no matter what he does, of reaching a durable happiness. What is happening to me, of course, has happened to a thousand others before me. No one is happy in this world—or nearly so—save the truly superior man or the fool. The first executes the wonderful things he meditates, and the second imagines nothing above the small things that he does.[4]

The very excessiveness of this harsh self-analysis is an accurate measure of his chronic extremity of spirit. Yet apart from the fact that he did execute some of the "wonderful things" he had meditated, it is a true prophecy. His claim that he was not an integrated personality is a central theme of his confessions:

> I am constantly an insoluble problem for myself. When I am agitated and aimless, the thought of inner calm charms my imagination. Back in ordinary ways, the monotony of existence kills me. I am overwhelmed by an inexpressible anxiety of heart. I need to be stirred morally and physically, even at peril of my life. These emotional needs become irresistible, and I gnaw at myself inwardly if I do not satisfy them. In the end there is not a being in the world I know less well than myself. . . . I have a cool head and a critical, even calculating spirit, yet alongside this are ardent emotions which lead me on without persuading me and dominate my will but do not capture my mind.[5]

His intensity had the paradoxical consequence of making both activity and repose insupportable to him; his categorical intellect fashioned a dualism out of what are simply complementary human needs. Beneath all the oppositions of his character he perceived a perpetual disjunction between reason and passion, mind and heart. Such was the fundamental problem of his life and his work and in his view the fundamental political and cultural problem of the modern world.

He saw himself, uncomfortably, as a man of pride, the anatomy of which he studied thoroughly. Pride, he believed, was the source of his willfulness, his perpetual restlessness and discontent; it lay behind his tendency to melancholy and the biting self-doubt from which he suffered. "You know that there are two distinct kinds of pride," he wrote to Kergorlay,

> or rather that pride has two faces, one sad one gay. There is the pride that revels in the triumphs it enjoys or believes it has had. That pride I would call presumption. Since God has seen fit to fill me with a strong dose of the vice of pride, he might at least have sent me the kind that belongs to this first genre. But my kind of pride is of a quite different character, it is always anxious and discontented, dark and melancholy, though not envious. It reminds me every moment of all the powers I lack, and fills me with despair at the thought that they are missing. The fact is that if I do have certain qualities, they are not the ones which are clearly needed in the career I have chosen, qualities I would enjoy having . . . quickness of understanding, facility of expression, a mastery of detail, coolness. I could add many others if I meant to paint my portrait as it constantly presents itself before my eye, but that's not necessary for the one who knows me best in the world.[6]

His ambitiousness was a matter of ambivalent fascination to him. Tocqueville sometimes thought that his distressing self-doubt was the result more of excessive ambition based on his "besoin de primer" (need to be the best) than of "pride turned in an odd way." Perhaps, he wrote to Beaumont, "this great distrust of my powers . . . results from the deep desire I constantly have to be the best possible and the eternal despair I feel that I will not be able to achieve that. I fall so low because I reach so high."[7]

Yet one suspects that the problem of ambition was a matter of uneasy introspection for him not simply because it was the cause of much personal pain. He was in truth ill-equipped for the great political role he desired. It was also the cause of an invidious animus that further distanced him from his contemporaries. He experienced what he called a "rage continuelle" at being overshadowed by glib and uncomplicated men who were decidedly his inferiors. It was also the expression of a heroic self-conception that generated his grandiose personal expectations. An undeniable messianic tinge emerges from Tocqueville's "beau rêve" of leading France from its moral and political morass, suggestive of the recurring Jeanne d'Arc fantasy nourished by French culture. It is possible also to interpret much of his behavior as an expression of his self-conception as a reincarnation of the true aristocracy of France. Whatever its full meaning, he certainly sensed the immoderateness of his ambition and recognized its destructive consequences." It is unreasonable, I admit," he wrote to Kergorlay, "to ask for something other than the ordinary human destiny. But such is the involuntary and all-powerful drive of my soul. There are certain aspects of humanity that seem to me so petty that I feel cool to them all even though they are mine too."[8]

"The true malady of my soul," he wrote late in life, "is the incessant restlessness of spirit that strives to go beyond limits in everything and becomes almost insensible to the good one has most desired when it has been grasped." Grandiosity has replaced self-distrust as his great malady, though the two are different faces of the same troubled psyche.

The issue of ambition was also resonant with class meaning. In the new democratic world, ambition had been tainted by the status-anxious, self-centered, middle-class entrepreneur, whose incessant striving for place could strike an aristocratic sensibility as nothing other than a sign of social and moral disorder. It had acquired the odor of a careerism devoid of principle and grandeur. Tocqueville was anxious not to appear to be driven by "petty" ambitions: "I wish, above all," he wrote to Beaumont, "that I not be thought to be driven by one of those petty but insatiable ambitions so common in our time."[9] In America he had been dismayed by what he saw as the general triviality of ambition in a society of free men on the make, all bent on the unworthy goals of getting and spending, accumulating wealth, and achieving security (though he also noted ironically that these security seekers were also extraordinary risk takers). To witness this harbinger of democratic debasement—ease and fatness as fulfillment—made him doubly aware that the same was happening in France.

His own need for success and fame was nevertheless insatiable. He was constantly tormented by the meaning of his need for praise and recognition, fearing especially that it made him seem a self-interested participant in the struggle for advantage and power rather than a disinterested man of principle. Ambition separated from a grand, selfless vision was contemptible. The only goal worth striving for, he said, was the good of humanity, not personal success.

Moved by a gigantic ambition to accomplish something great and to shape his world, he found that none of the means available, whether the law or writing or eventually politics, were satisfactory. No conventional career, one demanding long labor at modest, circumscribed tasks, seemed to offer what he needed. No common pursuit could have seemed adequate in the face of the visionary expectations he characteristically brought to everything he undertook. Even in what turned out to be his true calling, writing, he required "un grand sujet" before he could commit himself to a piece of work. He was always preparing himself for a great role in politics, the vocation he was least suited for by temperament and ability, as he himself ultimately recognized. The law and then literature were only means to the end of securing political power and influence. The law in its tedious daily mechanized routine was much too confining and could satisfy neither his intellectual interests nor his grandiose aspirations. While serving as assistant magistrate in Versailles, he and Beaumont avidly studied history and political economy: these broader disciplines offered the intellectual stimulation and spacious perspectives he needed. According to Beaumont, Tocqueville possessed all the qualities of mind and character, among them "his grave speech, the serious turn of his thought, the maturity of his judgment, and the elevation of his mind," that would have ensured a brilliant future in the law. But he was in a crucial way ill-fitted for the profession: "The mind of Alexis de Tocqueville would have suffered by being imprisoned within the limits of a specialty. The discomfort he experienced in the law grew as the exercise of judgment diminished; to the contrary, in proportion to the seriousness of the issue, his talent opened up, as if the bonds that had restrained his intellect had been relaxed or broken."[10] He found the theoretical study of law, especially in its relation to the culture and the social system of a people, deeply interesting but grew impatient with the constraints of legal practice. "I fear becoming in time a legal machine," he wrote to Kergorlay from Versailles, "like most of my colleagues, specialists if there ever were, incapable of understanding a major development and of conducting a grand plan, for they are fit only to deduce a train of truisms and to discover analogies and contradictions. I would rather burn my books than arrive at that."[11] His fellow junior magistrates were on the way to becoming "cuistres," pedants.

He found "le métier d'écrivain," as he called it, far more congenial and liberating than the law, saying, "It attracts me more than the profession of lawyer." Yet he long regarded writing as preparation for a life in politics. He carefully promoted his literary reputation, making sure that *Democracy in America* was published at the right time and in such a way as to provide a maximum boost to his political career. Literary success would ensure political reputation and prestige. If he was anxious to be elected to the Académie française for the glory, it was also because he saw it as a step toward his political ambitions. He told Beaumont that he regarded "the Académie as the entry into the political world" for him.[12] Not even the strong advice of Royer-Collard and Mill to stay out of politics for the moment and continue writing could deter him. He expressed vexed impatience that occasions for great actions seemed to elude him: "Oh how I wish that Providence would present me with a chance to do good and great things with this inner fire I feel within which doesn't know what will nourish it, whatever perils may follow," he wrote in 1835.[13] Yet at the very moment he sent this characteristic complaint to Kergorlay he had completed the first volume of his true "bonne et grande chose," *Democracy in America*, in which he acknowledged that Providence was flattening everything into the banality and mediocrity of democracy.

The multiple oppositions of his character thus made his ambitiousness a perpetual problem. If his desire for success, reputation, and influence was ardent, he remained at the same time retiring, scrupulous, and hypercritical, easily fatigued by the turmoil of social and political life. He was constantly strung out between equally strong drives for action and withdrawal. The price of success and power in the era of democratic politics and culture was high, painfully magnifying all of his inner contradictions. For so acute an anatomist of the waywardness and shallowness of public opinion, he was curiously sensitive to it and cultivated his public reputation as a means to gain influence. He craved fame and never succeeded in achieving a philosophical detachment from conventional rewards. When the Académie was debating the Prix Montyon in 1836 (*Democracy in America* won) he managed to be walking in the street outside when the decisive meeting ended and eagerly queried Lamartine about the results.[14] He frequently troubled Royer-Collard for advice about his career, at the same time apologizing for what he confessed must have seemed his hyperactive ambition and self-absorption. To Royer he wrote of the strain he felt between his role as a man of principle in politics and his desire for success. "I love to do good," he wrote, "but I also love the success it brings. That's my weakness."[15] He admitted that he felt deep dismay and self-doubt as a result of the silence with which the "grand public" had greeted volume 2 of *Democracy in America*, which he thought was "little read and poorly understood." Royer had to reassure him of the worth of his book but recognized that Tocqueville's immense ambition required more than a literary triumph for fulfillment: "The success the need for which torments you, is not literary success: you want to affect people, shape their thoughts and their feelings. It's a noble ambition, that of being a public man and a benefactor of humanity, and it is worthy of you because your spirit is as elevated as your mind. One does not achieve that through a talent for writing or by the excellence of the work but by a certain natural grandeur which manifests itself in favorable circumstances."[16]

Royer added that the circumstances were not favorable to the emergence of such "grandeur naturelle," and he several times advised Tocqueville to keep his distance from politics. He urged Tocqueville to devote himself for the time being to his literary work. After Tocqueville was defeated in 1837 in his first try for a seat in the Chamber of Deputies, Royer again, now a bit impatiently, recommended patience: "I certainly don't know why you lost, but I prefer that you did. You ask me why, and when, then, the time will be right. It seems to me that we have already discussed the matter: you are still young and destined to live through many events; it is not advantageous to be a participant when so young at the risk of being violently thrown from one's path, and so harshly that one can't return to it."[17]

5

MELANCHOLY

Tocqueville frequently spoke of his abiding melancholy, which sometimes paralyzed him. He knew moments of élan and joy, but he often saw himself as doomed to unhappiness. He succeeded in fulfilling this self-fulfilling prophecy. He saw life as something to be endured as bravely and as strenuously as possible and thought that happiness was a meaningless, even chimerical, goal in life. He cultivated his melancholy, believing it gave him a true view of the world and of his time. In his dark and turbulent emotional life and in his powerful sense of being different, Tocqueville resembles the archetypal romantic hero of his time. Nevertheless, he sharply condemned romantic melancholy as a decadent and useless turn in French culture.

Though Tocqueville was capable of seeing himself as a redemptive figure leading France to restored glory, his self-imagination was often suffused with a sense of marginality and impotence. Despite his openly critical detachment from the romantic movement, the sense of self he conveys is ironically a nearly perfect illustration of the romantic sensibility. Tocqueville seemed created for a leading role in the spiritual melodrama of romanticism: his vision of himself resonates with some of the deepest cultural impulses of his time. His confessional self-portrait curiously resembles the archetypal spiritually wounded, withdrawn romantic hero, burning himself out in a dark world of mediocrity, indifference, and spiritual inertia. To read his correspondence is to meet a son of Chateaubriand's René, a troubled spirit with no resting place in the world. In this context, his journey to America takes on additional meaning as a kind of bildungsroman, a romantic voyage in search of self. In fact during his travels in the United States he and Beaumont went on two spontaneous adventures (see part III, chapters 4, 5) that were reenactments of romantic fables, one of which had been let loose in French literature by Chateaubriand.

He described himself at various times as "un peu unhinged [*sic*]," perpetually "agité et troublé," "habituèllement sombre et troublé," suffering from a chronic "malaise morale," an "inquiétude vague," an "incoherente activité des désires," expressions he repeatedly used in his ongoing confessional self-analysis.[1] "I lack the most important of all the requirements of happiness," he wrote, "the capacity to enjoy tranquilly the goodness of the moment."[2]

Like Montaigne and Rousseau he fled the agitation and intensity of urban life, which shattered his composure, but he found no lasting tranquility in rural life and evidently no great pleasure in nature, or in what he called "la vie ani-male" of country life, at least not until the last years of his life, when failing health and his failure in politics, along with his dismay at the demoralization of France under Napoleon III, made the pastoral calm of the Norman countryside at last satisfying. He pays little attention to the texture and detail of rural life in his writing. His most extensive descriptions of nature in fact occur in his writing about America, especially in "Quinze Jours Au Désert" (see part III), a textbook specimen of romantic sensibility, full of echoes of Chateaubriand. In the country his gaze is almost fully turned inward on his unquiet, anxious self. Yet the same absence of descriptive texture is true when he writes about city landscapes. One looks in vain through his writings and his correspondence for excited or appreciative descriptions of urban life. His Paris remains a moral setting. He conveys no sense of the aesthetic, cultural, or social texture of the great city. For a sense of what life was like in the Paris of Louis Philippe and Louis Napoleon, Tocqueville is a useless guide.

To Kergorlay he wrote that "our two spirits are like two disengaged machines, one of which is immobile, the other spinning in the void," an image recurrent in his confessional writing that catches his sense of his failure to connect.[3] He characteristically saw himself as an isolated, marginal individual, a theme of his correspondence that becomes an obsession after 1851, when he found himself a despairing internal exile in the France of Napoleon III. The social world was alien and problematic for him. Though he was capable of sustaining warm, enduring friendships, he seemed to have regarded most others with either anx-ious mistrust, supercilious indifference, or snobbish scorn. His initial response both to his new legal colleagues in Versailles in 1828 and to his new fellow immortals at the Académie française was that they were oafs. Though he made some friends among the high-minded liberal opposition in the Chamber of Deputies, he apparently did not, as we have seen, know the names of many of his colleagues. Conventional social life had few attractions for him; it was a maze of deception and insincerity: "Who has not a hundred times visited some-one who bores you and who is bored by you in order to oblige him to come in his turn to be bored and to bore you chez vous?"[4] And though he made the rounds of the literary salons of Paris, these too were simply arenas of deception, "where honesty itself has a hundred artifices." Apart from his friendships, he was comfortable only in a few carefully cultivated epistolary relationships, as, for example, with Sophie Swetchine, the mystical Russian Catholic exile who nurtured a salon of such refined and subtle sensibility that Henry James thought her milieu couldn't be understood by anyone who hadn't participated fully in it.[5]

Tocqueville felt he was not only misunderstood by others, but also ultimately a mystery to himself. "Most people do not understand me," he wrote, "and that does not surprise me, because I do not understand myself." He could no more clearly see "the depth of my being than I could the center of the earth."[6] The problem of his identity became so absorbing to him that one senses he deliberately cultivated his puzzlement about it. He may well have valued whatever set him apart, a condition he had already achieved morally.

Undoubtedly his flimsy health and frequent physical collapses contributed to his self-perception as a marginal, doomed individual. His poor health, often "bien dérangée," kept him on the edge of despair and concentrated his sense of uniqueness. He was not like others. What he called his health he said "would be the illness of others." By his midthirties he felt he was disintegrating physically. "I confess to you," he wrote to Edouard, "that in this respect the future seems dark to me." "Health is a cannonball that I drag behind me," he said; "it is often quite heavy." In his mind it became a metaphor for his spiritual condition, the visible stigma of a profoundly wounded soul. The overwhelming effect on his psyche of his wavering and then worsening health—Tocqueville was, in effect, chronically ill—would have underscored his sense of difference as well as a subtle conviction of superiority. For the valetudinarian, survival can become a triumph of will and spirit. The chronic *malade* may even feel singled out by Providence for a special destiny. Tocqueville never claims that, but the comparison he often draws between himself and others stresses his sense of uniqueness.[7]

The persistent melancholy from which he suffered was also the focus of much self-analysis. It too served as a metaphor for his moral condition as well as a valuable perspective from which he viewed the world. Whatever its genesis, whether influenced by his depressed mother or a matter of genetic inheritance, like his flawed physical condition, it became for him a way of being in the world, a state of mind. He was as preoccupied with the problem and meaning of his "tristesse" as any romantic artist. If he often wrote of it as a malady to be overcome for the sake of effective action, it was also, he realized, a mode of perception, a kind of moral condition to be valued for the truths it yielded. While he prescribed work as an effective distraction from "all the sad thoughts that line the depths of my soul," he felt that the underlying melancholy of his life was too important a part of his way of seeing for him to change it. To Ampère he wrote that his melancholy was "a sadness without remedy, because though it makes you suffer, you don't wish to be cured of it. It is also of great value to you. It is sorrow that gives me a true view of my time and my country."[8]

6

SKEPTICAL ROMANTIC

In view of his own innate romanticism, Tocqueville's rationalist condemnation of romanticism illuminates another aspect of his complicated relationship to his culture and adds to one's understanding of him as a man awkwardly caught between two cultural eras, powerfully related to yet critically detached from both. He was a dangling man. His self-image is a collage of romantic motifs, yet despite his emotional affinities with this cultural moment he remained morally and intellectually hostile to it. His relationship to the Enlightenment was equally complicated. The divisions within were deep.

Tocqueville's emphasis on passion and heart, his tendency to invest freedom with redemptive powers, his admiration of daring and greatness of spirit and his disdain for bourgeois prudence, his longing for a life of heroic action, his praise of self-sacrifice in the pursuit of noble goals, his desire to reintegrate knowledge, religion, and morality and to reunite past and present, his celebration of the striving individual ready to stand alone against society to fulfill his vision, and his constant lament about the growth of uniformity in the modern world—all are deeply rooted in his temperament. These complex visions are central to his politics. And they are central to his art as well, for Tocqueville's histories are as much works of literature as political science. The dramaturgical turn of thought that adds power to his work has its source as much in a romantic sensibility that sought truth by exploring extremes as in the special taste for paradox of the ambivalent personality. Tocqueville was a romantic artist fascinated by upheavals, ruins, great events, dramatic confrontations, the idiosyncratic. His account of his first, spontaneous dash into the American West, "Quinze Jours Au Désert," is a fine example of romantic writing, reveling in the drama of wild nature, full of mystery, bold contrasts, violence, the sublime, the exotic, images of life and death intertwined, a sense of the ominous.

His self-image is constructed out of these same emotional elements. He is the melancholy, troubled, isolated, wandering, anxious hero, a kind of

misunderstood, visionary *malade* facing a tragic destiny, seeking love and meaning in the wasteland of modern life while at the same time trying to recover a
sense of lost wholeness by reconnecting with the past.

The romantic in Tocqueville would alone have been enough to make
America distasteful to him, as it sometimes was, except for the wilderness,
which raised the deepest reflections about man's destiny. He was appalled by a
people who, as he often said, were cold and completely rational, whose culture
expressed a coherent system of logically connected laws, institutions, and customs. The Americans were becoming more and more alike. In losing those
distinctive national and ethnic, or racial, as he called them, identities they had
brought to the New World, they were losing something vital, a source of
strength. His remarks, strewn through his travel notebooks, are perfect illustra-
tions of the romantic catechism about the preciousness of distinctive national
traits and the value of diversity. He thought the Americans were a people whose
imaginations were frozen, though oddly also grandiose.

Yet his intense absorption with self never became for Tocqueville an avowed
principle of politics or the imagination. He offered no affirmation of individualism and never argued that subjectivity was a privileged mode of perception. He
rejected sorrow, suffering, and disgust with the world as useless and morally
indefensible. Though he felt culturally and socially alienated, he did not flaunt
his otherness; and if he passionately guarded his independence, he made no
claim for unlimited liberty in the name of genius, conscience, or rights. His
idea of freedom was always moderate and always linked to notions of responsibility and order. The more florid manifestations of romantic exoticism did not
interest him, and he assailed the romantic fascination with the morbid and the
grotesque as a perverse tendency of modern, that is, democratic or romantic,
literature. Early literary manifestations of perceived decadence must have
appalled him if he read them. His critical detachment from romantic culture
was so striking that Ampère felt compelled to comment on it extensively in his
memoir of Tocqueville. It is an arresting analysis of Tocqueville by a literary
man who knew him intimately:

> In literature as in politics, he demanded reason and he loved grandeur. The
> ordinary disgusted him and the bizarre shocked him strongly. He did not
> admire the imagination if it wasn't sensible. Perhaps in this respect he car-
> ried his severity somewhat too far. His youth, which ended early, had shielded
> him from the twists and turns of thought and imagination through which
> many in our generation passed: although he much admired René and was
> related as well to the author, he never belonged to the family of René. His
> heart, fully capable of passion, never knew, I believe, the dream world of

passions. In all things he understood only the direct and the clear. He disliked subtlety in any genre, and all the wit in the world could not make it acceptable to him. He pushed his taste for clarity, spareness, and evidence until it almost became a kind of antipathy for philosophical discussion—he who was above all a philosophical spirit—and for theological controversy—he who was so strongly drawn to religious matters.

He never dwelled in that world of vague enthusiasms, innovations, modishness, and transient joys in which so many among us had dwelt. Perhaps therefore a number of misty, glowing horizons had been closed to him, but his had gained in clarity, in calmness, in just proportions, though not in immense and confused extent.[1]

Though Ampère was more sympathetic than Tocqueville to romanticism, he believed that Tocqueville's detachment from its unrestrained enthusiasms and innovativeness paradoxically helped his friend maintain a certain originality and clarity of vision:

These days everyone knows everything, has read everything, compared everything, understood everything. How often one successively admires and believes the most contradictory things. The intellect is certainly exercised in this way by all men, but it is often worn out and almost always the spirit is weakened. The visionaries who think this way and confuse everything, produce dazzlements, and dazzlements blind. The question is how to walk straight ahead, in effect, through a maze in which so many so diverse roads unroll before us. The result of considering all things in all their aspects is that one loses *la notion vraie des choses* [an understanding of the real order of things]; by wishing to comprehend everything one succeeds in understanding nothing at all.[2]

In these remarks Ampère was undoubtedly reflecting Tocqueville's own views about a cultural movement that in its promiscuous versatility and exultant subjectivity had obscured "la notion vraie des choses" and had compounded the moral and intellectual confusions of modernity.

7

SKEPTICAL PHILOSOPHE

By his own account, Tocqueville's encounter with the French Enlightenment shaped his mind enduringly. It bound him to a skepticism so strong that he turned it on enlightened thought itself. The qualities of precision and formality, of balance and directness that he aimed at in his writing, which impresses with its relentless logical pursuit of implication and its neoclassical clarity, makes him very much a voice of the eighteenth century, especially in its belief in the force and light of reason. So does his willingness to question everything—ideas, institutions, authority. He was a true liberal, believing that nothing was sacred, though he was not completely free of illusions and partialities. Yet if in many ways he was an heir of the Enlightenment, his critical disavowal of many of its central faiths and intellectual assumptions kept him awkwardly suspended between commitment and uncertainty.

As he sat at his desk writing, Tocqueville could look up and see a bust of Malesherbes, his illustrious eighteenth-century ancestor, his maternal great-grandfather, whose peculiar distinction it was to have been a defender of both the philosophes and Louis XVI. It was not simply a gesture of ancestral pride and piety that made Tocqueville look to Malesherbes more than anyone as a moral hero of the eighteenth century. A symbol of Tocqueville's own complicated relationship to the Enlightenment, Malesherbes was a supporter both of free inquiry and the scientific study of humanity and society and also of the "wisdom of the ages" as embedded in the complex institutions that structure human society. He acknowledged, that is, the claims of both reason and tradition. His ambiguous stance had been too much for the terrible simplifiers of 1793–94. For some, it has proven too much to accept or even understand about Tocqueville as well.

Tocqueville was no Joseph deMaistre seeking to erase the eighteenth century and to impose on society a fixed order derived from eternal truths. He thought that the Great Revolution initially had been a good thing, embodying noble aspirations until shanghaied by berserkers; and though he had been quietly opposed to the July Revolution he felt that the Restoration had seriously erred in its reactionary program. Enlightened reform, if moderate, was essential. He was deeply influenced by the philosophes and on the whole accepted their intellectual agenda. Their skeptic, critical disposition was very much his: truth was attained through free, rational, scientific inquiry in all areas of human life. There were few if any absolute truths; the effort to understand should not stand silent before vested interests and institutions; no myths or institutions were finally sacred. These are the traits of an essentially liberal mind, and such were his intellectual convictions. They did not always prevent him from being a passionate defender of the status quo or of institutions he believed were essential to social order and civilized life.

His historical and sociological inquiries, while critical of the spiritual damage done by the excesses of the Enlightenment, were meant to carry out the Enlightenment historicist program. They are fundamentally scientific efforts to pierce through mythologies and ideologies to establish a true understanding of laws of social and historical development. That is as true of *Democracy in America*, over which the shadow of Providence falls, as it is of the much more historically grounded *L'Ancien Régime et la révolution*. Tocqueville's mind is as skeptical, as relativist, as historicist as that of any of the philosophes. In fact he is in many ways more critical and less credulous than the eighteenth-century philosophers, for he brings to the scrutiny of intellectual and social processes an unremitting skepticism and self-reflexive tendencies that make him seem far less naive than the epigones of the Enlightenment or their nineteenth-century descendants the St. Simonians, Comteans, and other utopian socialists. He has gone a step beyond them and pierced the myth of reason, too. He was, as Mill said, an exemplary figure of the transitional era through which they were living, able to see through and evaluate both old and new truth claims and methods.[1]

Tocqueville's quarrel with the eighteenth century, which quietly shapes the whole argument of *Democracy in America* like a commenting chorus, surfaces powerfully in *L'Ancien Régime*. Though he is sympathetic to the philosophes' critique of the "absurd and unjust privileges" and "ridiculous and ramshackle institutions" that afflicted eighteenth-century France—but not sympathetic to their dream of instantly transforming them—his central animus against the philosophes is that, being "quite out of touch with practical politics," they had indulged in "abstract theories and generalizations regarding the nature of government" and had become "much bolder in their speculations, more addicted to general ideas, more contemptuous of the wisdom of the ages."[2] In their impetuous quest for a new rational order they had shattered not simply their society but a clear image of humankind. They had lost sight of "la notion vraie des choses"; they had left out too much of the truth about humans and society. They were the progenitors of the terrible simplifiers of the new age. Their fantastic emphasis on human rationality, ostensibly aimed at freeing the human spirit, had paradoxically created a new instrument of bondage, the belief in humans as machines.

Tocqueville's work is a prolonged debate with the central assumptions of the Enlightenment. His questioning quietly shapes *Democracy in America*, occasionally emerging openly. Recoiling from the burden of doubt that had resulted from his encounter with eighteenth-century philosophy, he struggled all his life to attain faith and belief and to escape the oppressive threat of an even greater Pyrrhonism. He stood at the edge of nihilism but even there experienced its horrors. Perhaps that glimpse into nothingness was an aspect of the "religious terror" he sometimes said he experienced.

One finds Tocqueville, far from regarding the past with serene, philosophic detachment, struggling, Laocoön-like, to free himself from the coiled ambiguities of his relationship to the Enlightenment. He did not wholly reject the Enlightened faith in progress, but he did not agree that the advance of rationality, knowledge, and technology could be equated with human progress and the advance of civilization. This skepticism flickers through his travel notebooks and *Democracy in America*, especially in his comments on the weakening of folk culture and instinctual life by the extension of human rationality; in his vision of the cold destructiveness of the so-called Anglo-American race, a people among whom he thought heart had become dominated by reason; and in his painful commentary on the subversion of the Native Americans by the more technologically advanced Europeans, whose claim to moral and cultural superiority was in his view untenable. He mocked the notion of human perfectibility and, like Emerson, refused to identify progress with material and intellectual advance.

Yet if Tocqueville's view of history was strongly shaped by a sense of human limitations and of the ironies and losses of progress and by a tragic conception of life, he was no cultural Luddite. The coming of the railroad to Cherbourg in 1853 did not fill him with rhapsodic visions of the future, but neither was his response a Gallic version of the machine in the garden. He accepted the reality and necessity of change and believed that on the whole the life of humanity was progressive and that the intellectual and material conquests of Western culture were liberating and productive. Indeed, an equally great fear expressed in *Democracy in America* is that democracy would breed so strong a love of well-being and material comfort that democratic peoples would lose the will and vision necessary for great effort and advance. Despite his piercing remarks about the destruction of the American Indian, his admiration of their culture and moral superiority, and his brooding about the losses entailed in the development of rationalist cultures, he could at the same time sound very much the Western chauvinist as he justified European domination of colonized peoples on the grounds of the superiority of Western culture.[3] He saw the impoverishment of a great portion of the laboring population as an inevitable, if regrettable, result of industrial development, which he quietly accepted as good or at least as Providential. If the extreme symbol of the Western thirst for progress was the cold and furiously destructive Anglo-American or the new, heartless destroyer of the Revolution who slew in the name of reason, an equally horrific counterexample was the moribund civilization of China, so locked in tradition and an enclosed system of ideas that it could make no intellectual or material advance at all.[4]

Similarly, he found the idea of happiness, especially the idea of happiness as a quest or a goal, chimerical. His ironic remarks in *Democracy in America* about the restless anxiety of a people blessed with all the conditions of happiness yet so fanatically committed to its pursuit that they were often driven to melancholy and madness were not simply ethnographic observations but also comments on the Enlightenment dream of happiness. He found happiness meaningless as a personal goal; remarks like the following are a silent counterpoint to *Democracy in America*: "Life then is neither a splendid nor a terrible thing," he wrote to his friend Stoffels,

> but (permit me to say) a middling [médiocre] thing. One shouldn't expect too much of it, nor fear it too much, but attempt to see it as it is, without resignation or enthusiasm, as what is given, not what one has made, that one will not be able to transform and that the question above all is to make it bearable. Don't think that I have arrived at this point of view without great struggle, nor that I hold it unwaveringly. Like you, like all men everywhere, I feel within me an ardent desire that drives me to regard happiness as the greatest good, but that—be sure of it—is a folly that one must struggle against. Such a sentiment is not manly and can lead to nothing that is manly [virile]. Life is neither a delight nor a sadness, but a grave responsibility that has been given us, and our duty is to do the best we can with it.[5]

This stoical view of life may have given him inner strength and helped him find "greater calm about what lies ahead, greater strength to bear the pain, the boredom, the monotony and the vulgarity of daily life, and fewer immoderate hopes for whatever."[6] The continued turbulence of his emotional life suggests, however, that he often failed to maintain the chastened resignation his ideal self recommended.

The Enlightenment's fantastic faith in reason, progress, perfectibility, and happiness was a minor issue compared to the scientific materialism, determinism, and skepticism it had fostered. It was against these threats that Tocqueville argued most desperately throughout his life. He rejected the sensationalist, mechanistic foundations of Enlightenment thought as philosophically inadequate and morally destructive approaches to a true understanding of humankind. The scientific materialism explicit in the work of thinkers like Claude Helvétius, Paul Henri Baron d'Holbach, and Julien La Mettrie was tacit in all Enlightened thought: it culminated in the man–machine image that was the ominous symbol of the age and was immensely threatening to human freedom and moral dignity. It had silenced or eliminated God, emptied the universe of moral meaning, and destroyed religious faith. Tocqueville's struggle against it was also a struggle within himself.

He rejected as well the eighteenth-century faith that a uniform theory of human behavior and thought, after the Newtonian model, was possible. The quest for great systems and general theories ultimately trapped men in fatalistic doctrines and denied the freedom of the human spirit. Such was the essential basis of his objection to the work of both Gobineau and G. W. F. Hegel and to a tendency in "democratic historians" to employ schemes of general causes to account for human behavior. "For my part," he wrote, "I detest these absolute systems which represent all the events of history as depending upon great first causes linked by the chain of fatality and which, as it were, suppress men from the history of the human race. They seem narrow to my mind, under their pretense of broadness, and false beneath their air of mathematical exactness."[7] *Democracy in America* is full of strictures against the mechanist and materialist conception of man. To ignore the unpredictable, incalculable dimension of human spirituality, he argues, would truly end the possibility of any kind of human progress. It would deprive the historian or those attempting to create a new science of society of a crucial means of understanding human behavior. More seriously, it would demoralize those who believed that values, will, and choice could intervene in history to guide the development of society.[8]

Yet in his own search for a comprehensive understanding of the historical development of democracy, the origins of the French Revolution, the rise of the centralized state, the causes of social change, and the ways in which social structure and social change affect culture, Tocqueville too sought to penetrate the varied surface of history to discover the general laws and forces that were shaping modern societies. Though the moral argument of *Democracy in*

America centers on the crucial importance of faith in human freedom and in the essential spirituality of humankind, his history is not only wholly secular but also, in its explanatory scheme, completely mechanistic; he tries to escape this problem by attributing to human nature a reservoir of unsocializable instincts, thirsts, and needs, as he does in his discussions of religion in America, or by claiming that the immense historical evolution he describes is ultimately the work of a guiding Providence. Apart from the extremely faint shadow of God over the whole human scene, about all that remains of the paradigm of Christian history in his work is the principle of linear development along with a growing apprehension of impending apocalypse. And even his apocalypse is a kind of anti-apocalypse. The nightmare vision of an inert society, or paradoxically of a culture without any sense of order and limits with which *Democracy in America* concludes, embodies the idea of a final failure to achieve any kind of transcendence. His democratic Hell could be either a tranquil, somnolent, secular scene in which society is an eternal barnyard, or a disorderly contest of competing, self-regarding groups struggling for advantage without a sense of the larger social good—Matthew Arnold's "ignorant armies clashing in the night." Both the argument and the structure of explanation of *Democracy in America* are shaped by the unresolved contradictions between Tocqueville's historicism and his belief in human freedom, between his science and his faith.

8

Skepticism and Religion: "Une Ombre Vaine"

Though Tocqueville's thought was not framed by religious concepts or expressed in religious language, his life was a continual spiritual quest that ended unresolved. He was permanently caught in the mazeway of reason and could avow no creed or unquestioningly accept anything on faith. Yet even if he was unable to give shape to his spiritual impulses, he was not a wholly secular man and was constantly moved by religious feelings even though he was not equipped to express them. He was outside of all organized, institutionalized religions and formal creeds and remained critical of them. He might be thought of as a sociologist of comparative religion. Yet on its deepest level *Democracy in America* constantly deals with religious questions: questions about man's powers and his fate and about the possibility of transcending history.

Tocqueville's struggle with the materialist and skeptical implications of Enlightenment thought was pitched most fiercely on the level of personal faith. His restless analytic consciousness and imperious intellectuality dissolved all certainties for him. After his birthright Catholicism was undermined by his early encounter with the philosophes, he spent the rest of his life searching for belief without resorting to the intellectually unacceptable strategies of dogma, mysticism, or sentimentalism. Doubt, however, was to remain a permanent plague for him. He had lost not only his Catholic faith but also the dream of certitude. He had early discovered—"it was the unhappiest time of my life"— that "the quest for absolute truth, like the search for perfect happiness, was a quest for the impossible." He was convinced that "for the great majority of questions that we must deal with, we have only approximations and probabilities." Though he learned to act in the face of uncertainty and to give existential reality to truths he couldn't demonstrate, doubt was a state of mind ill-matched to his passionate temper, a burden to his spirit. He considered doubt "one of the greatest miseries of our nature," and he placed it just below illness and death on his scale of evils, revealing how heavily his illness weighed on him.[1]

He did not have a skeptical temperament and remained a believer without beliefs. While he refused to indulge in metaphysical speculation he nonetheless pursued the phantom of exactitude to a degree that he admitted was pathological. "There is also another intellectual malady that troubles me ceaselessly," he wrote to Royer-Collard during his seemingly endless labor on the second volume of *Democracy in America,* in which he pursues the deductive parsing of his *aperçus* to an astonishing extreme: "and that is an irrational and unbridled thirst for certainty. Experience shows me that life is full only of probabilities and approximations, yet I constantly feel within me a taste for the absolute. I persevere in the pursuit of fleeting shadows that constantly escape me and that I cannot console myself for having failed to grasp."[2] In a world of "probabilities and approximate truths," belief for Tocqueville remained "une ombre vaine" (a fleeting shadow).

All of these intellectual and temperamental tendencies focused in his search for religious belief. On the deepest level his life was a struggle against meaninglessness, which he sought to resolve not by adopting any metaphysical system, but through an act of will. Neither the religious impulse he felt so strongly nor his quest for certainty found fulfillment in any system of belief. If he found doubt insupportable, he also regarded metaphysical and theological speculation as a gratuitous activity that only increased human intellectual and spiritual torment. "I have always thought that metaphysics and all the purely theoretical sciences that serve no purpose in real life," he wrote to Stoffels, "to be a torment that man voluntarily inflicts upon himself."[3] Though the religious beliefs he finally achieved resemble little more than the mild affirmations of rational religion, Tocqueville could sound almost as anti-intellectual as the most convinced fundamentalist who never questions the truths of divine revelation. But his fundamental truths were the self-evident truths of reason: "I would have had a passionate taste for philosophical studies . . . if I had been able to derive any profit from them. I always arrived at the conclusion that everything the sciences said concerning the truths of religion did not get me closer and often much less close to that very small number of very simple plain ideas that I arrived at immediately intuitively, and that all men, in fact, have more or less grasped."[4] On the major religious questions he found that "the most precise metaphysics" failed to provide him with clearer ideas "than the plainest common sense."[5] That his small inventory of religious truths originated in common sense was a claim he made often. In doing so he again identified himself with that current of eighteenth-century rationalism that culminates in Deism. Late in his life, in a now-well-known letter to his "confessor," the pious liberal Catholic Russian exile Mme Swetchine, he spelled out his credo. The "petit nombre d'idées simples" with which he started "easily lead directly to the idea of a first cause which is both self-evident and inconceivable; to those constant laws the physical realm reveals and that must be assumed hold also for the moral realm; to God's providence and by consequence to his justness; to man's responsibility for his acts once he recognizes that there is good and evil; and consequently to the thought that there is another life."[6] This statement of faith is straight out of the Deist catechism. "Le bon sens" was his refuge between skepticism and the claims of revealed religion. His beliefs were minimal assumptions he made to escape the absurdity and moral incoherence of life. In adopting this thin Deism he sounds very much like a disciple of his contemporary the philosopher Victor Cousin, whose eclectic commonsense system—derived in part from the Scottish realist philosopher Thomas Reid and in part from Cousin's predecessor at the Collège de France Royer-Collard—greatly influenced the serious "new youth" of Tocqueville's generation. But Tocqueville never listened to Cousin's lectures, and there is no evidence that he read much by the prolific Cousin. Yet it is impossible to believe that he was not thoroughly familiar with the ideas, the system, of the man who was the guru of Tocqueville's generation, a guiding spirit of the romantic, rebellious young who felt, like Tocqueville, that it was their destiny to redeem France. If Tocqueville's was a whole generation of Jeanne d'Arcs, the voice it heard was not that of God but that of Cousin—until they eventually became sober, responsible members of the established order, which sadly remained as imperfect as ever.[7]

Though such thin affirmations were scarcely satisfying to so passionate a spirit and to a mind with so unquenchable a thirst for certainty, he never moved beyond them. If he suffered from religious pain, one never senses that he was capable of making a Pascalian leap of faith in defiance of reason. At most he was left suspended in a perpetual encounter with mystery, with what he called "the depths which I cannot reach": "the purpose of creation; the destiny of creation of which we know nothing, not even of our body, much less of our spirit; the fate of that singular being we call man, to whom has been given just enough light to show him the misery of his condition and not enough to change it . . . such is the fundament, or rather the basic truths that my spirit thirsts to grasp but which always remain infinitely beyond my capacity to understand."[8] Neither Christian mythology nor Catholic dogma offered meanings that lay beyond his "ability to know the truth."

Yet neither did Tocqueville release his feelings in any devotional expression. A sense of religious piety is notably absent in his confessional writing, and passages in which he expresses religious emotion or even simply describes a religious experience are rare. He is no more than "profoundly moved," for example, when he reads the Gospels.[9] What was it that moved him? He does not say. It is improbable that he spent time in prayer or in religious meditation. His God was not at all a personal God, but rather, as he put it, "a first cause . . . immediately evident and inconceivable."

Indeed, Tocqueville's God is a God already horribly silent. When at the opening and conclusion of *Democracy in America* Tocqueville, viewing the turmoil and confusions of history, raises questions about God's intentions, the implied silence is immense. In the end, neither science nor religion has provided answers. A final, appropriate setting for these meditations was the deep silence of the American frontier forest. The idea of a silent god, this time refusing to respond to puzzled man, returns powerfully in an account of one of Tocqueville's wilderness experiences. He has been describing his encounter with a Nature that is clearly a hieroglyph packed with interwoven meanings of existence:

> We have often admired one of those calm and serene evenings on the ocean when the sails flap quietly by the mast, leaving the sailor doubtful whence the breeze will rise. This repose of nature is no less impressive in the solitude of the New World than on the immensity of the sea. At midday, when the sun darts its beams on the forest, one often hears in its depths something like a long sigh, a plaintive cry lingering in the distance. It is the last stir of the dying wind. Then everything around you falls back into a silence so deep, a stillness so complete, that the soul is invaded by a kind of religious terror. The traveler halts and looks around; pressed one against the other and with their branches interlaced, the forest trees seem to form but one whole; an immense and indestructible edifice under whose vaults eternal darkness reigns. On whatever side he looks, he sees nothing but a field of violence and destruction. Broken trees and torn trunks—everything testifies that the elements are here perpetually at war. But the struggle is interrupted. One would say that at the behest of a supernatural power, movement is suddenly halted. Half broken branches seem still held by secret ties to the trunks that no longer support them; uprooted trees have not yet had time to reach the ground, and stay suspended in the air. He listens and holds his breath in fear to better catch the least echo of life; no sound, no murmur reaches him . . . all is still in the woods, all is silent under their leaves. One would say that for a moment the Creator had turned his face away and all the forces of nature are paralyzed.[10]

There is probably more religious feeling in this passage than in anything else Tocqueville wrote. Here is Nature highly colored by Tocqueville's imagination. It is a tableau in which he finds objective correlatives for the deepest preoccupations of his spirit. In the midst of this profound stillness Tocqueville "the traveler" again experiences what he calls "religious terror." Nature offers images of every stage of life; the whole cycle of life, from birth to death to rebirth, is caught in a frozen or "paralyzed" chaos. Destruction and creation are blended into an enormous, mute reality; the old and the new hang together intertwined and make dramatically visible the question of change. The problem of meaning is posed, and the Creator, having "turned his face away," answers with silence.

He never said what he meant by "religious terror," a phrase he often used to describe his state of mind, or rather his emotional condition, during certain intense experiences when he felt he had arrived at the limits of his understanding and had to confront a reality that was either beyond comprehension or meaningless. If he meant that he had experienced the sacred, he did not use that term. He did not often explore his religious experiences. Perhaps they filled him with the kind of apprehensiveness that makes one mute, speechless at the edge of language. He gives no meaning to the transcendent, other than terror.[11]

Tocqueville's defense of Christianity was almost wholly ethical. It had been the major force for morality and civility in Western civilization. His test for the truth of Christianity seemed essentially to be that of historical survival: it had triumphed in the marketplace of competing ideas and faiths and had made men and cultures more humane.[12] When he read Pascal, he did not take notes on Pascal's "the heart has its reasons" justification of his faith, but on Pascal's pragmatic proof of the truth of Christianity: it had improved men and had survived. His notes on Pascal are in literal, commonplace-book style. They are neither reflective nor analytic; he asks no questions. They seem dutiful—or despairing.[13]

His test for the truth of other religions was equally pragmatic and enlightened. What were their moral effects? On such grounds, for example, he condemned Islam, with its doctrine "that salvation is through faith, that the greatest of all religious obligations is to obey the prophet without question, that holy struggle is the greatest of good works." "The violent and sensual tendencies of the Koran," he wrote, "are so striking that I can't imagine anyone of perception would miss them. The Koran is an advance over polytheism in that it contains clearer and truer ideas of divinity and in that it explains more extensively and clearly certain general obligations of humanity. But it inflames, and taking all into account I don't know if it hasn't been more harmful than salutary."[14] His judgments about Islam were constantly harsh, though it is doubtful he had more than a superficial knowledge of the religion.

He was far more a student of comparative religion and of religious behavior than he was of the truth claims or of the experiential dimensions of various religions, including Christianity. He was appalled by the squabbling of sectarians and religious fanatics, who, he said, "will finally make me a voltairian if I am not careful."[15] To his dismay he thought the terrible religious contentiousness and bitterness of European civilization was being reproduced even in America, where he noted that "six different religions or sects divide the faith of this nascent society," with the result that "disputes rage about the heaven that everyone claims as his exclusive heritage. Beyond that, even in the midst of the wretchedness of solitude and the troubles of the present, human imagination wears itself out inventing inexpressible sorrows for the future. The Lutheran condemns the Calvinist to eternal fire, the Calvinist the Unitarian, and the Catholic embraces them all in a common condemnation."[16] This kind of sectarian exclusiveness and self-righteousness was foreign to his temper and to his religious beliefs. He was equally critical of sequestering modes of piety, which in emphasizing "les vertus privées" lost sight of "les vertus publiques." When in the 1850s his good friend Corcelle slipped into a deeper religious piety, Tocqueville was alarmed. "I fear this will focus his whole life on religion," he wrote to Beaumont, "that is to say, on a realm that will increasingly make him a stranger to people like us. I even fear that (because he is an intense spirit) this will eventually somewhat distance him from the liberalism which is the only aspect of the old Corcelle that survives."[17] The sad example of Corcelle, he wrote, "alone suffices to explain to me all the follies and even the crimes into which the sectarian spirit has been able to seduce even the noblest and purest hearts."[18] He himself would never be touched by such zealousness.

Tocqueville showed only mild interest in or sympathy for the varieties of religious experience. He was more a rational student of religion and of religious sociology than he was a committed participant. His disgust with the kind of cloistral piety and sentimentalism then modish in the world of female "dévots" was milder than his bitter rejection of religious enthusiasm only because its malign political effects were passive. The "esprit excessif" that he saw seizing Corcelle is, after all, the natural impulse of an overflowing faith and it is at the heart of the religious experience. Tocqueville was simply appalled by it. It is no surprise that he failed to gauge correctly or even really to notice the great importance of evangelical religion in America, where he incorrectly saw the flow of religious life moving toward either rational religion (Unitarianism) or authoritarian religion (Catholicism), predicting that the authoritarian strain would triumph since the rationalist option was either too demanding or too unsatisfying for most men. He did note the emotional turbulence of American religious life but thought it might result in what he saw as madness. There were many reasons for Tocqueville's failure to appreciate the meaning and force of American evangelicalism, but among them was his insensitivity to emotional or experiential religion, which strongly repelled him. Though he had quickly seen how important religion was in American life, he thought that there was nevertheless something thin about it and that it was in danger of being commodified by the fatal touch of the larger culture, which brought a "trading taste" to everything.

Despite his personal religious longing and his metaphysical uneasiness, Tocqueville's tough intellectuality kept him trapped inside the rationalist cage. He was, all his life, preoccupied with the problem of faith in the age of democracy and science. He did not resolve that problem on the level of personal faith. It persisted as an unresolved issue that profoundly influenced all areas of his life. His effort to define a new kind of liberalism, one in which the realms of politics and morality were fused while avoiding zealousness, and his quest for a morally informed social science in which values were intrinsic to method were expressions, in his politics and in his literary art, of his inconclusive personal quest to unite faith and knowledge.

There is a cross on his gravestone in the cemetery at Tocqueville. It is not an emblem of his faith, but the last gesture of a seignieur who thought it his duty to encourage belief. But belief was beyond his own grasp, despite his spiritual longing. As he mourned his father's death in May of 1856, he wrote movingly to Corcelle of his father's many virtues and deep piety, which informed every aspect of his life: "The life and death of my poor father has been for me the greatest evidence of the excellence of religion. It has filled me with the strongest desire to believe. But alas, who is able to do so, if God does not move it?"[19]

9

Doubt and the Will to Believe

Tocqueville's will to believe was constantly at war with his all-pervasive will to doubt. At the end of *Democracy in America* he attempts to turn self-doubt into an escape from doubt and from the bleak view of the future of democracy he had inexorably arrived at. Self-reflexively he questions the scope of his knowledge and of his perspective, and he allows that his understanding of democracy may be shaped by his time and his culture. Objective understanding may be beyond reach: the observer becomes part of the problem. With this confession of his limitations, Tocqueville opens the door to belief and takes a Pascalian leap to a hope that humankind may be able to transcend its entrapment in history.

The problem of belief and the difficult relationship of knowledge, value, and action absorbed Tocqueville almost as much as the issues of political and social order and of personal and public morale on which his writing focused directly. In *Democracy in America* he occasionally turns his critical attention to the problem of knowledge itself. On perhaps its profoundest level *Democracy in America* is shaped by Tocqueville's continuing debate about the problem of belief and knowledge as well as about the Enlightenment doctrines of progress and happiness. To understand Tocqueville's personal struggle against skepticism and doubt, which oppressed him throughout his life, is to give richer meaning to the many passages in *Democracy in America* in which questions about knowledge and belief come to the fore and his central lines of inquiry shift temporarily out of focus.[1] He was a self-conscious, doubt-stricken observer, wrestling not only with complex social and political questions but also with the problem of knowledge. The uncertainty that dogged his personal search for belief appears also in his work.

The tension between doubt and belief is at the heart of the concluding chapter of *Democracy in America*, just as it is central to the chapter that begins the work. Tocqueville falters as he tries to take a last large view of his subject, "my vision hazy and my judgment hesitant."[2] "The world which is arising is still half-buried in the ruins of the world falling into decay," he goes on, developing a motif of the book's first chapter, "and in the vast confusion of human affairs at present, no one can know which of the old institutions and former mores will continue to hold up their heads and which will go under." Nevertheless, in the midst of all this uncertainty, in which "the spirit of man walks through the night," Tocqueville bravely tries a summary view of the vast transformation that has been his subject. But his effort collapses. He confesses that he only imperfectly understands the emerging new world, even though some of its salient characteristics can be clearly enough perceived.

He admits that he, the observer, is also the problem. The difficulty is not simply that the social reality he is trying to measure is extraordinarily complex; it is that his own prejudices as well as his intellectual limitations continue to obscure the truth. He sees much in the new world of democracy that "saddens and chills" him; he admits that he is "tempted to regret the state of society which has ceased to be." He recognizes his weakness in continuing to make judgments that may be irrelevant in a new age and acknowledges his inability to take a transcendent view of his subject, similar to that of the "the Almighty and Eternal Being, whose gaze of necessity included the whole of created things and who surveys distinctly and simultaneously all mankind and each single man," and whose conception of justice is broader than Tocqueville's own. There is nothing dogmatic about Tocqueville: he disavows any claim to know the complete truth about history and societies. He vows to do all he can "to enter into understanding of this divine view of the world and strive from thence to consider and judge the affairs of men." What Tocqueville means by this religious metaphor is not only that he must try to move beyond the limits of his understanding, but also that he has to rise above the limits of his judgments. And he offers a complex statement about the central dilemmas of social inquiry:

> No man on earth can affirm absolutely and generally that the new state of societies is better than the old, but it is already easy to see that it is different. Some vices and some virtues were so inherent in the constitutions of aristocratic nations and are so contrary to the genius of modern peoples that they can never be introduced therein. There are some good inclinations and some bad instincts which were foreign to the former but are natural to the latter. Some ideas spontaneously strike the imagination of the one but are repugnant to the other. They are like two distinct kinds of humanity, each of which has its peculiar advantages and disadvantages, its good points and its bad. One must therefore be very careful not to judge the nascent societies on the basis of ideas derived from those which no longer exist. To do so would be unfair, for those societies are so immensely different that direct comparison is impossible.

Thus at the end of his exhaustive inquiry into democratic civilization, Tocqueville describes himself as standing in doubt, caught between his own powerfully felt values and his awareness that his judgments might be relevant only for a world that was vanishing. The new world might not simply be eluding his understanding, it might in effect be leaving him behind, for he was a man whose ideas and imagination had been shaped by a society he thought would soon no longer exist. His hyperbole of a radical disjunction between old and new social orders ("they are like two distinct kinds of humanity") is an expression of a minor, yet important, strain in Tocqueville's thinking: the relativist view that there possibly were no laws, customs, or institutions absolutely valid for all peoples at all times. It is not a stance he consistently maintained, nor could he have, considering his frequently expressed conviction that there was a universally valid moral order even if modern men had lost sight of it. This conflict is a crucial source of strain in Tocqueville's social criticism; and it is a reflection of his personal struggle for belief.

Yet his extraordinary conclusion does not end on that note of doubt. Despite his deep bow before the inscrutability of history and his confession of failure, Tocqueville adds a characteristic assertion of faith when he argues that whatever darkness, constraints, and uncertainty humans may find themselves struggling in, what finally matters is the belief that will and effort can redeem the promise of democracy and that humans can master their destinies:

> For myself, looking back now from the extreme end of my task and seeing at a distance, but collected together, all the various things which had attracted my close attention upon my way, I am full of fears and of hopes. I see great dangers which may be warded off and mighty evils which may be avoided or kept in check; and I am ever increasingly confirmed in my belief that for democratic nations to be virtuous and prosperous, it is enough if they will to be so. I am aware that many of my contemporaries think that nations on earth are never their own masters and that they are bound to obey some insuperable and unthinking power, the product of preexisting facts, of race, of soil, or climate.
>
> These are false and cowardly doctrines which can only produce feeble men and pusillanimous nations. Providence did not make mankind entirely free or completely enslaved. Providence has, in truth, drawn a predestined circle around each man beyond which he cannot pass; but within those vast limits man is strong and free, and so are peoples.

It is with this pragmatic argument about the consequence of certain beliefs and with this statement of faith in the redeeming and creative powers of freedom that Tocqueville's long book about democracy ends. It is appropriate that it should, for throughout *Democracy in America* he raises questions about what human beings can know about societies and about social change, in fact, about knowledge itself. Throughout *Democracy in America* a continuing debate between doubt and belief frames Tocqueville's discussion about the prospects for democracy. That debate shapes the hesitant yet assertive, clinical yet impassioned tone that contributes significantly to the book's complicated and attractive moral tone. The unresolved struggle between mind and value, intellect and faith at the heart of *Democracy in America* is Tocqueville himself.

10

Exile: Voiceless in Cannes

The last decade of Tocqueville's life was spent in sad internal exile. He felt he was a stranger in his country, whose culture he no longer shared. He thought France was demoralized and corrupt and that it had cravenly surrendered liberty for prosperity and security. Just as bad, he was losing hope that America would serve as an example of the brighter possibilities of democracy as the increasingly violent struggle over slavery and the political instability of the republic worsened and as the darker, cruder aspects of American culture became more pronounced. Yet he would not give up all hope. Despite his failing health and increasing financial worries, this unhappy decade was also one of great accomplishment, above all, the writing of his pathbreaking study of the origins of the French Revolution. He also continued his defining debates with Gobineau about historical determinism, especially racial, and about the moral accomplishments of religion, mainly Christianity. Gobineau eventually goaded him into a final wan affirmation of humans' power to transcend history.

Tocqueville's "beau rêve" ended in nightmare. His political career and his dreams came to an abrupt end with Louis Napoleon's coup of December 2, 1851, and he spent the rest of his life in a kind of haunted internal exile in his own country, trying to nourish occasional flickering hopes for the future, slipping into an ever-deeper sense of isolation. It was a cruel and painful fate for someone who had so identified his own purposes with the life of his country— in itself an immense irony considering the deep alienation he felt. He now found himself an outlaw, as he put it. The great risk he had taken had failed.

This last, bleak decade saw the great accomplishment of his groundbreaking study of the origins and character of the French Revolution, *L'Ancien Régime et la révolution*. It also saw the final intellectual drama of his life: his long debate with Gobineau, in which he reaffirmed his belief in the power of will and intellect to transcend apparently fixed destinies. In the midst of his despair as he watched night descending on his country and on Western culture, he was provoked by Gobineau's radically bleak views of the condition of Western culture and of France into a last, Pascalian reaffirmation of his hopes for the human future and of what he avowed, despite the emptiness of the moment, was the enduring intellectual vitality and passion for liberty of the French people. His debate with Gobineau offers a fitting last look at the enigma of his struggle with doubt and belief.

Except for his writing and for the satisfaction he now occasionally felt as a gentleman farmer bent on improving his Norman estate, as well as for sociable, nostalgic moments at literary lunches and dinners with congenial old colleagues, these were difficult and painful years for him. They were darkened by growing financial worries and especially by the accelerating decline of his health, which now made nearly every day a challenge and a struggle.

The fate of his country caused him the greatest despair. If his imagination during his last years seemed fixed on the meaning of a terrible new figure (introduced in *L'Ancien Régime*) bred by the corruptions of a decadent culture—the audacious and desperate terrorist who had no conscience, no scruples, and no identity—he now also saw himself as the reverse of this "new species": the spurned representative of a dying culture, the relic of a species on the edge of extinction. His retreat from politics and society, the deepening solitude and inwardness of his life, his frequent illnesses and increasing physical debility, and finally his death—literally voiceless in Cannes—at the end of the 1850s reflect the moral isolation and spiritual disappointment of his last years. The central purpose of his life had been broken, and he declined with it. Not even his superb historical work sustained him, for he lost faith that in France's general moral collapse anyone would pay it attention. His personal writing in the last decade is full of a darkening apprehension that history, despite his remarkable effort to master it intellectually and psychologically, had deposited him by the wayside, a superfluous man.

Though he had always seen himself as "un homme bizarre," the idea of his superfluity became a more persistent theme of his self-imagination during his last years. "We are, both of us, of the ancient order, as one would have said eighty years ago," he wrote to Odilon Barrot in 1853. "Better yet, we belong to another epoch of life; we belong to an antediluvian species that will soon have to be collected in natural history cabinets to see how, in ancient times, those beings so singularly constructed as to love liberty, lawfulness, and honesty—strange tastes which suppose organs completely different from those which the inhabitants of this world are endowed—were constructed."[1] His sense of alienation and marginality was so intense that he repeatedly summoned up metaphors of radical racial transformation to capture it: "It isn't simply the times that have changed, it is the entire race which seems to have been transformed. I find myself an antique being in the midst of a new people."[2]

The idea of being one of the last survivors of a doomed culture persisted to the end. "We belong to an intellectual and moral community that is disappearing," he wrote to Victor Lanjuinais, an old friend and political comrade. He compared himself to a stranger just arrived at a place where everything is "new and unknown; the people, the language, the customs." In almost all respects he felt radically separated from his contemporaries: "I have noticed that there are almost no similarities between their way of thinking and mine. I have preserved strong tastes they no longer have; I still passionately care for that which they have stopped admiring; I have an increasingly invincible distaste for what seems to please them more and more."[3] Three years later he felt as isolated as ever: "My contemporaries and I more and more walk along ways so different, sometimes so opposed, that we almost never are able to share the same sentiments and thoughts. We live on good terms with one another without relating to one another. They have almost entirely stopped thinking about that which constantly and deeply preoccupies me; they no longer prize the values to which my heart remains attached. I feel indifference to, sometimes distaste for, the new values."[4] France had become a different country, the French another people.

What abyss separated him from his countrymen? Their demoralized and apathetic response to the Bonapartist assault on liberty was perhaps the worst of it. The apparent collapse of faith in free institutions struck him as "the most frightening symptom of our sickness," and he was doubly dismayed to see that even the best men had accepted their lack of freedom and had made their accommodation a virtue. "I am speaking," he wrote, "of the most upright [les plus honnêtes] because I am not concerned with the others, with those who now think only of how best to accommodate themselves to yet another regime and, what succeeds in plunging my spirit into unrest and a kind of horror, seem to make a taste for servitude an ingredient of virtue."[5] This remark echoes the vision of happy servitude in a benevolent tutelary society with which he had ended *Democracy in America* sixteen years earlier. He concludes his description of how, on his return from Germany in 1854, journals and newspapers had been confiscated from travelers, with a terse and bitter "I knew I had arrived in my country."[6] To live in even so moderate a police state as Louis Napoleon's and to experience the various inhibitions and precautions induced by the fear of surveillance was shocking. Even worse was the rubbery, ignominious response of the French to their loss of freedom. It was in the 1850s more than ever before that Tocqueville looked to England as the most responsible and stalwart model of freedom. His compatriots seemed bent on fulfilling his prophecy that in a crunch democratic people would surrender liberty for equality and security.

The warning he had sounded in *Democracy in America*, that liberty would be curtailed or sacrificed when a nation was at war or had succumbed to the hysterias and false declarations of danger that allow the extension of the powers of the state, was now being borne out in Bonapartist France, where imperialist ambitions had led to an ever-deepening repression.[7] A dark night was falling on France. To criticize the government openly was now dangerous. It was prudent to be circumspect even in one's private remarks: everyone knew that personal letters were scrutinized at random. It had been an act of considerable courage for Tocqueville to have published a letter in the *Times* of London sharply critical of Louis Napoleon, the new French despot. It was for his possibly hazardous public expression of dissent as much as for his intellectual accomplishments that he was celebrated and feted during his travels in England in 1857. That he had been foreign minister in one of Louis Napoleon's preimperial cabinets would not necessarily have protected him from the imperial police. Those who dared assail the policies or, perhaps worse, the quality of the regime were likely to be imprisoned as traitors. Such was the fate of the unfortunate Charles de Montalembert. It had become unpatriotic to speak one's convictions. In *Democracy in America* Tocqueville had written that "all those who seek to destroy the freedom of the democratic nations must know that war is the surest and shortest means to accomplish this." His contempt was great for those who had once contested Louis Napoleon's seizure of the imperial throne but now acquiesced in the new regime of order and power and quietly went about their business.

There were moments when he managed to hold on to the hope that the spirit of the French people would revive. In 1852, shortly after he resigned from the Chamber of Deputies and abandoned the political life which for so long had been the focus of his passions and ambitions, he composed a political testament, his final thoughts about the prospects for France and the only kind of constitution he believed possible for the country. After saying he had come to believe that in the future only a constitutional monarchy that combined France's traditional royal authority with "four necessary liberties," including freedom of the press, would save the nation from perpetual turmoil, he suddenly added that in any case France would never permanently submit to despotism or to any absolute power: "There is in our nature, in our defects, even in our vices something that is invincibly opposed to it."[8] He could not give up hope that France's spirit would some day revive and that its current debasement was accidental. But that hope was flickering. It revived somewhat during his last argument with the pessimistic Gobineau, but by then the late stirring of his hopes seemed subdued and tired.

Tocqueville's gloom about the condition of France was made heavier by the depressing spectacle of the self-destructive behavior of the United States as political life grew more violent there, in a nation Tocqueville had thought perhaps even more than England was a beacon of liberty. The United States seemed to be careening toward a violent breakup, a prospect that weighed heavily on his spirit. Another light was going out. His once-guarded hopes for American democracy had for some time been fading. Even before he had finished *Democracy in America* he had written to his American friends of his dismay about the growing political and economic instability and turmoil of the United States. He was especially troubled that the damaged moral prestige of the United States would strengthen the hand of European despots. In December of 1837 he wrote to John Quincy Adams,

> Though I've been thinking about the United States in a theoretical manner, you can be sure that I have continually had my eyes fixed on the daily procession of events there. I will not conceal from you that what has been occurring in America for several years troubles me deeply. The deplorable struggles that have taken place in several parts of the Union concerning the Negroes; the violent and illiberal principles enunciated and maintained by many of your political figures in these circumstances; the quarrel between the President and the Bank; and finally the commercial crisis from which you have just emerged, have notably diminished the moral influence the United States has exercised in Europe. This is an outcome that causes all true friends of humanity and of liberty among us to groan; and that from one end of our continent to the other delights the partisans of despotism.[9]

The principal damage to American repute was slavery and the increasingly violent struggle between antislavery forces and the "Slave-Power," especially over the issue of the expansion of slavery into new territory. Well before the bloody decade of the 1850s, Tocqueville was concerned that slavery might become even more deeply rooted in America. When Jared Sparks, the president of Harvard College and Tocqueville's principal guide to the history and culture of New England, praised his report of 1839 to the Chamber of Deputies on ending slavery in the French colonies—it had been translated by Mary Sparks—he replied, "It is for me a truly melancholy reflection to think that your nation has so incorporated slavery within itself that it will grow with her, and that as a result of her stupendous growth will take from humanity all the progress you have made and for which all civilized peoples have rejoiced."[10] He feared that if slavery, which he called "the worst of all social evils," were to spread it would be "an ineradicable pestilence" for "the rest of the world." Through his correspondence with Theodore Sedgwick, a scholar of constitutional law, Francis Lieber, the German-born American social scientist and journalist, and Charles Sumner, the abolitionist senator from Massachusetts, he anxiously followed the political struggles between North and South. To Sedgwick he wrote he was "violently opposed to the extension of this terrible evil beyond the already too great limits within which it is now contained. This would seem to me to be one of the greatest crimes that men can commit against the general good of humanity."[11]

The damage done by slavery to the moral prestige of the United States disturbed him perhaps as much as the crime of slavery itself. His last public word about the issue was a letter he sent in 1855 to the female antislavery journal *The Liberty Bell* in Boston in reply to a request for a statement from the antislavery activist Maria Weston Chapman, who was a Garrisonian abolitionist:

> As the persevering enemy of despotism everywhere, and under all its forms, I am pained and astonished by the fact that the freest people in the world is, at the present time, almost the only one among civilized and Christian nations which yet maintains personal servitude; and while this serfdom is about disappearing, from the most degraded nations of Europe.
>
> An old and sincere friend of America, I am uneasy at seeing Slavery retard her progress, tarnish her glory, furnish arms to her detractors, compromise the future career of the Union which is the guaranty of her safety and greatness. . . . As a man, too, I am moved at the spectacle of man's degradation by man. And I hope to see the day when the law will grant equal civil liberty to all the inhabitants of the same empire, as God accords the freedom of the will, without distinction, to the dwellers upon earth.[12]

This letter was later reprinted in William Lloyd Garrison's *Liberator*, though Tocqueville was not an advocate of Garrisonian abolitionism. He was a political abolitionist but never mentioned the antislavery Liberty Party or the Free-Soil Party in his correspondence. If his interest in the antislavery movement was intense, his knowledge of it was thin.

What troubled him as much as the prospect of the spread of slavery was the growing disorder and violence of life in the United States, which confirmed his earlier worst forebodings about the American character: its reckless disregard for limits, its ruthlessness, its inherent violence and moral disorderliness, qualities he had been concerned about but that he had soft-pedaled in *Democracy in America* with his deceptive emphasis on how chaste and respectful of the law democratic Americans were. He depended on his American correspondents for an understanding of political life in the United States, complaining that "unhappily I have few regular correspondents there." The most regular and informative were Sedgwick, Edward Childe, Lieber, and the Bostonian Sumner, the first three of whom were critical of American culture and politics, while Sumner was a leading abolitionist and prison reformer. Tocqueville had occasionally met Sumner in Paris when he was recuperating in Europe from the fierce beating he had suffered on the Senate floor at the hands of Congressman Preston Brooks, a South Carolinian enraged by his abolitionist taunting of the slave South. Sumner had also visited him at Tocqueville, where he no doubt explained the intricacies of American party politics of the 1850s. His closest American friends, almost all Bostonians, were themselves strongly disaffected by American life and severely critical of its values. Lieber longed to return to Europe. Sedgwick, born into an aristocratic Massachusetts family, was an acid critic of American culture. His letters confirmed what Tocqueville had believed for some time. Sedgwick's explanation of the economic crisis of 1857 made it far more than a matter of financial mismanagement or irrational exuberance on the bond market: it was a broad indictment of the American culture. The cause lay in the extravagance without limits of the Americans: "the combination of busyness, of intelligence, of presumptuousness, of energy, of religion, of indifference to all rules, of cold-bloodedness, of business acumen, along with carelessness and absolute neglect of good faith and morality, shameless fraud and brazen swindling."[13] This powerful combination of immense energy, great ability, and moral recklessness was exactly what had filled Tocqueville with foreboding when he was on the scene in 1831.

Although during the forties and fifties he had only a distant view of what was happening in the United States, he saw the large picture and understood what was at stake. French and European opinion of the United States during the Andrew Jackson years was increasingly savage, and he asked his American friends for reassurance. To Lieber, who had once signed on as the American correspondent to the ill-fated *Le Commerce*, he wrote,

> Please tell me . . . what you think of the present situation. I am not speaking particularly of the condition of the Parties, but of what is behind the struggle between them, the deeper political cultures and styles. I hear a majority of well-intentioned Europeans who return from the United States, or sometimes even Americans, saying things that trouble me. They say that the element of the population of the States whose culture is the most violent and whose manners are the crudest, more and more set the tone for the rest; that acts of personal violence performed to secure justice by one's self, have more and more become the customary way of justice.[14]

The European indictment of the violence of American culture as reported by Tocqueville, though he certainly shared it, became even broader. In early 1858 he wrote to Sumner,

> What is more damaging to European opinion, when it isn't preoccupied with the issue of slavery, is the behavior that one has begun to attribute to a great many of those who conduct the public business in America and who guide that of particular States as well as of the Union. We constantly hear tales, no doubt false or exaggerated but which lead opinion in Europe to believe that in America the majority of public figures lack moderation, sometimes probity, above all education, and that they belong to a species of political opportunists—energetic and shrewd, but violent, crude, and unprincipled.[15]

He added that he was not himself saying that this was the case, but he had made the same indictment in his notebooks in 1831.

France too seemed to have succumbed to the mind-deadening undertow of democratic culture and to be fulfilling other, darker visions of *Democracy in America*. It seemed absorbed in a spasm of materialist aggrandizement, totally produced by a frenzied pursuit of "le bien-être." "It's really sad," he wrote to his old political friend Pierre Freslon in 1857, "to live in such a time for those to whom the comfortable life isn't the main thing."[16] He thought the fact that *L'Ancien Régime* was selling well was meaningless, though its success was personally and materially gratifying. He thought it was mostly an item of consumption and a means of being *au courant* for a people whose lives centered on the "bourse" and their "toilettes," which remark ironically recalls what some critics of *Democracy in America* had said about the popularity of that book.[17] "One of the saddest effects of this regime," he remarked to Beaumont, "is to have made this nation at once frivolous and grasping. All those who aren't busy pursuing money by dishonorable means are determined to spend it in the maddest manner."[18]

Even discounting the orgiastic excesses of the moment, the culture suffered from the leaden touch of the hegemonic bourgeoisie. The utilitarian spirit of bourgeois democracy flattened everything with its "marteau de plomb." France was no longer the home of ideas. When Freslon wrote that he detected a certain revival of the intellectual life, Tocqueville replied, "I confess that I am happy to hear you say that, but I don't believe you at all. My impression is that, as for now, there is no public in France for literature. . . . From being the most literary nation in Europe, the one which inspired itself and inspired the rest of the world with the ideas esteemed in important books, there has come a generation that is not at all interested in the work of those who write, that attaches importance only to facts and at that to a very small number of facts: those which have a direct and immediate bearing on well-being."[19] The practical undercutting of the life of the mind that Tocqueville had argued in *Democracy in America* would be a formidable characteristic of any future democratic culture was well under way in France. Men were increasingly confined by their practical interests. They were lawyers, judges, farmers, or soldiers, interested only in the particular business that occupied them. The public man as well as the literary public and the cultural elite were vanishing. The death in 1855 of his relative the Comte de Molé, once president of the Council of Ministers, provided Tocqueville with the occasion to compose a cultural as well as a personal epitaph: "The death of M. Molé has lost to us one of the last examples of the old grand culture and style. He was also one of the last representatives of the old French taste for the pleasures of the mind, which seem more and more to be vanishing from among us. . . . M. Molé was one of those who believed that a strong and passionate love for the noble pleasures of the mind was compatible with all of life. He leaves no school."[20] Even the last métier from which he might exercise influence seemed to have lost power: "It is the literary elite that, of all elites, the Revolution has to the present most harmed."[21]

Yet although he believed that "we have almost completely ceased being a literary nation"—a judgment that reveals how isolated he was at a time of remarkable cultural creativity in France—and that "the influential classes are no longer those that read," he continued to write, believing that there was no more honorable way to spend one's life than to write "true and honest things that can draw the attention of the civilized world . . . and that even in a small way may serve a good cause."[22]

It was during this time, when the "good cause" seemed more and more hopeless to him, that he carried on an intense debate with Gobineau reaffirming his belief that the human spirit could lift itself out of its passive entrapment in history and, by an act of will, re-create society in the light of its moral ideals. Challenged by Gobineau's pessimism about the human moral condition and about the character of France, which he found intrinsically longing to be led by a despot, Tocqueville rose from his despair.

They had met in 1843, when Tocqueville had asked Gobineau to assist on a study of modern moral philosophies that the Académie des sciences morales et politiques had requested he undertake. Tocqueville asked Gobineau specifically to comment on whether modern moral systems had proposed anything new, that is, whether they were in any way an advance on Christian morality. His own view was that "it is really Christianity that seems to have accomplished the revolution . . . in all the ideas that concern rights and duties; ideas which, after all, are the basic matter of all moral knowledge."[23] Their disagreement was deep. Gobineau sharply disputed the argument that Christian morality, which Tocqueville thought had been the first and only advance beyond all previous moral codes, was still the basis of contemporary secular moral systems and even superior in adding a spiritual dimension to the idea of moral obligation. Gobineau, who said he was a practicing Catholic, was harshly critical of Christian morality, the gravest error of which was that it tied virtue and salvation to faith, thus suggesting that good works alone counted for nothing. Gobineau also argued that modern moral systems had greatly broadened the scope of rights and duties and expanded the notion of welfare.

The debate had not lasted long. Tocqueville replied quietly and briefly to a few points in Gobineau's passionate letters, arguing that "you consider the revolution of our times more original and beneficent than I do," and then put an end to it: "My dear Gobineau, you are an amiable, intelligent, and unorthodox adversary, with whom I do not want to battle. It is typical of philosophical debates that neither of the participants emerges dissuaded from his original opinions. Thus it is best not to dispute. It saves effort. Particularly useless are philosophical battles waged by the pen."[24] This was a curious argument from one who now lived by the pen. He concluded inconsistently by saying that there really weren't great differences between them about the above-mentioned issues, but that there were "more profound divisions" between them concerning other matters. "You seem to contest the social function of religions. Here we assume truly antithetical positions."[25] The "social function of religion" was of central importance to Tocqueville.

The next great contestations between the two did not occur until the following decade. Tocqueville was fond of Gobineau and admired his intellect. Though he was only eleven years older than Gobineau, he became something of a mentor to his fiery junior. When he became minister of foreign affairs in 1848 he appointed Gobineau his deputy, and he was ready to support him for membership in the Académie des sciences morales et politiques. Gobineau instructed Tocqueville about German culture, which he much admired, and informed him about the various cultures of the Middle East, where diplomatic service had kept him for many years. It was when Gobineau sent Tocqueville the first volume of what was to be his four-volume *Essai sur l'inégalité des races humaines* that the next of their serious debates erupted. The central issue was Gobineau's argument that the traits and capacities of races were inherent and permanent and that there were many distinct races, not simply evolving versions of the same underlying human species.

Tocqueville quickly disputed the scientific merits of Gobineau's thesis, taking the position of Jean-Pierre Flourens and Georges-Louis Buffon that there were diverse races but one human species, and that "human variations are products of three secondary and external causes: of climate, of food, and of manner of life." He cited Flourens's observation that the supposedly unique "black reticulum mucosum"—the "pigmentary stratum" of the Negro—supposedly, "the obvious cause of their inherent and specific blackness exists, in colors of varying intensity, in the American Indian and in a less pronounced but still very visible version in the Kabyl, in the Moor, and in the Arab, who belongs to the white race, and that traces thereof exist even in Europeans.[26] He felt that Gobineau's "doctrines" were "probably quite false": "Surely among the different families which compose the human race there exist certain tendencies, certain proper aptitudes resulting from thousands of different causes. But that these tendencies, that these capacities could be insuperable has not only never been proved but no one will ever be able to prove it since to be able to do so one would need to know not only the past but also the future. . . . What, in this whole world, is more difficult than to find the time and the composite elements that produced men who by now possess no visible trace of their mixed origins?"[27] It wasn't the technical dubiousness of Gobineau's theory that bothered Tocqueville most, nor was it his doubt that "by tracing the destiny of peoples along these lines" Gobineau could "truly clarify history." His profoundest objection to Gobineau's materialistic predestinarianism was that it demoralized men by persuading them that desire, will, and intellect could never overcome the trap and drag of their limitations and that the conditions in which they were immured were their immemorially destined fate. Its effect would be to undercut striving against injustice by telling subordinated and exploited peoples that their suffering was destined and permanent: "The lesson for lesser peoples living in abject conditions of barbarism or slavery [was] that, such being their racial nature, they can do nothing to better themselves, to change their habits, or to ameliorate their status." Worse, it justified injustices. "Don't you see," he asked Gobineau, "how inherent in your doctrine are all the evils produced by permanent inequality: pride, violence, the scorn of one's fellow men, tyranny and abjection in every one of their forms?"[28]

Even more broadly, Gobineau's theory undermined the essential belief that human will mattered and that the virtues that counted in an individual's life— "courage, energy, honesty, farsightedness, and common sense"—were also effective in the lives of societies "and that, in one word, the destiny of men, whether of individuals or of nations, depends on what they want to be." "There is," he added, "an entire world between our beliefs."[29]

Their debate over Tocqueville's objection that Gobineau's race theory was morally pernicious continued from these first remarks, in late 1853, through 1857 and in some ways until the end of Tocqueville's life. It seemed partially to lift Tocqueville out of the slough of despond into which he was sinking. In his very next letter, written on December 20, 1853, in St. Cyr, where he was working on *L'Ancien Régime*, Tocqueville picked up where he had left off, noting that the fantastic, exaggerated confidence that men of the eighteenth century had in their power to control their destinies was now gone:

> The weary aftermath of revolutions, the weakening of passions, the miscarriage of so many generous ideas and of so many great hopes have now led us to the opposite extreme. After having felt ourselves capable of transforming ourselves, we now feel incapable of reforming ourselves; after having excessive pride, we have now fallen into excessive self-pity; we thought we could do everything, and now we think we can do nothing; we like to think that struggle and effort are henceforth useless and that our blood, muscles, and nerves will always be stronger than our will power and courage. This is really the great sickness of our age; it is very different from that of our parents. Irrespective of your argument [that is, of its scientific truth], your book supports these tendencies; despite yourself, it promotes the spiritual lassitude of your already weakening contemporaries.[30]

He patently deplored the former excess as much as he did the later abjectness. Two years later Tocqueville greeted the last volumes of the *Essai sur l'inégalité des races humaines* by restating his fundamental objection to the work, namely, that its fatalism would worsen the current moral lassitude: "We have no regard for anything, beginning with ourselves; we have no faith in anything, including ourselves. A book which tries to prove that men in this world are merely obeying their physical constitutions and that their will power can do almost nothing to influence their destinies is like opium given to a patient whose blood has already weakened."[31] The implication of that argument was that all was not hopeless and that France might recover its nerve.

Gobineau's next provocation would soon force Tocqueville even more positively to struggle against the despair he constantly felt. In warmly praising *L'Ancien Régime* Gobineau had assailed the fantasies of the eighteenth century and the destructive consequences of the French Revolution, much as Tocqueville had. But he had also contemptuously denied that the French had ever wanted to be free, arguing that they were congenitally incapable even of understanding liberty. Tocqueville replied with a final, hopeful declaration that he refused to despair about the future of France. The verve of the French and their intrinsic love of liberty, he argued, would be restored. Gobineau responded,

> You very justly observe in your preface that with your love for free institutions you separate yourself from those who do not consider them practical because

of the low opinion in which they hold their fellow citizens. It seems to me to qualify by free institutions the mere mechanism superimposed on a society such as ours. A people like ours that, whether under the Republic, representative government or the Empire, will always maintain an immoderate desire for the intervention of the State in all of its affairs, that will be passively obedient to the gendarmerie, to the tax collector, to the surveyor, to the engineer, a people that does not understand true municipal administration, and to which absolute and irrevocable centralization is the last word, such a people not only will never have free institutions but will not even understand what they are.[32]

Tocqueville evidently took Gobineau's argument that the French were permanently incapable of understanding what constitutes true freedom and thus of creating free institutions to be an assertion that will and idea could never lift any peoples above their limitations. His powerful response broadened the grounds of argument—after which he called for an end to it:

I ask you to permit me, my dear friend, to discuss your political theories no longer . . . . where can our political discussions lead us? We belong to two diametrically opposed orbits. . . . You consider people today as if they were overgrown children, very degenerate and very ill-educated . . . I believe that a better upbringing could repair the wrongs done by their miseducation; I believe that it is not permissible to renounce such an effort. . . . You profoundly distrust mankind, at least our kind; you believe that it is not only decadent but incapable of ever lifting itself up again. Our very physical constitution, according to you, condemns us to servitude. . . . I do not think that I have either the right or the inclination to entertain such opinions about my race and my country. I believe that one should not despair of them. . . . No, I shall not believe that this human race, which is at the head of all visible creation, has become that bastardized flock of sheep which you say it is, and that nothing remains but to deliver it without future and without hope to a small number of shepherds who, after all, are not better animals than are we, the human sheep, and who indeed are often worse. You will forgive me when I have less confidence in you than in the goodness and justice of God.[33]

He had employed the same metaphor, of men as sheep, in *Democracy in America* as his gloom about the passive moral future of democracy grew thicker. Now, just as he had at the end of *Democracy in America*, Tocqueville has shifted the ground from what he had called Gobineau's "materialistic predestinarianism" to that of moral obligation as well as faith in providential intervention. He countered Gobineau's harsh science with a profession of religious belief.

In September of 1858, as his health began its terminal downward spiral, he offered a final, quiet refusal of Gobineau's pessimism in the last letter he wrote to him from Tocqueville. He was about to leave for Paris and then for Cannes in the south in what was a futile quest to regain his now-faltering health. Gobineau's continual belittling of the character of the French drove Tocqueville to an affirmation of French genius that is startling to read in view of his own mounting criticism of a France in which he now felt completely alien. In a way, it was also a declaration of faith, though finally a mild one. Its non sequitur and reservations are evidence of the conflicts he felt—his own criticism of the French culture of his time had been sweeping and bitter. Here was a curious about-face. As examples of a still brightly burning French spirit he effusively praises individuals whose work and ideas he had assailed. He declared that he was

> somewhat impatient when I hear you say that our nation has always been petty and mean [and] that it has never produced a genius. . . . As if some of the greatest works of the human mind did not come from our Nation? As if, above all, we had not produced a constant stream of great writers during the past three centuries, stirring and moving the spirit of mankind most power-fully—whether in the right or the wrong direction may be arguable, but their power one cannot doubt. . . . In your letter I find that you are . . . unjust to your contemporaries. When have [Louis-Adolphe] Thiers, [Abel-François] Villemain, and even Cousin done better than in their last works, despite the somewhat debatable value of their subjects? And so far as their intrinsic value is concerned, what European historian is more famous than Thiers, [who] more brilliant than Villemain, a better writer than Cousin? Is not Lamartine perhaps the greatest poet of our days, though he may no longer write anything but detestable poetry, and prose that is no better?

He again acknowledged that the present moment was bleak, but he refused to believe it was permanent:

> It is unfortunately only too true and sad that these very talented persons, who, to be sure, are not extraordinary geniuses, are getting old and that they are not being replaced by anyone. In the generations that come after those now in their fifties and sixties, after men of high intellect who are now becoming old dogs, who is there of any fame at all? . . . It is, I think, partly due to the widespread apathy of souls and to those clouds which hover above us, languishing every spirit. Strong hatreds, ardent passions, hopes and pow-erful convictions are, all, necessary to make human minds move. Right now nothing is strongly believed, nothing is loved, nothing is hated, and people wish for nothing but a quick profit on the stock exchange. Yet France has

never had a temper so permanently depressed as to be interested in nothing but material welfare, and I keep hoping that a new movement which will raise her will power will also reanimate her literature.[34]

It was a slight hope to hold onto. He found the unrelieved experience of extreme isolation a burden "under the weight of which I am often ready to succumb."[35] Though for various reasons, among them the demands of his research and writing, tightening financial resources, and his declining health, he lived an increasingly sequestered life, the solitude he felt was largely moral. In fact when his health allowed and when he was in Paris, he led a modestly active social life, attending lunches and dinners with friends and political colleagues. Nassau Senior's diary, which records the conversations at many of these lunches, makes it clear how great an effort Tocqueville made to maintain a social and intellectual life, mostly by participating in the noontime conversations of intellectuals, political figures, and notable visitors like Sumner. In 1857, for example, Tocqueville assisted at these literary and intellectual matinees regularly and had much to say. At one such gathering he would join Senior, Sumner, Earl Granville-Leveson-Gower, Guizot, Charles de Rémusat, Francisque de Corcelle, and Adolphe Circourt; at another, recorded not by Senior but by Lord Hatherton and attended by Senior, Prosper Merimée, Moncton Milnes, Sir George and Lady Lewis, he was "lively and talkative." (Hatherton described Tocqueville as "très simple, modeste et agréable; he is clearly in poor health; small, delicate, ashen-faced, dark, flat-chested and very thin.") These discussions were recorded by the ever-present Senior, who presided over a kind of traveling Anglo-French salon.[36]

When he could, Tocqueville also kept alive a social life at his home in Normandy, arranging visits by old friends like Stoffels and literary and political figures traveling in France, like Sumner. Yet his intimate friends Kergorlay and Beaumont, who did not live far away, rarely visited. He was miffed by Ampère's failure to visit despite much importuning. Ampère, in Rome, where he spent more and more time, was not able to tear himself away from yet another of his platonic amours. The effect on Tocqueville of Ampère's continuous postponing of a Norman rendezvous—such visits had been profoundly and joyfully mean-ingful to both—was to deepen Tocqueville's sense of isolation. He seems to have felt abandoned.

Though his triumphant visit to London in June and July of 1857 was satisfying in many ways, it added to his melancholy and intensified his sense of aloneness. The trip had started poorly with problems about accommodations. His favorite hotel, the York in the West End of London, was full because of a music festival being held at the Crystal Palace, and for awhile he went from place to place, "perdu dans cette immense ville," which increased his anxiety about where he would find the spirit-lifting letters from Marie he craved.[37] He had arrived during "un chaleur accablante," his English was rusty, his valet, Auguste, did not know the language or English ways and needed so much guidance that he felt he was the servant, Auguste the master. He turned to a metaphor he began to use in his last years: he was "more overwhelmed with a sense of isolation than I had felt in my youth in the midst of the forests of the new world." The long letters from London that he wrote to Marie every day are full of longing for "home, home," constant professions of his need for her, reflections on the meaninglessness of public acclaim compared to the quiet satisfactions of domesticity. To Marie he pleaded, "Tell me about all our little domestic affairs . . . it's what interests me more than anything in the world." Private life was "all that destiny has left open." Though there were satisfying moments during his monthlong visit, the dominant feeling in his correspondence is one of deep sadness: "My spirit is unseated," he wrote. He felt an abiding sense of aloneness even though he was not at all alone: he had been welcomed with "an avalanche of compliments" and greeted by the House of Commons, he had met Prince Albert and the historian Macaulay and was wined and dined constantly by the literate English aristocracy. Thoughts of the grim state of France haunted him as well: "Moreover, since my isolation saddens me, I see the bleak aspect of everything; the prospect of this society so free, so well-ordered, so prosperous, its principal elements so unified, instead of animating me with joyful ardor as it did twenty years ago fills my heart with sadness and envy."[38] To make matters worse, though he disciplined himself to work in the vast collection of materials on the French Revolution in the British Library, he was not satisfied with what he managed to accomplish and was sharply critical of the library's indifference to cataloging and organizing its materials.

   He was also preoccupied by growing financial worries as well as by his concern for the straitened financial condition of Beaumont and Kergorlay, a frequent subject of their correspondence. Money woes hung over the heads of these old aristocratic families, whose means were becoming less and less adequate as the commercially active middle classes were becoming prosperous and the cost of living rose. Quiet worry and sadness infuse their letters, which are full of concern about their children's prospects. Kergorlay had thrown himself into commercial enterprises to provide for his family's future. Tocqueville had almost completely lost hope that Kergorlay would ever fulfill his intellectual promise; he was now fearful that Beaumont, much depressed not only by France's bleak political situation and his own blighted dreams but also by the shabbiness of his estate and the prospect of an impoverished future for his children, also would abandon his intellectual ambitions. While his own gloom thickened, Tocqueville spent much time during these years trying to cheer Beaumont, reminding him of his accomplishments and of what he still had to offer. His efforts to brace his old companion even as his own spirits were sinking are moving. As for Kergorlay, it wasn't their political differences but Kergorlay's new devotion to the commercial life that finally put distance between them. Tocqueville sadly noted to Beaumont that theirs was now his sole surviving old friendship.[39]

The income from his tenanted lands, well managed by Marie, was adequate for his needs, but he had to live frugally. At times he was pressed—or felt pressed. When, in 1835, he returned from his travels in England and Ireland he was momentarily so strapped that he considered hocking his watch for funds.[40] Yet, according to Nassau Senior, he could count on a rental income of about twenty-five thousand francs a year from his tenants.[41] Money matters increasingly appear in all of his correspondence during these late years. He was much concerned about expenses when he visited England in 1857, though he was able to take Auguste along. Distressed by the cost of lodging and travel during the trip, he was always counting pennies. When he was in Paris in 1858 doing research for the planned second volume of *L'Ancien Régime* he wrote to Marie in Tocqueville that he was pleased to have found a decent room for five francs a night. Their friends were dismayed by the shabbiness of the last flat they rented in Paris before moving south to Cannes, his last move.

Ironically, though he had expressed contempt for the money obsession of the Americans, he had been seduced by the American railroad boom and as early as the 1830s had invested a substantial portion of his wealth in American railroad bonds. The depressions of 1837 and 1857 and the instability of the wild American economy caused him great anxiety. He frequently asked his American correspondents, Sumner among them, for advice and reassurance, confessing that a bond market collapse would cause "un veritable trouble [*sic*] dans ma fortune." He ultimately lost a quarter of his American investments, fuming about "ces voleurs de banquiers."[42]

The decade was marked by physical decline and occasional collapses, his health undoubtedly made worse by long hours of research and writing. Every day was a trial. His health, increasingly a subject of his correspondence, was severely tested by travel, by fatiguing sedentary labor in libraries and archives, by hot days and cold days, by thick urban air, and by the discomforts of a peripatetic, unsettled life which sometimes found him in shabby quarters. His letters to Marie are almost a clinical chronicle of his physical miseries ("mes maux"), many of them symptoms of the pulmonary and gastric ailments that finally brought him down. They are also full of anxiety about her health and pleas that she care for herself, not just for her sake but also for his. No detail of his daily physical life and of his nocturnal, increasingly sleepless, life went unreported, but there was no self-pity in his health bulletins. He would also report on good days and periods of energy, with the joyfulness that well-being produces—but such days became fewer. One hears in his correspondence someone retreating slowly into a dim last sanctuary. Nevertheless, despite his increasingly poor health, he never spared himself and continued to work and to travel to the limits of his strength.

By late 1858 illness had taken over both his and Marie's lives and driven them into an even deeper exile in Cannes. From then on his brief letters to family and friends are almost totally given over to the grim details of physical disintegration, Marie's as well as his own. Remissions were guardedly noted, but the story was one of relentless decline. Insomnia now bedeviled him. He suffered from bladder problems, constipation, "extreme faiblesse." Worst were the "crachements du sang," bloody coughing attacks that were especially terrifying because "they throw all bodily functions" into disorder and because of "the momentary derangement they bring about in the nervous system." At times he could speak for only a few minutes, in a barely audible voice, before lapsing into silence. This was especially trying when Hippolyte, a man of few words (and his sister-in-law Émilie, a woman of no words), came to care for him. He could walk short distances only, and they became shorter and shorter until finally he could manage just a few steps around the house. For awhile Marie was even worse: at one point problems with her vocal chords condemned her to "un mutisme absolu" for eight days. She suffered also from woes of bowels and gums along with various rheumatic disorders.[43]

All through his long, painful exile he tried in one grim image after another to catch the desolation of being a moral expatriate in his own country. He saw himself on "a deserted isle," "in the forests of America," "in the depths of the sewer in which M. Jaubert spent six months," or in a "burial vault" of which "one had just closed up the last opening." He felt distant enough to ask for news about "what's happening on earth." To Beaumont he confessed his despair at the prospect of growing old alone without a family, and his terror "of being attached to the world by only one soul and of what would remain for you should you lose her."[44]

To Sophie Swetchine he wrote, "You cannot imagine how painful and often cruel it is for me to live in such moral isolation, to feel myself outside the intellectual community of my times and my country. Solitude in a desert would seem to me less harsh than this sort of solitude among men."[45] All through this last decade of moral and intellectual isolation, during which he felt he had lost his country, he would most often compare the solitude he now felt to the solitude he experienced in the forests of America. Once more, at the end of his life, America presented him with a metaphor that illuminated his destiny.

Part II

THE CALLING OF POLITICS

1

VOCATION: POLITICS AS CALLING—TOCQUEVILLE'S "BEAU RÊVE"

For Tocqueville, politics was essentially a moral calling. The duty of political leaders was to guide the nation to fulfilling its ideals, keeping before the people the glory of France and the general good. Politics was far more than a battle of competing interests. He believed that his true task was to lead the nation from the swamp of middle-class politics that France had sunk into under the Bourgeois Monarchy, when the good of the society had been lost sight of as the dominant middle-class scrambled to secure its power and interests. He would recreate a politics of principle in which moral questions were central to political life. This was his "beau rêve," his great dream.

The ambitious Tocqueville was not about to accept Royer-Collard's counsel that because the time was not right he should delay entering politics. It would be some time before he realized that his true vocation was not political but literary. He saw himself as a disinterested leader of a lost and confused people—as a servant of humanity. If he admitted that he also craved success, he seems not to have understood that he also thirsted for power. When, after Tocqueville's death, François Guizot was asked if he could explain the various contradictions of Tocqueville's political life, for example, his tendency to support the left, which he distrusted, while he often opposed the right, with which he was temperamentally sympathetic, the answer was "because he wished to be where I was," that is, in the seat of power.[1] The roots of his passion for politics undoubtedly lay partly in what François Furet called his situation and in the turmoil that this situation, with its experience of loss, anger, and isolation, would have bred, especially in the resentment he felt as he watched his class being displaced by a crude, self-aggrandizing bourgeoisie. It took some time for him to realize that the French aristocracy had been decapitated long before 1789 and that even during the eighteenth century it was no longer France's ruling class. During the Restoration he had for a time served as an observant, proud secretary to his father when he was prefect of the Département of the Moselle. Hervé de Tocqueville was an effective, industrious, and shrewd political administrator, a bold, brave, and at times controversial political leader who, while a faithful and at times high-handed ultraroyalist, had also pushed through imaginative and moderately progressive social programs. For his admiring bright son it was a consequential apprenticeship.[2]

Tocqueville's political passion had a fundamental moral and intellectual foundation, clearly expressed in the idealized self-portrait he sent to Henry Reeve. While driven by a desire for power, not simply as class entitlement or by a familiar if inexplicable wish to shape history, he also dreamed of playing a redemptive role in French politics and of leading France out of the moral confusion and corruption it had fallen into after the noble aspirations of the Great Revolution had been betrayed. There is no reason to doubt that he truly regarded this redemptive role as duty and destiny. In this he was not singular. The dream of redeeming France from the moral miasma into which it had fallen was central to the self-understanding of his generation, a generation of young romantics whose values and passions he shared even though he had been raised in almost complete isolation from it.[3]

"My great dream in entering politics was to help reconcile the spirit of liberty and the spirit of religion." So he wrote in December of 1843, a third of the way through his active political life.[4]

He decidedly had not meant that he wished to see anything like a resurrection of clerical power in the state. He had in mind rather a restoration of a moral dimension to political life, a politics of conscience. It was this broken connection that he was convinced was one of the chief calamities of modern culture. Such remained a central problem of his political career. It is the issue he dramatically voices in the introduction to the first volume of *Democracy in America.*

Well before actively entering politics Tocqueville had clearly seen what his role was to be. "It's a most difficult task we are undertaking," he wrote to Beaumont in 1835. "To retain one's integrity amidst the parties that divide one's country; to restore honesty in politics in a nation which has become almost indifferent to right and wrong and that prizes only success. That's not a trivial undertaking. But what difference does it make? It's better to fail in trying this than to succeed in a different path."[5] There is something poignant and even defiant about this vision, which was not a realistic or a winning strategy for French politics. Though it is doubtful that Tocqueville had read Emerson at this time, if ever, his notion is Emersonian: the moral man in politics will be a converting presence; the bright light of his conscience will illuminate the truth for others; character will prove a greater power than the machinations of powerful men.

Did Tocqueville really believe this? What else can be assumed about a conception of politics that called for a disavowal of politics? or that transformed politics into transactions of consciousness in which those who had become "almost indifferent to right and wrong" would be awakened by a man of moral passion and eloquence, standing apart?

Tocqueville's model in all this was Royer-Collard, who from the start was an independent man of principle. But Royer had earned that role and knew how and when to use it. He knew that Tocqueville was not ready for it, hence had urged him to delay entering politics and to acquire greater authority through his writing. Royer had been prescient. Tocqueville immediately proved inept and ineffective. He lacked those powers essential for the role he dreamed of playing: a compelling presence, a warm and reassuring demeanor, and, above all, oratorical eloquence. His formal literary, painstakingly crafted speeches, nuanced and complex, over which he labored to find "le mot juste," illuminated minds but did not move men. Aloof, distrustful of others, transparently snobbish yet paradoxically unsure of himself, he lacked the charismatic qualities needed for the role he wanted.

It was when he joined others to publish a journal of opinion focusing on culture and politics that he might have come closer to solving his "difficult enterprise." The first half of the nineteenth century, beginning with the Restoration in 1815, saw an explosion of such journals, of all political and cultural persuasions. Some, like *The Globe*, were greatly influential. Tocqueville's *Le Commerce*, of which he was part owner and chief editorial presence, lasted little more than a year from mid-1844 through mid-1845. Its circulation, decent enough when Tocqueville and some friends had bought it, plummeted almost immediately.[6]

He returned to the idea of reintegrating a fragmented world in a letter of 1836 to Stoffels:

> What has always impressed me about my country, but especially for several years now, has been to see ranged on one side those who value morality, religion, order; and on the other those who love liberty and equality of men before the law. This struggle has struck me as the most extraordinary and the most deplorable that has ever been seen; because all these things we separate are, I am certain, indissolubly united in the eyes of God. They are all sacred things, if I may so express myself, because the greatness and the happiness of man in this life can result only from the reunion of all these at the same time.[7]

In politics as well as in other realms of life, the complex interdependence of these values had been lost sight of. This idea, of a calamitous disassociation of meanings and values, had been developed with great feeling in the introduction to *Democracy in America*, where it has often been obscured by the better-known passages that precede and follow it.

Well before he began his political years he had arrived at the view that the central issue of political life was essentially moral and that his political task would call for the infusion of values, not of religion, into politics. His journey to America had convinced him that the saving strength of the political life and culture of democratic America—the remarkable, pervasive presence of religion in all aspects of the life of that society. He thought it played only a superficial spiritual role in the lives of Americans but believed it was responsible for what he saw as the orderliness and respect for law that prevailed among them. There, however, the influence of religion had been strengthened by separating religion from politics, church from state. As much as the fact that the Americans had never had a true social revolution and thus had never suffered the bitterness of class divisions, it explained how the Americans were able to maintain a peaceful, orderly, nonrevolutionary Republic.

His view that French political life had lost its moral center was quickly confirmed by his experience in the Chamber of Deputies. In the last decade of his life, after his bitter, frustrated political career had been ended by Louis-Napoleon's seizure of power in December 1851, Tocqueville's brooding about France's moral collapse was given memorable shape in the figure of the revolutionary terrorist whom he introduces in *L'Ancien Régime et la révolution* at the end of his discussion of the influence of the "fierce, intolerant, and predatory" irreligion of eighteenth-century France on the Revolution. It was when "men's minds were in a state of utter confusion" that "revolutionaries of a hitherto unknown breed came on the scene: men who carried audacity to the point of sheer insanity; who balked at no innovation and, unchecked by any scruples, acted with unprecedented ruthlessness."[8] The appearance of such monsters was not just the transient horror of a brief, intense moment of crisis: "They were, rather, the first of a race of new men who subsequently made good and proliferated in all parts of the civilized world, everywhere retaining the same characteristics. They were already here when we were born, and they are still with us."[9]

Though they had first appeared in France, they were no longer local aberrations but "a race of new men" who had endured, proliferated, and, in a term that comes from the lexicon of prudent middle-class aspiration that seems peculiarly inappropriate for the triumphs of the berserk, made good. This new character was the product of "a new and unknown kind of virus."[10] Something new, malign, and incomprehensible had been released in the world and had taken hold. "We have seen violent revolutions in the world," he wrote in 1858.

"But the immoderate, wild, radical, desperate, audacious, half-mad, and especially the powerful and efficient character of these revolutionaries has no
precedent, it seems to me, in the great social upheavals of past Ages. Where
did this new breed come from? What produced it? What made it so efficient?
What perpetuates it?"[11]

He claimed not to understand fully the meaning of this terrible figure: "My
mind is worn out trying to conceive a clear understanding of this phenomenon
and in trying to find the best way to depict it. Apart from all that explains the
French Revolution, there is something inexplicable in its animus and in its
deeds. I sense what this reality is, but though I have tried hard, I cannot lift the
veil that hides it."[12] But he had long before grasped the meaning of the apparition so powerfully conjured by his imagination. This doom-laden figure represented many themes of his political and cultural thought. The spectre who was
"untouched by any scruples" was the dark, final incarnation of his apprehension that something had gone radically wrong in "le monde civilizé." This
figure of Tocqueville's imagination was the ultimate expression of the potential for moral disorder, for unrestrained individualism, for unbridled freedom,
and for the loss of a sense of limits—for all that he saw inherent in the main
tendencies of Western culture. It was the symbol of reason detached from
morality, of mind unhinged from any sense of a true and fixed order of things,
in fact another version of the vision of disorder and discontinuity with which
Tocqueville begins *Democracy in America*.

This "new man" was an extreme symptom of the spiritual crisis that underlay
many of the more banal disorders of modern political life, including the disassociation of politics and morality and the loss of the sense of self-restraint and of
social obligation that had resulted from the collapse of the old system of moral
and religious belief that he believed had hitherto provided a frame of norms
and sanctions that had restrained the human passion for power. A nightmare
version of the new pragmatic politician for whom the quest for personal power
had become the central goal of political life, he practiced a politics without
conscience, a liberalism not of principle but of self-interest.

Having made this diagnosis of what ailed politics in France, Tocqueville
plotted—or, rather, dreamily began—his political career, though *calling* is a
more appropriate word for it. Paradoxically, the two figures who most manifestly
expressed the pathology of modern politics, the revolutionary terrorist and the
bourgeois opportunist, regarded one another with fear and loathing; yet both
had been produced by the loss of a shared coherent moral frame of individual
and political behavior. The menaces of unrestrained individualism and of despotism alike were rooted in the same moral disorder, curiously just as the "twin

tendencies"—rather, the twin potential pathologies of democracy, toward anar-
chism and repressive conformity, that he ingeniously analyzed in *Democracy in
America*—resulted from the same underlying cultural movement.

The politician who in the eyes of Tocqueville most vividly represented the
moral malady of contemporary political life was Adolphe Thiers, the journalist,
historian, liberal deputy, prime minister in 1836 and 1840, leader of the left
opposition during the July Monarchy—and, well after Tocqueville's death in
1859, the first president of the Third Republic, the crowning moment of his
long political career. Oscillating between a politics of agitation and a politics
informed by fear of the people, Thiers seemed to Tocqueville to unite the revolutionary and the opportunistic bourgeois politico in one figure. Tocqueville
had been outraged by what he had perceived as the Jacobin bias of Thiers's
immense (ten volumes) *Histoire de la Révolution Française* when he read it in
1828—though he took notes on only the first twenty-eight pages of the first
volume without commenting on the moral drift of Theirs's narrative. Thiers's
emphasis on the confusion and inevitability of 1789 was a strange Jacobinism.
One must suppose that what Tocqueville found most offensive about Thiers's
history was the sense it conveyed that the Revolution was fated and not a matter
of will. For Tocqueville, maintaining the idea of choice was a moral imperative.

Tocqueville later said that at that time he had regarded Thiers "as the most
perverse and dangerous of men." Though he somewhat modified this violent
opinion, he continued to diabolize Thiers, whom he saw as the embodiment of
a degenerated, opportunistic liberalism the main impulse of which was self-
interest, a liberalism ready to sacrifice principle for power and advantage. To
him, Thiers was "the most complete example of insincerity and intrigue in
political life," one of the most adept practitioners of the new amoral theatrical
politics, the game of display and symbolism in which self-interest replaced principle and a genuine concern for the public good.[13] Such cynicism had understandably effected popular skepticism about politics. Between Thiers and the
so-called theorists, rationalists, and social engineers who were enlisting the
people in doomed crusades for instant freedom and justice, there was little to
choose. Thiers was the spiritual heir of the amoral, cynical Machiavelli. He was
the contemporary who came to mind when Tocqueville read Machiavelli's
History of Florence in 1838, while he was thinking through the prospects for
aristocratic liberalism—a leadership of principled men—as he struggled to
complete *Democracy in America*.[14]

The harsh judgment of Thiers as a man without a moral center undoubtedly
says more about Tocqueville's perception of politics and about himself than it
does about Thiers. He could easily have chosen someone else to serve as a

symbol of the moral confusion and hollowness of contemporary politics, for example, Guizot, the major voice and leader of French liberalism after 1830 and the dominant political figure of the July Monarchy. Yet it was Thiers and what he symbolized that preoccupied Tocqueville at this time. He was the new man of politics, Tocqueville plainly was not.[15] An ambitious, upwardly mobile, fiercely anticlerical member of the bourgeoisie, Thiers may simply have served to clarify more sharply Tocqueville's powerful animus against the spirit the now-dominant bourgeoisie had brought to political life, a spirit he described as a compound of unenlightened self-interest, petty materialism, resistance to change, and fear of the people. The ruling bourgeoisie had created a politics in which self-aggrandizement and fear were oddly yoked, a peculiarity of middle-class politics which Tocqueville explored at great length in the concluding volume of *Democracy in America* in his insightful, enduring analysis of how fear of change is combined with a thirst for change in bourgeois culture. His description in the *Recollections* of a fear-struck Thiers on February 24, 1848, "half mad" (Tocqueville's revolutionary terrorist was "presque fou"), "almost out of his senses," sighing, murmuring "incoherent phrases," being led home on an inconspicuous route through the Bois de Boulogne to avoid the crowds he thought were about to murder him, is an exercise in malice and aristocratic contempt.[16] It is also a political comment. The opportunistic politician lacked the courage to put his life on the line for what he believed, if he believed anything. Several anecdotes in Tocqueville's sizzling narrative of the events of 1848 emphasize his own courage in confronting danger when he faced down a potentially hostile crowd of citizens, a term he deliberately and ostentatiously refused to use while campaigning in 1848 for a seat in the Chamber of Deputies.[17]

Though the *Recollections* spares no one, not even Tocqueville himself, it is especially bitter about the moral tone the ruling bourgeoisie had given to the July Monarchy:

> The spirit peculiar to the middle class became the general spirit of the government. . . . This spirit was timid by temperament, moderate in all things except a taste for well-being, and mediocre; a spirit . . . that by itself never produces anything but a government without either virtues or greatness. Mistress of all, as no aristocracy has ever been or perhaps ever will be, the middle class, which must be called the ruling class, entrenched in its power and shortly afterwards, in its selfishness, treated government like a private business, each member thinking of public affairs only in so far as they could be turned to his private profit, and in his petty prosperity easily forgetting the people.
>
> Posterity, which sees only striking crimes and generally fails to notice smaller vices, will perhaps never know how far the government of that time

toward the end took on the features of a trading company whose every opera-
tion is directed to the benefit that its members may derive therefrom.[18]

This sweeping moral indictment, representative of everything that Tocqueville
wrote about the July Monarchy, could have been written by an angry Jeremiah.
Though it captures some aspects of the ethos of the July Monarchy, it is hardly
a fair or a thorough account of the politics or the theory of the "juste milieu,"
which was based on the idea that sovereignty resided not in the people or in
divinely appointed royalty but in reason, that is, reasoned judgments about the
general good. This theoretical foundation of the July Monarchy had been
worked out by Tocqueville's mentor Royer-Collard and the Doctrinaires, rationalist liberals for whom a politics of balance and compromise seemed to be the
surest way to achieve the general good and above all avoid revolutionary disorder. For Guizot and his party, however, reason identified the general good with
the interests of the ruling bourgeoisie.

But Tocqueville's jeremiad keenly expresses how he looked at political life.
It reveals what his calling meant to him, though he also had a modest practical
agenda with regard to social issues, labor policies, the problem of poverty, and
suffrage and strong ideas about foreign affairs and France's imperial ambitions.
The bitter critique of the politics of self-interest with which he begins the
Recollections sums up the views he had maintained even before his political
life began. He had continually assailed the opportunism and the timid conservatism, the readiness to abandon principle for short-term advantage, and
especially the narrowness of vision that characterized the July Monarchy. He
thought it a time of "license and servility" in which "most men in entering
political life seemed only to want to demonstrate the inconstancy and turpitude
of the human heart"; and he was disgusted by "the pathetic intrigues inflicted
on society these days, the miserable charlatans who exploit it, the pettiness that
reigns there almost totally." Political life had been emptied of generous ideals
and of any sense of the nobler purposes that had, from the Greeks to the Great
Revolution of 1789, formerly animated men. "What strikes me most about our
time," he wrote Royer-Collard, "isn't simply that there is so much pettiness, it is
that no one has any vision. A feeling for grandeur is absent, and one can say that
the idea of greatness is fading away."[19] Men seemed to have lost the capacity to
take the long view and to plan for it: "We live in a time and in a country which
has no taste for foresight. It is the time and the country of the unforeseen."

The chief villains in this piece were the triumphant liberals, who, led by
Guizot, had established a regime whose central aim was to consolidate and
justify the rule of the industrial and financial bourgeoisie, co-opting useful

intellectuals and tractable liberal aristocrats into a ruling elite of men known as notables. Moreover, they did so by means often at variance with the first principles of liberalism, not only by turning their backs on the evident need for social reform but also by repressing opposition and managing the political process. Emptying politics of ideas, passions, and real choices, they had turned it into a struggle of clashing personal ambitions.[20] "France has never seen," Tocqueville wrote in 1838, "ambition more brazenly displayed than in the behavior principally of the Doctrinaires. These men distress me with their aggressive and villainous behavior. To overturn the ministry in order to put in power M. Thiers or M. Guizot would be, for sincere friends of their country, to do the work of fools."[21]

For Guizot and his party, the interests of the ruling middle class were identical with those of the whole society. With the rise of middle classes to power, the Revolution had been fulfilled and the great historical movement for freedom and equality, the democratic revolution, had come to an end. Guizot went so far as to make it a personal matter. History had carried him to the top, and he was not about to relinquish the power that destiny had put in his hands. For Tocqueville, apart from however galling such crowing must have been, this effort to freeze the status quo, to declare the end of history, to confound the existing order with the ideal, and to rule in the name of freedom and equality while denying it was not only to defy history but to take a path that would lead to catastrophe.

Such confusion was also the sign of a deep cultural crisis, for ultimately the ills of contemporary politics seemed to result as much from a failure of the moral imagination as from a thirst for power. The moral clarity that had made it impossible to equate the interests of a class with those of a whole society, to confuse principles with what was useful, means with ends, the present with the future had been lost. The problems of politics became rooted in the ways men thought of life's purposes, of how they related to society, and limits they acknowledged as constraints to action. These were the problems that preoccupied Tocqueville as he wrote the second volume of *Democracy in America* and as he defined his purposes and strategies during the 1830s and 1840s while France drifted in "an uncertain state of perpetual drowsiness."[22]

If grandeur and vision were missing from political life, how might they be restored? Tocqueville hoped that fundamental principles and values would once again be raised in parliamentary debate and that "great parties," standing for different visions of the national future, would replace the many shifting, almost indistinguishable coalitions of politicians whose main aim was to acquire power. He thought that both the pride and the virility of France had to be reawakened by the vigorous pursuit of an imperial program and by the assertion of French power, even by military means if necessary, a view for which he was strongly criticized by Mill.[23] He did not answer Mill's chastising letter.

Eloquent leadership might also transform politics: the July Monarchy was a time in which oratorical power still counted for as much as political brokering and the corrupt management of seats in the Chamber of Deputies. It was a matter of deep frustration to Tocqueville that he lacked the eloquence that might awaken great passions. He was too self-conscious a speaker, noticeably unsure of himself and yet at the same time remote and icy, to be the tribune who could lead French politics out of the deepening swamp of self-serving pettiness.

Tocqueville called himself "un liberal d'une espèce nouvelle." Presumably he meant to distinguish himself from Guizotian liberals. But in some ways it is difficult to see how he was different, for he shared a great deal with them besides formal allegiance to the credal core of liberalism. Tocqueville's new liberalism has been adeptly and thoroughly analyzed by Roger Boesche in *The Strange Liberalism of Alexis de Tocqueville*. Boesche rightly emphasizes the way in which Tocqueville tried to restore moral and religious values to politics. This was his political vocation. He also had much in common with contemporary liberals. He shared Guizot's views on the desirability of a constitutional monarchy for France and shared his admiration for the conservative, orderly liberalism of England, as much Guizot's Mecca as his own. He believed also in governance by a moral and intellectual elite, and his thinking about suffrage was not much more generous than Guizot's, who also felt that the electorate should be slowly enlarged only as education prepared the people for the vote. But he thought the property qualifications argued for by Guizot were too stringent.

To a degree, he shared with the liberals of the July Monarchy a sense of need to balance the claims of liberty with the requirements of order. He thought that Guizot's stifling of press freedom and of freedom of association went too far, but his protests were mostly private. His idea of liberty was so complicated, so qualified by a strong regard for the demands and obligations of the community, by the need of loyalty to values beyond the self, and so restricted by the claims of the past and the future that in effect the moderate or regulated liberty he advocated seemed almost to converge with Guizot's standpat liberalism. He was not a bold or imaginative advocate of change and reform. If he called for a return of vision to politics, it was certainly not the vision of the utopians and radicals he scorned.

In some ways Tocqueville's new liberalism reveals a stronger democratic impulse than Guizot's establishment liberalism. He had a more generous, if abstract, sense of community, a broader idea of what constitutes human well-being, a larger idea of rights. He may have returned from America with a sense of the openness and possibility he experienced as such a striking aspect of American life. The lessons he drew from history were broader than those Guizot made the basis of his politics. Unlike Guizot, he believed that the democratic revolution was unfinished. It might be guided but not resisted. "Is it wise to suppose," he asks in *Democracy in America*, "that a movement that has been so long in train could be halted by one generation? Does anyone imagine that democracy, which has destroyed the feudal system and vanquished kings, will fall back before the middle classes and the rich? Will it stop now, when it has grown so strong and its adversaries so weak?"[24] Such questions were aimed directly at the reigning liberals constructing futile barricades against democracy. Yet so moderate was his view of the desirable pace of change that it is sometimes difficult to distinguish his practical politics from the timorous liberalism he scorned.

The crux of what he meant by his new liberalism is difficult to grasp unless one recognizes that Tocqueville's political agenda remains essentially that of a moralist. It lay not so much in the consistency of his advocacy of the principles of liberalism or in his recognition that the democratic passion was far from exhausted as in his conviction that there was an urgent need to restore integrity and clarity to the discourses of politics and to reintegrate values that the disassociative tendencies of modernism had sundered. His central aim as a new kind of liberal was to bridge the gulf that had opened between those who prized "morality, religion, and order" and those who loved "liberty and equality before the law." It was this integrative conception that he kept reaching for. When accused of advancing "théories radicales et presques révolutionnaires" he replied with another version of the same idea:

> I have shown and will continue to show an active and rational taste for liberty for two reasons: the first is that I profoundly believe in it; the second is that I do not want to be confounded with those friends of order who sell out the rule of freedom and the law so they can sleep peacefully in their beds. . . . I will thus frankly profess a love of liberty and a desire to see it develop in all the institutions of my country; but at the same time I will profess so great a respect for justice, and a true feeling for order and law and so profound and reasoned an attachment to morality and religious beliefs, that I can't believe that . . . I will be confused with the majority of the democrats of our time.[25]

2

VOCATION: THE RESPONSIBILITIES OF POLITICAL LEADERS

At the heart of the concept of aristocratic liberalism that Tocqueville worked out with Mill lay the question of who would provide democracies with the nonautocratic, benevolent moral leadership needed to overcome democracy's worst instincts. Where would this moral elite be found? how would it come to power? and how would it lead? Tocqueville's thinking about these questions, worked out in his correspondence with Mill and simultaneously in volume 2 of *Democracy in America* in the late 1830s as he prepared to enter politics, was vague. He offers no concrete ideas about how his aristocracy of merit is to be found, what class or group in society might fulfill that role, or, above all, how it was to go about re-creating a politics of principle and vision in which the quest for the general good would replace the politics of clashing interest groups seeking power and advantage for themselves.

If the central problems of democratic politics were essentially moral and cultural, what then was to be done? What prescriptions did Tocqueville's "new science of politics for a new age" offer to guide democracies through the perils they would inevitably face? His ideas often sound like the stoical musings of someone dealt a crippling blow by fate yet determined to make the best of it. The true task of political leadership was to restore soul to politics: to reinvest political life with a level of moral consciousness and with values that democratic culture would chronically undercut. Such was the calling that drew him to politics. Such was the essential aim of the aristocratic liberalism that Tocqueville elaborated in the second volume of *Democracy in America* as he contemplated the ills of French politics and as he discussed the problems of democracy with Mill in the late 1830s.

There were useful lessons to be learned from democratic America. Tocqueville was much impressed with how the remarkable religiosity of the Americans kept alive notions of moral order and of ordered liberty even among so fiercely individualistic a people—though he thought that in the long run democratic culture would weaken those aspects of religion that served as countervailing forces against democratic normlessness. He warned that the particular institutional and constitutional arrangements of the American Republic could not be adopted unaltered by peoples whose social systems and political cultures were deeply rooted in ancient experience and ritual. Certain broad principles, however, might be adapted in instructing other societies to guide a gradual and modest reconstruction of political institutions with the aim of maintaining a society which would remain free and liberal despite the ever-intensifying drive for democracy. These broad principles included the decentralization of government, the constitutional distribution and separation of powers, the broadening of the suffrage, the increase of political enlightenment through the popular sharing of civic responsibilities, and accountable, truly representative parliamentary government.

Like James Madison, whose *Federalist Papers*, that manual of the mechanics of politics, he had read, he thought that to a degree institutions might serve as engines or guarantors of virtue even when virtuous men were not to be found. He would have agreed with Madison's cool Calvinist observation that "enlightened statesmen will not always be at the helm" and that the Republic had to have an automatic pilot to survive, but the enduring aristocrat in Tocqueville was more inclined to think about the function and responsibilities of a moral elite in a democracy than about how to get along without one. The institutional resolution of the problem of virtue interested Tocqueville less. First on the agenda of his new liberalism was the problem of moral leadership. Who would lead the people out of the swamp of shortsighted expediency into which democracy was leading them? was it possible to create a party of virtue? It was an old French idea.

Tocqueville's thoughts about where such leadership was to be found were vague. The only contemporary example he could point to was Royer-Collard, who, as noted, had urged Tocqueville to stay out of politics until he had matured. In Tocqueville's opinion, Royer was the perfect model of the moral man in politics, very nearly the founding father of French democracy and its most eloquent and principled critic. He was "une grande âme," one of the last of the great political figures. "Original, grand, uniquely himself, influential over his time without having dominated it," he was above all a man of integrity whose practical political wisdom and ability to move men were unsurpassed. He had refused high office and power to retain his moral independence—his task was to lead by moral example and the force of argument. In his sketchy notes for a never-written essay on Royer, Tocqueville emphasized the man's disinterestedness and selflessness: "Powerful personality, indomitable yet not egoist. Able to become animated, passionate for or against issues unrelated to himself or his interests. The only man in politics to whom one could be devoted for that reason."[1] But Royer was a vanishing type: "He was the last of the great political figures, of the great political passions, of the great political characters. We no longer have anyone like him."[2]

The founders of the American Republic also illustrated his ideal, but they too were figures of the past. For Tocqueville (as for Guizot), George Washington was an icon of integrity and selfless statesmanship. He was "at the head of our race," an example of "true grandeur and true glory." But Washington's qualities were hopelessly out of date in France: "In France one would have found him dull: because we demand theatricality, high oratory and striking vices so long as they are audacious." Washington was a retroactive victim of democracy.[3]

The problem of leadership in democratic societies becomes the central issue of Tocqueville's correspondence with Mill (see part III, chapter 8). Though his aristocratic liberalism was elitist, he rejected any authoritarian or manipulative resolution of democracy, no matter how benevolent it might be. He had no illusions about the ability of the people to see wherein lay their happiness, and he knew that in all societies, except perhaps the United States, they fell short of the general enlightenment needed for self-governance; but he could not accept any version of elitism that called for forcing people to do what was best for them. The essential task was to prepare the people for self-governance and choice. "I am myself," he wrote to Mill, "a democrat in this sense. To lead modern societies by degrees to this point seems to be the only way to save them from barbarianism or slavery."[4] Muddling along in democratic confusion and turmoil was unthinkable.

What he had in mind was a forbearing, progressive paternalism that strove to educate the people and do as little as possible for them while awaiting their enlightenment, the kind of enlightenment he believed the Americans, whom he many times called "the most enlightened people in the world," had already achieved through extensive political experience and understanding. But if cultural change was to make that day ever more remote, then barbarianism or slavery would be the future. By the time he had finished thinking through *Democracy in America*, he had come to think that the culture of future democratic societies would lack the qualities needed to sustain independent critical intellect and liberty and that moral leaders who possessed such qualities would be ignored or rejected.

If he rejected the authoritarian solution, so too did he find the radical democratic dream of rule by the people nothing more than populist fantasy. Even an enlightened people would have to choose their rulers. To Mill he wrote, "For friends of democracy it's much less a question of finding a way for the people to rule than it is of finding a way of choosing from among the people those most capable of governing and of giving such enough power to enable them to direct their overall conduct and not the details of their lives, nor their means of execution. That's the problem. I am deeply convinced that the fate of modern nations depends on its solution."[5] It was Mill, however, who gave far more time than Tocqueville to the problem of how to choose the guiding elite by focusing on the issues of election and representation. Tocqueville was much more focused on quality of leadership and on the moral condition of the whole society. It was to Mill that he stated the issue most forcefully:

> I don't need to tell you, my dear Mill, that the greatest problem facing a people organized like ours is the gradual softening of the culture, the decline of spirit, the mediocrity of taste—it is here that the greatest dangers of the future lie. It is not to a nation democratically constituted like ours, where the natural weaknesses of "the race" coexist with the weaknesses of the "social state" [the kind of social and political order]; it is not such a nation that one can allow to be accustomed to the habit of sacrificing whatever nourishes its greatness to its comfort, great affairs to petty ones. It is not healthy to let such a people believe that its place in the world is smaller, that it has fallen from the rank its fathers had placed it so that therefore it's necessary to compensate for that by building railroads and becoming prosperous in the bosom of peace no matter how that peace was obtained.[6]

If the particular occasion that provoked this observation was what he thought was a growing spinelessness in France's foreign policy as other European powers flexed their imperial muscles, the deeper issue was the spiritual flabbiness of bourgeois culture. His desperate resort to jingoism was not characteristic of the way in which he generally thought about addressing the weaknesses of a materialist people grown soft and self-indulgent. Later, in the 1850s, he would write bitterly about the danger to freedom posed by the clamor for military preparedness and action. It was a danger he also had pointed out forcefully in the second volume of *Democracy in America*. One can't imagine him rallying behind any nationalist movement or military adventure for the sake of social solidarity, folk unity, or any kind of mystical national oneness. He detested great national celebrations and fetes as occasions for displays of irrationality, mind-deadening oratory, and the parading of false patriotism.

Tocqueville customarily had in mind a broader, more humane moral leadership that by example and precept would redress the moral shortfall of the culture. It was almost a priestly role he had in view. There are a number of striking moments in *Democracy in America* in which he comments on the responsibilities of the legislator; these responsibilities call for resisting the inclinations of the people by stimulating countervailing moral energies when the dominant tendencies of the culture threaten to upset the precarious balance between order and freedom—between individualism and social coherence, the pursuit of well-being and the pursuit of other values crucial to a thriving society.

The argument, stated in *Democracy in America*, is this:

> I have no doubt that the social and political structure of a nation predisposes a people in favor of certain tastes and beliefs which then flourish carefree; and the same reason, without deliberate striving and indeed almost unconsciously, keeps other opinions and inclinations out of mind.
>
> The essence of the lawgiver's art is by anticipation to appreciate these natural bents of human societies in order to know where the citizens' efforts need support and where there is more need to hold them back. For different times make different demands. The goal alone is fixed, to which humanity should press forward; the means of getting there forever change.[7]

If Tocqueville is Moses, he has a reserve tablet for other occasions. The duty of the legislator, who turns out in Tocqueville's view to be primarily a spiritual leader, a moral guide for his people, is to calculate and prescribe the right cure for the particular pathology or excess of the moment. And in his view there were many moral issues to be addressed: the skepticism and materialism of modern culture, the general debasement and trivializing of personal vision and ambition, the now-dominant focus on comfort, security, and the accumulation of wealth, and the threat to the difficult, creative balance between liberty and the passion for equality.

Whether it was a matter of urging or inspiring larger ambitions, longer-range vision, a greater willingness to postpone immediate advantage for future benefit, and a larger view of social connections and responsibilities, there was a broad range of issues that invited the moral leaders of a democratic society to apply countervailing strategies. He did not think that religion would do this. In *Democracy in America* he sees religion being more and more absorbed by the culture, abandoning its independent, transcendental values, unable to serve any countervailing role.

The argument from a strongly didactic chapter of the *Democracy* entitled "Why in Ages of Equality and Skepticism It Is Important to Set Distant Goals for Human Endeavor" applies to "men in power" and "rulers" as well as philosophers and moralists:

> In such a country where unhappily skepticism and democracy exist together, philosophers and the men in power should always strive to set a distant aim as the object of human efforts; that is their most important business.

The moralist must . . . constantly endeavor to show his contemporaries . . . that although the aspect of humanity has changed, the means by which men can obtain prosperity in this world are still the same and that, in democracies as elsewhere, it is only by resisting a thousand daily petty urges that the fundamental anxious longing for happiness can be satisfied.

The duty of rulers is equally clear.

It is at all times important that the rulers of nations should act with the future in view. But this is even more necessary in ages of democracy and skepticism than in any others. By giving such a lead, the chief men in democracies not only bring prosperity in public affairs but also teach individuals by their example to conduct their private affairs properly.[8]

And in another passage dark with the hint of the grim consequences that would follow should a society spin out of its moral orbit, Tocqueville warns "democratic legislators" that the future will be full of "strange vicissitudes" unless they apply corrective therapy to democracy's "fatal tendency":

When social conditions are equal, every man tends to live apart, centered in himself and forgetful of the public. Should democratic legislators not seek to correct this fatal tendency, or actually favor it, thinking that it diverts the citizens' attention from political passions and avoid revolution, it might happen that in the end they may bring back that very evil which they seek to avoid and that the moment may come when the unruly passions of certain men, aided by the foolish selfishness and pusillanimity of the greater number, will in the end subject the society to strange vicissitudes.[9]

Just how men of power, rulers of nations, lawgivers, moralists, philosophers, upright men, and legislators, the terms by which in *Democracy in America* he identifies the moral leaders he has in mind, were to apply corrective moral leadership to avoid the "strange vicissitudes" that lay ahead remains unclear in Tocqueville's writings. He did not envision the kind of coercive moral legislation for which he criticized the New England Puritans or the advocates of temperance laws in nineteenth-century America. He oddly shared some of the confidence of the American Transcendentalists (whose ideas, except for Emerson's, were still barely known in France), that to speak the truth would in the long run be a converting sacrament and that to stand on principle would ultimately prove an effective mode of practical politics. As he wrote to Royer-Collard, "For me, I have always believed that if men did not give up on their integrity so quickly they would succeed *à tout prendre* more surely in their plans than in abandoning their principles. But that's an opinion little shared."[10] Yet even such wan optimism was hard to maintain in the face of his acute and depressing analysis of the impermeability and inertia of public opinion in democracies in that despairing chapter of *Democracy in America*, "Why Great Revolutions Will Become Rare." He wrote this chapter in the spring of 1838, before he was elected to the Chamber of Deputies. In it he argued that it will be exceptionally difficult to divert or change or even challenge the prevailing drift of opinion in democratic societies, let alone transform values. Though democratic culture would give men a taste for the new and perpetually involve them in a kind of restless innovativeness, it would on a deeper level foster an immobility and a uniformity of belief that would block radical alternatives from the imagination. The inattentiveness and busyness of democratic peoples, the deep fear of radical change of any sort bred by the fear of loss, and the democratic suspiciousness of men who were different and superior, all conspired to produce a culture curiously resistant to fundamental change and deaf to radical challenge. The power of public opinion, the overwhelming consensus on values, and the hostility toward the exceptional to be found in egalitarian societies would intimidate the ordinary man and at the same time isolate those few who tried to challenge prevailing beliefs. Tocqueville's countervailing leaders would find themselves marching at the head of a parade whose momentum would make it extremely difficult to change direction. They would finally be swept along in the direction the crowd wanted to go.

It wasn't clear where the saving remnant was to be found. Tocqueville found it difficult to locate the source of such leadership in any social class or group, though its essential qualities—a capacity for heroic self-denial and for virtuous self-subordination to a code of honor—had been the chief virtues of the now-marginalized, powerless aristocracy. One could not count on finding such a saving moral force either among intellectuals, the bureaucracy, populist lovers of the people, or technological utopians nor among the now powerless and demoralized remnants of the aristocracy or among the bourgeoisie, whose values and compulsions were the source of the problem.

He had himself chosen "la vie de tête" and was closer to the intellectual class than to any other social element, but his deep suspicion of intellectuals, especially because of their tendency to lose themselves in fantasy and illusion and also because of their congenital skepticism, made it unlikely that they could provide the necessary moral guidance or serve as models of public spirit. They were as much a part of the problem as the bourgeoisie. Tocqueville's fantastic revolutionary terrorist, the radical, desperate, audacious, half-crazed new man, appears first in his bitter account, in *L'Ancien Régime*, of the destructive work of eighteenth-century intellectuals, who in their passionate quest for the truth had ironically lost sight of the true nature of things. In his *Souvenirs* intellectuals are, along with the self-centered and purblind middle-classes, the guilty fomenters of 1848, which in his view was not the result of real misery and political dissatisfaction but was the work of impractical theorists and mad ideologues leading a momentarily disoriented people astray. Impractical passionate dreamers, uprooted souls, dazzling self-promoters bereft of any faith except their dangerous faith in the power of ideas: not much could be expected of intellectuals, and much was to be feared from them. Perhaps it was some obscure self-insight that made him aware of how vulnerable they were to disorders of the self. One of the puzzles of Tocqueville's thought is his strange, recurring suspicion of ideas, which for him possess a dangerously deranging and corrupting power. It was not the intellectuals who would provide society with sensible, inspiring, countervailing moral guidance.

Nor would such leadership come from another social group synonymous with modernity, the bureaucracy. Tocqueville's distrust of this group was probably deeper than that he felt for the intelligentsia. It had no soul at all. His brief experience of it while working in the legal bureaucracy had made him fear he would become a "legal machine"; and when his nephew Hubert turned to him for career advice he warned him about the deformations of bureaucratic life. In such work, he wrote, "I have noticed that, in order to succeed . . . it was necessary to show a great deal of suppleness and obsequiousness with those who command you, and a great deal of deviousness and coerciveness toward those you command yourself."[11] Only in the magistracy was it possible "de rester soi" — to maintain one's integrity — and even then the pressure to conform was great. Beaumont had in fact resigned rather than knuckle under to oppressive, malevolent superiors, and Tocqueville had followed suit as a gesture of friendship and as a moral protest. One's integrity was not likely to survive in the bureaucratic world, in which the spirit of expedient careerism was bound to obscure a larger view of affairs. "In France," he wrote, "administration hardly ever conducts itself in the general interest of the country, but almost always in the particular interest of those who govern; and any man who isn't ready constantly to sacrifice the first of these interests to the other has no hope at all of succeeding."[12] Indeed, the bureaucracy, like the intelligentsia and the bourgeoisie, was responsible for much of the moral disorder and instability from which France suffered: "It is especially to it that we owe our incessant revolutions, our servility of manner, our continuing failure to create a moderate and reasonable liberty."[13] In bureaucracy Tocqueville finds his definitive image of modern despotism. He concludes *Democracy in America* with the vision of a bureaucratic state that stifles rather than liberates the spirit and that subtly transforms citizens into easily managed sheep rather than fostering independent, morally alert individuals.

Tocqueville's many references to a needed exemplary ruling elite only vaguely placed it socially. In discussing those who are to show the moral leadership democracy requires, he shifted between relatively clear functional types like lawgivers, legislators, men in power, leaders of the nation and an amorphous group consisting of philosophers, upright educated men, men of good will, as though he could not easily locate his moral elite specifically and saw it as a free-floating moral cadre. These would be odd, unaccountable men detached from any particular interest yet at the same time committed to the good of all, like the Tocqueville who, in his imagination, stood above history and apart from society.

Would such people appear in democratic societies? He increasingly thought it unlikely. And if they did, would anyone listen to them? He increasingly thought not.

Yet this was the public role he sought to fashion for himself in France's uncertain democracy. If there was something naïve and grandiose, even messianic, about his view of the political role he was called to play as a disinterested voice of "le bien general" and as an example of integrity in politics, it was based on a carefully thought through view of the moral state of the nation. As he wrote to Beaumont, the great task was that of restoring "political uprightness in a nation that has become almost indifferent to the good and the bad and that values only success." "Our interest and our duty," he added, "is to maintain wherever we can the principle of a wise and progressive liberty and not at all sustain without rhyme or reason the status quo, let alone a return to the ancient state of things."[14]

The Dead Sea of Politics

Tocqueville's political ambitions were intense. In local politics he carefully maintained the old aristocratic style of disinterested service while quietly working hard to promote his career and maintain his image as an independent man. He accepted the democratic need to work the hustings—in his cool fashion. In the role of democratic seigneur he succeeded admirably, and after an initial defeat in 1837 was elected to the Chamber of Deputies by his Norman constituents from 1839 until Napoleon III's seizure of power drove him from political life in 1851.

From the start, Tocqueville was ineffective in national politics. He was neither a passionate nor an eloquent orator, a major requisite for political effectiveness. He carefully guarded his independence, was so repelled by the leading politicians of the Chamber of Deputies and so scorned its ordinary members (as noted, he called them oafs) that he could form no working alliances. He was an isolated figure, admired for his intellect and his trenchant analyses of issues, but he did not come close to fulfilling the role he had hoped to play.

The Tocqueville who paid no heed to Royer-Collard's advice to stay out of the political arena, who ran unsuccessfully for political office in 1837, and who was elected to the Chamber of Deputies in 1839 was a more complex, realistic, and craftier figure than his ideal self-portrait suggests. Though he was politically inexperienced and naïve (on entering the Chamber in 1839 he had indeed been duped, as Royer feared he might be), he could be shrewd about the game of politics and knew how much success was a matter of image management. He was in fact independent but he also carefully managed his reputation, his image, as a man of principle beholden to no party. He gave finicky thought to where and next to whom he would sit in the Chamber and constantly wrote to the press to correct false statements about his positions and his alliances.

Tocqueville was never the disinterested, reluctant candidate who had to be sought by the office. Before he decided to seek a seat in the Chamber of

Deputies from Valognes near Cherbourg, close to his chateau in Normandy, he had canvassed possibilities in Versailles, several arrondissements in Paris, and in Cherbourg. In his first race for office he had been defeated, though not badly (247 to 210) by the incumbent, Count Jules Polydor Le Marois, the wealthy son of a general ennobled by Napoleon. Le Marois had spent freely and given the administration in Paris the necessary assurances that he could be counted on. Tocqueville had refused to do that, even though—or perhaps especially because—he was related to the then-president of the Council of Ministers in the Chamber, the Comte de Molé. Molé, who was genuinely fond of his young kinsman, had offered to support his candidacy if he would run as a candidate of the ministry. But Tocqueville had replied with a public manifesto, or credo, announcing his candidacy as a man with no strings attached. "The administration officially declared," he told Royer, "that since the tone of it seemed too independent and that the name of the King did not appear in it, it could not back the election of the person who had written it."[1]

In his accounts of his political campaigns he took every opportunity to burnish his image as an independent man of principle not ambitious for power. He had not, so he said, initiated his candidacy, was no party's man, and did not even know the electors who had, according to Tocqueville, spontaneously thought of him and who had asked permission to enter his name in the race, assuring him that he "needn't take any steps and that it was necessary only to give them permission . . . to let it be known officially that he would accept the office of Deputy."[2] In fact this proud account of his independence and come-hitherness, the traditional aristocratic story of the office seeking the man, was only partially true. He had subtly and quietly campaigned for office in many ways. That he should have seen fit to mask the truth of his first, failed political campaign, especially in his correspondence with the revered Royer, was a surprising departure from his customary veracity. His portrait of the reluctant candidate accepting a call to serve as a duty was written by the Tocqueville who saw himself as an ideal figure above it all, a man of no party rationally deciding what was best for the good of the nation. Even his realistic, frank, occasionally amused accounts of life on the local political campaign trail are tinged by a tone of noble detachment and noblesse oblige. They also make clear his disdain for democratic politicking.

Despite the abrasive and underhanded aspects of the campaign of 1837, he drew much satisfaction from it. He had lost by only thirty-seven votes and believed himself to have been supported by "the most enlightened, the most independent, and the most honorable members of the electoral college"; "nine-tenths" of those who had voted for him had never seen him, he said. The people had sought his candidacy.[3]

When he next ran, in March of 1839, he won easily, this time beating Le Marois, whose two-faced opportunism caught up with him. It was a deeply satisfying triumph for Tocqueville, granting him not only proof of the public esteem his fragile ego required, but also a real-world political identity. "This has been a grand success" he wrote to his old Metz schoolmate Stoffels, "and, I add, an honorable success, because it owed nothing to intrigue. I did not make one visit, I had not promised even one place. I limited myself to making an energetic appeal to the most honest and purest impulses of the human heart, and I succeeded. . . . This proves that the human race is not yet as bad as it has seemed to be."[4] This is a remarkable conclusion to draw from a small local election but also a clue as to what political life meant to Tocqueville: it was a morality play. But again, the story he prepared for his "honnête" friend Stoffels was not fully accurate. He had not stooped to intrigue, but he had worked the hustings and had made it clear that the traditional patronage responsibilities of a local notable would be honored.[5]

Despite the moments of warmth and the "proofs of public esteem" he had experienced during his campaigns, he remained an aloof, detached, somewhat Olympian figure whose relationship to the people of his arrondissement was distant and paternal. He had only briefly resided in Normandy and did not know the local folk or their culture. Though he sometimes professed fondness for the Norman people, he never felt at ease among them, though it isn't clear where, if anywhere, he felt at ease apart from his small cohort of friends. He observed the political and social life of the Normans who had put him in office almost with the sense of strangeness and detachment of an anthropologist commenting on a culture that wasn't his. The ambivalence he felt about the Norman people, the moral distance he felt from them, the sense of isolation he felt even in his own community are part of the picture of his alienation, a sense of conscious apartness, not antagonism. It is clearly put in the following candid commentary he sent to Royer:

> I have discovered here much goodwill and unending consideration. I am attached to these people without deceiving myself about their faults, which are large. The people here are honest, intelligent, quite religious, moral enough, very orderly. But they are not in the least disinterested. It is true that the self-centeredness of the people in this region is not like what one finds in Paris, so aggressive and often so cruel. It is mild, peaceful, and persistent about its particular interests, which gradually absorb all other feelings of the heart and thus dry up the springs of other values. They blend with this egoism a certain number of private virtues and domestic qualities which, taken together, make them honest men and poor citizens. I would, however,

excuse them for not being disinterested, if they would sometimes believe in disinterestedness. But they do not at all, and so, despite all the proofs of goodwill, I feel oppressed. Unhappily, only time will be able to rid me of this kind of oppression, and I am not patient.[6]

The moral standards to which he held the honest country men who were his constituents were the same as those he demanded of his sophisticated colleagues in the Chamber of Deputies. The deputies failed just as badly, with the result that Tocqueville continued to feel oppressed throughout his political life. There is a strong sense of otherness and of moral distance in his view of the people he is describing, and not a little naïveté. The closely circumscribed moral and social consciousness of Tocqueville's Normans made them seem like members of another tribe. The worldly Royer chided him: "Your Normans — they are like men everywhere!"[7]

Tocqueville found the tone and the level of ignorance of local public life deplorable: "What increasingly strikes me as I have further occasion to know these people is how little they are concerned with political matters. This goes so far as to make it impossible to talk about it myself. I have heard it said, and I believe it, that there are a good number of electors who don't know that M. Thiers is Prime Minister. Do all arrondissements resemble this one?"[8] Though he had been deeply impressed by the widely shared political awareness and savoir-faire of the Americans, which he thought was the saving strength of democratic politics in the United States, along with the orderliness and "chasteness" that religion brought to politics in the otherwise hurly-burly Republic, he does not mention what must have been a painful contrast for him.

The demands of democratic politics — when Tocqueville was first elected there were barely seven hundred electors in his college, consisting of those who could meet the steep property requirements — ill-suited his aristocratic temperament. He sometimes found amusement in the games of politics but did not really enjoy them. To the end he remained very much the seigneur, disdainful of emotional appeals, bonhommerie whether feigned or real, and opportunistic catering to public sentiment, all inescapable features of democratic politics. "In our time," he complained to Kergorlay, "it is not at all political acts or oratory that wins one voters, but establishing personal ties with them. It is a vicious system, I am convinced, but one can at least make it work to facilitate good works."[9] He regarded submission to the "vicious system" of democratic politics as a "kind of servitude," but he campaigned as vigorously as he could and played the game of public relations shrewdly, even assigning Marie the task of paying calls on the wives of the electors of his arrondissement. He drove himself to attend the endless circuit of political banquets, a joy of democratic politics, "because in this province it is only at table that one has occasion to find a number of men gathered and to get an idea of prevailing opinion." With obvious impatience he wrote to Beaumont of the miseries of his "tournée gastrononomico-électorale": "I have been completely worn out by the life I have been leading for more than two weeks. When I arrived here four months ago my friends overwhelmed me with dinner invitations. You know what passes for a dinner in the country: the whole day is spent at it, and the next day is spent recovering from the fatigue of the preceding day. . . . I have suffered prodigious boredom during this round, much impatience, and often irritation."[10] His patience may have been tried, but what was more seriously tried was his health, for he was beginning to suffer from chronic gastric ailments.

Tocqueville was also a somewhat grudgingly impatient but dutiful member of the Conseil Generale de la Manche, on which he served from 1842 to 1852 — as president from 1846 until he resigned in 1852 after Napoleon III's coup of December 1851. It was his last political office.[11] Even though his American experience had convinced him that it was crucial to strengthen local political institutions and civic associations and to broaden the political experience and sophistication of the folk, he was often bored and exasperated by "le petit côté de la vie politique," which robbed him of time to study, write, and think. To Royer he wrote,

I am so infuriated by this trivial activity which immediately follows the work of the Chamber that I feel myself prey to a passion for solitude and could try for myself the cell system I spoke about last winter. You have never lived, sir, in the region [*pays*] that has elected you Deputy; consequently, you cannot at all nor sufficiently sympathize with my misery. It is so great that though I really like these people and believe that they like me, I will finally wind up creating for myself a retreat in some remote corner of France where, far from them, I will be able to find time to reflect and, so to speak, to live, because I have no life here at all.[12]

Just as the daily, prosaic tasks of the law had bored him, so did the daily nitty-gritty of local political life. He needed broader horizons as well as greater intellectual stimulation than local interests and issues could offer. Moreover, he knew much too little about agriculture and too little about the economic and technical issues of the husbandry of his Norman farmers to represent them. He had to be tutored by Edouard about the effects that a reduction of the tariff on imported "bestiaux" would have on Norman cattle farmers and only then dropped his free-market objections to the tariff.[13] He was always inclined to take a national view of issues. Nevertheless, he was a dutiful member of the council, attended all sessions, and specialized in a few issues, such as harbor improvements for Cherbourg (to prepare for the war with England that he thought possible); farmer-friendly railroad routes in the Cotentin; the regulation of savings banks; community property; and especially questions having to do with abandoned children ("enfants trouvées"). Regarding this last issue, he chaired an investigating committee whose report harshly warned that continued public support of the irresponsible girls who abandoned their illegitimate children was simply making a moral problem worse: "La société se charge elle-même d'offrir au désordre des mères, un encouragement permanente et une sorte d'impunité par privilege," and thus contributed to social disorder. As André Tudesq put it in his preface to volume 10 of the *Oeuvres Complètes (Correspondance et Écrites Locaux)*, "This paper cedes nothing to Malthus. . . . Tocqueville's liberalism leads, in the name of 'public order,' to the same condemnation of *filles-mères*."[14] His views about poor laws and laws dealing with mendicancy were consistently severe: he tended to see poverty as more a moral issue than a social problem (see part II, chapter 4).

If he was at times impatient with micropolitics, he took such work seriously. However, his grand ambitions required a greater arena. Unfortunately, in that greater arena he suffered a greater misery.

In his *Recollections* Tocqueville composes a fascinating narrative of how he conducted his candidacy for reelection to the Chamber of Deputies after the Revolution of 1848, the first election held under a democratic suffrage. It says much about how he presented himself then and how he wished to be seen. The persona he presents, that of a courageously independent, principled individual who openly disdains the opportunistic and crowd-truckling modes of democratic politics, was not contrived for the occasion. It was an image he had nurtured and used whenever he could, though he always took care to disassociate himself from the now-defunct aristocracy. Nor was what he said to the people of La Manche about his political and social views untrue. But his brief narrative reminds one of the pride and self-satisfaction of Benjamin Franklin's *Autobiography*, which he had read. Though he had not meant to publish his *Recollections*, the text provides moral instruction for dignified survival and a guide to success in the intimidating, seductive world of democratic politics. It is a portrait of the aristocrat in the new world of democracy:

> The country began to fill with roving candidates hawking their republican protestations from hustings to hustings. I *refused* to represent myself before any other electoral body than that of the place where I lived. Each little town

had its club, and each club asked the candidates to give an account of their views and their *answer to any of these insolent questions*. Such refusals might have seemed contemptuous, but in fact they were regarded as dignity and independence in dealing with the new sovereign authority, and I got more credit for my revolt than others did for their obedience.

I limited myself to publishing an address and having it posted everywhere throughout the Department. Most of the candidates had resumed the old usages of '92. In letters they addressed people as "Citizens" and signed themselves "Fraternally yours." My circular began by calling the electors "Messieurs," and I ended by proudly assuring them of my respect.

"*I do not come*," *I said*, "*to solicit your votes*, but only to put myself under my country's orders. I asked to be your representative in quiet, easy times. *Honor forbids me* to refuse to represent you in a time of trouble with many possible dangers ahead. So then I do not ask for your vote, but *am ready to consecrate my time, my fortune and my life to you*. That is what I must tell you first."

I added that *I had been faithful to the end to the oath I had sworn to the Monarchy*, but that the Republic, which had come into being without my help, would have my energetic support, for I did not wish merely to tolerate its existence but to sustain it. I then went on:

"But what Republic is in question? There are those who mean by a Republic a dictatorship exercised in the name of freedom; who think that the Republic should change not only political institutions but reshape society itself; there are those who think that the Republic should be aggressive and propagandist. I am not that kind of Republican. If that were your way of being one, I could be of no use to you, for I would not share your opinion. But if you understand the meaning of a Republic in the same sense as I, *you can count on my devoting my soul to a cause which is mine as well as yours*.

"In times of Revolution, people who do not feel fear are like members of the royal family in an army, producing a great effect by very ordinary actions, for their peculiar position naturally allows no rivals and gives them great prominence. I was myself astonished at the success of my circular. In a few days it made me the most popular man in the Department of La Manche and the cynosure of all eyes. My former political adversaries, the conservatives and the agents of the old government, who had attacked me most and who had been overthrown by the Republic, came in a body to assure me that they were ready not only to support me but to follow my advice in everything.[15] [emphasis added here and below].

This was indeed royal behavior: a demonstration that fearlessness, integrity, conviction, and other qualities of character would carry the day. Tocqueville had not at all adapted to the American style of politics. But though he had been "astonished" at the response to his circular, he knew that he was dealing with a people who were in many ways predemocratic and whose culture still prompted them to defer to the self-assured behavior of the aristocracy.

His narrative proceeds to a triumphant finale:

> Meanwhile the first meeting of the electors of the arrondissement of Valognes took place. I appeared with the other candidates. The forum was a shed serving as a hall. The Chairman's platform was at the bottom, and at the side a professor's chair had been provided as a rostrum for the candidates. The chairman, a teacher at the college of Valognes, addressed me in a loud, authoritative voice, but very respectfully: "Citizen de Tocqueville, I am going to put to you the questions requiring your answer." To which I replied *in a slightly offhand way*: "Mr. Chairman, I am listening."
>
> "Why did you desert the opposition at the time of the banquets?" I was asked.
>
> *I replied boldly*: "I could find an excuse, but I prefer to give you my real reason. I did not want the banquets because I did not want a revolution. And I make bold to say that hardly any of those of you who sat down at those banquets would have done so if, like me, they had known what the result would be. So the only difference that I see between you and me is that I knew what you were doing, but you did not know."
>
> *This bold profession of antirevolutionary faith* had been preceded by one of faith in the Republic. The sincerity of one seemed to attest to the sincerity of the other, and the assembly laughed and cheered. My adversaries were ridiculed and I came out triumphant.

The ultimate step was Tocqueville's unabashed donning of the old virtues of the aristocracy:

> Question: "If a riot threatens the National Assembly, and bayonets invade it, do you swear to stay at your post and, if necessary, die there?" Answer: "My presence here is my answer. After nine years of unremitting, useless labor trying to steer the government that has just fallen into more liberal and honest paths, I would have preferred to have retired into private life and wait till the storm was over. But my honor forbade me to do so. *Yes, like you, I think that perils await those who want to represent you faithfully. But with the danger there is glory, and it is because of the danger and the glory that I am here now.*"

It had been in many ways a brilliant performance, bound to have a powerful effect among a people a good deal more ingenuous and less cynical than the politicos he was accustomed to addressing in the Chamber of Deputies, who were not moved by claims of foresight and courage.

Later, on election day, the first election with a greatly broadened suffrage, he marched with the people of his arrondissement to the polling place in Saint-Pierre Èglise, a village near his home. Though he had walked in the ranks ("They formed themselves into a double column in alphabetical order; I preferred to take the place my name warranted, for I knew that in democratic times one must allow oneself to be put at the head of the people but must not put oneself there"). At the appropriate moment (the procession had halted on a hill overlooking his chateau—he had delivered a paternal address to his flock, an amalgam of marching orders and civics lessons)

> I reminded these good people of the seriousness and the importance of this act they were going to perform; I advised them not to let themselves be accosted or diverted by people who might, when we arrived in town, seek to deceive them, but rather march as a united body with each man in his place and to stay that way until they had voted. "Let no one," I said, "go into a house to take food or to dry himself (it was raining that day), before he had performed his duty." They shouted that they would do this, and so they did. All the votes were given at the same time, and I have reason to think that almost all were for the same candidate.[16]

Indeed, they must have been. He was elected in March 1848 as representative to the Constituent Assembly of the Second Republic with 110,704 votes out of 120,000 cast in the Department of La Manche, approximately 93 percent of the votes cast. The frail, detached aristocrat evidently had a far greater appeal to the people of La Manche than had their democratic "courtiers."[17]

Whatever miseries and disappointments he may have suffered in local political life, they were far worse in the arena of national politics. As for the satisfactions he derived from lingering traditions of deference in Normandy, there was none of that in Paris. His fellow deputies on the national stage saw him as an odd, haughty character, remote and severe. His appearance itself must have made him almost seem an unearthly visitor seated high above his colleagues (literally, in the highest row of the Chamber) in saturnine, scowling judgment. Charles de Rémusat, who served for many years as a deputy and who knew Tocqueville very well, drew the following striking portrait of his colleague in the Chamber:

> He was a small man of agreeable and ordinary but pale appearance, crowned with a mass of curly brown hair, which made him look youthful; his unanimated and melancholy face became more expressive when he spoke; the ghastly pallor of his complexion was a harbinger of deep physical weaknesses, and caused those who wished him ill to suspect that he was bilious,

envious, and all that follows from that. He was none of that; he was only
somewhat wary, often in pain, often discouraged with himself. Coolly
received because he was the most distinguished in the Chamber except for
Royer-Collard, who did not counsel him to be accepting, he was on the
defensive. Since almost nothing took root in his mind that he himself had
not sewn, he thought a great deal, read little, and hardly knew what we
had written and what we had done. Hence the coolness that long reigned
between him and his colleagues, especially the most distinguished of them.[18]

Tocqueville succeeded in offending and alienating many, especially those who,
like Thiers, sensed his moral disapproval. Thiers thought him "a nasty man."[19]

The coolness and distance he showed were a matter not so much of class
disdain as of disdain for certain manners and values. He continued to value
character—generosity of spirit, integrity, wit, a degree of selflessness. Some of
the men he most admired were sons of the bourgeoisie, like Royer. What he
could not tolerate was vulgarity, that is, graspingness, opportunism, self-centered
ambition, and intellectual mediocrity. He was a moral and an intellectual snob.
Although he admitted that "no parliament (and I do not except the Constituent
Assembly of 1789) has ever contained more varied and brilliant talents than
ours of the closing years of the July Monarchy,"[20] the Chamber during the July
Monarchy was, not surprisingly, also heavily populated by ordinary talents and
partisan spirits and by functionaries who owed their places to their willingness
to obey orders and ignore conscience. His friend Charles Rivet observed that he
never noticed such men, never listened to them, didn't know their names.
Worse than that, he never paid them enough attention to be able to recognize
them, as he himself admitted. He never made the slightest effort to adopt any of
the ways of the tobacco-spitting, backslapping, first-name-calling pols he had
observed in the United States.

Tocqueville understood his shortcomings. With characteristically brutal
self-honesty he attempted, in the *Recollections*, to account for his political
impotence:

> The basic craft for a political leader necessitates his mixing continually with
> his own side, and even with his opponents, with a universal geniality and
> accessibility, lowering or raising the tone of his remarks as to be understood
> by men of every grade of intelligence; continually discussing and arguing,
> repeating the same things a thousand times in different forms, and always
> rousing himself to excitement about the same subjects. All things of which I
> am profoundly incapable. . . . As to getting on good terms with people, I
> could not do so in any general or systematic fashion, for there are so few

whom I recognize. Whenever there is nothing in a man's thoughts or feelings that strikes me, I, so to speak, do not see him.

He continues with a repelling admission: "I have always supposed that mediocrities as well as men of parts had a nose, mouth and eyes, but I have never been able to fix in my memory the forms that these features take in each particular individual. I am constantly asking the names of these unknown people whom I meet every day and constantly forget. It is not that I despise them, but I have little truck with them, feeling that they are like so many clichés. I respect them, for they make the world, but they bore me profoundly."[21] Tocqueville was not the only lover of humanity who has not cared for ordinary men.

Having such attitudes, he would have been doomed to ineffectiveness even had he been a powerful orator. Democratic politician he was not. Though he well understood the role that his ideal moral elite had to play in enlightening and leading the new democracies, he could not adapt his ways to the political style such a role called for. Beaumont implored him to behave more graciously toward the faceless, ordinary colleagues he would look through. He tried but always failed—he could not sustain the effort.

He did his best work as rapporteur for a number of parliamentary commissions dealing with issues he knew well: prison reform, the problem of slavery in the French colonies, Algeria. On such tasks he could give full rein to his talents. He was also a voice in debates about educational freedom and, especially, foreign policy. But he lacked the oratorical skills that count for much in large political assemblies. He was not confident enough to improvise well. The intensity of his passions would tie him in knots. His carefully crafted speeches, written out and delivered in a soft voice, had little effect. He could not be flamboyant or dramatic. Rémusat notes his inadequacy while praising the trenchancy of his speeches: "When he was on the platform, he was cold; nothing came to life, nothing took hold, nothing penetrated. His speeches, however, were remarkable, and are among those that most merit being read, although they lack color and movement; they always got to the heart of the matter. In the future they will seem like comments made during great events by a superb observer. However, they passed almost unnoticed."[22] Eventually he improved, but no matter how controlled he managed to become he lacked charisma. Beaumont felt that Tocqueville had failed to achieve "le premier rang" in politics because he was not "le grand orateur." He was physically too feeble and emotionally too brittle for the stress of intense political debate:

He spoke easily, with great elegance, but his voice sometimes lacked force: this was owing to his physical slightness. Perhaps getting started also unnerved him too much; he then became too emotional. With his fine and delicate nature, he was too susceptible to impressions. Platform struggles require of the orator, however, as much vigor and sang-froid as war demands of the soldier and of the General; because in assemblies he who speaks is at once General and soldier; it is he who fights and who leads. Such struggles were beyond Tocqueville's strength, who never engaged in them without his health being more or less shaken.[23]

His failure as an orator was the result of more than physical frailness or emotional stress: it was also a consequence of his fear that to speak spontaneously would destroy the concision he insisted on achieving. Moreover, his sense of mission must have burdened every speech he made with extraordinary meaning: every speech he gave was not simply a political speech but also a sermon. He was not good at the kind of improvisatory oratory that catches the mood of the moment and that moves people toward a goal rather than asking them to analyze it. Beaumont thought he was too literary: "Tocqueville came to the Chamber with the habits and methods of a writer; in his view, a speech was more a work of art instead of . . . an instrument of action. He strove never to say one word more than was necessary to express his idea and to make it clear to any mind sufficiently endowed with intelligence. He had for what are called platitudes an insurmountable repugnance, excellent disposition for one who is writing a book, but the most harmful of all for the orator speaking to great gatherings, where clichés are principally required."[24] There would be no talking down, no resort to ordinary speech which, though imprecise, nevertheless puts a speaker in the same world as his auditors. He must have seemed to many as he did to Rémusat: a curious, severe, remote, and tormented individual whose manner was condescending and whose speech was dead on arrival.

Another cause of his ineffectiveness, in Beaumont's view, was that he was ill-fitted for the role of opposition, which was uninspiring: "He was truly eloquent at the tribune only when he could mount it driven there by a powerful and profound emotion that inspired and sustained him. Now, the opposition role that all during this time his conscience prescribed for him, did not interest him at all. He was too circumspect for that role, too restrained, and perhaps too far-sighted . . . he naturally was more suited to govern than to oppose."[25]

Tocqueville understood his failings and his limitations. "You fill me with despair when you speak of such a great role," he wrote to Beaumont: "I know . . . what I lack for such a role, beginning with self-confidence."[26] But he also saw himself as someone who had been failed by his times and who felt himself floating helplessly on the "mer morte de politique": "It is great public passions that create great roles in political life. No one can struggle with spirit against the apathy, the indifference, and the despondency of a whole nation. Assuredly, I am not that man. I can easily set my own imagination on fire, but I feel the pervasive coldness penetrate all of me despite all my efforts."[27] Unhappily for him, this view of the deadness of contemporary political life, along with such self-knowledge, did not cause him to abandon his "beau rêve." He suffered all through his thirteen years in the Chamber.

He was repelled by the tone and pettiness of political life under the July Monarchy. Arriving in the Chamber with no illusions about what it would be like, he found it more calculating and sordid in its pettiness than he had imagined. His distaste for a political world in which everyone was coldhearted and purely self-interested grew deeper. He repeatedly refers to the "cold hearts" he encounters, a curious political criterion that says much about Tocqueville. "It is a sad side of humanity," he wrote to Stoffels after less than a year in the Chamber, "that is revealed in political life. One may say that no one there is pure or perfectly disinterested, that no one there is truly generous, that no one there feels free-spirited. In a word, no one in it is youthful, even the youngest ones. Something cold, calculated, and selfish shows itself even in the midst of the most passionate personal expressions. How could you not withdraw into yourself in such a scene and not instead seek a little open air where the spirit might breathe?"[28]

He attributed much of the baseness of political life to the thirst for wealth and power and argued that a certain indifference to one's political future was required to liberate the best in a man—a tough test for the insecure middle-class politico for whom politics was a career and not a moral calling. "The prospect of quitting political life without too much regret is possibly the best condition for playing one's role nobly and grandly."[29]

The profound aloneness he felt became even more intense because he found no party to which he could attach himself, nor anyone with whom he might collaborate. At times he found even Beaumont an unsteady colleague. "When I carefully look at our miserable political world and those who compose it," he wrote to Royer in September of 1842, "I nowhere see my place."[30] He knew that it would be impossible to form either a viable opposition or an administration without Thiers or Guizot. But he found both of them "fundamentally antipathetic to my way of thinking and feeling." "I mistrust them." Yet without them nothing could be accomplished, a prospect he found galling: "And what is politics without deeds? To participate in a public assembly but not work there on public business, nor join those who alone have the power to act, is that not a manifest absurdity? Isn't it to miss the main point of the nature of the thing, that one undertakes to accomplish something and yet only pretends to? Isn't it finally to carry one mode of life into another, theoretical observation into the life of action, to the great harm of both?"[31]

It wasn't just the powerful political chieftains he couldn't abide. There was no party with which he could ally himself without serious reservations:

> I feel an almost invincible repugnance about associating myself permanently with any of the political figures of our time, and among the parties that divide our country I don't see one with which I would want to establish a link. . . . Some seem to me to have an exaggerated, cowardly, and soft desire for peace, and their love of order is most often fearfulness. Others blend with their national pride and their desire for liberty (two things that I greatly prize in themselves) crude and anarchic feelings that repel me. A party that is liberal but not revolutionary, which alone would suit me, does not exist (and it certainly is not given to me to create it). I am therefore almost alone, and it remains for me only to express my own understanding and analysis of events.[32]

He did in fact find himself part of a small circle of compatible colleagues who stood for a moderate, progressive liberalism as opposed to both the static, conservative liberalism of Guizot's party as well as the radical egalitarian aspirations of the republicans and socialists. Though it provided a small community of the like-minded for Tocqueville, his sense of isolation was not much diminished. This independent moderate left was small and powerless. It was a fluid coalition of independent characters, not a united political party, and even had it been, one may doubt that Tocqueville would have been able to close the distance he felt from all but his intimate friends. His comments in the *Recollections* about his political allies are written with critical detachment and are sometimes acid. Even his hoped for alliance with Beaumont, with whom he had shared dreams of leading France out of the political–moral morass into which it had fallen, came to naught in the 1840s. Beaumont's ambition for power, his social facileness, his willingness to contemplate liaisons that Tocqueville could never accept, for example, with Thiers, and occasional moments of rebellion at being thought of as Tocqueville's lieutenant disappointed Tocqueville, who ruefully commented that Beaumont's quest for personal glory had occasionally led him to make opportunistic decisions.[33]

To be a man of principle in politics had condemned him to the role of a theoretical man in politics. This was his greatest agony in political life. He felt nailed to his bench; he compared himself to "a wheel which turns rapidly but, not being engaged, does nothing and is worth nothing."[34] It was an agony for which there seemed to be no adequate metaphor.

4

TOCQUEVILLE'S ARISTOCRATIC LIBERALISM

Tocqueville entered the Chamber with no clear, practical agenda of social and political reform and formulated one only late in 1847, when signs of the discontent that culminated in the Revolution of 1848 had become obvious. His progressive, nonrevolutionary liberalism was moderate, but it did propose gradual steps toward greater social equality and justice. He abandoned his reform program when the Revolution of 1848 struck, fearing the threat to property posed by all measures he considered steps toward socialism, believing that property was the ultimate bulwark of liberty. Nevertheless, he was keenly aware of and felt the growing social injustices of the new age of industrialism and capitalist expropriation and knew that these were the central political issues of the time.

What did Tocqueville have in mind when he called for a moderate, progressive, nonrevolutionary liberalism? He came to the Chamber of Deputies with no agenda of social reform. Despite Beaumont's belief that his friend did not fit the role of opposition, Tocqueville's politics were often countervailing. They recall his remark in *Democracy in America* that "the essence of the Lawgiver's art" is to know that "different times make different demands."[1] His position on all attempts to constrain or curtail freedom, whether of assembly, speech, or education, was almost always libertarian. He generally favored gradual extension of suffrage, to be accomplished in a way that enfranchised those who had some stake, that is, property, in society and were well enough educated to qualify. Universal suffrage would empower the ignorant masses and eventually lead to demagogic politics and socialism. Yet though he agreed that to ensure social and political peace it was necessary to extend the franchise slowly, he voted *against* every proposal to enlarge the suffrage that came before the Chamber during the thirteen years he sat in it. He gave much less thought to how the suffrage might be extended and to how equitable representation might be ensured than Mill, with whom he frequently exchanged general ideas about this issue.

During the July Monarchy his major work in the Chamber of Deputies concerned three issues: the abolition of slavery in the French colonies (he had long belonged to antislavery societies in France); the reform of France's prisons, concerning which he and Beaumont were the Chamber's acknowledged experts; and the subduing and colonizing of Algeria, which had become key to France's imperialist struggle for supremacy in the Mediterranean and the Middle East—a struggle gaining momentum as the Ottoman Empire disintegrated. He had long been interested in Algeria, having once even considered acquiring a plantation there with Kergorlay, who had taken part in the conquest of Algiers before resigning his commission in 1830. Though the idea of becoming a colonist was quickly dropped, Tocqueville's interest in Algeria remained intense. He published articles on it, visited it several times after entering the Chamber, and became rapporteur of a parliamentary commission on Algeria in 1847.[2] The question of Algeria, however, while absorbing for Tocqueville, did not bear directly on the questions of social and political and, above all, moral reform that were central to the sense of mission that had compelled him to enter politics. His hesitant progressivism coexisted oddly with an aggressive, almost jingoistic foreign policy.

Soon after having been elected deputy in March 1839 he was chosen to be rapporteur of a parliamentary commission set up in 1839 to report on a proposal to abolish slavery in the French colonies. It had been ended by the Revolution but reestablished by Napoleon. Of all the issues on the reform agenda of the time, Tocqueville was most straightforward and less conflicted about the abolition of slavery than any other.[3] After having returned from his journey to America and while he was writing the first volume of the *Democracy* he had joined the Society for the Abolition of Slavery, led by the foremost antislavery advocate in France, Victor de Broglie. Tocqueville's report called for the immediate emancipation of adult slaves, who would henceforth be paid wages by their former masters. These, in turn, were to be indemnified by the state, which would also prepare the freed slaves with suitable vocational and moral education. The report was never debated. When, in 1843, he served on yet another commission appointed to examine abolition, he quietly abandoned his earlier, immediatist view and lent tentative support to a proposal for the gradual preparation of the slaves for emancipation. For him, however, the goal was never in doubt—not only on principle and for humane reasons, but also as a prudent policy. The English had abolished slavery in their colonies, some of them almost in sight of France's Caribbean sugar islands, Guadeloupe and Martinique. The presence of freed blacks on nearby British colonies might well, he said, provoke insurrection and destruction. And in fact gradualism was more in keeping with his general approach to social and political change.[4]

His reports and speeches on prison reform concerned what on the surface seemed two technical questions: first, how much space per prisoner was required to ensure the health and sanity of each prisoner? and, second, what would bring about the moral reform of the inmates? Would collective life and labor along with strictly enforced silence be preferable to a system in which prisoners led an almost completely isolated life in their cells, with only a Bible to read, thereby being less likely to be further corrupted and where they thus had a better chance of moral healing? During their American journey Tocqueville and Beaumont had examined the outstanding examples of both systems: the regime of silence and collective life at the Auburn Penitentiary in upstate New York; and that of cellular and moral isolation at the Quaker-influenced Eastern State Penitentiary in Philadelphia. Tocqueville strongly favored the latter.[5]

The book that became the official report on his and Beaumont's mission to study the American penal system, *On the Penitentiary System in the United States and Its Application in France,* was almost wholly technical and barely touched on the question of whether reform and rehabilitation of the individual criminal were possible.[6] It offers little evidence of Tocqueville's deepest convictions about the possibility of the moral reform of men and their institutions. If by reform one meant "radical reformation," that is, "the radical change of a wicked person into an honest man" or the giving back "of primitive purity to a soul which crime has polluted," he thought there was no way of knowing success: "There exists no human means of proving this complete reformation. How can we prove with cyphers the purity of the soul, the delicacy of sentiments, the innocence of intentions? Society, without power to effect this radical regeneration, is no more capable of proving it if it exist."[7] All that could be proven was behavioral reform, and even here Tocqueville was pessimistic, doubtful that, without the help of grace, which remained a mystery, social intervention could do much to reform innately corrupt humans. He expected little of human beings, who were all flawed. An aphorism found in his papers—"Donnez-moi de la chair et de l'orgeuil, et je vous ferai un homme" (give me flesh and pride and I will make you a man)—expresses his Pascalian humor.[8] Yet while speaking during a parliamentary debate on a prison reform bill in 1844, Tocqueville interrupted his detailed cost-benefit analysis of the so-called cellular option with a powerful, passionate plea not to abandon the hope of reform by making the "idea of repression" the informing spirit of the penal code. This speech offers a glimpse of Tocqueville in the role of moral leader healing the rift between religion and secular concerns that he believed was his calling. It was the last speech of the debate on the prison reform bill introduced by Tocqueville as rapporteur. It was a response to critics and an exhortation to the jury:

So! You want to despair of reforming one of your fellow beings, however criminal he may be? You want to place the burden of eternal anathema on his head! You want to make him believe that he is incapable of ever raising himself, that the society into which he is going to return also believes only this; that it rejects him without respite or pity, that it endlessly pushes him toward crime! In a way you want to lock him in a legal hell from which there is no exit . . . you bind him to an indescribable, implacable, and terrible fatality in which one wrong turn forbids a single step backwards.

But what have you achieved but a return to complete paganism? Don't the ideas which underlie all Europe's beliefs derive from the conception of possible rehabilitation, of rehabilitation following atonement? Aren't these ideas the very basis of Christian beliefs? Why am I saying Christian beliefs? Aren't these the ideas of our time, of our age, of our civilization? Isn't the greatest glory of our French Revolution to have secularized Christianity somewhat by its results, to have taken its maxims from the religious sphere in order to make them inform the practical sphere of legislation? Isn't this the idea which animated all the great men who made the French Revolution? Only a few days ago I was reading a precious manuscript which the honorable Minister of the Interior had placed in my hands, a manuscript by [Honoré Gabriel Riqueti, comte de] Mirabeau. Well, what did I read in this manuscript? Mirabeau referred precisely to the introduction of the idea of amendment and rehabilitation into the body of the Penal Code as the first result of the French Revolution. He called it a great reaction against the Middle Ages. He was right: he wanted the code to be repressive but not merciless, and he said that his thought on this point was the result of the spirit of the century. He said this in a much more powerful and energetic style than I can phrase his thought.[9]

There is something abstract and historical about this plea not to abandon the goal of rehabilitation. Yet if his appeal was based on the authority of the past and on what conformed with "the spirit of the century," that spirit, summoned by Mirabeau, was also the spirit of the Enlightenment and of humane reform, always as much a part of Tocqueville as his skepticism.

After the Revolution of 1848 he was elected by the Provisional Assembly to serve on a committee of eighteen to draw up a new constitution. He fought successfully against a right to work provision which he saw as a step toward socialism; argued unsuccessfully for a bicameral legislature; and supported the popular election of the president as a safeguard against the power of a unicameral legislature.[10] In 1849 he served for five months as minister of foreign affairs, during which time he was preoccupied mostly with the problems created by the

French intervention in Italy to thwart Austrian influence and safeguard the Papal States during the republican uprising of Giuseppe Mazzini and Giuseppe Garibaldi in 1848.[11] Then failing health that required a long leave of absence and Louis-Napoleon's seizure of power in December of 1851 ended Tocqueville's life of public service. A political career that had begun with a dream ended in jail, where, along with many other deputies who had also protested Louis-Napoleon's coup d'état, he spent two nights, refusing special treatment and quick release.

Concerning the great social issues of the time—the immiseration of laborers, the growth of poverty, the right to work, public charity, poor laws as opposed to private charity, and all the social woes caused by industrialization and the disruption of rural life—Tocqueville was hesitant to take action. He seems to have paid little attention to the seriousness of poverty and social unrest in France, which he tended to underestimate until shortly before the Revolution of 1848. In January of that year he gave a famous speech warning his complacent colleagues that they were asleep atop a volcano, but in the years before that he seems to have said little about what was boiling up from below.[12] When it came to political responses to social ills he was not consistently progressive at all and seems to have thought more about warding off radical and utopian schemes for reform than proposing anything himself.

When by 1847 the gravity of France's social problems, especially in view of the Chamber's refusal to consider any reforms, had become evident, Tocqueville and his moderate progressive colleagues sketched a program of reform designed not only to avert political upheaval but also to relieve real misery. The very broad suggestions for reform proposed by Tocqueville included relief from financial burdens that were too heavy for the poor, such as legal fees, and a broad range of institutional reforms that would have constituted long-overdue steps toward a more equitable society. These ranged from state-founded and state-funded savings banks, credit agencies, free schools, and infant schools to more direct state intervention in establishing almshouses, direct relief to the unemployed, and even laws limiting the workday to ten hours.[13] But the Revolution of 1848 exploded before Tocqueville and his fellow liberals could act. The violence of the proletarian revolution of that year, which Tocqueville saw as a harbinger of the ultimate socialist assault on the right to property—the ultimate safeguard of individual liberty—interrupted his willingness to work for reform. Subsequently he voted against the ten-hour workday, against the abolition of the salt tax, and against amnesty for those responsible for the June insurrection, and he even approved of a measure allowing the hiring of substitutes by those drafted for military service. The need for order had trumped the need for reform.

However, if he had been slow to think about how to cope with growing social miseries and was long convinced that they were less severe in France than in England, he was not unaware of them. He was appalled by the overwhelming poverty of rural Ireland, which he saw as the result of the amassing of great estates by greedy aristocrats as well as rich bourgeois, creating a huge population of uprooted, starving peasants, then just starting to flee to America. He described this injustice and misery with undisguised anger in his Irish notebooks.[14]

His visit on the same journey in 1835 to the smoky, lurid hell of Manchester had also prompted some of his most vivid social commentary, in which he condemned not only capitalist destruction of human beings and the environment but also the social injustice of an economic system that made it possible for a few to grow wealthy by exploiting the many helpless poor. He had seen nothing like it in France, though there was no lack of urban misery to be observed under his nose, as in the Faubourg Saint-Antoine, a working-class quarter only a short walk from the Faubourg Saint-Germain, where in the attic of his parents' town house he wrote the first volume of *Democracy in America*. It was in the Faubourg Saint-Antoine that the worker uprising of 1834 culminating in the notorious massacre on the rue Transnonain, graphically immortalized by Honoré Daumier, occurred. At that moment Tocqueville was writing *Democracy in America*. He never mentioned it.

Even so, it would be incorrect to infer from his silence regarding the misery of the French proletariat and his underestimation of the number and condition of the working poor that he was indifferent to their pain or that he thought working folk had no rights. It may be that his apparent denial of a reality that was hard to miss resulted from an understandable fear, stirred by family memories, that urban unrest would lead to revolutionary disorder. He could take a more clear-eyed view of the miseries of the poor when he observed them elsewhere. Shortly after witnessing the horrors of Manchester, he lectured his friend the English economist Nassau William Senior, a moderate social reformer, that the welfare of the poor should not be narrowly conceived:

> I said that in English legislation the *bien du pauvre* had in the end been sacrificed to that of the rich. You attack me on this point, of which you are certainly a competent judge. You must allow me, however, to differ from you. In the first place it seems to me that you give to the expression *le bien du pauvre* a confined sense which was not mine; you translate it as wealth, a word applied especially to money. I meant by it all that contributes to happiness; personal consideration, political right, easy justice, intellectual enjoyments, and many other indirect sources of contentment. I shall believe, until

I have proof of the contrary, that in England the rich have monopolized almost all the advantages that society bestows upon mankind. Taking the question in your own restricted sense, and admitting that a poor man is better paid when he works on another man's land than when he cultivates his own, do you not think that there are political, moral, and intellectual advantages which are a more than sufficient, and above all a permanent compensation for the loss that you point out?[15]

Tocqueville's conception of what constitutes the well-being of the poor is certainly compatible with a refusal to consider any serious redistribution of wealth; but in his discussion of the problem of poverty with Senior he does reveal a broader idea of what constitutes oppression than apparently had occurred to his English friend. Tocqueville saw the English poor as so thoroughly expropriated and dominated by the wealthy that they were deprived of all opportunities for personal growth and satisfaction—robbed, as it were, of their individuality. In his view, they lacked the elementary freedoms and rights without which personality, the release and flowering of which was the chief value of civilization and possibly the greatest benefit of democracy, would wither. The human blight he had seen in Manchester, the lopsided distribution "of all that contributes to happiness" in an England in which capital powerfully and hardheartedly ruled, deeply disturbed him.[16]

England had also taught another lesson about the problem of poverty: how not to deal with it. Despite the appalling social injustice he had witnessed and denounced, the English reform experience spoke to the Tocqueville who tended to regard social and economic problems as moral issues. Efforts to relieve misery also had to be judged by their presumed moral consequences. The consequences of England's long experience with poor law legislation, culminating in the Poor Laws of 1833, made it clear to Tocqueville that legislated public assistance to paupers was bad social policy. Of the two possible ways of dealing with the spread of pauperism and misery, which he deemed inevitable, the work of Providence, he regarded private charity preferable since one's misery was not made a matter of public record, nor did it fix the individual in a permanent category. Since it was based on personal benevolence, it nurtured human relationships and was less likely than any socially organized system of welfare to deepen class divisions. Based, as charity had to be, on personal morality and private initiative, however, it could not be a matter for legislative action or social planning. Yet he admitted that private charity could not cope with so widespread a social ill.

His thinking about the problem of poverty, the subject of a paper he read before a learned society in Cherbourg in 1835, reveals much about the man.[17]

He had been astonished to discover that there were many more paupers in "le flourrisant royaume" of England than in much poorer countries like Spain and Portugal. The reason for this was that as the material needs and desires of a society rose and as "thousands of needs unknown" in less affluent times pressed to be satisfied, a larger and larger portion of the people had to leave their traditional agrarian occupations for industrial work. Tocqueville saw this displacement as an outcome not of class aggrandizement but of a more broadly based advance of human intellectual and technological power: "Each century, as it emerges from the hand of the Creator, extends the range of thought, increases the desires and the power of man. The poor and the rich, each in his sphere, conceive of new enjoyments which were unknown to their ancestors. In order to satisfy these new needs, which the cultivation of the soil cannot meet, a portion of the population leaves agricultural labor each year for industry."[18] While life for the majority had become "plus douce et plus commode . . . plus variée et plus ornée," the cost had been the deepening misery and dependency of a defenseless working class: the industrial worker, unlike the man of the soil, had nothing to fall back on.

Thus the spread of pauperism in the modern world had two dimensions, though one fundamental cause: the advance of material civilization, which was as irresistible as the rise of democracy. It was, according to Tocqueville, one of the three providentially ordained developments shaping the modern world: democracy, centralization, industrialization. And, like democracy, poverty seemed fated. It was "un maux inevitable," part of Providence's design for humankind: "I consider the industrial class as having received from God the special and dangerous mission of securing the material well-being of all others by its risks and dangers."[19] By enlisting in the new industrial army, the now-vulnerable poor were responding to a historical imperative. This was a remarkably benign view of the new, vast, and painful disruption of agrarian societies then under way. The fate of the poor had been ordained.

This is not to say that Tocqueville justified the exploitation of working folk, but his religio-historical view of the growth of poverty in the modern world may account for the modesty of his expectations about what might be done to solve the problem. If, in the future, life for the many was bound to become "easier, longer, more comfortable, more elaborate," so too the number of those dependent on society would ceaselessly grow. This "double movement" might be managed but not stopped. He concluded that it was necessary to find "the means of attenuating those inevitable evils which are already apparent."[20]

Of what might be done to attenuate the "inevitable" spread of misery he had no clear idea, except that private charity was far preferable to public assistance.

That the poor had a right to assistance was an attractive idea, but it was a "belle et séduisante théorie" bound to have "conséquences funestes": "Any measure which establishes legal charity on a permanent basis and gives it an administrative form thereby creates an idle and lazy class, living at the expense of the industrial and working class."[21] This "idle and lazy" class would sink into immobility, degradation, and barbarism: "The number of illegitimate children rises ceaselessly; that of criminals grows rapidly; the indigent population develops without limits; the sense of thrift and foresight increasingly abandons the poor."[22] In fact he saw public welfare leading to social and economic calamity — and then to revolution. It would not only deprave the poor and turn the wealthy into keepers of the poor, it would also dry up the sources of savings, stop the accumulation of capital, choke human industry and activity, and end by bringing about a violent revolution when the numbers of those receiving alms would become as large as those who gave it.[23]

What was to be done? Private charity could not adequately cope with the miseries and poverty produced by industrialism. Yet public welfare — "toute système regulière, permanent, administratif" — would in the end create more evils than it cured. Would it be possible, he asked, to prevent rather than cure the ills of poverty and social displacement? By raising this question Tocqueville found himself at the edge of a political and social prospect that challenged his convictions. He glimpsed the possibility of a far bolder intervention in economic life than anything he ever proposed or could have squared with his antipathy for bureaucracy and centralized government. He sensed, that is, the need for the kind of rational restructuring and management of society the Saint-Simonians had proposed, though a far more moderate version. Here too his vision of what might be necessary — at the end of his life he said that finding a more equitable distribution of wealth was the central task of the time — far outran his politics.

The Cherbourg paper was to have been followed by another dealing with the question, what is to be done? He never gave it, yet his draft offers evidence of the kinds of practical measures he was willing to consider that would not lead to the evils created by a system of public welfare and the deep threat to property and liberty posed by socialism. His preventive approach called essentially for the moral education of the working class, by encouraging thrift and "prevoyance" through the founding of savings banks ("caisses d'épargne"), which would be guaranteed by the state. In entertaining this idea, about which he also had doubts, Tocqueville even quoted Benjamin Franklin on the importance of thrift. Franklin's ideal of the thrifty, penny-saving laboring man with dreams of rising in the world through hard work appealed to his morality. It was a benign, docile, nonpolitical approach to the problem. He also considered the possibility of worker ownership by skilled workers of certain industries but dismissed it as not possible at the moment. Except for the somewhat more radical measures he had been willing to consider in 1847, which included direct aid to the impover-ished and out-of-work, he seems to have thought longest about the most bour-geois of the working folk, artisans with ancient craft and corporate traditions and names, such as the *ménusiers* (joiners) and the *boulangiers* (bakers). As William Sewell observes in *Work and Revolution in France*, such workers were recog-nized as part of the social or "nomenclatural" order. Those who were beyond that order were vaguely labeled *journaliers* (day workers), *manoeuvres* (physical or brute laborers), and *hommes de peine* (those who did hard and painful labor). Except for that moment in 1847, the moderate, prudential reforms just men-tioned seemed to have been designed by Tocqueville for the sufferers still in the human and social order, not for those who had fallen out of that order and become brutes with no name.[24]

But this occasionally flaring sense of injustice never led him actually to pro-pose any steps to deal with France's increasingly severe social ills. Though he had constantly been critical of Guizot's quickness to hear calls for reform as the first shouts of revolution and disorder—the result being that needed reforms were stifled while the July Monarchy became increasingly repressive—he too had opted for order in the turbulent first months of the Second Republic. As he said to the voters of La Manche while campaigning in early 1848, he had refused to attend the banquets held to support the right to work campaign because he too had "not wanted a Revolution," though it had by no means been clear that that had been a likely outcome.

Tocqueville eventually came to see the problems of poverty and the increas-ing distribution of wealth as the urgent issues of the time. But the economic and social miseries of a Europe in the throes of the industrial revolution that so aroused the indignation of Karl Marx and of the French socialists and utopians of the 1830s and 1840s preoccupied Tocqueville less than moral issues and ques-tions of political liberty and foreign policy. He was steady, if grudging, in his support of the movement toward political democracy and strongly opposed to the political status quo that France's new bourgeois rulers sought to maintain as the final resolution of the Great Revolution, but his economic and social views were conservative. He was quick to draw the line at any threat to property. In the same speech of January 1848 in which he castigated the Chamber for its unen-lightened selfishness, he uttered a passionate warning that the brewing social revolution was a threat to the rights of property. It was the need to defend the rights of property, not the rights of man, that at that moment fueled his eloquence.

It is too much to say Tocqueville was incapable of change or unaware of the need for taking greater steps toward social justice. There is enough complexity and inconsistency in his ideas to plausibly see him moving in time, with regard to social justice, in the same direction, if not nearly as far, as his friend Mill, toward accepting the need for a more equitable distribution of wealth, accomplished by state action. A few years before his death, when he had been liberated from politics, he would make the following unequivocal statement: "A more equal distribution of goods and rights in this world is the greatest aim that those who conduct human affairs can have in view."[25] He uttered this—an expression of the sense of social justice that had always informed his view of human rights—in 1856, well after the new bourgeois kingdom of inequality had been launched.

Part III

WRITING DEMOCRACY *IN* AMERICA

1

A MORAL LANDSCAPE

The first chapter of *Democracy in America* is ostensibly a bird's-eye view of the topography of America, but instead it mainly rehearses some New World myths and legends and announces some of the deepest historical and philosophical preoccupations of Tocqueville's imagination.

Tocqueville begins *Democracy in America* with a brief chapter innocently titled "The Physical Configuration of North America." But that title, like the matter-of-fact précis that heads the chapter, is deceptive. The reader does not encounter a straightforward geography, an inventory of resources, or even a rough ethnographic map. Instead, the reader immediately steps into a distorted and foreshortened landscape, rather like those old comic lopsided maps that reveal more about the strange consciousness of the parochial Bostonian than about the world as it really is. It is a landscape that says a good deal about Tocqueville and the forces of imagination that shaped *Democracy in America* and offers clues for understanding his trip to America and for exploring the various levels of meaning of his book.

The immense area north of the Great Lakes quickly slips off into arctic vagueness. The lakes themselves are curiously described: "Each is like a huge cup filled to the brim. The slightest change of global structure would tilt their waters to the pole or to the tropics."[1] If this is a magnificently designed world, as Tocqueville suggests, it is also a precariously balanced one. Of the area now covered by the United States, the West Coast stands in darkness; the South and the Southwest, with their distinctive terrains and resources, are not at all sketched; and the East Coast, which Tocqueville astonishingly calls "a tongue of arid land," an "inhospitable shore," is only briefly described; he does not mention the great differences between regions, including the variety of soils, climates, and flora, that would never have escaped the naturalist or the geographer. At the center of Tocqueville's map of North America looms the great Mississippi Valley, an area "about six times that of France." It is to this immense area and to the doomed Indians who live there waiting to be crushed by the westward-rolling tide of civilization that he devotes nearly the whole of the chapter. And even here what one finds is not an informative, thorough survey of the natural setting but a sketch more poetic than descriptive, with puzzling emphases. Tocqueville's description of the river system that fans through the valley is precise and detailed. River lengths are carefully recorded. But then one reads further:

> The valley watered by the Mississippi seems created for it alone: it dispenses good and evil at will like a local god. Near the river nature displays an inexhaustible fertility: the further you get from its banks, the sparser the vegetation and the poorer becomes the soil, and everything wilts and dies. Nowhere have the great convulsions of the world left more evident traces than in the valley of the Mississippi. The aspect of the countryside bears witness to the water's work. Its sterility as well as its abundance is their work. Deep layers of the fertile soil accumulated under the primeval ocean and had time to level out. On the right bank of the river there are huge plains as level as a rolled lawn. But nearer the mountains the land becomes more and more uneven and sterile; the soil is punctured in a thousand places by primitive rocks sticking out here and there like the bones of a skeleton when sinews and flesh have perished. The surface of the earth is covered with granite sand and irregularly shaped stones, through which a few plants just manage to force their way; it looks like a fertile field covered by the ruins of some vast structure.
>
> All things considered, the valley of the Mississippi is the most magnificent habitation ever prepared by God for man, and as yet one may say that it is still only a vast wilderness.

This is a highly artful and selective landscape, so obviously eccentric that one is prompted to look beneath its apparently random surface to discover Tocqueville's shaping intentions and to ask what he chose to see and to imagine, for he never visited the semiarid region west of the Mississippi. Though he says the valley is a "magnificent habitation," he oddly focuses on its desolateness. It is a scene in which the "great convulsions of the world" have clearly left their mark and in which sterility and abundance, good and evil seem to flow from the same source. Indeed, it is a landscape that reveals more about Tocqueville's moral and historical imagination and about the configuration of his feelings than about the "physical configuration of North America." On its deepest level it is shaped by his preoccupation with the nature and meaning of *change:* with the endless cycle, in nature and society, of death and rebirth; with the intimate relationship of life and death, good and evil; with the transience of human society and with the illusions of permanence and progress. In this strange map of North America he charts the topography of his psyche and illuminates some of the themes and ambivalence that pervade his work.

The New World, apparently rich and unspoiled, is, as Tocqueville sees it, haunted terrain — as indeed it was, having been populated by the phantoms and visions of the European imagination for so long. His landscape is laden with images of death and renewal. The Mississippi Valley, like the other "huge territories" of North America, might seem to be an untouched wilderness, occupied only by a few scattered and transient tribes of Indians, temporarily resident in the paradise that was awaiting the European; but it was already a graveyard, in which "the soil is punctured in a thousand places by primitive rocks sticking out here and there like the bones of a skeleton when sinews and flesh have perished." It was like "a fertile field covered by the ruins of some vast structure." And what Tocqueville sees in the great American forest is not so much a virgin wilderness of primeval trees but the awesome spectacle of change in which death and life seem to be blended and in which they work out their intricate relationship in silence:

> Here, as in the forest tamed by man, death was striking constantly, but it was no man's duty to remove the resulting debris, which piled up faster than time could reduce it to powder and make room for new growth. New growth, however, was constantly forcing its way through this debris, with creepers and plants of every sort struggling toward the light, climbing along fallen trunks and into the rotting wood, lifting the cracking bark, and opening the way for their young shoots. Thus death in some way helped life forward, as face to face they seemed to wish to mingle and confuse their functions.

It is also a landscape full of deception. Death lurks everywhere, even where nature in its richness and beauty, bursting with life, resembled the "fabled land of the poets." In a lyrical brief passage Tocqueville describes the West Indies as a kind of paradise:

> When the Europeans landed on the shores of the West Indies, and later of South America, they thought themselves transported to the fabled land of the poets. The seas sparkled with the fires of the tropics; for the first time the extraordinary transparency of the water disclosed the ocean's depths to the navigators. Here and there little scented islands floated like baskets of flowers on the calm sea. Everything seen in these enchanted islands seemed designed to meet man's needs or serve his pleasures. Most of the trees were loaded with edible fruits, while those which were least useful to man delighted him by the brilliance of their varied colors. In groves of fragrant

lemon trees, wild figs, round-leafed myrtles, a multitude of birds unknown to Europe displayed their bright azure and purple feathers and mingled the concert of their song with the harmony of a world teeming with vivid life.

Tocqueville's next comment about this gaudy paradise of plenty is remarkable: "Death lay concealed behind this brilliant cloak," he goes on, "but it was not noticed then."

The same mingling of life and death, the same overwhelming evidence of change and impermanence, is seen in the social realm as in nature. The only inhabitants of Tocqueville's landscape one sees are the Indians of North America, a people who, despite their great virtues—"no famed republic of antiquity could record firmer courage, prouder spirit, or more obstinate love of freedom"—but also because of those virtues, seemed fated to vanish: "Their unconquerable prejudices, their indomitable passions, their vices and perhaps more their savage virtues delivered them to inevitable destruction. The ruin of these people began as soon as the Europeans landed on their shores; it has continued ever since, and is coming to completion in our day." But the destruction of the Indian, sad transients in the New World Eden, was only the most recent version of an old story. This was not the first time on the spectacular terrain of the supposed New World that a society had died. North America had seen, in fact, a succession of vanishing societies. Tocqueville cites the evidence that "another people, more civilized and in all respects more advanced" than the nineteenth-century Indian, had long ago dwelled in the Mississippi and Ohio River valleys. However great they had been, nothing remained of them but "a dim tradition" and a few strange "manmade tumuli," apparently tombs: "When did they come there, and what was their origin, history and fate? No man can answer." Thus in the midst of this scene of splendid riches and unbounded possibilities—"the most magnificent habitation ever prepared by God for man"—one found the undecipherable scattered traces of a long-dead civilization, shrouded in mystery. "It is a strange thing," Tocqueville reflects, "that peoples should have so completely vanished from earth, that even the memory of their name is lost; their languages are forgotten and their glory has vanished like a sound without an echo; but I doubt there is any which has not left some tomb as a memorial of its passage. So of all man's work, the most durable is that which records his nothingness and his misery." Thus to the lament of his introduction about the intellectual and moral chaos that seemed to have been a by-product of the rise of democracy Tocqueville adds a reminder of the fragility of human aspiration and the vanity of humankind's quest for perfection and permanence. This is a curious way to begin a book about the New World Eden.

And yet he sounds another note. There is an echo in the first chapter of *Democracy in America* of the millennialist myth of America as the Promised Land where a chosen people would finally create a "new heaven and a new earth," the good society—a notion born again with the birth of the New Republic. Perhaps indeed something new, real progress and not simply a repetition of the old story of human striving and defeat, was about to appear on earth. Perhaps the Mississippi Valley, repository though it was of the ashes of earlier human dreams, would be the stage upon which the next great development of humankind was to occur. The very physical structure of the continent seemed a portent: "Land and water, mountains and valleys, seem to have been separated with systematic method, and the simple majesty of the design stands out amid the confusion and immense variety of the scene." Tocqueville employs the metaphor of special creation to convey his sense that there might be something unique about the scene he is describing: "The valley watered by the Mississippi seems created for it alone; it dispenses good and evil at will like a local god"; "All things considered, the valley of the Mississippi is the most magnificent habitation ever prepared by God for man." "Providence" has granted the Indians only a short lease in this paradise, which, despite their presence, "seemed the yet empty cradle of a great nation." The chapter in fact concludes on a powerful and positive teleological note: "It was there [in the New World] that civilized man was destined to build society on new foundations, and for the first time applying theories till then unknown or deemed unworkable, to present the world with a spectacle for which the past had not prepared it."

Plainly, this highly contrived landscape is a statement about the ambivalent feelings with which Tocqueville approached his subject. It establishes the structure of feeling that shapes the whole of *Democracy in America* and that, along with the articulated philosophical conflicts that run through the book, accounts for its great tension. It establishes the deep philosophical–historical themes of *Democracy in America*, all of which involve a testing of the dreams of the Enlightenment, for America was indeed the testing ground for the self-generative, self-redemptive aspirations of the new man of the West and for the Enlightenment faith in progress, knowledge, happiness, and freedom. Tocqueville has rendered a sketch that conveys something of that sense of extraordinary expectation almost universally felt about America, but also something of his sense of the fragility and mutability of life, of the deep ambiguity of existence, and of the illusoriness of human accomplishment. It is a background against which the proud claim that something new on earth was being created might be seen as a delusion. Its tone is one of quiet melancholy, the tristesse that results when one confronts the reality of impermanence.

Tocqueville seems suspended between a pessimistic persuasion that history is no more than a recurrence of the eternal, that progress is an illusion, and that men succeed finally only in building their own tombs; and the quiet hope that, in America at least, something new was to appear on earth, if it had not already done so. Was this a story of death? or of life? Were one to stop at the end of Tocqueville's moral and topographical introduction, his response to this question, which, by the end of *Democracy in America*, he has remarkably answered, could hardly be foreseen. Was America only an interesting version of the old? or was it truly something unique? Was it a monstrous deception, like the gaudy paradise of the Caribbean with its enchanted floating islands?

Tocqueville concludes his first chapter with the stunning remark that in America "civilized man" was about "to present the world with a spectacle for which past history had not prepared it," suggesting thereby that in the New World some grand act of transcendence or of redemption might possibly occur. He thus quietly announces the true subject of his book, which, more than it is equality or democracy, is freedom, its nature, dynamics, limits, and prospects. Would America be the place where humans finally break free from all that has bound them to misery and imperfection and where they return finally to Eden and, on terms more congenial to the Enlightenment, fulfill their human potential? Would it prove possible for humankind to escape history? or in pursuing the full freedom of which he had long dreamt would it discover that that, too, was a presumptuous, dangerous aspiration? Yet while drawn to America by the dream of freedom, Tocqueville is at the same time dragged away from the shores of the Promised Land by a powerful current of doubt. What is finally established in this unusual beginning is a deep ambiguity about the meaning of history and about the significance of America, that "great nation" the heartland of which was an immense valley that displayed not only "inexhaustible fertility," but also the ruins of an ancient civilization; a valley that was not only a cradle but also a graveyard; the home of a proud, gifted, but dying people who paradoxically had been undone by their unbounded freedom. *Democracy in America* starts by posing the problem of freedom; the book itself is a long meditation about freedom; and its final word is a sermon about freedom.

2

A MORAL HISTORY

Tocqueville's introduction to *Democracy in America* proposes yet another broad historical and philosophical context for his study of democracy. He makes clear his view that Western civilization is plunging into an ill-understood moral and intellectual transformation that has corrupted language and has torn social and political discourse from its old moral framework.[1]

Even before he unfolds the moral topography of his America, Tocqueville provides, in the introduction to *Democracy in America*, yet another immense context for what was ostensibly to be a book intended to tell the French what a fully developed egalitarian society was like and thereby to cast light on the democratic future. Yet what could his readers have thought they were about to read once they had finished the introduction, which opens with Tocqueville's breathless sketch of what he calls the providential design for "the Christian world"—the inexorable rise of democracy—and then goes on to deliver a long, impassioned sermon about the moral incoherence of modern life and a plea for the recovery of an uncorrupted language?

Nothing is better known about *Democracy in America* than the opening pages of the introduction, in which Tocqueville describes, with what he calls "religious terror," the all-conquering march of equality in the Western world. His comprehensive, synoptic account of the rise of democracy beginning in the Middle Ages, an account that reminds one of Marx's description, in *The Communist Manifesto*, of the similar and equally profound transformation of the feudal order by capitalism, immediately makes it clear that, even by the standards of historical writing in the early nineteenth century, the book that follows will be not a history but a historicized myth.

The transformation of the West, that is, of "Christian countries," has been all-encompassing and irresistible:

> The various occurrences of national existence have everywhere turned to the advantage of democracy. All men have aided it by their exertions, both those

who have intentionally labored in its cause and those who have served it
unwittingly; those who have fought for it and even those who have declared
themselves its opponents have all been driven along in the same direction,
have all labored to one end; some unknowingly and some despite themselves, *all have been blind instruments in the hands of God.*

The gradual development of the principle of equality is, therefore, a providential fact. It has all the characteristics of such a fact: it is universal, it is
lasting, it constantly eludes all human interference, and all events as well as
all men contribute to its progress. [emphasis added]

Tocqueville is awestruck by a historical transformation so sweeping that it
cannot be accounted for in any language other than a religious one:

Wither, then, are we tending? No one can say, for terms of comparison
already fail us. There is greater equality of condition in Christian countries
at the present day than there has been at any previous time, in any part of
the world, so that the magnitude of what has been done prevents us from
foreseeing what is yet to be accomplished.

The whole book that is here offered to the public has been written under
the influence of a kind of religious terror produced in the author's soul by
the view of that irresistible revolution which has advanced for centuries in
spite of every obstacle and which is still advancing in the midst of the ruins
it has caused.

This is a story not just of "the gradual development of the principle of
equality" but also of "ruins."

Almost ignored, however, has been what follows Tocqueville's sketch of providential history: an intense sermon about the loss of order and the pernicious
confusion of language in the modern world, consequences of the revolutionary
era, which distorted language by adding to it an ideological mission. The result,
he argues, has been deepening moral confusion and disorder. Was the right
naming of things, the reconnection of words to things and the restoration of
intellectual clarity and therefore of moral clarity, to be another aim of his book?

Tocqueville at the start accordingly proffers two immense themes for
Democracy in America. The first, his breathless account of the rise of equality as
providential design, shapes a story of continuities: the gradual, inevitable shaping of all aspects of life by a new principle of social organization. The second
great theme, which underlies his thinking about the possible sources of community and moral order in a democratic society of skeptical individuals as well
as his analysis of democratic culture, is opened by his account of historical
discontinuity. In this account, he presents a powerful view of a disoriented,

incoherent modern world radically disjoined from the past. For Tocqueville, if the rise of democracy has meant the enlarging of the state (or of the "social power") and the concentration of power greatly enhanced by modern technology, it has also meant the loss of social coherence and harmony and the disintegration of social order, a semblance of which is maintained now only by fear. It has also meant a devastating lapse into intellectual chaos, in which people mill about in "strange confusion," intellectually and morally disoriented. There is no longer a universal, patent, stable system of belief to bind people together in a moral community such as he believed had existed before. In the new world of "disorderly passions" and "wild instincts" in which a system of common belief is lacking, force becomes the ultimate argument, and even language is deranged:

> In the heat of struggle each partisan is driven beyond the natural limits of his own views by the views and excesses of his adversaries, loses sight of the very aim he was pursuing, and uses language which ill corresponds to his real feelings and to his secret instincts. Hence arises that strange confusion we are forced to witness. I search my memory in vain, and find nothing sadder or more pitiable than that which happens before our eyes; it would seem that we have nowadays broken the natural link between opinions and tastes, acts and beliefs; that harmony between the feelings and the ideas of man seems to have been destroyed, and one might suppose that all the laws of moral analogy had been abolished.

It is the realm of meaning and belief that lies in ruins. The old cultural system has been shattered, the old unity lost, and nothing has replaced it. Tocqueville stands near the end of that long process of "deconversion," as Philip Rieff called it, the gradual loss of the power and meaning of Western Christian culture, qualities which had not been replaced by anything of equal coherence or universality able to bind men in an integrated moral and social order and give them a sense of community.[2] It was, as Tocqueville saw it, a time without unifying belief or faith, a world in which men struggled with one another in "strange confusion," dimly understanding their plight while arguing strenuously in a kind of moral babble. In the midst of the disorder and incoherence of modernity, God, for Tocqueville, sits silently.

Such fragmentation and derangement of modern life, such loss of meaning and connection is summarized by Tocqueville in an eloquent comment which points to the deepest issues of *Democracy in America:* "Have all ages been like ours? And have men always dwelt in a world in which nothing is connected? Where virtue is without genius and genius without honor? Where love of order is confused with a tyrant's tastes, and the sacred cult of freedom is taken as scorn of law: where conscience sheds but doubtful light on human action? Where nothing any longer seems forbidden or permitted, honest or dishonorable, true or false?" Did he think America would provide an answer to these questions?

By the time he has completed *Democracy in America*, Tocqueville has fashioned disconcerting, in some ways ambiguous, answers to his questions. The central feature of modern democratic culture as he analyzes it in *Democracy in America* is its instability, its perpetual dynamism, its self-devouring energy. The restless genius of democracy destroys all it touches. He had discovered the America of Emerson, especially Emerson the archetypal American democrat who in "Circles" asserts, "I unsettle all things. No facts to me are sacred; none are profane; I simply experiment, an endless seeker with no Past at my back."[3] Emerson was the perfect embodiment of what Tocqueville saw as the unsettling spirit of modernity—though his literary career began after Tocqueville's visit, and there is no evidence that Tocqueville had read any of the work of this central figure of the new democratic culture, though he did briefly meet him in 1848. Emerson did read *Democracy in America* (in 1840), without comment.

One great underlying problem in *Democracy in America*, then, is this: what will succeed the shattered religious culture of the Christian world as a new basis of social order in the age of equality? Will a new culture capable of providing what he thought the old culture had fostered—a clear sense of moral order as well as the language to convey it—emerge from the ruins he saw lying about him? What will make social order and community possible in the new world of change, skepticism, and individualism when the old system of moral sanctions and rules, which had fused human beings in a harmonious system based on renunciation, self-restraint, and cooperation, has vanished? And since, in Tocqueville's view, freedom is not possible without order and a clear sense of limits, what will the future of freedom be in a world in which a kind of permanent, self-perpetuating disorder seems to be the likeliest prospect?

What is it, he asks in the introduction, that makes this society possible? what beliefs hold it together? how is its almost irresistible centrifugal dynamism contained? what bonds will unite the radically free individuals of the new world of democracy, locked, as Tocqueville put it later in *Democracy in America*, "in the privacy of their own hearts"? Will the old, lost harmony be recovered in the New World? Americans were asking the same question. James Fenimore Cooper, Tocqueville's contemporary, thought nature itself, the source of sublime sentiments and a vision of harmony, might successfully replace Christianity as a basis of moral order. Emerson, Henry Thoreau, and the Transcendentalists maintained that apparently isolated individuals belonged to a community of truth, one they would discover by fully accepting their uniqueness and trusting their subjectivity and individuality. The universalist impulse in American Protestantism found promise of the long-sought harmonious community, the peaceable kingdom, in the self-evident truths of rational religion. Biblical fundamentalists believed that the Kingdom of God on earth, a community of brothers and sisters in Christ, was taking shape in America. A legion of utopian thinkers and activists was planning and building communities based on new principles of order and new moral codes. Tocqueville's concerns were shared not only by French social thinkers but also by the people he had just traveled among.

3

Escape

Why did Tocqueville go to America? The Revolution of 1830 had put him in a tight spot personally, politically, and vocationally. For some time before 1830 he had been obsessed by the onrushing tide of democracy and deeply affected by the triumph of the bourgeoisie; but while America was the great modern model of a democratic middle-class society, it seems not to have been on his horizon as a destination for travel and study.

If his vision of broken time in the introduction to *Democracy in America* and the fantasy topography of its first chapter clarify Tocqueville's larger purposes, one should also be able to gain some insight into the origins and intentions of his book and its long, winding, complex argument by considering its genesis, his experience in writing it, and how he struggled to bring focus to his aims and ideas while it was in gestation and by considering as well his general ideas about writing, about literature, and about the writing of history.

It is a curious, unremarked irony that while the purpose of Tocqueville's journey to America ostensibly was to study the American prison system, the book that emerged from that journey was about freedom. He contributed nothing to the writing of *Du système pénitentiare aux Etats-Unis et de son application en France* (1833),[1] which, except for the notes and brief appendixes, was written by Beaumont.[2] He had contributed a great deal to its planning, to the laborious fieldwork it involved, and to its long thinking-through. The book unquestionably was the result of a genuine collaboration. But he did not write it. When it was time to write the official report, an act that among other things would surely bring their immense journey back to earth from the realm of mind, Tocqueville seemed not able to make that trip. In embarrassment he wrote to Beaumont, "During the past month I have begun to believe that I have been struck imbecilic. . . . We have thought it was a passing fit but through the days it has seemed more and more like a chronic malady. . . . You would laugh if you saw how I begin my intellectual efforts in the morning; I arise and seat myself in the huge armchair my father has imprudently given me; to the side I place a chair and on that I place an écritoire. On my lap I have a huge pad of paper, and nearby a pile of booklets. Thus prepared, I lean back in my armchair and, eyes half-closed, I await for the spirit of the penitentiary system to appear."[3] But his eyes remained half-closed. What is one to make of this writer's block and of its timing? was he simply exhausted? Circumstances in the France to which he and Beaumont returned in March of 1832 were not conducive to the calm that Tocqueville seemed to need when he tackled big subjects. A cholera epidemic had just swept into Paris, even into the aristocratic Faubourg Saint-Germain, where Tocqueville's parents were living at the time. He and they had to flee to Edouard's temporary home in St. Germain-en-Laye outside Paris. Urban rioting in the working-class arrondissements of Paris in protest of long-neglected miserable conditions, now made utterly insupportable by the scourge of the plague, at its most murderous in the slums, added to the terror of life in the city.[4] Simmering rumors of a legitimist insurgency must also have distracted Tocqueville, especially since Kergorlay was involved. A few months later Tocqueville would have to take time to defend Kergorlay at his trial for treason in Lyons, after the Duchesse de Berry's ludicrous Gilbert and Sullivan attempt at an insurrection had failed ignominiously.

But when he was aflame with a subject and clear about what he had to say, Tocqueville was able to work with great intensity even in the midst of turmoil and stress, as he did in 1834 when he was writing the first volume of *Democracy in America* while holed up in the attic of his parents' house in the Faubourg Saint-Germain, at a time when Paris was burning with another wave of workers' riots, bloodily suppressed. It was, as noted, the moment of the appalling massacre on the rue Transnonain, about which not a word appears in Tocqueville's correspondence.

Was the subject itself the problem? did it open up subterranean conflicts he couldn't yet manage? were his mind and psyche already absorbed by the larger meanings, historical, moral, and personal, of the amazing spectacle he had observed in America, out of which he was to shape *Democracy in America*? There surely was something incompatible in writing about prisons and thinking about America. For the same reason he found it difficult to fit his discussion of slavery in his book about the home of liberty. When he visited the immense Eastern State Penitentiary in Philadelphia, he had for the only time during his journey interviewed prisoners and taken notes: strangely, he had not inscribed those notes in the notebooks in which he recorded nearly everything about his journey. He had regarded his notebooks as the most precious of the resources he would bring back from the United States.[5]

It is not that he found the task meaningless or that he had failed to take it seriously. He and Beaumont had worked conscientiously as prison inspectors while in the United States and had gathered much material, though the notebooks he kept are full mostly of observations and reflections on politics, religion, law and class, character and social structure in America. His travel correspondence says comparatively little about the official mission of the two men. The fact is that that mission had been contrived: it was a pretext for advancing other purposes.

One of the notable aspects of Tocqueville's American adventure is that in many respects America seems to have been an accident in his life, almost an unpremeditated incident, certainly not part of the pattern of development that was shattered by 1830. There is little evidence to suggest that Tocqueville had thought much about America as an object of serious study and personal attention before 1830 (he certainly had not shown any compelling interest in it), though since the eighteenth century the French had been fascinated by America as a land of freedom and virtue—and before that century had contested with England and Spain to add it to their imperial domain as a source of potential great wealth. He undoubtedly was reasonably well informed about it. His family's home had long been a gathering place for many who had traveled in America or been exiled there, for former ambassadors to the New Republic, and even the former bishop of Boston. The Tocqueville home had been something of an American salon.[6] At the center of this au courant community was the dramatic François de Chateaubriand, whose exceptionally influential novels and philosophico-religio travel memoirs about the New World had helped launch French romantic literature.

Even so, though Tocqueville unquestionably had heard much about America, there is nothing to suggest that he had a big book on America in mind before the chance to visit the United States arose unexpectedly—unless, that is, one chooses to read his brief critical grumblings about Chateaubriand's *Voyage en Amérique*, published in 1827, as a declaration that he would do it right.[7] He later said he had been meditating a book on democracy perhaps five years before the opportunity to visit the United States opened up, but if that is so he had been remarkably mum about such plans. There is no hint of his intention in any of his correspondence. No word of it appears in anything he wrote to Kergorlay until the first volume of *Democracy in America* had been published in 1835. The explanation he offered to Kergorlay of the origins and character of his book is curiously on edge:

> It was not without thorough reflection that I made up my mind to write the book I am now publishing. I make no bones about the fact that my position

is in some ways vexing: it is unlikely to win the warm sympathy of anyone. Some will find that I do not like democracy and deal with it harshly, while others will think that I rashly encourage its development. The best thing for me would be if no one read the book, and indeed such good fortune may well be mine. Yet even knowing all this, I must tell you that some of the ideas that I shall soon be setting forth for you I have held for nearly ten years now. I went to America solely to clarify my thinking on the subject. The penitentiary system was a pretext. I used it as a passport that could gain me access everywhere in the United States.[8]

The notion that he thought it might be best if no one read his book because it was not likely to win "the warm sympathy of anyone" is not the only thing in his letter to Kergorlay that strikes one as odd. In fact he very much cared about winning the sympathy of others for his ideas. It is difficult to understand why he took so long to reveal to Kergorlay, who for a long while was his most intimate friend, what he had been planning for many years before his journey to America. Was this an ex post facto explanation? For some writers, perhaps most, it is difficult or even impossible to account for the origins of a book. Later, when writing about the beginnings of *L'Ancien Régime*, he gave that book an identical ten-year genesis. The origins of that book were so uncertain and confused that it is hard to say what he had had in mind other than a grand book on the French Revolution. He did not say and never did, though without being misleading he might well have, that he had been thinking about a book on the fate of the French aristocracy, a subject always on his mind.

If America had suddenly materialized accidentally in his life, his subsequent connections to it became remote, though he never became indifferent to the fate of the society he had come to feel represented the future of democracy and, along with England, the surest bastion of liberty. He evidently never considered traveling to America again: health would have made it difficult or impossible for him to return, as would his intensely busy and preoccupying political life in the 1840s and his consuming literary labors in the 1850s; but he seems never to have regretted that he couldn't. He continued to correspond with several American scholars, Francis Lieber, Jared Sparks, Theodore Sedgwick, and Senator Charles Sumner among them, but his American correspondence is sporadic, and though he asked his American friends to keep him informed about American politics, his knowledge of what was occurring in the United States was thin. He seems not to have read American journals and newspapers. What he did learn about the growing bitterness and violence of American politics, the struggle over the extension of slavery, and the increasingly unstable American economy much distressed him. By the 1850s his view of the American

future had become bleak. He returned in memory when he received an honor-
ary degree from Harvard in 1856 and was made a corresponding member of the
Massachusetts Historical Society that same year.⁹ On request, as mentioned
earlier, he contributed an eloquent antislavery testimonial to a Boston female
abolitionist journal, a journal that was a voice of Garrisonian, that is, immediatist, abolitionism, not Tocqueville's kind of antislavery politics. He had only a
distant view of political life in the United States, and he did nothing to keep up
with how the cultural life of democratic America was developing. He had visited America just before the great flowering of American literature in the 1840s
and 1850s, so his condescending view of that literature is perhaps understandable, but by the late 1850s—after Emerson, Thoreau, Hawthorne, Melville, and
Whitman had created what was to become an enduring American (and democratic) canon—he had not been curious enough to read this startling new
literature. He had heard rumors of it, however, and had cautioned François
Mignet, who in a speech at the Académie had made disparaging remarks
about American literature, that such a bleak assessment might no longer be
justifiable.¹⁰

Surprisingly, in the 1850s Tocqueville once said that in his view the most
ominous issue facing the American republic, one that he believed might
threaten its future, was not the increasingly bitter sectional dispute about slavery and states' rights or the ghastly prospect of a race war, both of which much
alarmed him, but the flood of immigrants, mostly Irish and German, from
Catholic and autocratic societies, who brought with them habits and a culture
ill-suited for a democratic society. He sounded then, in the 1850s, the alarm first
raised by American nativist movements in the 1840s, later powerfully organized
by the late nineteenth-century anti-immigration movement.¹¹ An equally
frequent topic of his American correspondence in the 1850s concerned his
investments, mostly in railroad bonds, about which he was at times anxious and
often asked for advice and information, including from Sumner.¹²

For what purposes, then, had Tocqueville gone to America? Was it mainly a
quest to examine democracy in its fullest development, to bring back news of
the future and lessons for his country? Though the journey certainly had intellectual and also political objectives, it was also an intense personal quest. It was
as much a journey in search of self and personal freedom as it was a fact-finding
mission in the service of reform, an intellectual undertaking to examine the
most advanced version of democracy, or an exercise in futurist speculation, the
last of which had been a staple of French writing for a century. And it was,
despite the cavalier remark he later sent to Kergorlay, a journey that Tocqueville
hoped would lead to a great book, literary fame, and political influence.

Apart from the carefully formulated objectives of this trip, Tocqueville had also journeyed to America—*fled* would not be an inappropriate term—to extricate himself from the impossible situation he found himself in after the Revolution of July 1830. Escape was the immediate motive for the trip. It is unlikely he would have gone to America had not the Revolution disrupted his life, at least not while an unimpeded career seemed to stretch out before him in France. It was a moment of great psychological stress for him, a moment in which his career seemed at an impasse, his sense of vocation unsettled, his political commitments unclear, his social and even familial relations disrupted by the political passions stirred up by the July Revolution. It was a time in which Tocqueville could not have felt remotely in control of his destiny and in which history might have seemed about to abandon him, as it had his family and his class. In taking the mandatory oath of allegiance to Louis-Philippe for the sake of his career, he had been subject to a profoundly humiliating coercion. His sense of alienation, isolation, and powerlessness was intense, his margin of freedom and choice narrow. In such circumstances, flight would have been a natural impulse, America an alluring sanctuary. It was not yet the hyperreality that so entranced later French voyagers like Jean Baudrillard, but even so it promised to be a land of marvels. Somewhere on the Atlantic during his thirty-day voyage Tocqueville had gazed in wonder at the phosphorescent ocean spume sparkling in the night and at the endless, empty daytime horizon and had anticipated with élan the great adventure that was to be a turning point in his life.

The New World: Fable, Romance, History

The New World had long fascinated Europeans, especially the French. It was the magical place where paradise might be restored, where the future would unfold and where dreams of abundance, freedom, and the recovery of moral purity might be fulfilled by a new Man living in unspoiled nature. No French person's imagination could possibly have escaped somehow being touched by these fantasies.

For many reasons it is understandable that Tocqueville turned to America to escape the prison France had become for him. For the French, America had always been more than a developing nation that might be exploited economically and geopolitically. The green Republic across the Atlantic was also a symbol resonant with all the dreams and aspirations of Enlightenment and revolutionary Europe and had long stirred the French imagination.[1] Even before the discovery of the New World during the Renaissance, the European imagination had been full of fantasies of an Eden or a Paradise to the West.[2] It was not the Enlightenment alone that had given America its special burden of moral significance; so too had sixteenth- and seventeenth-century Europeans, for whom it was not only contested ground for empire and an inexhaustible source of fur, fish, timber, immense noble estates, and possibly even gold and silk, but also a nest for all their dreams: that miraculous place where natural man in a natural environment (for millennialist Protestantism it was where salvation was to be found in a providentially chosen place) exhibited all those virtues that had been lost in a corrupt, overcivilized (or "fallen") Old World.[3] America and its native peoples had instantly become elements of a mythology that obscured its true contours and qualities. It served as a powerful instrument for testing, criticizing, and deflating the pretensions of European culture and society. The mythic–moral map of Tocqueville's first chapter expressed much of what the New World had long meant to the Old.

While all Europeans had played a role in the mythologizing of the New World, just as they had in its discovery and exploration, it was the French who were largely responsible for the myth of "le bon sauvage" as well as for "la rêve exotique" so central and so useful to the Western imagination well into the nineteenth century. By the time of Rousseau and Voltaire America was already a fabled place, a complex idea, a "mirage in the West."[4] In America one might see the future writ large. There the best aspirations of humankind might find fulfillment in a new order on earth. Above all, America symbolized freedom; and if in the minds of philosophers and moralists it stood for the idea of freedom, it also awakened personal dreams of freedom, as it always has, in those for whom the Old World promised only a constrained or meager future.

The Revolution of 1789 as well as that of July 1830 had lent renewed force to this old fascination. Now that the footsteps of democracy were heard more distinctly in France and now that the opportunity to remodel society had once again presented itself in all its bewildering and unsettling possibilities, America was more compulsively scrutinized than ever before. Its meaning and relevance became central issues of debate in French politics and literature.[5] By the time the first volume of *Democracy in America* had appeared, in 1835, French opinion of America had somewhat soured, but in the early moments of the July Monarchy its promise still seemed great, and French intellectuals studied the New Republic convinced that France had many lessons to learn from a people whose government stood for "virtue, justice, the rule of morality in politics."[6] It was still Washington's and Jefferson's America they had in mind. Andrew Jackson and his America would soon be discovered. Tocqueville would be dismayed when he did.

In this context, Tocqueville's journey to America can also be seen as a traditional pilgrimage in quest of a firsthand glimpse of Eden—or at least of the future. For it was to the New World, as to an oracle, that Europeans had turned for answers to fundamental questions. La rêve exotique had to some degree also been a mode of moral critique and prophecy. But apart from this deep-seated and pervasive European fascination with America, there were two more immediate inspirations for Tocqueville's journey to America.

The revival of the French preoccupation with the meaning of democratic America occurred when Tocqueville's deepening interest in the great social transformation of Western society from feudalism to democracy had been provided with a model of analysis and a sense of direction by the historical studies of François Guizot.[7] Whatever his subsequent criticisms of Guizot's frozen liberalism, Tocqueville was at this time an enthusiastic student of his histories. He read and discussed them with Beaumont, with whom he also attended Guizot's lectures at the Sorbonne.[8] Guizot was a major intellectual force for Tocqueville, who admired the historian's "esprit analytique" as a method of the broadest application, much as enthusiastic Marxists subsequently wielded the dialectic. He undoubtedly was much influenced by Guizot's project to uncover the guiding principles of the growth of civilization, his search for the structure beneath the fluid detail of history and for the master spirit of every civilization, by his grasp of the moral, cultural, and institutional unity of every society, his belief that the crucial, shaping component of civilization was religion. He was affected above all by Guizot's conviction that the major feature of Western history was the irrepressible rise of the bourgeoisie and of democracy.[9]

Guizot's influence, as the creator of a flexible, powerful intellectual system, would have served to make Tocqueville doubly conscious of the United States, where not so much the past but the future development of democracy might be read, since America, by habit of mind in France, was thought to be the future.

Also standing next to Tocqueville and pointing the way across the Atlantic was the immense figure of François René de Chateaubriand, the great romantic writer to whom Tocqueville was closely related: Chateaubriand was his uncle "par alliance," brother-in-law to Alexis's aunt, his mother's sister, who had been murdered by the Terror. In addition to its obvious and declared meanings, Tocqueville's voyage was also a romantic gesture in the style of Chateaubriand: the unhappy hero at the end of his tether seeks self, meaning, and freedom in exile, whether on a voyage to some exotic place or in the wilderness of the New World. Chateaubriand himself had made such a trip. There is much in his travel notebooks that strongly suggests this. At a moment of personal crisis in his youth, when, after the Great Revolution, his military career had seemed at an impasse, he had sailed for America with the avowed purpose of finding nothing less than the Northwest Passage. Tocqueville's great grandfather Malesherbes had pored over maps with the young Chateaubriand to help prepare him for this adventure. The fruit of that journey had not been the fabled passage but a number of books of colossal influence: *René, Atala, Les Natchez*, and, in 1827, his *Travels in America*.[10]

For a whole generation Chateaubriand stood as the very model of the romantic hero as writer, man of action, public figure. He was the dominant literary figure of his time, the Father against whom all the Sons would have to struggle through the first half of the nineteenth century. His work had achieved a kind of cultural centrality and power that made his ideas and his example inescapable even for those who had critical reservations about him, as Tocqueville did. His self-publicized adventures made him perhaps the first modern literary celebrity. If one aspired to a literary career—and especially if the dream was larger, combining literary accomplishment with heroic action and public influence—one had to contend with him, even though the struggle might not be overtly acknowledged. He was the major influence and, in Harold Bloom's meaning of the term, the main source of anxiety in French literary romanticism, shaping its sensibility and its imagination, filling it with enduring poses, motifs, and conventions, for example, his expressionistic, spiritualized word-painting of nature, designed to evoke the hallmark romantic sentiments of melancholy, loneliness, unrequited love, awe at the sublimity and mystery of the Creation, sadness at the fragility and fleetingness of life, all best released in dark, stormy, or moonlit scenes in which the imagination was freed from the constraints posed by bright light and precise objects. There are more than a few echoes of Chateaubriand in Tocqueville's prose. In his writing about America Chateaubriand refocused into powerful, luminous images the old rêve exotique and revitalized the myth of the noble savage, and it was his version of America that dominated the French imagination through much of the nineteenth century. His great hero René, who dies in exile in the exotic American South, became, along with George Gordon Byron's Childe Harold and Lamartine's Jocelyn (a trio cited as archetypal heroes of democratic literature by Tocqueville in *Democracy in America*), the model for a generation of suffering romantic writers and alienated youth.[11] Such pretenders appalled Chateaubriand by the ways in which they imitated René in prose or in personal style:

> If *René* did not exist, I would no longer write it: if I could destroy it I would. A family of René poets and René prose writers has been swarming about. We can hear nothing now but pitiful and disconnected phrases; they talk of nothing but winds and storms, and mysterious words whispered to the clouds and to the night. There is not a scribbler just out of school who hasn't dreamed about being the unhappiest man on earth, not an upstart of sixteen who hasn't exhausted life and felt himself tormented by his genius, who, in the abyss of his thoughts, hasn't given himself up to his vague passion, struck his pale and disheveled brow, and astounded men with sorrow which neither he nor they could describe.[12]

Was Tocqueville a son of Chateaubriand? Considering his critical reservations about Chateaubriand and his conscious effort not to be influenced by anyone, it seems unlikely. But influence, as Freud and Bloom make clear, often moves deviously and in disguises and can be expressed in complex oppositions as well as in literal reflections. That Tocqueville felt Chateaubriand's presence and reacted ambivalently to it there can be little doubt. The great man's power had even been directly and tangibly transmitted to him, for they were personally connected. The illustrious writer, already a semilegendary man of action and of letters, had sometimes stayed at Tocqueville's father's estate at Verneuil, on one occasion lost in work on his play *Moise* while Alexis and the other children played in the same study, on other occasions acting in family theatricals.[13] What can it have meant to a boy whose forte obviously was writing, to a boy who did not excel in the classics in his lycée years and was outstanding only in rhetoric and French composition, to have been on the same stage, as it were, also playing a role, alongside the Great Writer of the Age, a fellow actor? The family connection would also have the effect of transforming legends of exile and wilderness adventure into palpable items of family history, making them available for appropriation and imitation. It would have made America a place in the family history as well.

Tocqueville seems to have maintained a certain critical reserve about Chateaubriand. With a kind of genial, deflating mockery he called him "le grand homme," echoing Beaumont's "le génie sublime," uttered in the same tone. He objected to Chateaubriand's egoism and theatricality and also, finally, to his literary style, which he thought tended to smother reality in false colors. But certainly both Tocqueville and Beaumont as young writers had to struggle consciously against Chateaubriand's influence, which left its mark in their work. With Tocqueville's help Beaumont tried unsuccessfully to rid *Marie* of all traces of Chateaubriand. "There are still two passages that are reminiscent of Chateaubriand despite all the efforts I've made to avoid that," Beaumont reported;[14] and there are strongly imitative passages in Tocqueville's early writing and, more significantly, in his American notebooks, in which the impulses that informed his adventure rise to the surface,[15] and flower in melancholy, portentous prose. Chateaubriand in fact continued to be a kind of patron of Tocqueville. After the first volume of *Democracy in America* was published he introduced his young protégé to the literary world at Mme Récamier's salon; he had a hand in Tocqueville's election to the Académie française in 1841; and he maintained a benevolent, encouraging interest in his writing. Tocqueville's self-deflating account of an unexpected visit from Chateaubriand in 1839 makes it clear that even in his maturity (he was thirty-four) he still felt some awe for le grand homme:

> The day before yesterday I was astonished, confounded, confused and on top of that I don't know what else in seeing M. de Chateaubriand arrive at my place to hear, he said, some passages of my manuscript [the second volume of *Democracy in America*]. It was absolutely necessary to read to him from it. You can appreciate that, having made such a demand for I don't know what motives, he did not want to conclude with criticisms. So he complimented me effusively. I have discounted three-quarters of it, and enough remains for me really to hope that though his language was quite exaggerated, his

judgement was positive. At that moment I thus was much like a horse which, after having all four legs bound, is struck with a whip. Unfortunately the comparison is exact in every way.[16]

The image undoubtedly was exact. It conveys a sense of the conflict Tocqueville felt about Chateaubriand: between attraction and rejection, deference and criticism, a desire to imitate and a wish to supercede. Despite his deliberate effort to distance himself from Chateaubriand, he continued to be powerfully affected by the man. More generally, in its suggestion of a paralyzing ambivalence, it once again points at the deep inner struggle that Tocqueville constantly probed in his confessional writings.

Despite his antipathy to many of the cultural and psychological expressions of romanticism, Tocqueville nonetheless fashioned a self-image that resembled that of a tormented romantic hero. There was a good deal of René in him. He was himself aware of the deep split between his intellect and his passions. Their opposition, as he put it, is a persistent theme of his self-analysis. It seems plausible, then, to assume that Tocqueville may have identified emotionally with Chateaubriand and that the elder man continued to serve as an unconscious model for Tocqueville's career despite their intellectual and political differences. Whatever the other meanings and purposes of Tocqueville's journey to America may have been, it may also have been a reenactment of Chateaubriand's, in which Tocqueville, at a moment of crisis in his life, set out on his own search for a Northwest Passage, that is, for a glimpse of his destiny and the experience of freedom. Just as there was another, hidden Tocqueville within the public and literary figure, so there was a journey within the journey, another book within *Democracy in America*: a subliminal epic of self-exploration in which Tocqueville ranges through his own feelings and experiences in quest of his true self, to finally locate himself in history. The start of that journey begins in his passionate introduction and in his prefatory philosophical map of America, which key the inner, emotional voyage to come far more than they do the outer one, the combined practical, fact-finding junket and historical-philosophical expedition.

5

TOCQUEVILLE IN THE WILDERNESS

During their travels in America, Tocqueville and Beaumont twice ventured into what Tocqueville called the wilderness, the real America, the edge of civilization. These unplanned side trips reveal much about Tocqueville's self-imagination and the emotional subtext of how he saw and wrote about America. These journeys proved to be a source of images and metaphors for all his writing about America.

Tocqueville made three simultaneous journeys to America: one to examine the American prison system, the official expedition for which he was supplied with governmental sanction and a satchel full of letters of introduction; a second to study democracy in its most advanced development; and a third consisting of spontaneous adventures, journeys within the journey, in which he was most deeply responding to his personal emotional agenda.

There are several striking aspects to these improvised trips: they were undertaken suddenly, on impulse, or, as Tocqueville put it, they were "non premedité"; they both involved deep excursions into the wilderness; and he wrote about each three times, in his notebooks, then more elaborately in his correspondence, and finally in polished essays full of romantic conventions, essays which he did not publish as part of *Democracy in America* and which in fact were published only after his death. The very spontaneity of these trips suggests that Tocqueville was responding to motives and impulses beyond his conscious plans. These orthogonal journeys within a journey, much like the archetypal play within a play, further illuminate the meaning of Tocqueville's American voyage and are testimony to its inner richness.

Tocqueville felt that the real America lay in the interior, a notion he had suggested by focusing his map almost wholly on the Mississippi Valley, and it was to the interior that he obviously was powerfully drawn. It was there he had his most intense, almost dreamlike, even hallucinatory experiences, culminating in his interrogation of a silent God in the wilderness[1] and in his final transformation of the American Indians from the sad mendicants he had first encountered in upstate New York into noble, yet doomed, aristocrats with whom he had squatted and dined in mutual admiration.

As soon as it was possible, Tocqueville broke free from the confines of his schedule and his official itinerary to plunge, as he put it, into the wilderness. He had signaled his impatience to break away from urban America quite early in the trip. He and Beaumont had spent the first three weeks of their adventure entirely in New York City. Just before leaving the city to travel by steamboat up the Hudson River to Ossining to visit Sing Sing prison Tocqueville wrote the following:

> One can't imagine anything more beautiful than the North—or the Hudson—River. The great width of the river, the admirable richness of the north bank, and the craggy mountains which border its eastern shores form one of the most striking places in the world. *Nevertheless, this is not yet the America that I want to see.* Everyday we envy the first Europeans who, 200 years ago, discovered for the first time the mouth of the Hudson and mounted its current when both its shores were covered with vast forests and when one could see only the smoke of the savages rising above places where two hundred thousand people now buzz. And so it is that one is never contented.[2]

What was the America he so much wanted to see? and what meaning did it bear for him?

The first of his unplanned journeys occurred while he was on his way from New York City to Auburn Penitentiary in northwest New York. It was on this first major expedition to the interior, away from the urban coast, that Tocqueville's traveling sometimes became notably more a kind of impulsive exploration of the shadowy places of his psyche than a carefully planned investigation of American institutions and culture. This first brief deviation from their charted travels involved the story of a young French aristocrat who with his wife had been driven into exile, supposedly at Lake Oneida, by the violent turn of the Revolution of 1789.[3] Tocqueville's preliminary description of the visit to Lake Oneida is in notebook shorthand, but in its staccato directness he catches the on-the-spot immediacy and freshness of his emotions:

> Leave Syracuse at 2 o'clock. On horseback. Umbrella, gun, game-bag. We plunge through new clearings. We arrive at 6 o'clock at Fort Brewerton. General look round. The forest in permanent contest with man. Birds killed. View of Lake Oneida. Stretches beyond the horizon to the east between little wooded hills. Not a house or clearing in view. Monotonous, lonely look.
>
> We plunge through an immense forest where the path is barely traceable. Delicious freshness that reigns there. Sight wonderful and impossible to

describe. Astonishing vegetation. Enormous trees of all species. A disorder of grasses, plants, bushes. America in all her glory, waters running on every side, huge pines uprooted by the wind, twisted among plants of every sort.[4]

After a terse description of his search for the Frenchman's dwelling and his discovery of an old apple tree and wild vines that marked the spot, he concludes, "The house was [had been] there. There is no trace left of it. We wrote our names on a plane tree. We set out again. Profound silence of the island broken only by the birds that live there free. We traversed the whole island without finding any trace of the two beings who had made it their universe. This expedition is what has most vividly interested and moved me, not only since I have been in America but since I have been traveling."[5]

Tocqueville's curious remark that the "profound silence of the island" was "broken only by the birds that live there free" is an obvious and gratuitous comment that reveals how densely packed with personal meaning the experience had been for him. It had evoked the problem of personal freedom; and his remark, suggesting that freedom was found in flight, that is, in exile in a silent wilderness, hints at the urgency of the matter for him. He and Beaumont had ended their sentimental journey by carving their names on a tree, a gesture that symbolized their spiritual identity with the exiled young aristocrat, another wandering orphan of revolution. Small wonder that, having traced his own footsteps, as it were, to where they vanished in the silent wilderness, he added that no travel experience had ever moved him as much.

His subsequent accounts of this brief adventure further elaborate its personal meaning for Tocqueville. In a letter to his sister-in-law Émilie written in Batavia, New York, on July 25, 1831, almost three weeks after his visit to the lake, he reveals that he had known well in advance the drama of Lake Oneida, having read the story of a young French aristocrat living in exile there long before. What he hadn't known was that his route would take him "à quatre pas du lac Oneida"; nor had he known the fate of the young exile. Conceivably, at the start of the journey he thought he might encounter the nameless Frenchman, now an old man. In this first, simple retelling Tocqueville sharpens the hint that a question of identity was involved. He powerfully sentimentalizes the setting, after insisting that the story will make Émilie "dream while awake" for a week: "You should therefore know that about forty years ago a Frenchman whose name no one could tell me but who came from a wealthy noble family landed in America after having been forced by the Revolution to leave his country. Our fugitive was young, in good health, and he was never troubled by his stomach (note this); moreover, he had a wife he loved with all his heart."[6] The noting of differences simply points at the implicit identity. Again, he emphasizes the stillness and the emptiness of the place: "Imagine a calm and transparent lake several leagues in length, completely surrounded by thick woods whose roots it bathes; not a sail is to be seen on the lake, no dwelling on the shores; no smoke above these forests; a tranquility as complete as there must have been at the beginning of the world. A mile from the shore we discovered our isle; it was only a jumbled grove in which it was impossible to see the slightest trace of a clearing."[7] And in the midst of chaos, where nature battles back to stifle civilization, he discovers the ruins of the past:

> Here we found a sad and compelling spectacle; the very center of the isle clearly showed the unmistakable trace of man's presence. At first glance one noticed that the trees had been taken down; but passing time had already almost completely effaced this beginning of civilization. The offshoots of the surrounding forest had already pushed to the very center of the Frenchman's fields; parasitic climbing plants had already taken over the soil and had begun to link one to the other the new trees which were rising everywhere. It was in the midst of this disorder that we searched fruitlessly for the dwelling of our man; we found no more than traces of its lawns and gardens.[8]

Traces that were far more fragile monuments than those left behind by the Mound Builders of the Mississippi Valley.

Tocqueville continues his account with a melange of enigmatic personal comments, at once playful and somber, hinting that the experience had depths of meaning for him that could not be sailed over by witty navigation on the surface: "You others, dear sister, you suppose that because one wears a *bonnet carré* [that is, because one is a judge] and sends his man to the galleys, one is a reasoning machine, an incarnate syllogism. I am glad to inform you that you are mistaken, and that when a magistrate starts thinking of something other than the law, one doesn't know quite how far that will lead. Thus we left the Frenchman's isle with heavy hearts, wondering about the fate of this man we had never seen and whose name we did not know. Has there ever been a fate similar to that of this poor fellow?"[9] In response to that poignant question he briefly summarizes the exile's unhappy destiny and then suggests how strongly it has seized his imagination and how relevant it has seemed to *him*:

> Men drive him out from their society like a leper; he accepts his lot, creates a world for himself all alone. There he is, tranquil, happy. He stays there just long enough to be completely forgotten by his European friends; then his wife dies and leaves him alone in the wilderness, as incapable of living the life of a savage as of a civilized man; and in spite of everything, I say it

between us and quite low so that parents, people excessively reasonable by nature, do not treat us as mad, is there not something which captivates the imagination about a life hidden and cut off from the entire world which this poor couple led for so many years? Unfortunately, there are no doctors in the wilderness, and one must have the health of a peasant, or not commit to going there.[10]

This passage suggests that the whole experience was a kind of emotional rehearsal of deep exile for Tocqueville and that he had closely identified with the unnamed hero, who also found himself a dangling man, suspended between two worlds, between "la vie d'un sauvage," and "celle d'un homme civilisé." He speaks to his correspondent in a voice "tout bas"; it is essentially a meditation on "la vie cachée" that he is sharing. He finds the idea seductive. And if one looks ahead, one sees that in some ways this fable anticipates Tocqueville's withdrawal into deep isolation and internal exile in the 1850s, at which time he perceived himself to be alone in the world with Marie, living as if in a desert or in the forests of America, anxious about his health, anxious too about the total isolation he would face were his wife to die before him.

All of these themes of flight and freedom, isolation and solitude, the creative force of nature and the fragility of civilization find heightened expression in the literary version of this experience published in 1860, after Tocqueville's death. Years before, during his youth, Tocqueville writes, he had been powerfully impressed by a book called *Voyage au Lac Onéida*, which told the story of a young French aristocrat and his wife driven into wilderness exile by the Revolution. The tale had fixed itself in his mind and evidently had become a focus for his longings and fantasies:

How often have I envied them the tranquil joys of their solitude. Domestic happiness, the charms of conjugal union, and even love itself came to be merged in my mind with the picture of *the solitary island where my imagination had created a new Eden*. When I told my travelling companion [Beaumont] the story, he too was deeply moved by it. We often talked about it, and always ended by saying, sometimes laughing, sometimes sadly, "The only happiness in the world is on the shores of Lake Oneida." When events that could not have been foreseen took us both to America, this recollection returned to us more forcefully. We promised ourselves that we would go and see our two French people, if they were still alive, or at least visit their home. Consider how strange is the power of the imagination over the human mind; these savage parts, this silent immobile lake and these islands covered with greenery did not strike us at all as something new; on the contrary we seemed to be revisiting a place where we had passed part of our youth.[11]

Imagination and perception were so fused at this wilderness site, Tocqueville's "new Eden," that boundaries seemed to disappear, between France and America, past and present, self and the historical other. The scene is now embellished with various romantic literary flourishes and motifs made fashionable by Chateaubriand. "A stormy night that has been followed by a heavy day," Tocqueville writes. "Soon we found protection from the sun in the middle of one of those deep forests of the New World whose sombre savage majesty strikes the imagination and fills the soul with a sort of religious terror."[12] "Religious terror" (or "dread") is what Tocqueville says he feels, in his introduction to *Democracy in America*, as he contemplates the irresistible, providential sweep of history as it builds a new order of things out of the ruins of the old. It is religious terror he feels in the wilderness as he observes the apparently chaotic process by which life emerges from death and is absorbed by death, a mysterious struggle carried on in the midst of "a solemn silence," the meaning of which eludes him. Nature has become an emblem for the processes of history, a profoundly suitable background for the story Tocqueville is about to tell and for his own historical pilgrimage and personal quest. Is the religious terror he feels his way of expressing anxiety about self? "How can one paint such a sight?" he continues. "On marshy land where a thousand streams not yet hemmed in by the hand of man flow and are lost in liberty, nature has sown pell-mell in incredible profusion the seeds of almost all the plants that creep over the ground or climb above the soil."[13] There are echoes of the Creation in this scene of primeval abundance where chance seems to rule—that is, the meaning of which remains a mystery. How can existence emerge from "pell-mell"? In this version of the journey, streams have replaced birds as symbols of unrestrained freedom, "not yet hemmed in by the hand of man"; but the implied overarching question remains the same: what are the consequences of wild freedom, or natural liberty, for humanity? Will exile or escape to a new Eden and complete freedom lead to happiness and the true self?—one of the central questions of *Democracy in America*.

Tocqueville continues:

Over our heads stretched a vast dome of vegetation. Below this thick veil and amid the damp depths of the forest, there lay one vast confusion, a sort of chaos. Trees of all ages, foliage of all colors, plants, fruits, and flowers of a thousand species, entangled and intertwined. Generations of trees have succeeded one another there through uninterrupted centuries and the ground is covered with their debris. Some seem to have fallen yesterday; others already half sunk into the ground have but a hollow surface without depth, others are finally reduced to dust and serve to fertilize their last offshoots. Amid them a thousand different plants press in their turn and press toward

the light. They glide between these immobile corpses, creep over their surface and under their decaying bark raise and disperse their powdered debris.
It is like a fight between life and death. . . .

A solemn silence reigned in the midst of this solitude; one saw few or no living creatures; man was missing from the scene, but yet this was no desert. On
the contrary, everything in nature showed a creative force unknown elsewhere;
everything was in movement, the air seemed impregnated with the smell of
vegetation. It was as if one heard an inner sound that betrayed the work of creation and could see the sap and life circulating through ever open channels.

We walked on for several hours through these imposing solitudes in the
light of an unsettled day, without hearing other sounds than those of our
horses' hooves rustling the piled leaves of several winters, or forcing their way
through the withered branches that blocked the path. We, too, kept silent,
our souls filled with the grandeur and the novelty of the sight. At last we
heard the echoes of an axe-stroke, the first distant announcement of the
presence of a European.[14]

Whatever else one may say about this writing, it is not a precise description
of a North American forest but presents nature as metaphor, as the setting for a
transcendental drama of the spirit. Tocqueville and Beaumont ride in silence as
they approach hallowed ground—the new Eden where happiness may finally
be found—their ideas and expectations so intense that they hear a kind of metaphysical music ("It was as if one heard an inner sound that betrayed the work
of creation") and see the unseen ("and could see the sap and life circulating
through ever open channels"). The blending of elements and senses hints at
the overarching, all-encompassing unity of Creation, in which life and death
become simple phases of reality. This confirming epiphany, vouchsafed in the
silence that was the condition of insight, would have been understood by any
American Transcendentalist. Thus encompassed in hallucinatory anticipation,
Tocqueville rode through "America in all her glory," searching the oracle.

But now, in the rest of his account, Tocqueville underscores the blighted
dream of happiness and the futility of the quest for complete freedom. In images
that show the most delicate and creative aspirations of humankind being
devoured by a power that builds its own nonhuman order out of disorder, his
description of the exile's decayed island home fully plays out the motif of the
collapse of human dreams, the fleetingness of humans' effort to impose their
order and their truth in the great, dynamic surrounding chaos:

Weeds grew where once the exile's harvest ripened; brambles and parasitic
plants had come to take back possession of their former domain. One could
barely, at far intervals, discern the trace of enclosure or the mark of a field.

For an hour we searched in vain through the undergrowth of the wood and the brambles encumbering the ground for any sign of the abandoned dwelling. That rustic luxury which the fisherman's wife [encountered on the main shore of Lake Oneida] had just described to us, the lawn, the flower beds, the flowers, the fruits, those products of civilization which loving care had nourished in the depths of the wild, all that has vanished with the beings who lived there.[15]

All he finds is "an apple tree half dead with old age" and a vine running wild through the woods, to the very top of the trees. His new Eden has turned out to be not even a wild garden but a lost garden. The happiness to be found in complete freedom, in life outside society and its conventions, has turned out to be "wretchedness." One may escape "the European's bullet and the savage's arrow," but there is no escaping the imperious claims of nature, especially "the invisible blows of death." The next step after natural liberty *is* death. Natural liberty puts one at the brink. The peril is that one will be sucked into the all-surrounding chaos.

Tocqueville's melancholy conclusion brings the story back to its poignant personal meaning. He too, after all, had been forced into flight. His expedition had not been a jeu d'espirit, a lighthearted historical pilgrimage. One does not experience religious terror on such journeys, and it is with a reference again to some such feeling—his heart "racked by fear and hope"—that he finishes his account:

Perhaps those who read these lines will not understand the feelings they record and will treat them as exaggerated or chimerical. Nonetheless I will say that it was with hearts full of emotion, racked by fear and hope, and inspired by some sort of religious feeling, that we began our meticulous searches and followed up the traces of those two beings whose name and family and part of whose story was unknown to us; a story whose only claim on our attention was that in this very place they had suffered the griefs and joys that touch all men's hearts, because they have their origin in all hearts.

Is there wretchedness greater than that of this man! Here is an unfortunate whom human society has shunned: his fellows have rejected him, banished him, and forced him to renounce their intercourse and flee into the wilds. Only one being has remained attached to him, followed him into solitude, and come to dress the wounds of his soul and to give him, in exchange for the joys of the world, the more essential emotions of the human heart. There he is reconciled to his fate. He has forgotten revolutions, parties, cities, his family, his rank and his fortune; he breathes again. His wife dies. Death comes to strike her and spares him. Poor wretch! What can become of him?

Will he stay alone in the wilds, or will he go back to society where he has
been long forgotten? He is no longer adapted either for solitude or for the
world; he does not know how to live either with men or without them; he is
neither a savage nor a civilized man: he is nothing but a piece of debris, like
those trees in the American forests which the wind has the power to uproot,
but not to blow down. He stands erect, but he lives no more.[16]

And with that image of the uprooted man who belongs nowhere, Tocqueville's
tale of total loss ends. "It was not without sadness," he writes, "that I saw this vast
rampart of greenery retreating into the distance." The story was a paradigm of
his own life.

The second of Tocqueville's unpremeditated plunges into the wilderness
lasted much longer than the first—from July 19 to August 14. If it did not take
him to the heart of the wilderness or to the true frontier, it took him there in his
imagination, which made all that he saw luminous with meaning. This improvised dash to the west, which seems to have been Tocqueville's impulse rather
than that of an initially reluctant Beaumont, who at first tried to restrain his
enthusiastic friend, carried the prison inspectors from Buffalo to Detroit by
steamboat; then to Pontiac and finally Saginaw in the interior of Michigan by
horse; back to Detroit; and then by steamboat through Lakes Huron and
Michigan to Green Bay, Wisconsin, stopping at various places along the way,
including Sault Sainte Marie and Mackinac Island; once again back to Detroit,
whence they embarked by boat for Buffalo, Montreal, and Quebec. All in all,
by Tocqueville's estimates the excursion added a loop of fifteen hundred miles
to their journey, some of them arduous and hazardous. At its farthermost reach,
Tocqueville found himself briefly lost in the heart of America while hunting
alone along the Fox River in Wisconsin. He later wrote with quiet pride that he
believed he had been where no Frenchman had ever been. He had been alone
in the wilds of America.[17]

This journey too was a voyage of self-discovery, and Tocqueville's formal
account of it in "Quinze Jours au Désert" is his most passionate and personal
writing about America. It is full of dark insights that directly and indirectly
shaped *Democracy in America*. Certainly Tocqueville also had other, concrete
objectives in mind as he headed west. A trip so long and diffuse afforded opportunities to gather sociological and cultural data. Tocqueville and Beaumont
were anxious to see the native American in his natural environment after their
depressing encounter with the degraded remnants of the fabled Iroquois in
New York. They wished also to observe how settlement moved west and by
whom it was carried and even to test a classic eighteenth-century social hypothesis: that the closer one moved to the frontier of any society, the more primitive

the level of civilization one would encounter. A journey to the frontier would also be a journey backward through time—a venture in cultural archaeology.

But Tocqueville's accounts of this expedition, while full of detailed social and historical observations, are also powerful imaginative constructs in which he continues to work out the various themes of his intensely personal, sentimental journey to Lake Oneida. If moving to "the utmost limits of European civilization," as Tocqueville described his intention, was simply one version of "la rêve exotique" or a sociologist's fantasy, it was also the expression of a wish to divest oneself of one's cultural apparel and to free oneself from history as well, in other words, to find the natural self beneath the layers of convention and cultivation. Accordingly, there is a constant sense in Tocqueville's accounts of his wilderness expedition not simply of an encounter with the true physiognomy of civilization at its moment of confluence with nature, but also of confrontation with the essential issues of self and identity and with the basic meanings of civilization and nature. Indeed, on this journey too Tocqueville experiences religious terror while facing the giant enigma of the wilderness—"a silence so deep, a stillness so complete"—which he sometimes describes with Chateaubriandesque embroidery to emphasize its emblematic meaning, oddly pausing to justify his literary flourishes with the claim of exactitude: "Then darkness gave a new and terrible aspect to the forest. All around, one could see nothing but gathering or confused masses, without shape or symmetry, strange disproportionate forms, incoherent sights, and fantastic images that seemed to come from the sick imagination of a fever bed. (The gigantic and the ridiculous rubbed shoulders there as close as in the literature of our day.) Never had our footsteps raised more echoes; never had the silence of the forest seemed more fearsome. One might say that the buzzing of the mosquitoes was only the breathing of this sleeping world."[18] The footsteps of this journey into the wilderness continued to echo throughout his work.

In Tocqueville's pithy account of this trip in his notebooks, consisting of impressions seized at the moment, that is, good clues to what he consciously focused on, the Indian is the center of attention while the broader struggle between Nature and Civilization remains a muted theme to be fully amplified in "Quinze Jours au Désert." At this point the Indian seems to have replaced the exiled French aristocrat as the object of Tocqueville's quest, as the personification of his historico-philosophical concerns, even as a figure with whom he could identify. In a sense the Indian too was an exile, an uprooted figure constantly in flight; and while Tocqueville does not consciously draw the parallel, there is, during his ongoing account of his search for the real Indian, a noticeable merging of "savage" and "civilized," "red man" and "white," and even between Tocqueville's self-image and the image of the Indian hunter, guide, and warrior. The deeper Tocqueville penetrates the wilderness, the more confused identities become. Old distinctions and their meanings vanish. The visible signs of class, race, and culture are blended into a new wilderness semiotics in which symbols and meanings are scrambled. It was a perfect setting for visions. The social chaos of the frontier world—where French-Canadian pioneers looked like Indians; where Indians, according to Tocqueville, preferred speaking French to English and greeted travelers with a sonorous "Bonjour";[19] and where real racial fusion was producing a generation of exotic faces and styles—could easily have stimulated hallucinatory experiences, transcultural fantasies, and identity confusions. The collapse of old distinctions, this confused blending of civilized and savage, and the new reality produced by the simultaneously destructive and creative power of nature are themes that thread through all of Tocqueville's accounts of his trip to Michigan and Wisconsin. He experiences that new reality not simply as an observer but as a participant.

There are numerous instances in Tocqueville's wilderness writings of the inadvertent deceptions and misleading appearances that result from the collapse of distinctions on the frontier. "Strange character of the population," he writes in his notebook, "mixture of all sorts of blood. The most numerous, the French Canadians, *bois-brûles* or half-caste. Every gradation from European to savage."[20] For example, on the way from Pontiac to Flint and then Saginaw Tocqueville and Beaumont find themselves being shadowed by an Indian running noiselessly sometimes to one side of them then the other, sometimes behind or before them, through the forest. They fear an ambush: "While worrying about that idea, we saw in the wood in front of us the muzzle of another carbine. Soon we came up to the man who carried it. At first we took him for an Indian. He was dressed in another short frockcoat, which, fastened round his loins, outlined an upright, well made body; his neck was bare and there were moccasins on his feet. When we got near and he raised his head, we saw at once that he was a European."[21] They have a long conversation with this man, who expresses great admiration for the Indians, which Tocqueville fully records to introduce the "reader to a type of man whom we meet very frequently thereafter on the verge of the inhabited land. They are Europeans who, despite the habits of their youth, have ended up finding inexpressible charm in the freedom of the wilderness. Taste and passion draw them to the solitudes of America, while their religion, principles, and ideas attach them to Europe, so that they combine love of the savage life with the pride of civilization and prefer the Indians to their compatriots, without, however, looking on them as equals."[22]

On another occasion Tocqueville is waiting for a boat to carry him across the Saginaw River:

A few minutes later a faint sound could be heard and something approached the bank. It was an Indian canoe, about ten feet long, and shaped out of a single tree. The man who crouched in the bottom of this fragile bark was dressed and looked completely like an Indian. He spoke to our guides, who at his order hastened to take our saddles off and put them in the canoe. As I was getting ready to get into it myself, the supposed Indian came up to me and said in a Norman accent that made me jump: "Don't go too fast, sometimes people get drowned here." If my horse had spoken to me, I do not think I should have been more surprised. I looked at the man who had spoken to me and whose face, lightened by the first rays of the moon, shone like a ball of copper. "Who are you, then," I said to him. "French seems to be your language and you look like an Indian." He told me that he was a boisbrûlé, that is to say the son of a French Canadian and an Indian woman.[23]

The experience of confused identities and shocked expectations is repeated many times. He has a conversation with a "civilized savage dressed like one of our peasants"; meets a Mme Framboise, a "woman much to be admired," who, it turns out, has Indian blood; at another time mistakes the savage wife of a white settler as a Frenchwoman or an Englishwoman. Tocqueville himself certainly does not go native, but he does draw noticeably closer to the Indians, largely in sentiment (he concludes his journey full of admiration for the Indian) but even in behavior. All through the trip he is the hunter, shooting fowl and game at every opportunity, a bloody aristocratic sport he indulged in whenever he could during his travels in the United States, beginning with his jubilant birding expeditions in Ossining, New York. Such sport was now given extra panache by the experience of frontier freedom and perils. His elegant, engraved gun, much admired by the Indians, becomes a point of contact between him and them. They touch it. Like them he rolls himself in a blanket and sleeps on the ground, takes to roaming and shooting duck on his own, swims across a river, and squats in conversation, presumably in French, with a Chippewa chief with whom he establishes a kind of kinship:

> Dress of the chief: red trousers, a blanket, hair tied back on the top of his head. Two feathers in it. I fire my gun for him. He admires it, and says that he had always heard it said that the French were a nation of great warriors. I ask the meaning of his feathers. He answers with a smile of pleasure that he has killed two Sioux. He is a Saulter [Chippewa], a tribe always at war with the other. I ask him for one of the feathers, telling him that I will carry it to the land of the great warriors, and people will admire it. He takes it out at once from his hair and gives it to me, then stretches out his hand and shakes mine.[24]

That image of handclasping is repeated in another episode in which Tocqueville describes how, in the wilderness, roles are reversed and authority shifts to the savage. In the midst of the Michigan forest he writes of his Chippewa guides:

> We felt ourselves completely in their power. There, in fact, the order was reversed; plunged into deep darkness, reduced to his own resources, the civilized man walks like the blind, incapable not only of being his own guide in the labyrinth that surrounded him, but even of the means to sustain life. It is in the heart of the same difficulties that the savage triumphs; for him, the forest has obscured nothing; he walks with his head high, guided by an instinct more sure than the navigator's compass. . . .
>
> From time to time our Indians halted; they put their fingers to their lips to show that we must keep silent and signaled us to get off our horses. Led by them, we came to a place where one could see the game. It was a strange sight to see the scornful smile with which they took us by the hand like children and led us at last to the object they had seen so long ago.[25]

In the forest the Indian was master, completely in control of his environment. There he could see farther ahead than the civilized man, who became his childlike dependent, in a touching image led by the hand.

In a final minidrama, Tocqueville again implies a kinship with the Indian, who becomes a surrogate for his apprehensions about the future. It is a hot, sultry, mosquito-plagued midnight in Saginaw. Unable to sleep, Tocqueville steps outside his hut for some fresh air. A thunderstorm is approaching:

> The rain had not started yet, and the air seemed calm, but the forest shook already and was filled with deep groans and lingering wails. Now and again a lightning flash illuminated the sky. The tranquil flow of the Saginaw, the little clearing that edges its banks, the roofs of five or six huts, and the leafy fence that surrounded us appeared then for an instant like an evocation of the future. Then all was in the deepest darkness and the fearsome voice of the wilds was heard again.
>
> While I stood, struck by this great spectacle, I heard a sigh at my side, and in the flash of the lightning I saw an Indian leaning as I was doing against the wall of our dwelling. No doubt the storm had broken his sleep, for it was a fixed and troubled gaze that he cast around the scene.
>
> Was this man afraid of the thunder? Or did he see in the clash of the elements something beyond a passing convulsion of nature? Had the fugitive images of civilization which rose unbidden in the midst of the tumult of the wilds a prophetic meaning for him? Did these groans of the forest that seemed to be fighting an unequal battle strike his ear as a secret warning of

God, a solemn revelation of the final fate reserved for the savage races? I could not say.[26]

That is precisely the question Tocqueville had asked and already partially answered about the meaning of the advance of civilization, not for his race but for his class. In this fitfully lit and explosively stormy wilderness night, certainly the kind of scene in which personal terrors and fears begin to resonate with the external turbulence, the young aristocrat full of anxious questions about his future and the future of his class asks if the apparently troubled Indian sighing next to him has found "prophetic meaning" in this "passing convulsion of nature": that meaning ("a secret warning of God") being that "the final fate reserved for the savage races" was to be demolished like the surrounding forest by the onrushing power of civilization. Yet it has been Tocqueville who all along has been reading nature as a hieroglyph of historical and spiritual meanings; and it may well have been Tocqueville who had a clearer vision of the doom of his world than the Indian had of his. This transfer of meaning and identity illuminates in a flash how Tocqueville's imagination was working. The question he asked about the sighing Indian was just one version of the way in which he questioned America for clues as to his own destiny and as a way of thinking about his identity.

Indeed, shortly thereafter another storm breaks in the wilderness, this one wholly within Tocqueville's head. The following day, while making their way back through the forests to Pontiac and then Detroit without the aid of guides, Tocqueville and Beaumont momentarily find themselves lost. "Abandoned wigwam. Two roads. Doubt. We take the one to the right and cross the stream. The track seems little trodden. Unpleasant doubt for a long time." "Throughout the whole of that day we had not met a single human face. The animals too had disappeared," and they saw only a sparrow hawk on "the bare top of a dead tree." "Great was our distress," wrote Tocqueville.[27] And during this almost daylong experience of being lost Tocqueville has a "hallucination":

> It was in the midst of that profound solitude that we suddenly thought of the Revolution of 1830, whose first anniversary had just arrived. I cannot describe the impact with which memories of July 29 took possession of our minds. The cries and smoke of battle, the roar of guns, the rattle of rifles, the even more horrible ringing of the tocsin—that whole day with its delirious atmosphere seemed quite suddenly to rise out of the past and to stand before me like a living picture. This was only a sudden hallucination, a passing dream. When I raised my head and looked around me, the apparition had already vanished; but never had the silence of the forest seemed so icy, the shadows so sombre, the solitude so absolute.[28]

It is with this experience that Tocqueville closes "Quinze Jours au Désert," choosing, as it were, to bring the curtain down at this moment, as he stands in the "silence . . . so icy, the shadows so sombre, the solitude so absolute." This storm, too, whose tumult also breaks the silence of the wilderness, provokes a vision of the future, one for which the qualities of the wilderness serve as correlatives. While Tocqueville interprets the experience as an aberrant moment—an "apparition," "a passing dream"—it was a transparent surfacing of abiding personal concerns and historical anxieties. He had been traveling through the American forests with the Revolution of 1830 and all that it had meant and would continue to mean to him just below the surface of consciousness, where it nonetheless guided his imagination. Tocqueville's closing remarks about the wilderness reveal that the way in which he saw nature and the Indian was strongly shaped by his permanent personal as well as historical preoccupations. Indeed one can go a step further and suggest that the way in which Tocqueville interpreted his entire American experience—the way in which he saw America—was powerfully affected by his silent inward journey of self-exploration and by his personal dreams and nightmares. When he writes in the introduction to *Democracy in America*, "I admit that I saw in America more than America; it was the shape of democracy itself which I sought, its inclinations, character, prejudices and passions; I wanted to understand it so as at least to know what we have to fear or to hope therefrom,"[29] one may wish to add, without denying the truth of what he did say, that it was also a more complete truth about himself he sought, a better understanding of his "inclinations, character, prejudices and passions" and also of what he had "to fear or to hope."

The literal drama of the journey itself, full of danger, the exotic, and the sublime, is intensified by a movement of meaning on another level as Tocqueville records it in "Quinze Jours au Désert," his final literary version of the trip. In this account of the expedition Tocqueville compresses its full meaning into a much-amplified narrative of what was only its first leg, that from Detroit to Saginaw and back again. That particular jaunt lasted less than a week, while the whole expedition had taken three—yet he calls his narrative "Quinze Jours au Désert." Tocqueville has begun to pack this episode of personal history with meaning—one might say to mythicize it.

6

TRANSFORMATIONS

Just as the introduction to *Democracy in America* and its first chapter tell the reader about how Tocqueville's historical and philosophical imagination shaped his book, so do the various accounts of his wilderness trips, especially the ways in which he transforms the materials and symbols of his wilderness adventures. What began as ethnographic and naturalist observations became moral commentaries in which Tocqueville comments on the values and tensions of American life. These reveal Tocqueville's apprehensive insights into the American psyche and provide an emotional accompaniment to *Democracy in America*.

While the dynamics of imagination of Tocqueville's story are complex, two transformations seem especially significant, and these are related to the major questions that shape all of *Democracy in America*. "Quinze Jours au Désert," written aboard a steamboat as he headed west after his Michigan adventure, is his fullest account of his wilderness experience. It can be read, in fact, as a preliminary working out, a kind of thematic prefiguring, at least on the level of poetic imagination, of some of the main historical and philosophical issues that inform *Democracy in America*. The first of these shifts involves a remythicizing of the Indian, who as "Quinze Jours" unfolds regains some of his stature as the noble savage and begins to serve as a surrogate for values being lost to the onrushing tide of civilization. The other shift is that Tocqueville quietly manages to open up perplexing ambiguities about the meaning of progress and civilization, suggesting that these vaunted virtues destroy as much as they create, produce as much misery as happiness, and may be dehumanizing. He personifies much of this doubt about the value of the supposedly civilized life in his portrait of the grim, ferocious, relentless, angular, Bible- and axe-toting Anglo-American pioneer, in whom Tocqueville finds a powerful image of the spirit that drove westward-looking Americans through the wilderness. These two figures, the frontiersman and the Indian, grim antagonists, become the bearers of some of

Tocqueville's most disturbing insights into American civilization. They appear as full-blown creations of his imagination in "Quinze Jours au Désert" and reappear as part mythical, part historical figures in *Democracy in America*.

Tocqueville's initial encounter with the demoralized remnants of the Iroquois in upstate New York had been shocking. "I do not think," he wrote in "Quinze Jours," "I have ever suffered a more complete disappointment than the sight of those Indians. I was full of memories of M. de Chateaubriand and of Cooper, and I had expected to find in the natives of America savages in whose features nature had left the traces of some of those proud virtues that are born of liberty."[1] But instead of the noble, proud, lithe warriors he had anticipated, he found "weak and depraved beings," "small in stature," "the expression of their faces ignoble and vicious," with none of the graces he had imagined they would possess. "Their physiognomy," he wrote, "told of that profound degradation that can only be reached by a long abuse of the benefits of civilization. One would have said they were men from the lowest mob of our great European cities."[2] This comparison was becoming common in French literature in the 1830s.

Even more shocking to Tocqueville, however, was the callousness, the unfeelingness shown by the white man toward the Indian. It was a display of pitilessness and hypocrisy that, combined with Tocqueville's insight into the cold drive of the pioneer, darkened his vision of America. "In the midst of this society so well policed, so prudish, so pedantic about morality and virtue," he wrote, "one comes across a complete insensitivity, a sort of cold and implacable egotism, where the natives of America are concerned," a view that was grimly confirmed when he witnessed the brutal forced migration of the Choctaw in the bitter winter of 1831 on what would become known as the Trail of Tears.[3] With uncharacteristic sarcasm he sketched the convictions he repeatedly heard as justifications for the destruction of the Indian. "'The world here belongs to us,'" he was often told by the "honest citizens" with whom he discussed the matter: "'God, in refusing the first inhabitants the capacity to become civilized, had destined them in advance to inevitable destruction. The true owners of this continent are those who know how to take advantage of its riches.' Satisfied with this reasoning, the American goes to church, where he hears a minister of the gospel repeat to him that men are brothers and that the Eternal Being who had made them all in the same mold has imposed on them the duty to help one another."[4]

When he moved beyond his own stock responses and disappointed expectations and began to see the Indians with his own eyes, Tocqueville found much to admire: their "poetic manner"; their capacity for innocent gaiety; their independence and self-sufficiency; the honesty and directness that were a result of their "rude simplicity"; the proud ease of their power in nature. He found them far more attractive than he had initially, writing that an Indian in a serious mood had a "savage majesty" that "inspires fear" but that when the same man smiles "his whole face assumes an expression of naiveté and good will that gives it real charm." He was enormously impressed with the Indian's natural skills and powers; he possessed as much mastery in his environment as civilized people did in theirs.[5]

Above all, it was the Indian's indifference to wealth and comfort that most impressed Tocqueville, especially in contrast to the cupidity and acquisitiveness, the preoccupation with material well-being, shown by civilized man in America. The Indian he found to be "the most philosophic of all men. He has few needs and so, few desires. Civilization has no hold on him; he is unaware of or scorns its charms." "Sleeping in his cloak in the smoke of his hut," Tocqueville writes,

> the Indian looks with mistrust at the European's comfortable house; he for his part prides himself on his poverty, and his heart swells and rejoices at the thought of his barbarian independence. He smiles bitterly as he sees us plaguing our lives to get useless wealth. What we call industry he calls shameful subjection. He compares the workman to an ox laboriously tracing out a furrow. What we call the comforts of life he calls children's playthings or women's affectations. He envies us nothing but our weapons. When a man can find cover at night in a tent of leaves, when he can find enough to light a fire to keep off the mosquitoes in summer and cold in winter, when his dogs are good and the country full of game, what more can he ask from the Eternal Being?[6]

Tocqueville has hardly surrendered his disapproval of the Indian's willful primitivism, and even in his praise he remains distinctly ambivalent; but to someone who felt a good deal of contempt himself for the addiction of the middle classes to material well-being and comfort, the Indian's similar contempt as well as the real simplicity of his physical life must have seemed virtues that weighed heavily in the balance against his supposed backwardness. They suggested that the Indian's life had a dimension of spirituality and freedom that seemed to be ebbing from Western culture. Such indifference to the triumphant values of Western culture, especially to the passion for wealth and status, becomes a central attribute of the Indian as Tocqueville perfects his portrait. So too does the greater religious tolerance and peacefulness of this supposed savage. In contrast to the terrible religious contentiousness of the European that Tocqueville saw being reproduced even on the frontier, where "disputes rage about the heaven that everyone claims as his exclusive heritage," the

Indian showed himself less destructive, more joyful, more tolerant, vastly more charitable.

Tocqueville's portrait of the Indian in "Quinze Jours au Désert" was drawn largely by his moral imagination. A clue as to how far he had traveled in remythicizing the Indian after his disillusioning early encounters with the Iroquois in New York is that by the end of his wilderness journey he has apparently reversed himself and is now ready to *recommend* Chateaubriand as an accurate guide to Indian life and character: "One must read *Atala* before coming to America," he writes to Ernest Chabrol when he is back in New York City in October of 1831—a remark that suggests how strong Chateaubriand's influence remained throughout the trip.[7] If the Indian has not been exactly restored by Tocqueville to his former standing as nature's nobleman, he reasonably well resembles that old mythic figure. Tocqueville's view of the Indian, expressed with all his customary ambivalence, becomes a central item in his critique of both American and democratic civilization. As we shall see, in *Democracy in America* the Indian becomes even more thoroughly a focus of Tocqueville's moral criticism, among other things standing as a surrogate for the aristocracy and its doomed values and at the same time as a symbol for a kind of natural liberty imperiled by what he thought was its inherent tendency to disorder.

Tocqueville has partially resurrected the mythic Indian to serve as a foil to certain moral qualities of European, or Anglo-American, civilization that he saw accentuated on the frontier, especially the dark, destructive demiurge, the capacity for violence, that seemed to well from within the Anglo-American pioneer as he swept west destroying forests, animals, and Indians alike. His imagination also finds a figure to embody this destructive, acquisitive passion: the lean, cold-eyed killer of the frontier, the American frontiersman and pioneer, another memorable and central figure in Tocqueville's writing, portrayed most fully in "Quinze Jours au Désert."[8]

It was the spirit that animated a civilization that most fascinated Tocqueville; and it was in the gaunt, angular image of the pioneer that he caught a disturbing glimpse of the animus that drove American civilization westward and of the darkest and most destructive aspects of the American character, exhibited in more than the American's murderous disregard for the rights and well-being of the Indian. As moved as he was by the triumphant westward march of civilization, with all that it demonstrated about human power and creativity, he also saw the destructive consequences of that triumph. His ultimate judgment is full of foreboding, expressed in shocking images and terrible prophecies in "Quinze Jours."

Tocqueville saw the American pioneer as being driven by a cold passion: relentless, implacable, capable of making immense sacrifices, powerful in his "stoic stiffness," single-mindedness, and egoism. *Cold* is the word he uses most frequently to describe the frontier American, an attribute of mind and spirit that becomes central in his subsequent discussions of the American character. "It is the strength of his will," Tocqueville writes, "that has taken him to do work in the wilds to which he seems little adapted. But if his physical powers seem too slight for this undertaking, his features, lined by the cares of life, bespeak a practical intelligence, and a cold, persevering energy, that strike one at first sight."[9] The frontiersman-pioneer, Tocqueville's essential American, is

> cold, tenacious and relentless in argument; he attaches himself to the ground and snatches from savage life all that can be got out of it. He is in continual contest against it and daily despoils of it some of its attributes. Bit by bit he carries into the wilds his laws, his habits and his customs, and if he could, he would introduce everything down to the smallest refinements of advanced civilization. The emigrant from the United States [Tocqueville is referring to pioneers in the Michigan territory] is only interested in victory for its results; he holds glory but a vain clamor, and thinks that man has come into the world only to gain affluence and the comforts of life. He is brave nevertheless, but brave by calculation, brave because he has found out that there are several things harder to bear than death. An adventurer surrounded by his family, but one who sets little store by intellectual pleasures and the charms of social life.[10]

It is in what he symbolizes that this oddly heroic and terrifying individual gains his significance. Tocqueville sees him as "the representative of a race to whom the future of the New World belongs, a restless, calculating and adventurous race which sets coldly about deeds that can only be explained by the fire of passion, and which trades in everything, not excluding even morality and religion."[11] He is the torchbearer of a civilization the qualities of which Tocqueville for the most part finds repelling. He is bourgeois man in his most heroic guise, a figure whose virtues are limited and ultimately destructive; a calculating man who reduces everything to an object of trade, strangely narrow in his sympathies and imagination, and likely to produce a powerful but spiritually impoverished civilization. A future shaped by such a man, with his irresistible drive for wealth and power, very much troubled Tocqueville, who foresaw that it would be not only the wilderness and the Indian who would fall victim to the cold passion of such a "conqueror," but society and moral order too:

> A nation of conquerors that submits to living the life of a savage without ever letting itself be carried away by its charms, that only cherishes those parts of civilization and enlightenment which are useful for well-being, and which

shuts itself up in the solitudes of America with an axe and a newspaper; a
people who, like all great peoples, has but one thought, and presses forward
to the acquisition of riches, the single end of its labors, with a perseverance
and a scorn of life which one could call heroic if that were properly used of
anything but the strivings of virtue. It is a wandering people whom rivers and
lakes cannot hold back, before whom forests fall and prairies are covered in
shade; and who, when they have reached the Pacific Ocean, *will come back
on its tracks to trouble and destroy societies which it will have formed behind
it.*[12] [emphasis added]

Something was loose in this restless, dynamic civilization: a demiurge that
would eventually consume what it had created, restlessly unsettle the order it
had first imposed on the wilderness. Tocqueville does not again repeat precisely
this dark vision of a self-devouring civilization, but he continues to make this
restless and cold spirit, for which he has here found such memorable images,
central to his analysis of American society, which he sees doomed to a perpetual
and dehumanizing instability, a relentless, devouring destructiveness.

In the midst, then, of the American wilderness, listening to "the long fearsome war cry of civilization on the march," Tocqueville finds a more fearsome
force of destruction than the feared savage, whose war cry is by implication a
mere nothing. "So great is the force that drives the white race to the complete
conquest of the New World," he writes in "Quinze Jours," that the wilderness
and the Saginaw River (in Michigan), where he stood at that moment, would
soon be overwhelmed by the "noise of civilization and industry." It was a prospect that Tocqueville viewed with deep ambivalence. In flight himself before
that "long fearsome war cry of civilization on the march," he must in some ways
have seen himself as much a victim of the march of civilization as was nature or
the Indian. "It is this consciousness of destruction," he wrote,

> this arrière-pensée of quick and inevitable change, that gives, we feel, so
> peculiar a character and such a touching beauty to the solitudes of America.
> One sees them with a melancholy pleasure; one is in some sort of hurry to
> admire them. Thoughts of the savage, natural grandeur that is going to come
> to an end become mingled with splendid anticipations of the triumphant
> march of civilization. One feels proud to be a man, and yet at the same time
> one experiences I cannot say what bitter regret at the power that God has
> granted us over nature. One's soul is shaken by contradictory thoughts and
> feelings.[13]

"One's soul is shaken": so strong is the language of religious exaltation in
Tocqueville's writing about this wilderness experience that one feels he must

have been almost constantly in that peculiar state of intense consciousness that can find adequate expression only in religious language. His wilderness experience seems to have provided him with a chance to touch down on the deepest levels of his consciousness and to overcome that intense sense of alienation that had hitherto separated his sense of self from all that surrounded him. Hence his apparently extraordinary, exultant burst of activity in the forest, leaving the more robust Beaumont lagging behind, as it were. Doubt remains, yet he knows what he feels and who he is, and so even sorrow is expressed with a kind of serenity or even jubilation. In "Quinze Jours" his explorations of nature continue to provide metaphors for his spiritual and metaphysical journey, suggesting that the psychic soundings of the trip were profound. Once again, he evokes the Edenic theme to convey his sense of selfhood, or wholeness, regained, with its accompanying experience of equipoise and calmness. In the wilderness he escapes from history into a timeless and changeless world in which he experiences great inner harmony. He and Beaumont are canoeing alone one evening:

The sky was cloudless and the air pure and still. The river waters flowed through an immense forest, but so slowly that it would have been almost impossible to say in which direction the current was running. We had always found that to get a true idea of the forests of the New World one must follow up one of the streams that wander beneath their shade. The rivers are like main roads by means of which Providence has been at pains, since the beginning of the world, to open up the wilds and make them accessible to man. When one forces a way through the woods, one's view is generally very limited. Besides, the very path on which you walk is the work of man. But the rivers are roads that keep no mark of tracks. . . .

The wilds were there surely just the same as when our first fathers saw them six thousand years ago, a flowering solitude, delightful and scented, a magnificent dwelling, a living palace built for man, but which its master had not yet reached. The canoe glided without effort and without sound; the serenity of universal calm reigned around us. We, too, soon felt the tender influence of such sight. We talked less and less and soon found that we put our thoughts only into whispers. Finally we fell silent, and working the oars simultaneously, both of us fell into a tranquil reverie full of inexpressible charm.

Why is it that human language that finds words for every sorrow meets an invincible obstacle in trying to make the most gentle and natural emotions of the human heart understood? Who will ever paint a true picture of those rare moments in life when physical well-being prepares the way for calm of soul, and the universe seems before your eyes to have reached a perfect equilibrium; when the soul, half asleep, hovers between the present and the future, between the real and the possible, while with natural beauty all around and the air tranquil and mild, at peace with himself in the midst of universal peace, man listens to the even beating of his arteries that seems to him to mark the passage of time flowing drop by drop through eternity. Many men perhaps have seen long years of existence pile up without once experiencing anything like what we have just described. . . .

We were woken from our reverie by a gun-shot that suddenly echoed through the woods. The sound at first seemed to roll crashing along both banks of the river; then it rumbled into the distance until it was entirely lost in the depths of the forest. It might have been the long, fearsome war cry of civilization on the march.[14]

It was on these spontaneous trips, during which Tocqueville gave freest rein to his feelings and imagination, that he found himself more fully engaged with the meaning of his American experience than at any other time during his voyage. It was then that the meanings of his personal voyage of self-exploration and of his external journey were imaginatively fused. These purportedly exotic trips and the writings they inspired, so full of subjective musings and literary play—so full also of Chateaubriand—while apparently peripheral to the main objectives of Tocqueville's American travels, are in fact central to his experience and contain clues to the various levels of meaning as well as to the structure of feeling of *Democracy in America*. It was in the American forests that Tocqueville most fully explored his feelings about the meaning and prospects of the new democratic civilization he was witnessing; and it was in the wilderness that he developed some of his deepest insights into the spirit of American civilization. These insights continued to guide his imagination as he wrote about America and democracy, even when he was in a far more sociological than literary or poetic mode of mind.

Apart from his notebooks and letters, "Quinze Jours au Désert" is Tocqueville's first effort to give formal, literary shape to his American experience and to explore its meaning. Along with *Voyage au Lac Onéida* it contains, to use one of Tocqueville's most frequently used working phrases, the "point of origin" of much that appears in *Democracy in America* and is a useful guide to the full meaning of that work as well as to the fantasy work that prepared the way for it and the imaginative processes that produced it. Toward the end of "Quinze Jours," Tocqueville reflects on an earlier journey, this time not to the American frontier and the future but to the ruins of Sicily and the past:

One evening in Sicily we happened to get lost in a vast marsh that now occupies the place where once was the city of Himera; the sight of that once famous city turned back to savage wilds made a great and deep impression on us. Never have we seen beneath our feet more magnificent witness to the instability of human things and the wretchedness of our nature. Here too it was indeed a solitude, but imagination, instead of going backwards to try and get back into the past, went rushing on ahead and got lost in an immense future. It struck us as a peculiar privilege of fate that we who had been able to look on the ruins of perished empires and walk through wilds of human making, that we, children of an ancient people, should be brought to witness one of the scenes of the primitive world and to see the *still empty cradle of a great nation*.[15] [emphasis added]

It was with a vision of the Mississippi Valley as yet another "empty cradle of a great nation" that he would begin *Democracy in America*.

7

Beginning *Democracy in America*

Tocqueville returned to France uncertain about what he would write about America. For a while he and Beaumont had thought of writing a book together, but that idea was soon abandoned. He brooded about his book for two years, then wrote it (the first volume) in a terrific burst of energy and in high spirits in a year, finishing it late in 1834. The second volume took much longer, for many reasons, primarily because it was a work of far greater complexity and drew much more on his inner resources, what he called his "fantasie." The second volume traversed "un autre terrain," as he put it. This inwardness is reflected in the different qualities of the volume.

The idea for *Democracy in America* (henceforth I refer to the two volumes as *DA I* and *DA II*) took shape slowly in Tocqueville's mind, and the book itself developed even more slowly as he wrote it. From a certain point of view one can say that it was only when he was revising *DA II*, in 1839, that he finally understood the full scope and all the objectives of his work. So his correspondence makes clear. The creation of *Democracy in America* involved another long exploration not only of democratic culture and politics in America but also of the inner terrain of his psyche. Here, an account of his experience of the writing of what he hoped would be an original book and of his shifting ideas about how to construct it clarifies the range of its meanings and the sources of inspiration and imagination on which it drew.

The structure of the work itself warrants attention. Precisely when Tocqueville understood, or felt, that the book on America he had published in 1835 was incomplete and required a sequel is not clear. What is clear is that the experience of writing the second volume was almost wholly different from that of the first; that the scope and level of its cultural analysis are quite different; and that the book covers "un autre terrain," as Tocqueville put it.[1] That "autre terrain" was inner ground as well as unexplored intellectual territory. If there were two voyages to America—the official, or external, expedition to inspect democratic institutions and the democratic "social state" and the personal journey of self-exploration of which Tocqueville's wilderness trips were the most dramatic but not the only occasions—there were also two *Democracy in Americas*, the second much more an inner voyage in which Tocqueville draws his insights from much deeper within and in which his sociological commentary is colored more by his values, his self-imagination, and his feeling for the tragedy and ironies of history. Certainly the whole work is shaped by his sense of personal and historical catastrophe, which suffuses the introduction and the first chapter of *DA I*. There must have been very few moments or experiences throughout his American journey that were not personally resonant for him, so that in fact the two journeys to America were not intermittent but occurred simultaneously. But *DA II* is so decidedly different a book and so much more inward looking than its predecessor that its special character must become a key to its interpretation and meaning. One might say even that the writing of the second volume took him on yet another journey to America.

Tocqueville sailed from Le Havre with vague plans for writing a book on America jointly with Beaumont, in addition to whatever report would fulfill the responsibilities of their contrived official mission. His correspondence and Beaumont's as well make it clear that the idea of a collaborative work on American civilization, of comprehensive scope perhaps in the style and spirit of Guizot, had possessed them both perhaps even as early as the July Revolution itself, well on into the summer of 1831. Whatever their reasons, they both seemed persuaded even before arriving in the United States that the truth about America had not yet been caught despite the flood of writing about the New Republic that had already appeared in France, and that they would capture that truth, a double presumptuousness since they scarcely knew the literature and hadn't the vaguest idea at first of how to go about the job of finding the truth about this colossal new country. Beaumont wrote to his father, "All the time we are examining the penitentiary system we will be observing America; while visiting its prisons we will meet its people, visit its towns, its institutions, its 'republicans.' . . . how the government works is not at all known in Europe: we talk about it constantly and make false comparisons with nations which in no way resemble it; wouldn't it be a useful book that gave an exact idea of the American people, drew a large view of its history, the main traits of their character, analyzed their social state, and corrected all incorrect opinions on these matters?"[2] This surely was an agenda that would have daunted anyone who knew what he was doing and had a clear sense of the magnitude of the reality that lay ahead. Tocqueville is no less immodest. To Stoffels he writes that he and Beaumont were going to America not just to see "great cities and beautiful rivers": "We leave with the intention of examining in detail and as scientifically as possible all the resources of this vast American society about which everyone talks and *which no one knows*. And if events leave us the time we intend to return with the makings of a good book or at least of an original work because nothing yet exists on all this."[3] [emphasis added]

But by the fall of 1831, after the wilderness expeditions of July and August, the idea of a collaborative work seems to have vanished, and both now write of work they are planning independently. Their original intentions no doubt gave way for many reasons, among them the difficulty, as André Jardin suggests, of harmonizing partially diverging preoccupations as well as differences in intellectual style and temperament in a collective enterprise. But it also seems likely that the wilderness experience had something to do with the shift in intention: Tocqueville came out of the forest, as it were, with his way of looking at his American experience more fully fused with his personal imagination. He had connected America with his own vision, had placed his self at the center of the landscape he was describing, and henceforth found it more difficult to see America from any other point of view, though he certainly continued to share much ground with Beaumont, who may have experienced a similar intensifying of the personal imagination. That Tocqueville had started to look within for clues to the meaning of his American experience and observations is suggested in his letters to France after the summer of 1831. In October he writes to his mother as follows:

> I will leave America ready to understand the documents I have not yet been able to study. That is the clearest result of this journey. Beyond that, I have concerning this society only notes without order or development, full of various unrelated ideas to which only I have the key, isolated facts which bring back to me a crowd of others. Most valuable are the two small notebooks in which I wrote down verbatim the conversations I had with the most remarkable men of the country. These scraps of paper are of incalculable value to me, but only to me. The only somewhat generalized ideas I've expressed up to now I've sent to my family and to others in France. Will I ever write anything about this society? Truly, I don't know; it seems to me I have some good ideas but I do not yet know what form to give them, and the thought of making them public worries me.[4]

Beaumont has by now disappeared from his plans to write about America: the "we" has become "I."

At the very end of his journey he writes to his father from Washington:

> At the moment I am turning over many ideas about America. Several are still in my head; a great many are jotted down briefly on paper without any order,

or are opened up in the conversations written down at night after I returned home. During the last six weeks of this journey I have dreamed a great deal about what one might write about America. To attempt a complete view of the Union would be an absolutely impracticable undertaking for a person who has spent only a year in this immense country. I believe, moreover, that such a work would be as annoying as instructive. One might, however, present only those subjects that are more or less relevant to our social and political situation. Such a work would have both an enduring value and a contemporary relevance. Such is the broad frame; but will I ever have the time, and will I ever find the inner resources, needed to fulfill it? That's the question. There is, moreover, a consideration that is always in mind; I will write nothing unless I write what I believe to be true, and it is not always good to speak all the truth.[5]

Thus by the end of his visit he has only a very general conception of what his book will be. Its interpretive line will be shaped by the direct relevance of America to "our social and political situation," just as the meaning of America for him has increasingly been shaped by the way in which it has illuminated his identity issues—and he also has a much keener awareness that its execution will depend wholly on his judgment and strength. His last enigmatic remark, "I will write nothing unless I write what I believe to be true, and it is not always good to speak all the truth," intimates that he understood not only that this book would call for great tact, but also that the eternal problem of objectivity had been greatly complicated by his now-profound personal engagement with his subject.

DA I was written largely in Paris, in an intense burst of labor following a year or more of random and desultory activity. On November 1, 1833, shortly after his return from a trip to England, Tocqueville wrote Beaumont that he was in the midst of his "monomanie Américaine": "On arriving here I threw myself on America with a kind of fury. The seizure yet persists although occasionally it seems to let up. I believe that my writing is the better for it, though my health suffers a bit from the extreme turmoil of the spirit because I scarcely think of anything else. My ideas have expanded and become generalized. Is that good or is that bad? I await you to find out."[6] By July of 1834, manuscript in hand, he was negotiating with Gosselin for its publication, and by January of 1835 *DA I* was in the bookstores. The speed with which he wrote it is remarkable.

Tocqueville wrote *DA I* in circumstances, and in a state of mind and spirit, far different from those in which he composed *DA II*. If he suffered from the anguish of uncertainty about the fate of his book or from doubt about his ability to give shape to his ideas, he left no record of it, as he did so fully during the long haul of writing *DA II*. Probably the intensity with which he worked gave him little time for the morbidity he occasionally fell into while working on the second volume. It was an unusually bright and active year for Tocqueville, a period during which he found little time or incentive to dive deep within himself. The little that he said about his psyche suggests that the year he spent working on *DA I* may well have been, as he later claimed, the happiest of his life. The few letters he wrote are ebullient; his writing, he said to Beaumont, "moves my heart more than the law does." Moreover, though he had to have spent much time in a fury of writing, he was not nearly as isolated socially as he later was while writing *DA II*. Society, family, and friends—and Marie—were close at hand. He continued to attend various literary salons; maintained a study in his father's house in the Faubourg Saint-Germain, where for a number of months he kept a young American research assistant busy making summaries of federal and state statute books; immersed himself in a mountain of literature borrowed from the royal library, the American legation, and the American friends he met in Paris; consulted often with the young Theodore Sedgwick, who had been recommended to him by the American legation and whom, as it turned out, he had already met in Stockbridge, Massachusetts, when he stopped there in 1831 hoping to interview Sedgwick's sister Catharine Maria Sedgwick, the only American writer he made an effort to meet. Most important, he spent much time with Beaumont, to whom he submitted his work and who served as his chief critic, "mon juge," he said. The consultations were in fact mutual, Tocqueville simultaneously advising Beaumont on his work-in-progress *Marie*, a novel about slavery and race. Beaumont later happily recalled the time as one in which, "harnessed [as we were] to the same way of life, not a day passed without our seeing one another and submitting our work to one another."[7] Even the institutional focus of Tocqueville's writing, the copiousness of his data, the much greater clarity of the issues he was tackling in *DA I*, and his explicit intention of writing scientific history and not mythology kept him closer to the surface of his subject. He had little time for the intense, often melancholy self-scrutiny that usually accompanied all he did and little need to mine his psyche, to consult his "fantasie," for his material, as he often did when writing the second volume. Still, as the passionate introduction and dreamlike first chapter and much else of *DA I* make clear, even in such circumstances his work was strongly shaped by his self-imagination and by his mythicizing impulses. *DA I* turned out to be, in part, a moral fable.

The task of writing *DA II*, intrinsically more difficult, was complicated by various changes and disruptions in his life: his marriage to Mottley in 1835, an event that caused much family conflict and much strain for Tocqueville; the death of his mother in January of the following year; his acquisition in 1836 of the ancient family seat of Tocqueville, near Cherbourg, on the Cotentin in Normandy (the chateau, a wreck, abandoned since the revolution, required a great deal of restoration); travel for Marie's health; his own occasionally wavering health; his campaigns for a seat in the Chamber of Deputies in 1837 and in 1839. Until he settled down at Tocqueville in the later months of 1837 he was virtually without a permanent home.

With the end of his physical uprootedness came much greater isolation. Reaching inward for his ideas and inspiration and increasingly in need of the solitude and repose he required to engage in the arduous thinking his writing required, he turned his back on the turbulent and seductive city. *DA I* was begun in the heart of Paris, but it was finished in the silence of the Norman countryside.

Some of the volume that appeared in 1840 was written at Baugy, Edouard's estate near Compiègne, to the northeast of Paris. There, in a small study high in the house and overlooking the countryside in all directions, he found the quiet calm he needed. "It is here in this place elevated above all the miseries of the world that I retire to work," he wrote to Reeve.[8] If life there was not inspiring, it was agreeably tranquil. Baugy itself was unprepossessing. Describing it to Mill, he wrote, "You will not find one of your grand English estates but a quite comfortable small house nestled in the midst of a pretty park."[9] He continued to work there occasionally even after he had begun to make his own estate in Normandy habitable, in part because local politics threatened to absorb too much of his time at Tocqueville, in part because the various stimulations and stresses of Paris were becoming too distracting and unsettling. "I have torn myself away from the charms of Paris and of the whole political and literary world fermenting there," he wrote to Nassau Senior from Baugy in February of 1838, "in order to shut myself up with my books, pens, and paper in the midst of forests almost as dense as those of the New World and much less poetical."[10] Now and then he would visit Paris to obtain books, but he made such trips brief. His life at Baugy, as he described it, was "busy, monotonous but very agreeable." He was charmed by the placidity and order of his brother's household, precisely the environment he needed for his work: "It is charming to see the happiness that is the fruit of honesty and order. Everywhere in this house there is an air of reason and of morality that bit by bit penetrates you. Everything is comfortable, nothing is luxurious. Everything comes easily as if from within oneself without one ever perceiving the hand of the master. All around one sees contentment and benevolent glances and gestures of goodwill. In sum, all is well, so that a two-footed creature without feathers ought to be contented with it."[11]

Increasingly, however, he worked at Tocqueville as the dilapidated chateau was rehabilitated to suit his needs and as his attachment to the Norman countryside and to the Norman people deepened. He had once responded with a Parisian intellectual's shudder at the idea that he try country life: "I know very well that it would be easier for me to leave for China, to join the military, or to gamble my life on some hazardous and poorly conceived undertaking than it would be to condemn myself to the life of a potato."[12] But though it was only late in his life that he became fully adjusted to rural life, the tranquility it offered now began to captivate him. "I live here," he wrote Royer-Collard in 1837, "in a quite old, ugly, and uncomfortable chateau, but one in which, however, I am beginning to feel well and where I feel happier than I have been for a long time. An interior which pleases me; long roads mixed with grand promenades in the midst of fields in open country, these are the conditions of happiness; add to that few neighbors, much tranquility of spirit—at least as much of it as it is possible for me to bear—and you will understand that for the moment I have nothing more to ask of God."[13] There, in the round tower of his granite chateau, in the midst of an estate of six hundred acres, near the tenant-occupied granite *berceau* that he would point out to visitors as the first home of his family (he called it a hut), he finished writing *Democracy in America*.

Tocqueville had retreated to the countryside for many reasons. Apart from whatever domestic needs the move satisfied, it also provided him with a base for his political ambitions. To reoccupy the old family seat full of the ghosts of his heroic ancestors was also certainly an identity-confirming gesture. There was even something ideological about his withdrawal to the country: the move was also motivated by his growing moral uneasiness with the distorting hyperintellectuality of life in Paris. He felt that the overwrought, competitive intellectual life of Paris was out of touch with the true France, that it was increasingly abstract, artificial, and corrupting. The great distrust of intellectuals that shows up in his writings of the 1850s finds an early manifestation in his deliberate rejection of the Paris literary world. In his notes for a contemplated review of Henry Bulwer's four-volume *La France Sociale, Politique et Littéraire*, published in Paris in 1834–36, Tocqueville attributes Bulwer's many errors to the fact that the Englishman had spent nearly all his time in Paris, that heady entrepôt of wild ideas and prancing egos. The view from Paris was bound to be misleading: "There exists in the heart of Paris a floating mass of writers more or less disorganized in their habits, of females who write or are of compromised reputations, of artists of all sorts, of journalists, of odd enterprising characters who are drawn from all the corners of France by ambition or pleasure, a colorful multitude that exaggerates all the qualities and faults of the national character, but who represent perfectly only themselves. This society not only fails to give an exact picture of France, it doesn't even offer a true picture of Paris."[14] Just as he felt that the view from the American heartland revealed the real America, so Tocqueville seemed to think that one would be closer to the soul of France in some quiet rural sanctuary away from the city of lights that did not illuminate. The "floating mass in the heart of Paris" that in Tocqueville's view had misled Bulwer sounds much like the then-flourishing Parisian Bohemia that in all his writing about France and in his letters as well he managed to ignore. His own "picture of France," a France that was always in some ways "not me," did not have room for the effervescent, complex world of the great new Bohemia, part of which reveled in disreputability and scorned the bourgeoisie as much as he did, part of which ambitiously sought success and aspired to join the middle class when it left off the mime of mockery. Baudelaire slunk aimlessly through the streets of Paris, but he had also dreamed of becoming one of the immortals of the Académie française. (It is tantalizing to think how Tocqueville would have voted had Baudelaire ever become a candidate for immortality.)[15]

If Tocqueville's retreat was in part a reaction against the intellectual and moral noise of Paris, it was also a way of avoiding the emotional exhaustion that the intensity of his encounters with the highly charged intellectual life of that city usually led to—for here too his ambivalence would do its work, and he continually returned to the world of the salon. He would often return from his social forays agitated and disoriented. "Although pen in hand I often play the philosophe," he wrote Royer-Collard from Baugy, "unhappily I am far from viewing the affairs of the world philosophically. Deep within I feel a very great irritability, and I rarely enter into contact with my fellow human beings without experiencing a kind of general distress and profound anxiety. In Paris, when I return to my study, it is always a long while before I am able to eradicate as best I can the too vivid impressions of the evening, and I spend some of my day getting myself ready to work on the rest."[16] What does this confession reveal? More, perhaps, than Tocqueville intended. He returns from his social encounters shattered and profoundly troubled and needs a good deal of time to reassemble himself. By "semblables," whom could he actually have meant but those he in fact spent time with, the Parisian intelligentsia and the social elite that courted it? In this world his sense of identity is jeopardized. A more self-assured personality, one with a calm sense of self, would not have reacted to the stress and contrariety of social discourse with such intense anxiety. Tocqueville attributes his distress to an "irritability" of spirit, but that is simply a comment on symptoms, not causes. What his remark suggests is that he suffered so keenly from

doubt and uncertainty as well as from that same "besoin de primer" he had
written about to Kergorlay that he had to buffer himself against situations in
which these were likely to be intensified. His strategy for protecting himself
against the disequilibrium—the sense of self-disintegration—that intellectual
debate and social discourse seemed to produce in him was to withdraw into a
kind of intellectual isolation. When Royer-Collard once complimented him for
seeming so tranquil despite the turmoil of the time, he replied that for him
such tranquility, far from being an intrinsic trait of character, required a real
sequestration of the spirit:

> I have never been able to achieve that [tranquility] except by exercising a kind
> of physical violence on myself which for a while isolates my spirit from that of
> my fellows. That is my whole secret. I sequester myself; I lock myself up so that
> not the slightest breath from outside reaches me; I do not speak at all about
> what is happening in the world, and I succeed, I am embarrassed to say, in no
> longer thinking about it at all. Thus secluded, I easily imagine that I am the
> last of my species and that there is no longer any point in speaking about a
> human race that had once existed. I then feel inhibited by nothing, and I can
> then think freely and calmly. This condition is so much the fruit of my solitude
> and comes not from within myself that as soon as I find myself in the midst of
> the babbling crowd I again become completely agitated, irritated, troubled,
> and undone by thousands of contradictory emotions.[17]

There is certainly nothing unusual about a writer's need for solitude, in
which the imagination can unfold freely and follow its true course ("I then feel
inhibited by nothing, and I can then think freely and calmly"), but in Tocqueville
this need seems to have been extreme. Such deliberate and extreme sequestration was simply a deepening of that tendency to detachment and introversion,
of that fierce resistance to external influence, that made Tocqueville seem to an
observer like Charles de Rémusat to be living very much in a world of his own
even in the midst of so noisy a public marketplace as the Chamber of Deputies.
As noted before, Rémusat, who knew Tocqueville well, observed, "Almost nothing took root in his mind that he had not sewn himself; he thought a great deal,
read little, and scarcely knew what we had written or what we had accomplished."[18] This is the image of a self-contained, self-generative man, with a
glassy impermeability to external influence; a man not likely to be informed by
any ideas or illuminated by any experience not his own. When Tocqueville
writes about the terrible inwardness and alienation of individualism, the loss of
connection and the deep sense of isolation it entails, his own experience must
have been central to his insight.

Wherever he was, Tocqueville preserved a certain remoteness and distance, as if immediate influences might disorient him, compromise his ideas, or destroy the perspective he was seeking. He could scarcely bear to hear opinions about matters he was thinking through himself, so jealous was he of his independence of view and so fearful of losing it. While writing *Democracy in America* he refused to read anything his contemporaries had to say about America, sealing himself up with his own ideas. When Michel Chevalier's *Lettres sur l'Amérique du Nord* appeared in 1836, a book of considerable importance, Tocqueville would not read it but instead asked Beaumont to tell him about it: "I do not at all wish to read Chevalier's book; you know for me it's a matter of principle. Have you glanced at it, and if so, what do you think of it? What is its quality, and what is its aim? Finally, what impression has it made in the world, and in what way might it weigh against the philosophical-political work I am preparing?"[19] His refusal to read Chevalier's book may, however, have been more than a matter of "principle": Chevalier had once been a follower of Saint-Simon, whose utopianism Tocqueville scorned. In fact, Beaumont, one may guess with Tocqueville's backing, sought to block Chevalier's election to the Académie des sciences morales et politiques for that reason. Tocqueville may well have been indulging in some anticipatory personal and political censorship.

8

INFLUENCES: VOICES IN THE TOWER

Though Tocqueville strove to isolate himself from the stresses and urban cleverness that shook his confidence and from blows to his unstable psyche, he relied nevertheless on a circle of intimate friends for encouragement, criticism, and help with the tangled intellectual problems he kept encountering. Through this time he also shared ideas with Royer-Collard and Mill, the two major liberal philosophers of his time. Their presence is strongly felt in *Democracy in America*. Tocqueville's correspondence with Mill was especially important to him, as it was to Mill as well, though in many ways they were quite different. They unquestionably influenced one another: their ideas were nourished by their intense, if brief, correspondence.

As Tocqueville slipped deeper into deliberate self-isolation and into the world of his imagination, he continued to rely more than ever on a small group of intimate friends for information, criticism, and encouragement and for the kind of dialogue he needed to clarify his ideas. He carried them with him, as it were, into his intellectual solitude. They served as intermediaries between Tocqueville and the world. Of all those he depended on for stimulation and mediation, Beaumont, Kergorlay, and Ampère were especially important. He also listened to and debated with the more distant voices of Mill and Royer-Collard. They too played a part in the shaping of *DA II*.

What is striking about his trio of friends is its diversity. If each was a kind of alter ego for Tocqueville, fitting with one or another facet of his complicated personality, each of them was also a link with a different sector of the world of opinion and politics. Each possessed qualities that differed greatly from those of the other two but with all of which something in Tocqueville was resonant; each was the world, or part of it, transformed, miniaturized, made safe.

It was to Beaumont, with whom he had so long shared ideas, dreams, and experiences, that Tocqueville turned most often. Despite their differences in temperament and in personal style, their minor disagreements about political strategy, and a few rare flarings of personal rivalry, as well as Tocqueville's occasional dismay at Beaumont's slightly more flexible, pragmatic political liberalism, they had remained close. While the two men were living in Paris in 1834 they had met frequently (daily, according to Beaumont) to read their works-in-progress. Beaumont, as I mentioned above, was writing *Marie*. Their collaboration continued, though less intensely, while Tocqueville was writing *DA II* in his various rural retreats and Beaumont was doing research for and then writing a book on Ireland. Tocqueville relied so heavily on Beaumont's judgment and advice that he could write, "If we continue with the life we are leading I will end up by asking your advice on how to sign my name." While at Baugy or at Tocqueville, he would lament Beaumont's absence: though content with the solitude in which he had immersed himself, he needed someone with whom to share and to sharpen his ideas. "I lack only a good sounding-board for conversation," he wrote Beaumont. "I need you or Louis," he wrote from his tree-high study at Baugy. "I've been working since I've been here," he complained from Normandy, "but I work slowly and poorly. It's you that I need. Come then, and stay." To Tocqueville, Beaumont was "my invaluable Aristarque," comparing him jestingly to the ancient Greek editor of Aristotle: "I hope soon to submit to your severest challenges," he would write. Beaumont would be the judge of his work "above all others."[1]

Tocqueville's continued reliance on Beaumont is not difficult to understand. It was not simply a matter of the deep amity that had grown through shared experience. They tended to see things the same way and shared the same convictions about history, politics, and society. The extensive notes on American values and character Beaumont appended to *Marie* might well have been written by Tocqueville himself. One wonders if some of their shared ideas had first been formulated by Beaumont, who in some ways had a more rounded and better-informed mind.

In 1835, while on his journey through England and Ireland with Tocqueville, Beaumont offered in a conversation with Mill his views about the cultural effects of democracy, saying that this aspect of it raised "une ombre dans mon esprit." Democracy was good for the material well-being of the people, but he thought its intellectual consequences were likely to be destructive: "I think that the tendency of democracy may well be anti-intellectual." He thought democratic culture would sink toward mediocrity, that it would be inimical to literature, to the "high sciences," to speculative studies, to intellectual ambition. Mill had then commented, "I think that the tendency of democracy is exactly the opposite of the fear that you express."[2] When Mill reviewed *Marie*, in 1836, he noted that even though Beaumont was a "warm friend to the American

Government, and to popular institutions generally," his picture of life in the United States was bleak: he had "read no book which has represented American social life in such *sombre* colours, or which is more calculated to deter persons of highly cultivated faculties and lofty aspirations, from making that country their abode." Mill had concluded his review by suggesting that, except for the abomination of the "dark spot" of the deplorable race prejudice of the Americans, Beaumont's unfavorable picture of American life ought to be taken with a grain of salt as the culture-biased view of a Frenchman likely to take an unfavorable view of any other culture. Mill then astonishingly added that the same might be said of "a work of a far higher order of philosophy than M. de Beaumont's, the *Democracy in America* of M. de Tocqueville," which "will be apt, if read without this necessary caution, to convey a conception of America in many respects very wide of the truth."[3] It is not that Mill at this moment still held to his belief in the promise of democratic culture, which he did, but rather that Beaumont had already offered an even sharper critique of American culture than Tocqueville had yet formulated.

Beaumont understood Tocqueville's ideas and intellectual ambitions as well as Tocqueville did himself. Ampère with good reason said to Tocqueville that Beaumont was "un autre vous." Tocqueville highly prized his friend's qualities despite their differences in temperament and intellectual style—Beaumont was more sanguine, not as complex, more optimistic, hardly as moody—a kind of Horatio to Tocqueville's Hamlet (though in the fifties Tocqueville occasionally struggled to coax Beaumont out of a depression brought on by a sense of failure and uselessness, a sense he himself felt). Beaumont seemed to him to represent the contemporary man of common sense and good practical judgment, a person whose opinion he wished to shape and whose approval he wished to court. "You are for me not simply a good judge," he said, "but also the public personified. The spontaneity of your responses and the ardent way in which you give yourself wholeheartedly to the ideas and passions of our time, which you always bring to bear on whatever work one submits to you, make you, my dear friend, the most valuable of critics for me."[4]

He also continued to think of Beaumont as a kind of collaborator whose work both paralleled and completed his own: as the cocreator of a historical and political point of view. They had both started their joint intellectual life as Guizot's disciples, attending his lectures, reading his histories, discussing the principles of his historical vision in an intimate two-man study group. They had shared notes. From the start of their friendship, while young lawyers at Versailles, Tocqueville had thought of Beaumont as his "cher futur collaborateur," "bound together for life." He had hoped Beaumont's work would parallel and complement his and thus form a unity, and he had wanted to coordinate the publication of *DA II* with that of Beaumont's *l'Irlande*. He was as anxious to review and criticize Beaumont's manuscript as he was to have Beaumont advise him on his own. When, late in 1838, Beaumont seemed close to finishing his work while Tocqueville was still laboring to revise his, he wrote in some agitation, "I can't accept the idea that you will publish without our having been able to coordinate our work. Not that I believe I must advise you about details, but because it's important that we keep one another informed about our major ideas so that we are sure to appear before the public as in accord about what we say as we are in our hearts."[5] The image of presenting themselves to the world together united in word and heart suggests a powerful sense of intimacy.

Perhaps as important to Tocqueville, though in a different way, was Kergorlay. Tocqueville thought Kergorlay was the most intellectually gifted of his friends, in fact, of his generation, and it was a source of dismay and anguish to him that Kergorlay, an archlegitimist deeply opposed to bourgeois rule and to the values of the new order, had retreated to a wholly private existence in which he sullenly refused to put his great talents to use in any public service, even by writing. (Well after Tocqueville's death in 1859 he finally did enter political life, becoming first a deputy in the Chamber and eventually a life-senator.) "Not one of us," Tocqueville said, "has the intelligence and cultivation of Kergorlay. If he had come forward he would have been the first in the very first rank."[6] It was not ideological compatibility that drew the two together but the deep loyalty of an old friendship and common philosophical interests and pleasures. No other correspondence of Tocqueville's is as full of discussions of ideas, books, and religious and philosophical issues. Tocqueville's liberalism, moderate though it was, had little in common with Kergorlay's intransigent legitimism, though Tocqueville's view that the central problem of the time was the moral emptiness of political life was wholly shared by Kergorlay. Kergorlay's quick mind helped Tocqueville through many an impasse; even though he had little sympathy for his friend's practical politics, he could strike to the heart of issues and pose questions with a lucidity that freed Tocqueville time and again from the knots into which he had tied himself. There is a steadier and more probing exchange of ideas in their correspondence than in any other that Tocqueville kept up. Kergorlay was a country nobleman who was also an intellectual, widely read. From Baugy, while composing the early chapters of *DA II*, Tocqueville wrote to Kergorlay,

> There is so to speak hardly a day that I do not feel I need you. A multitude of imperfectly grasped thoughts sit in my mind because it is impossible for me to throw them into conversation with you and see how you react to them and

argue with them, or what new turn you give them in accepting them. There are three individuals who are with me a little everyday—Pascal, Montesquieu, and Rousseau; I need a fourth, and it is you. Although we often differ, on some matters seriously, there is in our general way of seeing and interpreting human affairs such great similarity that your conversation begins to awaken and animate me.[7]

Kergorlay spent much time with Tocqueville at Baugy and in Normandy. From Baugy Tocqueville wrote Beaumont, "Louis has just spent four days here. I was at that moment tangled in a web of ideas from which I was unable to extricate myself. It was a real intellectual cul-de-sac out of which he led me in a few hours."[8]

And from Tocqueville in December of 1838 he wrote in anguish to Beaumont that

> Louis, who has stayed with us almost all the fall, leaves tomorrow in order to harvest his wood. He has been very useful to me in my work. In return for this service I would have liked to get him going, but it would have been a waste of effort, and I begin to fear he will never get started. At this moment he is not deeply interested in any idea, and he reads and writes only to kill time. It is a painful sight to see someone with so many outstanding qualities condemned perhaps forever to miserable uselessness by petty weaknesses and small eccentricities. The sight of this touches me, chagrins me, makes me impatient and finally becomes so painful that despite all my fondness for him and the immense resource he is for us, I am not as distressed as I could be that he has left us. It is cruel to see this complete, willing self-annihilation of so strong and promising a being.[9]

It is difficult to doubt that Tocqueville's dismay and anger over the gifted Kergorlay's self-annihilation reflected his own anxiety about being useless. In view of his own struggle to create his identity and his refusal to accept the life of a nonentity, his brilliant aristocratic friend's deliberate self-immolation represented a threatening alternative to the path he had chosen despite his personal inclinations (Tocqueville was simply a more moderate and realistic legitimist than his friend and otherwise shared the same dark view of contemporary French culture). But so intransigent was Kergorlay all through the years of the July Monarchy that he could not accept, perhaps could not understand, Tocqueville's costly gamble or even his "beau rêve," and in the late forties and fifties, to Tocqueville's anguish, they somewhat drifted apart.

Kergorlay played an invaluable role in clarifying and shaping *Democracy in America* even though he was unproductive himself and self-destructive in his petulant retreat from a world in which he felt out of place. Whether his bitterness contributed to the darkening view about democracy that occurs in the latter chapters of *DA II* is not possible to say, though it seems unlikely. What the sad spectacle of the spiritual suicide of a brilliant aristocrat meant to Tocqueville as he struggled himself to come to terms with and to understand the historical and social forces that had so stunned his friend is also not clear; but Kergorlay's presence and active assistance during much of the writing of *DA II* may well have colored Tocqueville's mood as he shaped his comparison of aristocratic and democratic cultures and added to his feeling for what was being lost in the great transformation he was writing about. Kergorlay's detailed, honest, unsparing critiques of Tocqueville's writing (see below) were immensely helpful.

A third critic on whom Tocqueville depended was Ampère, the linguist, philologist, folklorist and mythologist, Egyptologist, student of Roman history and archaeology, student as well of medieval French literature who also wrote poetry, novels, and plays—a Renaissance man whose quickness of mind, gaiety, and ardent liberalism deeply attracted Tocqueville. Ampère was an alert, stimulating companion and a man of catholic tastes and interests, a joyful, passionate, mercurial alter ego. He was a familiar figure in the world of the Parisian literary salon, notably that of Mme Récamier, to whom he was devoted, and also in French academic circles. He lectured on French literature at the Collège de France and in 1847 was elected to the Académie française. His circle of friendships was broad enough to include individuals as diverse as the dandy Prosper Mérimée and the intellectually conservative Tocqueville, and his learning was cosmopolitan: he had studied with Friedrich Schlegel and Georg Niebuhr, and had so impressed Goethe with an essay he had written about the German poet that he had been invited to spend three weeks with him. If Tocqueville scornfully hovered high above the new Parisian Bohemia, that "floating mass" of writers, artists, female writers, and odd characters that he dismissed with contempt as unrepresentative of France, Ampère unquestionably knew those streets and kept him in touch with much of contemporary French intellectual life, even with its underground movements. But he had no lasting accomplishments. He was perhaps too amiably social and interested in too much. Henry James wrote that while Ampère was "an eminently appreciative and sociable mind . . . an accomplished scholar and a very clever man . . . [he was also] a striking illustration of the common axiom that between two stools one falls on the ground."[10] James's rueful judgment was that Ampère "travelled so much, moved so much in the world, formed so many personal and social ties, had such a genius for conversation and society and for friendship, that you wonder how he found time to open a book or mind his pen. . . . The verdict has been that Jean-Jacques . . . lacked exactness as a savant."[11] Whatever the justness of James's comments, it was the qualities he attributes to Ampère that made him so valuable as well as so attractive a friend for the less socially mobile Tocqueville and so astute and generous a critic.

They had met in the mid-1830s at Mme Récamier's salon and were quickly drawn to each other. Charles Sainte-Beuve, who knew them both well, called their friendship "une amitié passionnée." It was a passionate friendship that never weakened, even when Tocqueville in fury scolded Ampère for the enthusiasm with which he had at first greeted the Revolution of 1848. Their intimacy soon deepened to the point that Tocqueville even reconstructed one of the towers of his Norman chateau to suit the needs of his friend, who came often for days of writing and nights of reading. Ampère first heard Tocqueville read from the manuscript of *DA II* in May 1838. He was quick to perceive the profundity and originality of what he heard and saw that Tocqueville had advanced far beyond the first volume in the scope and depth of his work. His perceptive notes about the occasion express his enthusiasm and reveal something of the various sensitivities and the quick understanding he could bring to bear as a critic of his friend's work:

> May 15, 1838
> Lunch at Tocqueville's with [Claude-François Tircuy de] Corcelle. Before lunch T. read to us a chapter of his work. I was deeply pleased. The subject is this: on revolutions in democratic societies [undoubtedly chapter XXI, book III, vol. II, "Why Great Revolutions Will Become More Rare"]. The conclusion: revolutions in such are not to be as much feared as formerly. Revolutions in opinion more difficult, perhaps too difficult. All this is developed with great sagacity and profundity. It is full of originality and good sense, there is soul in it. The style has completely changed. It is now more spacious and steadier than in the first part, a bit too curt, in the style of Montesquieu. It has the solemn and drawn out unfolding of Rousseau along with some of the light touches of contemporary style. If there is a fault in it, especially for a casual reader, it is that it's a bit heavy. The whole book deals profoundly with change. Tocqueville's view is this: equality brings maladies against which only freedom can be a defense. With freedom, a democratic society is as capable as an aristocratic society. Without freedom it will be the worst of governments. Freedom of association is necessary in a democracy, where there are no prescriptive associations. Will there be progress? There is reason for doubt, but decline isn't certain. I admit that his picture of the society of the future saddens me, but he has helped me understand the benefits of equality. Family feelings become stronger. I am not persuaded that the human heart, the

human imagination, that our language, will not lose something, for the human spirit is a unity. I simply tell myself that there may flower from this intense material striving powerful and unified societies which may develop an unprecedented spirit and excitement. That would be the chapter about possibilities and dreams that I would have added to his book.[12]

That brilliant, challenging remark suggests the kind of positive reflections Ampère may have pushed Tocqueville toward, as a counterbalance to the gloomy, more pessimistic Kergorlay. Tocqueville did not add such a chapter, though a fleeting vision of what Ampère dreamt of—an unprecedented boom of cultural activity widely participated in by a striving democratic people on the make, free to try anything, uninhibited by old forms, uncowed by an authoritative cultural elite (there simply would not be one)—flickers throughout Tocqueville's analysis of the intellectual and cultural life of a society shaped by the dynamic of equality. Had conversations with Ampère made Tocqueville more aware of this possibility?

An increasingly frequent visitor at Tocqueville, especially while *DA II* was being revised in 1838 and 1839, Ampère happily placed his lively critical intelligence at the service of a work whose great importance he did not doubt. His commentary on the reading of May 15, 1838, suggests the kind of sensitive literary and philosophical questions he undoubtedly raised. By the time Tocqueville finished the book Ampère knew it by heart; and when it was at last published, he wrote a long poem celebrating the book and its author, verses in which he captures something of Tocqueville's complexity of spirit and vision and demonstrates how thoroughly he understood his friend and his book.[13]

These three men, whose diversity says something about the range of Tocqueville's imagination and sympathies and also reveals his Emersonian conviction that character mattered much more than politics, were Tocqueville's major advisors, as it were, as he wrote *DA II*. Each brought a different point of view and varied intellectual interests and sensitivities to the task. But they were not the only men Tocqueville leaned on for advice and encouragement. His father and brothers also read his work, though Tocqueville at times hints that his consultations with them were obligatory and useless. Their critical comments on the first volume, especially those of his discerning father, makes that rebuff seem unwarranted. A fourth close friend, Corcelle, spent much time at Tocqueville (he is one of the Muses in Ampère's celebratory poem about *Democracy in America*) and undoubtedly heard Tocqueville read much of *DA II*, but it is difficult to assess the contribution he made, if any. Curiously, Tocqueville does not acknowledge any critical assistance from Marie.

Through much of the time he labored on *DA II* Tocqueville regularly corresponded with Royer-Collard and Mill and with Henry Reeve. While none participated in the shaping of the *work* the way Beaumont, Kergorlay, and Ampère did, they constituted an important, if more distant, critical audience.

ROYER-COLLARD

Royer-Collard and Mill in a sense were the intellectual angels of *Democracy in America*. It was them Tocqueville most wished to satisfy with his work. Both had warmly greeted *DA I*. Tocqueville had met Royer-Collard in 1835 when Royer summoned him for an interview after the publication of the first volume, a copy of which Tocqueville had sent him. The distinguished older man had been full of praise for the work, which he had flattered with comparisons to Aristotle's *Politics* and Montesquieu's *L'Esprit des Lois*. He had found it "a beautiful work, not of our time."[14]

Royer was the grand old man of French liberalism: he had honorably survived the wars of politics since 1789 with his head still on his shoulders, his integrity intact, and his principles clear. He had been in the thick of the revolutionary struggle, had served in the National Assembly, had opposed the Jacobins, had negotiated with Georges-Jacques Danton for Louis XVI, had detested the empire and been an advisor to the exiled Louis XVIII. During the Restoration he was the guiding light and chief theoretician of the Doctrinaires, a faction of moderate liberals, among them Guizot, who were the major movers and shapers of the July Monarchy. Still a deputy from Champagne in the Chamber during the July Monarchy, he had become increasingly critical of the repressiveness and immobility of the bourgeois regime led by Guizot.

He had also been a major force in the intellectual life of France. He had lectured on philosophy at the Sorbonne, where he introduced the common-sense realism of the Scottish philosopher Thomas Reid to France, a philosophical baton carried on by his successor, Victor Cousin. At seventy-seven he was still in the Chamber of Deputies when the thirty-five-year-old Tocqueville joined it in 1839.

Though Tocqueville somewhat distanced himself from Royer after his political career began, he was profoundly influenced by the older man's political ideas. He admired Royer for having made moral issues once again central to politics and for having maintained a principled independence through a long political life. In Tocqueville's view, Royer was not simply an exemplary figure: he embodied France's past and present, having lived through and understood the history that Tocqueville himself was seeking to understand and master.

While Tocqueville was writing *DA II*, he corresponded with Royer about a great range of political and personal issues. At the start of his political career he read the powerful speeches Royer had delivered during the increasingly reactionary years of the Restoration under Charles X, speeches in which he eloquently defended liberty against encroaching power and articulated a liberal political philosophy of essential rights and of limits to power, the fundamentals of which were very much like Tocqueville's. Tocqueville took extensive notes on these speeches when he later read them (after he had completed the *Democracy*), occasionally adding admiring comments.[15]

Owing to the great similarity in their political thought, Royer's ideas illuminate much of Tocqueville's political thinking as well.[16] Royer was the intellectual leader of the Doctrinaires, whose moderate liberalism in theory shaped the July Monarchy. In his thought and politics he sought to fuse past and present, to unify a France that had been torn apart by the Revolution, and to retain as far as possible the values and institutions of prerevolutionary France while preserving the accomplishments of 1789. Despite his detestation of the court this meant accepting a constitutional monarchy: he was a reluctant legitimist, arguing that history, not ideal political considerations, made the monarchy a necessary institution for France. This was the view that Tocqueville, at the end of his life, said he finally accepted.[17] It also meant preserving the social reforms of the Revolution, including the abolition of the class system and all its legally created privileges and injustices. He rejected all old conceptions of sovereignty, which now resided not in divinely anointed royalty or in the people but in reason, that is, in reasoned judgments arrived at by a constitutionally managed political process involving debate and negotiation between interests that would arrive at agreements about the good of the nation. The very notion of sovereignty itself was unacceptable, for it implied unlimited power, which, whether exercised by a king or by the people, was certain to be abused and result in despotism. Power had to be hedged in by vigilantly guarded constitutional restraints such as the separation of powers and by clearly defined inviolable rights. Royer was an eloquent defender of such rights, arguing in many celebrated speeches for the crucial importance of freedom of the press and of speech, the suppression of which during the July Monarchy led him to break with his former fellow Doctrinaire Guizot. Royer also believed that the egalitarian, centralizing demiurge released by the Revolution also threatened the individual, and that for this reason, too, certain rights—"necessary liberties"—had to be maintained.

The political theory of the *juste milieu*, calling for rational negotiation between competing interests and values to determine the overarching (rational) interest of all, was in large measure Royer's creation. Theoretically it was an admirable conception, but, once put into practice by the ruling bourgeoisie led by Guizot, it was paralyzed by the fear that revolution lurked behind all proposals for change, an attitude which led to the corrupt practice of dealing out offices for support and to much repression; it had been corrupted too by the tendency of the governing bourgeoisie to identify its interest with the public good and to assume that with its rise to power the Revolution had been fulfilled. Royer's dismay with the immobility and the repressiveness of the July Monarchy was matched by Tocqueville's.

It is difficult to say how much Tocqueville was influenced by Royer-Collard's moral philosophy, which Harold Laski argued in an admiring essay was an essential element of his political thought. But it is striking how much Royer's great stress on the moral nature of humanity, and hence on the individual as an end in himself (and thus an essential instrument of moral progress), is echoed in Tocqueville's thought and in his ardent defense of the individual imagination against the power of public opinion and mass culture to oppress the singular mind. It was also Tocqueville's view that a society was to be judged by how much liberty the individual enjoyed in trying to achieve self-fulfillment. Royer was a Kantian as well as a follower of Reid. For these contra-Humian philosophers, humans were blessed with innate capacities that had to be unrestrained and fulfilled. Since for Royer mankind singularly possessed the faculty of judgment, essential for securing moral progress, the political consequence was that "no state can be adequate in which provision is not made for its exercise." Royer believed that "when you have described man as a member of the State you have not exhausted his nature. . . . He is not merely a member of the State" but a moral being whose conscience was of supreme value, for it was the basis of the good society.[18] The great aim of the state was thus neither wealth nor power, but the quality of life and mind it inspired, and it was to be judged by the degree to which it protected the rights and freedom of the individual. For Tocqueville too the good society was ultimately defined by how fully it made possible individual self-fulfillment, though it is doubtful that he would have unreservedly concurred with Royer in the daring moral argument that for the sake of the rare individual even the state might be sacrificed, an idea Laski says Royer contemplated. This conviction of the absolute necessity of individual freedom as a moral good and as the basis of moral progress informs *Democracy in America* explicitly and implicitly, from beginning to end. It is the threat to the individual imagination and to individual autonomy posed by the tendencies of democratic culture that partly accounts for the gathering darkness of the book.

No one in political life more closely fulfilled Tocqueville's ideal of the moral man in politics than Royer-Collard. As he began his own political career and as he wrote *DA II*, it was to the aging liberal philosopher-politician that he turned for counsel, not regarding specific issues he was writing about, but as if to his conscience embodied in a wiser, older, and more experienced figure. Perhaps he saw himself as Royer-Collard's heir in French politics. So seriously did he take his correspondence with Royer-Collard, which strangely combined personal frankness with great formality and courtliness, that he made rough drafts of his letters, the only instance, according to Beaumont, in which he was so fastidious. But, as was the case with Mill, a note of distance eventually entered their correspondence. Royer began to feel that despite his exceptional qualities Tocqueville was too full of himself, too driven by ambition and the desire for power, to be the truly selfless independent moral leader they had both thought he might be. With growing asperity he confided his disappointment to others, including the Duchesse de Dino, whose salon Tocqueville often attended, and the Comte Molé. To Molé he wrote of Tocqueville that "he craves success. I believe that if the good prevails and even dominates in his complex make-up, he lacks a certain grandeur of character that makes for complete integrity."[19] To Dino his comment was sharper: "He has a fund of honesty that is not enough for him, that he spends imprudently but of which something will always be left. I fear that because of his impatience to arrive he will stray into impracticable paths, trying to reconcile what is irreconcilable. He uses both his hands at once, giving the right to the left, the left to us, regretting that he hasn't a third which he would give invisibly."[20] What others might have called opportunism Royer called impracticability. In fact, the worst charge of this critique is the thought that Tocqueville might "stray," which is to say that he didn't know what he was doing.

Tocqueville's comment to Marie concerning Royer's advice was that "he told me my only defect was that I was too concerned with myself."

For his part, Tocqueville, his confidence bolstered after being elected to the Chamber, began to sense Royer's inadequacies, especially his deep skepticism about the possibility of an orderly democratic politics and his inability to conceive of a liberalism that would not lead to disorder. He also believed that Royer's understanding of the moment was somewhat limited and that he exhibited "a profound but exaggerated mistrust of the present times (the major aspect of which escapes him—he doesn't see that it is a transitional period").[21] Nevertheless, when the cool reception of *DA II* had much depressed Tocqueville he turned for reassurance to Royer, who read it through again and reaffirmed that he had in fact written a classic.

There is no better way to summarize Royer-Collard's political convictions as understood by Tocqueville than by quoting from a long letter about Royer that

Tocqueville sent in May of 1858 to his old political colleague Pierre Freslon, who had asked for a profile of the man. With some modifications it might well be a portrait of Tocqueville himself, though he takes pains to say that he did not always agree with Royer. Tocqueville's letter, a miniature essay, is a jewel of political portraiture and a deeply felt appreciation. Royer-Collard was, he wrote,

> a most original character . . . a singular combination of petty passions and of grand sentiments, of vanity that ignored itself, of grandeur of soul and of pride that knew how to assert itself: a noble and imposing figure above all, and one of those who, among all his contemporaries, most merited their attention and their admiration. All the principal acts of M. Royer-Collard were in effect linked mainly to two ideas, one greater and more command-ing than the other, but both expressions of his spirit.
>
> 1. Throughout his life, M. Royer-Collard firmly believed that we could and had to distinguish the liberal spirit from the revolutionary spirit. He had passionately wished for the destruction of the ancien régime, and had always feared it might return. He had passionately desired the abolition of privilege, the equality of political rights, the liberty and dignity of all. He always detested the spirit of adventure, of violence, of tyranny, of demagoguery, which is characteristic of the revolutionary impulse everywhere. He firmly believed that it was possible to overturn the ancien régime without following that spirit. He had hoped that the revolution would lead to something differ-ent from that revolutionary spirit. He never believed that it was necessary to destroy every aspect of France's old order, but to get rid of only that which was opposed to the modern spirit, to measured liberty, to equality of rights, to the opening of all careers and all destinies and to the dreams of all men. After the revolution he always sought to bind all institutions to this ideal, and as much as was possible and desirable to reunite the past and the present. Was there any aspect of his life that departed from this fundamental idea? I'm not aware of it.
>
> 2e The second fundamental idea of M. Royer-Collard, related to the first without necessarily following from it, was that the very same M. Royer-Collard had always maintained that the institution of Monarchy was, in France, a *necessary* institution; and it was pleasing to witness the unusual consequences sometimes resulting from this belief, combined as it was with the most intractably republican convictions I have ever encountered. Appalled by a court yet with a firm adherence to the idea of a Monarch! Among all the royals the one that seemed to him most likely to maintain the grand modern, liberal institutions he had hoped for and had spent his entire life defending now against the revolutionaries, now against the ultras and the émigrés was the royalty of the eldest branch. I have never known a man freer

from what one might call legitimist passions, less partisan for a race [*sic*] or a family, while believing at the same time that the best outcome for the revolution would be a monarchy of the *branche aînée* [eldest line], limited and kept in check by all the institutions that assured the triumph of new ideas. His life's dream was to unite the new spirit with this ancient family and to have them support one another. In the end, however, liberalism was for him the goal, a monarchy of the eldest line the means. I do not mean that these two basic convictions, key to the man, were equally important. I say only that these were his convictions, and that he had followed them from the start of the revolution when he had served as intermediary between the unhappy Louis XVI and Danton, up to his last speech against *le costume*, in 1836, I believe.

The passionate sincerity and the incomparable eloquence with which he defended these two convictions, which to the minds of most seemed contradictory, was always for me the most unusual spectacle I have ever witnessed. One had to hear him speak about the revolution: no one could better make clear the grandeur of that time and its superiority to our own despite its failings and its violence. The finest words I have ever heard uttered on what one might call the great achievements of '89 came from his lips. The harshest words I ever heard spoken about the vices of the ancien régime, the follies and the stupidities of the émigrés or the ultras, came from him. But when it was necessary to depict the violence, the tyrannical tastes, the disordered passions, the bloody follies and the intolerance of what he called the revolutionary spirit—he was Tacitus.

Though Tocqueville concludes this splendid portrait by saying that Royer "quite often failed to persuade me, but . . . always astonished me," he in fact shared the two *idées mères* he described as fundamental to Royer's politics. Tocqueville's egalitarianism, however, was somewhat qualified, and his support for the monarchy more tentative. Still, with regard to the monarchy, what may be construed as his ultimate view about the frame of government that would be best for France, a constitutional monarchy with the eldest branch restored—a view he seems to have arrived at by the midfifties—was precisely the same as Royer's.

MILL

His correspondence with Mill, equally formal, kept Tocqueville in touch with a man he regarded as the spirit of English liberalism. Tocqueville believed that England, which he called "le pays le plus civilisé du monde," was the true center of liberty in the world. As he later put it in the long letter he coura-geously (though anonymously) published in the *Times* in 1852 denouncing Louis-Napoleon's coup d'état and providing a detailed account of the event, "L'opinion publique anglaise, c'est le grand jury de l'humanité en matière de liberté." Mill's incisive review of *DA I* had deeply gratified Tocqueville, who wrote, "Of all those who have been good enough to pay attention to me, you are the only one who has entirely understood me, who has been able to grasp as a whole my general ideas, the ultimate drift of my thought and at the same time who has maintained a clear perception of the details."[22] He was attracted to Mill not simply because he had understood *Democracy in America* so well or because of the man's moral qualities, but also because through Mill he could keep in touch with the most advanced liberal thought in England. He well understood, as did Mill, how important the publicist, that is, the journalist, had become in the age of democratic politics, and Mill by the midthirties had become one of the most important political journalists in England.

They had met in May 1835, at the start of Tocqueville's second visit to England. Mill had already read *Democracy in America* and was deeply impressed. When Tocqueville left London shortly afterward to travel through England and Ireland, he arranged for a copy of his book to be delivered by hand to Mill along with a note expressing the hope that Mill would examine it— perhaps *examine* meant *review*. Mill had someone else in mind for that task, but when that plan fell through he himself wrote a praiseful review that made Tocqueville a celebrated figure in England.

In turn, Mill asked Tocqueville to contribute whatever he pleased to the *London Review*, the liberal journal of which he had just been appointed editor. Mill sent him a flattering, generous invitation: "The Review presumes to repre-sent the most advanced in democratic thought: which is precisely what you have—you yourself—either shaped or clarified, with a power hitherto unknown, out of known facts and principles. It is then you who must set conditions [for contributing to the Review] and not to be given them. Our hope is that you will truly wish to join us, and use the Review as a platform for your views."[23] Mill's wish was that Tocqueville would instruct and guide those who wrote for the *Review*, the purpose of which was to enlighten the English people about "questions de haute politique," or simply encourage the democratic spirit in a nondoctrinaire, open-minded way.

In his hesitant acceptance, Tocqueville explained what it was that attracted him to English liberals and in doing so underscored the ground they shared. He had arrived in England full of antipathy for "le parti démocratique," thinking it was like the French one, which was exploiting the democratic creed without understanding how to cultivate and guide democracy: "A French democrat is generally a man who wishes to confide the governance of society exclusively not in all the people but in a certain element of the people, and who, in order to achieve this result, clearly understands only the use of material force; unhappily there would be many other characteristics to add to this portrait. But those are the principal ones."[24] *La force materielle* was his delicate euphemism for *revolution*. English democrats, he was happy to discover, were not revolutionaries:

> On the contrary, everything I see in English democrats leads me to believe that if their views are often narrow and exclusive, at least their goal is the true goal that friends of democracy must maintain. In fact their ultimate goal, it seems to me, is to make the majority of citizens capable of governing and of being governed. Faithful to their principles, they do not presume to force the people to be happy in the way they consider most convenient . . . to lead societies step by step seems to me the only way to save them from barbarism or slavery. All my energy and desire will be devoted to the service of this cause, represented as it is in this country by honest and enlightened men. . . . I proceed to this goal resolutely, unhesitatingly, without enthusiasm and, I hope, without wavering.[25]

He was comfortable with English liberals because they were prudent, pragmatic reformers, gradualists and not revolutionaries, who in their quest for social and political reform maintained a sane reverence for what was strong and valuable in England's traditions and institutions. They were liberals and democrats, not revolutionaries. It was precisely this separation that he saw Royer-Collard ultimately failing to believe possible. Force was not on their agenda. Instead, they saw their task as that of educating the people and preparing them for self-governance. Tocqueville here states the central aim of "aristocratic liberalism": the conviction that the task of a responsible elite was to guide and enlighten a democratic people, not to coerce them or to impose doctrinaire notions of right order or of the good society on them. Such was the lasting common ground between Tocqueville and Mill.

Their subsequent correspondence, heaviest while Tocqueville was writing *DA II*, gradually grew thinner, lapsing after 1843 except for a letter from Tocqueville to Mill in 1847, a brief exchange in 1856, and a last letter from Tocqueville in February of 1859 sending thanks for the gift of *On Liberty*, which he had not yet been able to read because he was too weak with the tuberculosis that soon was to kill him. Sadly, he was never able to read the work in which Mill acknowledges the importance of Tocqueville's pioneering work not only in *Democracy in America* but in *L'Ancien Régime* as well. Their correspondence remained almost wholly on the level of ideas, was personally reserved, and full of polite conventions and repeated, though unquestionably genuine, acknowledgments of the importance of one another's work. Why it petered out is not clear because, except for one instance, disputes and differences between them were only obliquely expressed. It cannot be that their exceptional busyness prevented them from writing. Mill's correspondence with Auguste Comte flourished in the 1840s. Though Mill had strongly praised both volumes of *Democracy in America*, he also had much to say that was sharply critical: Tocqueville never responded to these criticisms or to Mill's requests for further discussions of the issues he raised. When Mill strongly rebuked Tocqueville's saber-rattling imperialism in 1843, he received no reply. Mill's wife, Harriet, strongly disliked Tocqueville, and that also may have had something to do with the cooling of their friendship.[26] Tocqueville's last letter to Mill, written from Cannes in February of 1859, concludes with the hope that the rumors of Harriet Mill's death were "mal fondé." She had in fact died a year earlier, in the south of France, not far from where Tocqueville now lay dying himself. Mill had not told him.

The two men's similarities and differences reveal much about Tocqueville. It isn't clear how much Tocqueville knew about Mill before they connected in 1835. Except for *Spirit of the Times* (1831) Mill had not yet written the major essays and books that made him the best-known and most articulate voice of English liberal thought. His essay "Civilization," which foreshadowed some of Tocqueville's analysis of democratic culture, appeared in 1836. Before that, he had written prolifically on French politics and culture, at first celebrating the Revolution of 1830, then denouncing the growing repressiveness and conservatism of Louis-Philippe's bourgeois regime. He had quickly traveled to Paris to witness and cheer the July Revolution and had enthusiastically sung *La Marseillaise* in the presence of Louis-Philippe — all this in contrast to Tocqueville's rueful viewing of the flight of Charles X from Versailles (rueful even though he had been critical of the absolutist follies of the last Bourbon monarch). The moment had displayed Mill's "redness," Tocqueville's "blueness."[27]

Though increasingly disillusioned by the failure of the ruling French bourgeoisie to broaden the domain of social justice and political equality, Mill had nevertheless enthusiastically welcomed the Revolution of 1848, the subsequent provisional government, and initially the Second Republic, before being bitterly disappointed once again. But he never abandoned his admiration for the provisional government that Tocqueville lambasted and ridiculed in his *Recollections*. The degree to which Tocqueville was aware of Mill's radical tendencies and his lapse into republican enthusiasm is not clear. They never discussed 1830 or 1848, though they did share their dismay about the immobility and repressiveness of the July Monarchy, and Mill was as critical as Tocqueville of Guizot's politics, calling Guizot a tool of the blindly selfish ruling French bourgeoisie.[28]

Mill was different from Tocqueville in many ways, and these differences by contrast highlight the political convictions they shared and illuminate the aristocratic liberalism that became their mutually fashioned response to the challenges that the rise of democracy posed: the growing power of mass culture and public opinion and also the growing power of the centralized state, both threats to the cultural and political freedom of the increasingly beleaguered individual.

Mill's extraordinary education alone would have made him a strange intellectual companion for Tocqueville, though until they were young men both were taught at home. Insulated from public education, they had missed the cultural experiences of their cohorts and had not benefited from making connections among their peers. In 1835 Mill was still struggling to free himself from the strict rationalism and utilitarianism of his upbringing. His essays on Jeremy Bentham (1838) and Samuel Taylor Coleridge (1839), which announced his liberation from Benthamite present-minded empiricism and Coleridgean backward-looking romanticism (though he retained something of both), lay a few years ahead. Mill was wider-ranging intellectually than Tocqueville. He was more open to the new, more experimental, and more responsive to the reformist impulses of the time. He was more visionary than Tocqueville and more distressed by the spread of the sooty poverty that was the gangrene of the early industrial revolution. He was even able, inspired by Harriet, to accept socialism as a plausible response to the deepening social crises created by industrialism, though he continued to argue for the inviolability of property rights as a necessary support for the aristocracy of merit he, like Tocqueville, thought crucial for democracy. In Mill this was a lingering Coleridgean conviction that a landed aristocracy, or at least secure landed wealth, might maintain the stability and continuity as well as the invulnerable independent leadership that democracy would require.

For the same reasons, among others, Tocqueville also thought the security of property was indispensable. For Tocqueville, the idea of socialism was simply a gleam in the eye of irresponsible social revolutionaries, though he tentatively accepted the need for a mildly more equitable sharing of wealth and for economic arrangements such as the limited worker ownership of factories that would make the right to well-being, to liberty, and to the full employment of one's abilities available to the working class. Tocqueville's ultimate response to the problem of pauperism was, besides encouraging private charity and discouraging mendicancy, the very Franklin-like notion of training the working poor in habits of thrift by opening savings banks for them. In fact, he quotes Poor Richard in making this argument. Mill would have accepted this idea, but he would have gone far beyond it.

By the time he met Tocqueville, Mill knew French literature and culture well. Many of his early ventures in journalism were, as noted, about the politics and culture of France. He thought the French public "the cleverest in the world" and that it was to France that one had to turn for truly original political and social thought. He confessed that he was "attached by tastes and predilections to France more than to my own country." By contrast to the French, the English, he said, were stupid and insular. He was deeply interested in French socialist and utopian thought. In the 1820s he had seriously studied the ideas of Saint-Simon and had even been fingered by Saint-Simonian missionaries, Barthélemy-Prosper Enfantin among them, as a possible leader of the movement in England. He drew back from their soliciting, but it was through his study of Saint-Simonianism that he became acquainted with the ideas of Saint-Simon's apostate deputy, Auguste Comte.[29]

Mill's correspondence with Comte, which ran through most of the 1840s side by side with his correspondence with Tocqueville but never touching—that is, neither Mill nor Comte ever mentions Tocqueville, nor do Mill and Tocqueville ever breathe the name of Comte—illuminates some of the differences that kept Mill and Tocqueville at arm's length despite their shared elitist liberalism. That contrast, between the intense, sometimes turbulent, and occasionally quite personal correspondence of Mill and Comte and the polite Mill–Tocqueville exchanges, is striking. Mill had written to Comte in 1841, presenting himself as a disciple, almost in the tone of a supplicant. Seeking to escape the Benthamite rigidity that took no account of history and of cultural progress, he had been taken by the Saint-Simonian and Comtean formulation of the stages of historicocultural development, especially by Comte's notion that the present moment was one of transition to the age of science, that is, to the positivist era of which he was the herald and chief theologian. For a while Mill took all that Comte said quite seriously; he even undertook the study of phrenology at Comte's urging, though a great many others were doing so also. Besides discussing aspects of Comte's positivism and issues of sociological method, Mill and Comte wrote about personal matters, even marital issues. (Sex and self were compellingly seductive and difficult subjects for the positivists.) They delved into aspects of the self with an openness that is missing from the correspondence between Mill and Tocqueville. Comte often vented his fury at the French intellectual and academic establishment, especially at Guizot, for failing to support him. Mill undertook to raise funds from admiring English supporters like the historian George Grote to aid the alienated and penurious positivist, until finally, appalled by Comte's intellectual egomania and his individual-stifling totalitarian system as it was finally presented to the world in *Le système de politique positive*, he ended the correspondence in 1847. Mill's affair with Comte reveals a quality of imagination, an intellectual adventurousness, and a willingness to explore even the most radical schemes for social reconstruction that is lacking in Tocqueville.

Did Tocqueville know of Mill's Saint-Simonian flirtation and his Comtean infatuation? Mill also much admired George Sand, regarding her as perhaps the outstanding contemporary continental writer. Tocqueville detested her. Mill also knew German philosophy and literature well. European thought seemed to him far in advance of that of his ill-informed countrymen, whose arrogant conservatism and narrowness he bitterly denounced. Both men were cosmopolitans, but beyond England and America Tocqueville's knowledge of other cultures was not as deep.

Whether Tocqueville knew much about *this* Mill is not clear. The Mill he met in 1835 was an influential liberal publicist with important liberal friends. It was not unreasonable of him to think of Mill as the leading public voice of English liberalism, of the pragmatic English liberalism that he wished to speak to. And they did share much. Above all, they agreed that the great issues raised by the advance of democracy were, first, the threat that mass society and central-ized power posed to individual liberty, especially to the different, boldly active, original individual; and, second, the need to foster and protect a moral, intel-lectual elite—an aristocracy of merit—that would prevent a society increasingly devoted to a quest for comfort and material well-being from sinking into a spiritually enervating cultural mediocrity, thus making it more pliable by power. The problems of liberty and leadership in democratic societies were the deep concerns that bound them despite their differences in background, temperament, intellectual inclination, and imaginative scope.

For Mill, what Tocqueville stood for was far more important than their polit-ical differences. Tocqueville was, in his view, an independent, critical thinker in an age of historical transition and displacement in which the shattered old order had not yet been replaced by a new. In an essay from 1836 on the poet and novelist Alfred de Vigny, Mill wrote that Vigny was a vivid example of a literary figure in a time of major social and cultural change whose complex sensibility and values kept him painfully yet fruitfully suspended between past and present and provided him with creative insights into, but also critical distance from, the passions, politics, and projects of the moment. Had he wanted to write about a social philosopher just as fruitfully suspended between two worlds, he added, he would have chosen Tocqueville as his representative figure.

Regrettably, Tocqueville seems never to have expressed so full an understanding of Mill, who was also coping with the demands of the past and the present in an equally poignant and ambivalent personal way. Of Mill it must be said, however, that in contrast to the cooler Tocqueville he was more vulnerable to the gusts of contemporary passions.

More specifically, what did they contribute to one another's thinking in the late 1830s while Tocqueville was writing *DA II*? Mill's review of the first volume had been laudatory, though not without reservations, which he muffled a bit. While he was preparing the review he wrote to Tocqueville that "my article will be, as you will see, a shade or two more favourable to democracy than your book, although in the main I agree, so far as I am competent to judge, in the unfavourable part of your remarks, but without carrying them quite so far."[30] When he later sent Tocqueville an "exemplaire" of his review he asked Tocqueville to send "all the observations that have been raised in your mind by the doubts I have expressed on only a few of your conclusions. I am far from having fixed ideas on the issues in question."[31] In reply, Tocqueville said that a full response would call for a book or a long conversation, not a letter, so he did not comment on Mill's reservations and doubts — nor did he at any time thereafter. Mill's delicacy and diffidence about his criticisms masked his numerous reservations, though he agreed with Tocqueville's major assertions about the possible hazards of democracy and believed that the book had immensely advanced understanding of democracy. The fact is that at this time and until he wrote *Civilization*, in 1836, an essay in which he noted that the progress of civilization had led to the development of a mediocre mass culture and to the empowering of an individual-oppressing public opinion, he had remained sanguine about the future of democracy.[32] Perhaps it was politeness as well as admiration for Tocqueville's accomplishment that led Mill to downplay his criticism, to stress his uncertainty and his readiness to change his mind. He was almost apologetic for having expressed doubts about aspects of Tocqueville's analysis of democracy.

What had he praised and what had he raised reservations about?[33] He had strongly underscored the significance of Tocqueville's assertions about the importance of local rights and of the American "municipal system," which both created and regulated "the spirit of independence in public affairs." "Local democracy" was "the school as well as the safety valve of democracy." (Mill here once again took the opportunity to pound "the herd" of supercilious and arrogant English travelers, who in their books on America had never noticed or mentioned this crucial institution.) He had also much praised Tocqueville's analysis of the crucial difference, in democratic systems, between delegation and representation. The danger of misunderstanding the difference was that the people would regard those they had elected to office simply as delegates committed to following their constituents' imperfect and biased understandings of issues, without sufficient freedom to follow their own judgment. Mill's criticisms, however, strongly qualified his praise. He posed several reservations about Tocqueville's assertions that in America merit was "rare among the governors," that "the most distinguished men are seldom called to public functions," and that "the race of American statesmen has decidedly *dwarfed* within the last half-century." At some length he raises qualifications to Tocqueville's argument that political leadership in a democracy is bound to become mediocre. Moreover, exceptionally able public servants were not always needed in a well-functioning, healthy society. In critical times "the first men in the country" will come forward as they did during the early years of the Republic and will be chosen to lead by the people; and, as the example of New England proved, a constantly advancing education, an enduring moral and religious heritage, an increasingly experienced and sophisticated people, and growing affluence will lead to the election of more able political leaders.

He more sharply criticizes Tocqueville's argument that a democracy is bound to miss the steady, informed, far-seeing guidance that a stable aristocracy would provide. "The only steadiness which aristocracy *never* fails to manifest, is tenacity in clinging to its own privileges. . . . In all other matters the opinion of a ruling class is as fluctuating, as liable to be wholly given up to immediate impulses, as the opinion of the people." Tocqueville's assertion about the political advantages of aristocracies "should have been predicated only of some particular aristocracies," which have "been very narrow aristocracies, consisting of so few members that every member could personally participate in the business of administration." In a numerous aristocracy "it is utterly impossible that there should be wisdom, foresight and caution in the governing body itself. . . . And it would be difficult for democracy to exhibit less of this willingness than has been shown by the English aristocracy in all periods of their history, or less than is shown by them at this moment."

Mill had reservations even about the issue that Tocqueville regarded "as the most serious of the inconveniences of democracy, and that to which, if the American Republic should perish, it will owe its fall. This is, the omnipotence of the majority." While acknowledging that Tocqueville was to be thanked for sounding a warning about this danger, Mill curiously spent most of his time minimizing it, at least as far as European nations were concerned. In America,

Mill notes, using evidence that Tocqueville himself provides in *Democracy in America*, a stratagem he uses all through his review, the majority in America has not oppressed the rich, and other minorities are so fluctuating that "it isn't easy to see what sort of minority it can be, over which the majority can have any interest in tyrannizing." The exceptions he allows are what he calls the antipathies that one part of the population may have for another, antipathies of religion or of race: and this danger, he argues, will exist "under any form of government." He was to repeat these comments five years later in his review of *DA II*. The truly serious issue raised by Tocqueville, that of a "tyranny exercised over opinions, more than over persons," which will stifle "all individuality of character, and independence of thought and sentiment," Mill minimizes by arguing that with the growth by means of education of "a highly instructed class" this evil may be averted and that in fact European civilization is sufficiently advanced to have produced a large, respected elite that can resist the views of the ill-informed many. He was soon to change his mind.

In raising such reservations about Tocqueville's alarms concerning political democracy and in all the other reservations he advances in his review of the first volume of *Democracy in America*, Mill is tenaciously writing as a defender of democracy, fending off antidemocrats ready to find in Tocqueville's book ammunition for their arguments. He agrees with Tocqueville about the hazards that lie ahead, but he remains more sanguine about prospects. Despite his praise, he seems to be resisting Tocqueville every step of the way. He quarrels with the idea that the people are always "unwilling to be guided by superior wisdom," and he finds certain aspects of Tocqueville's account of the weaknesses and dangers of democracy possibly "overcharged." In his review he raises so many reservations that it is hard to tell what he meant when he said there was only a "shade or two of difference" between them. At this moment his faith in democracy was stronger than Tocqueville's and would remain so.

He concludes his remarkable, complicated review with an optimistic look ahead:

> While, therefore, we see in democracy, as in every other state of society or form of government, possibilities of evil, which it would ill serve the cause of democracy itself to dissemble or overlook; while we think that the world owes a deep debt to M. de Tocqueville for having warned it of these, for having studied the failings and weaknesses of democracy with the anxious attention which a parent watches the faults of a child . . . we see nothing in any of these tendencies, from which any serious evil need be apprehended, if the superior spirits would but join with each other in considering the instruction of the democracy, and not the patching of the old worn-out machinery of aristocracy.[34]

It is regrettable that Tocqueville never fully replied to Mill's "humble" request for a discussion and for enlightenment about the many reservations he had regarding Tocqueville's assessment of democracy. In fact, Tocqueville did not reply either to the various reservations and criticisms or, with understandable modesty, to the very strong praise, of Mill's review of *DA II*.

Mill's optimism was based not only on his stronger hopes for democracy, but also on his conviction that European civilization was so advanced that it would not fully succumb to the evils Tocqueville warned about. It had an educated elite, a respected professional class, and a tradition of deference to merit, even if its aristocracy was now pathetically inadequate. But his view that the advanced civilization of European societies would provide a buffer against the hazards of democracy did not last much beyond his review of *Democracy in America* of 1835. It is in his essay "Civilization" of 1836 that Mill develops the idea that the advance of material civilization is likely to produce a mediocre culture that will stifle or ignore bold, energetic, different individuals, thus adding greater menace to the prospect of a tyranny of public opinion that Tocqueville had seen looming as an evil fruit of equality, a danger Mill had somewhat minimized in 1835. This is well before Tocqueville was to elaborate, in *DA II*, his vision of a mass culture intolerant of different, independent individuals, those who heard a different drummer, a culture inimical to intellectual progress.

"Civilization" marks the beginning of a darker phase in Mill's thinking about democracy. It may be that Tocqueville's shade darker view of an egalitarian society added fuel to his own growing antipathy for what he perceived to be and personally experienced as the growing mediocrity and intolerance of English middle-class culture. It may also be that Beaumont's very pessimistic view of the individual-suppressing consequences of America's democratic culture, which Mill discussed in his review of *Marie*, published before he wrote "Civilization," not only repelled him but also awakened him more fully to the potential power of mass prejudice and opinion.[35] For Mill, the extraordinary advance of material civilization had not produced comparable cultural advance, but in fact was leading to slow decline, which, when combined with the new power of mass culture and its slow smothering of individuality, was bound to have disastrous consequences:

> To meet this wonderful development of physical and mental power on the part of the masses, can it be said that there has been any corresponding quantity of intellectual power or moral energy unfolded among those individuals or classes who have enjoyed superior advantages? No one, we think, will affirm it. There is a great increase of humanity, a decline of bigotry, as well as of arrogance and the conceit of caste, among our conspicuous classes; but

there is, to say the least, no increase of shining ability, and a very marked decrease of vigour and energy. With all the advantages of this age, its facilities for mental cultivation, the incitements and rewards which it holds out to exalted talents, there can scarcely be pointed out in the European annals any stirring times which have brought so little that is distinguished, either morally or intellectually, to the surface.[36]

What was increasingly missing was a heroic elite willing, whatever the consequences, to educate and lead a people not yet ready morally or intellectually to wield power. The effect of "high civilization" on character was to weaken it by leading to a "relaxation of individual energy" and to an increasing focus on wealth and security, the result being that "the source of great virtues thus dries up." Just as serious was the fact that "the individual becomes so lost in the crowd, that though he depends more and more on opinion, he is apt to depend less and less on well-grounded opinion; upon the opinion of those who know him. An established character becomes at once more difficult to gain, and more easily to be dispensed with."[37] Such other-directed characters would lack the necessary heroic virtues, the willingness to stand alone, to make sacrifices, to face pain and uncertainty, at the very time the masses were attaining great political power and were in need of guidance from bold, energetic individuals. Mill does not say that the masses will ignore or suppress such individuals; but when Tocqueville, in DA II, suggests that the democratic future may well witness the ultimate individual-smothering triumph of mass opinion, Mill is ready to join him.

Mill powerfully praised DA II, though, as in his review of 1835, he had many reservations, not only about substance but about method as well.[38] He thought the book in places too abstract, a criticism also made by others, among them Edward Everett in the *North American Review*. Tocqueville's warnings about the dangers posed by the conformism and the mediocrity of mass society and by the power of majority opinion to repress the individual now struck home with great force. What he primarily objected to in the second volume was Tocqueville's attribution of this menace to democracy itself rather than to those malign effects of civilization he had first discussed in his essay of 1836 of that title. But his criticism surprisingly overlooked the fact that there was little difference between the culture of modern civilization he had earlier analyzed and the *culture* of democracy that Tocqueville had exhaustively examined in his increasingly pessimistic assessment of the strengths and weaknesses of democracy. This misunderstanding can be laid at Tocqueville's feet: he had failed to make the distinction between political democracy and the culture of democracy clear enough. Mill was unwilling to make democracy itself the villain.

After 1843, as I noted above, their correspondence dwindled and fell into long silences. It isn't entirely clear why. Their several disputes, especially about France's and Tocqueville's combative foreign policy, may have cooled their relationship. Both were occasionally ill for long stretches, with surprisingly similar ailments, and both were exceptionally busy men. Whatever the truth may be, the record makes it seem likely that Mill was a good deal more familiar with Tocqueville's ideas than Tocqueville was with Mill's. Unfortunately, Tocqueville did not reply to Mill's various challenges, perhaps because, as he said on another occasion, one couldn't satisfactorily discuss complex ideas in a language other than one's own. Mill's searching study of *Democracy in America* unquestionably sharpened his thinking about the problems of democracy and of mass society. What Tocqueville may have learned from Mill remains uncertain. Their increasing mutual focus on the need in democratic societies for leadership by a strong, independent, educated, morally courageous elite became central to their democratic theory. As Tocqueville was completing *Democracy in America*, Mill was in his mind as the critic he most wished to satisfy as well as a representative of the English liberalism he admired.

REEVE

Mill's relationship to Tocqueville was intellectual and quite formal. Though their correspondence was warm enough personally, it remained largely on the level of ideas. By contrast, Tocqueville's correspondence with Reeve, which began in 1835 and continued until Tocqueville's death in 1859, was not on the same intellectual level as that with Mill but more relaxed, informal, and familiar. However, Reeve understood the drift and significance of Tocqueville's ideas. It may have been Reeve who made Tocqueville even more thoughtful than he had been about the centralizing tendencies of democracy. When Tocqueville noticed that England's new Poor Laws (of 1833), democratic measures though they were, had extended the reach and powers of the government, he raised the specter of centralization with Reeve, who not only agreed but added that the then-pending prison reforms would have the same consequence. Tocqueville now ran with the idea: "Why is centralization an inevitable tendency of democracy?" he asked in his English notebook. He carried this new preoccupation to Mill, who agreed with Reeve's observation.

Reeve was strikingly unlike the smug, insular, arrogantly ignorant Englishman Mill scorned. He was a cosmopolitan man, thoroughly familiar with continental culture and politics, having been educated not only in England but also in Switzerland and Germany. He was fluent in German and French. He was a

lawyer, a grandson of the great English jurist John Austin. Just twenty-two when
he met Tocqueville, then almost thirty, in Paris in March of 1835, he was to
become an influential, widely connected journalist and eventually a premier
writer for the *Times* and subsequently director of the *Edinburgh Review*. He
fulfilled the role Tocqueville may have had in mind for Mill, as guide to English
politics and imperial ambitions.[39]

It did not take Tocqueville long after they had met to decide that the cosmopolitan, politically sophisticated Reeve, fluent in French, was the man to translate *Democracy in America*. After briefly thinking it over Reeve said no. Though
he realized that the book was "a work of the first rank ... perhaps the most
important work of political science since Montesquieu," he could not agree
with what he felt was Tocqueville's too-positive view of democracy. "I have
decided," he wrote in a letter to his mother, "not to write a word that failed to
agree with my profoundest convictions"; and though he admired the book he
did not wish to disseminate "a false doctrine." Reeve was a conservative Whig.
In the English political world he was somewhat to the right of Mill.[40]

A month later he changed his mind. He had come to see that his first impression of Tocqueville's book, based on a quick reading, "was completely erroneous" and that it was not tilted toward democracy.[41] He now understood that
Tocqueville's view was that democracy had to be accepted not because it was to
be preferred but because it was inevitable and had to be endured and civilized.
Reeve was not the only critic to be misled or confused by Tocqueville's ambivalences. Tocqueville would later gently chide Reeve at times for translating some
passages in a way that made him seem more positive about democracy than he
was, though it isn't clear what he specifically objected to.

Reeve would later also translate *L'Ancien Régime*, with which he was much
pleased. At first he had reservations about the book, telling Tocqueville that
while he found the subject full of interest, it was less fresh than *Democracy in
America*. But, as with Tocqueville's first book, Reeve's opinion changed. "You
have said many things that I have previously thought with less clarity and force."
He had had reservations about *Democracy in America* ("I was not always of your
opinion: I had less faith than you in ... [democratic] institutions, and I have
even less in them today"), but with *L'Ancien Régime* he found himself agreeing
"wholeheartedly with your thinking." He thought it was "a work of art."[42] He
had not read it until the completed work was sent to him to be translated, after
which he contributed only to the surprisingly lengthy and confused discussion
of what its title should be. When Tocqueville told him that the title tentatively
was to be *La révolution française*, Reeve wrote that that title inadequately
distinguished the book from the many others on the French Revolution and

perceptively noted that it failed to make clear Tocqueville's special emphasis on the state of France before the Revolution.

Reeve was more a facilitator than a stimulator, but as a perceptive critic deeply immersed in nineteenth-century English and continental political discourse and literature, as a basically sympathetic but independent reader, a very widely connected journalist, and a capable translator he was an invaluable friend. Far more than Mill, he kept Tocqueville informed about English politics and foreign policy. His name, as Tocqueville's first translator, is forever associated with *Democracy in America* no matter how many fresher, more learned, more linguistically sophisticated, more au courant translations supplant his. Mill was the first to tinker, apologetically, with Reeve's translation in the long quotes from *Democracy in America* he included in his reviews. Reeve's translation was soon allegedly improved by the great improver, the American Unitarian reformer Francis Bowen, professor of moral philosophy at Harvard.[43] The Reeve-Bowen version of Tocqueville's book, revised later by Philips Bradley, remained standard until the mid-twentieth century. It now shares the field with George Lawrence's lucid translation and with an elegant new translation by Arthur Goldhammer, a master modern translator of French scholarly works. Reflecting the usefulness of Tocqueville to all parties, there is also a new translation by the conservative political theorist Harvey Mansfield and Delia Winthrop, who present their version of *Democracy in America* as an effort to avoid the contemporizing of Tocqueville's language by recovering the meanings of the political lexicon and discourse of the early nineteenth century. Other recent new translations reflect how scriptural, how endlessly provocative a work *Democracy in America* has become. A new, deeply informed translation by the major American Tocqueville scholar James Schleifer has just appeared. But Henry Reeve will always be there, an abiding presence.

9

Writing as Moral Act

Writing did not come easily to Tocqueville. He was as obsessed with style and language as his great contemporary Gustave Flaubert, whose revolutionary Madame Bovary appeared the same year as Tocqueville's equally revolutionary Ancien Régime. Hoping to discover the source of their power and durability, he studied the works of classic writers, especially French, as models of what he called "le bon style." He wanted nothing less than to be counted among the great writers. His judgments about contemporary French literature were severe. For him, modern writers had become self-indulgent, their style decadent. His ultimate test of the worthiness of literature was moral. In *Democracy in America* he employs the full array of rhetorical and metaphorical techniques and subtly manages to create suspense and a dramatic sense of an approaching end.

Tocqueville constantly encountered the major writers of France's romantic literary renaissance, most of whom circulated through the same salons he attended. Some of them, including Hugo, Lamartine, Alfred de Musset, Charles Sainte-Beuve, Prosper Merimée, Ampère, and others, as well as many historians, were also members of the Académie française, which during Tocqueville's time as a member was also full of many now obscure poets.

He could not have been much at ease in the realm of the literary salon. Ambition for repute drove him to attend them, not the pleasures of serious conversation, which he seems to have found mainly at the salon of Mme Swetchine. He much enjoyed quiet, lengthy conversations in small gatherings of friends or like-minded colleagues, but intense, au courant conversation and displays of wit the purpose of which was to demonstrate cleverness and intellectual chic, sometimes barely masking erotic play, often left him emotionally distressed. He would then retreat to his rural sanctuary to compose himself and regain his bearings. When he was alone in his world, there was no challenge to his sense of superiority, nothing to derail the logic of his thought. The competition of ideas seems to have been extremely stressful for him, in part because of vanity, what, as before noted, he called his "besoin de primer."[1]

In his view, the world of the salon, each presided over by a favor-distributing "potentat," was an arena of highly charged competition for repute and primacy. He saw the salon as a battleground or, as he put it, "un jeu des coulisses." For the celebrated Mme Récamier, "to hold a salon was a game which she played well and almost always won; but she was sometimes defeated, and the effort occasionally left her exhausted."[2] The Duchesse de Dino, a close friend of Royer-Collard, battled tenaciously for primacy until she had vanquished her competitors. According to Tocqueville, "It was only after about forty years, when she had exhausted all her competitors, that she gave herself over to the joy of it."[3] At various salons he would occasionally encounter Stendhal, notorious for his spectacular ego-struts, performances designed to affront convention and twit a world that was not rewarding him sufficiently with either love or money. Tocqueville once even participated in a tableau with him. To imagine a conversation between them challenges the imagination. Compared to Stendhal, Tocqueville seems an unworldly, stiff-backed naïf. He never had anything to say about Stendhal in his correspondence, though *The Red and the Black* had been published in 1830 and *The Charterhouse of Parma* in 1839, by which time Stendhal's literary accomplishments had been recognized.

Nevertheless, despite his discomfort in the world of the salon, he continued to make the rounds, partly to maintain social connections, partly to sustain his repute, partly because despite his severe moral standards he in fact enjoyed gossip and could dish out his share of malevolent remarks. He advised Gobineau, whose career he sought to advance, to cultivate the connections he might make on the salon circuit.

Though he must have been au courant with the literary scene and could enjoy its gossip and biting badinage, he never set aside his disdain for what he saw as the disorderly, decadent culture of the romantics. There is no evidence that he read their work. He never mentions *Madame Bovary*, even though Flaubert's novel was not only a major literary but also a cultural and legal event, published in the same year as *L'Ancien Régime*. In his correspondence with his most intimate friends, which is full of personal confession and also moral commentary on the current cultural scene, he does not discuss any contemporary literary work, though he did chastise Gobineau for having written a long review of Musset's poetry for *Le Commerce*, the journal for which he was editorial director and guiding spirit. In his view Musset did not warrant such thorough attention. He was busy arranging reviews and seeking contributors for the literary pages of *Le Commerce*, trying, for example, to sign up Honoré de Balzac for a serialized novel.

Even though he sometimes wrote from a perch in the Faubourg Saint-Germain, a refuge for the aristocracy next to the beehive of Paris's booming Bohemia, that world was terra incognita to him. Not even curiosity drove him to inspect it. What he knew of France's surging democratic culture he learned mostly from adventurous friends like Ampère. If he did explore popular culture, it was at arm's length, by looking briefly at popular magazines, as he claimed he did. When, in his *Recollections*, he explained why he had not met Sand before he found himself seated next to her in 1848 at a literary lunch arranged by the witty English bon vivant and litterateur Monckton Milnes, described by Tocqueville as "un garçon d'esprit" but also as "un sot," he noted that it was because he had had nothing to do with "the world of literary adventurers" that was her milieu.[4]

His comments about Sand say much about not only his literary taste but also his views of the culture of the moment. He no longer read Sand, he said, because she was morally corrupt: "Despite the admirable qualities of her style, her plots and her characters are so outrageous and so unnatural, her moral sense so perverse, that we [he and Marie] no longer read her."[5] He also noted that "en dépit de sa brutalité" she had also enjoyed much power over a number of men and had been "la cause eloignée" of the death of Musset, who, as he seems to have believed, had drunk himself to death after having witnessed her embracing another admirer.

He offered another reason for disliking Sand: he said that he detested women writers who masked the sensibilities of their gender by writing as if they were men. The corruption he was complaining of was the unnatural behavior of women who were not being women. It was not because they aspired to write or even that they might write badly. They were violating the nature and sensibility of their gender. Still, by the end of their lunch he admitted that he finally felt some admiration for Sand, partly because she *had* behaved like a man: she had been forthright, decisive, forceful, factual. Evidently she had told him much about the life of the working class that he, unsurprisingly, had not known.[6]

What Sand thought of Tocqueville or of this encounter is not known. She may have enjoyed tweaking him by saying, when he asked her if she had read *Democracy in America*, that she read only those books given to her by their authors. Still, he was capable of enjoying her wit and her presence.

Even though he ultimately condemned Sand's work, he could appreciate "les grandes qualités" of her style. Aesthetic qualities, the beauty of good writing, counted in his literary judgments, as did wit and rhetorical skill, but his fundamental criterion for literature was moral. It was, finally, what the work-in-hand or the oeuvre revealed about the character of the writer and, more important, what its moral and social influences were likely to be that mattered most. The moral test was Tocqueville's ground of judgment for everything: individuals, historical works, religious and philosophical systems, novels, and politics. It was an approach to literature that he shared with Marie, who, for example, wrote to Lieber that she detested Eugène Sue's *The Wandering Jew* because of its scandalous "moral tendencies."[7] Tocqueville ultimately rejected Gobineau's sociology and race theory because it would lead to fatalism and resignation and would weaken men's will to improve societies and to transcend their condition. His judgment of Christianity and of Islam as well was made on the same grounds. Increasingly, this moral aim, namely, to inspire the will to transform the human condition, became the purpose that guided the writing of *Democracy in America*, despite the contradictory gathering fatalism of the book, with which it exists in great tension that is never resolved.

Tocqueville was keenly conscious of coming from a family of great literary accomplishment. He was also proud of its tradition of military service, but he lamented the high cost of the old feudal tradition and its readiness to battle unto death for France that had decimated the old nobility, his paternal ancestors among them, and had only briefly considered a military career. He never tired of talking about the intellectual liveliness, the wittiness, the sophisticated aesthetic taste, and the love of literature of the eighteenth-century aristocracy, who could, for example, lionize the brilliant though somewhat crude, by their standards, Scottish philosopher David Hume, who he thought would have been scorned by the pretentious pseudoaristocrats of Orleanist France as "un raseur," a bore.[8] That now-vanished aristocratic literary culture was most luminously exemplified for him by his maternal great-grandfather, the justly admired Malesherbes, who was important not so much as a writer but as, in Chateaubriand's words, a "patron de gens de lettres." Malesherbes was one of the two noble friends Rousseau had and carried on a correspondence with him and shared his love of botany. Rousseau's *Confessions* was written in an effort to reply to Malesherbes's request that he explain himself. It was Malesherbes who had saved Diderot's *Encyclopédie* from censorship, and it was Malesherbes whose liberal hand as censor when he was directeur de la librairie and secrétaire de la maison du roi had generously granted *permissions tacites* to subversive and scandalous publications.[9] Tocqueville had once planned to write a biography of his great-grandfather, whose bust watched over his writing desk.

As we have seen, Chateaubriand too was an enormous presence, in both person and spirit, in Tocqueville's life, however much the nephew tried to distance himself from the man he and Beaumont half-mockingly called "le génie" and however much he deplored the excesses of Chateaubriand's style.

Chateaubriand had introduced Tocqueville to the literary world at Récamier's salon and seems to have assumed the role of patron.

His family's rich literary culture, characteristic of the eighteenth-century French aristocracy who accumulated substantial libraries and enjoyed evenings reading aloud, also shaped his sensibility and his ambition. It was in Hervé de Tocqueville's library that the young Tocqueville first read Voltaire and the French philosophes. Hervé's aggressive, sometimes critical marginal comments on matters of style and diction and also on substantive accuracy in *DA I* show him to be a man of keen literary sensibility and of literary ambition as well: late in life he wrote a rather lumbering, conventional chronicle of the reign of Louis XV, a book about which Tocqueville seems to have written not a word.[10]

Tocqueville was not a facile writer. His calm, balanced prose did not flow easily from his pen. It was, rather, the fruit of enormous labor, of endless rephrasing and revising. Its lucidity and elegant formality were the achieved graces, not the spontaneous qualities, of his writing. They were wrested, as it were, from the chaos of his agitated and stuttering first drafts. He was a fastidious and demanding stylist, ever searching for the more precise, the more concise, the more graceful statement. While writing *Democracy in America* he would occasionally lecture himself about matters of style: as he composed the chapter on the condition of poetry in democratic culture, for example, he warned himself that it had been written in "un style affecté" and that he should suppress "le verbiage."[11] He would caution himself not to be wordy and oratorical. As he wrote chapter 9 of *DA II* he reminded himself to strive for "un style ferme, simple, court, coupé, didactique" and to avoid "la forme oratoire."[12] Avoiding the oratorical style cannot have been easy for him; his education had thoroughly trained him in classical rhetoric, and he had excelled in it. There are many oratorical moments in *Democracy in America*, when he turns to his readers and directly addresses them with a choice or a challenge, much as he did while speaking from the rostrum of the Chamber of Deputies.

He carefully studied the writers whose work had endured as much to discover their secrets of style as for their ideas and at great length described his quest to his old friend Stoffels: "Though my own style does not at all satisfy me, I have much studied and long thought about the style of others, and I am convinced about what I am now about to say to you: there is in the great French writers, in whatever era you choose, a certain characteristic turn of thought, a certain way of holding the attention of readers, that is unique to each of them. I believe that from the start one possesses an original cachet."[13] A memorable style was the result of character and of a way of thinking "unique to each"; hence imitation was the way to authorial death. However, he claimed to have discovered what great writers had in common: "that quality is quite simply *le bon sens*." ("Le bon sens" was a quality of judgment he applied to many things, for example, religious thought.) His explanation of "what then is le bon sens as applied to style?" was startlingly simple: ideas should be presented in an order simplest and easiest to grasp; an unambiguous point of view should be steadily maintained; the plain meanings of words ("leur vrai sens") were to be employed (that is, no riffling through a thesaurus simply to display one's versatility); precision was to be striven for.[14] He disliked the extravagant language of romantic prose, which he found imprecise and too often misleading and even false.

Above all, it was necessary to be precise and clear in one's figurative language. Illustrative figures like images and examples that stand for large ideas or underscore a point had to be used with great care. This is a curious caveat coming from Tocqueville: *sparing* is the appropriate word for his use of metaphorical language in *Democracy in America*, in which illustrative examples also are rare. One is almost startled to find Tocqueville reading *Henry V* in a log cabin in Tennessee or to catch a glimpse of Philadelphia's faux-classical waterworks in his chapter on democratic art as he explains why the democratic aesthetic is satisfied with imitation and with the appearance of the real. Figurative carelessness, he argued, was the sin of much contemporary writing: "I have spoken of this aspect of style more than the others because it is here that most writers of our time sin, and that leads us to label their style jargon."[15]

Though it wasn't until his political career foundered that he fully accepted the fact that writing was his gift and his vocation, he had always been ambitious for literary fame and had been a highly self-conscious stylist. Late in life, while enjoying the kudos for *L'Ancien Régime*, when the only road that remained open to him was that of literary accomplishment, he would reveal the reach of his ambition when he wrote to Kergorlay, "I know that between my style and that of the great writers there is a certain obstacle I must overcome to rise from the crowd to their ranks."[16] He had his eye on a place among the greats.

Though he was obsessive about being original, an expression of his profound need to be independent, he nevertheless frequently read his work-in-progress to his family and close friends, like Ampère, Beaumont, and Kergorlay, and asked them to critique his writing. The last two were astute, unsparing critics. Kergorlay was especially demanding: he would offer detailed, line-by-line commentaries, quarrel with word choice, jump on dull passages, and send overall evaluations of the tendencies of Tocqueville's style, helpfully focusing on its weaknesses. Tocqueville had sent him page proofs of *Democracy in America* a few months before the book appeared and received the following commentary on style, part of a longer critique and an example of Kergorlay's frank, tough criticism:

As for fine points, I find that your style, good on the whole and remarkable in certain passages, has a large enough number of small flaws some of which are negligence and incorrectness, others a painful and jerky pace in some stretches, others phrasings that in the end do not much please me. I believe that if you succeed in ridding yourself of all that, your work would shine with a steady light and would linger in the minds of many readers like a beautiful thing, a beautiful and remarkable account of the epoch, the century: be sure that it is by means of a style of a certain cast, a style that flows with unity, that the work of great authors has risen above repute for ingenuity and spirituality to that of genius and incontestable truth: if what you say passably well is a thousand-fold true one will say to you, "that is possible." If you speak in a style that arrests and dominates the reader, even if what you say is less profound, he will say, "It is certain, it is obvious, it is miraculously revealed, imaginative, insightful, etc."[17]

Kergorlay then advised Tocqueville to read some "maîtres," specifically Montesquieu, Rousseau, and Pascal, and to compare his prose to theirs, which he did while writing *DA II*, though as much as models of moral seriousness as models of style. Kergorlay then added many examples of faults or infelicities and was frank about what offended his taste. After the book appeared he sent the following evaluation of Tocqueville's style:

Your style decidedly has merit. It has its flaws, but also strengths; a somewhat rapid reading has led me to think that the second volume might have a stronger effect because of its style and by an enlarging of its scope. Your style opens up complex and remarkable ideas energetically and vigorously. It gives them a certain power. On the other hand, when the same style is applied to complex and concise matters . . . its concision compounds that of the subject [and] it exceeds that brevity that pleases and becomes a bit dry and jumpy. But the important thing is to succeed in the most elevated subjects, those that in the eyes of the many are the principal value of the book. Your style is a gift of great worth; it is necessary not to stop at this point but try to perfect it to the ultimate limit of your abilities.[18]

He added that he saw no reason to doubt that since Tocqueville was still young he would someday write "très bien."

When *L'Ancien Régime* was published, Kergorlay provided even more detailed, unsparing critical commentary, giving it three close readings, returning his eagerly awaited, densely annotated copy to Tocqueville, who was preparing a second printing. Kergorlay acknowledged the book's great accomplishment: he thought it was something truly new in the world: "It substitutes a profound study for the simple understandings that had appeared up to now concerning the transformation of autocratic European society during these last centuries. Mme de Staël said that it is despotism that is new and liberty that is ancient, but that had remained a brilliant undeveloped aperçu."[19]

However, he thought the book was too harsh on the eighteenth-century aristocracy and the old regime ("it is the strongest indictment of the old regime that has ever appeared"), and he urged Tocqueville to balance his harsh portrait with a few positive aspects of prerevolutionary France.[20] He also commented eloquently and sadly on what France had become; but most of what he had to say concerned Tocqueville's writing, saying that though his style had "gained in fluency and suppleness," it was still wordy, didactic, and overburdened:

> It seems to me that a fault of your style is to explain in too thorough and detailed a way an idea that is, and ought to be, complex because therein lies its truth. With regard to this I have picked out several of your most remarkable passages to demonstrate what I mean; I have removed some words, some incidental detail, some adjectives that only slightly modify, etc., and found that there remained a vivid phrase, a style that flows, finally something that recalls our great writers. I then asked myself if what remained was obscure or superficial and if it decidedly less illuminated the mind of the reader. It usually seemed to me not so, because I have noticed that those nuances and amplifyings I have excluded irresistibly follow from the central idea, and that, in a word, the reader, if he is not dumb, would divine what he does not see with his eyes.[21]

This was not simply abstract advice. Kergorlay proceeded to edit Tocqueville's text and send exemplary revisions: "When you will have my demonstration before you, you will see more clearly what I mean; but the advice I give you is this: take this or that phrase, this or that page; reread it aloud and all at once as if you were the first into whose hands had fallen a book without trouble and without great intellectual struggle. . . . That will be a great benefit."[22] He had also carefully noted various "négligences de rédaction." Tocqueville thanked him warmly for his proofreading and for the more serious suggestions about style. His reply makes clear how intensely invested he now was in his writing:

> Of all the correspondence that the publication of my book has led to between me and my friends and occasionally strangers, your letter is assuredly the most remarkable and the most useful. I can't beg you too strongly not to leave your task incomplete, but on the contrary to extend it as fully as you can. In doing this you will be rendering me the greatest service. Because, thrust back as I have been into the literary life, I have more reasons than ever to make myself

as outstanding as possible. I am astonished that you were able to find on a first reading as many real errors as your first letter claims. Because while the book had been written with much speed and energy, and above all in one breath in two months, before publishing it I had taken great care with its structure and had paid close attention to details of style. I am pleased that on a second reading the number of such faults has appeared fewer to you. But this time your criticisms aim higher and reach for the substantial aspects of style, that which completely escapes vulgar judges and which escapes all the learning of grammarians. I have always vaguely been aware of the problem you point out: that tendency to fold into the same phrase all sorts of intellectual nuances, in such a way that while completing and extending an idea, weakens it and enfeebles its expression. But never before has anyone so clearly demonstrated this fault to me. . . . hardly anyone has had the time or the sagacity to discover its cause. . . . This has been a very great service to me. The more you provide me with conclusive examples, the more you will succeed in curing me.[23]

Tocqueville understood that in striving for simplicity and clarity while at the same time trying not to bury the complexity of his thought, his prose itself had become clotted and jagged: "The defect that you have pointed out is, I think, generally the result of work done after the first effort. The first attempt is often better put than anything that subsequent reflection later adds. But the idea itself gains by being handled and deepened, reflected on again and again, all its implications turned over in my mind. Experience has shown me that it thus often gains its value. The trick is to combine the insight and force of the first writing with the thoroughly matured idea. I do not know if I will ever achieve that."[24]

L'Ancien Régime et la révolution was published in June of 1856, four months before *Madame Bovary* first appeared in serial form. It was in the bookstores by April of 1857, after Flaubert and his publisher had been unsuccessfully prosecuted for obscenity in a sensational trial. Though Tocqueville's opinion of Flaubert and of the novel (had he read it?) is not known, one can be sure he would have condemned the book for the same reason he rejected Sand's novels. Nevertheless, the simultaneous appearance of these pathbreaking works, books that truly broke the mold, reminds one of similarities between Tocqueville and Flaubert as far as their approach to style is concerned. Both were severe critics of bourgeois culture. Their literary styles—rejection of romantic ornateness; the quest for *le mot juste*; the endless rewriting of sentences in the search for exactness; the rejection as well of the commonplace and the cliché, which are instruments of commercial culture designed to hook the mass audience and increase sales—were judgments of a slack culture. In this sense, both were antidemocratic writers; that is, they rejected the two excesses of democratic culture, romantic formlessness and the commercialization of style and art. That two such dissimilar writers should have struck the same note at the same time and arrived at the same aesthetic, or counteraesthetic, says much about the cultural and countercultural currents of mid-nineteenth-century France.

Tocqueville constantly strove for originality and economy of expression in his writing. According to Beaumont, "He had an insurmountable repugnance for the commonplace," and he sought "never to say one word more than was necessary to capture his thought and make it intelligible to anyone endowed with adequate intelligence."[25] His later struggles with style as he was writing *L'Ancien Régime* resulted from his uncertainty about how to balance fact with argument, evidence with interpretation. Writing was a chore for him, and he professed not to like it. It was, he said, "a rude and detestable métier," and he claimed he was never satisfied with anything he wrote. His perfectionism could drive him to recast a sentence twenty times, and even his letters were pocked with corrections. "La forme," Beaumont said, "was his ruler, almost his tyrant. No idea, he used to say, ought to be presented in déshabille. To be received it must be presented in the fewest possible words consistent with perfect clearness."[26] Yet his desire to be precise and to capture every nuance of his thought paradoxically drove him to the excesses of elaboration that made him difficult to read. Beaumont believed this to be his major weakness as a writer: "The elaboration of his written style is excessive; it is too condensed. You cannot safely forget a sentence which is not necessary to the reasoning or to the narrative."[27]

"La forme was his ruler": in this Beaumont was absolutely correct. It was as central to Tocqueville's approach to writing as it was to his social vision. He believed that disregard for form was one of the failings of a democratic culture. What he perceived as the gaudy formlessness of romantic writing, that flowering of democratic style in literature, disturbed him as much as did the decline of social form, which filled him with terrifying visions of the rise of a shapeless mass society vulnerable to new kinds of domination and manipulation. Social tensions and conflicts had to be contained and resolved within carefully defined, though not rigid, social structures; similarly, the tension and struggle of ideas had to be subject to some kind of formal restraint and resolution. One of the most forceful qualities of *Democracy in America* is this sense of tension within form, as though considerable intellectual turmoil had been carefully controlled. There is rarely a direct expression of passion, but an artful and reflective shaping of it. He was sharply critical of romantic writing: of its excessiveness, its quest for sensation, its readiness to sacrifice meaning for effect. Romantic writers were literary showmen, seeking fame, not truth. His thoughts of the great romantic writers of his time—Hugo, Alfred Vigny, Musset,

Lamartine—do not appear in his correspondence, though he did say that though he had once read Lamartine with pleasure he could no longer tolerate his self-indulgent art, the aim of which was self-celebration. To Gobineau he cited Lamartine as a once-great writer whose style had become overripe. He did his best to squeeze any hint of Chateaubriand from his writing, usually, but not always, with success. Chateaubriand's writing was theater, in which performance overwhelmed meaning. His literary crime was that he was too ready to "decorate the truth." However, when Tocqueville listened to the old romantic read the latest installment of the *Mémoires d'outre-tombe* at Récamier's salon, he choked with emotion.[28]

Tocqueville's early prose style was restrained and plain, almost wholly devoid of vivid imagery, which explains the surface dryness, the abstractness, of *Democracy in America*. One rarely *sees* anything when traveling with Tocqueville. Detailed or lavish descriptions of landscapes, colorful sketches of individuals would have diverted the reader from the truths that lay beyond the language itself and that were not to be hidden by it. He was in fact capable of writing vivid descriptive prose: the notebooks of his travels in England and Ireland and his American notebooks as well, his often lively and gossipy correspondence, and especially his extremely theatrical *Recollections*, crowded with vividly drawn characters, demonstrate that he could. There are moments when he becomes the romantic writer reveling in the drama of nature as it speaks the language of signs, and he could write lavishly melodramatic descriptions of ruins and other evidences of a lost past. But in *Democracy in America* he had his eye on something else, on the truths that lay behind the surface. In this he was as much a transcendentalist as Emerson, though he did not often seek transcendent truth through its concrete embodiments, as Emerson did. The visible world did not entrance him. One sees nothing of Paris in reading Tocqueville; he never crosses a bridge, wanders through an arcade, pauses at a café, stops to admire a fine new building. More surprisingly, since the unfamiliar commands attention, one sees little of the American cities he visited and walked in. The streets of New York City in 1831 were as full of foraging pigs as they were of people, but Tocqueville does not notice them. He does briefly say in a letter to his mother that the buildings of the city were low and monotonous, that the streets were largely unpaved, and that there were "trottoirs" for pedestrians. What else did the booming city Walt Whitman was soon to celebrate look like, feel like? He says nothing of Philadelphia, nothing about the appearance or the architecture of Ben Franklin's city, other than that its streets are numbered rather than named after great men or events, which revealed, to him, a deeper truth about the Americans: that their minds or spirits were mathematical and coldly logical, not sentimental or passionate. His cities were moral and political realities, places in the mind. What did the streets of Paris look like during the turbulent days of 1848, when he walked through them on the way to the Chamber of Deputies? Don't ask Tocqueville.

Tocqueville's early prose style was, in addition, unrelentingly classical, that is, measured and balanced. In *Democracy in America* he argues, in his guise as teacher of democracy, that in order to counteract the utilitarian, industrial approach to literature characteristic of democracy, reading of the classics would be essential. The sensation of the day written in the wild style cultivated by democracy was good for the cash register but not for literary culture. "In democracies," he wrote, "it is by no means the case that all who cultivate literature have received a literary education, and most of those who have some acquaintance with good writing go into politics or adopt some profession which leaves them short, stolen hours for the pleasures of the mind. They therefore do not make such delights the principal joy of their existence, but think of them as a passing relaxation needed from the serious business of life. . . . Fine nuances will pass them by. . . . They like books which are easily got and quickly read, requiring no learned researches to understand them. They like facile forms of beauty, self-explanatory and easily enjoyable. Above all, they like things unexpected and new. Accustomed to the monotonous struggle of practical life, what they want is vivid, lively emotions, sudden revelations, brilliant truths or errors able to rouse them up and plunge them, almost by violence, into the middle of the subject."

His own prose would not be facile, easily understandable, or full of "sudden revelations." He would offer only "pleasures of the mind," though his book was rich with drama and a sense that revelation lay in the future.[29] He strove to avoid not only "les lieux communs," but also the attention-grabbing displays of wit and verbal virtuosity he accused romantic writers of cultivating. A random reading of nearly any paragraph or sequence of paragraphs in *Democracy in America* reveals an elaborate system of balances—parallel structures, antitheses, repeated phrases and rhetorical questions, balanced clauses—which lends a structural, an architectonic quality to his prose and creates the book's notable formality. In the macro and micro structures of his prose, Tocqueville relentlessly performs a balancing act that serves many purposes and creates a tone of great judiciousness that masks the inner turmoil of the author. "La forme" was his rule, but there was more to Tocqueville than that.

It is as though Tocqueville were making his way not willfully but by means of logically structured argument—as indeed he was. His prose moves step by step in reasoned progress toward what almost always seems to be syllogistically arrived at conclusions: conclusions or truths discovered not through insight or inspiration or empirically through the accumulation of evidence. This incessant balancing, on every level, in all structural elements suggests a certain structural aspect to his thought and to his way of perceiving and recording reality. It is thoroughly binary. His world was structured in opposites, the most striking of which, in *Democracy in America*, was the opposition of *aristocratic* and *democratic*, which stand for contrasting sets of spiritual and material values, social orders, political systems, even ways of relating to the natural world, for example, the poetic/religious/harmonious as opposed to the exploitive/materialist/individualist.

The consequences of this way of thinking and of representing reality are great. The ambiguous middle ground is lost to view. It leaves Tocqueville without the means of fully representing the uncertainties, the doubts, the tentativeness he sometimes felt as his experience of complexity made him aware of ambiguities that his structured parsing of that experience could not account for. With his balanced, structured prose Tocqueville builds an edifice of logic. It is a style that serves to impose order on even the most unruly reality, such as the churning, congenitally unsettled landscape, both social and physical, that he encountered in the United States, where change was the rule: a society constantly being transformed by a permanent revolution. His prose offers a contrast to the chronic cultural instability and disorder that he saw as the fate of democracy, and it contributes to the felt tensions of the book.

At times Tocqueville emerges from the redoubt he has constructed. Below the calm, orderly, restrained, even methodical surface of his prose—broken sometimes by his direct address to his readers, or by his occasional appearance as chorus commenting on the meaning of the drama of *Democracy in America* (a drama about man's fate), or by exclamations of astonishment at the marvels of the unprecedented reality he had witnessed—deeper currents of feeling are moving. These too determine the argument of the book. Tocqueville's literary art drew on the whole man; it is shaped by his inner conflicts, by the issues of identity that were especially intense at this moment of his life and by his continual effort to locate himself in history and to find a place for himself in society. In *History and Reading* Dominick LaCapra notes that Tocqueville was fully engaged emotionally in the writing of the scholarly *L'Ancien Régime*. The same was true for *Democracy in America*.[30]

Tocqueville the critic of romanticism was also a romantic. For him, the writer was not simply a disciplined craftsman willing to subordinate himself to the rules of the métier, seeking utmost fidelity to the *pensées* he aimed to express but also a heroic figure: independent, bold, risk-taking, visionary. This romantic notion of the writer was nourished by his idealized self-conception as heroic redeemer of France as well as by his belief that the greatness and glory and influence of France had been the work primarily of its great literary figures. He was quickly disabused of the dream that he might fulfill a redemptive role in politics, but even before the bitter, deflating experience of the 1840s his ambition, when it called for literary expression, took shape as the imperative to produce a heroic work of transformative power.

Apart from being an ambitious scientific study of the most extreme version of an egalitarian society, *Democracy in America* is also the work of Tocqueville as romantic hero. During his political years he kept lamenting the lack of the kinds of great occasions that call for heroic action—opportunities for him to slay the dragon. This he would do as tribune, a role for which he was sadly unsuited. The literary version of this need for heroic action was the great subject, the immense canvas, a colossal work in which he could perform, alone, an original, heroic deed. He often said that without a great subject he lacked the inspiration to write. Though he also realistically saw the writing life as a "rude and detestable métier" and could jest about it, for him the pen remained a sword. Undoubtedly, the writer was a figure of immense cultural and political power and significance in Tocqueville's France—it has always been thus in French culture. Historians were not just scholarly and literary figures but significant political and cultural voices. Tocqueville certainly shared this view of the importance and power of literature, but for him it had unusually intense personal meaning. It was in the writing life that his dream of heroism constantly sought fulfillment. As writer he could revivify the aristocratic ideal of a truly independent, original life, a life of no compromises in which he would be free of the "commonplace" and serve the "sacred cause" of freedom. Tocqueville's view of the heroic role of the writer as moral leader of the culture, as intrepid traveler encountering the immense unknown to return with the head of the dragon, fuels some of the energies of *Democracy in America* and makes it as much a dramatic narrative as a work of political science.

Whether or not Tocqueville's narrative strategy in *Democracy in America* was deliberate, his telling of the story of democracy, that is, of his encounter with democracy, is a dramatic work that moves, sometimes slowly, sometimes obliquely but always with a sense of inevitability and with a certain breathlessness, toward a tragic denouement. The tragedy is not that the author as hero fails, for he does return with his trophy. The drama lies in the fact that the realm that Tocqueville explores is for him, in Hayden White's words, "an arena of unremitting conflict," in which man's ideal nature and his rage for disorder struggle with one another toward an as-yet-undecided resolution, though Tocqueville holds out little hope that it will be anything but tragic.[31] His view of the fundamental moral and metaphysical struggle that is the deepest issue explored in *Democracy in America*—metaphysical in that it is rooted in man's nature—is stated in terms that seem to make it impossible for the struggle to end in a draw or in the apparent irresolution with which Tocqueville does end his book. If at the beginning of *Democracy in America* the future looks ambiguous to Tocqueville, by the end of his book he sees doom ahead.

Democracy in America can be read as a modern morality play—a didactic telling of a drama of doom with an immense cast of emblematic characters who represent certain moral qualities. The chief of these are Aristocratic Man and Democratic Man, who appear as expressions of values and ways of life. As a dramatic narrative, *Democracy in America* presents a double tragedy. It is the tragic story of a vanquished aristocracy whose demise is quietly lamented by Tocqueville as he spells out the consequences of its disappearance; and it is also the tragic story of democracy itself, whose fate is to succumb to self-indulgence and to refuse to acknowledge limits and thus fall victim to disorder and helplessness, a prey to the subtle, soft despotism whose shadow looms larger and larger as *Democracy in America* draws to its finale. The central tragedy of the book is the story of a self-destructive hero (an antihero), whose fateful flaw is his quest for comfort and happiness, but it is at the same time a lament for the missing aristocracy. *Democracy in America* is thus a drama with intertwined plots, a tale about a hero who loses his way and a tale about what happens when the other hero is vanquished.

Tocqueville's drama takes place on an immense stage over an enormous stretch of time. Consider the reflections about the prospects for the New World with which he begins his book and the long corridor of history down which he looks as a way of framing the story. The scope of the drama is as vast as its significance, for it is concerned with nothing less than humankind's past as well as its prospects. It is a drama about much more than democracy. The book's capacious, somewhat portentous beginning establishes a sense of the ominous—everything is at stake—and Tocqueville by various means keeps a sense of the foreboding alive to the end, for example, by saying again and again that fateful choices are at hand, as his drama veers from anthropology to prophecy, from scientific analysis to lecture and sermon.

As immense as the book is and as sluggishly as it occasionally flows, it nevertheless has great momentum, a force that is more strongly felt as Tocqueville approaches his conclusion. The deep tensions and central conflicts of the story, posed by Tocqueville at the start, are reiterated frequently throughout the book, often by Tocqueville himself stepping forward, much like the chorus in a Greek tragedy, to remind his readers of what is at stake in the choice between aristocratic sociopolitical systems and values and the democratic alternative. He seems to say it is still possible for them to choose even though in his view the triumph of democracy was inevitable. His slow demonstration of the fateful weaknesses of democratic culture also creates mounting expectations. As all the intellectual, sentimental, and social characteristics of democratic culture are gradually revealed and as their political implications are spelled out—as *Democracy in America* becomes a Dantesque journey through an increasingly unattractive landscape—Tocqueville's mood darkens, and he becomes apprehensive. He begins to express with increasing frequency his fears for the democratic future. The consequences of each option are progressively spelled out, and the evidence accumulates as the case is about to be sent to the jury. This constant repetition of the unresolved conflict of values that structures Tocqueville's drama adds greatly to its momentum, as does his enumerating of the dangers that loom ahead.

So do the several teleologies by which he structures his explanation of America. At first he is the terror-struck observer of the predestined work of Providence, which by definition is inexorable and all-determining. Throughout *Democracy in America* he never quite abandons Providence, which remains a shadowy presence hovering above the American story, but its role is soon taken over by those who established the enduring institutional, legal, and cultural design of the new society. These are, for Tocqueville, exclusively the Puritan founders of New England. Of them, he says, "When, after careful study of the history of America, we turn with equal care to the political and social state there, we find ourselves deeply convinced of this truth, that there is not an opin- ion, custom, or law, nor, one might add, an event, which the point of departure will not easily explain. So this chapter [chap. 2, bk. I, vol. I: Concerning Their Point of Departure and Its Importance for the Future of the Anglo-Americans] provides the germ of all that is to follow, and the key to almost the whole work."[32]

The "whole work" becomes a dramatic tale of discovery. Though he later qualifies his argument that in the Puritan origins of New England one finds the template for the institutions and culture of democratic America, he is carried away by his admiration for a people who abandoned their ancestral home not because they were forced to by necessity, but "in obedience to a purely intel- lectual craving." Tocqueville's passionate Englishmen were Pascalian in their willingness to gamble all "for the triumph of an idea."[33]

This genetic explanation is ultimately replaced, in *DA II*, by Tocqueville's rigidly applied typological analysis of the characteristics and the dynamics of American culture, yet another determinist mode of explanation. The all- determining deus ex machina now is the democratic "social state": the social and economic structure of the society, its culture and its "moeurs," that is, the habits of mind and heart of democratic man. This structural analysis, consis- tently and mechanically applied throughout *DA II*, again adds a strong sense of inevitability to Tocqueville's account of the development of American culture and politics. The origins of the democratic social state are so arbitrarily and briefly accounted for that they become very much like the Providence Tocqueville had at first evoked as an explanation for the rise of democracy.

In many other ways Tocqueville intensifies the sense of apprehension that envelops *Democracy in America* as he approaches the drama's finale. He leaves one with a sense of having ventured into a moral wasteland or rather a near-bedlam whose inhabitants wander about furrow-browed with anxiety, vulnerable to madness, especially religious madness, perpetually restless, made miserable by the futile pursuit of total happiness. They are increasingly rootless; deracinated culturally as well as physically; and, worse, they cannot orient themselves by means of a steady, realistic view of the future, whether it be the idea of a good society or simply an educated understanding of the long-range consequences of the acts of the moment. The classical tragic figure was undone by pride, democratic man, in his American guise, by a host of weaknesses. He is aggressively proud, increasingly isolated by a false sense of self-sufficiency, a victim of grandiose visions and unlimited desires, lost in culturally induced shallowness. Tocqueville's drama of a tragic figure ineluctably bereft of all that could guide him through the hazards and uncertainties of life unfolds slowly with growing force. The only hope is that he will be pulled back from the edge of disaster by the leadership of a wise elite, one which he is less and less inclined to heed even if it were to appear, which was unlikely.

Though they might have muted the growing ominousness of Tocqueville's drama, the book's many unresolved contradictions—or rather democracy's unresolved contradictions—instead add a note of uncertainty that intensifies *Democracy in America*'s unsettled, anxious denouement. Is democracy the story of the liberation of the individual? or of his ultimate subjugation by state power and by the many? Is it the story of a release of spiritual and creative energies? or of the trivializing of vision and aspiration? These and many other questions remain for Tocqueville, conflicting with his fear—with what I believe was his deepest conviction—that what lies ahead in the democratic future, despite the release of the individual from old thralldoms, is a new kind of subjugation to the many and suffocation in a banal middle-class culture.

In *Democracy in America* Tocqueville drew on all the resources of his mind and spirit. The questions he asked about the nature and future of democracy were not only theoretical or scientific or those of a curious observer. They had profound personal meaning. If he did not fully control all the resources he brought to bear on his book, they nonetheless shape it in ways that make it richer, that make it a dramatic work of art, and that reveal the whole man.

10

History as Moral Drama

Though Tocqueville was not a historian, his imagination was as much historical as it was philosophical and religious. It is difficult to know how extensive his historical knowledge was and what histories he had read. He was an *engagée* historian for whom the writing of history was a way to effect political change. Above all, for Tocqueville the writing of history was a moral act. Its central responsibility was to tell the story of what had strengthened or weakened liberty (not equality). On all levels, *Democracy in America* is a book about freedom, its conditions and perils.

Tocqueville was not a historian. He was not trained as a historian and did not think of himself as one. Not until he turned, in the 1850s, to the great subject of the French Revolution and its tumultuous aftermath did he begin serious, methodical historical research in sources. It was only while preparing to write *L'Ancien Régime et la révolution* that he became engrossed in the central historiographical problems of representativeness, quantitative adequacy, the value and hazards of primary sources, and the problematic usefulness of memoirs.

He called *Democracy in America* not a history, but "un ouvrage philosophico politique." Nevertheless, underlying his analysis of the new world of democracy and his professed intention of fashioning "a new science of politics for a new age" are immense questions about the meaning and direction of history. The whole work is informed by his powerful historical imagination, a habit of mind he shared with Mill, who, since his encounter with followers of Saint-Simon in England and his reading of Comte, had become deeply interested in the great transformations of history and the transitions between cultural epochs.

While Tocqueville was fundamentally a moralist in the classic French literary tradition, his imagination was essentially historical. History, not theology or any articulated system of philosophical belief, provided the informing metaphors of his thought, and it was within history that he sought clues about humanity's fate or the destinies of peoples. It was primarily through history that he sought to understand current political and social issues. The shock of the dislocations and radical transformations produced by the French Revolution, felt so keenly by Tocqueville himself and by his family, is registered on nearly every page of *Democracy in America*, throughout which one constantly feels Tocqueville's brooding sense of historical loss and his strongly felt need to restore the past to the present and to make time whole again.

Though he says of America that it has presented to an astonished world something new in the history of humanity, a nation that had sprung out of nowhere, he nevertheless tries to pull it back into history, that is, to account for its character and its institutions historically. But though he begins as historian, other intentions interfere, and his book becomes both an ambitious sociological study of the laws of social and cultural change and, finally, a moral fable.

Tocqueville begins his brief historical account of how democracy developed in America in the guise of a scientific historian. He remarks that America offers an unprecedented opportunity to study the growth of a society with clinical accuracy and thereby avoid the mythmaking that had hitherto characterized efforts to explain the origins and character of older societies whose beginnings lay hidden in an obscured and unrecoverable past:

> If we could go right back to the elements of societies and examine the very first records of their histories, I have no doubt that we should there find the first cause of their prejudices, habits, dominating passions, and all that comes to be called the national character . . . but up till now evidence is lacking for such a study. The taste for analysis comes to nations only when they are growing old, and when . . . the mists of time have closed.
>
> America is the only country in which we can watch the natural quiet growth of a society where it is possible to be exact about the influence of the point of departure on the future of the state. . . . Providence has given us a light denied to our fathers and allowed us to see the first causes in the fate of nations, causes formerly concealed in the darkness of the past.[1]

To say, in 1835, that "America is the only country in which we can watch the natural quiet growth of a society" was either a challenge to the major historians of his time, like Guizot and Augustin Thierry, the leaders of a historiographical revolution that called for myth-free historical studies of European nations based on ancient and medieval sources and for the recovery and vetting of such sources; or it may have been because he was not thoroughly familiar with their work. How well did Tocqueville know the historical literature of his time and the historiographical debates and issues of the 1820s and 1830s?

Tocqueville came of age intellectually at the time of a renaissance of historical scholarship and writing in France.[2] In a review from 1826 of new French histories, Mill, always deeply interested in French writers and intellectuals (who, as I have noted, he thought were much more likely to produce needed advances in social and political thought than the unimaginative, intellectually rigid, insular English), enthusiastically noted that "in the last five years France has produced many historical works of great importance; more than were ever produced by one nation within the same space of time."[3] The revolution in French historical writing, as it was later called by Lord Acton, was the work of the generation that came of age during the Restoration (1815–30), which sought as part of its dream of bringing about the moral regeneration and social healing of France to create a true, myth-free, empirically solid, politically relevant history. The problem of how to fit the Revolution into French history, whether to justify it as progress and fulfillment or reject it as destructive aberration, animated the new historical writing of the Restoration and the July Monarchy.[4]

Tocqueville says nothing about this turn in historical writing and rarely mentions the young, liberal historians such as Thierry who were excitedly attempting to create a usable history for postrevolutionary, postimperial France. Robert Gannett, whose *Tocqueville Unveiled* is the most thorough study of Tocqueville's historical methods and knowledge, has written that "Tocqueville's readings in history and philosophy were well developed by 1828"; but little is known of what histories he in fact had read.[5] He did read the major contemporary English historians. He does not mention the books of the young historians of his time, whom he knew: François Mignet, Edgar Quinet, Jules Michelet, or, as noted, Thierry, though it is hard to believe he did not know their work. Years later he wrote that he had read, with horror, Thiers's immoral history of the French Revolution (1826–28).[6] He does not mention at any time Mignet's two-volume history of the Revolution (1826), which Mill praised in the above-quoted review as a beautifully written popular narrative. He did read the anti-Whig *History of England* by the English priest John Lingard, a work that gave Macaulay fits, but apart from briefly mentioning Lingard's acidness in a long letter to Beaumont (a letter that was a potted history of England) he says nothing else about him, though it is plausible to think he had been influenced by Lingard's view that the English Reformation and the English Revolution had succeeded at the cost of much liberty.

There is no evidence that he paid any attention to another major turn in French historiography: the simultaneous boom in the historical study of law, stimulated in part by the stunning intellectual impact of the Napoleonic Code, which provoked questions about the ways in which law expressed the culture and the politics of a nation. New journals like the influential *Themis* were devoted to the historical and cultural study of jurisprudence, a field that dealt with many of the questions that deeply interested Tocqueville, but here too he is silent about what he may have read, though it is hard to imagine he had not at least heard about such work.[7]

He seems not to have been interested in another major debate of the moment, that concerning the origins of the French identity, that is, whether it was the Franks or the Gauls who had primarily shaped the French character. This was a debate not just about the identity of France, but also about the nature of race and the durability of race characteristics.[8] Later, during his search for the American character, Tocqueville had much to say about the various races that had peopled the New Republic; he employed the idea of race in a way that suggests he had not learned from the parallel debate among historians of early nineteenth-century France.

Nor did he have anything to say about the founding, by Guizot, Thierry, and others, of institutions such as the Société de l'histoire de France, created to support historical studies in France by gathering and storing the hitherto ignored and moldering documents of the past.[9] The exception to his general silence about the domain of history, apart from remarks in his correspondence about his readings in the history of England, is his well-known, admiring commentary on Guizot's celebrated lectures on European and French civilization, given at the Sorbonne from 1828 to 1830.

Though he seems to have written nothing about the work of the Restoration and romantic historians of his youth and maturity, there are similarities between their views of the proper uses of history and his own as implied in his own books. While historians like Thierry and Guizot aimed at dispelling the self-justifying and politically legitimizing myths and fables that over the centuries had been spun about national origins and character and sought to ground historical writing in carefully collected and verified sources, they also believed that historical writing was meaningful and useful only when the historian was engagée—only when it was the work of politically committed historians seeking to shed light on current issues and conflicts and thus shape politics and the course of history. The writing of history had to be a political act as much as it was the quest for the truth about the past. The historian's political and social passions had to shape his work: in fact, he ought to appear in his history, in voice and value.[10] The politically engagée historian need not necessarily be actively at work in politics, though, like Guizot and Thiers, he might be, as Tocqueville later was. In fact, historians then were public figures. Their work both as writers and as teachers had great political impact. A major historical work was a political event. Such was the ideal of historian as witness, cultural critic, and political actor, and it was an ideal that animated all of Tocqueville's writing, beginning with *Democracy in America*, even though in his later work he muted his engagement with the pose of ironic detachment.

The new liberal history also aimed at democratic inclusiveness: it sought to move beyond the traditional chronicling of the reigns of ruling elites and shed light on the lives of ordinary folk, to illuminate the mental and spiritual lives, the *mentalité*, of earlier ages and whole societies; and, above all, to tell the story of the development of liberty and democracy. To a degree some of this agenda was Tocqueville's as well.[11]

The French historian Tocqueville wrote about most extensively was Guizot. Tocqueville and Beaumont had been among the many entranced auditors, including Michelet, of Guizot's celebrated lectures.[12]

Guizot was a major intellectual influence on Tocqueville. His view of history as the story of the development of civilization—of more than just the political institutions of peoples but of their social systems and their culture as well— and the great scale on which his historical imagination played as he looked down the long corridors of time suited Tocqueville's intellectual tendencies, especially his thirst for the broad view and the long view and his holistic imagination. Tocqueville carefully took lecture notes, copied Beaumont's notes on lectures he missed, and subsequently read Guizot's *History of Civilization in Europe* and *History of Civilization in France* when they appeared. What had so inspired him? and what had he learned from Guizot? And in view of his initial enthusiasm for Guizot as well as the many similarities in their thought and politics, what accounts for his subsequent increasingly bitter disagreements with Guizot not just about political questions but also about issues of historical interpretation? Does Tocqueville's Guizotian apprenticeship illuminate anything about *Democracy in America*?

Two things about Guizot's approach to history seem to have struck and influenced Tocqueville the most: his *méthode analytique* and his argument that to fully understand the character of the institutions, especially the political institutions of a people and how they developed, it was essential to study their "social state," that is, their whole culture.[13] For Guizot this meant understanding more than the social system of a people, but also their *mentalité*, their literature, and, above all, their religious life. He thought that Montesquieu had focused too much on political institutions and practices and had not sufficiently recognized the importance of the "moral state" of a people. Tocqueville was enthusiastic about Guizot's analytic approach to history, essentially a technique of deconstructing events and institutions by analyzing how they were shaped by the culture of the time.[14] For awhile he went about applying the méthode analytique to everything, much as disciples of Marx would wield the dialectic.[15]

Aurelian Criautu, in his reflections about Guizot's impact on Tocqueville, believes that Tocqueville was more interested in Guizot's method than in the substance of his histories, and that may well be, in view of Tocqueville's increasingly angry, long-drawn-out disagreement with Guizot's celebration of the bourgeoisie as the torchbearer of liberty from the Middle Ages on.[16] Yet he fully agreed with Guizot's assertion that Christianity had played the central role in the advance of European civilization and in assuring its supremacy. Guizot's lectures and his histories made a profound impression on Tocqueville, whatever their subsequent disagreements.

What of Guizot is there in *Democracy in America*? Tocqueville's book begins as an exercise in the *esprit analytique*, and in its early chapters it seems also to be an application of the concept of the social state to the study of the development of American institutions. His second chapter, "Concerning Their Point of Departure and Its Importance for the Future of the Anglo-Americans," and the third, "The Social State of the Anglo-Americans," do begin to explore the cultural baggage of the early Americans as well as the class systems of the colonies. Though he soon abandons his examination of the mental world of the founding generations, which focused heavily on that of New England, and quickly shifts to an account of the laws and institutions of the United States and more or less abandons any discussion of the mores of the Americans (until he returns, at the end of *DA I*, to an analysis of race in the United States), he does seem to be applying Guizot's broad cultural conception of the social state. But he does not carry that approach forward very long. Beaumont noted in his foreword to his novel *Marie, or Slavery in the United States*, written at the same time Tocqueville was composing the *Democracy*, that Tocqueville in his forthcoming book "has described the institutions" of America, while "I myself have tried to sketch the customs." Throughout *Marie* as well as in its appendixes Beaumont discusses concretely, in detail, many aspects of American culture, not just the issues of race that are central to his book.[17] Tocqueville himself noted in *Democracy in America* that a more thorough examination of American society was to be offered by Beaumont. It was indeed. In fact, many of Beaumont's observations about American culture are repeated, at greater length and with less empirical support, four years later in *DA II*, which suggests questions about how much of Tocqueville's subsequent commentary on American culture drew on Beaumont's insights, or on the observations they must have endlessly shared and mulled over during the intense togetherness of their nine-month journey through the United States. Was Beaumont a collaborator, albeit a silent one in the writing of *Democracy in America* after all? It is difficult to say how much he contributed to Tocqueville's understanding of American culture, but he seems to have been more keenly interested than his colleague in understanding the social values and behavior of the Americans, while Tocqueville initially focused on their political institutions and more directly on the story of liberty in America. In reading *Marie* one encounters, though more briefly, much that would appear later in Tocqueville's second volume.

Tocqueville's initial study, in *DA I*, of the social state of the Americans is scanty, even allowing for the fact that materials for such a study were themselves scanty and just then becoming available in a few pioneering collections of historical documents. In a rare departure from his customary practice of saying little about the books he had read to prepare for the writing of his own, he added full bibliographical notes to his "point of departure" chapter (the second). His probing of the culture of the Puritans asks no questions about the spirit and the political implications of radical Protestantism or the meaning of the millennial imagination that was the English inheritance of the New England Puritans and that a knowledge of English history, even at that time, would have suggested. A Guizotian analysis would have more thoroughly studied the available English literature and documents and would have thought more about the relationship of religion in England and New England to the political culture of the early Americans. Tocqueville's discussion of the culture of New England does catch something of the spirit of the Puritan mind, but after briefly pointing to the political implications of the moral culture of the English founders, he quickly moves on to his analysis of American institutions and laws, to return to the social state, the cultural world, of the Americans only in *DA II*, and then in a method that cannot be called analytic. He later said, in explaining why he felt compelled to write the second volume of the *Democracy*, that he had not at first understood that he had to more thoroughly base his study of the political institutions of the Americans on a deeper probing of their culture, a much more thorough understanding of their "habits of the heart."[18] He had initially applied Guizot's historical methods with a light hand. He was interested not only in the questions about democracy and society that he was mulling over: he was also a young man in a hurry, with political ambitions and a keen desire to make a name for himself.

Despite his early admiration for Guizot, he soon became a bitter critic. This was in part because of Guizot's politics, but it was also because of the bourgeois slant of Guizot's histories, which Tocqueville felt falsified the history of liberty and by doing so badly confused the true foundations and the politics of freedom. Politically, though, Guizot was a liberal, one of the shapers of the ideology and the political program of the Doctrinaires, whose ideology shaped the July Monarchy. Tocqueville was infuriated by Guizot's repressive, order-oriented liberalism, by his argument that the middle classes had always been the torch-bearers of liberty, and by his claim that the bourgeoisie represented the whole nation, which meant in practical terms that to serve its interests was to serve the interests of all and the common good. To maintain the new bourgeois political and social order (which Guizot regarded as the culminating triumph of French history since it represented the triumph of the sovereignty of reason over com-peting claims to power), Guizot was willing to play fast and loose with the free-doms the securing of which his histories had chronicled. A man whose temporizing politics has overshadowed his considerable accomplishments, he was detested by Tocqueville almost as much as that other historian and politi-cian Thiers, who at least was not such a hypocrite. The disgust he felt was shared by Mill, who in 1836 would write of Guizot in a review of the *History of Civilization in Europe,*

> Despite the honorable character which he has earned for himself as a profes-sor and as a literary man, he is known in England chiefly as one of the prin-cipal instruments of the profoundly immoral, as well as despotic *régime* which France is now enduring. One of the detestable arts of that system, as of the system of Napoleon, of which it is an imitation, is to seek out, and place in stations of eminence, all the most distinguished abilities in the nation, provided they are willing to prostitute themselves to its service. In the capacity of a tool of this system, though we believe him to be greatly more sincere than most of the other tools, we have nothing to say for M. Guizot.[19]

Tocqueville detested Guizot's stratagem of co-option and struggled against even seeming to be a "tool" of the ruling elite. He just as strenuously rejected Guizot's argument that the history of the middle classes beginning in the Middle Ages was the history of liberty, which was not the work of the aristoc-racy, as Tocqueville was convinced. Guizot further argued that the spread of liberty had been given notable momentum by the English revolutions of 1640 and 1688 and then fulfillment by the French revolutions of 1789 and 1830, espe-cially the latter. Tocqueville believed that the idea that the English Revolution was a paradigm of the French, and that the latter had further and fully devel-oped the liberties won by the former—a central argument of the liberal histori-ography of the Restoration and the July Monarchy—was incorrect, a grotesque, catastrophic oversimplification. This was far more than a clash over historical interpretations.

He kept up this particular historiographical (essentially political) dispute until the end of his life. As late as 1852, when both men had been driven from political life, Guizot by the Revolution of 1848 and Tocqueville by Napoleon III's coup d'état in 1851, Tocqueville used the occasion of the presidential speech he was obligated to give at the annual public session of the Académie des sciences morales et politiques to assail what he believed to be the false linking of 1688 with 1830 that was central to Guizot's history and to his politics as well. It was a bit of malicious public mockery, designed to point out the disastrous political consequences of erroneous history. He argued that science and theory are not always helpful in "l'art du gouvernement": "Even the study of history, which often illuminates current realities, sometimes obscures them. How often don't we encounter among us those who, their minds full of scholarly ghosts, have seen 1640 in 1789 and 1688 in 1830, and who in the aftermath of a revolution have always wanted to interpret the second in the light of the first, resembling those learned physicians who, quite knowledgeable about the old maladies of the human body, remain ignorant about the specific new illness from which their patient suffers and succeed in killing him with erudition!"[20]

Guizot had the last word, attacking Tocqueville publicly when there could no longer be a reply. In 1861, concluding the customary welcoming reply to the inaugural speech of the Abbé Dominique Lacordaire, elected in January of 1861 to succeed Tocqueville in the eighteenth *fauteuil* of the Académie française, Guizot turned to comment on Lacordaire's predecessor. His lengthy remarks on both the *Democracy* and *L'Ancien Régime* were generous, but he finished with a stinger: it had been Tocqueville's brief moment of political responsibility and commitment in 1848, when he had served as minister of foreign affairs and had also struggled fruitlessly for his ideas as a member of the Constituent Assembly's committee to draft a constitution for the Republic, that had finally taught him the true difficulties of securing liberty. He subtly turned the tables on Tocqueville, suggesting that during his first ten years in politics, when he was basically an observer and a critic, he himself had been free to base his judgments on theory and not on practical knowledge: "For ten years following his entrance into political life, M. de Tocqueville enjoyed, in easy and pleasant circumstances, privileged pleasures; he offered moderate and loyal opposition to the political powers of the time, and with full freedom gave full rein to his ideas, free of having to struggle against obstacles and of any responsibility for consequences."[21] Though Guizot had not directly confronted Tocqueville's mocking rejection of the thesis that 1688 was linked to 1830, he was suggesting that Tocqueville's ignorance of the real world of practical politics lay behind his historical judgments. In his view, the far more realistic *L'Ancien Régime* reflected the triumph of fact and experience over theory. Until his painfully won political maturity, Tocqueville had been one of those "doctes médecins" who, applying ancient remedies to misdiagnosed illnesses, was likely to kill the patient. Of *L'Ancien Régime*, Guizot wrote that it was "a less brilliant book, less confident and more rigorous than the first [the *Democracy*], but superior because of its intellectual elevation and precision, firmness of political judgment, and its understanding of the essential conditions of liberty; a book that reveals all that the mind of M. de Tocqueville, already so lofty and rare, had absorbed in so little time experiencing the difficult exercise of power while under the weight of responsibility."[22]

The historical issue over which Tocqueville and Guizot bitterly differed was central to the way in which Tocqueville judged the worth and the truth of all histories. Robert Gannett Jr. has called this Tocqueville's "liberty test." No history was acceptable that did not have as its central concern the way in which men, ideas, and events enhanced or weakened liberty. As Gannett puts it, "Tocqueville insisted that the writing of history must support the instantiation of his view of liberty's essential components. Therefore, to the extent that bourgeois history segued into an endorsement of statist history, be it in the work of Guizot, Thierry, Mignet, or Thiers, Tocqueville took exception to this aspect of it. To the extent that populist history arrived at a similar conclusion, in the work of Michelet or Lamartine or Blanc, he similarly rejected it. The way a writer judged liberty became the sine qua non of Tocqueville's historical judgment."[23] There is no evidence that Tocqueville was familiar enough with the work of most of the historians mentioned by Gannett to "reject" or debate their historical interpretations, for nowhere does he write about their books or even mention them in his correspondence. But the idea that he applied a "liberty test" in his judgment of historical works is well illustrated by remarks he made in 1857 about Henri Martin's very popular multivolume history of France, the most recent edition of which had just appeared, when he was asked for his opinion of Martin by William Nassau Senior. Martin was a Republican by persuasion and a supporter of Thiers, to whose chair at the Académie française he succeeded in 1878. Tocqueville agreed that Martin's history deserved to be well received because he was conscientious and hardworking and "his historical account was not superficial," but he should have blushed when he went on to accuse Martin of being partisan and of always allowing "ses amours et ses haines" to influence his historical judgments:

> He belongs to that unfortunately important class of theoreticians we call, perhaps incorrectly, demagogues, whose political ideal is the absence of any political check on the will of the people; he had been thinking of a hereditary monarchy, a permanent president, an independent judiciary, an

established church, free of all privileged institutions, bodies, or classes. Their goal is equality, not liberty or security. They are centralizers and absolutists. An all-powerful legislature, elected by universal suffrage, seated for a year or more, and governing like the Convention, through the intermediary of committees or a single despot, chosen for a week and not reeligible, is the style of governance that they would prefer. The past five years have possibly disabused Martin about his Asiatic democracy, but his earlier volumes are throughout imprinted with his prejudices against any system that calls for a separation of powers and independent authorities that control and balance one another.[24]

One can't read *Democracy in America* without immediately noticing that it is really a book about the fate of liberty in the modern, that is, the democratic, world. In fact, Tocqueville right away announces that such is his true subject. His preoccupation pervades *Democracy in America* and shapes it in many ways: in his analysis of how the political institutions of the Americans affect their liberties; in his examination of how democratic culture enhances but also menaces individual freedom, especially intellectual freedom; and in his view that liberty is in peril when a society loses its aristocracy. With regard to method, it appears in his struggle with the deterministic implications of his social science; and also in the way in which his emblematic figures, the actors in *Democracy in America* as morality play, represent different lessons about the blessings and hazards of liberty. He had once thought to title his book *On Equality in America* but *On Liberty in America* would have more truly reflected the book's central preoccupation. Throughout his life, all his work—his political work and his writing—was shaped by what he called his "passion for liberty" and by his instinctive loathing of equality as well as by his conviction that whatever the benefits of equality might be, it would ultimately prove to be a destructive demiurge.

In every way *Democracy in America* is a book about the nature of freedom. This ultimate concern shows up constantly even in the way in which he spins the historical facts he uses to construct his narrative. Consider how he constructs one of his emblematic figures, the Puritan, to convey a moral lesson that he all but preaches overtly. In his treatment of the Puritan, Tocqueville makes as clear as possible the moral as well as the purportedly scientific purposes that history could serve. One might choose other figures who were packed with symbolic meaning for Tocqueville: the Indian, the American woman, the slave—but the Puritan, first to appear as moral messenger in *Democracy in America*, will best illustrate this aspect of the book.

The Puritans especially fascinated Tocqueville, in part because they seemed to be the key to understanding the dynamism and also the peculiar contradictions of

American civilization.[25] They were the founders of the institutions that were the basis of America's thriving republicanism, especially the traditions of local independence and personal liberty. Tocqueville believed that theirs was a triumph of spirit and mind. They stood for certain admirable moral qualities, and it was to these qualities, as much as to any objective social and historical realities, that he attributes their power and their creative triumph. Above all, they stood for a conception of liberty, as freedom-within-order, that was identical with Tocqueville's own.

"I think I can see the whole destiny of America," he writes as he begins *Democracy in America*, "contained in the first Puritan who landed on these shores, as that of the whole human race in the first man." He notes that his account of the Puritans will provide "the germ of all that is to follow" and will be "the key to almost the whole work." For Tocqueville, "the originality of American Civilization," by which he meant its system of ordered freedom and of the untrammeled freedom it enjoyed to innovate *within limits* carefully defined by a clearly understood moral and religious code, stemmed from its Puritan roots. With the arrival of the Puritans in the American wilderness, as Tocqueville describes it, "democracy more perfect than any of which antiquity had dared to dream sprang full-grown and fully armed from the midst of old feudal society."[26]

This is extraordinary history. In fact, it is mythology and could have been written only by someone with an imperfect understanding of the history of English radical Protestantism (and by someone who had not read Lingard's histories very carefully). It was in the New England colonies that the "principle of liberty" was most completely developed and applied and where "the two or three main principles now forming the basic social theory of the United States were combined." The dynamism and freedom, the innovativeness and "moral chasteness" of American life were rooted in the culture of the Puritans, whose "influence now extends . . . over the whole American world." New England civilization, he writes, perhaps consciously elaborating an old Puritan metaphor, "has been like beacons on mountain peaks, whose warmth is first felt close by but whose light shines to the furthest limit of the horizon." Later transformed into the Yankee, then the westward-trekking pioneer, and finally into that all-powerful figure of Tocqueville's, the Anglo-American, the Puritan was destined, he thought, to sweep triumphantly over all of North America, dominating all other Europeans already there as well as the natives of North America. He would conquer all because he was "far superior . . . in civilization, industry, and power." This superiority Tocqueville attributed to what he called the "purely intellectual and moral qualities" of the Puritan founders.[27]

Such intellectual and moral qualities were of supreme significance to Tocqueville, more important as explanatory factors than the Puritans' practical policies or political institutions. He admired their idealism, their practical spirituality, and their "marvelous combination" of "the spirit of freedom and the spirit of religion." They were not moral models in every respect. He was critical of the harsh coercive mechanisms the Puritans, in their "passion for regulation," had constructed as they sought to maintain an orderly and godly Bible Commonwealth. Their laws, which "constantly invaded the sphere of conscience," were often "ridiculous and tyrannical."[28] But their virtues were far more important than their failings. They were a people of vision, moved by a passion for freedom, and they understood that true liberty requires order to survive and flourish. As middle-class Englishmen shaped by the "intellectual battles" and the religio-political turmoil of the English Reformation they had developed a "more profound culture" and had brought to the New World "wonderful elements of order and morality."[29] For Tocqueville even more the heart of the matter, and the basis of his very great admiration for the Puritans, was that they had in a sense transcended history. "No necessity forced them to leave their country," he says of the settlers of New England in an extraordinary and revealing passage: "they gave up a desirable social position and assured means of livelihood; nor was their object in going to the New World to better their position or accumulate wealth; they tore themselves away from home comforts in obedience to *a purely intellectual craving*; in facing the inevitable sufferings of exile they hoped for the triumph of an *idea*" [emphasis added].[30]

Tocqueville's heroic visionaries had founded a society in which "the boldest speculations of humanity were put into practice" and where "free rein" was given to the "natural originality . . . [of] the human imagination." Thus America originated, as he put it, as "the fantasy of dreamers"; it was a place "where innovators . . . [were] allowed to try out experiments in freedom."[31] The historical impulse with which Tocqueville began his book has quickly been replaced by the moralizing imperative, announced in his introduction, that guides his imagination throughout *Democracy in America*. By the time he completed the book several years later, he had unhappily come to the conclusion that democracy threatened to stifle the originality, the bold speculations, and the freedom to innovate enjoyed by the founders. In fact, the Puritans almost completely disappear in *DA II* as the creators of American culture and institutions.

What Tocqueville admired about the Puritans as much as their powerful commitment to an idea was their conception of liberty as disciplined freedom, not as license but as principled action involving obedience to moral law. In commenting on their concept of liberty Tocqueville waxes ecstatic. He quotes John

Winthrop's distinction between natural liberty and civil or moral liberty, the latter being "a *liberty* for that only which is just and good . . . maintained in a way of *subjection* to *authority*"—a "fine definition," he thought.[32] The Puritan was simultaneously an innovator, a dynamic political experimentalist fashioning a new order of things on earth, and a profoundly religious and moral man who understood that were he to violate moral limits he would destroy his freedom. It was this "marvelous combination of the spirit of religion and the spirit of freedom" that made the Puritan, the first American, so powerful and so meaningful a figure to Tocqueville.[33] The Puritan represented the vital truth of Tocqueville's dream of a "new kind of liberalism" for France, one in which freedom and religion, liberty and order were essential to one another and made orderly progress to a more just society possible. This was excellent didactic history.

Tocqueville's historical and cultural profile of the American Puritan is a sketch informed by some learning. It would be pointless to belabor its inadequacies. Despite these he managed very well to grasp the spirit and the contradictions of the Puritan mind, just as he also achieved startling insight into the psychological engine that drove American capitalism well before the American capitalist system was fully formed. It took another century before a full, relatively objective understanding of the Puritans was finally achieved. He read much in early American literature, especially chronicles and histories, studied charters and early codifications of laws, though it is not clear how thoroughly, since some of these apparently had been summarized for him by an assistant who for some reason he kept in the dark about his project. He also consulted authorities, notably George Warden, whose large library of Americana he consulted in Paris; and especially Jared Sparks, the president of Harvard College, later the notorious bowdlerizer of Washington's letters, but also an informed guide to the history and institutions of the New England town, enormously important in many ways to Tocqueville's understanding not only of the evolution of American political institutions but also to his evolving views of the necessary conditions of liberty. He tried to see the Puritan with historical accuracy and made much in his notebooks of the crucial importance of the "point of departure" or the "point of origins" of the Americans—having been strongly encouraged to take this view by the New Englanders he had interviewed during his long and consequential stay in Boston, which he visited longer than anywhere else in the United States. But his proud New England informants also freed the moralizing impulse in Tocqueville, for they were culturally inclined to interpret the American past in the same way. Indeed, American historiography was still largely in its hagiographical stage, as in the work of George Bancroft, for example, whom Tocqueville later met and read. Tocqueville's ultimate concern with freedom also appears in his struggle with the moral implications of historical and social science method, a struggle that pervades his book.

Democracy in America is far more a work of social science than it is a history. But when Tocqueville does turn to social science in his quest to create a "new science of politics" the better to understand democracy, he still finds himself dealing with the demon of determinism, from which he only partly escapes. In the *Democracy* he persistently seeks to gain a clear understanding of the laws of social and political change and of the necessary connections between social structure and culture, culture and politics. Yet while he seeks to understand the laws of social evolution, he refuses to accept the deterministic implications of the historical and sociological schemata that were his explanatory mechanisms, and he continues to insist, most notably at the conclusion of the book, that humankind's will is free to shape its destiny. There is no mistaking this fundamental conviction of his thought. His avowal of the effectiveness of human will was his ultimate act of faith. Freedom was the foundation of moral order; unless one assumed that humans are free, even though it was a freedom within circumstances one could not control, then they are simply an instrument of history without moral quality or responsibility.

In this way he rejected the fatalism of determinist philosophies of history. It was more to the fatalism of Thiers's history of the French Revolution than to its Jacobin bias that he objected. And such was the point of his objection to Gobineau's racial historical theory, which he rejected not just because it simplified history and reduced a complex of causes to one—that is, on methodological and theoretical grounds—but also because its moral consequences were destructive. He argued that Gobineau's fatalistic doctrine was especially dangerous in an age when men, morally and intellectually exhausted in the aftermath of a great revolution and a great cultural upheaval, believed themselves "capable of nothing." That the prospect of moral exhaustion and an absence of will was no marginal fear on his part is suggested by the frequency with which the nightmare vision of democracy collapsing into a kind of terminal inertia recurs throughout *Democracy in America*. Yet while he offers a profound objection to his own social science, he does not abandon it.

Much the same point about the moral implications and consequences of historical theories emerges from his critical discussion, in *Democracy in America*, of the tendency of historians in the era of democracy to subordinate particular influences to general causes, to lose sight of how individuals shape history, and to see peoples rising and falling according to some fixed and inexorable destiny, their history determined by an "inflexible Providence."[34] This is a view that ironically he himself takes in the *Democracy* and from which he unsuccessfully struggled to extricate himself. He offers no specific examples of such democratic historians, but no doubt he would have said that many of his contemporaries would have fit the bill. While in aristocratic eras the historian's attention is always drawn to dominant individuals and much less to the web of events itself, "the historians of democratic epochs, seeing the actors less and the events more, can easily string facts together in a methodical order."[35]

However, there are few individual actors in *Democracy in America* shaping the history of liberty in America. For Tocqueville, that history, enacted on a grand stage of vast spaces and unparalleled abundance, is the story of how social forces, the qualities of the dominant Anglo-American race, the disappearance of an aristocracy, and collective passions were shaping the destiny of a people. The actual political and social battles and the roles played by forceful, dominating individuals like James Madison, John Adams, and Thomas Jefferson, all as important in the story of liberty in America as its ingenious Constitution, are not mentioned in his book. He would later learn—and confess that he learned late—that liberty was secured in the arena of political struggle, for which theory prepared one inadequately.[36]

To ask about Tocqueville's knowledge of history and about his historical literacy, that is, to know what historical works he had studied by the time he sat down to write *Democracy in America*, is to encounter the almost impenetrable veil he cast over his intellectual life. The title of Gannett's revelatory study, *Tocqueville Unveiled*, is itself suggestive: to veil oneself is a deliberate act or a habit of mind, to unveil is to remove a cover or reveal a hidden truth. In writing about "the intellectual origins of Tocqueville's thought," François Furet commented as follows:

> [Tocqueville] was remarkably discreet about his reading, not only during the period of his studies but indeed throughout his life, as can be seen from his correspondence. His was a mind convinced of, not to say obsessed by, its own originality. Even in places in his major works where he clearly drew on one or another of his predecessors, he generally remained silent about what he was up to, as in his failure to mention Madame de Staël in the chapters of the second part of *Democracy in America* dealing with the influence of democracy on intellectual tendencies in the United States. In fact, Tocqueville's "discretion" is so thoroughgoing that even a question as simple as whether Tocqueville read a lot or a little in his youth and later life is hard to answer unequivocally.[37]

The question of what histories he had read at any time of his life is also hard to answer. Those who have studied his intellectual life have often had to guess about this matter on the basis of what it would be incredible to think that Tocqueville, who was an intense intellectual most comfortable in the world of ideas and who moved among and knew most of the writers and historians of his day, didn't know. When André Jardin, in his thorough biography, turns to the question of the histories Tocqueville had read or been guided by as he prepared to write *L'Ancien Régime*, he resorts to such dodges as "it would be quite extraordinary if he had not read it [Michelet's *Histoire de la Révolution*]"; and "it is less certain Louis Blanc's history [*Histoire de la Révolution*] was among the books of Blanc he was familiar with." Jardin writes that Tocqueville "could not have been unaware of the *Histoire de la Révolution* by his friend Mignet, or of the *Histoire du regne de Louis XVI pendant les années ou l'on pouvait prevent la Revolution* by François-Xavier Droz . . . who had presented a copy of the book to him." Similarly, "he was not unaware of the forty volumes of *l'Histoire parlementaire de la Révolution* by Buchez and Roux (1833–1836), which in fact provoked a veritable revolution in the historiography of the period." Tocqueville mentions none of these books or any others in *L'Ancien Régime*, though Jardin adds that "the problematics" of Droz's book, published in 1839, "are somewhat comparable to those of *L'Ancien Régime*." He also asserts that although Tocqueville "never spoke" of Madame de Staël's *Les Considérations sur la Révolution française* "there are some resemblances that seem to prove that he had read it attentively."[38] The need for such "must have been aware of" assertions and for the scanning of texts for evidence of what Tocqueville had read is the result in part of what Furet called Tocqueville's remarkable discretion about what he had read, at any time in his life.[39] The practice of acknowledging the work of others, especially work that has been inspirational or influential or drawn from, was not routine in French historical writing in Tocqueville's time; but he seems to have gone to extremes in veiling his indebtedness to the work of others. Gannett makes it clear, in *Tocqueville Unveiled*, that in the planning and writing of *L'Ancien Régime* Tocqueville drew heavily on the research of other scholars without openly (that is, in his book) noting his indebtedness to them.[40] After largely giving up the idea of studying the origins of the Revolution through the witness of observers and participants as recorded in memoirs, that is, by visiting that time through the eyes of others, he had done an immense amount of archival research himself, about which he wrote extensively in his notes to *L'Ancien Régime*.

But in those notes he failed to mention the work of other scholars on whose work he had heavily leaned. Why had he been silent about such intellectual indebtedness? He was far from being a dishonest man. Furet's remark about Tocqueville's obsessive need to be original seems more to the point. Whatever he wrote was as much an act of self-definition, part of his unending quest to secure his identity, as it was an effort to discover the truth about democracy or about history. His work had to be his alone. He could not bear to be dependent on others. As close as he was to Beaumont, it was inevitable that their plan to collaborate on a big book on America would fall through. He left the writing of *On the Penitentiary System in the United States* entirely to Beaumont. When he sent the final page proofs of *L'Ancien Régime* to Reeve to be translated, he proudly told him that no one else had read the entire work, proof of its originality. Throughout his correspondence with Kergorlay from 1853 to the publication of *L'Ancien Régime* he dwells on the originality of his project, which he discusses with both excitement and apprehension about the historical territory he is exploring. The same is true concerning his quest for an original style. To improve his writing he has studied the literary masters, but "I have striven to remain myself and to imitate no one, not even this or that great writer." His quest for originality was unlimited. Something deeper than "aristocratic pride or snobbery" was involved in his obsessive pursuit of originality.[41]

The puzzle of what Tocqueville knew and when he knew it, of what he had read and when he had read it, holds for much of his intellectual life, not just for his knowledge of history. Saint-Beuve famously said of Tocqueville that he had begun to think before he had read anything: had he continued to think without reading very much? So thinks Françoise Mélonio. Rémusat claimed he did not know what his colleagues in the Chamber of Deputies had written, and they were exceptionally literate and accomplished, as he himself admitted. Tocqueville never mentions anything written by the prolific Rémusat, who was a fellow member of the Académie française and who would later write about Tocqueville. Those seeking to understand his indebtedness to Pascal, for example, have for the most part had to point at parallels and similarities in their thought. He undoubtedly knew Pascal, but it is not clear what he read, for he does not refer to text or title or anywhere write at length about Pascal's ideas. One mainly finds only shimmering reflections of Pascal, of Pascalian thoughts, in his writings.[42] The notes he took on Pascal's *Pensées* are simply straightforward reading notes, without elaboration or the interjection of his reflections. They have no life.[43] The same is true of his complex indebtedness to Chateaubriand, which Marc Fumaroli has commented on by pointing at suggestive parallels in their thought and language. With regard to Chateaubriand, the intellectual indebtedness seems to have run both ways, the aged romantic reading his nephew's work as confirmation of his fears about democracy.[44]

By his own testimony, Tocqueville continually read Rousseau while he was writing *DA II* (Kergorlay had suggested that he do so as a help for style), but he never specifically says what Rousseau he was reading, though of Rousseau's works it seems certain that he must have read *The Social Contract*. He does not directly comment on any of Rousseau's ideas, which by the early nineteenth century were so much part of the French intellectual brew that he might well have quietly drunk them in simply by imbibing the discourse of the time. Had he read *Émile* or *The Confessions*? Beaumont knew *The Confessions*: he wrote about them to Tocqueville in a way that suggests he assumed Tocqueville would know what he was talking about. His remarks on the great books he read as he labored on the second, difficult volume of *Democracy in America* in the late 1830s, seeking to understand the moral and literary qualities that had made Plato, Machiavelli, Montesquieu, and others immortal, are brief and thin. He never wrote reviews, though as the guiding mind of *Le Commerce* he ran the literary pages as well as setting its general editorial policy, for example, trying unsuccessfully, as noted, to induce Balzac to publish a serial novel in the journal. What he had read of Balzac is not known. He almost always read for what he needed, less for the pleasure of learning or of knowing other minds intimately, though there were occasionally evenings, at Tocqueville with Marie, of reading for the joy of it. When he wrote about literature, it was usually in his familiar esprit analytique. He seems more a sociologist or historian of literature than a lover of the beauties of prose and poetry, though it is hard to imagine that someone as passionate as Tocqueville would not have responded to these as well.

Tocqueville is notably unrevealing about what contemporary writers he had read and about his views of the intellectual debates and developments of his time. He associated with or encountered most of the major literary and academic figures of midcentury France and knew almost all of its significant historians, but he rarely comments on their work or even mentions them. He surely must have been thoroughly familiar with the ideas of the philosopher Victor Cousin, whom he knew well, as they were both members of the Académie française and the Académie des sciences morales et politiques and the Chamber of Deputies, and they were personally friendly. Through Cousin alone he must have heard much about the intimate life of the literary and intellectual world: Cousin and Flaubert had shared a mistress, the poet Louise Colet. However, he never discusses Cousin's ideas, though one might plausibly argue that there are similarities between Cousin's idealistic, pragmatic, eclectic, spiritualized commonsense philosophy and Tocqueville's thought. Cousin was the best-known French philosopher of his time. He had been the student of Royer-Collard, whom he succeeded in the chair of philosophy at the Sorbonne; he had studied with Hegel, who had intervened to rescue him from Prussian detention as a suspected revolutionary; and he was the guru of Tocqueville's generation, an intellectual of great influence and notoriety. Tocqueville and Beaumont jestingly called him "our Platon," a mixed compliment considering Tocqueville's ambivalence about Plato. But apart from occasionally mentioning his name, often in connection with a political issue, Tocqueville has nothing to say about Cousin's ideas.[45]

One can say the same about the major literary figures of romantic France and about its notable artists and musicians as well. If Tocqueville ever heard Frédéric Chopin play, or listened to a symphony by Hector Berlioz, or gazed at a painting by Eugène Delacroix, or enjoyed the very lively theater of Paris, he recorded no such experiences. As Paris resounded with the music of Wolfgang Amadeus Mozart and Gioacchino Rossini, he had to consult his friends about which operas were worth hearing. This dimension of his life is inaccessible.

Does it matter that large areas of his intellectual life remain veiled and that questions about the breadth and depth of his knowledge must remain unanswered? Is the question of what he drew discreetly from others or of how obliquely derivative some of his ideas may have been important? It may be that the originality he has been credited with is to a degree the result of his discretion about what he had read, of his failing to acknowledge his intellectual debts. The idea that the rise of democracy was inevitable and unstoppable was old hat by the time Tocqueville, in *Democracy in America*, announced its arrival as the work not of man but of Providence. Almost fifty years earlier Chateaubriand had said the same. By Tocqueville's time the idea that democracy was the destiny of humanity had long been a staple of French political thought. Similarly, the idea that democracy was more a social state than a political system had been made central to French political discourse by Royer-Collard as well as by Guizot decades before Tocqueville's book. It was Royer-Collard who, in Pierre Rosanvallon's words, "stated—in terms that would remain classic for an entire generation—the new sociological meaning of the word 'democracy'": "The semantic shift was established by the beginning of the 1830s." "Democracy is in the mores," wrote Abel Villemain in his introduction to the 1835 edition of the *Dictionnaire de l'Académie française*. "Naturally it was Tocqueville who spelled out the situation with the most talent and éclat, even if he was only following in the footsteps of Royer-Collard."[46] Furet noted that "the interpretation of the French Revolution in a long-term historical setting, an interpretation that stresses the weight of the past and reduces the significance of the change for which the Revolution wanted to take credit, did not originate with Tocqueville,"[47] though the fact that he was mum about what he had read and about other studies of the origins of the Revolution may have made it seem so. Had he successfully created the myth of his originality? Does the question of his intellectual influences matter? If one wants to understand Tocqueville's ideas as thoroughly as possible, it does.

11

The Birth of a Book

In view of the continuing intensity of his relations with friends and mentors, Tocqueville hardly seems an isolated figure laboring in solitude, pulling his master-piece out of his head like a golden thread. Yet the detailed account he left, in his confessional vein, of his struggle with the second volume of *Democracy in America* leaves little doubt that his writing of it involved a profound inward turning—as he put it, a journey over "un autre terrain," the country of his inmost self, and that on this journey he was quite alone. He describes the experience of writing *Democracy in America* in a way that makes it seem like a colossal emotional struggle, which it was: a great labor concluding with something very much like a birth.

The second volume of *Democracy in America* proved especially difficult and unsettling. The problem was not simply the pressure of other commitments: especially local political life and his responsibilities in the Chamber of Deputies, to which he was elected in 1839, and also his wavering health. The book had become intrinsically more complex. He had embarked on an exploration for which no one had cut a trail, and too often for his fragile confidence he would lose his way and bog down in uncertainty. He put it as follows: "In the first part of my work I focused on the laws, which are fixed and concrete matters. Now it sometimes seems to me that I am up in the air and that I fall into common-places, the absurd, or the boring without being able to stop myself."[1] The second volume was less well planned than the first; it slowly unfolded as he wrote it, and he did not always see clearly where he was going. He had no exact idea of the scope of his work and kept discovering its hidden dimensions as he pro-ceeded. "My subject is much greater than I," he wrote plaintively to Royer-Collard.[2] He was on a true voyage of discovery, this time not through America but through his mind. He constantly miscalculated the time his book would require. At times he even despaired that he would finish. Though he did attempt to outline the book in advance, his vague plans were simply sketchy roads into the wilderness along which he groped his way with a flickering candle.

Attempting to account for the slowness of his work on *DA II*, he explained his method to Reeve and Mill: "Every day I discover that I have been mistaken in my expectations," he wrote to Reeve: "You ought easily understand this since you know that it is not my practice to prepare a subject in advance, but only to set the general framework and establish the principal idea and thereafter follow the course of my thoughts: quickly or slowly depending on whether they slow down or speed up. Thus I don't know in advance if what remains to be done will require very many or very few pages."[3] To Mill he wrote from Baugy in September 1836 that

> my subject begins to weigh on my mind the way a nightmare does on a sleeper's stomach; I feel my mind full of ideas among which I do not clearly see any order and which I am able to develop only one by one. I would like to move on quickly but I can only drag myself along slowly. You know that I do not start to write with a firm intention to follow a system and to move on no matter what toward a goal; I give myself to the natural movement of my ideas, allowing myself to follow one implication or another in good time. Thus so long as the book is not finished I do not know precisely where I am going and if I will ever get there. This uncertainty becomes insupportable.[4]

The book continued to take shape slowly and in ways he had not foreseen. It seemed to have no limits. "I could never have imagined that a subject so many facets of which I have turned over would show me so many new aspects," he wrote to Reeve in the fall of 1836. In the summer of 1837 he was still expressing dismay, now to Mill, that "the scope of the book has grown much larger." He was still not fully in control of his work when in February of 1838 he wrote to Nassau Senior, "The subject is much more difficult and infinitely wider than I supposed when I undertook its treatment. I should probably have recoiled from the task had I been aware of its extent"[5] He was still struggling to see his work with the clarity he insisted on even as he began working on the last chapter: his thought had shifted to that most difficult terrain in which it was at last imperative for him to resolve, or at least to deal with, the ongoing debate within him between science and doubt, knowledge and faith, that is the profoundest issue of his book and the true frame in which he had tried to think through the questions he had raised about democracy and its future.

It seemed to him, he complained to Kergorlay in October of 1838, "that ideas appear and disappear before my eyes like Chinese shadow puppets and that I see them only through a veil that prevents me from fully grasping them. It's a question of the final chapter, about which we have had so much to say."[6]

Democracy in America was a burden that gave him no rest. As he put it to Ampère, "You know that it has never been a comfortable mistress." At times his chronic anxiety sank into a deeper kind of apprehension: "There are moments," he wrote to his friend A. M. Bouchitte, "in which I am seized by panic-stricken terrors."[7] He was often overwhelmed by a sense of inadequacy and overreaching, which he analyzed in detailed descriptions of what was, for him, becoming a nightmare: a prolonged experience at the edge of endurance and mind. "I often work with passion," he wrote,

> but rarely with pleasure. Awareness of the imperfection of my book over-whelms me. I constantly have before my eyes an ideal that I can't approach and when I am quite worn out trying to get there I stop and retrace my steps full of despair and disgust. My subject is much greater than I, and I am distressed to see how little I have made of ideas that I think are good. There is another intellectual malady that torments me incessantly, and that is an unlimited and irrational passion for certitude. Experience shows me every day that life consists only of probabilities and approximations, yet nevertheless I feel the taste for the certain and the definitive growing without limit in my soul. I doggedly pursue a fleeting shadow which always escapes me, and which I can't console myself for not having grasped. All these diverse feelings make my work agitated, painful, and erratic, full of angry soul-searching, momentary euphorias, and sudden depressions.[8]

His accounts of his long effort to deliver himself of his book catch something of the turbulence and even the irrationality of the experience. However serene his rural retreat may have been, he appears not to have matched it with a corresponding inner tranquility. He unpredictably swung in wild arcs between hope and despair, experiencing "several leaps of real happiness which occur from time to time in the midst of my habitual malaise, much discouragement, irritation, disgust, and then suddenly bright hopes. All this at the heart of my solitude makes my existence troubled and agitated by violent and contradictory emotions, some of which are good and sound, others of which don't matter much because I can't deceive myself. The book moves on very slowly amidst these difficulties."[9] Despite his doubts and inner turmoil, he drove on with his task, demanding so much of himself that occasionally his health broke down. His personal as well as intellectual intensity allowed no evasions. He was not, he said, "his own dupe." Neither did his literary scruples permit easy-going escapes. He believed that a writer owed his subject and his audience all his strength and ability, and he accepted this duty as a matter of honor, rather like a professional or literary manifestation of noblesse oblige. His sense of the greatness and urgency of his subject also carried him along. Slowly writing and rewriting sometimes for seven hours a day for months at a stretch, he was engulfed by what he called his "monomanie." "My life has been so regulated and so focused during the whole period of which I speak," he wrote to Royer-Collard, "that in a way I haven't felt alive. At the moment it all seems to me to be just one day devoted to one thing."[10] His drivenness enabled him to roll on through periods of despair and difficulty, but it was also an additional burden, tightening the tensions of an already high-strung, complex, self-critical personality. He was too intense to relax: "I need repose, and for me repose is intolerable," he complained to Beaumont when fatigue had momentarily forced him to suspend his writing for a few days. When he wasn't at work, he thought compulsively about it. To Reeve he wrote that he had returned to "cette damnée Démocratie," which he said he wore like a pair of glasses on his nose and through which he saw everything. A degree more fanaticism and his family would have "to intervene and take me away to Charenton" (a madhouse near Paris).[11]

On September 15, 1839, he wrote to Reeve that he had returned to Paris the day before with his completed manuscript. "Mon livre est enfin terminé," he wrote, "terminé définitivement; alléluia![12]

It was in many ways a remarkable accomplishment. When one considers the circumstances of his life from 1835 to 1840—his strenuous journeys to England and Ireland, much physically draining travel to and fro in France that involved days of body-jolting travel by coach to get from Paris to Valognes, his unsettled itinerant domestic life, the dilapidated, uncomfortable condition of the chateau at Tocqueville, the death of his mother, his marriage to Mary Mottley despite much opposition and subsequent occasional marital stresses, Marie's periodic illnesses, his strenuous, time-consuming, emotionally draining political campaigns in 1837 and 1839, and, above all, his fragile health and physical collapses, not to speak of his emotional and intellectual struggle with *DA II* as he swung from élan to depression and worked intensely to think through and conclude his increasingly complex argument—the book seems a heroic feat. It *was* a heroic feat. It had called for physical courage, force of will, a great dream, unflinching self-confrontation, and powerful ambition.

Years after having finished his "grand ouvrage" he claimed never to have read it again.[13]

Part IV

TOCQUEVILLE'S AMERICA

1

Tocqueville's American Notebooks and *Democracy in America*

The notebooks Tocqueville kept during his American journey record his immediate, powerful reactions to his encounter with every aspect of American life as well as the many conversations he had with leading American figures and his preliminary reflections about American politics, religion, and culture.[1] They were the most important source of what became *Democracy in America*. His first views and judgments of America, vividly recorded in the many notebooks he excitedly filled, were often darker and more critical than those that ultimately appeared in his book. Had he not written *Democracy in America*, what picture of Tocqueville's America could one draw from his notebook remarks? How much of the darker, more apprehensive view of American life that appears in the notebooks (and in his other writings of the moment) vanishes in his book? And which of his observations and judgments served as the bases for his later analysis? How did he get from the notebooks to *Democracy in America*?

Tocqueville was not the first Frenchman to journey to America in search of the future, and a long file of his countrymen has followed in his footsteps. Yet he was, and still is, the most insightful and influential of them all, principally because he raised questions about democracy that are enduringly meaningful and also began to develop a view of democratic culture rich with insights that continue to illuminate where the country is now. How he shaped that view and how he achieved those insights are questions I examine in this book. The fruit of his journey, *Democracy in America*, has become a fundamental work of social science. Beyond that, it is a masterful literary accomplishment. Of all travelers' accounts of the reality and the future of America, it has been enduringly meaningful.

Tocqueville did in fact discover the future in the furiously industrious people who, as he described them, were relentlessly hacking their way across the still-green continent while shedding all restraints, customs, traditions, and inherited identities in a colossal social experiment in self-fashioning. In effect he discovered

America for a second time (which is what he said the Americans were doing every day—as they still are). One might say he is one of the inventors of America: the celebratory version of the country's past and prospects is usually supported by an abundance of quotes from *Democracy in America*. (His dark comments are almost wholly ignored.) He has become a participant in the national dialogue about what America is and about the choices it faces as it struggles with the exigencies of its troubled political and cultural life in a time far less optimistic than the boom years of the young Republic.

Since his voyage of discovery, an apparently endless stream of hyperarticulate French travelers has followed Tocqueville to this hyperreal land of wonders and portents, a society of dreamers and utopians where the future of all humankind can be read, perhaps to be shuddered at as French scrutinizers of the United States often do.[2] Regrettably, their reports have seldom been serious works of cultural analysis. Recently, they have been media events and have vanished like media events; or demonstrations of critical or social theory; or simply ventings of dismay and anger that France is no longer lighting the way for humankind. Whatever originality they sometimes have is that they do report on the unending originality of American culture. And for that matter, few homebred studies of America have added much to what was essential in Tocqueville's view of American culture. If, for example, as some recent major histories of the United States have it, the signal fact about America is that from the start it was a nation of hustlers, Tocqueville said the same thing less dramatically by pointing out how thoroughly it was dominated by the industrial–entrepreneurial spirit.[3] If, during his brief, breathless visit, he missed or ignored a good deal, he nevertheless got the essential facts right and gained profound insight into the driving spirit of the culture.

Tocqueville's notebooks, his detailed record of the nine-month journey he and Beaumont made in 1831–32 to America, sometimes display the same cultural superciliousness and contempt recorded without embarrassment by his imitators. He now and then offers equally hyperbolic accounts of his encounters with the new. However, the notebooks mainly reveal a serious mind struggling to grasp the meaning of the still-new society and to answer the great questions raised by the transition from the age of tradition and authority to the age of reason and experiment: questions about possible new foundations for human community, about the future of liberty, about what the culture of democracy would be like, and about the chances of managing or even transcending history, which seemed to be arcing toward the future with a will of its own no matter what anyone did. The notebooks are treasuries of the raw material, the thoughts and observations out of which grew his socio-philosophico-historico "grand oeuvre," *Democracy in America*. In them he banked the material that was transformed and elaborated as he shaped it into responses to the questions he asked. These are questions Americans are still asking, which accounts for the continuing relevance and power of *Democracy in America*. That continuing power is the result also of the almost-mythic standing of his journey, like those of Marco Polo, Columbus, Captain Cook, and Lewis and Clark.

Tocqueville traveled in America during the boom-time of the young Republic. It was a moment of explosive change and irresistible expansion, of great optimism yet great uncertainty, of rapid progress toward political equality (for white males) but also of dangerously intensifying political tensions. The struggle over slavery was fast growing more intense. Though it was an unsettled time, it was also an exuberant time, when the perfectionist, millennialist, immediatist impulses of American culture had been released, and Americans set about to transform all the institutions of their society—and of humanity itself. A powerful sense of possibility had taken hold: everything was up for reform. "What a fertility of projects for the salvation of the world," Emerson wrote in *New England Reformers*, listing a fantastic range of reform crusades. Though he ostensibly was writing about the overflowing of the passion for reform in New England, his comments were true of the whole society. Bible societies, Sabbatarian societies, temperance societies, Sunday School societies, Intentional (Utopian) communities, domestic and sexual reform societies, diet and health movements, agricultural and ecological reform societies, and antislavery societies, all devoted to the perfection of human-kind and to the complete, immediate fulfillment of human possibilities, were springing up like mushrooms in the remarkably fertile social soil of the new Republic. A new person was in the making, even as the old one ran about omniv-orously devouring the land and its creatures in freedom's great modern binge.[4]

It was also a time of cultural flowering. The American literary renaissance was about to find its great early voices, and a distinctive American culture with its Barnumesque exuberances, its wild, tall-tale-inspired vernacular, and its confidence men had burst upon the land, bringing excitement and danger.[5] The "common man" was feeling his power and expressing it in every way. The country seemed to be bursting at the seams. Change was not only sweeping but rapid. The adolescent Republic suddenly outgrew its old clothing. If the Revolution had been the Republic's big bang, then the decades following Jefferson's democratic revolution of 1800, the Louisiana Purchase, the triumph of Andrew Jackson, and the launching of the westward movement constituted its inflationary period. The possibilities of democracy were being rapidly explored and fulfilled. How much of this did Tocqueville see or understand? Though he cannot be given high marks for his fieldwork, he nevertheless remarkably managed to catch the poetry of the emerging American culture, by which I mean he sensed the inner life behind the visible, exhilarating material boom of American life; he not only glimpsed but also understood those impulses of the imagination that were shaping the emerging new American culture. It was for this accomplishment that he was praised by the pioneering student of the American Renaissance, F. O. Matthiessen.

Tocqueville's notebooks, along with the letters he wrote to family and friends in France, record his first effort to make sense of America and to answer the questions about what democracy means for human community, for the human spirit, and for the future of liberty. They are made up of immediately transcribed interviews, collected data, comments on codes of law, American politics and religion, cultural observations, reminders of future research, and occasional summary reflections on the issues he had been thinking about. They constitute a portfolio of preparatory sketches for the great tableau that was to follow.

The notebooks, the field notes of a philosophical anthropologist and political theorist, offer a view of what he was thinking and feeling as he traveled through the United States. They allow one to see his doubts and ambivalences, convey something of the intensity with which he pursued various lines of inquiry, and make it possible to see how his tentative answers to the questions he was asking either grew more complex or did not. They reveal how he came to see the contradictions and paradoxes of democratic culture, because from the start America was where democracy itself could be tracked to its lair. (He thought he had finally cornered it in Ohio.) The notebooks offer a glimpse of Tocqueville at work.

Looking over his shoulder, one senses something of the excitement he felt, of his puzzlements and uncertainties, and of the shock of discovery he experienced as he encountered the bizarre, unprecedented society he had come to study. His reactions ranged from astonishment to revulsion. The passionate Tocqueville was so high that it was almost always he who pushed the expedition beyond prudent or planned paths, pulling an occasionally reluctant Beaumont along, as on their spontaneous monthlong trip to the West. At other times Tocqueville went off by himself into the American forests to shoot birds or in search of religious epiphanies, while his more robust, though more cautious, companion stayed behind to sketch the startling new world. In the midst of the bitter winter of 1831–32 Tocqueville's health briefly broke down: Beaumont later thought that that anxious, though transient, moment was when the seeds of the pneumal catastrophe that finally did him in were sown. However, one has to be careful not to construe the excitement so palpable in the notebooks as admiration.

Tocqueville's notebooks also raise the question of what he did not see or perhaps chose not to record. The United States in 1831 and 1832 was sizzling with unrest. Tocqueville is quiet about this. The notebooks say nothing about workers' first efforts to form trades unions and about employers' efforts to suppress them legally as alleged conspiracies or by extralegal means such as blacklisting. These first stirrings of the labor movement in the United States were especially strong in New York, where Tocqueville spent much time, and in Philadelphia. The notebooks say little about the abolitionist movement, though abolitionist and antislavery societies were among the most notable of the associations that he saw springing up to push every conceivable cause and reform. He does mention temperance societies as an example of the American penchant for association and a Baltimore association the purpose of which was to found and manage a racetrack. They don't mention Nat Turner's uprising, which occurred in Southhampton County, Virginia, in August of 1831, but he and Beaumont were on their long, spontaneous side trip through Michigan and Wisconsin and then back to Quebec when this fearsome bloody event occurred. Yet he was in Philadelphia when Turner was finally captured and executed. There is no mention of William Lloyd Garrison or his newspaper *The Liberator*, though Garrison in January of 1831 launched his fiery paper in Boston, where Tocqueville spent more time than anywhere else in the United States. Garrison was national news in 1831.

There is little mention of many of the central issues of Jacksonian politics, such as monopoly, banking, imprisonment for debt, and suffrage, though he notes the struggle over westward expansion, the forcible resettling of the Indian, and the expansion of slavery. There is nothing about the political turmoil he surely must have heard about during his stay in Washington in January of 1832 (when he briefly met Jackson) as the bitter struggle between the Jacksonians and the National Republican Party, which would become the Whig Party in 1834, intensified. But he has much to say about the physical crudeness of the nation's capital.[6]

Of course, he had just so much time. He was pressed by the commitments of his official mission and spent much time traveling over a vast country by crude and sometimes painful means. His physical courage was exceptional. His health finally collapsed in a drafty log cabin in Tennessee in the midst of the brutally icy winter of 1831–32. It was a moment of mortal danger for Tocqueville, one that he and Beaumont recalled in correspondence almost fifteen years later, when Tocqueville expressed his gratitude to Beaumont for not having abandoned him. He also interrupted his inspection tour of democracy, as we have seen, with a lengthy excursion into the wilderness, to experience firsthand the impress of nature on society and the human spirit, long a preoccupation of French writing about America and a central theme of Chateaubriand. Pressed for time toward the end of his journey, he sped almost nonstop through the slave South from New Orleans to Washington, closely passing Montpelier, the home of the still-living though very old Madison, as well as Jefferson's already disintegrating Monticello, where, a mere five years after Jefferson's death, he would have found goats grazing the lawns and grain being stored in the beautiful sunlit rooms of Jefferson's great house. It would not be surprising if by then he was too exhausted to absorb more. Still, the omissions and silences are striking and worth noting because they raise the question of what he may have chosen not to record or selectively had not noticed, as, for example, the urban violence it is hard to imagine a European traveler not observing or not hearing about.

The America of the notebooks differs in significant ways from the America he presents in *Democracy in America*. The portrait of America rendered in his book is more positive, though ultimately its view of the future of democracy becomes increasingly pessimistic. In some ways the *Democracy* is his American dream book, with some of the darker aspects of American life scanted, except for slavery, which is much more fully discussed, as is the cruel uprooting of the Indians.[7] Nevertheless, the notebooks do contain the nub of everything that is in *Democracy in America*. By the time he left the United States in February 1832 every element of his theory about the politics and culture of democracy and every observation about the effect of the democratic "social state" on cultural life was in place in some shape or other in the notebooks, ready to be organized and elaborated into a large work of analysis and theory. Shortly before he returned to New York City from Washington he wrote to his father, "Right now I am mulling over many ideas about America. A great many are as yet in my head; the germs of many have been thrown down without order on paper, or have been expanded in conversations written out in the evening upon returning home."[8]

The darker perceptions that underlay the growing pessimism of *DA II* are also scattered throughout the notebooks, ready to be organized into a coherent argument.

In many instances Tocqueville drew on the notebooks for more than ideas and illustrative examples. Lines and even passages reappear almost verbatim in the *Democracy*. For example, a good deal of what he has to say in the book about the Indian is based on discussions with French Canadians in Quebec and on his long interview aboard a Mississippi River steamboat with Sam Houston. Some of Houston's comments, or rather Tocqueville's transcriptions of Houston's remarks, show up almost word for word in the dramatic chapter called "The Present State and the Probable Future of the Three Races that Inhabit America."⁹ The notebooks were more than sourcebooks; they also contain his first efforts at setting his ideas down on paper.

Had Tocqueville not been able to write *Democracy in America*, what picture of America could one reconstruct from the notebooks and from his letters to France? What, in effect, was the starting point for the book he would begin to write two years later? One might perhaps assume that he did not record *all* his thoughts and observations in the notebooks and in the careful letters packed with observations he sent to family and friends, but it is unlikely that much he had in mind or observed is missing. He was an assiduous, methodical, and self-reflexive journal keeper. Just before he sailed back to France he had written to his mother that of all the material he was bringing back, it was his notebooks that really mattered: these contained everything he would need for the big book he hoped to write, the shape of which he still only vaguely saw. If they alone, along with his correspondence, which he asked everyone to save, were the only resources he could count on, he would have all the necessary "idées mères" and data for his future work.¹⁰

In some ways, the America of the notebooks is a dark place. Some of the notes' harsh judgments of American character and culture are given milder, more detached, and nuanced expression in *Democracy in America*, and some disappear, though it is doubtful he had changed his mind. The understandably terse and more ambivalent notebooks do not prepare one for the burst of enthusiasm with which, at the end of *DA I*, he describes the dynamism of the Americans or his almost awed vision of the energetic, imperial Anglo-Americans sweeping over the continent, subduing the French in Canada and the Spanish to the South and then sailing stormy seas more boldly and speedily than anyone to establish a commercial empire. No more powerful hymn to Manifest Destiny and to the American spirit was ever written. As he concluded *DA I* in 1834, he was carried away by this vision of an all-conquering America:

> It must not be thought possible to halt the impetus of the English race in the New World. The dismemberment of the Union, bringing war into the continent, or the abolition of the republic, bringing tyranny, might slow expansion down, but cannot prevent the people ultimately fulfilling their inevitable destiny. No power on earth can shut out the immigrants from that fertile wilderness which on every side offers rewards to industry and a refuge from every affliction. . . . Thus, in all the uncertainty of the future, one event is at least sure. At a period which we may call near, for we are speaking of the life of nations, the Anglo-Americans alone will cover the whole of the immense

area between the polar ice and the tropics, extending from the Atlantic to the Pacific coast.[11]

There is little of this in the notebooks. And by the time he finished *DA II* in 1839 this vision of a bold, dynamic, almighty Anglo-American Republic has disappeared.

He and Beaumont had been shocked by the crudeness of American manners; by the cruel graspingness and "iciness" of the people; by the destructive rapaciousness of the Americans toward their astonishingly abundant environment; by the bombast and triviality of political life in the great democracy; and by the shallowness of the religious life of the Americans. They were especially troubled by two dark aspects of American life: the barbarous, inhuman, in effect genocidal race prejudice of white Americans toward blacks and native peoples and the overwhelming materialism of the Americans, who were obsessed with money to the exclusion of almost all other values. They had been not at all surprised by the thinness of American literature, art, and intellectual life, which they evidently had assumed was either nonexistent or derivative and thus didn't bother seriously to inquire about. (Though Mill had much admired *Democracy in America*, he had criticized Tocqueville and Beaumont too for having examined life in America too much with the same smug assumption of superiority with which he thought the French viewed all other cultures, including the English.[12] He might have been appalled by the notebooks, though he surely would have found them fascinating examples of the strategy and of the logic of social analysis, the subject of his *Logic*.)

Yet even as he was filling his notebooks with incredulous and skeptical comments, doubts, and even open condemnation of certain aspects of American culture, Tocqueville increasingly balanced his negative judgments with what he found positive and promising about America, whether it was aspects of democratic politics or religion or the general level of American intellectual life, which he found to be higher than that of the French. His exploration of America was also an exploration of himself, a quest for identity, as open-minded as his cultural spectacles and his felt urgencies would allow. If he was skeptical about democracy, he was not out to prove anything, unless it was to show why an aristocracy was culturally indispensable. He had no ideological errand. Nothing better illustrates his ability, so evident in his notebooks, to challenge his observations and to modify his judgments than the self-reflexiveness, or the dialogue with himself, that runs throughout the notebooks, the mark of an essentially liberal mind. He was freer to do this in America than he usually was at home, where the weight of his cultural inheritance, the exigencies of politics, and the keenly felt psychological anxieties and wounds he suffered as a vicarious victim of the Revolution were inescapable. His mind and his spirit opened up in America. The America that emerges from his notebooks is a dynamic world of paradoxes, the future of which he caught glimpses of but would not finally see until he pulled all his ideas and insights together in the late 1830s as he wrote the second volume of *Democracy in America*.

2

TRAVELING THROUGH THE NEW REPUBLIC WITH
TOCQUEVILLE AND BEAUMONT

As Tocqueville and Beaumont traveled the New Republic, Tocqueville did not fail to
note what he found admirable about American life, including its egalitarian informality and its practical political sophistication.¹ But he also walked on its dark side.
He sensed a strain of violence, a ruthlessness, an inhumanity toward non-European
races, and an overwhelming cupidity in the wild new democracy as well as an almost
unredeemed cultural crudeness and looseness that he began to feel was congenital
to democracy, primarily because it lacked an aristocracy, a permanent elite. This
idea becomes central to his later analysis of the characteristics of any democratic
culture. He gingerly recorded his first thoughts about slavery in the United States
almost as if he were simply a curious observer, even though he was a fervent antislavery activist in France. His comments on American slavery are amplified in *Democracy
in America*, in which he vents his anger and disgust with the dehumanizing institution. His discussion of slavery in *Democracy* is awkwardly placed, well toward the end
of the first volume, almost as an appendix, suggesting that he found it hard to place
such radical inequality in the radically egalitarian New Republic. He has much to
say about religion, class, politics, the power of money, American aspirations; and he
writes too about the emerging American identity, reminiscent of Hector St. John de
Crèvecoeur's earlier commentary. Some of his observations are the kernels of his
analyses in *Democracy in America*, some he suppressed, though it isn't clear why.

As Tocqueville and Beaumont traveled through the United States Tocqueville
began to see a quality in the American spirit that deeply troubled him and that was
a quietly abiding specter in all that he later wrote about American life and culture:
a coldness and implacability, a powerful acquisitiveness, a ruthlessness toward
nature, a fierce competitiveness, a cruel racism, and a heartlessness about the lives
of the different, that is, native Americans and Africans—traits that, in combination
with the deeply rooted messianic assumptions of American self-understanding,
whether religious or secular, could become an awesome engine of violence.²

All this is much subdued in *Democracy in America*, and one must ask why. Tocqueville never openly integrated his sense of the demonic and destructive in the American psyche with the rest of his cultural analysis but mostly persisted in seeing the Americans as remarkably peaceable and law-abiding. Yet he was not blind to the strain of violence in American life. In the midst of the wilderness that he called the real America, which, as we have seen, he describes as a scene in which death competes with life in a never-ending struggle, he places a powerful image of the American as a character of enormous energy, cold and determined, an axe in one hand and a Bible in the other, destroying everything before him, forests, animals, the Indians, while creating a civilization he would in turn destroy perhaps to re-create once again. No word appears more frequently in his description of the emotional makeup of the Americans than *cold* — unless it is *icy*. Even the frontiersman pushing through the forests uprooting or destroying all that thwarts him is animated by "a cold, persevering energy"; he is "cold, tenacious and relentless in argument; he attaches himself to the ground and snatches from savage life all that can be got out of it."[3]

He felt that the Americans suffered from a deficiency of heart. There was something frigid, logical, and calculating about them, qualities which stood out in sharp contrast to the French Canadian people among whom he traveled for several weeks in August of 1831, people who, though "inferior to the Americans in knowledge," were "superior in qualities of the heart": "The French of Canada seemed prodigiously like the French people, or rather . . . still are French people, trait for trait, and consequently entirely different from the English populations surrounding them. Gay, lively, joking, fond of glory and renown, intelligent, eminently sociable, their manners are gentle and their characters are obliging. . . . the Englishman and the American are either *coarse* or *icy*."[4]

Tocqueville saw the American people, whom he described as a "restless, calculating, adventurous race which sets coldly about deeds that can be explained only by the fire of passion," sweeping in triumph across the continent and then returning "on its tracks to trouble and destroy the societies which it will have formed behind it."[5] This vision of destructiveness will later appear transmuted in the specter of the self-devouring culture that darkens *DA II*. The demonic impulse he had intuited and remarked upon in the notebooks is later given form in the powerful description of the New World landscape that opens his book, where in the midst of unparalleled abundance and beauty he sees death struggling with life. A deadly snake lay coiled and waiting in Paradise.

Tocqueville seems to have struggled to suppress this grim insight, perhaps because it was too ominous or because he did not wish to say that democracy inevitably led to disorder, violence, chaos. In fact, in an impressive act of denial he asserts quite the opposite, by claiming that the Americans were remarkably peaceful and showed "extreme respect . . . for the law," which "alone and without public force . . . commands in an irresistible way." "I am inclined to believe," he wrote, "that there is something in the complete confidence in the law which leads men not to take advantage of it."[6] Remarkably, he would still be saying, in his preface to the twelfth edition of the *Democracy* (1848), at a time when political and social life in the United States was becoming ominously violent, as he well knew, that while European nations had been ravaged by war, revolution, and civil strife, "America has not even suffered from riots." On the whole, despite his troubling intuition of the demonic in the American spirit, the America that appears in *Democracy in America* and to some degree in the notebooks as well appears as a peaceable kingdom in which busy men, enjoying unparalleled abundance and opportunity, live in harmony under the law. One might credit Tocqueville with advancing a scarcity theory of social conflict, except that even by the 1830s there was a great deal of social conflict and violence afoot in the United States. And though the outlaw, a term Tocqueville knew, had not yet appeared, his subtle analysis of the democratic psyche catches glimpses of the antinomian strain in the American spirit.

He traveled in the United States during a time of growing urban unrest and political turmoil. Rioting was a familiar occurrence there in the 1830s, as it long had been, caused by a great range of rising angers and social tensions: nativist prejudices, growing class bitterness, culture wars even about language and accent and the ethnicity of actors in the theater (battles as violent as the ones that sometimes occurred in the parterres of the politically volatile French theater), and efforts to organize labor. Elections were especially turbulent. Tocqueville's visit to New York City in 1831 was sandwiched between two notably bloody election riots in 1828 and 1834.[7] In New York City there had been furious protests, sometimes leading to bloody street violence, even about the enforcement of laws prohibiting the free foraging of pigs in city streets. Had he walked much about the city he certainly would have had to dodge wandering porkers. He doesn't mention them. These riots expressed not only antagonism to authority, but also race angers, pitting the mostly Irish pig owners against the mostly black wardens whose job, often the only employment free Negroes could get, was to corral wandering pigs.[8] Tocqueville took no note of such turmoil while he was in New York City. Neither the notebooks nor *Democracy in America* take note of the violence that more and more often boiled to the surface of American life.

More surprisingly, there is not one word about the long and continuing history of slave unrest and insurrection. Concerning the agony of slavery, the grimmest aspect of life in America and the great contradiction in a society devoted to the principle of equality, Tocqueville in his notebooks is curiously subdued, though he constantly probed for information about slavery and its social and economic effects. He observed and noted instances of race prejudice so profound that a hint of Negro ancestry would exclude passably white octo-roons from white society: the "drop of blood" curse that became the seed of Beaumont's *Marie*; and he comments on the many ways even free blacks in the North suffered cruel treatment and were denied their rights. Yet the problem of race and of slavery is given less attention than other issues in his notes, even though he thought slavery was an abomination. The notebooks make it clear that whenever he could he pressed his informants about slavery, but his notes are for the most part restrained summaries of his interviews. He started to ques-tion Americans more insistently about slavery only toward the end of his visit, when he began his perilous midwinter journey down the Ohio and Mississippi rivers from Cincinnati to Louisville and then Memphis and New Orleans. Perhaps he had been reluctant to probe so explosive an issue, though there was nothing tentative about his judgment that slavery was a brutal violation of human rights and an assault on human feelings.

It was something said by a Georgia planter, a Mr. Clay, whom Tocqueville met in September in Boston, that gave him a phrase he used in a question he put to John Quincy Adams. Clay had said that the introduction of blacks was "the one great plague of America" (in Clay's view it was a plague because the two races would never get along and the whites would leave the South when the more numerous blacks inevitably gained their freedom). A few days later Tocqueville asked Adams if he saw slavery "as a great plague for the United States." Adams replied, "Certainly," adding that slavery had "altered the whole state of society in the South" by creating a culture in which work was felt to be suitable for black slaves and not for whites, who had become a lazy aristocracy. The idea that "slavery was more prejudicial to the Master than to slaves," a judg-ment he heard several times repeated, became a central focus of Tocqueville's interviews.[9] It shaped his own comments about the economic and moral conse-quences of slavery, especially his well-known, though not fully informed, expla-nation of the differences between the cultures of Kentucky and Ohio. It was the ruinous economic and moral effects of slavery about which Tocqueville seems most preoccupied in his notebooks. The horrific effects of slavery on the slaves themselves he comments on only in *Democracy in America*.

He persistently solicited opinions about the future of slavery in the United States, prompting various grim, sometimes bloody scenarios from those he que-ried. The abolitionist movement was, by the time of his visit, gathering force and roiling politics, but there is no mention of it in his notebooks. Neither does he mention Garrison, who by the time of Tocqueville's visit was so notorious that he had been threatened with hanging should he appear in Virginia. He says not a word about Nat Turner's bloody uprising in Virginia in August of 1831. Turner had finally been caught in October and hanged in early November. It is possible, but unlikely, that Tocqueville had not heard of this later while he was in Philadelphia or in Baltimore, a city in which urban slaves mixed with a large population of free blacks. Nor does he have anything to say about the immense commotion caused by David Walker's *Appeal . . . to the Coloured Peoples of the World*, then being printed in Boston and smuggled into the South, which called for a slave rebellion, though, again, it may not have come to his attention.[10]

Nevertheless, though it became clear how immense the issue of slavery was and despite the insight he gained into the enormous impact of slavery on southern character and culture and into how it imperiled the southern economy, Tocqueville made no effort to investigate slavery firsthand. Perhaps he was unable to do so because he traveled through the South during an especially bitter winter. He had been appalled by a number of revealing racial encounters, especially in Baltimore and New Orleans, and his notebooks record observations about the lives of American blacks, slave and free. But his fieldwork, as it were, did not involve the close study of a plantation, of the southern master class, of the slave economy, or of the lives of slaves. Accurate though his remarks about slavery and the southern character were, they were either secondhand or derived by a quick, imaginative mind from a few discussions or from a few sharp perceptions recorded by an artist with a powerful sociological imagination. It is a good example of the technique of his qualitative social science. He also believed that one could rely on the educated elite of a society for accurate cultural and social analysis. Except for his prison research, empirical analysis was not his style at this time. Even when later, in the 1850s, his research and writing became much more empirical he remained uncertain about how to blend fact with analysis and how much data were needed.

At any rate, Tocqueville never visited a plantation to witness slavery directly, and if he ever spoke to a slave or a free black man or woman he doesn't mention it in the notebooks. (He did interview several Negro prisoners at the Eastern State Penitentiary in Philadelphia, but his prison interviews are not mentioned in the notebooks.) He was ready to make judgments about many aspects of American life, but his notebook comments about slavery seem to be more those of an inquisitive observer than of a moral witness. Nevertheless, there is no doubt that the America he pictures in the notebooks is suffering under the great wrong of slavery and race prejudice, a judgment that Tocqueville lets the Americans make themselves, though it was his as well.

He struggled to understand the anomaly of slavery in so fervently egalitarian a society. It so contradicted the democratic ethos that when he wrote *Democracy in America* he turned to the issue of the brutal exclusion of blacks and Indians from American society only at the end of the first volume, in a chapter that fits so awkwardly it seems almost like an appendix, as if he didn't quite know how to fit it in, just as the black man and the Indian did not fit in a society shaped by the principle of equality. They seemed not to be part of the democratic society to which he had devoted his book. In explaining why he was turning to the issue of slavery and the fate of the Negro and the Indian only toward the end of the *Democracy*, he wrote, "It was above all democracy that I wished to portray," as if to say that democracy as practiced appeared to be relevant only to white Americans and that the exclusion of blacks was primarily a problem of race prejudice.[11]

Though he confronted the anomaly of slavery in an egalitarian society only late in *Democracy in America*, Tocqueville unquestionably felt, as I have noted, that it was an abomination. His long discussion of slavery in *Democracy in America* makes it apparent that he thought it was a vicious system based on the false assumption that the character of the Negro was innate rather than having been created by the monstrous deprivations that had twisted him out of shape. The Negro as slave had been constructed, not found. Moreover, the powerful and appalling image of the black slave he draws in the *Democracy* could not have been based on Tocqueville's own observations, for he had not observed slave communities or plantation life. Instead, he had heard many claims that the Negro was inherently inferior, obviously advanced to justify slavery, and drew from these his image of the slave-as-grotesque to illustrate what can happen to human beings when they are totally deprived of freedom (just as the portrait of the Indian that immediately follows that of the slave illustrates the consequences of unlimited freedom).

In *Democracy in America* Tocqueville turns the slavery advocates' justification for the brutal institution upside down and uses it to show what slavery can do to human beings. Some of his remarks seem cruel in their depiction of the slave as less than fully human in his passive acceptance of his subservience, but Tocqueville's description of the slave as a being devoid of human feeling is in fact Tocqueville's comment on the heinousness of slavery itself, an evil so horrific that it could apparently rob a human being of his humanity and turn him into a grotesque. The worst deformation caused by slavery, in his view, is that it can create a being with no purpose of his own, without a sense of self, and without those passions and feelings common to humanity. He does not claim these are inherent characteristics of the Negro. Concerning the intellectual capacity and the moral sensibility of the Negro he is agnostic, much as Jefferson was. This may be racism in the guise of doubt, but in a notable passage in *Democracy in America* he suggests that it is the white man's prejudice that has transformed the Negro and turned him in imagination into what his oppressor feared and loathed, suggesting that race differences were to some degree a question of perception.[12]

Tocqueville joined the Société française pour l'abolition de l'esclavage in 1835, after the first volume of *Democracy in America* had appeared. He would begin his Report on Abolition (1839), delivered to the Chamber of Deputies by the new deputy from Normandy, by denouncing the racist justification for black slavery: "It has sometimes been assumed that Negro slavery had its foundation and justification in nature itself. It has been declared that the slave trade was beneficial to its unfortunate victims, and that the slave was happier in the tranquility of bondage than in the agitations and the struggles that accompany independence. Thank God, the Commission [appointed by the Chamber of Deputies to report on Destutt de Tracy's proposal to abolish slavery in the French colonies] has no such false and odious doctrines to refute."[13]

Though it was by far the ugliest aspect of American life, slavery was not the only thing that troubled Tocqueville. In his notebook portrait of America he condemns the overwhelming materialism and cupidity of the Americans, a judgment he later elaborates in *Democracy in America* when he analyzes the roots of that materialism, which by then becomes an aspect of democratic, not just American, culture. From the start he describes with obvious revulsion a society that is so consumed by the pursuit of wealth that it is blind or indifferent to other values. Throughout his visit he never modulates his harsh, scornful commentary about a people obsessed with money. The Americans, he found, were feverishly industrious, engrossed in commercial activity. Shortly after he arrived he sent his old Versailles colleague and roommate Ernest Chabrol the following comment: "Nothing is easier than to enrich oneself in America. Naturally the human spirit, which needs a dominating passion, ends by turning all its thoughts towards gain. It results from this that at first appearance this people seems to be a company of merchants gathered for trade; and as one digs further into the national character of the Americans, one sees that they have sought the value of all things only in answer to this question: how much money will it bring in?"[14] He never changed this judgment, even though he encountered in Boston what was to him a far more engaging society, in which one did not always find intellectual and spiritual values overshadowed by money values, culture by commerce (though it was Boston merchant-capitalists who were then beginning to drive the soon-to-boom American industrial economy). He had also observed in the South a strange kind of New World chivalry, more sentimental than practical, as much concerned with honor as with commerce. Vastly more powerful in America than these idiosyncratic regional cultures was the dominant "industrial turn of mind." It was in Ohio that he finally tracked down what he thought was the essence of American—or rather, the purest specimen of a democratic—society: "The whole of society is a factory!" The material, acquisitive, entrepreneurial, industrial imagination touched everything: "the mercantile spirit obtrudes in all the activities and sayings of an American." Even American ministers seemed to him to be "entrepreneurs of a religious industry."[15] This bleak view of the distortions of cultural life in democratic America is not subdued in *Democracy in America*. It provides some of the basis for his elaborate theory of what any democratic culture is bound to be like, whatever its starting point.

All through the notebooks his remarks about American formal culture are, with few exceptions, withering. Despite his lengthy sojourn among the literati of Boston, where he met individuals who valued leisure and knew how to use it, and though he met many remarkable, learned, and perspicuous individuals throughout the United States, he found the life of the mind and the arts sadly wanting. American culture was dull, mediocre, trivial. The rapidity with which he rendered this judgment suggests that he had come prepared to find barbarians. He would later say in *Democracy in America* that Americans were completely uninterested in the theater, even though while he was in New York City theatrical life there was booming and audiences were large and lively.[16] In New York and elsewhere cultural wars about the theater were as hot as they were in Paris. Though he and Beaumont had seen several plays in Philadelphia, his notebooks record only one visit to a theater, in New Orleans, where he saw a French play: "Strange scene presented by the auditorium: dress circle, white; upper circle grey. Colored women very pretty. White ones among them, but a trace of African blood. Gallery: black. Stalls: we felt we were in France; noisy, blustering, bustling, gossiping, and a thousand leagues from the United States."[17] They were not in France, however, but in the United States. The "noisy, blustering, bustling, gossiping" audience could not really be American.

In New York Tocqueville and Beaumont had visited a museum, where, as Beaumont wrote home, they "had laughed like the blessed" when, instead of the paintings they had expected, they had seen a "magic lantern and some stuffed birds."[18] Perhaps Tocqueville had not laughed all nine months, but he saw nothing to praise during that time. He had nothing to say about American architecture, which had already evolved a distinctive vernacular style and a modest classical style felt to be suitable for a democratic republic. The shadow of Versailles, a shadow that had fallen over him for many years, fell over the whole American architectural landscape. If he could call his chateau "une bicoque" (a shack) and "une masure" (a hovel), no building in America could have seemed worth noting. Not even the beautiful simplicity of Charles Bulfinch's buildings, so distinctive in Boston, caught his attention.

His notebooks show not a glimmer of curiosity about writers and painters, of whom there were in fact quite a few, including some remarkable women, for example, the writer Catharine Maria Sedgwick, Theodore Sedgwick's sister, whose work had been translated and published in Paris by the late 1820s. She was, as noted, the only American writer he made an effort, unsuccessful as it turned out, to meet. By 1831 there were New Yorkers who might have spoken about the painters Thomas Cole and Washington Allston, had he asked. One shouldn't take an inflated view of the condition and quality of the arts in America at this time. Americans themselves were lamenting the thinness and derivativeness of American culture. Emerson's Phi Beta Kappa oration at Harvard in 1836 would challenge Americans to develop an original culture. It was 4 a.m. in the American literary renaissance; Thoreau, Hawthorne, and Whitman were still dormant, and Emerson had not yet quit his Boston church for a larger pulpit. One wonders what Tocqueville would have had to say had he visited the United States twenty-five years later. In 1831 he found it easy or perhaps convenient to believe those conservative Americans, still largely in thralldom to the culture of the metropolis, that is, England and the Continent, who spoke of a decline in American cultural life caused by democracy.

To a degree this neglect to inquire more fully than he did can be explained by his preoccupation with the political and legal aspects of American democracy and by the pressures of the official mission he and Beaumont fulfilled scrupulously even though it was a cover for other purposes. It can also be accounted for by the natural bent of his mind. But his conviction, expressed from the beginning of his visit until he sailed away, that Americans were "a people with very little feeling for the pleasures of the mind" and that they took "too little account of intellectual questions"—judgments bluntly repeated in *Democracy in America*—must have damped any inclination he might have felt to probe American cultural life, which he continued to see as a flat, gray wasteland. After nearly six months in the United States he sent the following scornful judgment from New York to his cousin Mme de Grancey: "In the United States they have neither war, nor pestilence, nor literature, nor eloquence, nor fine arts, nor revolutions; no great excesses, nothing which awakes attention in Europe. They enjoy . . . the most insipid happiness which can be imagined."[19]

With regard to social behavior and manners, the culture of a utilitarian, money-crazed society that had no time for form and ceremony was bound to strike a French aristocrat as crude, even barbarous. Tocqueville's remarks about American manners were sharp and remained so, though if he never overcame his revulsion he balanced his judgment by noting certain positive aspects of democratic manners, especially the forthrightness of the Americans and what he called their chasteness, by which he seems to have meant an apparent moral orderliness based on what he believed was the admirable sexual morality of American women.

He had immediately been appalled by the chauvinism of the Americans. "Up to now," he wrote on May 15, having spent four days in New York City, "we have formed the impression that the Americans carry national pride to an altogether excessive length. I doubt if we could extract from them the smallest truth unfavorable to their country. Most of them boast about it without discrimination, and with an impertinence disagreeable to strangers that bears witness to but slight enlightenment."[20] "These people," he wrote to his mother, "seem to me stinking with national conceit. It pierces through all their courtesy." He quickly noted a streak of "small-town pettiness in their make-up." Their manners were crude—though not bad. "Up to now [again on the fifteenth of May!], it seems to me that this country illustrates the most complete external development of the middle classes, or rather that the whole society seems to have turned into one middle class. No one seems to have the elegant manners and the refined politeness of the upper classes in Europe. On the contrary, one is at once struck with something vulgar, and a disagreeable casualness of behavior."[21] At the end of June he was still dwelling on the same disagreeable casualness: "I hope that we shall never adopt the carelessness that reigns here. The public prosecutor speaks with his hands in his pockets, the court chews, and the lawyer picks his teeth while interrogating witnesses."[22] By the late fall, in Philadelphia, the shock of American crudeness had not worn off. He wrote to Kergorlay that "the inhabitants of the country are not all the most agreeable company. A great number smoke, chew, spit in your beard." However, he was sensible enough to quickly put the matter in perspective: he also found American manners "sober, poised and reserved, neither refined nor formal but exactly what one would expect from a cold, practical middle-class people accustomed to treating one another as equals and as opportunities."[23] They had not yet refined the art of pretense, though he had noticed at the same time that, envy being the dominant emotional driving force behind the passion for equality, their egalitarian principles had not overcome the thirst for status and the habit of making invidious distinctions.

Despite the crudeness of the Americans, he thought that "they do not the less form a race of very remarkable men. Besides, they don't stand on ceremony, they bear the same conduct in others admirably. . . .They lack refinement, grace, and elegance; at each instance in America you are aware of the absence of a superior class which, if it existed, would give the example to all the rest. But after all, that's a superficial thing at which it is not reasonable to halt."[24] Ultimately, when he came to write *Democracy in America*, he saw virtue and even the potential for a new kind of social unity, in the naturalness and informality of American, that is, democratic, behavior.

More significant was his recognition that "the absence of a superior class" would have decisive consequences for democratic culture. This social fact became central to his analysis of that culture, accounting not only for its formlessness, casualness, and the abandoning of traditional, customary modes of social address, but also for every aspect of the arts, crafts, language, and literature.[25] The question of the qualities—the strengths and weaknesses of democratic culture—later became crucially important to Tocqueville when he turned, in *DA II*, to shape his final thoughts about the future of democracy.

3

DEMOCRATIC RELIGION: MAD MESSIAHS AND CHASTE WOMEN

Except for the politics of the Americans, nothing interested Tocqueville more than their religious lives and the role that religion played in politics. A strong note of skepticism about the depth of American religious life runs through his notebooks. During his travels he had little direct experience of American religious practices and institutions; instead, he conducted many interviews with the articulate elite, his customary way of gathering information for social analysis. He was not equipped to understand American experiential evangelical religion, which appalled him. He was much impressed by the way in which religion, whether shallow or "mad," helped maintain order in a society of aggressive individuals and kept it "chaste," a word he often used. Women played a major role, by their family work, in religion's social function. Their spirituality kept the family tranquil and was the major source of social decorum. Some of his ambivalence about American religious life disappears in *Democracy in America*. There, he dwells on how religion helps maintain order and liberty in the United States, much less on its spiritual aspects.

Of all that is perhaps best known about Tocqueville's view of democratic America, perhaps the foremost, especially these days when the ideology of faith-based politics is much heard in the United States, is his assertion that democracy and liberty cannot survive without the support of religion. However, by the end of *Democracy in America* he had quietly raised so many doubts about the quality of religion in a democratic culture and so thoroughly pointed out its weaknesses that he seemed to have abandoned the argument that it would be an effective guardian of liberty. In *Democracy* he sees religion in democratic America as a powerful, potentially oppressive force—one of those opinions denied at one's peril. More significant, he says that it has so capitulated to the central values of democracy's materialistic, acquisitive culture that it provides no countervailing alternatives, no sacred sanctuary, to which the anxious and bewildered might turn to find more satisfying meanings and no sense of a fixed moral order with limits not to be crossed.

In view of Tocqueville's positive, occasionally enthusiastic comments in *Democracy in America* about the power and political benefits of religion in America, the doubts he expressed about it tend to be regarded as secondary. But an even stronger note of skepticism about the religious lives of the Americans runs through his notebooks. Most Americans professed belief, he observed, but he thought their religious lives were indifferent and shallow. They paid little attention to the real claims of religion.

From the start of his journey Tocqueville recognized that the Americans, so absorbed by the pursuit of material gain and well-being, were at the same time an astonishingly religious people—or seemed to be. However, the pervasiveness of religion in America struck him as especially important because of its function as a means of social control and its importance in bringing order to a busy society constantly pressing against limits in its self-aggrandizing turmoil. "Never before have I been so conscious," he wrote to Kergorlay in June while still in New York, "of the influence of religion on the social and political state of a people since my arrival in America. It is impossible not to recognize the necessity of this motivation and regulation of human actions."[1] Except for questions about politics, law, and class and also about penal policy, no subject so thoroughly held his attention as the religious culture of the Americans and the function of religion in a democratic society. He turned to it in nearly all the interviews he recorded in his notebooks. Religion had been at the center of the great transformation wrought by the French Revolution, which in some ways it had precipitated. Its future role in French political life was still undecided and a matter of intense debate. For Tocqueville, the issue of the relation of religion to politics was crucial.

As was his customary practice, his anthropological investigations were largely carried out through interviews with the knowledgeable elite rather than in the field. His firsthand experience of American religious life was limited. When he did get out to sacred places—when, for example, he observed a Shaker service in the village of Niskayuna, New York, near Albany—he seems not to have understood and was strongly repelled by what he witnessed. He was by virtue of temperament, experience, education, and religious upbringing ill-equipped to understand any version of the spiritual enthusiasm so vividly evident in American religious life. When he did write about it, it was with a kind of appalled mockery. Though he twice wrote about the Shaker service, once in a letter to his mother and a second time in a fable he later wrote about a stranger wandering through the American religious landscape, it seems to have been no more to him than a bizarre show, a terrifying demonstration of human frailty.

His first comments about the Shakers, sent to his conservative Catholic mother, consisted of a brilliantly described, condescending, incredulous,

amused but also horrified description of a long service that included the strenuous, ecstatic yet formal ritual dancing along with the chanting and singing for
which the Shakers were to become famous. He had not taken seriously or struggled to understand the meaning of the ecstatic yet disciplined, democratic yet
socially structured communal religious expression he had witnessed. He
thought it was madness, a demonstration of the "aberrations into which the
human spirit can fall if abandoned to itself."[2] Ironically, he did not see that what
he had observed was also an expression of the chasteness and orderliness that he
thought religion had brought to American culture.

A summary translation of his letter: "The community files in, men and
women through different doors, wearing ceremonial costumes, women all in
white. Among them some very old, some very young, some pretty, some very
ugly. The oldest first, the younger ranged behind. Males and females sit segre-
gated at opposite sides of the hall. Silent meditation. Long discourse on the
religious and moral obligations of the Shakers. All join in high-pitched chanting, the shrillest I have heard in my life. The most fervent mark time with their
heads, nodding like Chinese porcelain figurines. The chanting lively and fast,
the young and the old male and female dancing until breathless. Not amusing
but pitiful to see white-haired old men exhausted from heat and fatigue still
joyfully leaping about. Hand clapping. Dance interrupted by a spontaneous
talk. More dancing and speaking. Like the other Quakers, no priest." He goes
on as follows:

> They placed themselves two by two in a curving line so that the men and
> women made but a single circle. They then held their elbows against the
> body, stretched out their forearms and let their hands hang, which gave them
> the air of trained dogs who are forced to walk on their hind legs. Thus pre-
> pared, they intoned an air more lamentable than all the others, and began to
> turn around the room, an exercise they continued for a good quarter of an
> hour. After which one of them made a brief talk to assure us that the Shaker
> way was the only route to salvation, and made an effort to convert us; after
> which the community withdrew in the greatest order and in silence. I imag-
> ine that the poor devils (les pauvres diables) needed rest.[3]

Tocqueville does not mention that he had visited the Shaker mother church
in America, founded by the English immigrant Mother Ann Lee in 1780.

He found himself in the United States during one of the many religious
awakenings that periodically sweep the country, this time the red hot outburst
of spiritual fervor known as the second Great Awakening. If one had to judge
from his notebooks and his letters, he seems not to have noticed it or been told

about it, though what he does say about American religion in his notes and especially in the *Democracy* suggests that he did have a broad sense of what was happening and what it meant. He had journeyed through upstate New York when that region was in such religious and social turmoil that it became known as the "burned-over district." It was where yet another outburst of evangelical Christianity, ignited and then fanned ingeniously by the great revivalist Charles Grandison Finney, had burned fiercely.[4] (It was there too, in Palmyra, New York, close to Rochester, the scene of Finney's first great revival success, that Joseph Smith in 1823 had his revelation and discovered the buried scripture that was the beginning of the Church of Jesus Christ of Latter-Day Saints.) Judging from his notebooks, Tocqueville passed through this region without feeling the heat, as if he had walked through a house on fire while discussing whether rational religion (Unitarianism) or Catholicism would be the dominant religion of the American future. Though by the time Tocqueville visited western New York Finney had moved away to the bigger markets of New York City and Philadelphia, the fields and small towns of the burned-over district were still smoldering with the fires he had lit, and the memory of Finney must have been stalking every parish and precinct. Auburn, where Tocqueville and Beaumont spent days visiting the important Auburn Penitentiary, was also where Finney had conducted a triumphant two-month revival in 1827.

There is no mention in his notebooks of what in *Democracy in America* he calls the "various forms of religious madness" produced by "the impassioned, almost wild spiritualism that one seldom encounters in Europe."[5] He is referring there, in chapter 12 of the second part of volume 2 ("Why Some Americans Display Enthusiastic Forms of Spirituality" which had replaced his first title, "Concerning the Bizarre Sects that Spring Up in America"), to the enthusiastic camp meeting revivals that had spread like wildfire through the woods of the frontier states during the second Great Awakening. For that chapter or perhaps some other he did write but did not include a short "morceau" titled *Les Sectes en Amérique*: a fable about what was bizarre and presumably characteristic in American democratic religious life in the form of a tale told by someone wandering through the forests and villages of America encountering first a Quaker meeting, then a Methodist revival service, and then a Shaker service (evidently the same one he wrote about to his mother).[6]

With the exception of the Shaker service in Niskayuna, it is not clear what religious meetings Tocqueville had actually observed or what he had heard or read about. (He did attend a few Catholic masses.) His fable can't be read as a report on cultural fieldwork. However, it reveals the disdain he felt for enthusiastic modes of religious experience and expression. The three vignettes are written with a mixture of mockery, astonishment, humor, and barely disguised contempt. He makes it clear that it is indeed both madness and pretense that he is writing about, both qualities of the enthusiastic egalitarian revivalism that, oddly, along with rationalist religion, was the essence of democratic religion.

Tocqueville's traveler jests about the lengthy, silent Quaker meeting, which he thought at first was a gathering of the deaf and the mute. He laughs at the claim that revelation has authorized the sameness of dress he describes at great length as well as at the pompous assurance of salvation promised by his guide, a salvation guaranteed by following prescribed behavior and dress. He is angered by the self-righteousness with which he is talked down to. In the next vignette, Tocqueville's innocent, wandering onward in the strange religious landscape of democratic America, happens upon a tumultuous Methodist service, which he describes with mock incredulity: he is about to rush to the aid of a man moaning and shrieking in contorted agony, until he suddenly realizes that the moaner is preaching to a crowd of wildly gesticulating, heaven-beseeching, breast-beating, head-pounding, terror-struck auditors driven to the edge of madness by the preacher's vivid descriptions of the hell that awaits the unrepentant and the unconverted:

> He spoke of the perversity of man and of the inexhaustible abundance of divine vengeance. . . . He explored one by one the dreadful mysteries of the next life. He drew a picture of the Creator ceaselessly busy piling up generations in the pits of hell while just as indefatigably inventing torments as in creating sinners. I was transfixed by anxiety, the congregation even more than I: terror was expressed in a thousand ways on their faces, on which repentance showed itself as despair and frenzy. Women lifted their children in their arms and uttered mournful cries, others beat their forehead on the ground, men writhed on the benches or rolled in the dust while loudly confessing their sins. As the preacher's movements became faster and his descriptions more vivid, the congregation's passions seemed to grow, and it was often difficult not to believe that one was in one of the infernal places the preacher was describing.
>
> Penetrated by horror and full of disgust, I fled. Creator and Guardian of all things, I thought, would you recognize yourself in the horrible portrait that your creatures here made of you? Is it necessary to debase men through fear in order to raise them to you?[7]

Lost in such reflections, the horrified traveler flees through the forest until he comes to a beautiful village, built on newly cleared land, evidently a planned community, at the center of which stood a great hall which served as a church.

He has happened upon the Shaker community that Tocqueville so vividly and uncomprehendingly described in the letter to his mother. Tocqueville's traveler describes the same astonishing, frenzied religious service, but the fable concludes with biting irony: after the hectic dance one of the eldest members of the community, after wiping the sweat from his forehead, delivers himself of the following prayer: "My brethren, let us give thanks to the all-powerful, who in the midst of all the diverse superstitions that disfigure humanity, has deigned finally to show us the way to salvation, and let us pray he will open the eyes of that crowd of unfortunates who are still plunged in the darkness of error and save them from the eternal torments that perhaps await them."[8] In his earlier comment on what he had witnessed in Niskayuna, it was the Shaker service itself that Tocqueville had found to be a disfiguring superstition, a demonstration of "the aberrations into which the human spirit can fall if abandoned to itself."

Chapter 12 of part 2 of *DA II* is Tocqueville's remarkable gloss on enthusiastic religion. It is in this chapter that he famously remarks that "forms of religious madness are very common" among the Americans. His curious explanation for such madness reveals much about Tocqueville's limited understanding of American religious life and much about his view of human spirituality. He attributes the outburst of enthusiastic religion only briefly to the pervasive evangelical Christianity then flaming in the United States ("In every state of the Union, but especially in the half-peopled lands of the West, there are preachers hawking the word of God from place to place"), but more fully to an unquenchable human "taste for the infinite and love of what is immortal," to "sublime instincts" implanted in the soul that cannot be fully satisfied by "the good things of this world." To acquire the good things of this world was, in his view, "the dominant passion among Americans." The longings which drive the religious mad along "extraordinary roads to eternal happiness" are thus, in Tocqueville's account, not really aberrations, but rather the expressions of man's profoundly spiritual nature: "The soul has needs which must be satisfied. . . . If ever the thoughts of the great majority of mankind came to be concentrated solely on the search for material blessings, one can anticipate that there would be a colossal reaction in the souls of men. They would distractedly launch out into the world of spirits for fear of being too tightly bound by the body's fetters."[9] "I should be surprised if," he goes on to say, "among a people uniquely preoccupied with prosperity, mysticism did not soon make progress." Tocqueville is here ignoring the cultural basis of religious life and substituting his own mystical explanation of the modes of American religion. The power and pervasiveness of evangelical millennial Christianity are given scant mention, as is the Bible-saturated imagination of the American people, who by the early nineteenth century had been shaped not only by the Old Testament and its Prophets, as it was for the Puritans, but also by the New Testament and the mythos of Jesus. As Tocqueville focuses more and more in *Democracy in America* on the evolving "social state" of the Americans and on how it shapes their spiritual and intellectual lives, evangelical and messianic Christianity appears as only a minor shaping force in American life, if that.

His comments in *Democracy in America* on the religious life of the Americans are inconsistent, confused, and preachy, a blend of theory, superficial observation, and his own admonitions about the importance of cultivating belief in the reality of spirit and "a taste for the infinite" among democratic peoples to divert them from becoming increasingly focused on material pursuits and on comforts. Evidently he did not think that enthusiastic religion would accomplish this. In chapter 9 of part II of *DA II* he argues that it is mainly self-interest, not deep spirituality, that draws Americans to religion, suggesting that there is something calculating and prudential about the Americans' avowals of belief. He inappropriately quotes Pascal to make his point: "If we make a mistake by thinking the Christian religion true," Pascal has said, "we have no great thing to lose. But if we make a mistake by thinking it false, how dreadful is our case."

The religion of the Americans is a prudential means of achieving success in this world:

> They practice their religion . . . without shame and without weakness. But in the very midst of their zeal one generally sees something so quiet, so methodical, so calculated, that it would seem that the head rather than the heart leads them to the foot of the altar. . . . Preachers in America are continually coming down to earth. Indeed they find it difficult to take their eyes off it. The better to touch their hearers, they are forever pointing out how religious beliefs favor freedom and public order, and it is difficult when listening to them whether the main object of religion is to procure eternal felicity in the next world or prosperity in this.[10]

Yet in chapter 12, "Why Some Americans Display Enthusiastic Forms of Spirituality," discussed above, he notes that it is not always self-interest that draws the Americans to religion. His explanation of the occasional upwellings of "enthusiastic forms of spirituality" among the materialist Americans also reveals how much he continued to discount the continuing power of evangelical postmillennial Christianity in the United States.

One can't escape the poignant irony that it is Tocqueville himself, in the lecture-chapter (chapter 15) that culminates this sequence of chapters on religion in democratic America, who argues that those who legislate for a democratic people must urge such societies to heed distant goals and spiritual realities, and that in doing so they too will in effect be applying the doctrine of self-interest, which will be to maintain social order and the conditions of liberty, not to foster true belief.[11] He too is stressing the practical benefits of religion.

Thus, to explain the Americans' occasionally enthusiastic religious behavior, Tocqueville resorts to generic modes of spirituality and to deep, universal spiritual longings in human nature, rather than to the evangelical, millennialist, Christian imagination that had saturated the culture. He did not see in American religious life all that would provide the seedbed for the fundamentalism and the messianic imperialism that would flower later in the nineteenth century and explode in the next.

Tocqueville was ill-equipped to understand evangelical Christianity or pietist religion. He scorned religious "devôts," was later, in the 1850s, appalled by Edouard's and his close friend Corcelle's embrace of Catholic piety. It is unlikely that he knew much about the bizarre forms of religious superstition and folk belief that had flourished under the noses of the Enlightened in the eighteenth century, though he had to have caught glimpses of that persisting religious underworld in rural Normandy. His own religion was a religion of the head. Forms of enthusiastic, ecstatic religion that led to loss of control and unseemly, inarticulate, undignified, emotive speech and behavior could only have horrified him, which was his reaction to the Shaker service he witnessed.

While he did not understand American experiential religion, there is much in his comments on religion and morality in both his notebooks and *Democracy in America* that clearly shows he well understood the social function of religion in America. Finney's revival movement, apart from being a flaming of Christian piety, demonstrated that religion could also serve as an instrument of social control and order, which function it had performed by calming the social and economic turbulence boiling over in upstate New York after the building of the Erie Canal, completed in 1825. The merchants and manufacturers of Rochester had good reason to strongly support Finney and even to demonstrate their piety by attending his services. Finney, with his fake boastful sinners planted in the audience, soon to be reduced to fake tears by the great evangelist, with posters plastered everywhere to announce coming meetings, and with his front-row "anxious bench" for troubled souls teetering on the brink of conversion, had perfected the business of promoting and organizing revival meetings and the techniques of inducing conversions. He was the very model of the minister-as-industrialist described by Tocqueville in *Democracy in America*. Had Tocqueville heard of this aspect of Finney's work? There were plenty of people in Auburn, where Tocqueville had stopped, who would have denounced it.[12]

Tocqueville's remarks on the crucial role women played in American religious life also reflect a cultural development of the moment: the feminization of many aspects of American cultural life.[13] It was mostly women who were swelling church membership and swooning in the woods. Whether or not Tocqueville knew this to be so, he may well have heard it or sensed it. His notebooks record comment after comment about the moral superiority and the greater spirituality of American women, all culminating in his assertion in *Democracy in America* that religion "reigns supreme in the souls of women."[14]

Though doubts about the religious culture of the Americans occasionally appear in *Democracy in America*, he subordinates them to the major line of his argument about religion, which is that it is the essential prop of order for a materialistic, acquisitive people who are highly innovative and adventurous, given to flights of fantasy yet at the same time skeptical about authority, culturally indisposed to ceremony, form, and tradition or to reverence for the past. It is in *Democracy in America* that he says, after having described how "religion keeps the Americans within certain limits and moderates their passion for innovation," that it is more needed in democracies than in any other kind of society, for "how could society escape destruction if, when political ties are relaxed, moral ties are not tightened?" Religion was a stronger restraint on the American demiurge than politics or policing.[15]

In the notebooks, however, Tocqueville's skepticism about the spiritual depth of the religious life of the Americans runs through his inquiries. He didn't doubt its importance as a source of order and a safeguard of liberty, though there is evidence in his notebooks that he thought it might be an oppressive force, especially if wielded by public opinion. One couldn't be a doubter and hope for a public career. Religion might be an essential bulwark of liberty but at the same time might menace spiritual freedom. His American acquaintances challenged his skepticism about one or another aspect of the religious life of the Americans. Late in his journey, in November, he told Richard Stewart of Baltimore that he was "inclined to see a profound indifference beneath all religious beliefs." Stewart denied this, arguing that the vast majority of Americans were truly believing.[16] When the head of the Presbyterian seminary in Auburn, New York—"an old man whose piety seemed to us sincere and even *ardent* (a rare thing in America)"—claimed that the "religious principle" was making headway, Tocqueville quietly added in his notebook, "I am much afraid that he deludes himself." His American informants failed to allay his doubts.[17]

After six months in the United States he was still asking if religion there was "only superficial? Or is it deeply rooted in men's hearts?"[18] He wondered how the pluralism and tolerance of American religious life could fail to breed indifference. And though he came to see that religion strongly regulated the lives of the Americans not only in appearance but also in fact, he also felt that in some ways their religious lives were empty. In a letter to Kergorlay he described the Americans: "A practicing but indifferent population, which lives from day to day, accustoms itself to surroundings that are satisfying but hardly tranquil, and whose appearances are satisfied. These people live and die *on the surface*, without ever bothering to get to the bottom of things. They no longer replenish themselves."[19] He sensed that in becoming a civil religion—that is, in becoming so thoroughly identified with the dominant values of American culture and in winning the kind of universal allegiance that made it a unifying force—religion in America had lost its transcendental dimension. It had become a kind of industry; ministers in America, he thought, were "entrepreneurs of a religious industry."[20] Religion in America was fervent but shallow and made little real difference in people's lives. It suffused the culture and the American imagination but was no longer a sanctuary for the spirit.[21]

Some of the reservations and doubts expressed in the notebooks are muted in *Democracy in America*. Perhaps in retrospect the strengths of American religious life simply outweighed what had disquieted him when he was on the scene. In the *Democracy* he offers a quite positive view of American Catholicism, which even though it was a hierarchical religion was so imbued with democratic values that it thoroughly upheld the principle of equality and defended religious toleration. It was also an ardent advocate of the separation of Church and State. In his notebooks, however, Tocqueville had argued that the egalitarianism of the Catholic Church in America was a matter of circumstance and not of conviction. It reflected the fact that American Catholics "are poor and almost all come from a country where the aristocracy is Protestant." Even sharper was his conviction, perhaps reflecting his view of French Catholicism, that American Catholic support for liberty of conscience was superficial and that Catholics would "persecute if they found themselves the strongest."[22]

Tocqueville thought that American Protestantism, "a mixture of reason and authority," was an unstable compromise, unsuitable for the masses. He also believed that in the future both Catholicism, the religion of authority and dogma, and Unitarianism, the religion of reason and freedom of conscience, would rapidly gain adherents at the expense of the evangelical Protestantism that for the moment was spreading like a firestorm across the country. He was persuaded that most people needed a dogmatic religion to guide them through life. Neither evangelical Protestantism, with its trying demands on individual conscience and will, nor rational religion, with its insistence on reasoned judgment, could serve as a democratic, or mass, religion.

In Boston he challenged William Ellery Channing, the Unitarian pope, with his skepticism. In a way their discussion appropriately was a reenactment of much earlier arguments between Calvinists and Arminians, more polite but equally at odds. The aristocrat looking down on the masses challenges the democratic faith in the abilities of man: "Allow me to raise one objection, said I. It applies not only to Unitarianism but to all Protestant sects, and even has a great bearing on the political world: do you not think that human nature is so constituted that, however education and the state of society may be perfected, one will always find a great mass of men unable by the very nature of their situation to make their reason work on theoretical or abstract questions, and who, if they have not a dogmatic faith, will believe in precisely nothing?"[23] Channing's reply, that religious questions were not too difficult for everyday reason and that God had "put their solution within the grasp of everyman," struck an incredulous Tocqueville as "more specious than solid." Channing, whose politics were Whiggish, challenged Tocqueville by arguing that it was not the great questions of religion but the complexities of politics and social policy that were beyond the grasp of the ordinary mind. Tocqueville also argued that religion could not be democratically governed and that Catholicism's rule by elite and dogma better fit human capacities, again revealing his lack of sympathy with, or his failure to understand, the basic impulse of Protestantism: its hallowing of the individual conscience as a means of salvation. Again, social order had priority.

How did religion fulfill its critical function as a means of social control? Tocqueville thought that America was not only the most enlightened nation on earth, by which he meant politically literate, it was also the most moral. American morals, he noted, were "the most chaste that exist in any nation." These dual superlatives, hardly the result of comparative studies of national character, run through the notebooks and are repeated in the *Democracy*. What did he mean by *chaste*? To Tocqueville, it meant moral orderliness, soberness, humility, all the virtues that Franklin, whom Tocqueville admired, had so unhumbly striven to perfect. What Tocqueville had found was a middle-class society in which the absence of class barriers had unleashed ambition and the dream of rising in the world. It was a society in which the middle-class ethos, namely, high valuation of work, order, thrift, sexual restraint, self-denial, reproval of idleness, set clear and necessary rules for a people who were constantly tempted to overstep old bounds and limits in their eagerness to succeed. In democratic America one found no flâneurs or idle rich. Such was the moral condition of the great majority of the overwhelmingly middle-class population, at least in the northern states, where it had not been weakened by the culture of slavery.

The basic source of the moral chasteness of the Americans was the sense of limits that religion brought to the culture; and if one can judge from the notebooks, sexual restraint was a crucial element of the chasteness he found so strong in American life. All the elements of it are in the notebooks, in which *chaste* means not only sobriety and seriousness but also sexual restraint. This is made clear by Tocqueville's many comments about the sexual mores of the Americans and the sexual dignity of American women. Tocqueville's pure woman appears full-blown in *Democracy in America*, but glimpses of her can be caught in the notebooks. It is she who establishes the moral tone of the society.

What is the source of his image of the pure, sexually strict American woman? Had the women he met seemed icy and remote, too serious for flirting, unskilled at the sexual games perfected in the social milieu Tocqueville knew? It would appear that he interpreted her sexual remoteness as an expression of intense religiosity. If manners in general were cruder in America than in Europe, he saw none of the looseness of sexual behavior that he thought was characteristic of societies with deep class divides. "Morals are pure," he wrote on June 9 while in New York City, very early in his stay, "that much is undeniable. The European roué is absolutely unknown in America."[24] This early observation was forcefully reinforced by Joel Poinsett, a U.S. representative from South Carolina, during their prolonged conversation en route from New Orleans to Washington in January of 1832. Poinsett spoke of "the prodigious respect for the marriage tie among us" and replied to Tocqueville's request for an explanation of "the extreme chastity" (not virtue) of the American people by saying that "the chastity of our morals is due more to particular circumstances and especially to the complete absence of men with the time and means to attack women's virtue. Besides, I think that the race of women is very remarkable in America. I find them much superior to our men."[25] Tocqueville would repeat that last remark almost verbatim in *Democracy in America*.[26]

In the *Democracy* the most important source of the moral chasteness of the American people lay in what Tocqueville thought was the stability of middle-class family life, which he describes in rosy colors. It is a highly idealized picture, and he would later privately admit that it was.[27] The stable, contented family, at the center of which was the extraordinary, self-denying, sexually pure American woman, was the source of the moral chasteness that so struck him:

I do not doubt for an instant that the great severity of mores which one notices in the United States has its primary origin in beliefs. There, religion is often powerless to restrain men in the midst of innumerable temptations which fortune offers. It cannot moderate their eagerness to enrich themselves, which everything contributes to arouse, *but it reigns supreme in the souls of women, and it is women who shape mores.* Certainly of all countries in the world America is the one in which the marriage tie is the most respected and where the highest and truest conception of conjugal happiness has been conceived.[28] [emphasis added].

Religion "reigns supreme in the souls of women"; women determine the moral tone of the family; the "order and peace," the innocence and "regularity" she is responsible for within the family translates into the chasteness, "the love of order," of the world beyond the family:

> When the American returns from the turmoil of politics to the bosom of the family, he immediately finds a perfect picture of order and peace. There, all his pleasures are simple and natural, and his joys innocent and quiet, and as the regularity of life brings him happiness, he easily forms the habit of regulating his opinions as well as his tastes.
>
> Whereas the European tries to escape his sorrows at home by troubling society, the American derives from his home that love of order which he carries over into affairs of State.[29]

Democracy in America describes American women as perfectly educated to serve as mainstays of moral order in a society constantly careening toward disorder. They are the chief vessels of self-denial, exemplars of restraint and self-sacrifice. Their training, not convent walls or chastity belts, has made them so. More important, they are guardians of moral order because of their greater natural spirituality. They keep society in touch with the idea of a moral order because they are not engrossed in the material concerns of their husbands and because they are sexually contained. Tocqueville had a great deal to say about the religiosity and social function of American women, but there is no evidence that he interviewed any or even had lengthy conversations with them. What he thought he knew about them was constructed from observation and from the testimony of the male elite who were his primary source of social data.

How to understand this extraordinary view? Can Tocqueville have been unaware of the sexual turmoil and the confusions about sex resulting from the passion for equality, then seething below the surface of American life? Such turmoil was soon to burst forth in an astonishing number of utopian experiments in gender relations as well as in sexual and family practices, of which John Humphrey Noyes's notorious Oneida Community was just one of many. At the same time, French feminists had also become articulate advocates of gender equality and sexual freedom, to Tocqueville's dismay. The American chasteness he constantly refers to was, he thought, the contribution of American women to social order and resulted from their sexual restraint and renunciation.

When Tocqueville speaks admiringly of the power of religion in America, he is praising the effect that religion seemed to have on maintaining social order and decorum and a sense of limits rather than the spiritual quality and character of that religion. In fact, the vital religious life he caught glimpses of, the disorderly religion of enthusiastic individuals reaching for heaven, he deemed madness. It was practiced by lunatics running loose in the woods or by strange communards dancing spastically while moaning and shrieking. The evangelical Christianity that was just then in the midst of one of its periodic blooms left him cold. In the United States he could shake his head in amused dismay at it. In France, however, he worried that the energies of piety would suck up the energies of politics. A Great Awakening there would have seemed a disaster to him, the wrong direction for a democratic France to take. For Tocqueville, salvation lay not in democratic enthusiasm and openness, but in order and chasteness: it would be achieved through politics, not piety.

In *Democracy in America* the focus of his discussion of religion in America shifts largely to its function as a guarantor of liberty and as a bond that unites civil society. It serves this task by establishing a moral order that is not to be violated and at the same time by backing away from political entanglements. which meant that it would not be weakened by political strife. Yet confusion undercuts Tocqueville's argument: how could religion fulfill its role as liberty's ultimate defender if it could survive in democratic cultures only by surrendering its transcendental dimension and becoming businesslike and pragmatic, that is, by adapting to the dominant values of the culture? That was one fate he foresaw for democratic religion. The other was the religious madness he also saw lying ahead in the democratic future as the inevitable challenge of human spirituality to the materialist vision of life, with men and women bursting forth in wild new modes of spiritual expression as a way of coping with an increasingly dominant material culture that did not satisfy spiritual needs they no longer understood. It is in underscoring these possibilities, rather than in arguing for religion's indispensable service as guardian of liberty, that Tocqueville deserves to be called farseeing. He feared that religion would be so transformed by democratic culture that it could no longer serve as a countervailing force in a culture that knew no limits.

4

CLASS IN AN EGALITARIAN SOCIETY

Tocqueville looked at American society through spectacles accustomed to seeing a European social landscape. He was astonished by the fluidity of status and wealth in democratic America and so impressed by the informality of manner and the absence of old forms of deference that he failed to note deepening social divisions or the extent of poverty and misery in the United States. He thought the whole society was middle class. He records no conversations with working folk—artisans, laborers, servants, new immigrants—and no observations of their manner of life and their views of the land of promise. He does perceive social distinctions but notes that these are created by the indelible human craving for social distinction and by easily accumulated (or lost) wealth.

At first glance, the brave new egalitarian world of democratic America must have struck Tocqueville as a utopian fulfillment of the eighteenth-century dream of liberty, equality, and brotherhood. He obviously was fascinated and overwhelmed by what at first appeared to be the complete triumph of equality in American life. In his notebooks he jotted down example upon example of the ways in which the passion for equality had transformed every aspect of social life.

He was astonished to have found a society that "seems to have turned into one middle class." Middle-class manners and style of life prevailed. The old class markers were gone: "All wear the same clothes." "An incredible external equality prevails in America," he wrote: "all classes [what were these?] endlessly meet and there does not seem the slightest indication of social positions. At Canandaigua [in upstate New York] I saw a district attorney shake hands with a prisoner." Public officials were granted no special status or esteem: "They shake everybody by hand." President Jackson was addressed in a public letter as "Dear Sir." The governor of New York lived humbly in "a very small wooden farmhouse of one story" and was "occupied in personally supervising the cultivation of his fields." "It is clear that white servants regard themselves as their masters' equals. They gossip on familiar terms." "They sit at the same table, do not serve but help."¹ The authoritarian or hierarchical principle had disappeared from all social relationships. From style of dress to status before the law, equality was the rule. Belief in equality was almost universally avowed with a passion that stifled doubt or opposition. Though a person wasn't hanged for expressing antiegalitarian sentiments, he could count on being either ignored or scorned, yet another example of the oppressive power of public opinion.

That he should speak of "all classes" while commenting about the triumph of equality suggests that his social perceptions were still organized by the social template he had brought with him. Hence the astonishment with which he viewed the extreme social leveling that led him to load his notebooks with example after example of his democratic anthropology instead of limiting himself to one or two telling images or anecdotes, as was his customary style of social analysis. Even though the France he knew was changing dramatically, the social model he had vividly in mind was that of traditional France. He put it succinctly in the notebooks:

> In France prejudices of birth still hold very great sway. Birth still puts an almost insurmountable barrier between men. In France, the profession a man exercises still to a certain extent places him socially. These prejudices are the most fateful of all to equality because they make permanent and almost indelible distinctions, even when wealth and time are against them. Such prejudices do not exist at all in America. Birth is a distinction, but it does not in the least place a man socially; it carries with it no right and no disability, no obligation towards the world or towards oneself; classification by professions is also almost unknown; it certainly does make a definite difference to the position of individuals, a difference of wealth rather than of standing, but it does not create any radical inequality, for it by no means prevents the intermarriage of families.²

The absence of such prejudices in part explained the amazing degree of social mobility in America. Individuals were not locked into social positions by ancient prejudices. The much greater freedom of marriage illustrated this fluidity: "When one wants to judge the equality between the different classes of a people, one always comes to the question of how marriages are made. That is the root of the matter."³ In America, marriage was a decidedly more democratic institution than in Europe, where class considerations still weighed far more heavily than individual preferences. The openness and freedom of marriage demonstrated the classlessness of democratic America. What evidence Tocqueville had for the absence of class boundaries in marriage is not clear. His long visits to New York and Boston should have provided ample evidence that such boundaries were still powerful, unless he regarded even these elite societies as thoroughly middle-class.

Other factors contributed to the triumph of equality as well. In *Democracy in America* he fully develops his historical explanation, but the nub of it appears in the notebooks when he writes, "In the United States, it is said, society has been built from a clean slate. One sees neither victor nor vanquished, neither plebeian nor noble, neither prejudices of birth nor prejudices of profession."[4] In other words, American society had been middle class from the start, and it had been kept that way by inheritance laws that made it difficult, so he thought, for families to establish themselves by accumulating and preserving huge landed estates. His visit to New York, where great estates passed on from generation to generation, should have disabused him of this notion. A cluster of other circumstances such as the abundance of land and of opportunity, the fluidity of fortunes, and especially the power of money had kept it that way. The middle classes *were* America for Tocqueville. They were the history, the destiny, and the norm of the society through which he was traveling in search of the future.

But many did not appear in the social landscape he sketched: laboring people, the poor, the black man, the red man, and all those wounded by the social pathologies and the economic dislocations of an aggressively competitive society. Except for the Negro and the Indian he paid hardly any attention to the nonbelongers, who remained largely invisible. He was not much interested in the evidence or extent of inequality in the society sworn to the principle of equality. The inequality of women is completely smothered by his dreamy praise of the essential moral and spiritual role they played. He paid little attention to the issue of how many of those who in principle enjoyed equal rights were denied the vote because of property requirements in various states, assuming perhaps that the dogma of the sovereignty of the people meant that universal suffrage had been achieved or, what he argued in *Democracy in America*, would inevitably be achieved.[5]

With regard to poverty, he and Beaumont were more interested in how the various states coped with it than in its causes and incidence. In their one subsequent statistical exploration of the matter, in an appendix to *Le Système Pénitentiaire*, they calculated on the basis of figures derived from their close study of the State of New York that there was "un pauvre" per 107 inhabitants in New York, compared to 1 in 16 in France. Perhaps this was the basis for their statement that there were few poor in America.[6] In another appendix, citing the lamentable example of England, which had created a system of public charity, they lectured the State of New York for its indulgent support of paupers, warning that in England such a policy had created a class of feckless social freeloaders, whom they described with a metaphor that would be meaningful to their Parisian readers: "We tend to believe that any law that provides regular and assured aid for the miseries of people will almost certainly result in the ceaseless increase in their number. Such a law moreover always degrades the people it is meant to aid. We know what enormous sums the poor tax in England has already raised. This has been the practice for half-century, and one can say accurately that in that country, the proletarians enjoy the ground floor while the owners *are their tenants*."[7] At the Auburn Penitentiary he and Beaumont observed inmates at work but evidently did not interview them, talking instead at great length with the warden, Elam Lynd, then well known as the leading exponent of the system of silent, communal, as opposed to solitary, hard labor and as a hard-nosed defender of the use of *le fouet*, or the whip. Then, in a startling departure from his customary mode of social observation, Tocqueville interviewed, during a stretch of twelve days, forty-four prisoners at the new Eastern State Penitentiary at Cherry Hill in Philadelphia. He did not record the notes he took on these interviews in his notebooks, perhaps because they were too lengthy, perhaps because they were material for his joint enterprise with Beaumont and not for his use alone. But these interviews were central experiences of his journey. The notes from his interviews with occasionally articulate and at times tearful prisoners, who undoubtedly were moved to have found an apparently sympathetic ear in the realm of Quaker silence, are detailed and nonjudgmental. Tocqueville may have been touched by such pathetic characters, but he was most interested in learning if silent, solitary confinement led to moral reform or religious conversion. He asked about each prisoner's personal history and about the crime that had led to his imprisonment (there was one woman, "une negresse"). His notes are most detailed about what the prisoners had to say, guided by his questioning, concerning the psychological, moral, and physical consequences of the solitary, silent confinement he and Beaumont were contrasting with the system of partial isolation and enforced total silence practiced at Auburn. This was to become a major issue, along with the question of cost, when the Chamber of Deputies debated prison reform just before the Revolution of 1848.[8]

Tocqueville appears to have been most concerned about the connection between style of incarceration and the prospects for the moral reform of the individual. He had nothing to say then or later about what the lives and fates of the prisoners revealed about the society that had extruded them and was punishing them. If these exceptional, intense encounters had provoked any reflections about the extent of equality in democratic America, he did not record them or draw any conclusions about the society that had produced such people and that was making them suffer. In another appendix to *Le Système Pénitentiaire* he and Beaumont do offer scathing comments on the cruelty and the heavy-handedness of the Anglo-American practice of imprisonment for debt.[9] However, the Eastern State interviews would not have told him anything clear about class in America, for among the forty-four who opened their hearts to him a number were professional men, some had once been prosperous, several were guilty of crimes of passion, one was eighteen, another an octogenarian, and six were black.

Tocqueville's interviews with convicts at Eastern State Penitentiary were the closest he came to the mind and heart of the common man in the Age of Jackson. He had visited the unhappy underside of American life. He came back from this American inferno of weeping losers, all desperate for the companionship of others, with no poetry but instead a technical report on prisons and some life stories that showed not all Americans had done well in the pursuit of happiness.

Even though Tocqueville appears to have been oblivious to evidence of social anger offered by urban unrest, there are signs that he was aware that there was a troubled underclass of losers and dissenters, the nonchosen or nonelect. One catches glimpses of this in some of the questions he asked Jared Sparks about how order was maintained in those essential elements of the polity, the towns: "Is there among you an animus of the poor classes against the rich classes which often leads the former (always in the majority) to oppress and humiliate the latter so that they are not chosen for public functions? If this disposition exists, what do the rich classes do?

"Does one often see agitators exercising strong influence in the towns? By what means do they usually acquire such influence? To what class of society do they belong? How is this problem remedied?"[10] Sparks assured Tocqueville that the towns were not troubled by class tensions and intrigues because everyone could participate in elections and because merit was the quality all voted for. Tocqueville appears to have believed him. Perhaps he had heard echoes of "pas de nobles" and thought of his own political hopes as he asked these questions. The good of the community, according to Sparks, guided everyone. He also assured Tocqueville that despite stringent laws about alcohol and the extensive surveillance imposed by local moral codes, town life was not made morally oppressive by snooping town officials, one of Tocqueville's concerns. He was troubled by the moral vigilantism of the Puritans and their social and cultural heirs and was on the qui vive for ways in which democratic mores and politics might oppress the individual.

Despite his suggestive questioning of Sparks, he seems not to have been concerned about "intrigants" in the cities he visited, which, as I have noted, he

thought were remarkably peaceful and orderly though they were in fact simmering with tensions of all sorts and frequently riotous. Though the social composition of the major contending political parties of Jacksonian America, the
Jacksonian Democrats and the Whigs, was somewhat blurred and shifting,
there were nonetheless visible class and ethnic divisions in American politics,
and these by the 1830s had become deeper. Political turmoil and violence
provided ample evidence of social conflict. Local and national elections in
New York City, where the newly founded, Irish-dominated Tammany Hall was
already active, were constantly marred by riots.[11] The cities Tocqueville visited
had huge, turbulent slums, none of which he says anything about, though he
must have seen them. There were inescapable marks of every kind of social
pathology. A booming number of well-publicized philanthropic organizations
and religious societies had sprung up to care for and reform the poor, the sick,
the unemployed, delinquents, prostitutes, unbelievers. In Boston and New
York, at least, there was abundant statistical proof of the extent of poverty, some
of it in fact cited by Beaumont and Tocqueville in *Le Système Pénitentiaire*. In
short, the evidence that the United States was becoming a two-class society, or
an increasingly divided society, was inescapable.

Tocqueville took little note of this. Why was that so? It might in part have
been a matter of perspective. He spent almost all his time in the United States
with wealthy conservatives and well-educated, well-off professionals. However,
the articulate, socially observant members of the American elite, like the New
Yorker Philip Hone, were well aware of the growing misery and anger that surrounded them in the cities, where smelly slums overflowing with immigrants
were engulfing their mansions and forcing them to move to the still-green out-
skirts of the cities. The uptown migration of New York's wealthy out of the
increasingly rowdy, crowded, unkempt lower Manhattan northward to Gramercy
Park and up Fifth Avenue was under way by 1831.[12] Tocqueville's personal propen-
sity for keeping the poor at arm's length unless it was to think about the problem
of poverty and poor relief—or to hand out alms—may also have continued to
keep them semivisible. Would recognition of how much distress and real misery
existed in the egalitarian utopia he was visiting have undermined his theory of
democracy or weakened the positive things he wished to say about the Paradise
of Opportunity he was visiting, in which traditional barriers to rising in the world
supposedly had vanished? He did not wish to furnish European reactionaries
with evidence of the failures of democracy. Still, the question remains: how
could so alert and perceptive a social observer have apparently missed so much?

Though he was quick to note all the signs of equality's triumph, especially all
the openness and flexibility and mobility that abundance and the relative absence

of ancient social prejudices had made possible, he knew that American society was nonetheless stratified and fragmented. It was not an undifferentiated society, and, he would later add in *Democracy in America*, it never would be: equality would be forever unattainable because of the inevitable natural inequalities among men, and also because envy, in his view the deepest of all democratic emotions, the passion for distinction, the thirst for wealth, and the fluctuating breaks of life ensured that inequality would be the rule.[13] The impossible quest for equality had already led to the social anger he failed to detect in the United States.

Tocqueville saw that the passionate egalitarians he traveled among separated themselves into groups that shared a common style of life and the same economic status. "One must not suppose," he wrote in a reflective summary essay in his notebooks, "that in America all classes of society mix in the same drawing rooms. . . . People in the same profession, with the same views and the same education, seek each other out by a sort of instinct and come together to the exclusion of others."[14]

Besides the passion for equality another was at work: the passion for distinction, which led to the practice of invidious exclusion. Tocqueville never accuses the Americans of hypocrisy concerning their egalitarian principles, but he is clear about the ways in which the society fell short of the ideal. Real incquality did exist in American life. He never took its full measure, and he seems even to have averted his eyes, but there was, he acknowledged, an "inequality born of wealth and education."[15] Even so, he constantly blurred the significance of such disparities. Again, it was a comparative matter. Such class differences, as he noted, did not seem to matter as much as they did in France. Invidious social clustering was largely confined to private life and was, he thought, "less felt [in the United States] than anywhere else."[16] The era of private clubs and exclusive communities had not yet begun. The founding of excluding institutions, the purpose of which was to establish social distinction and identity, would begin after the Civil War and the onset of the much greater flood of immigration that so terrified the Anglo-Americans who were Tocqueville's normative Americans.

Moreover, the American class structure was vastly more flexible than the European: "The difference is that no arbitrary inflexible rule prescribes this arrangement. . . . there is nothing final in it for anybody, and no one can be hurt by it."[17] Invidious social practices were the result of what Tocqueville calls "a sort of instinct," the passion for social distinction, a passion as deeply rooted as that for equality. Tocqueville had begun to transform class into as much a psychological as a socioeconomic reality. He had noted that phenomenon of social behavior that Thorstein Veblen a half century later would call "invidious distinction."

In fact, the passion for distinction, the need to stand out and to appear to be better than, not just equal to (an expression of the *envy* Tocqueville believed was the driving force of egalitarianism), not only survived but flourished in egalitarian America. He wryly remarked upon the strange fascination that a democratic people who refuse to admit that anyone is any better than anyone else and who had banned titles and legal social ranks can show for nobility and for the ancient paraphernalia of aristocratic display. "In this republican country" he noted, "they are a thousand times more fond of nobility, of titles, of crosses, and of all the inconsequential distinctions of Europe than we are in France. The greatest equality reigns here in the laws. It is even in appearance here in the customs. But I tell you that the Devil loses nothing by it."[18]

In that the continuing fervor of the Americans for social distinction could not satisfy itself with ermine or titles, money became the most powerful marker of difference. Tocqueville's mocking of egalitarian craving for social distinction is mild when compared to the fury that boils forth in his comments on the power of money in American society, where it has become the sole effective instrument of stratification and distinction, the major source of power and influence. Here, all of his loathing for the bourgeoisie and its values is vented with undisguised disgust. His observations about the lust for money and its social power in the United States, beginning with the notebooks and continued in *Democracy in America*, bristle with moral vehemence and social anger. In few other places in his writings on democratic America is he more personally engaged.

Ultimately, when he turned to *Democracy in America*, his remarks shift from the startled anthropological comments in his notebooks on the visible characteristics of an egalitarian society to reflections on the psychological impulses behind the Americans' passionate quest for equality, concluding with his warning that equality would never be achieved and that the pursuit of equality was bound to make men perpetually unhappy and restless and lead to social turmoil.

5

Born-Again America: The Creation of an American Identity

In his search for the American identity, that shared character and culture without which there could be no enduring nation, Tocqueville wrestled with the question of whether the traits and values of races are indelible. He only gradually abandoned the view that physiognomy fixed the identity of a people. He did not find unifying national traits in any American regional culture or even in the Anglo-American culture that was the basis of American institutions and values he found dominant. He found it instead in the Americans' extraordinary invention of a new culture, characterized by the belief that reality is endlessly malleable, that the past can be completely shed, and that individual identity can be chosen at will. He had discovered the American Dream. That dream eventually struck him as a great and possibly fatal cultural weakness. He also discovered that the Americans shared a common belief system as well as a common democratic epistemology or way of thinking.

Tocqueville's journey to America was more than a fact-gathering mission and a search for the soul of democracy. It was also an intellectual adventure, in the course of which he wrestled with a number of questions about race and national character, about the permanence of racial characteristics, about the sources of national unity, and about whether it would prove possible to forge a nation with a new identity out of the diverse European peoples that had poured into the New World. If he had not precisely formulated these questions before his journey, they nonetheless clearly were on his mind from the start. His notebooks record his repeated return to them and his changing responses. Was there an American character?

What drove his search for the essential American culture was the assumption that a multicultural society could not long survive. It had long been assumed that a nation could not survive with more than one church and one culture. The long history of repression and intolerance was witness to that. That assumption shows

321

up in various ways in Tocqueville's inquiry, primarily in his constant reflections and observations about the so-called races that had peopled the New World as well as in his view that in the future America would be either Unitarian or Catholic, unstable Protestant sects having self-destructed.[1] Was his quest also a nostalgic search for a cultural and social unity that Europe and France had once enjoyed, a search for a lost wholeness? One might say that such was also the goal of his plea for a return to a morally and politically uncorrupted language, for the recovery of a wholeness of language and culture, that rings out in anguish in his introduction to *Democracy in America*.

The notebooks also record his ultimate startled realization that the Europeans, in becoming Americans, had transcended their origins and the cultural or what he called the racial endowments they had brought to the New World and had remade themselves. They had been, as it were, born again.[2] Such was Tocqueville's profoundest discovery about this new ultraegalitarian people: they were constantly remaking and renewing themselves and their culture. Society was not something given and fixed in which individuals found their places. It was to be remodeled and improved. The same was true of every individual: not only spiritual but also social rebirth was possible and imperative.

This is the eureka one hears in the notebooks. Tocqueville increasingly saw the Americans as a thoroughly rational people, a word he often uses in describing them, a people who were constantly transcending the limits posed by custom, folk culture, race identity, a sense of the past. This deepest radicalism of the Americans, that is, their disavowal of all inherited identities and cultures, finally troubled him. It reinforced his view that the fatal flaw of democratic cultures would be that they would lack any sense of limits or acknowledge the claims of the past. And it troubled his belief, characteristic of his romanticism, that the continuing vitality and creativity of a people required that they remain rooted in their folk origins—that to fashion themselves by the light of reason rather than being guided by the voice of blood and by felt connections to their cultural roots would be enervating.

The intensity of Tocqueville's quest to discover an allegedly American identity, initially focusing on race, partly explains how it was that Tocqueville was able at times to overlook or minimize existing divisions within American society. The American who finally comes into focus for him and who represents the whole society is the white, middle-class Anglo-Saxon male with his auxiliary wife—though all newcomers quickly enough become American whatever their origins. It is this American about whom *Democracy in America* is written. The America his focus finally centers on is the America that dominated all public discourse and all proclamations of national identity and purpose, whether uttered by Whigs or Jacksonians: a white, Anglo-Saxon, Christian America with a providential destiny in which other races did not count. In this America, women were to play a "better-half" role as separate and sequestered voices whose suffrage was spiritual. The black man and the Indian were excluded, beyond the pale. In defining the American, Tocqueville leaves many out.

Three entries in the notebooks written over a period of half a year illustrate the questions about race and national character he wrestled with and trace the evolution of his thought:

> American society is composed of a thousand different elements recently assembled. The men who live under its laws are still English, French, German and Dutch. They have neither religion, morals nor ideas in common; up to the present one cannot say that there is any American character, at least it is the fact of not having any. There is no common memory, no national attachments here. What then can be the only bond that unites the different parts of this huge body?
>
> 29 May, 1831, Sing-Sing, New York[3]

> The Americans, in coming to America, brought with them all that was most democratic in Europe. When they arrived they left behind on the other side of the Atlantic the greater part of the national prejudices in which they had been brought up. They became a new nation which adopted new customs and new mores and something of a national character.
>
> 2 December, 1831, Cincinnati, Ohio[4]

> Spirit coldly burning, serious, tenacious, selfish, cold, frozen imagination, having respect for money, proud, industrious, rationalist.
>
> 13 January, 1832, Washington, D.C.[5]

Why he should for a time have posed the problem of American identity in terms of race is something of a puzzle. He was not thinking of the Negro and the native American. From the start it was clear they would remain unassimilable. At the time of his visit in 1831 and 1832 the United States was still a heavily English society, and it did not take Tocqueville long, in his search for the American character, to focus on the country's English heritage. When Jackson was first elected in 1828 the United States culturally was still strikingly homogeneous, except for the excluded peoples. The great wave of Irish and German immigration that would transform the country by the 1840s had just begun. In 1828, thirty thousand Irish immigrants had entered the country; in 1832 it was fifty thousand, and by the end of the decade half a million. The new Americans, largely Irish and German (and Catholic), ended the cultural uniformity and peace that had made democratic reforms possible, especially with regard to the suffrage. Nativist sentiments had begun to stir in the early thirties, soon to erupt in violence and in a powerful nativist political movement, but the new and different immigrant had not yet become a political or an economic issue while Tocqueville traveled the country.[6] Why then did he pose the question of national unity in terms of race?

He had begun his anthropological commentary by overestimating the racial heterogeneity of the American people and by asking what bond could unite a people of such diverse origins. The problem posed by such diversity eventually gave way to another: given their intense individualism, the newness of the society, the rapidity with which social institutions and manners changed, and the astonishing mobility that kept the whole society in seemingly permanent flux, what kept the Americans together? His first response had been that their unity was calculated, that it was based on interest (he would later call it enlightened self-interest). Shortly before he sailed back to France, he jotted down some of the elements of that American character he initially had said did not exist. He would soon add more, eventually drawing a fantastic portrait of the American as a dreamer who had fully broken free from the past and was constantly reshaping his identity and renewing himself and his world every day, living out a dream of endless progress.

The background for Tocqueville's initial questions about what made the Americans a nation was the long-running debate in France about the origins of the French nation and French culture. At issue was the question of the racial origins of the French nation, which had blended contributions from Franks, Gauls, and Romans into the unique society that was modern France. The debate, which was intensely political, turned on judgments about the qualities, or gifts, of each race, which, though based on physiognomy, were essentially moral, political, and cultural. Were race traits enduring and unchanging? could various races blend into one, mixing their flavors into something new and unique? had the Franks subdued the Gauls, thereby impressing their culture and their political institutions and inclinations on the emerging new nation?

It isn't fully known how familiar Tocqueville was with this debate. It may have shaped his reflections, which he conducted in the same anthropological terms. The quest to understand the spirit, or genius, of each nation intensified as European romantics reacted against the cosmopolitan, rationalist universalism of the eighteenth century, and it was conducted in the language of race. The major historians of early nineteenth-century France, including Thierry, Michelet, Mignet, Guizot, Quinet, all of whom he knew well, had taken positions on the issue, which had powerful political implications. To favor one race was to vote for a particular politics and cultural style.

Tocqueville does not seem to have acknowledged or commented on this historical–anthropological debate. Yet while he was in the United States he for a time carried on a parallel inquiry, which in the end also had political implications when he realized that the new nation was basically Anglo-Saxon and was thus destined to be the new home of liberty and free institutions. He too thought of races mainly in terms of their moral and cultural qualities, and the distinctions he drew among them were invidious. His ranking of supposed races by their moral and intellectual qualities was conventional and made it possible for him, as it did for many others, including Mill, to justify the European conquest and repression of morally underdeveloped peoples, which he argued was a good thing for their sake and for the general advance of civilization.

Later, though he argued against the race theories of Gobineau's *Essai sur l'inégalité des races humaines,* he did not deny that there were moral and intellectual differences between races. Instead, he argued that it could not be *proven* that racial traits were congenital and permanent and that Gobineau's theory of racial determinism was not only unscientific but, more important, fatalistic and thus morally ruinous. Nevertheless, despite his conventional race ranking and his acknowledgment that there were significant moral and intellectual differences between races, Tocqueville eventually disavowed the idea that the races of humanity were fundamentally, decisively separate. There was a deeper unity to humankind than the apparent differences between races suggested. In his presidential address of October 25, 1851, to the Académie des sciences morales et politiques on "l'unité de l'espèce humaine" he expressed the conviction that "nations, tribes, classes . . . are only parts of a unity, and Man finally appears through the varied multiplicity of men."[7] Both in *Democracy in America* and in his speeches and writings in the effort to end slavery in the French colonies, he had argued that the traits ascribed to the Negro to justify his enslavement were not indelible race characteristics but the results of that enslavement.

Nevertheless, he began his search for the American assuming that race played a powerful role in determining the character and culture of a people. Even though he believed that by conscious choice he himself could transcend *his* historical destiny, it was inevitable that no matter how much of the cosmopolitanism of the eighteenth century he had absorbed he would begin his journey deeply conscious of the constraints and limits that shape a people's ways of life, their politics, even their worldviews. Immemorial custom, deeply rooted habit, a web of institutions and laws, languages, and literatures shaped the destinies of a people. Tocqueville used race and physiognomy as shorthand for the idea that the culture of a people was an enduring force in their lives.

In the notebooks he occasionally asserted that race was permanent. In the small frontier settlement of Saginaw, Michigan, he met inhabitants of French and English ancestry who remained French and English: "The people inhabiting this little bit of cultivated plain belong to two races who for nearly a century have lived on American soil and obeyed the same laws. But there is nothing in common between them. They are English and French, just like those one finds on the banks of the Seine or the Thames."[8] The Frenchman, even though clad in "moccasins, otterskin cap and woolen cloak" and even though he had become "an unwearying hunter" who "sleeps in the open and lives on wild honey and bison flesh," was still unmistakably French: "gay, enterprising, haughty, proud of his origin, passionate lover of military glory, vain rather than mercenary, a man of instinct following his first inclination."[9] Nothing of the sort could be said of his neighboring English frontiersman, who, facing the same difficulties, had hardened himself against them. "The Englishman," said Tocqueville, "is cold, tenacious and relentless in argument; he attaches himself to the ground and snatches from savage life all that can be got out of it. . . . Bit by bit he carries into the world his laws, his habits and his customs, and if he could he would introduce everything down to the smallest refinements of civilization."[10] What is at point here is not Tocqueville's remarkable analysis of the differences between the traits of the French and the English, but his argument that race is fate. "Some philosophers have believed," he wrote in August as he steamed west on Lake Huron toward Wisconsin,

> that human nature, everywhere the same, only varies according to the institutions and laws of different societies. That is one of the opinions to which the history of the world seems to give the lie on every page. In history, all nations, like individuals, show their own peculiar physiognomy. Their characteristic traits reproduce themselves through all the transformations that they undergo. Laws, morals, religions alter; dominion and wealth change hands; external appearances vary; the dress is different; prejudices vanish or are replaced by others. Through all these diverse changes you always recognize the same people. Something inflexible shows through in spite of all man's adaptability.[11]

Initially, then, Tocqueville sought the source of the originality and character of a people not in its peculiar mode of adaptation to circumstance, not in the circumstances themselves, but in some irreducible quality, vaguely identified with its origins or with its physiognomy. Though he gradually relinquished this view, it remained a plausible hypothesis for him and continued to bedevil his thinking about the sources and nature of the American character. A December entry in the notebooks expresses doubts about the confident cosmopolitanism of the Enlightenment by wondering if the vigor and originality of a people might not depend on the maintenance of their racial or folk identity. He here gives voice to the romantic persuasion that vitality and identity might be lost if a people followed reasonings rather than customs, no longer "took as a model a certain ideal perfection peculiar to it" and were no longer "concerned to do as its fathers did."[12] Tocqueville the romantic debates Tocqueville the philosophe.

The idea that race characteristics were permanent persisted even as he was working out a new sense of what was American about the character of the people he was observing. For a while he remained fascinated by the apparent indelibility of national character and the tenacity of what is now called ethnic culture. The American was in a sense a truer European, the inessential dross removed, the core purified: "America gives the most perfect picture, for good and for ill, of the special character of the English race. The American is the Englishman left to himself" (January 15, 1832).[13] The same was true of the French in America, who were "to the French of France as the Americans are to the English. They have preserved the greater part of the original traits of the national character, and have added more morality and more simplicity" (August 29, 1831).[14] He was intrigued by the way in which the Germans of Pennsylvania kept alive "the spirit and the ways of their fatherland" (November 25, 1831).[15] Out of the crucible of the New World experience came not something new but an intensified version of the old. The transforming power of the frontier, in this view, is reductive, not creative.

But a different view began to emerge. It isn't surprising that this shift seems to have occurred as Tocqueville ventured farther west, which he found to be a truly new world, unlike anything he had known in Europe, not only in appearance but also in the character of its inhabitants. So advanced there was the process of cultural and political change, so unusual its inhabitants, that he began to think that something new was being created. The first step in this change was to see the American as a decultured European, without any singular character other than a powerful individuality that took idiosyncratic shape depending on circumstance. "There is," he wrote of the American he met in Ohio, "no memory that attaches him to one place more than another, no inveterate habits, no spirit of routine. . . . many have come from Europe and have left their habits and their memories there."[16] The web of memory and culture linking past to present, Europe to America, seemed to have been broken. He began to see that the cultural transformation he was witnessing involved a good deal more than the divestment of old traits and traditions and more than the freeing of the individual from the grip of custom and prescription. It meant the emergence of a new culture and a new "social state" based on a new world of abundance, open space, and exhilarating freedom and on the principles of democracy. He had momentously discovered the culture produced by "democracy without limits."[17] A people could leave their past behind. It had become clearer to him that there was a real unity to this new society. Peoples initially quite different were being transformed by the New World.[18]

He had already discovered regional subcultures with distinct characteristics, first revealed by the striking contrast between the New Yorker and the Bostonian, then manifested even more clearly by the westerner, who in some ways became the essential American for Tocqueville, and then by his encounter with southern culture, shaped by slavery. His notebooks record detailed observations of these regional cultures: they were larger unities, but they could not serve as the essential democratic culture, which was the fowl he was stalking.[19]

The American slowly emerged. His character was unprecedented and difficult to recognize. "As yet there is no American outlook" he would write, even as he described what he called an American outlook. He had thought that the incredible mobility of American society made the emergence of a unified culture unlikely, but this mobility turned out to be the key to the emergence of an American identity. The American "has inhabited twenty different places and has nowhere formed ties that hold him" and consequently was a free cultural agent, continually remaking himself and his world. There were a few traits common to all: industriousness, fervent acquisitiveness, and a love of change or, as he alternatively put it, "instability of character." As he wrote in an eloquent mini-essay in his notebooks, "Often born under another sky, placed in the middle of an ever-moving picture, driven himself by the irresistible torrent that carries all around him along, the American has no time to attach himself to anything, he is only accustomed to change and ends by looking on it as the natural state of man. Much more, he feels the need of it, he loves it, for instability instead of causing disasters for him, seems only to bring forth wonders around him."[20]

By the time he had spent half a year in the United States he had developed a more precise sense of a distinctively American character. It had also grown out of his recognition that the culture, the social state, of the Americans was overwhelmingly English. Other races had had little influence on the development of the American character. His long stay in New England, from early September to nearly mid-October of 1831, had persuaded him that the culture and institutions of the United States were essentially English. Such was the message forcefully delivered by the articulate New Englanders he had met. Tocqueville thoroughly absorbed their view of America's past and destiny. They constituted the kind of aristocratic elite he was already convinced democracies could not do without. In *Democracy in America* he powerfully emphasizes the Anglo-Saxon inheritance of the United States with great eloquence: the *Democracy* concludes with a vision of energetic, shrewd, bold, self-confident Anglo-Americans triumphantly sweeping over the whole continent, subduing the French to the north, the Spanish to the south, and eventually conquering even the seas. It was the message of Manifest Destiny spoken by a Frenchman.

Whatever institutional imprint the English had left on American life, the Englishness of the Americans would go through a double refinement, in his notebook reflections, to produce a truly extraordinary national character unlike anything on earth, including England itself, where the voice of the past was always strongly heard. This new American character was powerfully optimistic; it had broken free from the past and was giving shape to a new, ever-changing culture. The transformation occurred as Tocqueville sharply shifted his search for the source of national character away from race and toward the New World, which had created a new character.

It was the first English settlers, he had noted in December while in Ohio, where his understanding of the sources and the qualities of the American character seems to have been decisively transformed, who had shed their national traits and had become a different people, with "new mores and something of a national character."[21] That transformation was being repeated in the great westward migration then under way: "Today a new migration has been producing the same effects. The new emigrants bring to their adopted country principles of democracy even more disengaged from any ties, habits, even less stamped by convention, and minds even freer than the former ones."[22] The elemental Democratic man had finally appeared: the American character had been born. Environment, more than race, determined the character of a people. All that had remained of the English inheritance had been the English "instinct for liberty" and certain qualities of spirit—they were profoundly rational and logical. Other cultural traits and habits, all other ordinarily slow-changing "moeurs," were quickly shed. Tocqueville's ultimate view of the transformative power of the frontier was not quite as sweeping as Frederick Jackson Turner's, but otherwise he believed that a new man and a new culture had been born on American soil. Though there is no evidence that he had read Crèvecoeur, he sounds very much like his French predecessor, who a generation earlier had called the American a new man.

By now he was convinced that there was an inner unity to American culture and society and that this new society was a coherent entity rather than a mass of busy individuals alike only in their individuality. There was a "logical unity," an

uncoerced coherence, to American culture because it had, as it were, been created from scratch and was not a synthesis of the disparate cultures that had
flowed into the New World. While it was true that the point of departure had
not been a void—Tocqueville argues in *Democracy in America* that the English
had initially been the chief architects of American institutions and culture and
had arrived with a crucially important cluster of intellectual, political, and religious values and practices—the society that had been created in the New World
was something fresh and new. It was, above all, the conscious creation of a
remarkably rational and logical people, not the result of the slow evolution of
inherited institutions. "One of the most striking features of American institutions," he wrote while in Washington, close to the end of his visit, "is that they
form a perfectly logical chain. That is a merit to which very few peoples can
aspire. . . . the fact is that there are pretty few peoples who can be understood
from one end to the other. The special reason that has put the Americans in a
state to be understood is they have been able to build their social edifice from a
clean start."[23]

One aspect of the rationality of the Americans lay in the freedom with which
they could respond to new circumstances and new problems with new solutions. Though he had scoffed at the geometrical and numerical approach of the
Philadelphians to city planning, the Americans' response to the possibilities of
the environment was an illustration of the "perfectly logical chain" that linked
all aspects of American life. Reason and not sentiment guided them. He would
have perfectly understood Jefferson's imposition of a geometrical planning
grid on the uneven, curving terrain of the United States. The Americans were
rationalists: even in planning their government they had applied the laws of
mechanics.

Yet there was another source of the newness of the American character. The
completely new, ever-changing world of apparently endless abundance in
which there were few restraints to ambition had unleashed the imagination.
The Americans found themselves in a sunlit world of limitless possibilities in
which there were no barriers to the pursuit of happiness. It was a world changing so rapidly that it seemed new everyday. If their attention was riveted on the
opportunities granted by a materially abundant environment and intensely
focused on the task of making nature yield its wealth, it was also unfettered by
a sense of limits. The European mind, by contrast, seemed rigid in its restraint,
its respect for form, its reverence for custom, its greater awareness of complexity
and limits. To the American, everything seemed possible, nothing was fixed,
all could be improved. His imagination had not been chastened by the experience of scarcity or by the powerful restraints of ascriptive statuses. Instead,

the experience of constant change encouraged him to imagine a future of unbounded possibilities.

If the American was notable for his rationality, he was also a dreamer. Here too Jefferson, driven by his visions, might have been a model, constantly measuring, constantly improving the land—a rational dreamer. In a remarkable passage in his notebooks Tocqueville captures the visionary quality of the American character:

> By a strange inversion of the ordinary order of things, it is nature that changes, while man remains unchanging. The same man may give his name to wilds that none has witnessed before him; he has been able to fell the first tree in the forest and built in the midst of the solitude a planter's house round which a hamlet has formed and which is now surrounded by a huge city. In the short space between birth and death he has seen all these changes. And a thousand others like him have been able to do so. In his youth he has lived among tribes who now live only in history; during his life rivers have changed or diminished their course, the climate is different from what it was before, and all that is still in his imagination only a first step in an endless career. Howsoever powerful and impetuous the course of history is here, imagination always goes in advance of it, and the picture is never large enough. *There is not a country in the world where man more confidently takes charge of the future, or where with more pride that he can fashion the universe to please himself.* It is a movement of the mind which can only be compared with that which brought about the discovery of America three centuries ago. *And in fact one might say that America has been discovered for a second time.*[24] [emphasis added]

Such was not the mind-set of a visionary few. The whole society had been released to its dreams: "One must not imagine that such thoughts only take shape in a philosopher's head; the artisan thinks them as much as the speculator, the peasant as much as the town-dweller. They belong to every object. They form a part of all feelings; they are palpable, visible, felt and, in some sort, strike all the senses."[25] Tocqueville here has caught the optimistic, confident, perfectionist spirit of this exuberant moment in American life, when, having landed on the shores of a new world, Americans set about creating a new society—a novus ordo seclorum.: "The idea of a possible improvement, of a successive and continuous betterment of the social condition, that idea is before him in all its facets."[26]

Had Tocqueville grasped how pervasive the spirit of evangelical Christianity was in the United States he might have understood that the conviction that the

material and social worlds could be endlessly improved applied to the individual as well. For the religious imagination, however, it was a matter not only of
"continuous betterment" but also of instant transformation by means of conversion and faith. If this intense born-again moment in American religious life was
in part the result of anxiety caused by uprootedness and rapid social change and
by the Protestant quest for salvation by conversion, it was also an expression of
the perfectionist, utopian mood that had gripped all Americans, a mood that
had deeper, permanent sources. It is doubtful that Tocqueville could have
imaginatively entered the evangelical mind even had he seriously studied the
radical Protestantism that was still blazing in both rural and urban America, but
he quickly perceived the everything-is-possible faith that touched every aspect
of American life. The world was to be remade, and, in a democratic society, all
were to be saved.

This faith in the improvability of everything was just one aspect of that "common outlook" he initially had felt was missing. Along with enlightened self-
interest, it was a bond that united Americans. The astonishing number of reform
societies was made possible because many shared the faith that the world was to
be refashioned. The whole society, not just exceptional individuals, had become
visionary.

He would discover other elements of a common outlook. This remarkable,
broadly shared faith that the world was to be remade was one aspect of a larger
community of belief that unified what at first glance seemed to be a society—or
rather a crowd—of striving, competitive individuals. The fact that the Americans
were united by a common belief system became apparent from the start. "What
strikes me," he wrote to Kergorlay at the end of June, after just one and a half
months in the United States, "is that the immense majority of spirits join
together in certain *common opinions.*"[27]

From the start he had begun to discover an unparalleled uniformity of belief
in a society that seemed to lack any unifying character except for a startling
sameness of appearance. So remarkable was this ideological unity that he confessed it moved him to envy; by contrast, France was torn by social divisions and
bitterly opposed political persuasions. His envy did not last. It did not take long
for him to understand that the striking uniformity of belief and opinion of the
radically individualistic, deracinated Americans not only was a source of community but also could be and was an oppressive force that might intimidate and
silence individuals. "I know of no other society in which there is so little intellectual freedom," he would write in *Democracy in America*: the devastating
consequence of a system of belief so broadly shared that it stifled difference and
dissent.[28] The "immense majority" in America believed that "the republican is

a good form of government . . . natural to human societies"; it had faith in "the wisdom and good sense of humankind" as well as in "the doctrine of human perfectibility." This common creed maintained that "necessarily it [the majority] will be right" but that "one cannot enlighten it too much"—hence the universal faith in education.[29] An optimistic, perfectionist republicanism based on faith in man and on the rationality of majority rule unified this society of fiercely independent individuals who lacked common traditions, a common religion, common ethnic origins, and class and local loyalties.

Even those conservative Americans with whom Tocqueville spent most of his time and who heavily shaped his views of the culture and politics of the United States would have assented to much of this creed, with some reservations about human abilities and considerable doubts that the time was right for universal suffrage. A conservative like Chancellor Kent, whose *Commentaries* Tocqueville studied carefully while in the United States and read again in Paris, might fiercely oppose the extension of the suffrage, but other doubters remained silent or gave up the struggle. In a notebook entry dated September 30, 1831, he added to his inventory of the common creed: "The two great social principles which seem to me to rule American society and to which one must always return to find the reason for all the laws and habits which govern it, are as follows: 1st. The majority may be mistaken on some points, but finally it is always right and there is no moral power above it. 2nd. Every individual, private person, society, community or nation, is the only judge of its own interest, and provided it does not harm the interests of others, nobody has the right to interfere. I think that one must never lose sight of this point."[30] Tocqueville here began to construct a dilemma that he never resolved and that in fact the society had not—and still has not—resolved. The democratic credo is that the majority is "finally . . . always right"; at the same time, the religious faith of the Americans as well as a constitutionally established cluster of rights set limits to what is permissible and accordingly establishes that there is a "moral power above" majority judgment. Would an increasingly pragmatic, experimental, competitive culture fascinated by "the new" be able to maintain these limits, this unity of belief? Such was the great question Tocqueville constantly asked as he thought about the prospects of the young American democracy—and the fate of all democratic societies.

In *Democracy in America* he would explore the intellectual foundations of this shared democratic moral and political creed by arguing that the democratic mind also had a common way of looking at things, a general philosophical method, as it were. There was a democratic temper, a democratic intellectual style. The democratic mind was empirical, skeptical, pragmatic, and uneasy about intellectual authority. Tocqueville thought that the age of democracy would not be an age of faith. Yet the skeptical individual would find it difficult to stand alone. In need of some source of authority, the skeptic would find it in the many. And beyond this, certain ideas had immense power in America not simply because they were broadly maintained, but also because they were elements of a deeply rooted worldview and were the logical consequences of an episteme that was natural to a democratic people.[31]

One suspects Tocqueville would not have been surprised had he been told that in the future the characteristic philosophical styles of the Anglo-American people would express their radically empirical temper and that they would reject idealisms and Hegelisms of all sorts. Such would not be the future of his countrymen.

6

POLITICS: ORDER AND DISORDER
IN THE NEW REPUBLIC

The central question for Tocqueville was whether the political life of a fully democratic society could function well enough to secure liberty and preserve the unity of the nation. Would democratic culture preserve the strengths that a free, egalitarian people needed? His notebooks record his dismay at the evident decline in the quality of political leaders as democracy advanced as well as what he saw as the fading of a sense of the common good and a concern for posterity. The self-centered passions, the cupidity, and the cultural wildness fostered by democracy foreshadowed problems for the future of democratic freedom. He greatly amplified this argument in the *DA II*. He was impressed nonetheless with the way in which the Americans, through vigorous local political activity, their pragmatic, nonideological way of dealing with issues, and their skill at forming associations devoted to particular interests, developed a broad range of competences and great political astuteness. In this respect he found the Americans the most enlightened people in the world.

All the elements of Tocqueville's later, fully developed political theory of democracy and of all he has to say about democracy and its prospects in *Democracy in America* are to be found in the notes about democratic culture and institutions scattered throughout his notebooks. His curiosity ranged over every aspect of American life, but the notebooks make it clear that, apart from the American penal system, his attention was most focused on five matters: politics, religion, class in an egalitarian society, whether there was an American character or identity, and whether this striving, multifarious republic of competitive individuals would endure or fly apart. There were other questions, too: for example, could the middle classes govern. that is, could a society without an aristocracy be well governed or even governed well enough? But the matters above were what he focused on.

Tocqueville was a thoroughly political man. His intellectual life centered around political questions. His ambitions too were political. It was in politics that he saw the destinies of humanity and nations being decided; and it was in political life that the greatest of all questions, whether human will and belief could take control of history, would be answered. He saw the political life of a people as the clearest expression of its laws, culture, and spirit. For all the broad range of his curiosity, he was, during his visit, most keenly interested in the political institutions and civic practices of the United States. Apart from how the American democratic political system worked, the questions that most focused his thinking, both during his visit and later, concerned the durability of the New Republic and whether democracy would maintain the moral qualities needed to preserve liberty. What factors augured well for its future? what seemed to threaten its prospects? He toted up lists of advantages and disadvantages, strengths and weaknesses, as if trying to calculate the odds of survival.

Beginning with the notebooks, his critique of American political democracy is taut with ambivalence. He had arrived when the democratic revolution of which Andrew Jackson was both symbol and leader was in full flood, and much that he observed disturbed him. Jefferson and Adams had only recently died; Madison was still alive, though ancient. Yet the quality of most public officials, from the president on down, already seemed appallingly low. Jackson, whom he met shortly before he left, was in a sense a paradigm. Tocqueville thought him "a very mediocre man" who truckled to majority sentiment and, with majority support secured, acted with astonishing ruthlessness and high-handedness.[1]

He was sharply critical of the continual toadying to majority sentiment that he thought was the heart of democratic politics. In a scathing chapter in *Democracy in America* he describes this as a reincarnation of the old "courtier spirit" of Louis XIV's court, where flattery and groveling flourished as techniques for gaining power. The old court toads were now democratic politicians.[2] He was astonished at the surprising degree of power allowed democratic officials with majority support behind them. His heaviest indictment of democratic politics was that the quality of political leaders was appallingly low.

This last criticism came repeatedly from his American acquaintances, most of whom were not Jacksonians, though it was a judgment he surely would have arrived at on his own. He characteristically drew from it the most sweeping and dramatic questions. "Why," he asked in Baltimore in early November, "as civilization spreads, do outstanding men become fewer? Why, when attainments are the lot of all, do great intellectual talents become rarer? Why, when there are no longer lower classes, are there no more upper classes? Why, when knowledge of how to rule reaches the masses, is there a lack of great abilities in the direction of society? America clearly poses these questions. But who can answer them?"[3] Even though he met many able, responsible, even learned and virtuous public servants, some of whom he relied on heavily for information that was vital to *Democracy in America*, he continued to argue that democracy had led to a decided lowering of standards since the early days of the Republic, when cultivated, honorable men like Jefferson, Adams, and Washington guided the nation. "When voting rights are universal," he wrote while in Memphis, "and deputies are paid by the State, it is a strange thing how low the people's choice can descend and how far it can be mistaken."[4] This remark was prompted by what he had just learned about the spectacular career of Davy Crockett: "Two years ago the inhabitants of the district of which Memphis is the capital sent to the House of Representatives an individual called David Crockett, who had received no education, could read only with difficulty, had no property, no fixed dwelling, but spent his time hunting, selling his game for a living, and spending his whole life in the woods. His competitor, who failed, was a fairly rich and able man."[5] A Tocqueville–Crockett interview would have been memorable, and it is tempting to wonder what Tocqueville would have thought or said had Colonel Crockett introduced himself with the splendid frontier tall-tale boast with which he had announced his arrival in Washington in 1827 as a newly elected representative from Tennessee: "I'm David Crockett, fresh from the backwoods. . . . I can wade in the Mississippi, leap the Ohio, ride a streak of lightning, slip without a scratch down a honey-locust, whip my weight in wild-cats, hug a bear too close for comfort, and eat any man opposed to Jackson." However, it is unlikely he would have agreed to meet this marvelously articulate rustic, who back in Normandy would have been regarded as a poacher and a dangerous, rootless man. Moreover, if he had heard more about Crockett, he chose in his notebook to focus on Crockett's "unwashed" illiteracy, not on the man's politics, which involved a career in which he began as a fierce antibank Jacksonian and ended as an ally of Nicholas Biddle, the polished director of the "Monster" Bank of the United States and mortal enemy of Crockett's fellow frontiersman Jackson.[6] Tocqueville did not examine the local life of democracy on his expedition and seems not to have been interested in talking to the people's politicos. His major source of information about politics in the United States, as about everything there, was the American elite. There is no evidence he spent much time reading American newspapers, though he later devoted two chapters of *Democracy in America* to the role of newspapers in a democracy.[7]

He did, however, interview Sam Houston, a fellow Mississippi River steamboat passenger with whom by chance he traveled for four days from Memphis to New Orleans. Houston, who had been governor of Tennessee and had also been elected a Creek Indian chief, was a combat friend of Jackson. He was no

ordinary man. Tocqueville's description of Houston's graceful, almost aristocratic bearing, lithe strength, and moral energy is admiring, as were his comments about the white stallion Houston was riding. That interview, which took
place on December 31, 1831, the day before they arrived in New Orleans, is one
of the longest recorded in the notebooks, surely an accolade from Tocqueville.[8]
It was concerned solely with the Indians of the South, whom Houston knew
well. Though Tocqueville recognized Houston's physical and intellectual powers, he nonetheless was incredulous that someone with so wild a personal life,
which included having sought refuge among the Creek after allegedly having
killed someone, could have succeeded in politics. "I asked what could have
commended him to the people's choice. 'That he came from them,' I was told,
and had risen by his own exertions."[9] But the remarkable Houston was not one
of the ordinary new, crude pols of the age of Jackson.

It was not only the people's preference for representatives cut from the same
cloth that kept "men of distinction" out of politics. The rough and tumble campaigning of mass politics, in which a candidate had to sell himself as one of the
boys ("one must haunt the taverns, drink and argue with the mob"), repelled
good men even before the voters had a chance to reject them. Chancellor
Kent's argument against the popular election of judges provided Tocqueville
with a conclusive quote: "'The fittest men,' Kent says frankly in speaking of
judges, 'would probably have too much reservedness of manners and severity of
morals, to secure an election resting on universal suffrage.'"[10] In the election of
1848 in La Manche Tocqueville would face this challenge without abandoning
his aristocratic manners.

The same decline had occurred in other aspects of American political life.
Democracy had trivialized political debate. Politics had become a clashing of
petty interests, with principle and a well-defined sense of the public good abandoned. Why he thought the central political issues of the Jackson years—the
seizure of Indian lands, the expansion of slavery, the tariff, internal improvements, the power of the Bank of the United States, the right of labor to
organize—were trivial is not clear. In fact it isn't likely that he did. They involved
provisions or principles of the Constitution, and he knew how momentous the
issue of slavery was. He seems to have meant that political debate was not conducted on the level of principle: "America has had great parties, but they exist
no longer; there has been a great gain in happiness, but in morality, I doubt it.
I cannot conceive a more wretched sight in the world than that presented by the
different coteries (they do not have the name of parties) which now divide
the Union. In broad daylight one sees in their breasts the excitement of all the
little shameful passions which ordinarily are careful to keep themselves hidden

at the bottom of the human heart. As for the country's interest, no one thinks about it, and if it is referred to, that is for form's sake."[11] "Great parties" were those attached to "generating principles and not to their consequences, to general conceptions and not to particular cases, to ideas and not to men."[12] Political debate conducted by newspapers that served as party mouthpieces was little more than a noxious flow of "coarse insults," "petty slanders," and "impudent calumnies."[13] "There are men of integrity in all parties," he wrote, "but there is no party of integrity."[14]

This dismayed criticism of democratic politics in America is exactly what he would soon be saying, nearly word for word, about French political life during the July Monarchy. In fact, he was soon condemning French politics for the same deficiencies, even though he appears not to have commented on them before his American experience. In Philadelphia he asked Biddle, the Jacksonians' chief ogre, to explain why there were no longer great parties in the United States like the ones that were still to be found in France. That was in 1831.[15]

In a politics whose ruling animus was the pursuit of private interest and in which the ruling practice was that the end justifies the means, the idea of the public good grew feebler. Political passions in democracy focused not on the general interest but on self-interest. Politicians at every level fought for office and power and were rarely concerned for the common good, if they took time to think through what that might be. Tocqueville doubted that the American faith that the sum of private interests would always "harmonize with the general interest" would prove well founded. "A sort of refined and intelligent selfishness seems to be the pivot on which the whole machine turns," he wrote. "These people here do not trouble themselves to find out whether public virtue is good, but they do claim to prove that it is useful."[16] In the hullaballoo of American politics, in which a host of petty interests battled for attention and satisfaction, it was difficult for citizens to think clearly about the public good. In a democracy one's politics became increasingly self-centered, and one's political vision tended to reach no farther than one's grasp. He would soon be saying the same about France.

The surge toward universal suffrage seemed full of perils to him. Though in 1831 a number of states, including North and South Carolina, Virginia, Rhode Island, Tennessee, Connecticut, and New Jersey, still maintained some property qualifications for the vote, he took no note of ways in which the suffrage was still limited. He was certain that full suffrage would inevitably be achieved, as he wrote in *Democracy in America*.[17] Mass politics in effect meant the rule of mass man. The exceptional man was either ignored or driven from political life. A recurring lament of the notebooks is that an aristocracy of merit, so important in his later political theory, was disappearing from American political life. This bitter observation would later be given memorable expression in those bleak, despairing pages of *Democracy in America* in which he discusses the power and the inertia of mass opinion and the unlikelihood that the individual whose ideas differed from the values and opinions of the masses would ever gain a hearing, let alone exercise influence. Heroic generals and politicians who were like the people would always triumph over eggheads.[18]

The dogma of popular infallibility, he wrote in his notebooks, was just as absurd as the old faith that "the King can do no wrong."[19] This was true even in the United States, where, as Tocqueville acknowledged, the people were much more politically experienced and astute than anywhere else. Nor was it simply a matter of the demonstrable fallibility of majority judgment. He also believed there was a justice that transcended majority judgment, and a public interest that transcended individual or group interests. Majority opinion might have political priority, but it could not automatically be granted moral priority. Its power, however, could scarcely be doubted.

His notebooks and letters bear witness to how increasingly troubled he was by the power of public opinion in democratic America—a society with an immense, relatively undifferentiated public still lacking the historically evolved diversity of European societies. In *Democracy in America* he memorably formulated his observations and fears about the power of public opinion in the various chapters devoted not only to the tyranny of the majority but also to all that contributes to the uniformity of opinion and to cultural uniformity in democratic societies.[20] By the time he concludes *Democracy*, however, it was not the potential oppressiveness of mass opinion that loomed as the great danger for freedom in the future. Other qualities of democratic culture, among them its increasing normlessness and its refusal to accept limits, alarmed him even more.

Other weaknesses of democratic politics preoccupied him throughout the notebooks. Democratic governments, he wrote in Philadelphia, were decidedly less efficient than aristocratic governments: "When the detractors of popular governments claim that in many points of internal administration, the government of one man is better than the government of all, they are, in my view, incontestably right. It is in fact rare for a strong government not to show more consistency in its undertakings, more perseverance, more sense of the whole, more accuracy in detail, and more discretion even in its choice of men, than the multitude."[21] He observed how democratic politics interfered with the sound administration of institutions that should have been left to the governance of experts; and he noted the disadvantages that were the results of the decentralization, the lack of continuity, the party competition, and the constant surface turmoil and instability that were characteristics of American politics. The least serious of these concerned efficiency: "In what concerns criminal justice, roads, prisons and generally for all undertakings that demand rapidity of execution or continuity of conception, the lack of centralization makes itself felt in America."[22] Far more serious was a weakened capacity for the sustained pursuit of high ideals and large purposes. "The principle of the sovereignty of the people," he wrote, "often gives the nations that adopt it an energy that the others lack. However, the people does not always know how to impose the necessary sacrifices on itself," and he proceeded to quote Alexander Hamilton's *Federalist* 31, in which Hamilton discusses popular resistance to taxation as proof of the point.[23] Tocqueville's American observations suggested that a democratic people would lack the discipline and the foresight to make disagreeable, if necessary, laws. In America he encountered a people who "live from day to day and are much less able to impose painful exertions on themselves for the sake of the future." "One cannot know exactly how much energy and great power of self-control American democracy could show in time of crisis," but he doubted there would be much.[24] His apprehension—that democracies are prone to suffer from a failure of vision and will and that a democratic people engrossed in the pursuit of material happiness will be unable to make those great efforts and sacrifices sometimes required of a people—is strongly registered in the notebooks. It later casts a cold shadow over *Democracy in America*.

Such were the aspects of politics in democratic America that most offended his high-minded elitism: the low quality of leadership; the continual blurring of principle in a politics that appealed primarily to interest; the feeble sense of the public interest; an inability to take the long view (*prévoyance*); and the tendency to identify majority judgment with the right and with moral law. He thought these were likely to prove congenital defects of democratic politics. Neither in his notebook reflections nor in *Democracy in America* does he resolve the conflict he had raised between the ideal of the local control of the peoples' affairs and centralized guidance of national affairs with the general good in mind. Later in his life, it was these defects and conflicts, along with the increasing violence of American political life and the instability of a dynamic, aggressive economy, that loomed larger the longer he thought about the prospects for American democracy.

Tocqueville's American sojourn also opened his eyes to much that was positive in democratic politics, recorded with admiration in his notebooks. Universal suffrage led to the flaws discussed above, but it also had "wonderful advantages,"[25] and there is no doubt that to Tocqueville these were exhilarating. The chief advantages of democracy were that it led to an enormous increase of political activity, a tremendous release of energy, and a level of political savoir-faire that led him often to say that the American people were the most enlightened in the world, one of his characteristic hyperboles. "The wonderful effect of republican governments (where they can subsist)," he wrote in his notebooks, "is not in presenting a picture of *regularity* and *methodical order* in a people's administration, but in the *way of life*. Liberty does not carry out each of its undertakings with the same perfection as an intelligent despotism, but in the long run it produces more than the latter. It does not always and in all circumstances give the people a more skilful and faultless government; but it infuses throughout the body social an activity, a force and an energy which never exist without it, and which bring forth wonders. It is there one must look for its advantages."[26] These qualities might counterbalance democracy's inefficiency and inability to take a long view of the social good.

The spread of suffrage led to a more alert, a more aware people, more jealous of their liberties than they were before. It greatly raised the level of political consciousness in the nation, and by transforming the people from spectators to participants it strengthened them as individuals. It was democracy as *participation* that he discovered in the United States. If Tocqueville would later emphasize the cultural tendencies that threatened to subordinate the individual to society and that led to excesses of all sorts, he found that democracy as participation could strengthen the individual. It was the way of life he found admirable. The whole of society was infused with a vigor and a force lent to it by independent, active individuals making decisions about all matters vital to themselves, free to act and thus to develop a broad range of competencies that in turn enhanced their freedom. For Tocqueville, democracy's gift to a people fortunate enough not to abuse it is competence. Democracy might be inefficient, but it opened up the possibility of individual self-fulfillment and of an enhanced moral identity for individuals (possible only through choice and action). The question was, would other tendencies of democratic culture—especially the intellectual laxness and the quest for present pleasure he thought it was likely to produce—undercut that gift of competence?

It was not just the dogma of popular sovereignty and its fulfillment in universal suffrage that was responsible for the vitality of politics in democratic America. The remarkable looseness of government, the decentralized political structure, along with the great freedom of association the people enjoyed and the astonishing frequency with which they took advantage of it, also encouraged that vitality. In January of 1832, while in New Orleans, he summed up this discovery with a rueful glance at the France to which he was about to return: "The greatest merit of the government of the United States is that it is *powerless* and *passive*. In the actual state of things, in order to prosper America has no need of skilful direction, profound designs or great efforts. But need of liberty and still more liberty. It is to nobody's *interest to abuse it*. What point of comparison is there between such a state of affairs and our own?"[27] Such was the potential moral effect of democracy that most impressed Tocqueville. He forcefully recorded this view in a notebook entry of September 20, 1831, after a conversation with Josiah Quincy Jr., the president of Harvard College:

> Note: One of the happiest consequences of the absence of government (when a people is happy enough to be able to do without it, a rare event) is the ripening of individual strength which never fails to follow from it. Each man learns to think and act for himself without counting on the support of any outside power which, however watchful it be, can never answer all the needs of man in society. The man thus used to seeking his well-being by his efforts alone stands the higher in his own esteem as well as in that of others: he grows both strong and greater of soul. . . . the influence of such a state of affairs on the moral and political character of a people would more than make up for all the inadequacies if there were any.[28]

His encounter with the New England character and the New England way profoundly impressed and influenced him. Powerful individuals like Quincy, John Quincy Adams, Jared Sparks, and above all the remarkable Rev. Joseph Tuckerman, the saintly yet practical Unitarian minister who had devoted himself to a street and prison ministry and who instructed Tocqueville and Beaumont on penal issues, embodied the New England tradition of intellect, conscience, and responsibility. They were models of the aristocratic liberal leadership he thought democracies would need if they were to thrive. Their flinty New England individuality could not have been to his taste, but he greatly admired their sense of civic responsibility and their profound knowledge of the people, the culture, and the history of New England. What he learned from them became essential and enduring elements of his political thought. There he found a political system that had, as it were, grown from the ground up, one in which the small community was prior to central government not only historically but politically as well. It was a politics that relied on strong, independent individuals and that went on producing them. But would democracy continue to develop such strong, inner-directed citizens?

This was to a degree an ideal view of New England politics, though the Quincys and the Adamses were still there. In *Democracy in America* Tocqueville notes the surviving tradition of deference to the community's aristocracy, that is, to the best families and the best men, very much like the continuing deference to notables in French local politics. Quincy was a Boston notable. Yet if in the early nineteenth century New England's seventeenth- and eighteenth-century institutions and culture were still significantly alive, the prerevolutionary, preindustrial past was fading fast and becoming legend. Tocqueville encountered New England through its sage mythmakers.

If he learned anything about the realities of rural and urban poverty, about growing class inequalities and divisions, and the new ethnic turmoil in the cities, he chose not to record it. His notes about his conversations with Tuckerman touch not on the social pathologies Tuckerman was working to heal but on institutional problems.[29] If he did encounter the realities of the new New England, he may have chosen to ignore them to preserve the ideal example that was to be an important element of his democratic theory. When he was told that there were perhaps two thousand prostitutes in Boston, he refused to believe it, even though they lived within a stone's throw of Boston's Brahmins.[30] His sojourn in New England seems to have convinced him even more that government in the United States was remote and feeble. He had witnessed "the spectacle of a society proceeding all alone, without guide or support, by the single fact of the concourse of individual wills. It is useless to torment the spirit seeking for government; it is nowhere to be perceived, and the truth is that it does not, so to speak, exist."[31] That bit of hyperbole was set down in Hartford, Connecticut, just as he was leaving New England, where he had become persuaded of the crucial importance a triad of institutions played in American life: the town, the jury, and the association. These first appear in the notebooks. It was through these, Tocqueville believed, more than through state and national political bodies, that the individual will was felt and political education delivered. It was a splendidly decentralized system, with many occasions and levels on which the individual might act, in fact was called upon to act. Local government was so important in America that Tocqueville was moved to say, in another characteristic hyperbole, that "the town is the ultimate individual in the American system."[32]

In *Democracy in America* the town will acquire an aura of sanctity as the seedbed of virtue. It becomes a school of liberty and individual rights as well as of social feeling and community solidarity.[33] His view of the town as the ultimate expression of individuality and as the most creative institution in American life makes Tocqueville an early celebrator of an idea that still carries much charm in today's American culture. Town and family, about which he will have much to say in *Democracy in America*, were the central, shaping institutions of democratic America.[34] In view of the immense importance he thought they had, it is remarkable how little he observed of either during his journey through the United States.

He was equally impressed by the jury as a critical political institution. He thought it was "the most powerful and direct application of the dogma of the sovereignty of the people . . . because the jury is nothing but the people made judge of what is allowed and what is forbidden to do in society."[35] The jury, like the town, will appear in *Democracy in America* not only as an instrument of popular power, but also as a school in which the people develop political awareness, a sense of responsibility, and that attachment to the law so crucial in a society composed of aggressively competitive individuals.

No less important than the town and the citizen-jury was the association, which he also discovered in New England. The New England diaspora and example had already begun to carry it throughout the country. This is certainly the best-known aspect of Tocqueville's critique of American democratic institutions. For him it was the most important source of strength in American political life, for it was where individuals, united in small, intentional communities, were freest to act to make their interests and their values felt. Associations were not part of the formal structure of political institutions, which would exist whatever the will of the people. They had to be willed into existence, and they depended on the voluntary participation of men and women with common interests. "The power of the association," he wrote while in Boston, "has reached its highest degree in America. Associations are made for purposes of trade, and for political, literary and religious interests. It is never by recourse to a higher authority that one seeks success, but by an appeal to individual powers working in concert."[36] Associations were admirable not simply because they pulled citizens out of self-absorption and isolation; it was through associations, including corporations, that Americans had been able to harness effectively their energies in a prodigious number of enterprises social and economic. "It is by this means," he wrote, "that a country where capital is scarce and where absolutely democratic laws and habits hinder the accumulation of wealth in the hands of a few individuals, has already succeeded in carrying out undertakings and accomplishing works which the most absolute kings and the most opulent aristocracies would certainly not have been able to undertake and finish in the same time."[37] Their most important virtue was that they served as barriers to the power of governments. They were modern substitutes for those now-vanished or greatly weakened institutions that had once stood between the state and the individual. They were instruments of power and at the same time guardians against its abuse. This understanding of the crucial importance of the association became even clearer to Tocqueville when, in *Democracy in America*, he took the long view of the development of democracy, which was increasing the power of the state and making individuals more vulnerable. This function of the association, that is, as a guardian of liberty, loomed largest in *Democracy in America*, in which he greatly expanded the initial remarks recorded in the notebooks. So did its importance as a school in which the social imagination was extended. At a time when traditional social structures were crumbling and when, except for town and church, individuals were isolated the freedom to form intentional communities was of enormous importance.

There was much else he found healthy and promising in American political democracy, well noted in his political anthropology. Though he was appalled by the finger-poking-the-chest, spit-in-your-beard style of democratic politics, there were good things about its informality. Public officials were not deified or truckled to: "They are absolutely on the same footing as the rest of the citizens."[38] The old black magic of deference that so cowed Europeans was missing from American politics. Citizens didn't simper before political figures; political figures less often acquired an unrealistic, inflated view of their power and importance. Yet however much Tocqueville appreciated this aspect of egalitarian politics, he reverted to the style and expectations of deferential politics when he returned to France. There, he behaved as if he expected his middle-class supporters in Normandy and even his middle-class colleagues in the Chamber of Deputies to defer to him—though he did not demand it. New England also pleased him because the politics of deference was still alive there. Old and honored families with social and political pedigrees were still expected to govern, and did.

Equality honored the office, but the man who occupied it was no better than anyone else. The idea pleased Tocqueville. The spirit of democracy was antipaternalistic, which led to a healthy suspicion and jealousy of power in all areas of American life. He saw that "paternal power, which was so prominent a feature of the republics of antiquity . . . is reduced almost to nothing in American institutions. American laws seem to look with as jealous and suspicious an eye on the power of a father as on all other powers that can interfere with human liberty. Customs, morals, and opinions are, in this, in harmony with the laws. Paternal power is an aristocratic institution. It makes old men into a privileged governing class. It gives them a sort of patronage by making their descendants depend on them, all things antipathetic to democracy."[39] He here sounds the spirit of Jefferson, the radical democrat, who went so far as to argue that the writ of one generation ought not to extend to the next.

On principle Tocqueville did not regret the demise of "paternal power," which had often throttled human liberty, even though instinctively and by social training he remained a paternalist and despite his belief that democracy was not likely to survive without aristocratic leadership. He rejected paternalism as a political principle. He would still shepherd the folk of Valognes to the polls and lecture them on their duties, but at the same time he insisted on walking in the ranks and not at the head of the voting procession.

He was highly critical of the politics of expediency that he thought democracy fostered, but there was a nondoctrinaire, pragmatic quality to American political life that he admired. The Americans might play fast and loose with principle or ignore it, but neither were they slaves to it. In his notebooks he comments that they were not inflexible laissez-faireists, as Europeans believed. The basic rule of American government might be to remain as passive as possible in all areas of national life: "It makes no claim to foresee everything and carry everything out; it gives no subsidies, does not encourage trade, and does not patronize literature and the arts. But where great works of public utility are concerned, it seldom leaves them to the care of private persons; it is the State itself that carries them out." What seemed important to Tocqueville about this was that "there is no rule about the matter. The activity of companies, of parishes and of private people is in a thousand ways in competition with that of the State. . . . So then no exclusive system is followed; in nothing does America exemplify a system of that uniformity that delights the superficial and metaphysical minds of our age."[40] The pragmatic rule of whatever works had its dark consequences, but its great advantage was that it tended to nourish diversity and variety, essential to a healthy and a free society. For Tocqueville and Mill, the defense and maintenance of diversity became a crucial aspect of the democratic theory they mutually worked out in the 1830s and 1840s. Tocqueville believed there had once been a politics of principle in America, and he thought democracy needed a stronger sense of form and limits; but he also thought that the Americans' refusal to be systematic or to insist on uniformity was an advantage. It protected individuality and diversity: "Everything adapts itself to the nature of men and places, without any pretension to bend them to the strictness of an inflexible rule. From this variety springs a universal prosperity spread throughout the whole nation and over each of its parts."[41]

Could the middle classes govern? Tocqueville had arrived with the aristocrat's conviction that the bourgeoisie was not fit to rule. He didn't fully surrender his contempt for the abilities and the moral qualities of the middle classes, as many notebook comments reveal, but he also recorded his grudging recognition that an enlightened bourgeoisie could govern successfully. "There is one thing which America demonstrates invincibly," he wrote at the end of November as he began his journey south aboard the steamboat *Louisville*, "and that is that the middle classes can govern a State. I do not know if they would come out with credit from thoroughly difficult political situations. But they are adequate for the ordinary run of society. In spite of their petty passions, their incomplete education and their vulgar manners, they clearly can provide practical intelligence and that is found to be enough."[42] Though they lacked the virtue of the aristocrat, which was the ability to rise above self-interest, the enlightened self-interest the middle classes brought to the challenge of governance would be adequate. Can he have thought that the Revolution had not been a "thoroughly difficult political situation" or that the Constitutional Convention had been an assembly of aristocrats?

Running through the notebooks is a fascinating discussion of the nature of virtue. In a way, it is the heart of Tocqueville's study of democratic politics in the United States, for he therein deals with the prospects for the disinterested, honest leadership he believed democracies would in the future require. He came to see that America demonstrated that "virtue is not, as had long been claimed, the only thing that maintained republics." An enlightened though not necessarily virtuous people could do the same if they had understanding of public affairs, knowledge of the laws and of precedents, feeling for the well-understood interests of the nation, and the faculty to understand them.[43]

This experienced, practical, shrewd, hard-driving people seemed to be making the American Republic thrive on the basis of enlightened self-interest, not because they were virtuous in the classical sense of the term. Having failed to find the classical Republic, Tocqueville had discovered the liberal Republic.

Virtuous the Americans were not, except for a virtuous individual here and there, like Washington, John Adams, Jefferson — perhaps the whole founding generation. At the end of his stay in Washington Tocqueville set down his definitive judgment of the American character:

> When one considers the chastity of their morals, the simplicity of their manners, their habits of work and the religious and settled spirit which prevails in the United States, one is tempted to believe that the Americans are a virtuous people; but when one considers the commercial fervour which seems to devour the whole society, the thirst for gain, the respect for money and the bad faith which appears on every side, one is soon led to think that this pretended virtue is only the absence of certain vices, and if the number of human passions seems restricted here, it is because they have all been absorbed in just one: the love of wealth.[44]

He wrote this immediately after having commented on what he called "one of the greatest stains on the American character," the bad faith of their commercial practices demonstrated by the "great number of insolvencies and bankruptcies which take place every year in the different States of the Union." In other words, the Americans lacked honor. He would return to this judgment in the late 1830s and again in the 1850s when his confidence in the United States was shaken not only by the growing violence of the struggle over slavery but also by the economic collapses of 1837 and then 1857, brought about, he thought, by American carelessness with credit, deceptive business practices, the unrestrained ambitiousness of a people lusting for wealth, and a breakneck ethos. Credit was as much about honor as it was about paying one's debts. Curiously, in *DA II* he argued that while democratic people, exemplified by the Americans, might no longer follow traditional codes of honor, they nevertheless had a sense of honor, as demonstrated by how scrupulous they were in their commercial dealings—an instance of how deductive reason can sometimes ignore the facts or how the logic of theory can overwhelm experience.[45] Despite the long chapter on honor in the *Democracy*, Tocqueville's encounter with the excesses of American entrepreneurial practices, which threatened to ruin him, drove him at times to despair about the future of the dishonorable Republic in which he had invested a considerable part of his wealth.

If enlightened self-interest could reasonably well substitute for virtue in maintaining an orderly, peaceful society, it was immensely assisted in this by the federal Constitution, which Tocqueville thought wholly admirable. It was, he thought, a great work of political ingenuity and vision. He carried a copy of the *Federalist Papers* all through his journey and studied them when prompted by questions or observations. Back in Paris he read them with renewed intensity as he prepared to write *Democracy in America*. In addition to what he learned from the *Federalist Papers* about how to construct a government that would both control power and enable it—lessons he tried to apply when, in 1848, he was a member of the Provisional Assembly's committee to draft a constitution for the Second Republic—he also quickly realized that only a very politically experienced people could have invented so remarkable a piece of political machinery and made it work. The success of the Americans was the fruit of long experience in practical politics: "The Constitution of the United States is an admirable work, nevertheless one may believe that its founders would not have succeeded had not the previous 150 years given the different States of the Union the *taste for and practise of, provincial governments*, and if a high civilization had not at the same time put them in *a position to maintain a strong, though limited, central government*."[46] At this point, he knew little about the history of constitutional thought or of the experience of constitution writing in England and England's North American colonies, But he was correct to note that the genius of the Constitution was the fruit of long experience in the exercise and control of power in "provincial governments." The founders were enlightened in two ways: they were the products of "a high civilization," that is, of the Enlightenment, and also of centuries of experiment in self-governance.

Toward the end of his journey, when his mind had already set sail for France even though he was still in Washington, he summed up much that he had learned in the still-new Republic and also confronted what he was returning to in a remarkable and passionate notebook entry praising the strengths of the American Republic while indicting the French for having failed to create a true republic or even to understand what one was. His rage about the betrayal of the French Revolution poured out as his blows fell on Royalists and Republicans alike. It was a jeremiad, a masterpiece of rhetoric, which he began strangely by referring to himself in the third person, as if he was as much the subject as the sad history of republicanism in France:

> He knew very exactly what he could hope and fear from liberty. That in France for [?200] [editor's comment: "the figure is uncertain"] years we have had anarchy and despotism in all its forms, but never anything that looked like a republic. If Royalists could see the internal functioning of a well-ordered Republic, the deep respect professed there for acquired rights, the power of those rights over the crowds, the religion of law, the real, effective liberty enjoyed there, the true reign of the majority, the natural ease with which everything progresses, they would see that they were including under a single name diverse states that have nothing analogous between them. Our republicans on their side would feel that what we have called the Republic has never been anything but a monstrosity that one does not know how to classify, a [missing word] covered in Blood and filth, dressed in rags to the noise of the quarrels of antiquity; and what does it matter to me whether tyranny is clothed in a royal mantle or in a Tribune's toga? If I feel its heavy hand on me? When Danton had wretched men whose only crime was not to think as he did, slaughtered in the prisons, was that liberty? When later Robespierre sent Danton to the scaffold because he had shown himself his rival, there was justice in that no doubt, but was that liberty? When the majority of the Convention proscribed the minority, when the arbitrary power of proconsuls took from citizens their goods, their children and their life, when an opinion was a crime, and a wish expressed in the sanctuary of the domestic hearth merited death, was that liberty? But, some one might say, I am looking into the blood-stained annals of the Terror. Let us pass over the time of *necessary* severities, shall I see liberty reign in the time when the Directory destroyed the newspapers, and sent the members of the majority that was going to overturn it, to die in the wilds of Guiana? When Bonaparte as Consul substituted the power, the tyranny of one man for the tyranny of

factions? Again, was that liberty, was that a Republic? No, in France we have seen anarchy and despotism in all its forms, but nothing that looked like a Republic.[47]

For all his misgivings and doubts about American democracy and about democracy itself, he had encountered in the United States something that resembled a republic.

Would the American Republic survive? Tocqueville brooded over this question in his notebooks and then in *Democracy in America*. He was never quite sure. The longer he wrestled with the question, the less certain he became. The guarded optimism—or barely suppressed anxiety—he felt while in the United States had very nearly become despair by the time he had finished his big book eight years later, as his thinking about the culture of democracy and its political consequences deepened. The scattered aspects of what finally became a coherent theory of democratic culture and politics were carried back to France in his notebooks. His loss of confidence in the prospects for democracy was further deepened by his witness of the troubled political life of France during the July Monarchy as well as by his growing dismay over the violence and disorder of American politics and economic life in the late 1830s and during the 1850s.

"What maintains a Republic in the United States?" he asked in Washington as he prepared to leave. Of the "thousand reasons" that maintained republican liberty in the United States, he cited just a few. The prevailing equality of condition and the consequent absence of social bitterness and divisiveness was one. The abundant, inexhaustible environment, which provided an "immense field to human activity" as well as many alternative ways of satisfying ambition, was another. The structure of the Republic was a third: "The division of the Union into little States reconciles internal prosperity and national strength; it multiplies political interests and weakens party spirit by breaking it up."[48]

Far more important than these conditions was the general enlightenment of the American people and the fact that their practical political education was more advanced than any other people's. "It is this truth," he said, "in which I firmly believe, that inspires in me the only hope I have for the future happiness of Europe."[49] At this point in his thinking, it was the enlightenment of the many, their broad experience and practical abilities, and above all their highly developed political consciousness—all this and not an able elite—that would safeguard the Republic. The future of the Republic and of political democracy depended on the culture of the people. However, it would not be long before he, along with Mill, had turned to the central maxim of their "aristocratic liberalism": that the health of democratic societies would depend on the wise guidance of a disinterested elite, not on the good judgment of the people, which was likely to remain a dream. When he later thought through the dynamics of democratic culture and its political implications, the focus of *DA II*, his hope that the general enlightenment of the people would preserve democracy flickered and faded.

As he sat in New York in February 1832 awaiting the delayed sailing of the pacquet that would take him and Beaumont back to France, he added to his speculations about the future of the American Republic the cultural and social insights he had gathered from his experience of the western states and territories. These already prompted a darker vision of the perils of growth and of potential cultural collapse. He had seen democracy at its "extreme limits." He saw danger to the Union in its extremely rapid growth not only because "speedy change and shifts in wealth and power cannot take place without bruising interests or without arousing violent passions," but mainly because such growth might too greatly weaken those cultural conditions necessary to the healthy functioning of a democracy. The influence of the older, more stable, more settled population in the older states could restrain a culture of extreme limits, the implication being that should the whole culture find itself perpetually pushing to the limits and then beyond, as Emerson urged it to do, the disorder of the "half-savage, uncultivated" West might become the future. The whole society would find itself back in the wilderness, the kind of wilderness which the Puritans had found on their errand, now become as much cultural as it had been religious:

> Now, not only do the new States of the Union, by the simple fact of their existence, increase the difficulty of maintaining the federal bond, but they also provide much slighter guarantees of wisdom and moderation than do the older States. The new States are generally made up of adventurers. The progress of society is so rapid, one might say so impetuous, that everything there is in disorder. Nothing there in morals, ideas or laws betrays an appearance of order or stability. In a word, they have the half-savage uncultivated minds which are characteristic of the first inhabitants of wildernesses, combined with the power which generally belongs to older societies.[50]

The threat to the Republic and to liberty came not from the bitter social and nationalist strife that Europe knew too well, but from a disordered and unstable culture. Democracies, or republics, did not depend for their survival on virtue, as Montesquieu had thought, but on the culture of the people. General enlightenment as well as order and stability in morals, ideas, and laws was essential.

He took a last hesitant look into the troubling unknown. Would America's material abundance be enough to maintain a stable democracy and a republic without those cultural strengths he believed essential for maintaining and even understanding the conditions that made freedom possible? A comparative look at South America, which enjoyed extraordinary abundance, suggested not.[51] Were the fundamental requirements for a free democracy as much cultural as they were material? He found this a "great insoluble question." But by 1840 he had a grim answer to that question.

7

A Dark Vision of Democracy's Prospects

Democracy in America lay embedded in Tocqueville's notebooks. Though in some ways his book offers a milder view of America than appears in the notebooks — he omits or softens some of his harsher judgments — by the time he turns to the second volume his thoughts about the future of democratic culture and politics, wherever it develops, become darker. He foresees a culture out of control, without a sense of limits, guided by the expedient, disturbingly unrealistic, without a strong concern for the future or a deep sense of the past, a culture that did not foster true virtue, which he said America lacked. These characteristics of democratic — or modern — culture greatly endangered liberty, which was his main concern. He shared this vision of cultural derangement with many in his generation, the romantic generation, though ironically he thought romanticism itself was decadent. He was equally concerned about the apparently inevitable growth of state power, also a menace to liberty. This and the following chapters attempt to account for how his observations of American society and his finally evolved theory of democratic culture led him to his pessimistic view of the future of democracy.

The question is, how did Tocqueville get from the observations, reflections, and judgments recorded in his notebooks, which can be regarded as a sketch of his first thoughts about American democracy, to *Democracy in America* itself and to the darkening skies with which it ends? Three years intervened between his return to France and the publication of *DA I*, another four before he completed *DA II*. During the book's long gestation, further reading and study, debate with friends and colleagues, his crucial correspondence with Mill and Royer-Collard, and further dismaying experience of the culture and politics of bourgeois democratic France all went into the shaping of *Democracy in America*. Yet the main lines of his thinking, culminating in his increasingly bleak view of the prospects for democracy, are present in the notebooks. The end lay embedded in the beginnings. Tocqueville concludes *Democracy in*

America with a cautionary fantasy shaped out of his worst forebodings about democracy. Though he presents it as a possibility rather than as a prophecy, it is difficult to escape the conclusion that it represents his ultimate persuasion about the moral destiny of democracy.

How does one account for this descent into pessimism about the democratic future? His thinking had taken such a somber turn partly as a result of his troubled observations about the growth of state power in Europe and about politics and culture in the new age of middle-class power, partly also as a result of insights he derived from his theoretical exploration of the probable lines of development of any future democratic culture. They were derived as well from the insights gained from his remarkable venture into the bizarre inner world of the democratic psyche, insights based on earlier observations of American culture recorded in his notebooks but not at all developed in *DA I*. The unhappy prospect he finally saw was that the undisciplined passions of democracy and especially the unintentional cultural revolution created by the advance of equality would not strengthen but rather undermine freedom, which was his chief value. Tocqueville thought that democracy had many strengths but in the end might prove itself to be self-destructive. He had failed to think through the consequences of much that he had noted during his travels in democratic America. What he had quietly suppressed came back to haunt him. The balance between strengths and flaws became increasingly precarious.

What had returned to haunt him was a vision, slowly but inexorably developed in *DA II*, of a new despotism, more suffocating, more far-reaching, and more powerful than any history had previously known, in which men are caught in a kind of "orderly, gentle, peaceful slavery" while apparently enjoying perfect equality and an illusory freedom. It is a vision of human life reduced to inertia, coolly luminous perhaps, but unspeakably trivial. In his fantasy Tocqueville dwells less on the power of the tutelary state than on the passiveness of life under it. "I see," he writes, "an innumerable multitude of men, alike and equal, constantly circling around in pursuit of the petty and banal pleasures with which they glut their souls. Each one of them, withdrawn into himself, is almost unaware of the fate of the rest. . . . they are near enough but he does not notice them. He touches them but feels nothing."[1] This is a nightmare vision of a futile, anaesthetic, and, finally, meaningless future. The "immense protective power" that smothers everything in its benevolent embrace is also described in subhuman images. Like some killing growth it "covers the whole of social life with a network of petty, complicated rules that are both minute and uniform." It "does not break men's will, but softens, bends and guides it . . . does not destroy anything, but prevents much being born . . . is not at all tyrannical, but it hinders, restrains, enervates, stifles and stultifies so much that in the end each nation is not more than a flock of timid and hard-working animals with the government as its shepherd."² It is a world without belief or conviction, inhabited by mild, will-less ruminants. Worst of all, it is a world without freedom.

This was hardly the reality he had encountered in the uninhibited scramble of life in Jacksonian America, where the danger seemed to lie rather in the excesses of an unrestrained people hell-bent on exploiting their freedom and where there was nothing that remotely resembled a tutelary state. Tocqueville had also noted tendencies in democracy that would have served as the basis for a brighter prospect than the vision of benevolent despotism with which *Democracy in America* ends. He had occasionally caught sight of the possibility of a democratic future of unparalleled political and cultural activity, new forms of community, a broader idea of humanity, and warmer, more natural human relationships. Though he foresaw the growth of an extensive cultural meretriciousness, he also believed that in the culture of democracy the expression of feeling would be more truthful and direct. He had written, with appreciation, of a future in which the disappearance of constraining conventions, forms, traditions, and elites would lead to an awesome release of intellectual and material energies, to a dynamic, innovative culture that could create a society of aggressively active and uninhibited individuals, all bounding with hope and fantastic visions of unlimited progress. Democracy might produce a society of believers with great faith in themselves. There are moments in *Democracy in America* in which Tocqueville seems to suggest that the massed energies of a strivingly ambitious egalitarian people might lead to great accomplishments, though these generally would be collective, not individual.³

Yet he ends his inquiry into the prospects for democracy with a vision of a constantly unstable, endlessly innovative culture without a sense of form or limits, in other words, a culture of extremes, along with his apprehensions about a twilight future in which the anomic undertow of democratic life would lead to further cultural disorder and to the loss of a sense of community. The force of his own theoretical analysis of democracy and his experience of democratic culture led him to this dark view of the democratic future, but he was also borne along by the central impulses of the romantic movement. The specters of decline, decadence, and enervation, of death in conformity, of egalitarian tyranny, of a violent future or of an utterly boring future, all of which haunted the romantic era, were especially nourished by fears of the cultural and social derangements thought likely to follow from the loss of faith, that is, from the rationalist destruction of Christianity. As faith declined, freedom's perils would grow, claimed the great romantic guru Chateaubriand, who saw human individuality and creativity blighted in a skeptical future; Tocqueville shared these apprehensions, arguing frequently that the only way to ensure freedom, creativity, and justice in the democratic future was to find a new basis for religion or for the sense of moral order he believed had formerly been nourished by Christianity, in the desacralized modern world.

Along with Tocqueville's foreboding about the threat to freedom posed by the cultural derangements of democracy, another historical development endangered liberty. By the time he had turned to the conclusion of *Democracy in America* (part 4 of volume 2), Tocqueville was so convinced that centralization of power was the master trend of history that he began to describe the process with the same awed sense of witnessing the work of Providence he had expressed years before in his account of the advance of democracy. The skeptic, he had written, needed only to reflect "about what was happening daily in his life": and the historian would see that in the last half century centralization has increased everywhere in a thousand different ways: "Wars, revolutions and conquests have aided its advance; all men have labored to increase it. In the same period, while men have succeeded one another at a tremendous rate at the head of affairs and while their ideas, interests and passions have shown infinite variety, yet all have desired centralization in one way or another. The instinct for centralization has proved the one permanent feature amid the usual mutability of their lives and their thoughts."[4] This sounds very much like those opening passages of *Democracy in America* in which Tocqueville describes, with what he calls "religious dread," the inexorable progress of democracy, which seemed fated to enlarge its domain no matter what humankind did: "Everywhere the diverse happenings in the lives of peoples have turned to democracy's profit; all men's efforts have aided it, both those who intended this and those who had no such intention. . . . All have been driven pell-mell along the same road, and all have worked together, some against their will and some unconsciously, blind instruments in the hands of God. . . . The gradual progress of equality is something fated. . . . Every man and every event helps it along."[5] Now what seemed fated was not so much democracy but the centralization of power. In the five years that elapsed between the writing of the introduction to *Democracy in America* and its concluding chapter, Tocqueville had discovered an even deeper current in the providential tendency of human affairs.

There would be no exceptions. Even the Americans, whom he had been astonished to find living virtually without a central government and who had never experienced the kind of bitter, prolonged social struggle that inevitably led to the centralization of power, would suffer the same fate. Their traditions of individual rights and local freedom would only slow, not avert, the process;

nor would their religious faith save them, for it too would be weakened by the secular temper of the democratic mind and its passionate pursuit of wealth and well-being. The deepest "general and permanent tendencies" of democracy would lead even that singularly blessed people toward the centralization of power. The apparent uniqueness of America would finally prove to be only a different route to a common destiny—the ever-increasing power of the state— for the moment more clearly seen in the Old World than in the New.

The process of centralization was more visible and advanced in Europe, especially France, "where," he wrote, "the Revolution of which I speak has gone further than in any other country."[6] America may have given him his first glimpse into the future of democracy; France reinforced it. The most powerful currents of democracy everywhere were those that led to the growth of central- ized power: of the sovereign, the state, the social power, as Tocqueville variously called it. Freedom was not the natural destiny of a democratic people. Much might be done to limit the reach of the social power, but to do this would require conscious, steady effort and indeed a new science of politics, certainly a much profounder understanding of the conditions both of social order and of freedom than humans had yet fashioned. "In the dawning centuries of democ- racy," he wrote, "individual independence and local liberties will always be the products of art. Centralized government will be the natural thing."[7] Certain conditions or causes might retard or hasten the centralization of power, but these were adventitious—peculiar or accidental factors, as Tocqueville described them—not the supreme tendencies of democracy. Henceforth free- dom would be an artifact involving the contrived and painstaking re-creation of conditions that were not the natural expression of the egalitarian spirit.

In his account of the advance of centralization, Tocqueville stresses eco- nomic factors far more heavily than he had earlier in *Democracy in America*, reflecting, as Seymour Drescher has suggested, his growing anxiety about con- temporary manifestations of French economic statism.[8] The entire process of political and social centralization was based, he saw, on an irresistible and irre- versible economic revolution, every consequence of which augmented state power. His account of the political consequences of the transformation of prop- erty from land to fluid capital, of the ways in which the growth of industrialism had provided government with opportunities to intervene in economic life— and of how the "new and complex relations" among men created by capitalism had also vastly multiplied the regulatory functions of government—would serve as a suggestive primer for a technological interpretation of the origins of the modern state. American economic life had not yet reached the stage of devel- opment where Tocqueville's analysis of French economic statism would apply.

He saw it as an economy of petty entrepreneurs and speculators whose fortunes rose and fell as they struggled in constant competition, so that they were not likely to accumulate great wealth and power. Industrial capitalism—just taking off when he visited the United States—was to develop spectacularly after the Civil War, leading to the growth of concentrated economic power, matched then by the growth of state power. Tocqueville only glimpsed this reshaping of the American economy. In his view, the greatest danger to the America Republic came from the omnipotence of the majority, not great wealth or concentrated economic power.

But the heavy attention Tocqueville gives to economic factors, so unusual an approach for him that it is startling, constitutes a partial deflection from his primary intention, to examine the political implications of his prior analysis of democratic culture. Though he incompletely fulfills that intention in his concluding chapter, the whole weight of his prior inquiry bore heavily on his final judgments about the prospects for freedom in the democratic future.

8

The Democratic Psyche and the Hazards of Equality

Tocqueville's brilliant analysis of the psychology of democratic man depicts a society of alienated, unstable, self-absorbed, anxious individuals caught in impossible-to-fulfill quests, not the rational citizens democratic societies will require if they are to flourish. In *Democracy in America* he does note possible new forms of community: intentional communities (for example, associations and towns) and communities of opinion (for example, newspapers); but he does not finally see these as overcoming the isolation of the individual. In *Democracy in America* he elaborates his picture of a society of lonely individuals withdrawing into smaller and smaller circles, ultimately into families and then each into his own heart. The ultimate consequence would be a weakening and a narrowing of the social imagination.

Tocqueville's exploration of the turbulent and paradoxical passional life of "democratic man" is a considerable work of the imagination and one of the achievements of *Democracy in America*. It provided him with some of his most important insights into the psychopolitics of the new world of equality. As the psychologist of democratic life, anatomizing the astonishing configurations of the tumultuous democratic psyche, intensely scrutinizing each "queer twist" of the "human heart," his work displays the imaginative richness of Balzac's La *Comédie Humaine*—imaginative in that Tocqueville's psychology, or social psychology, was the least systematic and the least theoretical aspect of his work on democracy. It depended more on the play of his sensibility, well trained to interpret almost reflexively the complex semiotics of social gesture and behavior and to detect the faintest nuance of motive, than on the kind of semisystematic reflection that went into his effort to derive the lines of development of any future democratic culture. The roots of his growing gloom about democracy may be traced in what he saw as the major pathologies of the democratic psyche and especially in what he thought their political bearing was likely to be. His portrait of democratic man is not flattering.

Tocqueville had in fact visited the Purgatory in which he finally leaves the readers of *Democracy in America*. Below the busy surface of democratic life, with all its swelling affirmations and energy, he had penetrated a restless psychic underworld of fear and anxiety. If incessant change was the chief feature of the democratic social condition, uncertainty was the ruling principle of the democratic psyche. Tocqueville's growing sense that the loss of social order would be followed by psychological disorder (he noted that madness was reputedly the chief affliction of the Americans) and ultimately by moral and spiritual disorder drove him to the dark finale of *Democracy in America*. It would be the pervasive psychological as well as cultural derangements of democracy that would in the end create the tutelary state.

Of the psychosocial disorders that seemed endemic to democracy, three stood out. The first was an increasing psychic isolation of the individual, resulting in an impoverishment of the social imagination and a pervasive social indifference: "They are near enough but he does not notice them. He touches them but they feel nothing." The second was a phobia about anarchy and disorder resulting in a compulsive grasping for order. The third was an increasing intolerance of difference, manifest in fear and envy of others and in repressiveness toward the deviant, a consequence of the anxiety and uncertainty about identity experienced in the fluid, egalitarian society. All of these, he thought, would add up to a politics of assent to state power.

Though Tocqueville saw numerous countertendencies to the fragmenting forces of equality, it was democracy's potential for weakening the social bond that seemed greatest to him. He thought that the disaggregative tendencies of democracy, its antipathy for fixed social boundaries, in fact for any fixed social order, would increasingly isolate individuals socially and psychologically. As their attachments one after another were broken, individuals would begin even "to think of themselves in isolation."[1] Preoccupied with comfort and security, focused tightly on their private affairs, they would increasingly be shut within the narrow confines of their immediate interests. To escape the dreadful anonymity of mass society, they would withdraw into "a multitude of small private circles," little intentional communities the fundamental purpose of which was to establish some kind of distinctiveness by excluding others.[2] This they would do by active choice. What would seem most real to such people would be their immediately experienced private worlds. Their self-centered emotional commitments would leave little room for more than fleeting concern for public affairs. The radical shift of psychic energy from public or communal to private affairs and the atrophying of social consciousness caused by the egalitarian transformation of society would produce a massive social and even political indifference. Even those most powerful engines of community, intentional associations, were expressions of individual, private interests. They were devoted to special interests, not to the general good.

Even in the United States, where in many respects public life continued to engage a great many enlightened individuals, especially at the local level, and where a legion of well-organized middle-class reformers and transcendentalist visionaries energetically sought to create a purer, more humane, and more orderly society, the same tendencies were gathering force, weakening social bonds. The temptations, hopes, and fears of an unsettled world thrust everyone into perpetual motion.

Frantically active in personal affairs, haunted by anxieties about loss and at the same time preoccupied by great expectations of success, withdrawn from competitive or different others, "democratic man" was in danger of losing sight of himself as a social being with social obligations. The "breathless cupidity" Tocqueville saw as one of the psychic disfigurations bound to be produced by equality would prove to be an alienating mechanism. Though the general apathy that he called the "fruit of individualism" could easily lead to anarchy, he thought it more likely that it would enhance the power of society. "It is always an effort," he wrote, "for such men to tear themselves away from their private affairs and pay attention to those of the community. The natural inclination is to leave the only visible and permanent representative of collective interests, that is to say, the State, to look after them. . . . In times of democracy private life is so active and agitated, so full of desires and labor, that each individual has scarcely any leisure or energy for political life."[3] The sundry torments and resentments unloosed by democracy would have much the same effect. Tocqueville's psychological profile of "democratic man" is a portrait of a mistrustful, jealous, anxious being, dangerously uncertain of his identity. Envy was the driving force of equality, a restless, agitating demon responsible for the chronic invidiousness, the anxious, vigilant attention to the differentiating symbols of status so characteristic of middle-class life. Paradoxically, envy grew more intense with the advance of equality. "Men's hatred of privilege increases as privileges become rarer and less important," Tocqueville wrote. "The flame of democratic passion apparently blazes the brighter the less there is to feed it. . . . when conditions are unequal, no inequality, however great, offends the eye. But amid general uniformity, the slightest singularity seems shocking, and the more complete the uniformity, the more unbearable it seems."[4]

Envy was at least a moderately complicated passion. It could lead either to the slaying of the exceptional and the privileged or to their emulation or indeed to both, the democratic feat superbly performed by the essential democrat

Emerson in *Representative Men*. There was also another psychological mechanism responsible for the repressiveness and the manifold intolerances of democratic life, such as pressures to conform and refusal to accept or even to acknowledge differences, whether manifest in social behavior or in ideas.[5] This was democratic man's increasingly desperate defense of his fragile, arbitrary identity in an uncertain world of perpetual motion and change from which the old rituals and attachments that had once provided a reasonably secure sense of identity were gone. Differences thus become intolerable not only because they are threatening to identity. What Tocqueville had located in the stressful inner world of democracy was a source of that powerful anxiety about deviancy that is one of the familiar psychological effects of intense social change.

The intolerance of the different produced by both envy and the uncertainties of democratic selfhood would accelerate the growth of what Tocqueville at times called the social power. As democratic intolerance of diversity increased, curiously intensified, so too would the social power, called on to enforce the uniformity craved by the democratic psyche. Since the demand for full equality would never be fully satisfied ("men will never establish an equality that will content them") and since democratic culture in other ways would be a hothouse of deviancy, the powers of the state would be constantly augmented as it was called in repeatedly to respond to the insatiable demand of the egalitarian temper for uniformity.[6]

An exaggerated fear of anarchy was the third potentially destructive compulsion of the democratic psyche. Tocqueville identifies democratic apprehensions about disorder largely with middle-class property anxieties, but he suggests that the thirst for order of people wandering in the shifting, featureless desert of postmedieval life stemmed from profound problems of selfhood and identity. He suggests even that property becomes a symbol that, for the socially and psychologically alienated individual, stands for psychic security; money is a major identity marker for democratic man. As Tocqueville describes the process, property is increasingly identified with the individual and loses its social, even its physical, character. It becomes a symbol of self.[7]

As he wrote *DA II*, Tocqueville no longer sought to attribute the moral chasteness, respect for law, and remarkable orderliness of the Americans to the continuing force of the Puritan tradition, which in the first volume he had argued was "the key to the whole work."[8] And while he continued to attribute it to the influence of religion and women, as he had in his notebooks, he increasingly sought to account for all patterns of behavior sociologically and psychologically. Ideas have vanished. In doing so, Tocqueville grasped what has for a long while now been recognized as a distinctive cluster of contradictions at the center of American, or, for Tocqueville, democratic culture: an affinity for change and a fear of change; a perpetual thirst for the new, expressed some-times simply as a passion for action or in a restless innovativeness, coexisting with repugnance toward any fundamental challenge to the existing order.[9] What he had indeed seen was that ambivalence about norms that shows up in American culture in, for example, certain chronic confusions about the law: does freedom lie beyond it—a persisting cultural dream—or in obedience to it?; or in the uncomfortable tension that finds simultaneous expression in both antinomian fantasies and nightmares about anarchy. The distressing psycho-logical uncertainties and losses of democratic life would bring people close to the insupportable prospect of chaos, from which they would recoil. The wilder-ness the Puritans dreaded would reappear in the disorder of the democratic psyche.

Involuntary disturbers of the status quo, democratic people would anxiously resist any efforts to alter it deliberately—in fact, they would cling to it stub-bornly. Afraid of all threats to property, now invested with immense psychic meaning, impatient with anything that might disturb their private concerns, and anxious to avoid the unsettling shocks to identity caused by encounters with radically different others, they would desire nothing more than public order and tranquility. If their self-aggrandizing lusts and pragmatic innovative turn of mind drove them, in their endless pursuit of "complete felicity," to adventurous, risky behavior, such boldness would find only economic, not political, expression. Quite the contrary, the antipathy of a society of ambitious petty entrepreneurs for social turmoil and instability would find fruition in a politics of law and order, thereby further enhancing the powers of the state and speeding the centralization of power. "They love change," Tocqueville wrote, "but they are afraid of Revolutions." For such people, "love of public peace is often the only political passion they retain, and it alone becomes more active and powerful as all the others fade and die."[10]

This longing for order, rooted in the psychological disorientations of demo-cratic life, struck Tocqueville as a greater menace than the potential dangers of anarchy or revolution, for it was the dominant political emotion at loose in societies in which power was already rapidly being centralized. "I freely agree that public tranquility is a very good thing," he wrote. "Nevertheless, I do not want to forget that it is through good order that all peoples have reached tyranny."[11]

Tocqueville did not see the psychological tensions and torments of "demo-cratic man" leading directly to the madhouse, at least not immediately. His analysis of the egalitarian temper is complex: the inner terrors and anxieties of democracy in part fascinated him precisely because they were so much at variance with the cheerful bombast, the noisy exuberance, the amazing busyness, the strong sense of promise of American life. He had fully noted both faces of the democratic psyche in his notebooks. Democracy would be psychologically liberating and stimulating, too. The disappearance of a fixed social order would lead to a sense that there were no longer fixed limits to human effort or aspiration and thus to a psychic buoyancy that would be a source of great vitality. It would release power. But increasingly it was the strains of the endlessly deracinated life that drew Tocqueville's attention. He saw that while democracy would release people's dreams, the uncertainty and perpetual striving that accompanied the fading of traditional limits and social bonds would exact a high psychic price. He saw the Americans laboring under an immense psychological burden. It was with some irony that in his notebooks he called them the happiest people on earth—and he does so at greater length in the *Democracy*.[12] If they were no longer consigned to a fixed place in society and were remarkably free to shape their own destinies and dream incessantly of success and glory, they were also haunted by nightmares of loss and failure and by identity anxieties that would be expressed in various forms of social and intellectual intolerance. They were, he thought, a strikingly serious people suffering from a strange, unsettling malaise.[13]

Throughout *Democracy in America* Tocqueville masterfully analyzes the fears and anxieties, the unrequitable restlessness, the grim drivenness—the whole range of psychological drives and disturbances—of democratic life. These add up for him, when combined with the growing power of mass opinion and the enhanced power of the state, to a politics of order, resentment, and indifference, to slow, petty, bitterly contested change (he had commented on the pettiness of American politics in his notebooks) but not to anything like the permanent revolution fancied by Jefferson.

9

A Culture of Extremes: The Prospects for Freedom in a Culture Without Limits

Tocqueville's thinking about what were in his view the crucial questions—what kind of culture would democratic societies in the future create? and how would that culture affect the political life and the freedom of democratic peoples?—was guided by his observations of the cultural life of the Americans; by his experience of the increasingly materialistic and timid culture of bourgeois France; and by his theoretical working out of the relationship of the social structure of a people to their culture and their politics. With regard to America, the Puritans, so important in *DA I* in shaping the culture of democratic America, have vanished, replaced by the laws of social development and by a vague Providence. Crucial for Tocqueville was the disappearance of a fixed elite, that is, an aristocracy. He saw the development of a money-oriented culture that lacked a sense of limits and form, was endlessly expedient, living for the moment, having a feeble sense of the past and also the future, craving change yet craving comfort and security. It would be a culture that despite its many strengths would weaken independent critical intelligence and threaten liberty. A new aristocracy was needed, a democratic elite that would set standards for society and would provide moral guidance.

Tocqueville's ideas about the future of democracy are derived even more from his theoretical exploration of the probable lines of development of any future democratic culture than from his complex analysis of the democratic psyche. The former was in fact to a degree based on his analysis of what was likely to be permanent and what transient in the democratic "social state," the base to the cultural superstructure. His observations—his painful experience—of the degradation of French culture also shaped his thinking about the future culture of democracy. In all this, he uncovered even more fully the hitherto secret or hidden forces of democratic development.

Tocqueville understood that the political prospects for egalitarian peoples, above all, the prospects for liberty in the democratic future, ultimately depended on the cultural and moral consequences of the rush to equality that he saw as the dominant feature of modern life. On a number of occasions in *DA I* he had briefly raised questions about the culture of democracy that are fundamental to any full inquiry into the stability of democratic societies and democratic politics. No account of American democracy and its possible futures would be satisfactory, he had suggested, unless "the whole moral and intellectual state" of the Americans was examined.[1] Such had been his mentor Guizot's prescription for a full, deep study of a people's political institutions and the development of liberty. He turned to this task in the second volume, but there, as he seems finally to have realized when he neared the end of his four-year struggle to complete his work, his inquiry had broadened into an effort to fashion a general sociology of democratic culture. It was during the interval between the first and second volumes of the *Democracy* that his exchange of ideas and forebodings with Mill both confirmed his thoughts and helped develop them. But it was by means of his general sociology that he sought to discover the central features of any democratic culture, thereby fulfilling his original intention of seeing "in America more than America," of seeing, that is, the "shape of democracy itself."

His exploration of the idea of a democratic culture is structured by four sets of questions: the first has to do with the character of the social base, or social state; the second with the major characteristics of the frame of mind produced by that social state; the third with cultural forms and styles whether material (for example, craft work), symbolic (for example, literary, scientific, or artistic), or social (styles of personal relationships and social behavior); and, fourth, with the dialectical relationship between culture and politics or, more broadly, with the interplay between consciousness and values and the social state. Despite his occasional demurrals that the relationships he so methodically draws can be stated with any precision or indeed that equality "is the sole cause of everything that is happening now," one of the notable aspects of *DA II* is the way in which Tocqueville invariably seeks to demonstrate how the social condition of a people shapes every facet of their culture, from their manners to their language, from the themes of their imagination to the formal qualities of their art and literature.

At every step of the way, democratic America provides the basic evidence — the *données* — for his speculations. Though he warns of the error of confusing "what is democratic with what is only American," it is with few exceptions America, where one encountered democracy "without limits," that was his model for what the democratic social state and democratic culture would in the future be like. For all his comments about the uniqueness of America and the nontransferability of its institutions, he seems also to have assumed that all democratic societies would grow increasingly alike and that with the possible exception of politics it was in America that one might see the future most clearly.

With regard to the American or democratic social state, Tocqueville is not as interested in the genesis of that social condition as he is in providing a structural analysis of it as a given. This approach in some ways sharply restricted his understanding. The questions he asks have to do with class structure, social and economic mobility, the fluidity of wealth, and the general level of wealth. Tocqueville's conclusions about all of these led to the crucial point of his analysis of democratic culture: there would be no fixed ruling class or permanent cultural elite to establish norms. Though early in *Democracy in America* he does discuss the law and economics of land in attempting to account for the origins of the social state of the Americans, he devotes on the whole little attention to the material basis of American life, apart from making rather general assertions about it, especially its remarkable abundance. It would not be accurate to say he was uninterested in how Americans made their livings, and he saw clearly that the economy does powerfully shape the social state; but his analysis of American economic life, accurately reflecting the little time he actually spent investigating it, is sketchy. He was more interested in the culture and psychology of work and in the motivations that drive men to labor and to accumulate wealth than in the conditions and organization of labor and its relationship to capital. He was far more interested in the impulses that led Americans to use their resources and technology in a way that revolutionized their society than in the technology itself. He draws a portrait of the informing spirit, rather than the structure, of American capitalism. The consequence is that while he had a good feeling for the inner dynamics of American economic life, his understanding of the structural characteristics of that economy and of the developments that presaged the accelerated industrialization that followed the Civil War was poor. As before noted, he did not see the beginnings of the concentration of capital and failed to detect the process through which capital extends its domination over politics and an economic ruling class emerges.[2] But England and France, too, where a very wealthy and powerful bourgeoisie had developed, could have provided a different model.

Why did European industrial developments not influence his thinking more? He saw the rich in America as timid, deferential, and without much influence in a society of small-scale enterprises in which wealth was unstable and risk great. His picture of the economic base of the American social state is static; it is a world of restlessly busy small entrepreneurs locked in a perpetual stalemate of competition, by means of which power and wealth remain widely dispersed. But if he missed the mechanisms that would make the concentration of wealth and power possible, he keenly understood the spirit that moved the machine.[3]

Tocqueville saw the United States as a highly mobile, fluid society in which everything was moving toward equality of condition, which, while never fully achieved, remained the norm. And the more one considers Tocqueville's portrait of American society, the more one sees that change, impermanence, and mobility were even more the basic facts to be grasped about America than equality of condition. Equality was simply the norm. In *Democracy in America* he has moved beyond that initial astonished inventorying of the evidence of equality jotted down in his notebooks. If the flux of democratic life occurred largely within certain limits, it was nonetheless more significant than the limits themselves. Tocqueville does not in fact describe the United States as a classless society. Social differences and levels, though much less extreme than in Europe, remain, but they are now placed on shifting and unstable economic foundations, not on the permanent foundation of birth or of legal order. Moreover, they play a considerably diminished role in public life. What Tocqueville in effect describes is simply a shift from a rigidly to a fluidly stratified society, from one of fixed orders of men in which birth and prescriptive right determine social destiny to one in which standing in the social order is determined by will, energy, and character. "In democracies," he wrote, "men never stay still; a thousand circumstances make them move from place to place, and there is almost always something unforeseen, something if one may put it so, provisional about their lives."[4] Nothing was fixed. There were no permanent ranks, orders, classes of men; and this social fluidity, the result of a complex cluster of causes lying in both circumstance and law, had immense cultural consequences.

The most important of these consequences for Tocqueville as he worked out his cultural analysis stemmed from the fact that there would be no permanent and stable elite of cultural producers, consumers, or arbiters to dominate the cultural life of democratic societies. With this traditional source of authority lost, the dynamics of the cultural process were bound to be radically transformed. Here, Tocqueville has come to what for him was the nub of the matter: the crucial, fateful social transformation that would shape the culture and the politics of future societies, either sooner or later but in any case inevitably.

The incessant circulation of people in society meant that each generation would see new ones at the top, as it were, and these would lack the tastes, inclinations, and sense of form of a permanent aristocracy. Moreover, Tocqueville thought that intellectual and cultural authority was not likely to be located in any particular profession which, because of its prestige, might exercise some sort of cultural hegemony. No group, either by virtue of its expertise or by any social or cultural authority would serve as cultural arbiter or establish the cultural tone for the whole society. The fluidity of democratic life meant that there would be no permanent model at the top.

Tocqueville did not think that the absence of a permanent leisure class free to devote itself fully to formal cultural and intellectual pursuits would necessarily lead to cultural stagnation, for the disappearance of such a class would be accompanied, as it had been in America, by an extension of cultural participation and by an explosion of cultural activity. If the absence of a leisure class meant a change in the spirit of cultural life—for example, a relaxed adherence to formalities of craft and style, a drift toward utilitarian approaches to knowledge and art and to an abandoning of tradition—it also meant that cultural life would be freer to develop in ways that had hitherto been restrained by the presence of a dominating cultural elite. But that the demise of such an elite would make a great difference in the cultural life of any society was certain. In *Democracy in America* he traces the consequences of the absence of a stable, tradition-minded, formality-loving elite through every aspect of cultural life, whether it be social manners, language, craftsmanship, or literature.

"Take the case of an aristocratic people interested in literature," he wrote: "in that case the labors of the mind as well as the business of government are controlled by a ruling class. Literature as well as politics is almost entirely confined to that class or those nearest it. That gives the key to all the rest."[5] The dominant values and tendencies of the literature will reflect the values, the social condition, and the consciousness of the class that produces it. "When a small unchanging group of men," he goes on, "are concerned at the same time with the same subject, they easily get together and agree on certain guiding principles to direct their efforts. If it is literature with which they are concerned, strict canons will soon prescribe rules that may not be broken. If these men occupy a hereditary position in their country, they will naturally be inclined to invent rules for themselves but also to follow those laid down for their ancestors. Their code will be strict and traditional."[6] The qualities of the literature produced and consumed by such an elite would be formal, full of elaborate conventions, shunning anything too explicit or lively. In democratic societies, to the contrary, literature takes quite different tendencies. Writers do not come from a class with stable, clear social and cultural traditions but from "a heterogeneous, stirring crowd": "They are not guided by the same lights, do not resemble their own fathers; and they themselves are changing every moment with changing place of residence, feelings, and fortune. So there are no traditions, or common habits to forge links between their minds, and they have neither power nor the wish nor the time to come to a common understanding." The literature of a democratic society reflects the looseness, the fluidity, the turbulence, the tendency to constant self-renewal of the society itself: "In these circumstances one will not expect to find many of those strict conventions accepted by writers and readers in aristocracies. Even if a few conventions are accepted by one generation, it does not follow that the next will observe them too, for in a democracy each generation is a new people."[7]

Just as important as the loss of a social base for a cohesive, traditional, and formal literary culture is the fact that writers now respond no longer mainly to their own inclinations and traditions but to the values and sensibilities of their middle-class readers, who constitute a huge and voracious and profitable market. In the democratic society it is the taste of the marketplace that dominates and shapes literature, and the taste of the marketplace is the taste of the middle class. In a literature responding to such an audience—practical, busy, informal, craving the new, demanding quick answers and vivid entertainment—"the order, regularity, skill and art characteristic of aristocratic literature" will vanish: "Formal qualities will be neglected or actually despised. The style will often be strange, incorrect, overburdened, and loose, and almost always strong and bold. Writers will be more anxious to work quickly than to perfect details. Short works will be commoner than long books, wit than erudition, imagination than depth. There will be a rude and untutored vigor of thought with great variety and singular fecundity. Authors will strive to astonish more than to please, and to stir passions than to charm taste."[8] If the literature of a people was thus shaped primarily by its general social condition, so too were all other aspects of its cultural life. The culture of a society with a fixed elite centers on that elite, which is not only the chief cultural consumer but the ultimate cultural arbiter. It sets the standards, maintains a sense of proper form, which only slowly changes. And in every way he can Tocqueville seeks to demonstrate how the middle-class frame of mind produces a culture of what he calls the middle zone, the chief characteristics of which are utility, practicality, immediacy of result, impatience with form, perpetual innovativeness, and a quest to astonish.

It was in his exploration of what he saw as the strongest features of the democratic imagination that Tocqueville caught his clearest glimpse of what the culture of democracy would be like. Three qualities of that imagination seemed especially significant to him. First, it would increasingly be oriented toward the present. The sense of the past would be attenuated, though obviously it would continue to shape the imagination more strongly in some societies than in others, depending on the strength of old habits of mind, the tenacity of class structures and institutions, and the pace at which change eroded all of these. The chief cause of this loss of the past is the chronic mobility characteristic of democracy, weakening all the social links, links to class, family, guild, community, that formerly kept the past vividly in mind. Tradition, if it is not entirely lost to sight, loses its authority. Democratic man even deliberately turns his back on it: "Equality stimulates each man to want to judge everything for himself and gives him a taste in everything for the tangible and the real, and a contempt for tradition and formalities. . . . Aristocracy naturally leads the mind back to the past and fixes it in the contemplation thereof. But democracy engenders a sort of distaste for what is old."[9] For Tocqueville, there was no more regrettable deficiency of the democratic imagination than this loss of connection with the past, which for Tocqueville had intense personal poignancy. It was as if his ancestors were twice to be rubbed from history. *Democracy in America* does in fact have an agenda: it is at once a lament for the lost aristocracy, a celebration of its virtues and accomplishments, and a demonstration of its crucial role as a cultural force—and a comment on the cultural pretensions of the bourgeoisie.

The counterpart to this antitraditional, antihistorical turn of the democratic imagination was the enhanced power of the idea of progress. The past not only faded from mind, it was positively rejected as a guide for the future, which democratic man believed would surely be different and better. The faith in progress; the confident belief that man's ingenuity and power would transform life; the whole powerful thrust of secular utopianism released by democracy, all made the past seem irrelevant, except perhaps as a point of departure; people would "treat traditions as valuable for information only."[10] Yet the confidence in progress that was one result of the demise of a static social order would not necessarily be translated into an alert consciousness of the future or into a concern with distant goals, however oriented toward change democratic society was. The democratic imagination would be oriented to the future, alive with optimistic anticipation of perpetual improvement. Yet in a way the future would trouble democracy's thinking as little as the past in that there would be little inclination to sacrifice either present advantage or present comfort for future considerations. A culture without a sense of history, Tocqueville implies, would have no clear vision of the future either.

Tocqueville also saw the democratic imagination as possessing a feeble sense of transcendence, a diminished sense of the sacred. The age of democracy was demonstrably no longer an age of faith. Tocqueville may have believed that human spirituality, based on an innate inclination of human nature, was ineradicable; but he saw that nearly all aspects of democratic life and culture threatened to smother it. The radically empirical bias of the democratic mind, which loved to anchor itself in facts, and the democratic passion for material well-being and for the useful focused attention so much on this world that the possibility that other dimensions of reality existed tended to drop from mind.[11] Places where one might seek the presence of the sacred were now factories in which the sacred was brought to earth. He saw the progress of equality accompanied by the progress of secularization, again occurring at different rates and with varying thoroughness depending on the strength of the religious traditions of different societies. It is not that a democratic people would be without beliefs, but these would increasingly be secular. Their source would no longer be transcendental authority. Goals and standards of good would be wholly internal. In democracy, it was human beings who would indeed be the measure of all things.[12]

The unappeasable acquisitive drive of the democratic temper seemed to him likely to lead to a dangerously narrow philosophical materialism, against which the leaders of democratic societies would have to struggle. But to keep even a pale spiritual consciousness alive in such societies would require a deliberate effort that ran counter to the central tendencies of democratic culture, the power of which makes his proposed remedies seem desperate, even hopeless. He saw that it would be self-destructive for religion to challenge the dominant spirit and style of democratic culture. It would have to simplify its ritual life radically and restrain its challenge to the overwhelming passion for material comfort that was the democratic "mother of all desires."[13] Religion would pose no serious, vital challenge to the ruling spirit of democracy but would have to enter into that spirit. But this would simply speed the transformation of religion into the mechanism for validating the culture's central values that it was becoming.

If a sense of the past and a sense of the transcendent were fading from the democratic imagination, so too was a sense of the tragic and of limits. The democratic imagination would be profoundly optimistic, Tocqueville thought, even though he perceived the many ways in which people living in democratic societies would become vulnerable to a great many anxieties and strains, to persisting, anguishing uncertainties largely absent from aristocratic societies, in which people did not suffer so much from the psychological torments that inevitably accompany limitless hopes. Had Tocqueville been more familiar with the terrors of the Protestant imagination, he would have understood that it cultivated its own inescapable anxieties—about salvation. He had in mind the dream of earthly salvation, that is, success.

A society from which traditional limits were vanishing would develop a culture without a sense of limits. The view of human power and of the power of reason, the dream that society and even man himself could be indefinitely transformed for the better, would be greatly magnified by democracy as the old social restraints that had served to chasten hopes fell away. Resignation would not be a democratic emotion, nor would acceptance of one's destined place. If in the democratic era the past, as a real presence shaping motives and consciousness, drops away, the future opens up as a vista of gaudy possibilities. Tocqueville locates the source of such rising expectations not so much in the actual experience of material, technological, or intellectual progress as in changes in the structure of society, which becomes fluid, unsettled, without any fixed order or permanent social boundaries.

For what is most deeply characteristic of democracy, Tocqueville saw, is that it erases all traditional boundaries that formerly had led humankind to feel that there were permanent and insurmountable barriers to change. If well-defined, fixed social boundaries and the constant experience of limits were compatible with only modest ideas of progress and improvement, the new fluidity of democratic social relations inflated such ideas to a new order of magnitude. The democratic imagination would recognize no limits. Democratic people would be permanently innovative, driven on by a socially based confidence that change for the better was not only inevitable but limitless. They would, he thought, exhaust themselves in the "pursuit of . . . complete felicity."[14]

The culture of democracy, reflecting the fluidity and changeability of a society which had lost its traditional moorings, would thus be a culture in which regard for traditional canons of form, and even a sense of the importance of form, were severely diminished. As aristocratic societies vanished, so did the notion of good form; and as those crafts, professions, and elites whose social function was to conserve and transmit the formal aspects of culture lost their coherence and power, the sense of form was increasingly rooted in the larger, turbulent society itself, the primary experience of which was instability and change. In *DA II* Tocqueville offers abundant commentary on this process, from the development, in democratic societies, of "a certain incoherence of manners" to the way in which language stretches and grows beyond old forms and limits and becomes spectacularly innovative. In all formal aspects of democratic culture, "the rules of style are almost destroyed," and disorderly and often wildly contradictory development occurs.[15]

With great ingenuity and insight Tocqueville traces out the multiple contradictions of the democratic culture to come. It is one of the major achievements of *Democracy in America* and a triumph of theory. He sees that democratic society will be a society without extremes, a society in which a kind of prosaic sameness, a chilling "universal uniformity," prevails.[16] Variety, he frequently laments, is doomed to disappear as the steamroller of equality flattens all differences. In America one already found, he wrote, "a multitude of people with roughly the same ideas."[17] At the same time, the culture of a society without extremes is potentially a culture of extremes. It will be a culture without a sense of limits, free to push on in a never-ending exploration of possibilities, unrestrained by tradition or convention of any sort. Thus Tocqueville sees democracy unleashing the imagination, which, no longer attached to a fixed reality, will push on in many different and contradictory directions. Democracy would develop a culture of contradictions.

There would be a tendency in democratic culture toward superliteralism, so that in striving to see reality with a fidelity so perfect that nothing was left in the shadows people would "often employ their talents in the exact delineation of everyday life" and "copy trivial objects from every angle";[18] but there would also be a striving after the bizarre, the melodramatic, and the grandiose. Democratic culture would be a culture of the bigger-than-life, characterized by huge public monuments, bombastic oratory, and sweeping visions of national destiny — by a pervasive giganticism.[19] Democratic poets, he thought, "finding no stuff for the ideal in what is real and true," would abandon truth and reality and "create monsters."[20]

The democratic imagination would focus powerfully on the individual, exploring the recesses and pathways of the individual consciousness with a passionate intensity, making the individual sensibility a central guide to reality. Yet at the same time, as people in fact became more alike, it would grow increasingly fascinated with the collective destiny of humans and, in its search for general laws and causes, lose sight of the individual. Tocqueville thought, for example, that the historical imagination in the democratic era would not be concerned so much with individuals as with the collective destinies of groups, classes, nations. It would emphasize, not the individual will, not the freedom of the individual to choose and thereby to make a difference in history, but those forces and movements that sweep individuals, whatever their wills, toward destinies not of their choosing. For democratic historians it would not be individuals that mattered but masses of people, not the will and vision of individuals but the system that shaped their lives. In effect, the democratic imagination would be sociological.

Democracy would also lead poetry in two directions: toward an emphasis on "the nation itself," on collective destiny, on the whole of society as a complex, mysterious entity; and at the same time toward an exploration of the inner life of the individual and "the dark corners of the human heart."[21] The democratic imagination would in this manner move toward two extremes: a preoccupation with subjective consciousness as creative force and source of law and a fascination with society as a system in which the individual is a subordinate and will-less mechanism and with laws that account for social change and behaviors.

What Tocqueville saw as the central features of democratic culture all become now-familiar aspects of what moderns have come to mean when they speak of modernity: its ever-accelerating exploration of the new; its disassociation from the past and from all convention and tradition; its simultaneous hyperliteralness and flight from literalness; its celebration of technique; its tendency to seek the real in the hyperbolic and the fantastic; its radical individualism and its tendency at the same time to quantify human experience, to turn humans into abstractions and to see them as parts of systems. A society whose central experience was that of chronic change and rootlessness would produce a culture surging wildly in many different directions—"immense," "incoherent," "over-drawn"²²—full of distorted visions caused by the loss of a sense of fixed proportions and by the collapse of a permanent order of things. Though literal reality would be seen with an ever-increasing clarity and though men would seek to measure it with painstaking exactitude in the conviction that truth was to be found in the most perfectly literal reproduction of reality, they would also rely on their personal vision as a way of knowing the most real. Both hallucinations and systems would be the fruit of democracy.

The prospect of this new and in many ways creative cultural freedom did not, however, at all diminish Tocqueville's anxieties about the political and moral destiny of democracy. For what democratic man needed above all was to create new sources of inner discipline to replace the limits and sanctions once provided by the lost older order, for freedom could not survive without discipline and formality. But it was just this shift that seemed unlikely to occur. The democratic culture he saw emerging would offer little sense of limits. It would be a culture with a powerful quest for change, with the result that forms, conventions, and rules would lose their authority.

And it is precisely on the consequences of the democratic disdain for formality and its chronic disregard of limits that Tocqueville dwells in the dark final chapters of *Democracy in America*. It is the problem he finally encounters in his search for new sources of moral order and new defenses for freedom. The idea that the age of equality, preeminently an age of change, would be a time of moral uncertainty and expediency informs all of *Democracy in America*. As we have noted, even more powerful than his account of the providential rise of equality is the lament about the intellectual and moral disorder of his time with which he begins his book. One might argue that this was the true subject of his work, and it bears repeating: "Have all ages been like ours? And have men always dwelt in a world in which nothing is connected? Where virtue is without genius, and genius without honor? Where love of order is confused with a tyrant's tastes, and the sacred cult of freedom is taken as scorn of law? Where conscience sheds but doubtful light on human actions? Where nothing any longer seems forbidden or permitted, honest or dishonorable, true or false?" He continues to say that he cannot believe that the Creator will allow man "to struggle endlessly through the intellectual squalor now surrounding us"; but by the end of his work his quest to discover new sources of order in an egalitarian world to replace the old order lost has failed. The worst prospects were that democratic contempt for form—for rules of conduct, political due process, even social decorum—would slowly lead to disregard of the moral principles that underlay such rules and were the basis of the idea of rights. As Tocqueville warns in his conclusion, in the democratic future the principle of utility would replace all other principles of order. The political results would be devastating. Without rules and formalities to protect them, individuals would be helpless before the aggrandizing thrust of the social power. The rule of utility would justify their subordination in the name of political necessity. The chief casualty of the widening intellectual disorder of democratic culture would be freedom.

Such were the sources of Tocqueville's harrowing, pessimistic view of the democratic future—from which, it must be said, he averted his eyes at the last minute, as he did in the desperate, unconvincing affirmations of his conclusion to *Democracy in America* and even in his debates with Gobineau in the late 1850s. The aim of all his work was to see how the present had been shaped by the past, the better to judge what might be done to escape the apparent inevitabilities of history. In reaching back into the past as he wrote *Democracy in America*, what most preoccupied him was the evidence of deeper tendencies in modern culture, those great transformations of society, culture, and spirit both he and Mill were struggling to understand. The social forces and cultural changes he found already under way dashed his hopes. America simply afforded him the most vivid glimpse of what lay ahead. He feared that a cultural dark age was approaching, a dark age paradoxically produced by the brilliant flowering and wild freedom of fully developed democratic culture.

CONCLUSION

Tocqueville was convinced that the necessary antidote to the weaknesses of democracy—among them its permanent cultural and social disorder, its weak sense of a common good, the moral effects of hyperindividualism, the development of an anti-intellectual mass culture, its inability to make sacrifices for the long-range good—was an aristocracy of merit, rising from the people and chosen by the people, that would provide the needed countervailing guidance. But it was just such a democratic aristocracy, the sources and role of which he and John Stuart Mill had struggled to think through, that he found missing in the United States and that he thought unlikely to arise.

There already was abundant evidence, recorded in his notebooks in 1831 and then discussed in *Democracy in America*, that the quality of political leadership in democratic America had seriously declined from the remarkable generation of Washington, Jefferson, and Madison to the time of Andrew Jackson, whom Tocqueville saw as a demagogue. He did not think this decline had happened by chance. It was the inevitable result of the dynamics of democratic social and cultural change. The same lamentable decline was occurring in France as well, more slowly but just as surely. He thought the admirable Washington would be mocked in the France of the 1830s as a dull character in a political world that had become theatrical, full of unprincipled power-seeking spellbinders.

The detailed, critical observations of American politics and culture recorded in his notebooks and in his letters were somewhat muted in the first volume of *Democracy in America*, which was devoted mainly to an examination of American institutions and laws, but they were fully opened in the second volume, in which his initial observations of American culture and politics were structured by his theoretical analysis of democratic culture, especially by his analysis of the relationship of "the social state" of a people to their culture and politics. It was at this point that "what was American" blended with what was essentially democratic. He had thereby arrived at a deeper understanding of what he had observed in America. His first apprehensions and criticisms were now grounded.

Tocqueville had come to see that democratic culture had a built-in dynamic of incessant change—social, cultural, economic. This was true of all democratic societies, but it was especially intense in America, where it was given a powerful spin by the unprecedented circumstances of American life, which had led to a culture of excess. For many reasons America was ill-equipped to deal with the hazards created by the ill-disciplined freedom democracy was bound to produce. The first volume of *Democracy in America* is dominated by the spirit and influence of the Puritans, above all by their devotion to the idea of freedom and order within the law, but it concludes with an almost admiring account of the risk-taking spirit of the Anglo-Americans as they swept West and then looked for worlds to conquer. He thought this spirit was bound to conquer all that lay before it. It was the expression of a recklessness, an abandon, that ran deep within the culture. This temper, or distemper, of American culture troubled him. If it was creative, it was also destructive. He alludes to it in many ways at different times, though not always directly. Curiously, though he traveled much on riverboats at a time when they were swarming with gamblers and confidence men—once spending four days on the Mississippi in the company of Sam Houston—he never mentions these characters, though he could hardly have missed them. But he nonetheless well noted the spirit that animated them. They were Melville's "confidence men."

The penchant for risk taking, muted in the first volume of *Democracy in America* except for its uncharacteristically exhilarated conclusion, was related to a democratic weakness Tocqueville deplored. That was democracy's inability to take the long view, to note or care about the long-range consequences of policies and actions. To Tocqueville this lack of *prévoyance* was the result not simply of the diverting temptations of American life and of fantasies of unlimited abundance but also of an inherent democratic inability to make present sacrifices for future good.

In every aspect of American life, the risk-taking spirit as well as the fantasy of constant renewal, of beginning again, pushed Americans beyond limits. Their lives were experimental. They quested for immediate satisfactions and the "big pot."

The characteristics of democratic culture that most troubled Tocqueville were the already visible decline in the quality of political leadership and the weakening of a sense of the common good. An aristocracy of merit had not appeared—and it wasn't likely to. The people would elect only those who were most like them, who spoke their lingo, who were shortsighted and focused on present profit and staying in office. Such leaders would cater to the people's clamoring wants instead of calling for restraint and self-discipline, reminding them of their highest ideals, counseling them to make sacrifices for the sake of a future good—instead of, above all, constantly stressing the common good. A disharmonious, fractured society, increasingly diverse in many ways, was bound to lose a sense of the common good. A society in which the experience of difference was compounded by the alienating ethos of individualism, an ethos that bred social indifference (much stressed and deplored by Tocqueville), would be composed of a myriad of private and local worlds in which a larger common good would be hard to discern. The continuing absence of the kind of aristocratic elite Tocqueville called for, a leadership that focused the eyes of the nation on broader social interests and on more distant goals, would be fatal for the brighter possibilities of democracy. Tocqueville saw all this already happening.

The long-range prospects for democracy were not encouraging. By the 1840s and 1850s he was further alarmed by developments in the United States, namely, by the increasingly disheveled culture of the Americans and the growing turbulence and fracturing of their politics, especially the profound, bitter division over slavery and its expansion. Worrying also were the apparently unrestrained excesses of their risk-taking, unstable economic lives, which affected him directly.

Tocqueville unquestionably knew some of the voluminous writing by eighteenth- and nineteenth-century French moralists, and literary figures like Stendhal and Chateaubriand (whose work he knew intimately), speculating about the meaning and promise of the New World. Much of this literature expressed the hope that America might provide humankind with a chance at moral redemption—with a chance to escape the corruption and moral confusion that had come to plague Western civilization, an indictment powerfully and influentially expressed by Rousseau, whose views were not singular. Would America be the place where humankind, nurtured by an undefiled nature, might regain the purity and harmony that had been fouled by Western institutions?

Tocqueville was too much the skeptic, too much the critical thinker to entertain seriously the many new French versions of the old European myth of an Eden to the West. But if some part of this dream had tinged his thinking as he looked West despite his doubts about democracy and the repugnance it caused him to feel, then great was bound to be his disappointment. There is enough in *Democracy in America* to suggest he was more than simply commenting on the Dream of Redemption, but also subtly giving voice to it. The first chapter of *Democracy in America* asks a great question: would humanity in the New World finally succeed in transcending history and create a society that truly was exceptional? Tocqueville may have come with that question in mind, but by the time he finished *Democracy in America,* and even more by the end of his life, that question had become simpler: would this new society survive? and if not, would the prospects for democracy go down with it? Tocqueville did not fully give up on democracy, but he left himself little ground for confidence in its future.

A Brief Chronological Narrative of the Life of Alexis de Tocqueville

1805

Alexis-Charles-Henri-Clérel de Tocqueville was born in Paris on July 29, 1805, the youngest and third son of Hervé-Louis-François-Jean-Bonaventure Clérel de Tocqueville and Louise-Madeleine Le Peletier de Rosanbo, both from ancient noble families. Tocqueville's father was a descendant of the founding Norman nobility; a Guillaume Clérel had fought alongside William the Conqueror at Hastings. His mother was a descendant of a great network of very old "familles de grande robe"—noble servants of royal power, the most illustrious of whom was Guillaume-Chrétien de Lamoignon de Malesherbes, who as friend of the philosophes, defender of freedom of the press, and critic of many royal policies also served in many royal offices, especially that of director of the library, that is, chief censor, in which position he was notably liberal. He was in many ways a model for Tocqueville.

1805–14

His family lived quietly in Paris and Verneuil-sur-Seine, as it had since 1794, after Hervé and Louise had been released from prison. Hervé worked to regain family lands that had been seized by the revolutionary government.

1814–24

These were the Restoration years following the end of Napoleon's empire. An unsettled life as Alexis accompanied his father, an ultraroyalist prefect, from one département to another, six all told, the last being Seine-et-Oise (1826–30).

Hervé was an often arbitrary and manipulative ally of royal power and prerogative in its struggle with the bourgeoisie as well as more radical groups in all the départements in which he served. He was later called by the liberal journal the *Globe* "one of the most reactionary Prefects of the time," though he was an energetic administrator and was moderately progressive with regard to economic development, social, and educational issues. After the July Revolution of 1830, Hervé de Tocqueville retired from public life, refusing to accept the bourgeois monarchy of Louis-Philippe, which enthroned popular, in effect, bourgeois, not royal, sovereignty.

1821–24

Tocqueville's formal education began when he was sixteen at the "collège royal"—the lycée in Metz, the governing seat of the Département of Moselle, where his father was prefect. He attended this school until 1824. Prior to his formal schooling he had been tutored at home, mostly by the family chaplain, the Abbé Lesueur, whose Catholicism was strongly tinged by Jansenist Predestinarian Calvinism and its dark views of man. Lesueur sought to turn Alexis away from a life of military service, the ancient family vocation, toward a career in politics, as a statesman, or toward a life of the mind.

At the Metz lycée, Tocqueville excelled in rhetoric but little else. He studied no English and no history, his studies in mathematics and Greek were rudimentary, but his Latin education was serious. In rhetoric, great emphasis was placed on oratory in public service, an irony considering Tocqueville's later failure as an orator, which he much lamented. He fought a duel, the cause of which is unknown. In his father's library he read much in seventeenth-century French literature, in translations of classical authors, and, most significantly and consequentially, in the eighteenth-century French philosophes and writers, including Voltaire, Rousseau, Montesquieu, Gabriel de Mably, Georges-Louis de Buffon. This was a first-rate solo education that he later said had destroyed his Catholic faith, although it unquestionably prepared him to understand the intellectual background of the Revolution. He was educated in relative isolation and in the sticks, as it were, which perhaps contributed to the isolation he felt and lived in throughout his life and to his sense of difference.

1824–26

Law school in Paris, when he was eighteen to twenty-one. He lived briefly by himself in the Latin Quarter, then with his mother in the Faubourg Saint-Germain, an aristocratic sanctuary. The legal curriculum was conservative, the reforms of 1819–22 having been abandoned because law schools had become recruiting grounds for liberal and revolutionary secret societies such as the Carbonari. Tocqueville became the secretary of a private discussion group whose participants were mostly noble. He did not distinguish himself in his legal studies.

1826–27

He traveled in Italy and Sicily with his brother Edouard, and he wrote a meditation on Sicily much influenced by François René de Chateaubriand.

1827–32

He was appointed *juge auditeur*, or apprentice lawyer, rather like an intern, in Versailles, in which position he served from June 1827 to mid-1832. An extra position was opened for him as the son of the prefect, on the assumption that he would provide a useful link between the judiciary and the départemental administration. He moved into the prefecture and later moved into his own room on the Rue d'Anjou, living with Gustave de Beaumont, a more affable and sociable individual than he, then already one rung up as a deputy public prosecutor. After Beaumont moved on and up to Paris in September of 1829, he lived with Ernest de Chabrol.

He did not like judicial work or the legal life as then practiced, and his service was undistinguished, perhaps in part because he was often disdainful and cold toward others though curiously abject about himself and his abilities, but also because his interest in the law was historical and philosophical rather than practical. He did not speak fluently or always intelligibly. His first biographer, André Jardin, described him at this time as "slight and thin; his face was at once childish and rather sickly, framed by long, silky black hair and brightened by large dark eyes. He was often silent, with a sort of stiffness that was taken for pride and disdain, though distrust, shyness, and distraction also entered in. He himself agreed that he was rather 'icy' and 'not especially outgoing.'" In 1830 he was denied promotion to deputy public prosecutor and continued as *juge suppléant* with the same minor functions as before, still without salary.

1828

He met Mary Mottley, a young Englishwoman perhaps twenty-eight years old then living in Versailles. After a lengthy acquaintance and courtship, a period of doubt, and against much opposition, he married Mary—thenceforth Marie—in October of 1835, after he had published the first volume of *Democracy in America*.

1830

Tocqueville was in Versailles during the July Revolution of 1830, which was provoked by Charles X's reactionary policies, feared to be a resurrection of the royal divine right absolutism of the ancien régime. The Duke d'Orléans became Louis-Philippe I, not as king of France but as king of the French, symbolizing the great shift of sovereignty from the Crown to the people.

In effect, the collapse of the Restoration Monarchy and the inauguration of the Bourgeois (Orleanist) Monarchy meant the triumph of the bourgeoisie and not of the people, the displacement of the aristocracy by a plutocratic bourgeoisie, an extremely limited advance of equality, and the suppression of republican hopes. Tocqueville had thought that Charles's arbitrary effort to restore the full royal prerogative was madness. Although he belonged to the hastily restored National Guard, a citizens' militia, he did not take up arms to defend the king. Sadly, he watched the royal person's lengthy caravan leave Versailles as it began its long, slow trip to Cherbourg (and then to England), passing through Valognes in Normandy, a few miles from the chateau at Tocqueville that Alexis would inherit in 1836. (In 1839 Tocqueville would be elected to the Chamber of Deputies by the handful of electors of the arrondissement of Valognes.)

After a brief but agonizing pause, Tocqueville took the oath of loyalty to the bourgeois king, required of everyone in public service. His brothers resigned from their military commissions, and his father left his civil commission. His closest friend and cousin Louis de Kergorlay, lieutenant of artillery and just back from the military conquest of Algiers, turned in his commission and was soon involved in a failed royalist insurgency. His new colleague and friend Beaumont did take the oath. Tocqueville had broken with his family's ultraroyalist traditions, not feeling as strongly about the old feudal fealty to the royal person or race, while thinking that perhaps the Revolution had inaugurated a true constitutional monarchy, which he was willing to serve and guide, and not the repressive oligarchy it quickly became. It was the first of his many declarations of independence.

1831–32

On April 2, 1831, Tocqueville and Beaumont sailed from Le Havre, beginning their now-famous journey to the United States. Uncomfortable in their sworn roles as servants of the Bourgeois Monarchy and with Tocqueville also suspect because of his ultraroyalist relations and connections, they contrived to be sent on an official mission to inspect and report on the prison system in the United States, at that time thought to be the most advanced and humane in the world. Permission to take leave was granted reluctantly, and they were to travel at their own expense, though with official letters.

The true purpose of their expedition was to discover the future by studying the world's most advanced democratic society and jointly to write a major book that would make their names. After a five-week sea voyage, their journey began in New York City, from whence they traveled north through New York State, visiting Sing Sing and Auburn penitentiaries, then via the Great Lakes to Michigan and Wisconsin, back to Quebec, then down the Hudson Valley to Albany, thence through Massachusetts to Boston for the longest and most consequential stay of the journey. From Boston they traveled through Connecticut to New York City, then to Philadelphia, Baltimore, and Cincinnati. They then headed south, traveling down the Ohio and Mississippi rivers to Memphis and New Orleans, which they visited briefly in January of 1832. The last leg of their journey took them rapidly through the South, barely pausing anywhere, to Washington, D.C., where they stayed for two weeks, and then back to New York City, from which port they sailed back to France on February 20, 1832.

They had interviewed many prison officials, political figures, and members of the American elite, people who deeply influenced Tocqueville's understanding of the United States and its culture. The Bostonians they met, including John Quincy Adams, Jared Sparks, the president of Harvard College, Josiah Quincy, and Joseph Tuckerman, powerfully shaped their ideas about the importance of local institutions (especially the town) and of the Americans' point of origin, that is, their originating culture—the culture of New England and of the Puritans—in the making of the American Republic. Such is a major theme of the first volume (1835) of *Democracy in America*; in the second volume (1840) emphasis shifts to the social condition, the "social state," of the Americans as the primary factor in accounting for their culture, and the Puritans largely disappear. Tocqueville unsurprisingly later said that he felt most at home in Boston, the only American city (in the North) with anything resembling a polished, self-assured aristocracy. He was invigorated by the trip, went shooting ("fowling") when he could, and except for one episode of illness on the rugged trip was in rare good health almost throughout the journey.

The most valuable record of the journey is found in Tocqueville's travel notebooks and in his and Beaumont's letters home.

1832–33

Tocqueville and Beaumont returned to France in February 1832, well before their eighteen-month leave was up. Beaumont quickly got to work writing *Du Système Pénitentiare aux États-Unis et de son Application en France*, which was published in January 1833. Tocqueville contributed notes and comments, and at Beaumont's request he inspected a few Swiss and French prisons but otherwise seemed to have fallen into a funk and did little or none of the writing. In 1833 their book won the Prix Montyon, given by the Académie des sciences morales et politique. The book established them as serious public figures with considerable expertise about prisons.

Beaumont was dismissed from the judiciary for refusing to serve as prosecutor in a sordid sex, murder, and money case on the borderline between the aristocracy and the bourgeoisie, with complicated political meanings. Tocqueville immediately resigned in sympathy and solidarity, glad to quit the judiciary. He later participated in the defense of Louis de Kergorlay, on trial for treason as a participant in a pathetic, farcical uprising of ultras in Provence. Tocqueville's passionate speech defends his friend Kergorlay as an example of the nobility's tradition of service to France and of the virtues of the old aristocracy.

Tocqueville traveled to England in August and early September of 1833 to see how the English aristocracy was making the transition to democracy after the Reform Bill. In October he started writing *Democracy in America* in an attic room of his parents' house in Paris in the Faubourg Saint-Germain.

1834

Tocqueville wrote the first volume of *Democracy in America*, finishing it by October, when he delivered it to the publisher Gosselin. Tocqueville discussed various aspects of his work with the American Theodore Sedgwick, who became an important correspondent, and he hired a young American diplomat, who was at the moment between assignments, to copy out many passages from American statute books and legal commentaries. He visited Mary Mottley in the evenings.

1835

Democracy in America was published in January and by midyear had been reprinted seven times. He was introduced to the literary world at the celebrated salon of Julie Récamier by his uncle-in-law François de Chateaubriand. The book won the Prix Montyon, worth seven thousand francs, having been championed against opposition by the celebrated philosopher and politician Pierre-Paul Royer-Collard, much admired by Tocqueville and a great influence on his thinking despite a few differences. They began a correspondence that lasted until Royer's death in 1844. Tocqueville met Henry Reeve, who translated both *Democracy in America* and *L'Ancien Régime* and became Tocqueville's closest English friend, along with the economist Nassau William Senior. In London he met John Stuart Mill and asked him to review *Democracy in America*. Mill wrote a highly laudatory review, which made Tocqueville's name in England. They began a consequential correspondence, important in shaping the ideas of both men and the history of political thought, though it tailed off in the mid-1840s for reasons unclear. He traveled through England and Ireland and was appalled by the brutality of industrial Manchester and the poverty of the land-deprived Irish peasantry. Shortly after his return, he and Mary Mottley were married. She converted to Catholicism. He began volume 2 of *Democracy in America* while living at his brother Edouard's chateau in Baugy, near Compiègne, north of Paris. It was completed four years later at Tocqueville, his estate in Normandy. He also published two major essays in 1835: *Mémoire sur le paupérisme*, and (at the request of Mill), *L'Etat Social et Politique de la France avant et après 1789*, which appeared in Mill's *London Review*.

1836

Louise-Madcleine Le Peletier de Rosanbo de Tocqueville, Tocqueville's mother, died in January of 1836. He inherited the family estate at Tocqueville, on the Cotentin peninsula in Normandy, in the arrondissement of Valognes, which he represented in the Chamber of Deputies from 1839 until 1851. The chateau at Tocqueville, barely habitable at the time, became his home until his death in 1859, although he and Marie continued to live with Edouard until the following year. He spent much time and money repairing it and improving it, turning it by the 1850s into something like an English park and sheep run. His admiration for the English aristocracy and its style of life grew ever stronger. He began to sound out local feelings about the nobility and about his family and to cultivate the voters of his arrondissement, although his initial plans for entering politics focused on a seat elsewhere.

1837

He published *Deux Lettres sur l'Algérie* in a Versailles newspaper in which he owned an interest. He had long been interested in Algeria as a focus of

French imperial ambitions and had even considered acquiring an estate there with Louis de Kergorlay. He later became a fierce advocate of French imperial domination of North Africa.

His political career began in earnest. Plans for taking a seat in the Chamber of Deputies, first from Versailles, then from various arrondissements in Paris—the quartier de Notre Dame, the quartier Saint-Louis, and then the 10th arrondissement, which included the Faubourg Saint-Germain—all fell through. The next possibility was the arrondissement of Cherbourg, in which he actually was a resident. That plan also failed. He finally agreed in late 1837 to enter the contest for deputy from Valognes. His very wealthy opponent, Comte Jules Polydor Le Marois, spent heavily and played a two-faced game, secretly promising the government he would no longer oppose it while saying quite the opposite at home. Tocqueville refused the support of the prime minister, the Comte Molé, a cousin, testily saying that he wished to remain independent. Marois conducted an unscrupulous campaign and won, 247–210. Tocqueville's defense of Louis de Kergorlay in 1833 was used against him, as it was every time he ran for the Chamber of Deputies.

He was named to the Legion of Honor. He hesitated, not wanting to appear "coopted" and less than independent, but then accepted. Also "coopted" in 1837 were Michelet, Hugo, Sainte-Beuve, Musset, Alexander Dumas.

1838

He was elected to the Académie des sciences morales et politiques. He grudgingly accepted, fearing it might be a detour on the road to the Académie française, which it was his great ambition to join. He later carefully planned and managed his election to the Académie.

1839

Tocqueville was elected to the Chamber of Deputies from Valognes in October after a nasty campaign, defeating the incumbent, Marois. He was chosen rapporteur of the Chamber of Deputies' Committee on the Abolition of Slavery. After much hesitation, involving the game of appearances—he was careful about whom he sat next to—he took a seat on the center-left of the Chamber of Deputies. He was chosen rapporteur of the Committee on the Prison System.

1840

Volume 2 of *Democracy in America* was published in January.

1841

After intense campaigning, during which he lined up and asked for votes, Tocqueville was elected to the Académie française. He served on the Committee on Liberty of Teaching.

1843

He was rapporteur of another Committee on the Prison System.

1844

He became part owner and codirector of the journal *Le Commerce*. He guided its policies, even its literary pages. He had a major yet temporary falling-out with Beaumont. The journal steadily lost circulation and was sold in November 1845. He was reelected to the Chamber of Deputies. He gave a speech on liberty of teaching in which he favored variety in the school system, including some freedom for religious schools, and a modernizing of the curriculum.

1846

A second visit to Algeria, this time accompanied by Marie for the urban part of the trip.

1847

He was chosen rapporteur of the Chamber's Committee on Algeria. Tocqueville and a small group of liberal deputies began a discussion of measures to be taken to respond to the numerous social miseries and rising unrest of industrial France. These involved a work program, some abatement of taxes and fees burdensome to the working poor as well as other steps, all of which Tocqueville abandoned after the Revolution of 1848 began.

1848

Just prior to the eruption of the Revolution of 1848 he gave a well-noted speech to the Chamber of Deputies in which he warned that it was sitting on a volcano. He was elected to the Constituent Assembly charged with drawing up a new constitution for France and was chosen by that assembly to serve on the committee to draft the constitution. His proposal for a bicameral legislature was rejected. In December he was easily reelected to the Chamber of Deputies in France's first experience of universal suffrage.

1849

In the new Legislative Assembly he served as minister of foreign affairs from May through October.

1850

The onset of the tuberculosis that afflicted him through his fifties began to drive him from active political life. In December he traveled to Italy in the quest of health and there completed his *Souvenirs*, a memoir of the Revolution of 1848.

1851

Napoleon III's coup d'état took place on December 2. Tocqueville, along with many protesting deputies, was arrested and jailed for two nights. He rejected the offer of special treatment. The *Times* of London published his detailed account (and denunciation) of the coup, anonymously.

1852

He refused Napoleon III's offer of the Foreign Ministry and completed his withdrawal from politics by resigning from the Conseil de la Manche, on which he had served for thirteen years. He began serious research for *L'Ancien Régime et la révolution*, which he carried on strenuously despite failing health, an unsettled life resulting from the need to find a climate suitable for his health, anxiety about his finances, and deepening gloom about France. He began the major phase of his correspondence with his onetime research assistant (and later aide in the Foreign Office) Arthur de Gobineau, disputing Gobineau's race theories. *L'Ancien Régime* was published in 1856. The book was a great success. He was despondent about the political and cultural condition of France and the United States. He also began his correspondence with Mme de Swetchine, the spiritual high priestess of an esoteric salon.

1857

He continued research for a planned second volume of *L'Ancien Régime* and traveled for a last time in England, where he worked in the British Museum and was much celebrated. He visited Parliament. A British naval ship carried him back to Boulogne.

1858

His health badly failing, he continued to work on *L'Ancien Régime* but finally sought a restorative climate in Cannes in Provence.

1859

He died in Cannes in April and was buried in Normandy at Tocqueville.

NOTES

Works frequently cited have been identified by the following abbreviations:

CW   John Stuart Mill, *The Collected Works of John Stuart Mill*, vols. 18 and 20, introduction by Alexander Brady. Toronto: University of Toronto Press, 1985.

DA   Alexis de Tocqueville, *Democracy in America*, ed. J.-P. Mayer, trans. George Lawrence. New York, 1951.

JA   Alexis de Tocqueville, *Journey to America*, ed. J.-P. Mayer, trans. George Lawrence. New Haven: Yale University Press, 1959.

OC   Alexis de Tocqueville, *Oeuvres Complètes*. Paris: Gallimard. All quotations from the *Oeuvres Complètes* are cited as *OC* followed by specific edition, volume, and page number. Unless otherwise specified, all translations from *OC* are mine.

OCB   Alexis de Tocqueville. *Oeuvres Complètes*, ed. Gustave de Beaumont. Paris: Michel Levy Frères. 1861. All quotations from Beaumont's edition of Tocqueville's works will be cited as *OCB* followed by specific volume and page number. Unless otherwise specified, all translations from *OCB* are mine.

Recollections Alexis de Tocqueville, *Recollections*, ed. J. P. Mayer, trans. George Lawrence. New Brunswick, N.J.: Transaction Books, 1987.

I.1. IDENTITY IN A TIME OF HISTORICAL TRANSITION

1. OC VI, 1:37–38.
2. The quotations from Tocqueville's letters to and from Gobineau found in John Lukacs's *Tocqueville: The European Revolution and Correspondence with Gobineau* are translated by Lukacs; those from *OC* are mine. OC XIII, 2:233.
3. Tocqueville, *The Old Regime and the Revolution*, trans. Stuart Gilbert, 140. *L'Ancien Régime* is Tome II of *OC*. Edited and heavily annotated by François Furet and

Françoise Mélonio, with all of Tocqueville's notes, and translated by Alan Kahan, it was published in 1995 as *The Old Regime and the Revolution* by the University of Chicago Press.

4. OC VI, 2:487.

I.2. CLASS

1. Henry James, "The Two Ampères," in *Literary Criticism: French Writers; Other European Writers* (Library of America). Lord Hatherton, who spent days with Tocqueville in 1857, thought his manners and intellectual style were more English than French (*OC* VI, 2:481–86).
2. Furet and Mélonio, eds., *The Old Regime and the Revolution*, 181.
3. OC VIII, 1:233.
4. Tocqueville's hostility to the values and morality of the bourgeoisie bristles all through his *Recollections*, which is a Balzacian book but without charity or nuance.
5. Maza, *The Myth of the French Bourgeoisie*, chap. 2. According to Maza, virtually all (87 percent) of the aristocratic prefects serving during the Restoration were replaced by middle-class bureaucrats.
6. See OC XIII, 1:60 n. 2.
7. OC VI, 1:326. See also OC VI, 2:273.
8. OC XIV, 331.
9. OC VI, 2:301; OCB 2:353.
10. OC VIII, 1:262.
11. Ibid., 1:49.
12. Ibid.
13. OC VI, 1:39.
14. OC XIV, 480.
15. OCB 1:284.
16. OCB 2:388–89.
17. OC X, introduction by André-Jean Tudesq; to Edouard, OC XIV, 232–33, 235.
18. OCB 1:442.
19. Furet, *Interpreting the French Revolution*, 153. See also Gannett, *Tocqueville Unveiled*.
20. OC VI, 2:429.
21. Review of the first volume of Tocqueville's *Democracy in America*, in CW 18:78–79.
22. OC VI, 2:429–30.
23. OC XI, 32.
24. OC XIV, 376.
25. Beaumont's "Notice" (his biographical introduction to his 1861 edition of Tocqueville's *Oeuvres Complètes*), OCB 1:44–45.
26. OC XIV, 214.
27. OC XIII, 2:327.
28. OCB 2:284.

29. *OC* XIII, 1:464.
30. Ibid., 1:464–65.
31. Ibid., 2:47–48.
32. Ibid., 1:471.
33. *DA*, vol. 2, pt. III, chap. 11, p. 599.
34. *Recollections*, 5.
35. *OC* VI, 2:430.
36. *OC* XIII, 1:320.
37. *JA*, 257.
38. *OC* VI, 2:301.
39. Ibid., 2:305.
40. Ibid.
41. On women in *DA*, see *DA*, vol. 1, pt. II, chap. 9, p. 291; and vol. 2, pt. III, especially chaps. 9, 10, and 12.
42. *OC* XV, 2:292. See also *OC* VI, 2:302; *OC* VIII, 3:536. Tocqueville's last letters to his nephew Hubert (in *OC* XIV) are full of reflections about women and marriage.
43. *DA*, vol. 2, pt. III, chap. 12.
44. Ibid.
45. *OC* XIV, 251–52.
46. On the Duchesse de Dino, see *OC* XI, 17 n. 1, 21, 28, 30, and *passim*.
47. *OC* XV, vol. 2. Tocqueville's extremely confessional correspondence with Sophie Swetchine is, despite its exaggerated deferential politeness and spirituality, rich with all themes of his lifelong self-analysis and his religious and moral speculations. For a critical view of Swetchine, see James, *Literary Criticism: French Writers; Other European Writers*.
48. *OC* VII, 301.
49. Ibid., 293.
50. Ibid., 301 n. 4.
51. Neither Emerson nor Tocqueville says anything about this meeting in May 1848.
52. *DA*, vol. 2, pt. II, chap. 1, pp. 505–6.
53. Ibid., chaps. 8–9.
54. *The Old Regime and the French Revolution*, trans. Stuart Gilbert, pt. II, chap. 8.
55. *OC* VI, 2:273–74.
56. Tudesq, introduction to *OC* X, 7–11.
57. *OC* XIII, 2:203–4.
58. Ibid., 2:472–73.

I.3. INTIMACY

1. *OC* XI, 40.
2. *OC* VIII, 1:89.
3. *OC* XI, 161, 163, 169–70.
4. Ibid., 424.

5. Beaumont's "Notice," *OCB* 1:101–2.
6. *OC* XIII, 2:46; *OCB* 1:244.
7. *OC* XI, 152.
8. *OC* XIII, 1:430–31.
9. Ibid., 1:431.
10. Editor's introduction, on Tocqueville's often harsh and cruelly deflating criticisms of his friends. *OC* XV, vol. 1.
11. See Palmer, *The Two Tocquevilles*, on Hervé as historian and writer.
12. *OC* XIV, 278–79.
13. *OC* VIII, 1:603.
14. *OC* XIII, 2:35.
15. *OC* VIII, 3:478.
16. Jardin, *Tocqueville*, 53.
17. Ibid.
18. Ibid., 52.
19. *OC* VII, 97, 102, 112.
20. Jardin, *Tocqueville*, 52.
21. *OC* XIV, 476.
22. Ibid., 478–79.
23. *OC* XIV, 485.
24. Jardin, *Tocqueville*, 51.
25. *OC* XIV, 408–10.

I.4. AMBITION

1. *OC* XV, 2:313–14.
2. *OC* XIII, 1:346.
3. On early nineteenth-century French thought on self and psyche, see Goldstein, *Post-Revolutionary Self; OC* VI, 1:30.
4. *OC* XIV, 395–96.
5. Ibid., 396.
6. *OC* XIII, 2:106.
7. *OC* VIII, 1:95.
8. *OC* XIII, 2:28.
9. *OC* VIII, 1:449–50.
10. Beaumont's "Notice," *OCB* 1:8–9.
11. *OC* XIII, 1:108.
12. *OC* VIII, 1:174–75.
13. *OC* XIII, 1:377.
14. Ibid., 1:377; *OC* XI, 87.
15. *OC* XI., 109.
16. Ibid., 93.
17. Ibid., 53.

I.5. MELANCHOLY

1. *OC* XV, 2:309. Tocqueville constantly used these words to describe the troubled state of his psyche—including, curiously, the English "unhinged." He obsessively tried to describe and to account for his mental disequilibrium and depressions. See also *OC* XV, 2:313, for another specimen of what he called his "unpitying" self-analysis. With his friends he was relentlessly frank about his psychological disabilities. To cheer his depressive friend Stoffels he would either chide Stoffel's gloominess and weak sense of civic duty—or describe his own flaws at length.
2. *OC* XV, 2:309.
3. *OC* XIII, 2:318; *OCB* 1:396.
4. *OC* VIII, 1:144.
5. James, "The Letters of Mme Swetchine." James's portrait of Swetchine is unflattering. She comes through as a religious mountebank.
6. *OC* XIII, 2:127.
7. *OC* XIV, 320; *OCB* 1:447. By his midthirties his correspondence is full of bleak comments about his premature aging as well as his chronic melancholy.
8. *OC* XI, 364.

I.6. SKEPTICAL ROMANTIC

1. *OC* XI, 446–47.
2. Ibid., 447.

I.7. SKEPTICAL PHILOSOPHE

1. "Alfred de Vigny," in *Mill: Essays on Literature and Society*, ed. Jerome Schneewind (New York: Collier, 1965).
2. Tocqueville, *The Old Regime and the French Revolution*, trans. Gilbert Stuart (New York: Doubleday, 1951), 141.
3. See, e.g., his correspondence with Mill and Reeve about India.
4. *DA*, vol. 2, pt. II, chap. 25, p. 464.
5. *OCB* 1:448.
6. Ibid.
7. *Recollections*, 62.
8. An excellent discussion of this issue in Tocqueville is Mitchell, *Individual Choice and the Structures of History*.

I.8. SKEPTICISM AND RELIGION

1. *OC* XV, 2:313.
2. *OC* XI, 59–60.
3. *OCB* 1:440; *OC* XI, 55.

4. *OCB* 1:441.
5. *OC* XV, 2:312.
6. Ibid., 2:314–15.
7. On Cousin's ideas and influence on Tocqueville's generation, see Spitzer, *The French Generation of 1820, passim*; Siegel, *The Idea of the Self*; and Goldstein, *Post-Revolutionary Self*.
8. *OC* XV, 2:314.
9. Ibid., 2:323.
10. *JA*, 383.
11. Tocqueville speaks of the "religious terror" he feels in the introduction to *DA*, vol. 1, and on many other occasions, e.g., when writing in 1827 to Kergorlay about the barren, ruined countryside around Rome (*OC* XIII, 1:96). It is one of his stock phrases, and it hides more than it reveals.
12. This was the basis of his defense of Christianity in his debate with Gobineau. See below, 91–92.
13. Tocqueville's notes on Pascal are in *OC* XVI (*Mélanges*), 551–54.
14. *OC* XIII, 2:25–29. Tocqueville and Kergorlay often discussed Islam, and there is much about it in his correspondence with Gobineau. But his knowledge must be considered thin, though he told Kergorlay that he had read the Koran.
15. Ibid., 1:474.
16. *JA*, 308.
17. *OC* VIII, 3:501.
18. Ibid.
19. *OC* XV, 1:162. The disagreement about whether Tocqueville embraced Catholicism (perhaps only sacramentally) cannot be resolved, for it is not possible to enter his spirit and mind at his last hour. However, on the basis of what is known about his views of religion and of Catholicism, it seems unlikely he underwent a deathbed conversion. Mignet, a close friend (the only French historian to be such) thought not: he said Tocqueville was a "philosophical Christian," not a *dévot*. Beaumont dealt with this question by saying that Tocqueville had not undergone a conversion since he had been a Christian all his life. He said Tocqueville did accept the last sacrament, but it was to placate his wife, who wished to avoid scandal. (See Nassau William Senior, "Conversations After Tocqueville's Death," in *OC* VI, 2). See Tocqueville's letters of 1856 to Corcelle, a *dévot*, after his father's death, about the example of his father's piety and saintliness and his own inability to follow his father and believe, though he wished to.

I.9. Doubt and the Will to Believe

1. In those passages in *Democracy in America* in which Tocqueville discusses epistemological questions and issues of religion, belief, and skepticism in democratic culture, he is highlighting his own convictions though struggling to be the objective social scientist. His preface to volume 2 and part I of volume 2 is veined with dissonance

between his convictions and the democratic realities he is reporting. His concluding "General Survey" directly addresses this dissonance.

2. This quotation and the three that follow are from the final chapter ("General Survey of the Subject") of *DA*, vol. 2, pt. IV.

I.10. EXILE

1. Qtd. in Jardin, *Tocqueville*, 473.
2. *OCB* 2:230–31.
3. Ibid., 2:238.
4. *OC* XV, 2:298.
5. *OC* XVI, 298.
6. *OC* XV, 2:120.
7. *DA*, vol. 2, pt. III, chaps. 22–26, esp. pp. 649–50.
8. *OC* III, 3:465–70. This "position paper" was sent to the Count de Chambord, representative of the branch *aînée* of the Bourbons, who found Tocqueville's screed interesting but did not reply. Tocqueville's last thoughts about France's political future closely resembled Royer-Collard's. See also *OCB* 1:436.
9. *OC* VII, 68–69.
10. Ibid., 83.
11. Ibid., 195.
12. Ibid., 163.
13. Ibid., 224.
14. Ibid., 214–15.
15. Ibid., 226–27.
16. *OCB* 2:254.
17. See Françoise Mélonio's essential *Tocqueville and the French*, trans. Beth Reps (University of Virginia Press, 1997), originally published as *Tocqueville et les français*.
18. *OC* VIII, 1:452.
19. *OCB* 2:254.
20. *OC* XV, 2:157.
21. *OC* VI, 2:301.
22. *OC* XIII, 2:303.
23. The following quotations from the correspondence of Tocqueville and Gobineau are from Lukacs, ed., *Tocqueville: The European Revolution and Correspondence with Gobineau*. I have used Lukacs's translations. The Tocqueville–Gobineau file is *OC* IX, edited by M. DeGros and J-J. Chevallier.
24. Lukacs, *Tocqueville*, 210–11.
25. Ibid., 211.
26. Ibid., 222.
27. Ibid., 227–28.
28. Ibid., 228–29.
29. Ibid., 229.

30. Ibid., 231–32.
31. Ibid., 270.
32. Ibid., 301–2.
33. Ibid., 308–10.
34. Ibid., 225–26.
35. OC XV, 2:268.
36. OC VI, 2:481. Senior's written record of his conversations with Tocqueville (and others who knew him well) is a major source for any study of Tocqueville and his ideas (and of his Norman chateau and domain). He asked Tocqueville to read his journal for accuracy. Tocqueville occasionally said that Senior had missed some nuances or that he would have had more to say, but on the whole he seems to have approved of Senior's record of their conversations. See OC VI, 2:269–70, 420, and 436, for examples of his comments. Senior sometimes disguised Tocqueville by referring to him with different initials. On the whole, Senior's record of Tocqueville's views and those of others can be assumed to be accurate.
37. OC XIV. This account of Tocqueville's last visit to England is based on his letters to Marie, all in OC XV, 596–626. All quotations are from his letters to Marie. He evidently spoke of the isolation he felt in London to Sophie Swetchine (OC XV, 2:322).
38. OC XIV, 606.
39. OC VIII, 3:527.
40. Ibid., 1:155.
41. OC VI, 2:280–83.
42. On Tocqueville's investments and his correspondence about them, see OC VII, letters to Sumner and E. Childe; and OC VIII, 3, letters to Beaumont, in 1857–59.
43. Details of Tocqueville's health in the fifties and especially in his last two years are found in his letters to Marie and in his correspondence with Beaumont, Kergorlay, Ampère, Corcelle, and Edouard. His health, whether he was well or not, but especially when he was disintegrating, was a constant subject throughout his correspondence from his thirties on.
44. OC VIII, 3:434.
45. OC XV, 2:268.

II.1. Vocation: Politics as Calling

1. OC VI, 2:513.
2. See Jardin, *Tocqueville*, 18–35, for Hervé de Tocqueville's work as prefect of various departments from 1815 to 1830.
3. See Spitzer, *The French Generation of 1820*. Spitzer's cohort was born between 1792 and 1804, hence Tocqueville himself is not discussed, but he shared much of the culture and aspirations of this generation; moreover, he knew nearly everyone discussed by Spitzer, some of them very well, including their literary journalism. It was the generation for whom Victor Cousin (Tocqueville and Beaumont jestingly called him "notre Platon") was the intellectual and moral guru.

4. *OCB* 1:434.
5. *OC* VIII, 1:162.
6. On *Le Commerce*, see Roger Boesche, "Tocqueville and *L'Commerce*: A Newspaper Expressing His Unusual Liberalism," *Journal of the History of Ideas* (April 1983), 277–92. Boesche discusses Tocqueville's ideas rather than the internal politics of the journal. See also Jardin, *Tocqueville*, 388–96; and *OC* VII, 93–113, for Tocqueville and Marie's letters to Francis Lieber, the journal's American correspondent. Important also is Tocqueville's troubled correspondence with Beaumont in *OC* VIII, 1:521–55.
7. *OCB* 1:437–38.
8. Gilbert, trans., *The Old Regime and the Revolution*, 157.
9. Ibid.
10. Ibid. Tocqueville uses these very same words in a letter to Kergorlay, *OC* XIII, 2:337.
11. Ibid., 337–38.
12. Ibid., 338.
13. *OC* XI, 25.
14. Ibid., 19–21.
15. Tocqueville's view of Thiers gradually became somewhat more moderate, especially after Royer-Collard pointed out Thiers's virtues. See *OC* XI, 27.
16. *Recollections*, 57–58. All through this angry work Tocqueville portrays Thiers as a vacillating opportunist.
17. Ibid., 90.
18. Ibid., 5.
19. *OC* XI, 61.
20. On Guizot, see Douglas Johnson, *Guizot*; and Pierre Rosanvallon, *Le Moment Guizot* (Paris, 1988).
21. *OC* XI, 61.
22. *OC* VI, 1:325.
23. Ibid., 336–38.
24. *DA*, vol. 1, introduction, p. 12.
25. *OCB* 2:455.

II.2. Vocation: The Responsibilities of Political Leaders

1. *OC* XI, 102.
2. Ibid., 103.
3. *OCB* 2, 436–37.
4. *OC* VI, 1:294.
5. Ibid., 303–4.
6. Ibid., 204.
7. *DA*, vol. 2, pt. II, chap. 15, p. 543.
8. Ibid., 548.
9. Ibid., 545.
10. *OC* XI, 146.

11. *OC* XIV, 291.
12. Ibid., 291.
13. Ibid., 294.
14. *OC* VIII, 1:163.

II.3. THE DEAD SEA OF POLITICS

1. *OC* XI, 46–47. On the campaign see annotations to *OC* VIII and XIII, and Jardin, *Tocqueville*.
2. *OC* XI, 46.
3. Ibid., 45–47.
4. *OCB* 2:439.
5. On the role of notables in local politics, see Tudesq, introduction to *OC* X.
6. *OC* XI, 64.
7. Ibid., 89–90.
8. Ibid., 90.
9. *OC* XIII, 1:476.
10. *OC* VIII, 1:316.
11. On Tocqueville's service on the Conseil de la Manche, see Tudesq, introduction to *OC* X; and L'Hommedé, *Un département français sous la monarchie de juillet.*
12. *OC* XI, 118.
13. *OC* X, introduction and "On Tariffs"; *OC* XIV, 232–33, 235.
14. Tudesq, introduction to *OC* X, 22–23.
15. *Recollections*, 88–89.
16. Ibid., 95.
17. Jardin, introduction to *OC* VIII.
18. Rémusat, *Mémoires*, 4:45.
19. *Recollections*, 25 n. 17.
20. Ibid., 10.
21. Ibid., 82.
22. Rémusat, *Mémoires*, 4:45.
23. *OCB* 1:61.
24. Ibid., 62.
25. Ibid., 63–64.
26. *OC* VIII, 1:487.
27. Ibid.
28. *OCB* 1:411.
29. Ibid., 432.
30. *OC* XI, 107.
31. Ibid., 107.
32. Ibid., 108.
33. Jardin, introduction to *OC* VIII, 1:31–32.
34. *OC* XI, 107–8.

II.4. Tocqueville's Aristocratic Liberalism

1. *DA*, vol. 2, pt. III, p. 543.
2. On Tocqueville and Algeria, see Pitts, ed., *Alexis de Tocqueville: Writings on Empire and Slavery*; also Richter, "Tocqueville on Algeria," *Review of Politics* 25; and Jardin, *Tocqueville*, 316–38 and *passim*.
3. For a comprehensive study of Tocqueville and slavery, see Jennings, *French Anti-Slavery, 1802–1848*; and Drescher, ed., *Tocqueville and Beaumont*, 98–173.
4. For more on Tocqueville and slavery, see part IV, chap. 1.
5. On the question of prison reform in France and in Tocqueville's time, see Drescher, *Tocqueville and Beaumont*, 60–97; and OC IV, introduction to vols. 1 and 2.
6. *On the Penitentiary System in the United States*, which won the Montyon Prize, immediately established Tocqueville and Beaumont as central authorities on prisons and penal reform. The data-packed appendixes are to be found in OC IV, 1. From 1832 on, their correspondence is full of prison affairs.
7. Drescher, *Tocqueville and Beaumont*, 79.
8. OC XVI, 572.
9. Drescher, *Tocqueville and Beaumont*, 80–81.
10. On Tocqueville and the Constitution, see Jardin, *Tocqueville*; OC XV; and OC VIII, 2.
11. On the intervention in Rome and on papal reform, see OC XV, 2; also Jardin, *Tocqueville*.
12. Tocqueville's speech of January 27, 1848, is in appendix III, 749–58, of the Mayer-Lawrence edition of *DA*.
13. OC III, 2; notes to Dufaure.
14. Tocqueville's Irish and English notebooks, OC V, 1, have been translated by Lawrence as *Tocqueville's Journeys in England and Ireland*.
15. OC VI, 2:70.
16. Tocqueville's shock on seeing Manchester perhaps lies behind the bleak chapters on the human and social effects of manufacturing in *DA*, in which he fears the possibility that industrialism might turn workers into automata and rob them of their humanity.
17. Tocqueville's paper on pauperism from 1835 is in OC XVI, 117–39; and in Drescher, *Tocqueville and Beaumont*, 1–28.
18. Drescher, *Tocqueville and Beaumont*, 7.
19. Ibid., 9.
20. Ibid., 11.
21. Tocqueville had already slammed the idea in one of the appendixes to *The Penitentiary System*. See part IV, chap. 4 below. See also his reports on *enfants trouvées* for the Counseil de la Manche in OC X, 593–692.
22. Drescher, *Tocqueville and Beaumont*, 19.
23. Ibid., 25.
24. See William H. Sewell, Jr., *Work and Revolution in France: The Language of Labor from the Old Regime to 1848* (Cambridge: Cambridge University Press, 1980).
25. OC XV, 2:291–92.

III.1. A Moral Landscape

1. All quotations in this chapter are from the first chapter of *DA*.

III.2. A Moral History

1. All quotations in this chapter are from Tocqueville's introduction to *DA*.
2. See Philip Rieff, *The Triumph of the Therapeutic: Uses of Faith after Freud* (New York: Harper and Row, 1966).
3. See Ralph Waldo Emerson, "Circles."

III.3. Escape

1. *OC* IV, 1. *Du Système Pénitentiaire* was published in 1833. See the Tocqueville–Beaumont correspondence from 1832 to 1833 (*OC* VIII, 1) for their exchanges about this work. It has been edited and translated by Thorsten Sellin as *On the Penitentiary System in the United States* (Berkeley: University of California Press, 1975). This edition lacks the original appendixes.
2. *OC* VIII, 1:279.
3. Ibid., 1:111–12.
4. On the cholera in France, see *OC* VIII, 1:111–15; and *OC* XIII, 1:247–49.
5. *OC* XIV, 144.
6. Jardin, *Tocqueville*, 94–95.
7. Fumaroli, *Chateaubriand: Poesie et Terreur*, 721.
8. *OC* XIII, 1:374.
9. *OC* VII, 199.
10. Nolla, ed., *De La Démocratie en Amérique*, by Alexis de Tocqueville, 2 vols., 44–45 note g.
11. See *OC* VIII, 3:240, for dangers of the "new" (post-1830s) immigration.
12. See ibid., 247–49, on his investments.

III.4. The New World

1. Durand Echeverria, *Mirage in the West*; and Fumaroli, *Chateaubriand*, pt. III, chap. 1, pp. 323–37.
2. A. Bartlett Giamatti, *The Earthly Paradise and the Renaissance Epic*. Princeton: Princeton University Press, 1966.
3. Millennialist fantasies about the New World were largely English, not French.
4. See Echeverria on myths about America in eighteenth- and early nineteenth-century French literature. The old myth of America remained alive as late as Stendhal.
5. Rémond, *Les États-Unis devant l'opinion Française, 1815–1852*.
6. Ibid., 132.
7. On Guizot, see Douglas Johnson, *Guizot*, and below, 256–62. For Guizot's influence on Tocqueville, see Melvin Richter, "The Deposition of Alexis de Tocqueville,"

Tocqueville Review 26, no. 1; Gannett, *Tocqueville Unveiled, passim*; Jardin, *Tocqueville*, 81–82; and Furet, "The Intellectual Origins of Tocqueville's Thought," *Tocqueville Review* 7: 120–24.

8. *OC* VIII. Tocqueville's letters to Beaumont in 1829 and 1830 are full of enthusiasm for Guizot's lectures and his *Histories*.

9. On Guizot's historical vision and analytic method, see Gannett, *Tocqueville Unveiled, passim*.

10. François de Chateaubriand, *Mémoires d'outre-tombe*, 1:375; 2:146; and Fumaroli, *Chateaubriand*, part III.

11. *DA*, vol. 2, pt. I, chap. 17, p. 487.

12. Quoted in Richard Switzer, *Chateaubriand* (New York: Twayne, 1971).

13. Op. cit., and *OC* VI, 2:301.

14. *OC* VIII, 1:145.

15. Ibid., 145. Beaumont on their effort to get rid of traces of Chateaubriand.

16. Ibid., 337–38.

III.5. TOCQUEVILLE IN THE WILDERNESS

1. See *JA* for his essays as well as his notes.

2. *OC* XIV, 96–97.

3. For source of the Oneida story, see *OC* XIV, 119 n. 1.

4. *JA*, 127. All quotations are from this edition of *JA* translated by George Lawrence.

5. Ibid., 127–28.

6. *OC* XIV, 119–20.

7. Ibid., 120–21.

8. Ibid., 121.

9. Ibid.

10. Ibid.

11. *JA*, 345–46. Tocqueville wrote this piece sometime before 1838.

12. Ibid., 343.

13. Ibid.

14. Ibid., 343–44.

15. Ibid., 348.

16. Ibid., 348–49. This story became the basis in part for Beaumont's *Marie*.

17. Tocqueville surely must have known that many Frenchmen had been on the ground he was walking. French place names and French-speaking Indians must have made that evident, but in his romantic reverie he had moved beyond the reach of France.

18. *JA*, 350–403.

19. *JA*, 144–46.

20. Ibid., 143.

21. Ibid., 374–75.

22. Ibid., 376.

23. Ibid., 388.

24. Ibid., 144.
25. Ibid., 381.
26. Ibid., 401–2.
27. Ibid., 140.
28. Ibid., 403.
29. *DA*, introduction.

III.6. Transformations

1. *JA*, 351.
2. Ibid., 204.
3. *DA*, vol. 1, pt. II, chap. 10, p. 324.
4. Ibid., 329.
5. *JA*, 393–94, 396.
6. *DA*, vol. 1, pt. II, chap. 16, pp. 327–31.
7. Tocqueville to Chabrol, October 1831 from New York City.
8. *JA*, 363–64. This cold killer of the frontier appears first in Tocqueville's notebooks.
9. Ibid., 363.
10. Ibid., 393.
11. Ibid., 364.
12. Ibid.
13. Ibid., 395.
14. Ibid., 397–98.
15. Ibid., 399.

III.7. Beginning *Democracy in America*

1. *OC* XI, 44.
2. Quoted in Pierson, *Tocqueville and Beaumont in America*.
3. *OCB* 1.
4. *OC* XIV, 144.
5. Ibid., 166.
6. *OC* VIII, 1:136.
7. Ibid., 323.
8. *OC* VI, 1:31.
9. Ibid., 313–14.
10. *OC* VI, 2:82.
11. *OC* VIII, 1:150.
12. *OC* XIII, 1:356.
13. *OC* XI, 34.
14. *OC* VI, 1:318–24, esp. 323.
15. See Jerrold Siegel, *Bohemian Paris*.
16. *OC* XI, 29.

17. Ibid., 51.
18. For Rémusat on Tocqueville, see *Mémoires*.
19. OC VIII, 1:193.

III.8. INFLUENCES

1. OC VIII, 1:284.
2. Quoted in Nolla, *De La Démocratie*, 2:59 note c.
3. *CW*, 18:95–96.
4. OC VIII, 1:317.
5. Ibid., 326.
6. Ibid., 329.
7. OC XIII, 1:418.
8. OC VIII, 1:279.
9. Ibid., 2:329.
10. Henry James, "The Two Ampères," in *Literary Criticism: French Writers; Other European Writers.*
11. Ibid.
12. OC XI, quoted xvi–xvii.
13. Ibid., 139–45.
14. Ibid., quoted v.
15. Ibid., 97–104.
16. The following account of Royer-Collard's political ideas and moral philosophy is based on Laski, *Authority in the Modern State*; Lamberti, *Tocqueville and the Two Democracies*; Rosanvallon, *La démocratie inachevée*; and the editorial annotations to OC XI.
17. OC III, 3:465–70 .
18. Quoted in Laski, *Authority in the Modern State.*
19. OC XI, ix.
20. Ibid., ix.
21. Ibid., 103.
22. OC VI, 1:295–96.
23. Ibid., 292. Mill often wrote to Tocqueville in French, Tocqueville rarely in English. Mill had studied in France as a youth, was fluent in French, and was widely read in French literature and history.
24. Ibid., 294.
25. Ibid., 294–95.
26. Packe, *Life of John Stuart Mill*, on Harriet Taylor's biting comment on Tocqueville.
27. On Mill, see Packe, *Life of John Stuart Mill*. On Tocqueville's London encounter with Mill, Mazlish's *James and John Stuart Mill* is helpful.
28. *CW* 20:370.
29. On Mill and Comte and the Saint-Simonians, see *The Correspondence of John Stuart Mill and Auguste Comte*, ed. and trans. Oscar Haac (New Brunswick, N.J.: Transaction Books, 1995).

On Mill and French culture, see John C. Cairns's introduction to CW 20.
30. *OC* VI, 1:299.
31. Ibid.
32. See "Civilization," in *CW* 18:118–47.
33. Mill's review of *DA*, vol. 1, is found in *CW* 18:47–91. All quotes are from that edition of his work.
34. *CW* 18:86.
35. Ibid., 95–96.
36. Ibid., 125–26.
37. Ibid., 132.
38. Mill's review of *DA*, vol. 2, is found in *CW* 18:153–204.
39. On Reeve, see introduction to *OC* VI, 1.
40. Quoted in introduction to ibid., 1:9.
41. Reeve to Tocqueville, quoted in ibid., 10.
42. Ibid., 169–70.
43. On Bowen, see Daniel Walker Howe, *The Unitarian Conscience* (Cambridge: Harvard University Press, 1970).

III.9. WRITING AS MORAL ACT

1. *OC* XIII, 2:106; *OC* VIII, 1:95.
2. *OC* VI, 2:493, also 301.
3. Ibid., 494.
4. *Recollections*, 133.
5. Ibid., 134.
6. Ibid.
7. *OC* VII, 112.
8. *OC* VI, 2:430.
9. On Malesherbes, see Robert Darnton, *The Literary Underground of the Old Regime*. On Malesherbes and Rousseau, see Jean Guéhenno's biography of Rousseau (London: Routledge and Kegan Paul, 1966).
10. On Hervé de Tocqueville as a writer, see Palmer, *The Two Tocquevilles*.
11. Nolla, *De La Démocratie*, 72 note b.
12. Ibid., 44 note g.
13. Ibid., 63–64 note r.
14. Ibid.
15. Ibid.
16. *OC* XIII, 2:309.
17. Ibid., 1:366.
18. Ibid., 1:371.
19. Ibid., 2:300.
20. Ibid., 305–6.
21. Ibid., 305.

22. Ibid.
23. Ibid., 308.
24. Ibid., 308–9.
25. *OCB* 1:62 (Beaumont's biographical introduction to his edition of Tocqueville's *Oeuvres Complétes*).
26. *OC* VIII, 1:379.
27. *OCB* 1:320.
28. *OC* VIII, 1:152.
29. *DA*, vol. 2, pt. I, chap. 13, pp. 473–74.
30. LaCapra, *History and Reading*.
31. White, *Metahistory*.
32. *DA*, vol. 1, pt. II, chap. 9, p. 279.
33. *DA*, vol. 1, pt. I, chap. 2, p. 36.

III.10. HISTORY AS MORAL DRAMA

1. *DA*, vol. 1, pt. I, chap. 2, pp. 31–32.
2. On French historical writing in the early nineteenth century, see Gossman, *Between History and Literature*.
3. *CW* 20:18.
4. On French Restoration historians, see Mellon, *The Political Uses of History*.
5. Gannett, *Tocqueville Unveiled*, 28–29.
6. *OC* XI, 25–27. Tocqueville's notes on Thiers's *History* are in *OC* XVI, 537–40.
7. On the new historiography of law and jurisprudence, see Kelley, *Historians and the Law in Postrevolutionary France*.
8. See Barzun, *Race in France*; and Krzyzstof Pomian, "Franks and Gauls," in Pierre Nora, ed., *Realms of Memory*. Also Gossman, *Between History and Literature*, 100–101.
9. Gossman, *Between History and Literature*, 94.
10. Ibid., 86–88.
11. Ibid., on Thierry, Guizot, and Michelet.
12. On Guizot, see Johnson, *Guizot, Aspects of French History*; and Rosanvallon, *Le Moment Guizot*.
13. On Guizot's influence on Tocqueville, see Gannett, *Tocqueville Unveiled*.
14. *OC* VIII, 1:90–92.
15. Ibid.
16. Criautu, introduction to *The History and Origins of Representative Government in Europe* by Guizot.
17. Beaumont, *Marie*, 3–4, 6–7.
18. *DA*, introduction, vol. 1, pp. 19–20.
19. *CW* 20:370.
20. *OC* XVI, 229–42.
21. Ibid., 244.
22. Ibid.

23. Furet, quoted in Gannett, *Tocqueville Unveiled*, 24–25.
24. *OC* VI, 2:478–79.
25. Chapters 2 and 3 of *DA* are devoted to the Puritans. His reading in seventeenth-century American sources and histories is noted in appendix I of *DA*. See also Nolla, notes to his edition of *De La Démocratie*.
26. *DA*, vol. 1, pt. I, chap. 2, p. 39.
27. Ibid., chap. 2.
28. Ibid., vol. 1, pp. 42–43.
29. Ibid., 36.
30. Ibid.
31. Ibid., 39.
32. Ibid., 46.
33. Ibid., 46–47.
34. *DA*, vol. 2, pt. I, chap. 20, pp. 495–96. On Tocqueville's thinking about the issue of moral choice and will in history, see Mitchell, *Individual Choice and the Structures of History*.
35. *DA*, vol. 2, p. 495.
36. *OC* XVI, 230–31.
37. Furet, see above, note 23.
38. For Jardin's discussion of Tocqueville's knowledge of the historical works of his contemporaries and of his failure to acknowledge their influence, see Jardin, *Tocqueville*, 483–84.
39. On Tocqueville's "remarkable discretion" about his reading, see Furet, *Interpreting the French Revolution*, 135.
40. See Gannett, *Tocqueville Unveiled*, for more on the work of others Tocqueville had used without acknowledgment.
41. *OC* XIII, 2:302.
42. Luis Diaz del Corral, "Tocqueville et Pascal," *Revue des Travaux de l'Académie des sciences morales*, 1965, 2d semestre, 70–83.
43. *OC* XVI, 551–54.
44. Fumaroli, *Chateaubriand*, 758–60.
45. On Cousin's influence, see Spitzer, *The French Generation of 1820*; and Siegel, *The Idea of the Self*.
46. Rosanvallon, *La démocratie inachevée*, chap. 3.
47. Furet, *Interpreting the French Revolution*, 135.

III.11. THE BIRTH OF A BOOK

1. *OC* VI, 303–4.
2. *OC* XI, 59.
3. *OC* VI, 1:35.
4. Ibid., 2:314.
5. Ibid., 82.

6. *OC* XIII, 2:47.
7. *OCB* 2:344.
8. *OC* XI, 59.
9. Ibid., 64
10. Ibid., 45
11. *OC* VI, 1:30.
12. Ibid., 47.
13. *OC* VIII, 3:374.

IV.1. Tocqueville's American Notebooks and *Democracy in America*

1. Tocqueville returned from the United States with fourteen notebooks, which he appears to have used randomly. Some of the notebooks were topical, some primarily contain quotes in commonplace book style or his transcriptions of interviews held earlier in the day. The notebooks, published in the *Oeuvres Complètes* (Tome V), were edited by the pioneering Tocqueville scholar J.-P. Mayer, translated by George Lawrence, and published as *Journey to America* (New York: Doubleday, 1971). All references are to the paperback version of 1971 and are cited as *JA* + page number(s). I have used the Lawrence translation throughout.
2. Recent notable examples are Jean Baudrillard, *America*; and Bernard-Henri Lévy, *American Vertigo*. Both look back to Tocqueville.
3. Exemplary interpretations in this vein are Walter McDougall, *Freedom Just Around the Corner: A New American History, 1685–1828* (New York: HarperCollins, 2004); and Daniel Boorstin, *The Americans: The Democratic Experience* (New York: Random House, 1973).
4. An outstanding guide is Ronald Walters, *American Reformers, 1815–1860* (New York: Hill and Wang, 1978). See also Emerson's essay, "New England Reformers."
5. Still the most penetrating study of the early nineteenth-century American cultural coming of age, by an admirer of Tocqueville, is Francis Otto Matthiessen, *American Renaissance* (New York: Oxford University Press, 1941). Also illuminating is Irving Howe, *The American Newness* (Cambridge: Harvard University Press, 1987), which catches the hopes and fantasies that burst forth at the time of Tocqueville's visit.
6. For a comprehensive, detailed, and lucid history of the political, social, and cultural history of the United States from the late eighteenth century to the Civil War, see Sean Wilentz, *The Rise of American Democracy* (New York: Norton, 2005). Wilentz's endnotes and bibliography constitute a thorough guide to the historical literature of the past half century. Wilentz describes the America that Tocqueville could have known had he been more thorough and less hasty.
7. See below, pp. 290–294.
8. *OC* XIV, 166.
9. *DA*, vol. 1, pt. II, chap. 10.
10. *OC* XIV, 144.

11. *DA*, vol. 1, conclusion, p. 411.
12. *CW* 18:95–96.

IV.2. TRAVELING THROUGH THE NEW REPUBLIC WITH TOCQUEVILLE AND BEAUMONT

1. Pierson's *Tocqueville and Beaumont in America* is a detailed narrative analysis of Tocqueville's and Beaumont's journey, thoroughly documented with quotes from their correspondence and notebooks. A paperback reprinting (Baltimore: Johns Hopkins University Press, 1997), though otherwise unchanged, is regrettably and misleadingly titled *Tocqueville in America*. Beaumont was with Tocqueville every step of the way: they discussed everything, shared observations, and shaped one another's thinking. I believe Beaumont was a major influence on Tocqueville's thinking.
2. I focus largely on Tocqueville in my discussion of their journey through the United States, avoiding the cumbersomeness of referring to "Tocqueville and Beaumont."
3. *JA*, 363, 393.
4. Ibid., 197–98.
5. Ibid., 364
6. Ibid., 263. Also see *DA*, vol. 1, pt. II, chap. 5, pp. 224–26.
7. On the riots of 1828 and 1834 in New York City, see Wallace and Burrows, *Gotham*.
8. On pig riots, see Paul A. Gilje, *The Road to Mobocracy: Popular Disorder in New York City, 1763 to 1834* (Chapel Hill: University of North Carolina Press, 1987).
9. *JA*, 46, 49.
10. On Turner, Garrison, and Walker, see Wilentz, *The Rise of American Democracy*, 340–41.
11. *DA*, vol. 1, pt. II, chap. 10, pp. 316–17.
12. Ibid., 340–43.
13. See Drescher, *Tocqueville and Beaumont on Social Reform*, for Tocqueville's "Report on Abolition," 1839.
14. Tocqueville to Chabrol, June 9, 1831, quoted in Pierson, *Tocqueville and Beaumont in America*, 130.
15. *JA*, 276.
16. *DA*, vol. 2, pt. I, chap. 19, pp. 492–93.
17. *JA*, 165.
18. Beaumont, quoted in Pierson, *Tocqueville and Beaumont in America*, 50.
19. Quoted in ibid., 356.
20. *JA*, 402.
21. *OC* XIV, 83.
22. *JA*, 113.
23. *OC* XIII, 144.
24. Ibid.
25. *OC* XIII, 1:232. The absence of a fixed superior class is central to Tocqueville's analysis of the culture of democracy. It especially shapes all of vol. 2, pt. I, of *DA*.

IV.3. Democratic Religion

1. *OC* XIII, 1:225.
2. *OC* XIV, 117.
3. Ibid., 116–17.
4. See McLoughlin, *Modern Revivalism*; and Whitney Cross, *The Burned-Over District: The Social and Intellectual History of Enthusiastic Religion In Western New York, 1800–1850*.
5. *DA*, vol. 2, pt. II, chap. 12, p. 534.
6. Nolla, *De La Démocratie*, appendix III, "Les Sectes en Amérique," 2:318–20.
7. Ibid., 319–20.
8. Ibid., 320.
9. *DA*, vol. 2, pt. II, chap. 12, pp. 34–35.
10. Ibid., chap. 9, pp. 528–30.
11. Ibid., chap. 15, pp. 542–46.
12. On Finney's techniques, see William McLoughlin, *Modern Revivalism* (New York: Ronald Press, 1959). On Finney in Rochester, see Paul Johnson, *A Shopkeeper's Millennium: Society and Revivals in Rochester, New York, 1815–1837* (New York: Hill and Wang, 1978). On the minister as entrepreneur of a religious industry, see *JA*, 183.
13. See Ann Douglas, *The Feminization of American Culture* (New York: Knopf, 1977).
14. *DA*, vol. 1, chap. 9, p. 291.
15. Ibid., 294.
16. *JA*, 70. Stewart, however, argued that religion had become an oppressive force in American life in that popular opinion did not tolerate skepticism or disbelief and thus silenced dissent. Tocqueville is silent about this in *DA*, though he may have had it in mind when he wrote about the power and oppressiveness of public opinion in America.
17. *JA*, 61.
18. Ibid., 70.
19. *OC* XIII, 1:229.
20. *JA*, 189.
21. *DA*, vol. 1, pt. II, chap. 5, pp. 447–49; vol. 2, pt. II, chap. 9, p. 530.
22. *JA*, 54.
23. Ibid., 53.
24. Ibid., 61.
25. Ibid., 109.
26. *DA*, vol. 2, pt. III, chap. 12, p. 603.
27. Nolla, *De La Démocratie*, vol. 2, chap. 16 (Tocqueville's notes).
28. *DA*, vol. 1, pt. II, chap. 9, p. 291.
29. Ibid., 291–92.

IV.4. Class in an Egalitarian Society

1. *JA*, 225, 290, 191, 200.
2. Ibid., 273; see also 231.

3. Ibid., 275.
4. Ibid., 245.
5. *DA*, vol. 1, pt. III, chap. 5.
6. OC IV, vol. 1, appendix III, 319–22.
7. Ibid.
8. Tocqueville's notes on his Eastern Penitentiary interviews are in OC IV, vol. 1, appendix VII, 329–41.
9. OC IV, vol. 1, appendix IV, 323–24.
10. OC VII, 29.
11. See Wilentz, *The Rise of American Democracy*; Burrows and Wallace, *Gotham*.
12. See Burrows and Wallace, *Gotham*.
13. *DA*, vol. 2, pt. III, chap. 13, pp. 537–38.
14. JA, 273–74.
15. Ibid., 225.
16. Ibid.
17. Ibid., 274.
18. OC XIII, 1:226.

IV.5. BORN-AGAIN AMERICA

1. JA, 52–53.
2. Tocqueville does not use this expression, but he discovers to his astonishment that the Americans have quickly forged a new identity, a new "esprit."
3. JA, May 1831.
4. Ibid., December 1831.
5. Ibid., January 1832.
6. For U.S. immigration statistics and history, see Herbert Klein, *A Population History of the United States* (Cambridge: Cambridge University Press, 2004).
7. OC III, 3:233.
8. JA, 392 ("A Fortnight in the Wilds").
9. Ibid.
10. Ibid.
11. Ibid.
12. Ibid., 163–64.
13. Ibid., 179.
14. Ibid., 193; also 197–98.
15. Ibid., 162.
16. Ibid., 186–87.
17. Tocqueville uses this expression in JA, 275–77. It had earlier appeared in Royer-Collard's writings about democracy.
18. Just before he left the United States, Tocqueville reviewed the factors that shaped the "social state" of a people. See JA, 185.
19. Tocqueville's observations about the various regional cultures of the United States are acute. His comments on the differences between the cultures of New York and Boston

remind one of Henry James's views. Tocqueville was most comfortable in Boston. On New York, see *JA*, 208; on Boston, see *JA*, 36, 43, 209; on southern culture, see *JA*, 49, 62, 88–92, 169–80, 275–84.

20. *JA*, 186.
21. Ibid., 187.
22. Ibid., 89.
23. Ibid., 177.
24. Ibid., 186.
25. Ibid.
26. Ibid., 183.
27. *OC XIII*, 1:226.
28. *DA*, vol. 1, pt. II, chap. 7, pp. 254–55.
29. *OC XIII*, 1:226–27.
30. *JA*, 148.
31. Tocqueville explores the intellectual effects of democracy in *DA*, vol. 2, pt. II, and the power of public opinion in *DA*, vol. 1, pp. 250–59.

IV.6. Politics

1. *JA*, 158. Tocqueville has equally harsh comments about Jackson in *DA*, 393–94. In his notebooks he astonishingly calls Jackson "a heartless despot" and a "desperate political gangster" (*JA*, 161). Was he repeating some Jackson-hater's words?
2. *DA*, 257–59.
3. *JA*, 161.
4. Ibid., 267.
5. Ibid., 267–68.
6. For a sketch of Crockett's complicated political career, and for the quotation from his frontier tall-tale bombast, see Wilentz, *Rise of American Democracy*, 432–33. The adventurous Crockett died at the Alamo, after he had had enough of political life.
7. *DA*, vol. 1, pt. II, chap. 3 ("Freedom of the Press in the United States"), and vol. 2, pt. II, chap. 6 ("On the Connection Between Associations and Newspapers"). Curiously, he was advised by Marie to say as little as possible about journalism in the United States because he was not well informed (Nolla, *De La Démocratie* 2:107–10).
8. *JA*, 251–57.
9. Ibid., 268.
10. Ibid. (quoting Kent), 268.
11. Ibid., 251; see also 170–72 and *DA*, vol. 1, pt. II, p. 175.
12. *JA*, 171.
13. Ibid., 251.
14. Ibid.
15. Ibid., 80–81.
16. Ibid., 218.

17. On constitutionally established suffrage limits in the several states in 1831–32, see Alexander Keyssar, *The Right to Vote: The Contested History of Democracy in the United States* (New York: Basic Books, 2000).

18. *DA*, vol. 2, pt. III, chap. 21, with its despairing pages on the power and inertia of masses, who scorn or will not listen to different voices.

19. *JA*, 155.

20. *DA*, vol. 1, pt. II, chaps. 7 and 8; also vol. 2, pt. III, chap. 21. In fact, the power of public opinion, bearing with it the possibility of majoritarian tyranny, is the implicit subject of the whole of volume 2 of *DA*.

21. *JA*, 155.

22. Ibid., 244.

23. Ibid., 262–63.

24. Ibid., 263.

25. Ibid., 171.

26. Ibid., 155.

27. Ibid., 167.

28. Ibid., 38–39. It was in New England that Tocqueville wrote (to his friend Chabrol, October 7, 1831) of "the spectacle of a society proceeding all alone, without guide or support, by the single fact of the concourse of individual wills."

29. *JA*, 209. On Tuckerman, see Howe, *The Unitarian Conscience*. Howe is a lucid analyst of the intellectual and moral milieu of Unitarian Boston and Harvard. He also writes about Francis Bowen, a professor of moral philosophy at Harvard who provided a moral revision of Reeve's translation of *Democracy in America*.

30. *JA*, 231.

31. Ibid., 78–79.

32. Ibid., 152.

33. *DA*, vol. 1, pt. I, chap. 5.

34. Ibid., vol. 2, pt. III, chap. 8, and the subsequent chapters on women.

35. *JA*, 152, 229.

36. Ibid., 219.

37. Ibid., 266.

38. Ibid., 199.

39. Ibid., 269.

40. Ibid., 287–88.

41. Ibid., 288.

42. Ibid., 271.

43. Ibid., 272.

44. Ibid., 257.

45. Tocqueville included a long chapter on democratic honor in the second volume of *DA*. It somewhat masked his critical views (see my part I, chap. 10). Honor had been perhaps the central value of aristocratic cultures. He consulted his father about the nature of aristocratic honor—and received a lengthy analysis. For Hervé's essay and for comments by his brother Edouard, see Nolla, *De La Démocratie* 2:192–202.

46. *JA*, 260–61.

47. Ibid., 178–79.
48. Ibid., 245–46.
49. Ibid., 246.
50. Ibid., 247.
51. Ibid., 245–46.

IV.7. A DARK VISION OF DEMOCRACY'S PROSPECTS

1. *DA*, vol. 2, pt. IV, chap. 6 ("What Sort of Despotism Democratic Nations Have to Fear"), p. 692 and *passim*.
2. *DA*, 464–65; also 534, 632, 645. Tocqueville discusses the inertial tendencies of democracy and the prospect that they might lead to spiritual emptiness throughout the second volume of *DA*. It is a murmur that grows louder as his book unfolds.
3. *DA*, vol. 2, pt. I, chaps. 10 and 11.
4. Ibid., 687–88.
5. Ibid., 11–12.
6. Ibid., 679.
7. Ibid., 674.
8. See Seymour Drescher, *Dilemmas of Democracy: Tocqueville and Modernization* (Pittsburgh: University of Pittsburgh Press, 1968).

IV.8. THE DEMOCRATIC PSYCHE

1. *DA*, 508, 671.
2. Ibid., 604.
3. Ibid., 671.
4. Ibid., 673.
5. See *DA*, vol. 1, pt. 2, chap. 7; and vol. 2, pt. 3, chap. 21.
6. Ibid., 537.
7. Ibid., 52–54, 614–15.
8. Ibid., 32.
9. See Marvin Meyers, *The Jacksonian Persuasion* (Stanford: Stanford University Press, 1957), and especially *DA*, vol. 2, pt. III, chap. 21.
10. *DA*, vol. 2, pt. III, chap. 21, pp. 638, 671. The major development of this idea is in *DA*, pp. 634–45.
11. Ibid., 540.
12. Ibid., 535–38.
13. OC XIV, 19–25.

IV.9. A CULTURE OF EXTREMES

1. *DA*, 159.
2. Ibid., vol. 2, pt. II, chap. 19.

3. Ibid., vol. 2, pt. II, chap. 20.

4. Ibid., 611.

5. Ibid., 472.

6. Ibid., 473.

7. Ibid.

8. Ibid., 474.

9. Ibid., 549, 483–84.

10. Ibid., 429.

11. Ibid.

12. Ibid., 534–46, 547–49, 429–34.

13. Ibid., 542–46.

14. Ibid., vol. 2, pt. II, chaps. 15, 16.

15. Ibid., 536.

16. Ibid., 704.

17. Ibid., 56.

18. Ibid., 468.

19. Ibid., vol. 2, pt. I, chaps. 12, 17, 18.

20. Ibid., 489.

21. Ibid., 487.

22. Ibid., 489.

BIBLIOGRAPHY

PRIMARY

This study of Tocqueville is based largely on his *Oeuvres Complètes*. The many "Tomes" of this ultimate edition of Tocqueville's writing are listed below, along with their editors, whose introductory essays and detailed annotations have been immensely helpful. The *Oeuvres* comprise all his writing: books, essays and political papers, huge correspondence, speeches and notes about various matters, and some reading notes. They are a model definitive Collected Works—though the indexes are not conceptual or topical, and one must look elsewhere for bibliographical guidance. Taken together, the introductory essays and the notes constitute a biography of Tocqueville and a history of his time. Especially valuable is his abundant correspondence with friends and colleagues. It is in the correspondence, much of which is candid and confessional, that one gets close to this elusive and complicated man and thus can begin to understand the roots of his ideas and the dynamics of his imagination. Valuable too are the minibiographies, embedded in the notes, of many of Tocqueville's political and literary contemporaries.

I have also utilized Gustave Beaumont's edition of Tocqueville's *Oeuvres* (1861), which made important correspondence (sometimes heavily edited and misdated) available before Antoine Redier's *Comme Disait M. de Tocqueville* (1926) and then the *OC* (1951—) appeared. Beaumont's edition is cited as *OCB*, the complete modern edition as *OC* followed by Tome number (I, II, etc.), volume number, and page number.

For those who wish to read Tocqueville in English, I also list translated editions of his major works, to which my citations refer. I have used George Lawrence's translated versions of *Democracy in America*, *The Old Regime and the Revolution*, his notebooks (published as *Journey to America*), his England and Ireland travel notes (published as *Journey to England and Ireland*), and his *Souvenirs* (published as *Recollections*). I have used Thorsten Sellin's version of *On the Penitentiary System in the United States*. My note citations are to the editions Lawrence translated. Translations of Tocqueville's correspondence in the *Oeuvres Complètes*, unless otherwise noted, are mine. Translations from the works by Seymour Drescher and John Lukacs are theirs.

There are excellent, more recent translations of Tocqueville's major works, especially Arthur Goldhammer's superb translation of *Democracy in America* as well as Alan Kahan's translation of *The Old Regime and the French Revolution*, but I have long admired the great clarity and straightforwardness of Lawrence's translation, which I read as a graduate student long before I read Tocqueville's French. Lawrence seems to me to capture Tocqueville's meanings and tone, though he occasionally flattens Tocqueville's elegant style, which Tocqueville had worked thoughtfully to perfect, modeling himself on classic French writers, hoping to produce an enduring work. However, Tocqueville also sought to be a journalist, though he failed to achieve the style du jour in his writings for the press and in his speeches and was sometimes mocked and parodied for the ornateness and pomposity of his prose. I was tempted to use Goldhammer's eloquent version of the *Democracy*, but my familiarity and satisfaction with Lawrence decided the matter. I have also listed other available translations below. These all have their virtues, and their readers will understand Tocqueville well enough with any of them. The long history of Tocqueville translations, beginning with Henry Reeve's, is an interesting subject in itself, as are the introductory essays about the continuing relevance of *Democracy in America* that have accompanied all the new editions (or volumes of selections) that have appeared regularly since the late nineteenth century.

The most recent edition of the *Democracy* has just been published in four volumes by the Liberty Press, edited by Edouard Nolla and annotated as well as newly translated by the Tocqueville scholar James Schleifer, who knows Tocqueville intimately and whose work has long been devoted to his thought and life.

Oeuvres Completès (OC) I, 2v, *De La Démocratie en Amérique*, ed. Harold Laski.
OC II, 2v, *L'Ancien Régime et la Révolution*, ed. J.-P. Mayer.
OC III, 3v, *Écrits et Discours Politique*, ed. André Jardin, Françoise Mélonio.
OC IV, 2v, *Écrits sur le Systeme Pénitentiaire en France et à l'Étrangère*, ed. Michelle Perrot.
OC V, 2v, *Voyages*, ed. J.-P. Mayer.
OC VI, 2v, *Correspondance Anglaise*, ed. Hugh Brogan and P. Kerr.
OC VII, 1v, *Correspondance Étrangère*, ed. Françoise Mélonio, Lise Quéffeleque, Anthony Pleasance.

OC VIII,3v, *Correspondance d'Alexis de Tocqueville et de Gustave de Beaumont*, ed. André Jardin.

OC IX, 1v, *Correspondance d'Alexis de Tocqueville et Arthur de Gobineau*, ed. M. Degros and J-J Chevallier.

OC X, 1v, *Correspondance et écrits locaux*, ed. André-Jean Tudesq and Lise-Quéffelec-Dumasy.

OC XI, 1v, *Correspondance d'Alexis de Tocqueville et Pierre-Paul Royer-Collard; et d'Alexis de Tocqueville et Jean-Jacques Ampère*, ed. Andre Jardin.

OC XII, 1v, *Souvenirs*, ed. Luc Monnier.

OC XIII, 2v, *Correspondance d'Alexis de Tocqueville et de Louis de Kergorlay*, ed. Jean-Alain Lesourd.

OC XIV, 1v, *Correspondance familiale*, ed. Jean-Louis Benoit and Andre Jardin.

OC XV, 2v, *Correspondance d'Alexis de Tocqueville et de Francisque de Corcelle; de Tocqueville et Madame Swetchine*, ed. Pierre Gibert.

OC XVI, 1v, *Mélanges*, ed. Françoise Mélonio.

OC XVIII, *Correspondance d'Alexis de Tocqueville avec Adolphe de Circourt; et d'Alexis de Tocqueville avec Mme Circourt*, ed. A. P. Kerr.

Edouard Nolla, ed., *Alexis de Tocqueville, De La Démocratie en Amérique*, 2 volumes, annotated, with Tocqueville's notes and marginal comments, excerpts from Tocqueville's letters, and letters to him, and various appendixes. This heavily annotated version of the *Democracy* includes many of Beaumont's travel sketches as well as marginal comments by family members and friends who read the manuscript.

Translations

Alexis de Tocqueville, *Democracy in America*, ed. J.-P. Mayer, trans. George Lawrence. New York, 1951 (paperback, 2 volumes in 1).

——— . *Journey to America* (Tocqueville's American Notebooks), ed. J.-P. Mayer, trans. George Lawrence. New Haven: Yale University Press, 1959.

——— . *The Old Regime and the French Revolution*, ed. and trans. Stuart Gilbert. Garden City, N.Y.: Doubleday, 1955.

——— . *Recollections*, ed. J.-P. Mayer, trans. George Lawrence. New Brunswick, N.J.: Transaction Books, 1987.

——— . *Journeys to England and Ireland*, ed. J.-P. Mayer, trans. George Lawrence. New York, 1968

Alexis de Tocqueville and Gustave de Beaumont. *On the Penitentiary System in the United States and Its Application to France*, ed. Thorsten Sellin. Carbondale: University of Southern Illinois Press, 1964.

John Lukacs, ed. *Correspondence of Alexis de Tocqueville and Arthur de Gobineau*, in *The European Revolution and the Correspondence of Tocqueville and Gobineau*, intro. and trans. John Lukacs, Garden City, N.Y.: Doubleday, 1959.

Roger Boesche, ed. *Alexis de Tocqueville: Selected Letters on Politics and Society*, trans. Roger Boesche and James Toupin. Berkeley: University of California Press, 1985.

OTHER AVAILABLE TRANSLATIONS OF DEMOCRACY IN AMERICA

Henry Reeve, Francis Bowen, and Phillips Bradley (Anchor)
Arthur Goldhammer (Library of America)
Harvey Mansfield and Delba Winthrop (University of Chicago Press)
James Schleifer (Liberty Fund)
Gerald Bevan (Penguin)

OTHER PRIMARY

Gustave de Beaumont. *Marie, or, Slavery in the United States*, trans. Barbara Chapman, introd. Alvis Trinnin. Berkeley: University of California Press, 1958.
——— . *Lettres d'Amérique*. Paris, 1973.
John Stuart Mill. *Collected Works*, vol. 18, *Essays on French History and Historians*, introd. Alexander Brady. Toronto: University of Toronto Press, 1985.
——— . *Collected Works*, vol. 20, *Essays on Politics and Society*, ed. J. M. Robson, introd. Alexander Brady. Toronto: University of Toronto Press, 1977.
François de Chateaubriand. *Mémoires d'Outre-Tombe*.
Charles de Rémusat. *Mémoires de ma vie*.

SECONDARY

The Tocqueville literature is now a flood and is increasing rapidly. Since 1990 alone perhaps three hundred books about the man and his ideas have appeared, and the periodical literature is immense—manageable only by specialized reading. On the selective bibliography below I have listed only the books that I have in various ways found especially illuminating and that have informed my thinking about Tocqueville. I have learned much from many other scholars, and some of their work is cited in my notes. A bibliography of all the books and articles I have consulted would make too long a tail for this study. Even a quick search on the Internet will yield an abundance of books and articles for those who would like to pursue any aspect of Tocqueville's life and thought. Many of the books in my secondary bibliography offer extensive bibliographies.

These three outstanding studies appeared too late for me to benefit from them, followed by my list of secondary sources:

Criautu, Aurelian. *Tocqueville on America after 1840*. Cambridge: Cambridge University Press, 2009.
Damrosch, Leo. *Tocqueville's Discovery of America*. New York: Farrar, Straus and Giroux, 2010.
Goldstein, Jan. *The Post-Revolutionary Self: Politics and Psyche in France, 1750–1850*. Cambridge: Harvard University Press, 2009.

Barzun, Jacques. *The French Race*. New York, 1932

Baudrillard, Jean. *America*. New York: Verso, 1989.

Boesche, Roger. *The Strange Liberalism of Alexis de Tocqueville*. Ithaca: Cornell University Press, 1987.

——— . *Selected Letters of Alexis de Tocqueville on Society and Politics*. Translated by Roger Boesche and James Taupin. Berkeley: University of California Press, 1985.

Brogan, Hugh, *Tocqueville*. London: Fontana Press, 1973.

——— . *Alexis de Tocqueville, A Life*. New Haven: Yale University Press, 2007.

Burrows, Edwin G., and Mike Wallace. *Gotham: A History of New York City to 1898*. New York: Oxford University Press, 1998.

Criautu, Aurelian, ed. Introduction and notes to François Guizot, *The History and Origins of Representative Government in Europe*. Indianapolis, 2002.

Darnton, Robert. *The Literary Underground of the Old Regime*. Cambridge: Harvard University Press, 1982

Drescher, Seymour. *Tocqueville and England*. Pittsburgh: University of Pittsburgh Press, 1968.

——— . *Dilemmas of Democracy: Tocqueville and Modernization*. Pittsburgh: University of Pittsburgh Press, 1968.

——— , ed. *Tocqueville and Beaumont on Reform*. New York: Harper and Row, 1968.

Echeverria, Durand. *Mirage in the West*. Princeton: Princeton University Press. 1957.

Eisenstadt, Abraham, ed., *Reconsidering Tocqueville's Democracy in America*. New Brunswick, N.J.: Rutgers University Press, 1988.

Fumaroli, Marc. *Chateaubriand: Poésie et Terreur*. Paris, 2003.

Furet, François, "The Intellectual Origins of *Democracy in America*." *Tocqueville Review/ Revue Tocqueville* 26, no. 1, Numéro special bicentenaire (1805–2005), 2005.

——— . *Interpreting the French Revolution*. Translated by Elborg Foster. Cambridge: Cambridge University Press, 1981.

——— . *Revolutionary France: 1770–1880*. Oxford: Oxford University Press, 1992.

——— . "The Ancien Régime and the Revolution." In Pierre Nora, ed., *Realms of Memory*, vol. 1, *The Construction of the French Past*. Translated by Arthur Goldhammer. New York: Columbia University Press, 1996. First published as Pierre Nora, ed., *Les Lieux de Mémoire*. Paris.

——— , and Françoise Mélonio. Introduction and notes to *Tocqueville, the Old Regime and the Revolution*. Translated by Alan Kahan. Chicago: University of Chicago Press, 1998–2001.

Gagnon, Paul. *France Since 1789*. New York: Harper and Row, 1972.

Gannett, Robert T., Jr. *Tocqueville Unveiled*. Chicago: University of Chicago Press, 1973.

Gargan, Edward. *Alexis de Tocqueville: The Critical Years, 1848–1851*. Washington, D.C.: Catholic University Press of America, 1955.

Goldhammer, Arthur. "Translating Tocqueville." *Tocqueville Review/Revue Tocqueville* 26, no. 1 (2005).

——— . "Translator's Note." *Democracy in America*. New York: Library of America, 2002.

Goldstein, Doris. *Trial of Faith*. Amsterdam: Elsevier, 1971.

Gossman, Lionel. *Between History and Literature*. Cambridge: Harvard University Press, 1990.

Guellec, Lawrence, ed. "Tocqueville et l'esprit de la démocratie." *Tocqueville Review/Revue Tocqueville*. Paris: Presse de la Fondation nationale des sciences politiques, 2005.

Henri-Lévy, Bernard. *American Vertigo: Travelling America in the Footsteps of Tocqueville.* New York: Random House, 2006.

Herr, Richard. *Tocqueville and the Old Regime.* Princeton: Princeton University Press, 1962.

L'Hommedé, Edmond. *Un département français sous la monarchie de juillet.* Le Conseil général de la Manche et Alexis deTocqueville (correspondence inedité). Preface by A. Coville. Paris, 1933.

James, Henry. "The Two Ampères" and "The Letters of Mme Swetchine." In *Literary Criticism: French Writers; Other European Writers.* New York: Library of America, 1986.

Jardin, André. *Tocqueville: A Biography.* Translated by Lydia Davis with Robert Hemenway. Baltimore: Johns Hopkins University Press, 1998.

——— , and André-Jean Tudesq. *Reaction and Reform: 1815–1848.* Translated by Elborg Forster. Cambridge: Cambridge University Press, 1983.

Jennings, Lawrence C. *French Anti-Slavery: The Movement for the Abolition of Slavery in France, 1802–1848.* Cambridge: Cambridge University Press, 2000.

Johnson, Douglas. *Guizot: Aspects of French History, 1787–1874.* London: Routledge and K. Paul, 1963.

Kahan, Alan S. *Aristocratic Liberalism: The Social and Political Thought of Jacob Burkhardt and Alexis de Tocqueville.* Oxford: Oxford University Press, 1992.

Kaledin, Arthur. "Tocqueville's Apocalypse: Culture, Politics and Freedom in *Democracy in America.*" *Tocqueville Review/Revue Tocqueville* 26, no. 1 (2005).

Kelley, Donald R. *Historians and the Law in Postrevolutionary France.* Princeton: Princeton University Press, 1984.

LaCapra, Dominick. *History and Reading: Tocqueville, Foucault, French Studies.* Toronto: University of Toronto Press, 2000.

Lamberti, Jean-Claude. *Tocqueville and the Two Democracies.* Translated by Arthur Goldhammer. Cambridge: Harvard University Press, 1989.

Laski, Harold. *Authority in the Modern State.* New Haven: Yale University Press, 1919.

Lively, Jack. *The Social and Political Thought of Alexis de Tocqueville.* Oxford: Clarendon Press, 1962.

Lukacs, John. Introduction and translation, *The European Revolution and the Correspondence of Alexis de Tocqueville and Arthur de Gobineau.* Garden City, N.Y.: Doubleday, 1959.

Maza, Sarah C. *The Myth of the French Bourgeoisie: An Essay on the Social Imaginary, 1750–1850.* Cambridge: Harvard University Press, 2003.

Mazlish, Bruce. *James and John Stuart Mill: Father and Son in the Nineteenth Century.* New Brunswick, N.J.: Transaction Books, 1988.

Mellon, Stanley, *The Political Uses of History: A Study of Historians in the French Restoration.* Stanford: Stanford University Press, 1958.

Melonio, Françoise. *Tocqueville and the French.* Translated by Beth G. Reps. Charlottesville: University of Virginia Press, 1995.

Mitchell, Harvey. *Individual Choice and the Structures of History*. Cambridge: Cambridge University Press, 1996.

Nolla, Edouard, ed. *Liberty, Equality, Democracy*. New York: New York University Press, 1992.

Norton, Charles Eliot. "Alexis de Tocqueville." Review of Tocqueville's *Oeuvres Complètes*, ed. Gustave de Beaumont. *Atlantic Monthly*, November 1861, 551–57.

Packe, Michael St. John. *The Life of John Stuart Mill*. New York: Macmillan, 1954.

Palmer, Robert R. *The Two Tocquevilles: Father and Son: Hervé and Alexis de Tocqueville on the Coming of the French Revolution*. Princeton: Princeton University Press, 1987.

Pierson, George Wilson. *Tocqueville and Beaumont in America*. 1938; reprint, Baltimore: Johns Hopkins University Press, 1996.

Pitts, Jennifer, ed. *Alexis de Tocqueville: Writings on Empire and Slavery*. Translated by Jennifer Pitts. Baltimore: Johns Hopkins University Press, 2001.

Rédier, Antoine, *Comme Disait M. de Tocqueville*. Paris, 1925.

Rémond, René. *Les États-Unis devant l'opinion Française: 1815–1852*. Paris, 1962.

Richter, Melvin. "Tocqueville's Contribution to the Theory of Revolution." *Nomos* 8 (1966).

——— . "Tocqueville on Algeria." *Review of Politics* 25 (1963).

——— ."A Debate on Race: The Tocqueville-Gobineau Correspondence." *Commentary* 25 (February 1958): 153–60.

Rosanvallon, Pierre. *La démocratie inachevée: histoire de la souverainete du people en France*. Paris, 2000.

——— . *Democracy: Past and Future*. New York: Columbia University Press, 20.

——— . *Le Moment Guizot*. Paris: Gallimard, 1985.

Ryan, Alan. *J. S. Mill*. London: Routledge, Kegan Paul, 1974.

Schleifer, James. *The Making of Democracy in America*. Chapel Hill: University of North Carolina Press, 1980.

Scott, David H. T. *Semiologies of Travel, from Gautier to Baudrillard*. Cambridge: Cambridge University Press, 2004.

Shiner, L. E. *The Secret Mirror: Literary Form and History in Tocqueville's Recollections*. Ithaca: Cornell University Press, 1988.

Siegel, Jerrold. *Bohemian Paris*. New York: Viking, 1982.

——— . *The Idea of the Self: Thought and Experience in Western Europe Since the Seventeenth Century*. Cambridge: Cambridge University Press, 2005.

Spitzer, Alan, *The French Generation of 1820*. Princeton: Princeton University Press, 1987.

——— . *Old Hatreds and Young Hopes: The French Carbonari Against the Bourbon Restoration*. Cambridge: Harvard University Press, 1971.

Tudesq, André-Jean. *Les Grandes Notables en France, 1830–1848*. Bordeaux. 1964.

Welch, Cheryl B. *De Tocqueville*. Oxford: Oxford University Press, 2001.

——— , ed. *The Cambridge Companion to Tocqueville*. Cambridge: Cambridge University Press, 2006.

White, Hayden. *Metahistory: The Historical Imagination in the Nineteenth Century*. Baltimore: Johns Hopkins University Press, 1973.

Whitman, James. *Harsh Justice: Criminal Punishment and the Widening Divide Between America and Europe*. Oxford: Oxford University Press, 2003.

Wilentz, Sean. *The Rise of American Democracy*. New York: Norton, 2005.

Wolin, Sheldon. *Tocqueville Between Two Worlds*. Princeton: Princeton University Press, 2001.

INDEX

Abolition. *See under* Slavery

Académie des sciences morales et politiques, xxxiii, 91, 92, 207, 261, 271, 325, 388, 390

Académie française, xxxiii, 56, 172, 205, 213, 236, 271, 390–91

Acton, Lord, 255

Adams, John, 268, 378

Adams, John Quincy, 87, 291, 343

Agoult, Comtesse d', 33

Algeria, colonization of, 138, 390

Alienation: from class/culture, 9, 22, 37; vs. common good, xv; of democratic man, 362; and friendship, 38; and individualism, xiv, 6–7, 206, 360, 380; of Tocqueville, 6, 7–10, 22, 33, 53, 64, 83, 84–85, 125, 167, 195

American character: the American as dreamer, 265, 280, 324, 331; common traits, 321, 328, 332–33, 379; cultural transformation in, 327–29; democratic mind of, 333–34; emergence of, 8; as enlightened, 342, 351; rationality as trait, 8, 28, 64, 68, 322, 323, 327, 330–31; risk taking as trait, 248, 379, 380; self-interest as trait, 324, 332, 348; stereotypical, 323–24; Tocqueville's dark view of, 286, 288–89, 294–95, 297. *See also* Democratic man

American Dream, the, xv, 284, 321

American identity, and emergence of a "born-again" culture, 322, 329–32

American Indians: authority in wilderness, 186; conquering of, 193; noble savage myth, 168–69, 171, 189, 192; prejudice toward, 190, 286, 293; racial fusion, 184–85; Tocqueville's views of, xxiii, 69, 154, 155, 175, 183–87, 190–92

American journey, 288–98, 386–87; accidental, 164; and emerging American culture, 281–82; as inner journey, 59, 173, 182, 199; as intellectual adventure, 321; and meaning of America, 201; notebooks from, 279–87; as pilgrimage for French, 169; purpose of, xxxii–xxxiii, 162, 165, 166–67, 173, 200, 279, 321, 387; Tocqueville's dark view of Americans during, 288

American notebooks, 279–98; on American character, 8, 64, 286–87, 322, 324; on American Indians, 284; on aristocracy of merit, 339–40; balance in, 286; as basis of *Democracy in America*, 279, 280–81, 284, 285, 287, 354; Chateaubriand's influence on, 170, 172; contents of, 282; on democratic culture, 282, 335–36, 351; on equality, 315; omissions from, 283–84, 290–92, 295–96,